Anglo-Scandinavian Occupation at 16–22 Coppergate: Defining a Townscape

By Richard A. Hall

with D. T. Evans, K. Hunter-Mann and A. J. Mainman

and contributions from S. J. Allen, D. Hamilton, M. Holst, C. Tyers and J. Hillam

Illustrations by Lesley Collett

Published for the York Archaeological Trust by the
Council for British Archaeology

2014

Contents

List of Figures

List of tables

Richard Hall at the Coppergate excavation with HRH Prince Charles, October 1977

Volume 8 Fascicule 5

Anglo-Scandinavian Occupation at 16–22 Coppergate: Defining a Townscape

By Richard A. Hall

with D. T. Evans, K. Hunter-Mann and A. J. Mainman
and illustrations by L. E. Collett

and contributions from S. J. Allen, D. Hamilton, M. Holst, C. Tyers and J. Hillam

Key words: Anglian, Anglo-Scandinavian, burials, churches, coins, dendrochronology, domestic, industry, land use, radiocarbon dating, rivers, sculpture, streets, structures, timber, topography, trade, urban, Viking Age, York

Preface
by P. V. Addyman

> *In my beginning is my end. In succession*
> *Houses rise and fall, crumble, are extended,*
> *Are removed, destroyed, restored, or in their place*
> *Is an open field, or a factory, or a bypass.*
> *Old stone to new building, old timber to new fires,*
> *Old fires to ashes, and ashes to earth*
> *Which is already flesh, fur and faeces,*
> *Bone of man and beast, cornstalk and leaf.*

> T.S. Eliot, *East Coker*

This monumental publication is the culmination of a research design conceived by the founders of York Archaeological Trust in 1972. Forty years on, it completes, for one period at least, the broadly-based archaeological study of the whole process of urbanisation in York that they had in mind for the Trust. They were aware of the remarkably comprehensive range of archaeological deposits available in the city. They also knew of the exceptional ground conditions in some areas that make it possible to recover a suite of unusual materials, not just artefacts but once-living organisms, and the potential of such evidence to document the city's development, changing land use, environment and the impact of humans upon it. The Trust, always working within the framework of rescue archaeology, declared a policy of selecting for prolonged careful area exca-

vation sites where development was some way off and which might be typical of general neighbourhoods in York. Once selected these sites were to be investigated intensively not just by the then conventional techniques of archaeology but laying equal stress on reconstructing the environmental and occupation history of each area from non-artefactual evidence (Addyman 1975, 201–3).

In its early years the Trust carried out a scoping exercise, excavating numerous small sites which between them revealed the strengths of particular zones within the city for the purpose in mind, while laboratories were developed capable of addressing the problems of conservation, particularly of artefacts of organic materials, and of carrying out a wide range of palaeoecological research on the sediments, often organic-rich, from the excavations. The main sponsor of the work was the Department of the Environment whose Chief Inspector of Ancient Monuments, Andrew Saunders, urged the Trust to concentrate efforts on major projects where York could make a unique contribution to urban archaeology. He pointed especially to the need for study of the origins of urbanisation in the 9th and 10th centuries, and the opportunities York offered to recover details of urban houses of the period, then virtually unknown.

By that time the Trust had recruited to its staff a young scholar, Richard Hall, whose doctoral research on Viking towns and deep personal commitment to the period suited him eminently to the task. It had also carried out excavations underneath the still-standing buildings of Lloyds Bank in Pavement, York, which demonstrated the quality and depth of archaeological deposits of the period in that area, the presence of structures of the 9th–11th centuries, and their remarkable state of preservation. When a comprehensive redevelopment was proposed by the City of York Council of land it owned nearby in Coppergate, the former site of the Cravens sweet factory, the Trust recognised the opportunity, negotiated the demolition of the buildings on the site well before the proposed start of development, and began excavation in 1976. The work eventually went on for five years and four months and is the subject of this report, the main account of the excavation and the structures found. There are 20 preceding reports on particular aspects of the site.

The 16–22 Coppergate excavations (Fig.130) comprehensively achieved all that was expected of them. They documented the development of a substantial swathe of the centre of York from the Roman period to the present, but especially showed how urban life regenerated in the 9th century, how the general layout and detailed sub-division of this part of York was achieved by the early 10th century, and how in essence it determined patterns still present today. Generation after generation of buildings were uncovered – houses that rose, fell, crumbled, were removed, destroyed, restored – more than enough to satisfy the Department of the Environment's 1975 hope. Timbers submitted to fires, fires to ashes, ashes to earth, earth that was full of flesh, fur, faeces, bones of man and beast, cornstalk and leaf – more than enough to chart,

through the efforts of a huge team of archaeological specialists, the everyday life and conditions of urban dwellers of 10th-century York ... and in a way never achieved before.

The project became world famous as 'The Viking Dig', and was inspected possibly by upwards of one million people, locals and visitors from round the country and the globe. Eventually it generated the construction of the Jorvik Viking Centre on the site of the excavation, a new departure in public interpretation of the results of archaeology, which itself, after 30 years, has been enjoyed by over 17 million visitors. More importantly in the long term, perhaps, the project has provided for the first time details of a large swathe of Viking Age York, still unmatched in other contemporary towns in Britain. The material culture from Viking York is also similarly difficult to match. The evidence for all this is now fully available in published form in this and the supporting reports, and in the collections and archives held by York Archaeological Trust and the Yorkshire Museum at York.

The Coppergate excavation, along with other major excavations being undertaken in York in the 1970s, required resources well beyond those at that time available from the Department of the Environment and its successor English Heritage. York Archaeological Trust, working with its consultants Borodin Communications, therefore undertook a resource-gathering campaign to support the work. Fortuitously, the first exploratory excavations in Coppergate, below the floors of Victorian cellars along the ancient street frontage, produced a series of spectacular finds: timber buildings surviving to a considerable height; artefacts of the Viking Age; a range of objects in leather, textile and wood of a kind only rarely recovered before. Borodin, led by its owner W. J. Kingston and coordinated for the Trust by its account executive Christopher Martins, mounted a publicity campaign on the project in advance of the opening of the site as a paying attraction for the public. It rapidly became apparent that the discoveries, representing the archaeology of the Viking colonial age, were of as much interest in Scandinavia as in Britain, prompting regular visits from Danish, Norwegian and Swedish media.

The case was made for much more extensive excavations. For these, much enhanced resources

Fig.130 *The Coppergate site looking towards All Saints' Church*

were required. To obtain them a 'special development campaign' was initiated under the chairmanship of Magnus Magnusson, then at the height of his TV fame as host of the popular television quiz programme *Mastermind* and himself a writer and scholar on Viking Age themes. The special development campaign had patrons from Britain and each of the Scandinavian countries: The Prince of Wales and Queen Margrethe II of Denmark, both of whom had read archaeology at Cambridge, Crown Prince Harald of Norway, King Carl XVI Gustaf of Sweden and from Iceland President Kristjan Eldjarn, himself a distinguished archaeologist and former Director of the Icelandic National Museum. The Scandinavian ambassadors and the Archbishop of York became presidents of the campaign and a working committee chaired by the Prince of Wales began assembling resources. With backing of this calibre York Archaeological Trust was able to negotiate a loan of £76,500 from the Scandinavian Bank – a vast sum at the time for a small charity – to insert sheet piling to facilitate deep and extensive excavation. Enthusiastic help from British ambassadors in the Scandinavian countries laid the groundwork for support there, Dame Anne Warburton, HM Ambassador in Copenhagen, becoming a particular enthusiast for a project which she saw as underlining Denmark's age-old community of interest with Britain. A grant from the Tjæreborg Foundation to create a new conservation laboratory to handle the burgeoning finds was one of many from Danish supporters.

Publicity about the Coppergate finds caught the eye of C. Ian Skipper, a Lancashire entrepreneur whose enthusiasm for the project soon turned to practical help. With his support the visitor facilities at the Coppergate site were brought up to a high standard and the commercial opportunities of the site maximised. He established Cultural Resource Management Ltd, a trading arm of the York Archaeological Trust charity, transferred to it Borodin's roles and account executive Major A. E. Gaynor. The on-site commercial operation, a mail order service for related merchandise and the associated publicity, brought substantial supplements to the excavation funds. Meanwhile fundraising extended to the United States where establishment of the Foundation for the Preservation of the Archaeological Heritage Inc, a not-for-profit American foundation, enabled the many Scandinavian expatriates in the United States to make their own donations in support. Exhibitions were held in New York and Minneapolis and a Waldorf Astoria fundraising dinner was hosted by Vigdís Finnbogasdóttir, who had succeeded Kristjan Eldjarn as President of Iceland and as a patron of York Archaeological Trust.

In due course the extended periods that the City of York Council was able to make the 16–22 Coppergate site available to the Trust came to an end. Faced with the potential closure of a highly successful and widely-known tourist attraction that was generating a handsome income for the Trust, Ian Skipper suggested that the site be made a permanent attraction in the centre of York. After several unsuccessful proposals a scheme was eventually agreed with the City of York and the site developers Wimpey Construction Ltd. What is now the Jorvik Viking Centre was to be built in a basement constructed on the site of the excavation below the city's new shopping precinct. This involved another phase of fundraising. Grants were obtained from the English Tourist Board and from Ian Skipper himself, and loans from Wimpeys and a consortium of seven banks. In the event the Centre, using innovative display techniques, proved so successful commercially that the entire loan for its construction was paid off within four years. The Jorvik Viking Centre, encapsulating in an accessible form the vast fund of new knowledge about the Viking Age obtained in the Coppergate project, became a national asset, recommended by the National Curriculum as the main resource for study of the Viking contribution to Britain's history, and still, after 30 years, generating funds for further archaeological research in York. For his contribution to archaeology and other charitable work Ian Skipper was appointed OBE and received the British Archaeological Awards 'Award of Awards' – the Golden Trowel – in recognition of his achievement in changing the way archaeology is presented to the public.

The opening of the Jorvik Viking Centre in 1984 did not mark the end of the Coppergate project. It was scarcely more than the beginning. York Archaeological Trust over the next almost 30 years has been carrying out research on the vast product of data recovered from the site. Specialists in a huge range of fields have prepared reports on their findings. Illustrators and editorial teams have turned those reports into publications that between them constitute what will always be a bedrock in the study of the development of English towns and of Viking Age archaeology. The work, supported throughout by English Heritage, has been the collective labour of a host of collaborators, many acknowledged below, others perhaps unsung. Throughout the whole time, however, almost until the very end, the process has been overseen by the young scholar whose arrival at York Archaeological Trust in the 1970s ensured that the very best was made of the opportunity presented by the Coppergate site. With this report his great work is now complete, a tribute to a great archaeologist but, in the event, sadly, also a memorial.

Foreword

by Ailsa Mainman

This report completes the publication of the discoveries made at 16–22 Coppergate during the five-year campaign of excavation from 1976 to 1981, and subsequent watching brief (see Fig.131). The site produced archaeological evidence from the 2nd to the 16th centuries but it is best known for the stunningly preserved remains of Viking Age York; these are the subject of this report.

This is the final publication in the post-excavation programme as originally conceived (see below for full publication list), and deals with the site itself. As such it represents the culmination of a programme of analysis and research on the physical features and structures belonging to a 500-year period between the end of Roman occupation in the city and the Norman Conquest. A period of post-Roman abandonment was followed by the gradual establishment of a new urban landscape of streets, dwellings, workshops and churches in what was an important area of Anglo-Scandinavian York. The excavation was in the core of this area, offering a rare opportunity to examine a great swathe of early townscape at a crucial point in the rebirth of towns in western Europe. This fact, combined with the extraordinary preservation conditions encountered at Coppergate, makes the site of national significance.

The report is the legacy of Richard Hall, who directed the excavation and who oversaw the programme of research and publication, but who died before completing this final element of the work. He left a well-advanced text including instructions regarding illustrations, both drawings and photographs, and this text has formed the basis of the current report. His final thoughts, which would have formed the overall discussion of the significance of the discoveries at Coppergate, were, sadly, incomplete. Fortunately, however, his extensive discourses published elsewhere, and his numerous presentations and discussions with colleagues, provide insights into his thinking and thus inform the final discussion section presented here.

A few points regarding authorship need to be made. Firstly, new information regarding the initial post-Roman periods (Periods 2–3), in the form of C14 dates of early burials, has allowed a reconsid- eration of the immediately pre-Viking Age levels on the site. The section which deals with these phases, therefore, is an amalgam of Richard Hall's original text and this new material, presented and discussed by Ailsa Mainman. The sections dealing with Periods 4A–5C which cover the late 9th/early 10th to late 11th century are substantially the work of Richard Hall with the gaps filled in, as far as possible, by the project team. Sections of text written by Ailsa Mainman appear on a grey background, those by Kurt Hunter-Mann on a brown background. Work to bring the archive collected during the subsequent watching brief on the site to publication has been carried out by Kurt Hunter-Mann, with the assistance of Karen Weston. Individual specialist reports are the work of the named specialist authors.

In the unfortunate circumstances of Richard Hall's death, it was agreed that it was important to present the information in the most comprehensive, and comprehensible, way possible, together with what is believed to be his interpretation and understanding of it, thus ensuring that this significant body of data is available for future scholars to consider and to challenge. 16–22 Coppergate was a large and complex site, the outstanding preservation conditions providing a wealth of data recorded without the benefit of computer technology, which created a challenge during post-excavation work. The team of digging staff, which worked over a continuous five-year period, included individuals with a range of skills and experience from professional archaeologists and archaeology students to volunteers and inmates from the open prison system. The site archive is vast and challenging but records details of activity and occupation which spanned, in total, 1500 years of occupation from the Roman period to the 15th/16th century (see Table 25).

The importance of the site for understanding Anglo-Scandinavian York can hardly be over-stated and its contribution to the wider context of Viking Age studies is no less significant. Richard's premature death denied him the satisfaction of seeing the publication of the site through to completion, but he would have been profoundly grateful for the hard work and determination of his colleagues in doing so. Especial mention must go to David Evans who worked with Richard on the site and assisted throughout in all aspects of the post-excavation analysis; to Kurt Hunter-Mann whose understanding of the site was gained initially by his work with Richard on the medieval period (*AY* 10/6) and who was able to pull together the watching brief material and to elucidate the stratification of the main site; and to Lesley Collett whose formidable skills in converting complex plans and sections into clear and meaningful drawings have made a vital contribution to this report. Painstaking work by several specialists underpins the results, and thus the interpretation of the site, and their reports are included in the volume with additional material available online (www.yorkarchaeology.co.uk). Many others were involved in the project and warm thanks are given to them in the Acknowledgements section, but without this core team the publication would not have been completed.

Introduction

The archaeology of Anglo-Scandinavian York before the Coppergate excavations

The potential richness of York's Anglo-Scandinavian/Viking Age (mid-9th–mid-11th century) archaeological deposits has not been in doubt since Dudley Waterman (1959) catalogued and discussed the Anglo-Scandinavian artefacts found in the city. His pioneering catalogue demonstrated that the large number and wide variety of objects attributable to this period was unusual within the understanding of English urban development then current. Inevitably, his distribution map showing where these objects had been found reflected in part no more than the locations of the principal road and building works of the 19th century, for it was those operations that had brought most of the objects to light. They were thus without any archaeological context. Nevertheless, Waterman's map highlighted the concentration of discoveries in the area south-east of the Roman fortress, on the neck of land between the Rivers Foss and Ouse, around the approaches to Ouse Bridge (see Fig.132). This was the only medieval bridging point across the Ouse, and Waterman equated this concentration in part with the abandonment of the Roman bridge over the Ouse, which had stood 250m upstream, on the central axis of the fortress, and its replacement with a ford or bridge here, where the present Ouse Bridge stands. He argued that this repositioning attracted a cluster of occupation along and around the routes leading to this key topographic feature.

Subsequently, through consulting antiquarian reports and undertaking a series of watching briefs in the streets of Ousegate and Pavement, near Ouse Bridge, Jeffrey Radley (1971) was able to show that organic remains, including structural timbers and evidence for various industrial activities, survived *in situ* in the vicinity. This led him to suggest that the Micklegate-Ousegate-Pavement axis was the main commercial thoroughfare of Anglo-Scandinavian York and that the focus of commercial activity might have been at the junction of the streets Pavement, Ousegate and Coppergate (*ibid*, 39) (Fig.132).

The first archaeological excavation in this vicinity took place in 1972, when York Archaeological Trust excavated four shafts, each 2m square, below Lloyds Bank at 6–8 Pavement (Addyman in *AY* 8/3; see Fig.131, **8**). This operation demonstrated the presence of up to 9m of archaeological deposits, many of them dating from the Anglo-Scandinavian period. It also confirmed that the deposits were anoxic, with consequent good preservation not only of artefacts (*AY* 17/3) but also of environmental evidence in the form of botanical, entomological and other remains (*AY* 14/4). Having prospected the area with this small-scale excavation and gained a greater understanding of its archaeological potential, the next requirement was for a more extensive sampling of this part of Anglo-Scandinavian York.

The Coppergate site and the circumstances of its excavation

The opportunity to investigate this part of Anglo-Scandinavian York more thoroughly than had previously been possible arose with York City Council's proposal to redevelop adjacent sites bounded by Coppergate, Piccadilly, Castlegate and the River Foss, encompassing a total of 2.02ha (Fig.131). Having secured the Council's far-sighted agreement to make the area available for excavation, York Archaeological Trust chose to excavate a site on the Coppergate frontage, some 75m from the investigations at 6–8 Pavement. Immediately beyond the excavated site the street Coppergate skirts around All Saints' church. The street was altered in 1782 when parts of the church were demolished and the outer edge of its graveyard was attenuated in order to widen the road. In contrast, the survival of 15th- to 16th-century buildings at 26 and at 28–32 Coppergate, immediately adjacent to the excavation site (Fig.131), indicated that this part of the street's south-eastern frontage has not altered its alignment or position since the late medieval period. The alignments of property boundaries between Coppergate and the River Foss vary from plot to plot, in order to take account of the curving courses of both the street and the river; this variation is mirrored in the precise alignment of individual structures within each of the plots.

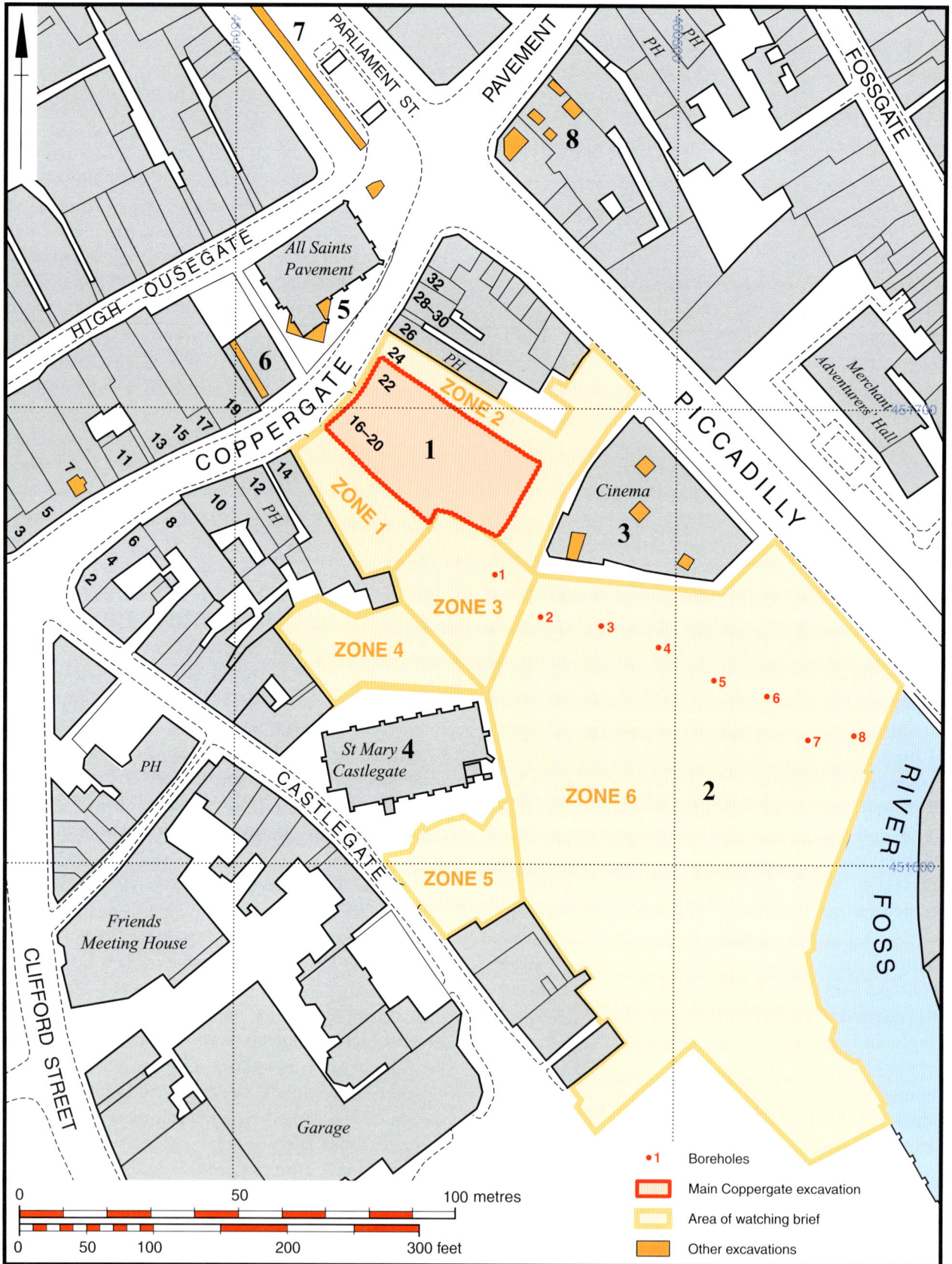

Fig.131 *Site location plan:*
1, 16–22 Coppergate; 2, area of Watching Brief, Zones 1–6; 3, 22 Piccadilly; 4, St Mary's Church Castlegate; 5, All Saints' Church Pavement; 6, Watching Brief, Zone 7; 7, Parliament Street sewer; 8, 2–4 Pavement and Lloyds Bank, 6–8 Pavement. Scale 1:1250. © Crown copyright 2014 Ordnance Survey Licence No. 100018343

Please Note: To avoid the need for constant and long-winded compass-based definitions of alignment, a simple system is employed here which reflects the presentation of plans. The position of features such as walls, fences etc. will be described in terms of their relationship to the street frontage of Coppergate. The street frontage, therefore, becomes Site North and all descriptions of site features conform to this. Discussion of Coppergate in the wider context of the city will adhere to True North. To aid the reader there will be a double north point on plans, with Site North being 45° to the west of True North. Where a wider sweep of the area is under discussion, for example in the context of the watching brief report, the discussion reverts to using True North.

York Archaeological Trust began investigations on the site in May 1976 with agreement from the owners, York City Council, that excavation could proceed for two and a half years without interruption. Initial grants to fund the work did not include an allowance for any large-scale safety measures to support the sides of the excavation, such as the piled vertical steel sheets that were eventually positioned around the perimeter. Thus, at the start, adequate safety margins had to be left undisturbed at the sides of the excavated area, buttressing the modern street Coppergate at the north-west end of the site as well as nearby structures on adjacent plots to the north-east and south-west. The limits of these unexcavated strips were defined by pragmatic considerations. A suite of cellars, belonging to the demolished Craven's Sweet Factory and the White Horse Public House which occupied the site, stopped approximately 7.5m short of the street frontage, leaving a block of soil beyond them that was adequate to support that frontage in the earliest stages of excavation. Similarly, to the south-west and north-east, the side walls of the outer cellars defined adequate margins between the excavation edges and adjacent properties; the unexcavated strip to the south-west also acted as an entranceway for the heavy machinery which was required intermittently.

After the first year's work had revealed structures and artefacts of demonstrable importance, a generous loan from the Scandinavian Bank provided the necessary funding to meet the cost of installing sheet piling around the perimeter of the excavated area and extending it up to the street frontage. This was put into position in July 1978 and thereafter archaeological excavation could continue in safety without endangering staff and the surrounding area. At this time, however, another threat to the excavation's progress emerged. From early 1979 onwards it became clear that neither the site itself nor the finances to enable excavation to carry on would be available for more than a further few months. Nevertheless, despite constant uncertainty, excavation continued steadily until the developers were finally ready to begin their work in September 1981.

In total, approximately 1000m² was excavated within the properties at 16–22 Coppergate, previously occupied by the White Horse Public House and Craven's Sweet Factory (1982 revision of Ordnance Survey 1:1250, sheet SE 6051 NW) between May 1976 and September 1981 under the writer's direction. The entire area was excavated down to its mid-10th-century levels, but earlier deposits were seen in a more restricted area comprising two long, contiguous strips, one behind the modern street frontage and the other down the site's western half. Subsequently, during redevelopment of the site and its environs, when most of the remaining archaeological deposits were summarily removed or heavily disturbed, a watching brief was undertaken by N.F. Pearson which allowed the investigation and recording of structures and features lying beyond the limits of the excavation. This watching brief embraced the whole of the 2.02ha area of the Coppergate Shopping Centre redevelopment from the Castlegate frontage in the west to Piccadilly in the east. Observation and recording was carried out in often adverse conditions as ground preparation works by the construction company were undertaken largely by machine. Where significant archaeological deposits were disturbed, construction work was suspended to allow recording, or, where appropriate, small-scale excavation. To facilitate recording the redevelopment area was split into discrete zones (Zones 1–7; Fig.131, **2** and **6**). The results of the watching brief are incorporated in this report where relevant.

The excavated area extended from the Coppergate street frontage down a natural slope of 1 in 10 towards the River Foss; the underlying sub-soil was sandy clay. Figure 135 shows the build up of deposits and their sub-division into periods, highlighting the thinning out of deposits downslope, prior to the major dumping episodes ascribed to Period 6 (post-Conquest).

The earliest activity or occupation on the site (Period 1) took place in the Roman period (Table 25). At that time the Roman legionary fortress lay 160m to the north-west; this extra-mural area is known to have been occupied by temples, and probably also contained a variety of commercial establishments. Evidence for Roman buildings constructed of timber and stone was recovered, but the precise uses of these structures have not been deduced. Timber structures and fences dated from the 2nd century AD (*AY 6/2*, 201), while the stone building belonged to the later 3rd century but was abandoned, and partially demolished in the mid-4th century (*ibid,* 237), a process which continued during the Anglo-Scandinavian period. Subsequently, set back and roughly parallel with the Coppergate street frontage, a small number of 4th-century Roman graves were aligned more or less with one of the principal axes of the legionary fortress. These formed part of a pattern emerging elsewhere in the city of burials encroaching onto vacant land (*ibid*, 214–17, 373).

There is no evidence that Romano-British activity continued on the site beyond the conventional date of c.400 or shortly after, and from then until the mid-9th century the site seems to have been largely unoccupied. This period (Period 2) was marked stratigraphically by the accumulation of up to 0.85m of grey silty clay loam soils. These, it is thought, had accumulated as a result of natural agencies. At various horizons in this build up occasional ephemeral features were noted, some of them apparently pits (recorded as 'shallow cuts' or 'depressions') and others of unexplained purpose. The great majority of the pottery in these layers and cuts was Roman, although sporadic hand-made sherds, usually attributed to the Anglian period, were present. There was no compelling evidence for structures, domestic or otherwise, to comple-

Table 25 Summary of archaeological development at 16–22 Coppergate

Period	Date	Characteristics
1	late 1st–late 4th century or later	Roman timber and stone buildings; late Roman cemetery. Limited survival of organic remains
2	5th–mid-9th century	Apparent desertion. Homogeneous loamy deposits which did not preserve organic materials
3	mid-9th–late9th/early 10th century	Rubbish disposal, suggesting occupation close by. Post/stake and wattle alignments, possibly boundaries. Organic materials preserved only in pit cuts.
4A	late 9th/early 10th century–c.930/35	Realignment of boundaries, suggesting that Coppergate was laid out by this period. Possible buildings at Coppergate frontage. Organic materials preserved mainly in pit cuts
4B	c.930/5–c.955/6*	Four tenements distinguishable, with post and wattle buildings at Coppergate frontage. Evidence for iron working and other trades on a commercial scale. Organic-rich deposits nearer to Coppergate; organic content thinning to zero towards River Foss
5A	c.955/6*	Near Coppergate frontage only. Layers between structures of Period 4B and 5B; probably mixture of dump deposits and soil from 5B semi-basements
5B	c.955/6*–early/mid-11th century	Perpetuation of boundaries. Introduction of 'sunken-featured' structures in double row at street frontage. Organic-rich deposits as in Period 4B
5Cf	mid–later 11th century	Organic-rich deposits at street frontage, associated with buildings which survive only in Tenement D
5Cr	mid–later 11th century	Post-built structure sealed by earliest in a succession of dump deposits. Little organic material surviving
6	later 11th–16th century	No remains surviving at street frontage, but area to rear increasingly built up above later dump deposits. New methods of building and rubbish disposal, leading to reduction in organic content of deposits

* In previous publications this date was c.975 but has been revised as a result of refinements to the dendrochronological determinations.

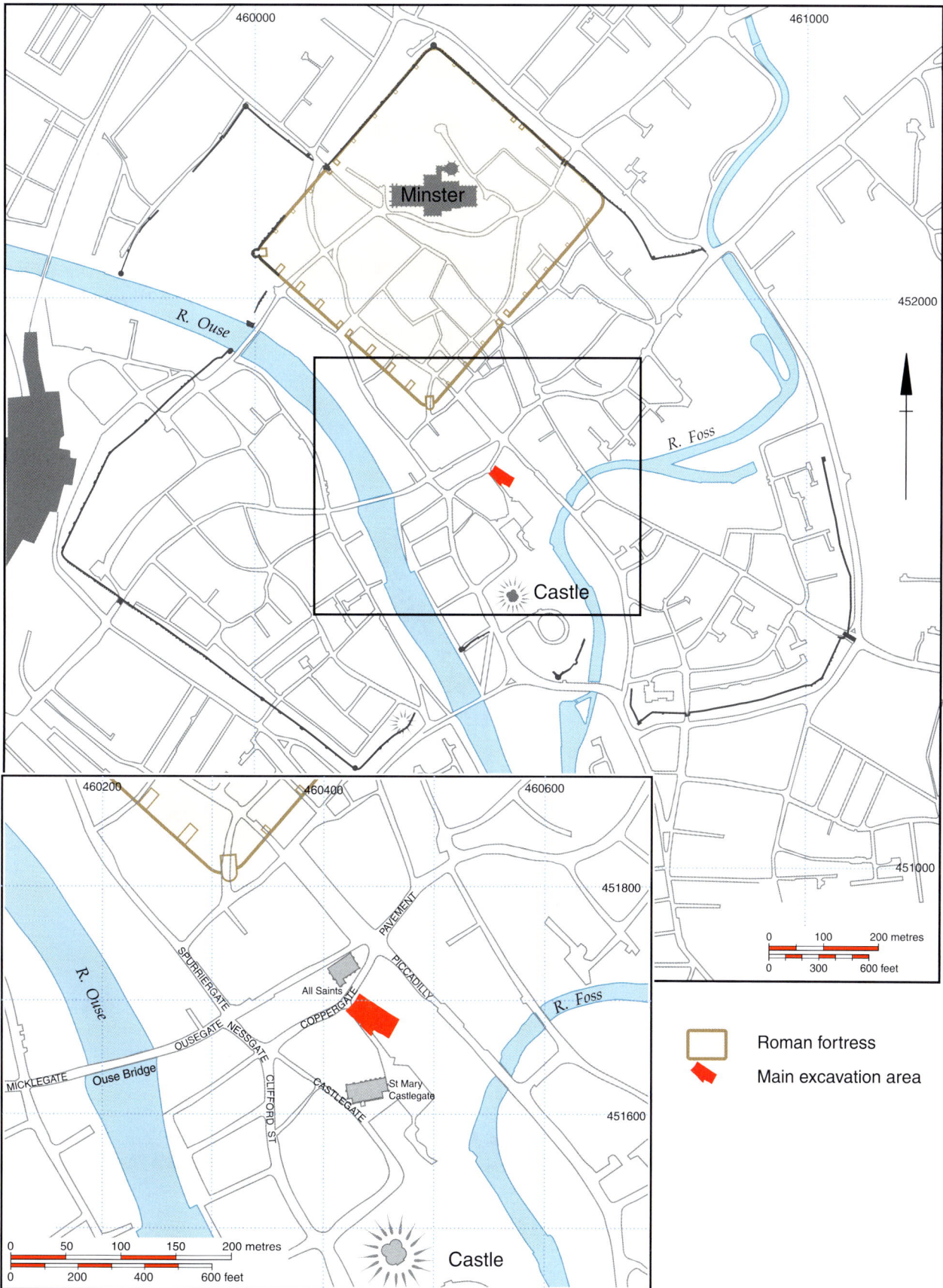

Fig.132   *Location of Coppergate within York. Scale 1:10 000/ 1:5000.* © *Crown copyright 2014 Ordnance Survey Licence No. 100018343*

533

ment the discovery of an 8th-century helmet and spearhead in a wood-lined shaft only 9m beyond the perimeter of the excavation during construction work in 1982 (see Pit 1778 on Fig.136). Indeed, there is reason to believe that the helmet and spearhead were deposited in the Anglo-Scandinavian rather than the Anglian period (*AY* 17/8).

The Anglo-Scandinavian era is conveniently dealt with as a unit in this report not only because of its historic identity, but also because the archaeological remains of the period were for the most part clearly distinguished from preceding and succeeding material. As it is clearly of prime importance to establish the basis for the chronological framework of this report, the evidence which has led to the adoption of these principal temporal divisions is described here, even though it previews some of the material presented below.

In the eastern half of the strip excavated behind the modern street frontage, the latest Roman levels were sealed by layers of very dark grey silty clay loam, for example 30890 (not illustrated), up to 0.2m thick, upon which a multi-phase hearth/oven/furnace had been constructed. An archaeomagnetic determination relating to a medial phase in the feature's use was centred on AD 860. This feature and a number of associated pits were interpreted as marking a re-commencement of activity on this part of the site in the mid-9th century even though, with the exception of only a handful of sherds, all the pottery associated with the hearth is of Roman date. *Stycas* of the Northumbrian kings Eanred (808–41) and Aethelred II (841–48) were found in contexts stratigraphically just a little later than the hearth (*AY* 8/1, 17, 52–3), and this, together with other strands of evidence described below, argues for some Anglian activity prior to the mid-9th-century burst of activity which marks the start of Period 3, the Anglo-Scandinavian occupation.

The complementary sequence in the western half of the frontage strip, beyond the zone of pits and other cuts approximately contemporary with the hearth, showed that the 4th-century cemetery and some subsequent ill-defined activity there was covered by a layer of very dark grey silty clay loam with mixed inclusions, up to c.0.85m thick. The disparity between the depth of Period 2 deposits to the north and to the south of the site is due to

a large, but poorly defined cut, 37152. This cut, recognised in post-excavation as belonging to early Period 2, measured 4.5m east–west by 5m north–south and truncated some of the later Roman material towards the south-west but not towards the north-east as a result of the prevailing natural slope of the ground.

Above the silty clay loam a range of features, apparently contemporary with broadly similar features above the hearth, were examined, and it is the appearance of these features which is taken as marking the start of Period 3 here. The intrusion of later features makes it impossible to link the hearth on the north-east with a precise stratigraphic equivalent to the south-west; this leaves open the possibility that the uppermost parts of the very dark grey loam are strictly contemporary with the hearth. This cannot be proved, however, and those uppermost parts did not contain any artefacts to link them to the hearth. All of the clean grey soils in the south-west part of the frontage strip are here assigned to Period 2.

In summary, at the modern street frontage, features of mid-9th-century date which mark the inception of Period 3 lay above or were cut into the uniform, relatively clean grey silty clay loam of the underlying Period 2, and they clearly attest an intensification of activity. Further south, i.e. further behind the modern street frontage, where evidence for similar activity became less intense and quickly petered out altogether, the distinction was not so obvious, and undifferentiated soils continued to accumulate within Period 3.

At the termination of this Anglo-Scandinavian phase, at the Coppergate street end of the site the uppermost Anglo-Scandinavian levels, those ascribed to Period 5C, were truncated by modern disturbance which had removed virtually all traces of later medieval occupation there (*AY* 10/6, 791 and *passim*). Downslope, nearest to the River Foss, a rapid accumulation of rather homogeneous dark grey silty loam, up to c.1.8m thick and dated to the 11th–mid-12th century, protected the Anglo-Scandinavian deposits from all but a few intrusions (*ibid*, fig.398). Only in the centre of the site was there no clearly defined upper limit to the Anglo-Scandinavian levels, but here relative stratigraphy allows them to be identified.

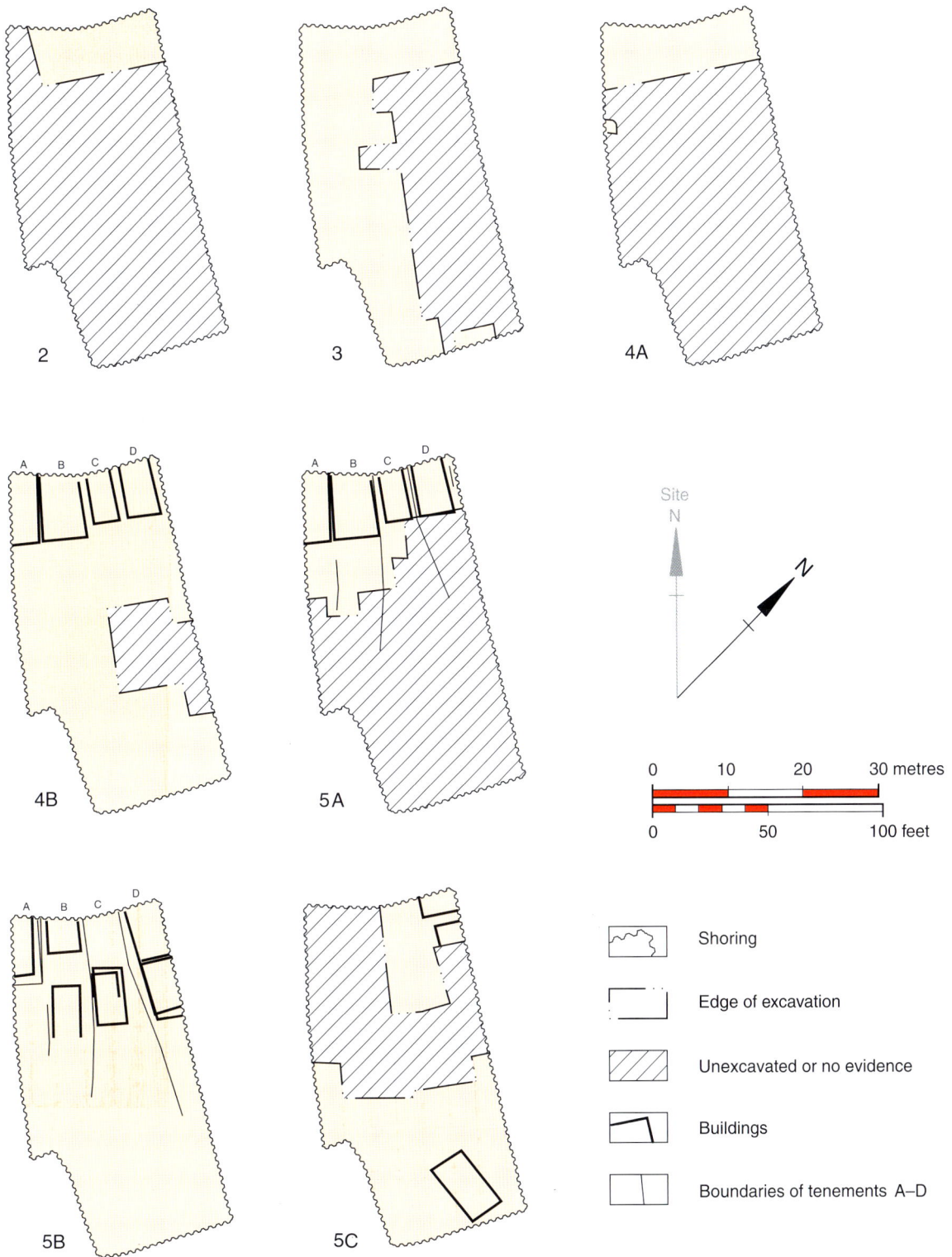

Fig.133 *Plans of the site showing the area of deposits excavated for each period. The variation is due either to restricted excavation or the limited occurrence of the relevant deposits. Scale 1:800*

Three principal periods of activity have been isolated within the Anglo-Scandinavian era, Periods 3, 4 and 5 (Table 25 and Fig.133). Initially, from c.850 to c.900, there is evidence for glass working, a scatter of haphazard burials (see pp.548–51), the disposal of rubbish, and the erection of post and stake alignments (Period 3). Then, c.900, a new series of post and stake alignments sub-dividing the area was established on the axes which defined all subsequent activity, but these alignments, ascribed to Period 4A, do not appear to form coherent structures. Property divisions separating four plots (designated Tenements A, B, C and D) and recognisable buildings of post and wattle construction were initiated c.935 (Period 4B). The watching brief revealed evidence that similar plots lay to each side of the excavated area, the most complete of which, continuing this layout to the east, was designated Tenement E (see p.573).

Subsequently, c.955/56, the latest post and wattle structures within the excavated area were covered by up to 1m of soil (Period 5A), and into this were cut sunken-featured structures which respected the earlier plot boundaries (Period 5B); in some cases a second building stood behind those on the street frontage. On one plot where later stratification survived, a sunken structure was replaced in the early to mid-11th century by buildings erected at ground level (Period 5Cf). The sole building found at the riverward end of the site was erected using timbers that have a combined felling date in the range 1013–49. Contexts lying statigraphically between this building and the band of rather homogeneous dark grey silty clay loams referred to above are designated Period 5Cr.

The site is located on a broad spur of higher ground above the River Foss which drops from 10.5m OD at the top left-hand corner to 5m OD at the lowest point (Fig.134). The route which the street of Coppergate was to take sat upon this highest ground, and this in turn dictated the arrangement of the buildings along its course. Except in one case (Structure 5/12), the buildings in both Period 4B and 5B hug this higher ground; Figure 134 goes some way to explaining why this is. There is evidence that the sloping land created constructional challenges and in some cases contributed to the collapse of individual second-rank buildings; it also discouraged further construction behind the second rank of later 10th-century buildings. Figure 134 also helps to illustrate why the backyard deposits thinned out further away from the street frontage, making them difficult to ascribe to distinct periods with any certainty.

Thanks to the preservation of organic materials induced by a rapid accumulation of permanently moist soils gradually infilling this natural slope from the early 10th century onwards, structural remains of all types survived; they provide a view of pre-Conquest timber buildings unparalleled in Britain. Three, arguably four, distinct building styles were recognised (see p.709), together with fences and drains, pits and wells lined with planks, wattle and barrels. Possible pens and enclosures were identified, complementing environmental and faunal evidence for animal husbandry and horticulture, together with features associated with all manner of industrial activities. The survival of organic and inorganic artefacts and environmental data across the site adds detail to the picture.

The circumstances of the excavation decreed that the Anglo-Scandinavian remains of each period described here were not exposed, recorded and excavated as a single operation. Instead, separate blocks of Anglo-Scandinavian stratigraphy in different locations were excavated semi-independently over the entire five-year investigation. This less-than-perfect approach was dictated by several factors. One was that the depth of medieval deposits covering the Anglo-Scandinavian layers consistently increased along the axis from the street frontage towards the River Foss, a reflection of the site's position over the downward slope of the river terrace. The excavation of these post-Conquest deposits inevitably became increasingly protracted in areas closer and closer to the river, thus incrementally delaying the time when the uppermost Anglo-Scandinavian deposits were exposed in each area (Fig.135). Secondly, adverse weather conditions made excavation impossible for six months or more each year except within confined areas that were protected from the elements by a polythene cover. In most years financial and logistical considerations limited the area that could be covered to a strip at the current street frontage, although in some winters an area across the southern end of the site was also protected. Unfortunately, the width of the area at the frontage that could be covered on these

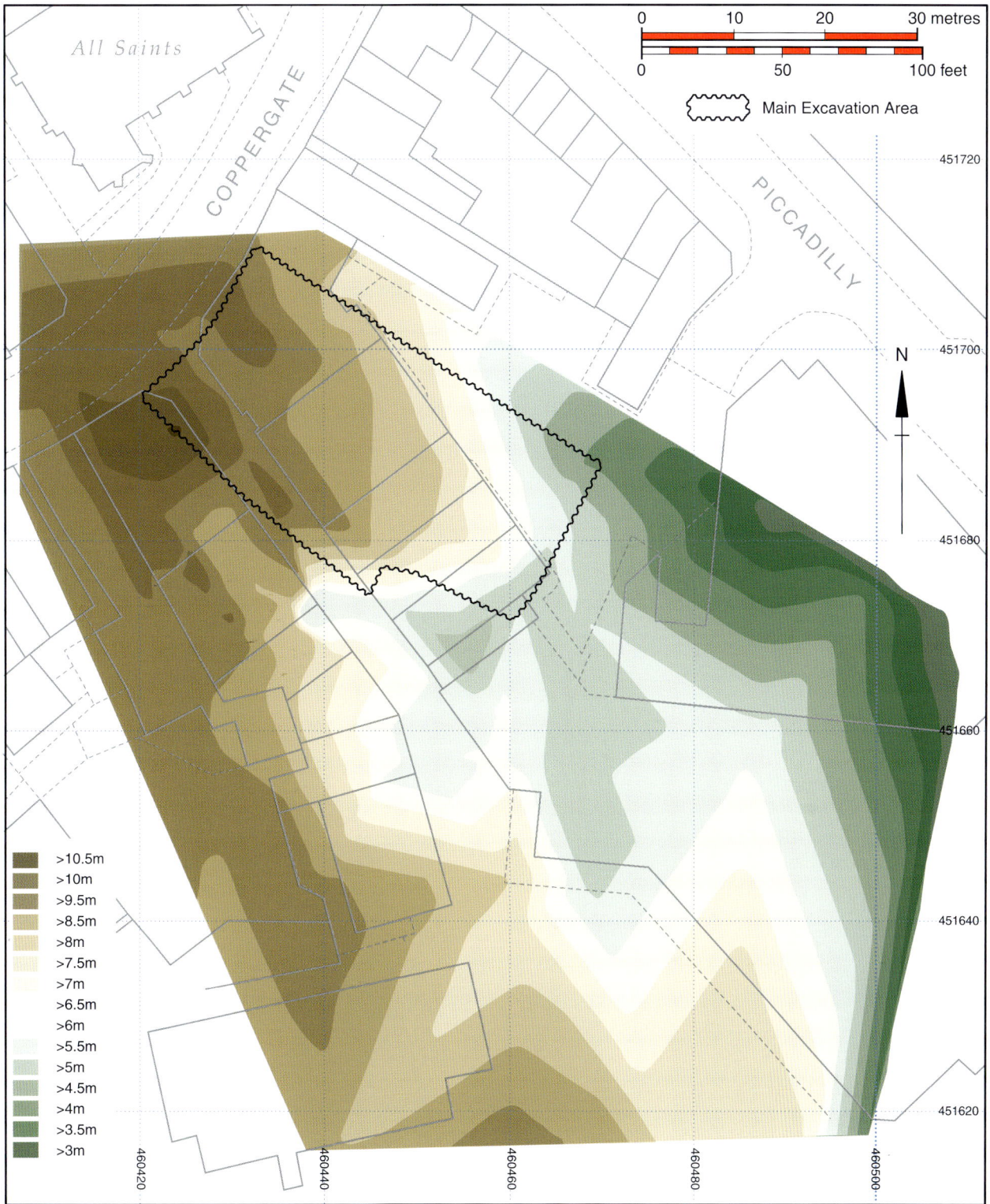

Fig.134 *Topographical survey derived from levels recorded in the area of the watching brief. Scale 1:625*

© Crown copyright 2014 Ordnance Survey Licence No. 100018343

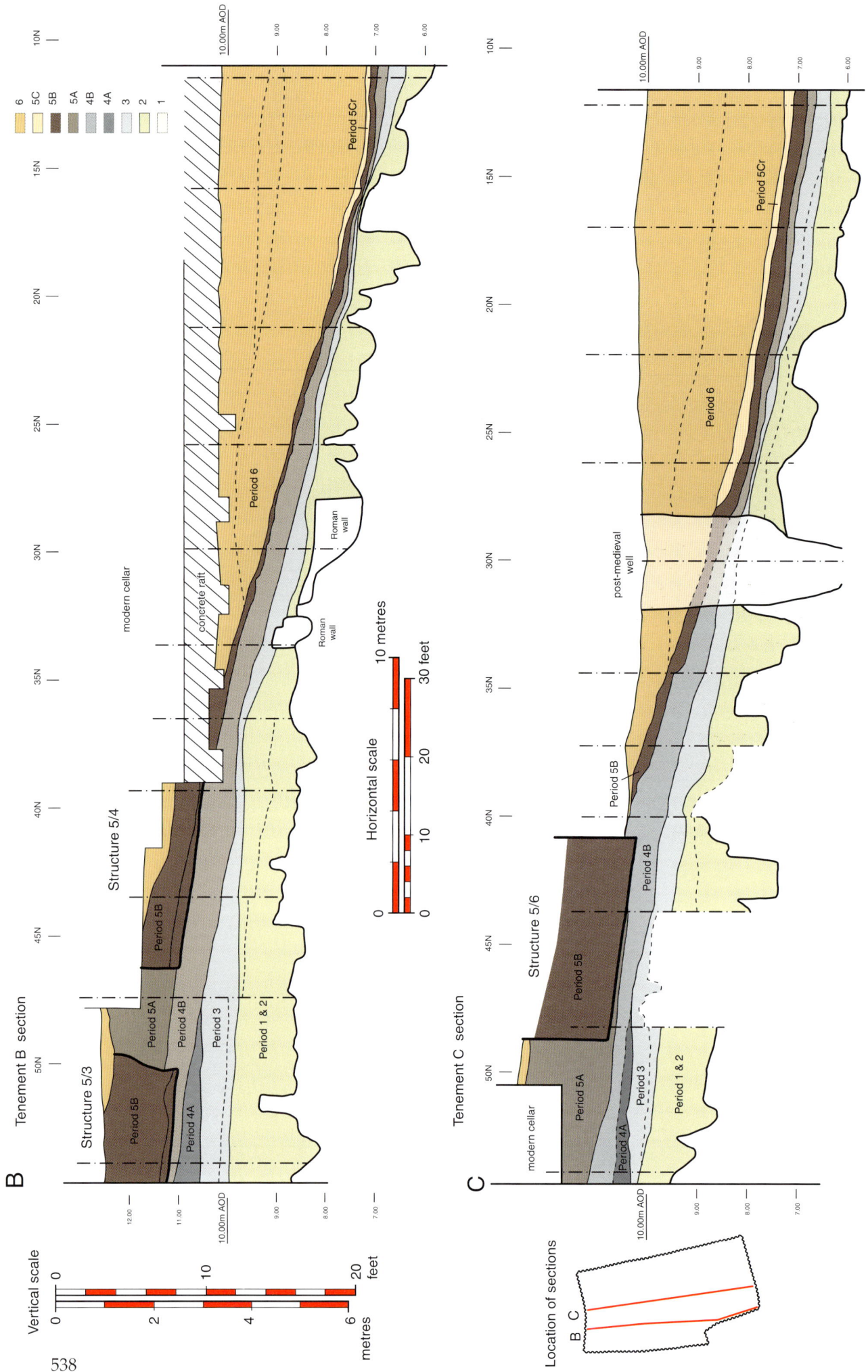

Fig.135 *North–south sections through the site with deposits identified by period. Horizontal scale 1:200, vertical scale 1:100*

B Tenement B section

Structure 5/3

Structure 5/4

modern cellar

concrete raft

Period 6

Roman wall

Roman wall

Period 5B

Period 5A

Period 4B

Period 3

Period 1 & 2

Period 4A

Period 5B

Period 5Cr

6
5C
5B
5A
4B
4A
3
2
1

Horizontal scale

10 metres

30 feet

Vertical scale

feet

metres

538

12.00

11.00

10.00m AOD

9.00

8.00

7.00

10.00m AOD

9.00

8.00

7.00

6.00

10N
15N
20N
25N
30N
35N
40N
45N
50N

C Tenement C section

Structure 5/6

Period 5Cr

Period 6

post-medieval well

Period 5B

Period 4B

Period 5A

Period 4A

Period 3

Period 1 & 2

modern cellar

Location of sections

B C

10.00m AOD

9.00

8.00

7.00

6.00

10N
15N
20N
25N
30N
35N
40N
45N
50N

occasions did not coincide with the length of the structures partially exposed underneath it, particularly when the post and wattle structures of Period 4B were under examination. From the winter of 1978 onwards, therefore, the frontage strip was always at an earlier level of excavation than the area behind it, even though individual buildings spanned the two areas.

The threat of imminent deadlines to terminate the excavation so that redevelopment could commence, ever present from early 1979 onwards, also affected the scheduling of excavation. The obvious preference to expose and investigate contemporary developments within the post and wattle structures across the entire frontage simultaneously had to be sacrificed to expediency. Thus at the west end of the frontage, where the sunken structures had destroyed more of the post and wattle structures, these remains were excavated and lower levels examined while later phases of post and wattle buildings were still being dissected to the east.

At the outset it was found that construction of the modern cellars had removed virtually all deposits later than the early/mid-11th century in their area, thereby providing immediate access to Anglo-Scandinavian deposits below them. Thus the later phases of the southern rank of sunken-featured structures described below were uncovered in 1976–77. To avoid any possibility of the sides of the excavation collapsing, the earlier buildings below these could not be excavated until after perimeter shoring was installed in 1978; and to ease interpretation, their excavation was further delayed until the block of previously undisturbed soil across the street frontage of the site was excavated to their depth. This work at the frontage, in progress from mid-1978 onwards, brought to light first a series of sunken-featured structures and then an underlying series of post and wattle structures that presumably fronted onto the Anglo-Scandinavian street. Modern widening of the road and the establishment of the pavement has encroached over the fronts of these structures, which were therefore inaccessible beyond sheet piling. It was only in 1980 and 1981 that the earlier phases of sunken-featured structures in the southern rank, and underlying layers immediately behind the post and wattle buildings, were excavated; 1982 saw the recording of a previously

truncated wall of a building at the western edge of the excavation and the investigation of a building on Tenement E beyond the east side of the excavation.

The divisions between different levels of progress were made along what were interpreted as fence lines, which interrupted the stratification; individual structures were excavated in phase across their width, even when an axial baulk crossed them. The south (back) walls of these structures, however, lay to the south of the winter-covered frontage strip referred to above, and thus these southern parts of the buildings were excavated separately, after the remaining area had been investigated.

Eventually, shortage of resources halted excavation of a large strip in the north-eastern part of the site. Thus layers earlier than c.930 were excavated only in the strip across the Coppergate frontage and in the western half of the site (Fig.133).

Continuity in excavation/recording techniques and standards was provided by the permanent and semi-permanent members of the archaeological team. Direction throughout was by the principal author, assisted by Area Supervisors D.T. Evans (1976–81), M.J. Humphreys (1976–78), S.A. Power (1976–79) and I.G. Lawton (1978–81). A small number of experienced excavation assistants provided the nucleus of the excavating team, some of them working on the site continuously for several years; they were supplemented by generally inexperienced teams recruited for one-year periods under successive government-sponsored Manpower Services Commission employment schemes from 1979 to 1981, by moderately experienced summer 'volunteers' who included students of archaeology and related disciplines from Britain, Scandinavia, Europe and North America, and occasionally by labour from other sources, including Askham Grange Open Prison and Rudgate Open Prison. In evenings and at weekends members of York Excavation Group excavated and recorded an area within the site as an integral part of the project, and their results are also incorporated here.

Over 35,000 contexts were recorded and excavated altogether, of which more than 20,000 relate to the Anglo-Scandinavian era: the sheer quantity of data dealt with by a small team in the pre-field computer age was itself a major challenge. Post-excavation analysis has resulted in the synthesis presented here: the excavation and post-excavation archive upon which it is based resides at YAT, while remains of some of the structures reported here are displayed in the Jorvik Viking Centre, York.

Reporting and discussion of the multifarious data recorded throughout and after the excavation is published in *The Archaeology of York* series; a list of published titles featuring the findings of the excavation is given below (Table 26).

Recording methods

The excavation utilised the then standard York Archaeological Trust methodologies, adapting and enhancing them as necessary. Each stratigraphic unit was given a unique number identifier (the *context number*) which is the key reference point for stratigraphic, artefact and palaeoenvironmental studies. The methodology for recording timbers

involved the assigning of a context number to each individual wooden upright. Horizontal woven wattle rods were not automatically given a context number, either singly or collectively, although for particular recording purposes a number might be assigned. Pieces of worked wood resting on the ground surface were given an individual context number only if their position, unusual size or other exceptional characteristics suggested deliberate emplacement rather than casual disposal.

In addition, each series of wooden uprights that seemed to form an integrated, homogeneous alignment was given an individual context number which referred to the whole ensemble. An alignment might contain as few as three upright elements, although considerably more components were usually identified. Several criteria were used to identify alignments. The most reliable was the presence of wattle rods woven between the upright elements. In some cases where no rods remained

Table 26 Publications in the *Archaeology of York* series featuring the 16–22 Coppergate excavation

Series No	Title	Author	Date
AY 6/2	*Archaeology in the Environs of Roman York: Excavations 1976–2005*	P.J. Ottaway	2011
AY 8/4	*Aspects of Anglo-Scandinavian York*	R.A. Hall *et al.*	2004
AY 10/6	*Medieval Urbanism in Coppergate: Refining a Townscape*	R.A. Hall and K. Hunter-Mann	2004
AY 14/7	*Biological Evidence from 16–22 Coppergate*	H.K. Kenward and A.R. Hall	1995
AY 15/3	*Bones from Anglo-Scandinavian Levels at 16–22 Coppergate*	T.P. O'Connor	1989
AY 15/5	*Bones from Medieval Deposits in York*	J.M. Bond and T.P. O'Connor	1999
AY 16/5	*Anglo-Scandinavian Pottery from Coppergate*	A.J. Mainman	1990
AY 16/8	*Roman Pottery from York*	J. Monaghan	1997
AY 16/9	*Medieval Pottery from York*	A.J. Mainman and A. Jenner	2013
AY 17/5	*Textiles, Cordage and Raw Fibre from 16–22 Coppergate*	P. Walton	1989
AY 17/6	*Anglo-Scandinavian Ironwork from Coppergate*	P.J. Ottaway	1992
AY 17/7	*Non-Ferrous Metalworking from Coppergate*	J. Bayley	1992
AY 17/8	*The Anglian Helmet from Coppergate*	D. Tweddle	1992
AY 17/11	*Textile Production at 16–22 Coppergate*	P. Walton Rogers	1997
AY 17/12	*Bone and Antler from Anglo-Scandinavian and Medieval York*	A. MacGregor, A.J. Mainman and N.S.H. Rogers	1999
AY 17/13	*Wood and Woodworking from Anglo-Scandinavian and Medieval York*	C.A. Morris	2000
AY 17/14*	*Finds from Anglo-Scandinavian York*	A.J. Mainman and N.S.H. Rogers	2000
AY 17/15*	*Medieval Finds from York*	P.J. Ottaway and N.S.H. Rogers	2002
AY 17/16*	*Leather and Leatherworking from Anglo-Scandinavian and Medieval York*	Q. Mould, I. Carlisle and E. Cameron	2003
AY 18/1	*Post-Roman Coins from York Excavations 1971–1981*	E.J.E. Pirie	1986

*Publications available to download from the York Archaeological Trust website

540

in situ, other characteristics indicated that a series of uprights might be grouped together and considered as an alignment. These characteristics included the linear positioning of uprights; their simultaneous or nearly simultaneous exposure as overlying soil layers were excavated; and near uniformity in their absolute height. The case for such a grouping together would be further strengthened when the uprights in question were regular in their form, size and spacing, and/or when they defined a boundary between recognisably distinct deposits to either side.

Some of the alignments recognised during the excavation had both stakes and posts attributed to them; post-excavation analysis has sometimes re-attributed such diverse elements to separate alignments, unless there is compelling evidence, such as interwoven wattle rods, to demonstrate that they were integral.

The circumstances of excavation mean that what may be component parts of an individual alignment were sometimes exposed months or even years apart, and recorded under separate alignment numbers. Here, a single number has been used for each integral alignment.

In terms of integrating and analysing the overall stratigraphic record, the principal difficulty encountered during excavation and analysis concerned posts or stakes with no apparent posthole or construction trench to provide a guide to the layer into which they had been inserted. Sometimes the disposition of adjacent layers provided a clue, but there remain very many instances where stratigraphic certainty is not possible. Later intrusions of all sorts cut into alignments, while decay of individual elements and stretches of alignments compounded the difficulties, as did the essential similarity of many of the layers of dark brown peaty loam, which were often differentiated only by the most subtle variations of colour, texture or content.

Stakes (as opposed to posts) are defined in site records as upright timbers with a maximum cross-sectional dimension not exceeding 50mm; the vast majority had a circular cross-section and retained their bark. Posts are defined as upright timbers of larger scantling, which may or may not have been dressed. The term beam is used here for a substantial squared horizontal timber, whereas a plank is a horizontal timber that is relatively thin in relation to its width. A plank positioned vertically as a structural member is here termed a stave.

Historical Context

The historical evidence for York in the Anglo-Scandinavian period, including the sources and how they can be used and interpreted, has been described elsewhere in this volume of *The Archaeology of York* (Rollason in *AY* 8/4, 305–24) while the sources themselves have been presented and discussed in Volume 1 of *The Archaeology of York* (*AY* 1). The reader is referred to these publications for a survey and discussion of what historical sources can reveal about the city during this period but a basic time line is presented here.

Table 27 Historical Events in York

Date	Events
866	Viking Great Army captures York
876	Viking Great Army settles in Yorkshire
876–927	Viking kings rule York
927–39	English king controls York
939–54	English, Dublin Vikings and Scandinavians compete for power in York
954	Expulsion of Eric Bloodaxe, last Viking king of York
954–1066	English control York through earls and archbishops
1066	Battles of Fulford and Stamford Bridge
1069	William the Conqueror subdues York

Period 3

2010

2002

2061　2165

1986

1976

1687

Site N

N

post-hole
pit
scoop
gully
wood

Pit 1778

0	10	20	30 metres

0	50	100 feet

Fig.136 *Plan of 16–22 Coppergate and the watching brief showing Period 3 activity. Scale 1:250*

Periods 2 and 3
Introduction

Richard Hall left an advanced, but incomplete, text relating to these two initial post-Roman periods, highlighting the questions he hoped to resolve and with the bare bones of a discussion. Where possible the queries have been addressed and the results are incorporated into the text below, together with additional information gleaned from specialist reports. The discussion which follows puts flesh on the bones of his draft text, following the themes he had indicated, drawing inspiration from his published works and from conversations between himself and other colleagues, and combining these with the results of new research.

Period 2 represents a period of post-Roman abandonment. While there is no evidence for occupation on the site between the 5th and the 9th centuries there are indications that there was activity in the area prior to the second half of the 9th century when the first property boundaries were established. The division between Periods 2 and 3 must, therefore, be seen as ill-defined. It seems likely that there was activity on the higher ground, along the course of what was to become the street of Coppergate, a century or so before the street itself existed, and possibly on the excavated area; and the evidence indicates an intensification throughout the 9th century. A case can be made for occupation in the form of putative structures and pits containing both human waste and a range of domestic and industrial debris in the decades before the arrival of the Viking Great Army in 866 and, as was the case in the late Roman period, the site was used sporadically for the interment of the dead. These burials have recently been dated by C14 (see pp.719–22); as these results were not available when the draft text was written, new sections of text have been added discussing their implications.

Restraints of time and resources meant that it was not possible to investigate the entire excavation area down to the earliest levels. Two adjoining areas, together forming an L-shaped cross-section through the site's main axes, were excavated down to and through levels ascribed to Period 3 (Figs 133 and 136). They were 35m long north–south and c.20m west–east, and were each c.9–10m wide, sloping down at gradients of approximately 1 in 10 towards the River Foss, and approximately 1 in 20 from west to east, away from the ridge along which the street Nessgate/Castlegate runs (see Fig.131).

Excavation showed that after Romano-British occupation (Period 1) (*AY* 6/2) the area had been virtually abandoned for some four centuries (Period 2). During this time soils accumulated for depths of up to 0.85m (Fig.137), masking the Roman deposits which had incorporated parts of at least two stone structures. One of them, towards the north-western part of the site, was represented only by robbing trench 31754 (*AY* 6/2, 211, fig.139). It appeared to have been thoroughly demolished in the Roman era, is sealed by Period 2 deposits, and therefore had no effect whatever on subsequent developments. Traces of a more recognisable structure further to the south included both robbing trenches (e.g. 28039) and short lengths of surviving foundations and footings capped by up to three courses of stonework (Figs 138 and 139).

Three factors make it difficult to separate with certainty the layers of Roman, Anglian and early Anglo-Scandinavian date around this structure (*AY* 6/2, fig.138). The first is the near uniformity of layers attributed to these periods in this part of the site. The second is the high proportion of Roman pottery in the ceramic assemblage of all these layers; even contexts likely, on stratigraphic

Fig.137   *Sterile, uniform soil which built up during the Anglian period over part of a collapsed Roman building. Scale unit 0.1m*

Period 3 (front)

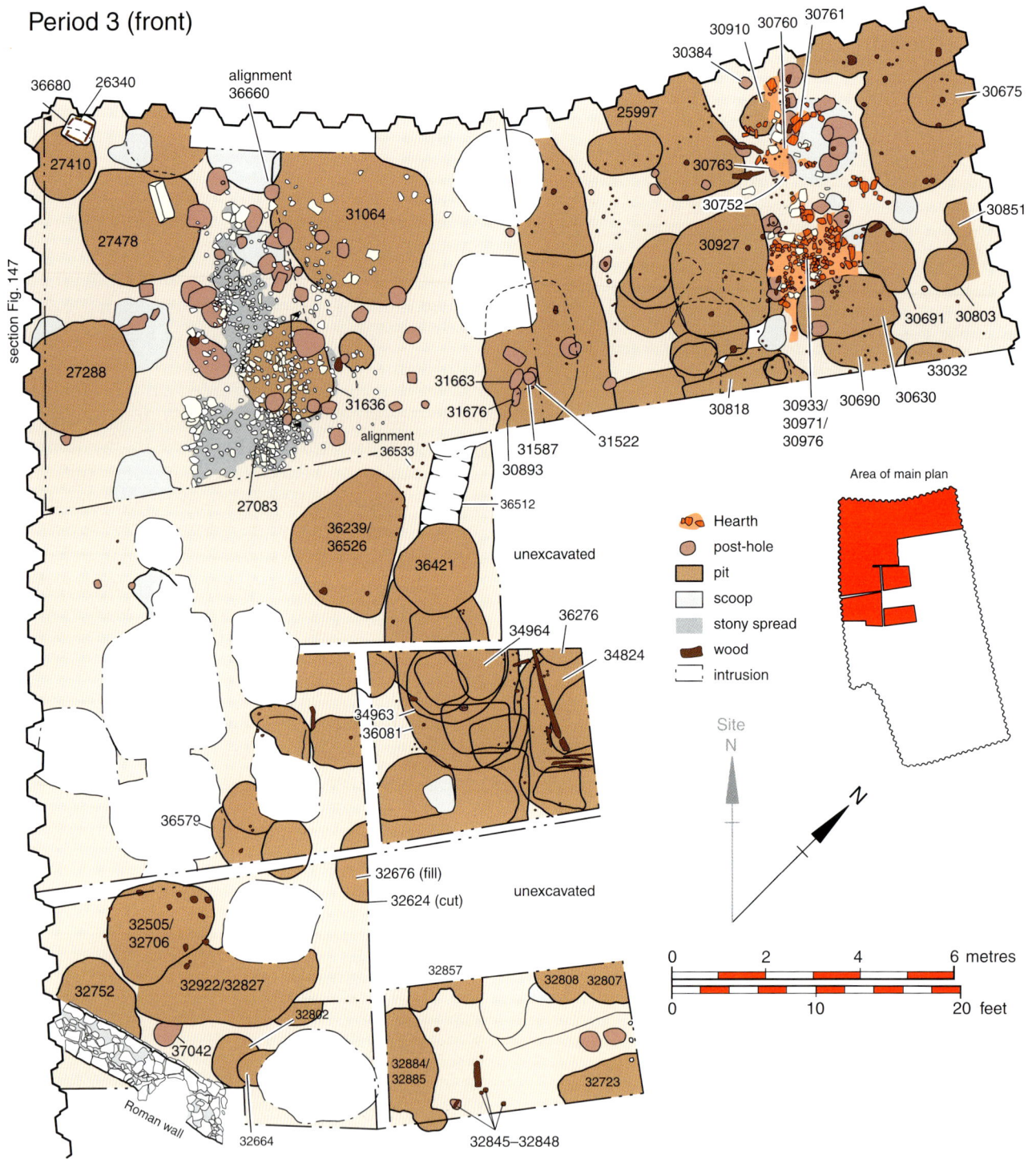

section Fig. 147

36680   26340

alignment
36660

30910 30760 30761

30384

25997

30675

27410

27478

31064

30763

30752

30851

30927

31663

31676

31587

30893

31522

31636

27288

alignment
36533

27083

36512

30818

30933/
30971/
30976

30690

30630

33032

30691 30803

36239/
36526

36421

unexcavated

34964

36276

34824

34963
36081

36579

32676 (fill)

32624 (cut)

unexcavated

32505/
32706

32752

32922/32827

32802

37042

Roman wall

32664

32857

32808 32807

32884/
32885

32723

32845–32848

Legend

Hearth

post-hole

pit

scoop

stony spread

wood

intrusion

Area of main plan

Site
N

0   2   4   6 metres

0   10   20 feet

Fig.138   *Plan of Period 3 pits and features at the front of the site. Scale 1:125*

Period 3 (rear)

Roman wall

32691

37133

3706

28542

32994

Roman wall

3731

32973

28573

32918

28190

28385

28355

26943

28387

3700/3717

28065

28038

28039

28958

28777

24950
36682
28039

26787

26789

26014

26784

26709

26221

27070

28283

28050

26708

26713

20581

26714

27225

27228

28446

alignment 28199

28324

gravel

28794

alignment 36683

Area of main plan

post-hole
pit
scoop
stony spread
wood

Site
N

0 — 0
2
10
4
20 — 6
feet metres

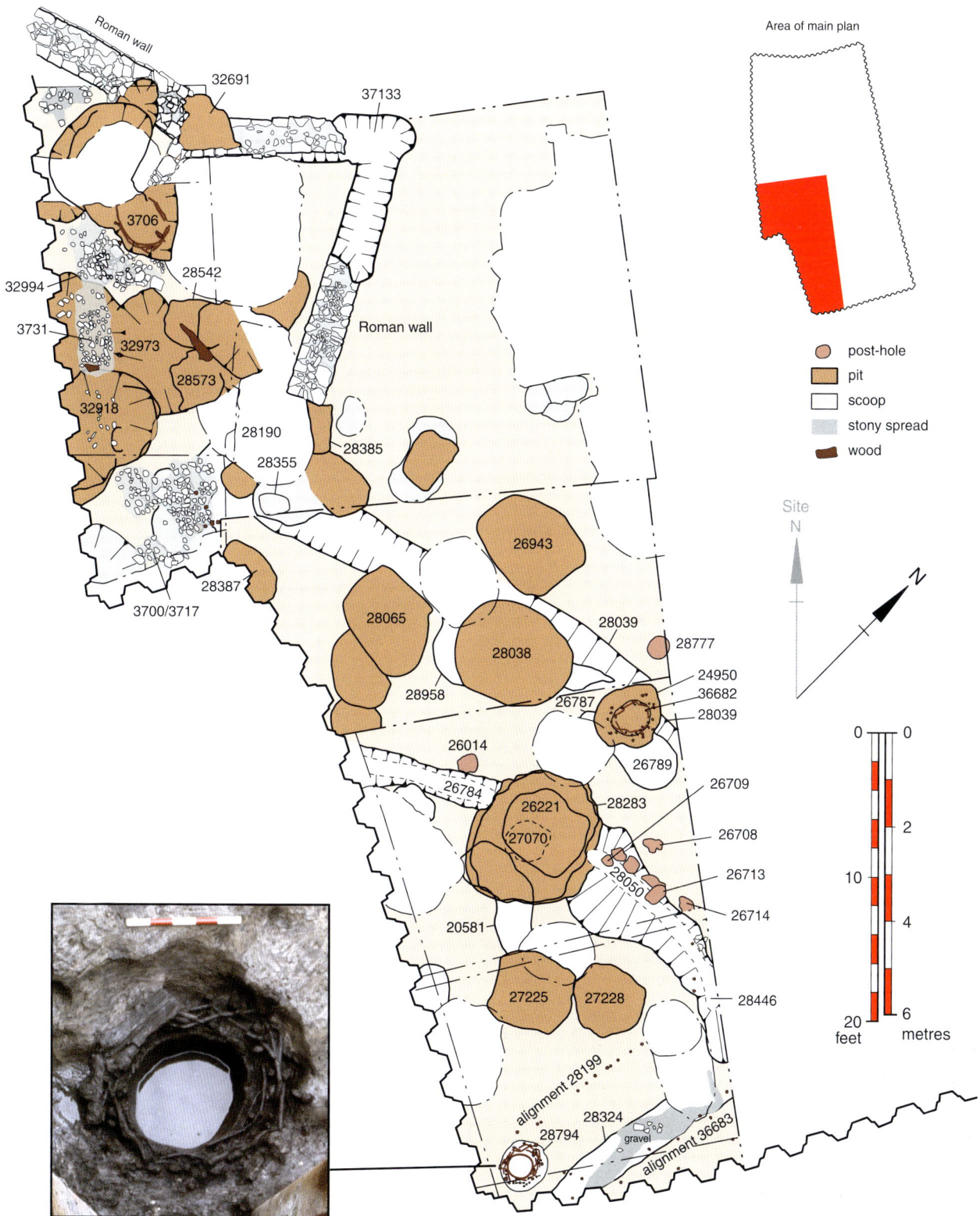

Fig.139 *Plan of Period 3 pits and features at the rear of the site; inset shows lined pit 28794. Scale 1:125*

grounds, to belong to Period 3 often contain only Roman pottery (*AY* 16/5, fig.144). Thirdly, at the southern end of the site only very shallow robber trenches were encountered, cut directly into or from only just above natural soil; this may suggest that the upper parts of these trenches and adjacent stratification had been removed in a large-scale earth-moving operation of unknown purpose.

Given all these circumstances, it is impossible to make definitive statements about the date of the robbing episodes, although it appears that at least some of them may have taken place immediately before the later 9th-century activity described below, rather than when plots were established in the 10th century. Indeed, the division between the robbed portion of the Roman building and the structure still partially surviving *in situ* does not correspond to the 10th-century plot boundary, as might be expected if robbing was later than the establishment of the boundary. Those parts of the Roman building which were upstanding in the south-west were sealed by accumulating deposits during either Period 3 or Period 4, but they can have protruded only marginally above the late 9th- or early 10th-century ground surface, and will not have affected development in their vicinity.

The main focus of activity in the mid-9th century appeared to be on the higher ground in the northern part of the excavated area, along what was to become the Coppergate street frontage. It was marked by a transition from the uniform, mid- to dark grey-coloured silty clay loams which represent the Anglian era to a build up of predominantly dark or dirty grey silty clay loams, within which a sequence of features could be isolated (Figs 138 and 150).

One of the earliest of these, if not the very first, was a shallow cut 33252, probably originally circular in shape, in the north-east corner of the site. It marked the primary phase in a series of intercut hollows, the largest of which was over 2m in diameter and up to 0.2m deep. The depressions

Fig.140   Shallow trenches defining the area of hearth 30761. Scale unit 100mm

were filled with mixed layers of ash, charcoal and clay loam that frequently showed signs of heat. At least three principal recuttings could be identified; it seems that smaller and, in the case of cut 30910 (Fig.138), deeper cuttings on the north side of the complex alternated with large depressions to the south. In the same area, a number of post-holes contemporary with one or other of these recut depressions were also recognised, although not all existed simultaneously, and later intrusions may well have obliterated others. Approximately 1m to the south of this complex was a broadly contemporary surface or surfaces of generally small limestone rubble and tile fragments (30971), with some slightly larger fragments at the base (30933/30976) (Fig.138). The surface was cut away in places by intrusions, particularly at its southern end. Further to the south some of the larger pits which can be assigned to the late 9th century may have co-existed with the features described above, but intrusions combine with the lack of precisely datable associated artefacts to make certainty impossible.

Above the uppermost of the depressions a small area of clay had been deposited, into which were

Fig. 141 *Glass fragments found near the Period 3 hearth*

set re-used Roman tiles (30761). They had marked traces of burning on their upper faces. To the north, east and south there were slight indications of shallow trenches defining a sub-rectangular area which enclosed the tiles, which have associated post-holes, for example 30764, at opposite ends of the gullies (Fig.140).

Fig.142 *Hearth 30933/30971 cut by burial 30944. Scale unit 0.1m*

The process for which this sequence of features formed the setting clearly involved the use of intense heat; they can be interpreted as representing successive hearths, kilns or ovens. A cache of 29 small fragments of glass was found in a spread of sandy clay (30752, Fig.138) just off the south-west corner of the tile setting in the uppermost hearth. The fragments (shown on Fig.141) include pieces of Roman vessel glass, a possible Roman gaming counter, and several threads and blobs of glass. The latter have been identified as waste from glass melting (Bayley 1987, 254), and the whole cache suggests that waste glass was being collected, presumably for remelting. It is possible, therefore, that the succession of hearths and the associated features may represent the structural setting for the recycling of cullet. Scientific dating evidence for this activity comes from a thermoremnant magnetic determination taken from context 30760, a layer forming part of one of the recuttings in the middle of the sequence of hearths. This has provided a date of c.AD 860 ± 20, and thus indicates that the hearth and its associated features were in use in the mid- to later 9th century, although whether before or after the Viking seizure of York in 866 is impossible to say.

Relatively soon, perhaps immediately, after the latest of the hearths had fallen into disuse, a phase of pit digging in their immediate vicinity began, and pits were also dug further to the west (Fig.138). In some cases later Anglo-Scandinavian and medieval activity had disturbed and destroyed many of the upper layers of pits and deposits, and there was a great deal of recutting and intercutting across much of the site, while in other areas later intrusions had removed all deposits relating to this period.

Two of the earliest of these north-eastern pits, lying within 1m of each other, contained human remains, and the fragmentary, disarticulated remains of another skeleton were recovered from a third pit. Skeleton 30944 lay in the southern part of a large but relatively shallow sub-rectangular cut with steeply sloping sides, 30927, with maximum dimensions of 2.4 x 2.1 x 0.4m (Figs 138 and 142). The skeleton lay on an approximately east–west alignment (40° east of true north), with its skull at the east. The legs were slightly flexed, as was the right arm; the left arm was found in an unusual position, with the hand below the skull and the radius/ulna and humerus forming two sides of an upstanding inverted V of bone with the elbow joint at its apex (Figs 143 and 146). The right femur was found lying above the flexed right arm, its head at the right shoulder and its distal part just above the wrist. The right half of the pelvis lay inverted beyond the right elbow, and some of the metatarsals were also found displaced. The absence of disturbance to the bones immediately adjacent to these indicates that displacement occurred after linking

Fig.143   Skeleton 30944. Scale unit 0.1m

Fig.144   *Skeleton 30979. Scale unit 0.1m*

Fig.145   *Skeleton 36318. Scale unit 0.1m*

tissue had decayed. A raking cut from foot to pelvis and beyond, continuing just above the right arm, could have disturbed and redeposited these bones, but no such cut was detected archaeologically. The skeleton was initially identified by Mrs J. Dawes as that of a male aged 35–45 and further analysis by Malin Holst confirmed this: 'The dental wear, rib ossification and left auricular surface suggested an age of 36–45 years, whereas the right auricular surface and pubic symphyses suggested an age of 26–35 years. Considering the widespread degenerative joint disease in this individual, it was decided that the older age was more plausible, indicating that this was an old middle adult' (see below, p.725). Holst went on to confirm that it was a male of 1.615m

(± 29.9mm) height who also suffered from osteoarthritis and exhibited congenital abnormalities. Fragmentary textile remains found adhering to the mandible and extending over the area of the chest and below the vertebrae and scapulae are discussed in *AY* 17/5 (pp.331–2, fig.138); they may represent a garment or shroud placed around the body before burial. None of the other artefacts found in the pit could be associated definitively with the skeleton.

Approximately 1.8m to the south, and largely inaccessible below an unexcavated area, part of a second skeleton, 30979 (Figs 144 and 146), lay within a shallow declivity or cut 30818 (Fig.138). Apparently articulate, it was aligned approximately

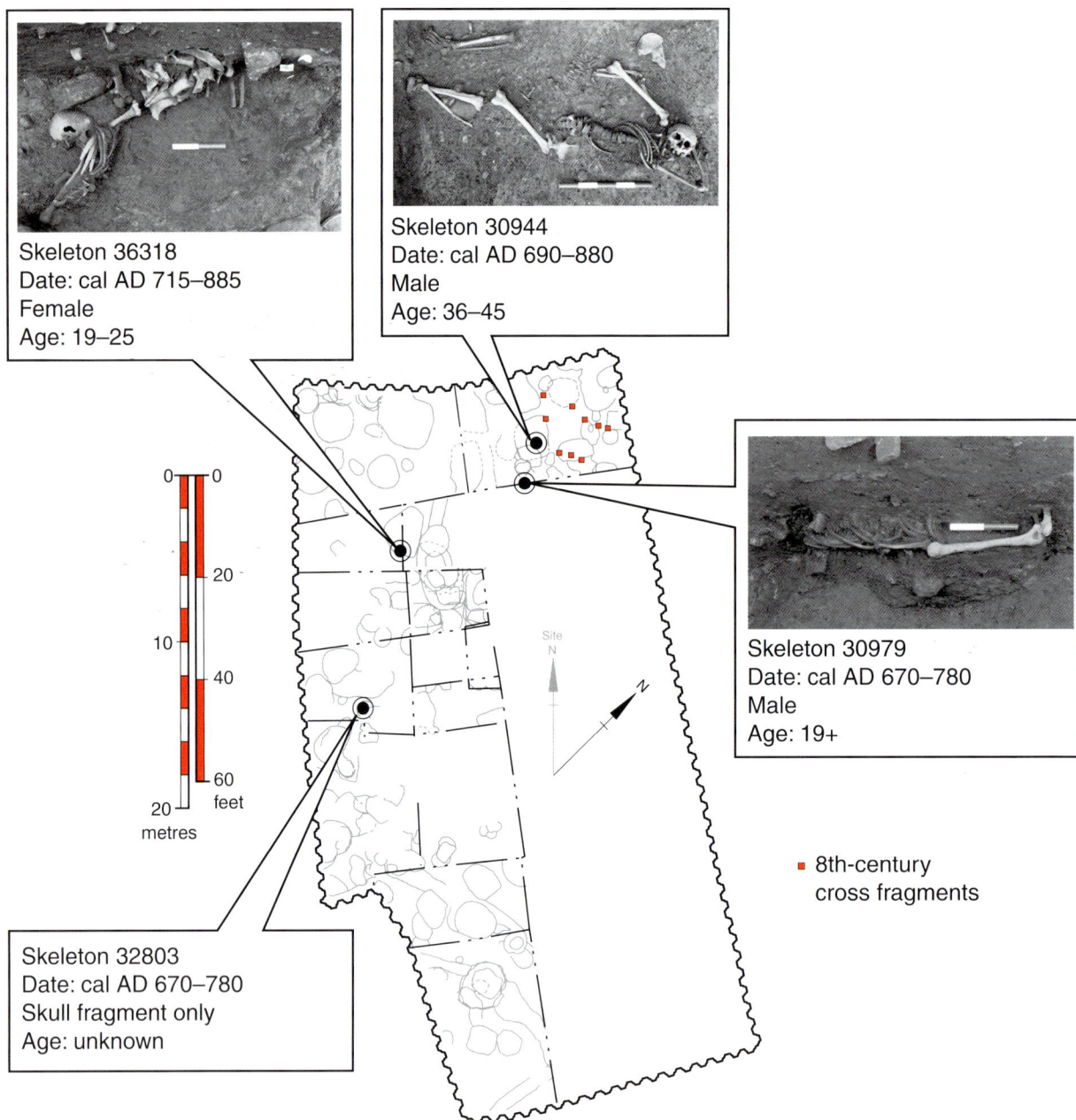

Skeleton 36318
Date: cal AD 715–885
Female
Age: 19–25

Skeleton 30944
Date: cal AD 690–880
Male
Age: 36–45

Skeleton 30979
Date: cal AD 670–780
Male
Age: 19+

Skeleton 32803
Date: cal AD 670–780
Skull fragment only
Age: unknown

■ 8th-century
cross fragments

0
0
20
10
40
60
feet
20
metres

Site
N

Fig.146   *Location of early burials (scale 1:400), also showing distribution of late 8th-/early 9th-century stone cross fragments*

east–west (20° east of true north); the skull, if present, would have been to the site west. Only some ribs, part of a clavicle, a humerus and the proximal/distal ends of a radius and ulna were exposed, with the upper arm extending back beyond the head and the fore-arm bent at an angle to it (Fig.144). On the evidence of the humerus, which was fully fused, this individual was aged nineteen years or older and the humeral head suggested a male (see below, pp.725–6).

Further west, portions of a third skeleton, 36318, identified as the cranium, upper arms and trunk of a possible female aged 19–25 years (see pp.725–6), were found in another partially excavated pit (36239, Fig.138), 7m to the south-west of skeleton 30979 (Figs 145 and 146). This pit, like the others, was considered as belonging to the late 9th century. The disturbed condition of these remains shows that they are not precisely *in situ*, but their condition suggests that the original burial position was close by. A fragment of a skull (skeleton 32803), found in the base of a Period 3 pit (Fig.146), was also recovered from the centre of the site, towards the western edge of the shoring.

Since this text was drafted these skeletons have been subjected to C14 dating, refined using Bayesian analysis, and the results indicate that they could be earlier than had previously been thought. Figure 146 shows their distribution across the site and gives a summary of gender, age and date. Details of the analysis appear in the Radiocarbon Dating Report (pp.719–22) and the implication of these new dates for the interpretation of the burials is included in the discussion section below (pp.560–1).

In addition to the human remains noted above, several isolated human bones or small groups of bones were retrieved from 10th-century levels in the centre and south-west of the site, which was occupied at that time by the backyards of plots. They were principally limb bones, from a minimum of one man, one woman, one young man and one adolescent or juvenile. Their source was not identifiable, and while the disturbance of further graves in the small Roman cemetery is one possibility (see AY 6/2, 214–17), some may have derived from other unlocated burials of Anglian and Anglo-Scandinavian date.

The two semi-articulated skeletons, 30944 and 30979, were both recovered from features slightly later than the latest phase of the hearths that had the archaeomagnetic determination of c.860 ± 20 (see p.561 for further discussion). Both had been placed not in purpose-dug graves but in pits already opened for some other reason; this is indicated by the shape of the cut or by the nature of the layers covering the human remains. Skeletons 30944 and 30979, although close to each other and apparently contemporary, were buried at alignments varying by 20°, and were apparently placed with their heads at opposite ends.

This small number of pre-Scandinavian burials at Coppergate might be explained by their being on the periphery of a cemetery that had its focus beyond the excavated area. Such a cemetery might have been associated with the church of All Saints, Pavement, which lies on the opposite side of the modern street of Coppergate (Fig.131, 5). Traces of

a small, possibly two-cell church, tentatively dated to the 10th century, have been uncovered in investigations below the western end of the present south aisle (Paula Ware, pers. comm.), just 25m from the Coppergate burials. There is, however, no known structural evidence for any earlier church building, notwithstanding speculations based on the inscription of the 8th-century Anglo-Saxon helmet (Binns *et al.* 1990). An early foundation, however, provides a context for a late 9th- to mid-10th-century grave cover recovered, upside-down, from the fabric of the vestry during its demolition (Lang 1991, 79–80) and, perhaps, for other sculptural evidence recovered on site (see Fig.324).

Alternatively these rather scattered burials could be unassociated with any churchyard which would by no means be unusual at this time (Hadley and Buckberry 2005, 126–7). In that way they may be compared to those from Dublin (McMahon 2002) although the phenomenon of Scandinavian settlers interring individuals close to settlements, but not in regular or long-lived cemeteries, is also known from rural sites in the York area such as Riccall (Hall, 2002, 5; Hall 2005, 1–4). The use of irregular, pre-existing cuts to house the Coppergate burials, however, raises one important point. The pits in which the corpses were placed do not have the regularity of purpose-dug graves, and the burial rites, as represented both by these pits and by the orientation and disposition of the corpses within them, appear irregular and improvised. A 'cleaning up' operation after large-scale violence suggests itself as one set of circumstances that might have necessitated such an unusual approach to burial. The *Anglo-Saxon Chronicle*'s description of the Northumbrian counter-attack on the Vikings in York 867 tells how they '…gathered a great army and sought out the raiding army … at York city and broke into the city, and some of them got inside, and an immense slaughter was made of the Northumbrians there, some inside and some outside …' (Swanton 1996, 69). This disastrous enterprise may have left numerous corpses in the city to be disposed of in the summary fashion recognised in these skeletons, although there might equally have been other, clandestine or unrecorded, slayings earlier in the 9th century which would also have prompted hasty burial of the type implied by the archaeological evidence here, and any connection with the documented events is speculative.

The dates now available for these burials do just about allow for this interpretation in the case of 30944 (cal AD 690–880, see Table 31), but the weight of probability is that these burials are earlier, and this is certainly the case with skeletons 32803 and 30979 (both cal AD 670–780). See discussion below (p.561).

A series of other pits, contemporary with and slightly later than the pits containing skeletons, were mostly circular in shape, e.g. 27288, 31636 and 27410 (Figs 138 and 147). They were not all open simultaneously; some shows signs of recutting, others seem to have been sealed quickly, while others were left open long enough to be colonised by abundant beetles and flies (*AY* 14/7, 528). Pit 27478 (Fig.138), although containing no pottery, was notable for having at its base a human skull, almost certainly from a disturbed Roman skeleton 34147A which

lay within the contiguous Roman grave 34133 (*AY* 6/2, 215, fig.141). The pit also contained a large rectangular limestone block, presumably from an adjacent Roman structure. Wedged below the block was a length of wood which may have been used by stone robbers in an attempt to lever the block out of the pit (cf. a 12th-/13th-century instance noted at The Bedern, York; *AY* 3/3, 171–2, fig.101). Where such recycled stone would have been deployed is an interesting question, with church building being perhaps the most obvious answer.

Most of these pits contained fill layers which, on the basis of their colour, texture and aroma, were interpreted during excavation as cess. Subsequently, study of the insect, plant and parasite remains in these pit fill layers has confirmed that in many cases they comprise, *inter alia*, deposits of human faeces, animal manure, and the sweepings from houses or

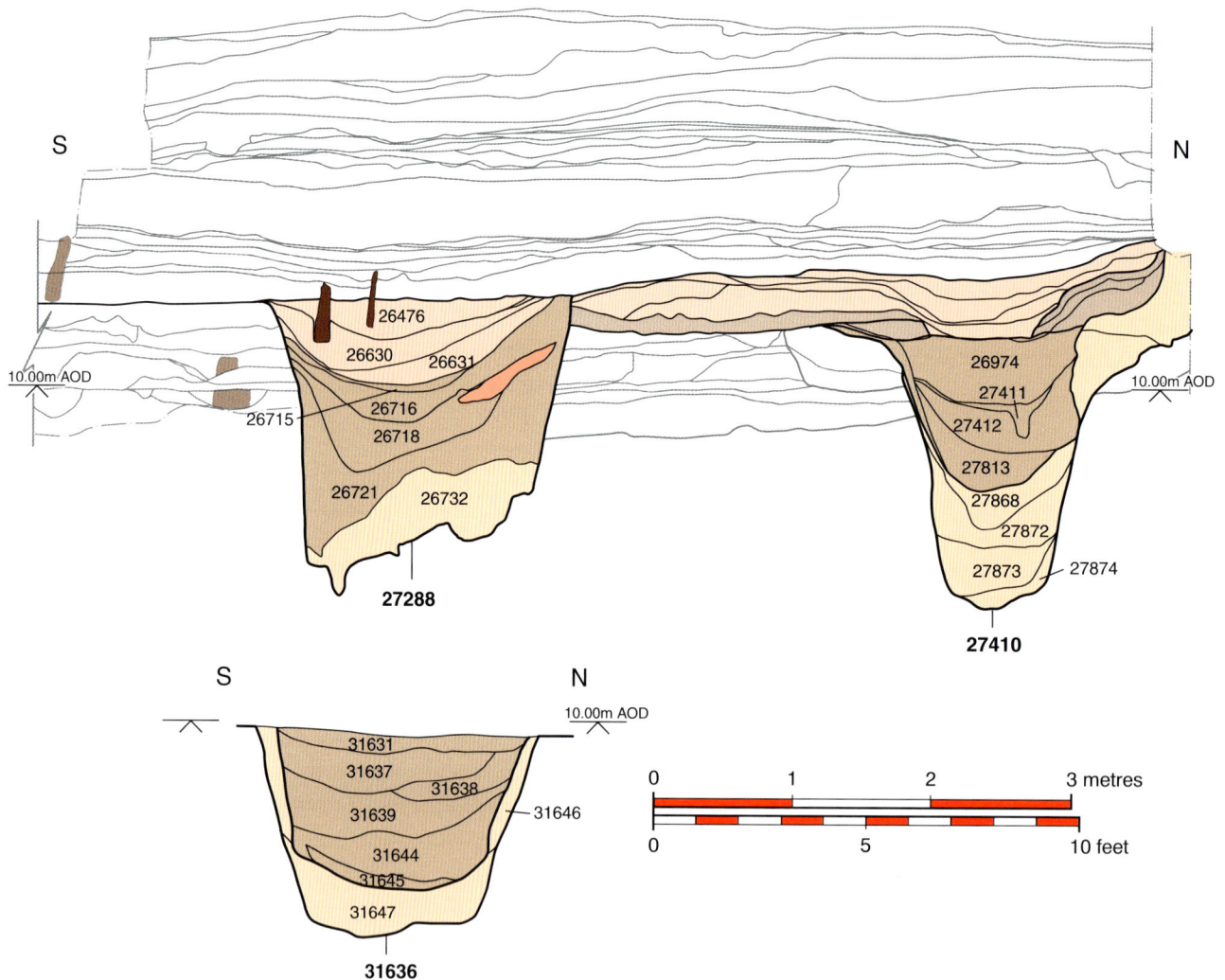

Fig.147   *Sections through pits 27288, 27410 and 31636 (for plan see Fig.138). Scale 1:50*

animal pens (*AY* 14/7, 514ff), indicative of occupation nearby. Some of the pits, particularly those with wattle linings, for example 34824 and 36276 (Fig.138), may have been constructed specifically to serve as open-air latrines (*ibid*, 748) and contained little other than cess; post-holes observed in the section of, for example, 27410 and 27288 (Figs 138 and 147) might have served to support toilet seats. Other pits may have been dug for other particular purposes that cannot now be detected, and yet others dug for the disposal of more general rubbish (see pp.559–60).

Unique on the excavation site among the features of this date was a cut, 36680, dug into the backfill of pit 27410, and lined with a 0.45m square wooden shaft 26340 (Fig.138). It was just under half the size of the undated but similarly lined pit at the riverward end of the site which contained the Coppergate Anglian helmet, a pit which is tentatively identified as a well (*AY* 17/8, 864–81) (Fig.148). In the case of 36680, however, both its smaller dimensions and the fact that its abutted sides survived to a maximum height of 0.19m suggest that it was constructed for some function other than as a well. The shaft's charcoal fill, 26202, contained a Roman tile recut to make a mould for casting metal-working blanks (*AY* 17/7, 771, 831, *3991*). No other contemporary infrastructural traces that could be associated with metal working were detected, although at a slightly later date a small, shapeless tile setting surrounded by ash, 24418 (not shown on plan), 2.8m southeast of the shaft and also above the remains of an infilled pit (27478), may have been a hearth. Artefactual evidence (*AY* 17/7, fig.329) indicates that low-intensity non-ferrous metal working may have taken place on this part of the site at this date. These pits in the north-west corner are broadly contemporary with a group of post-holes to their east (which include 31584, 31585, 31599, and 31600 and which varied in depth from 80 to 310mm) (Fig.150).

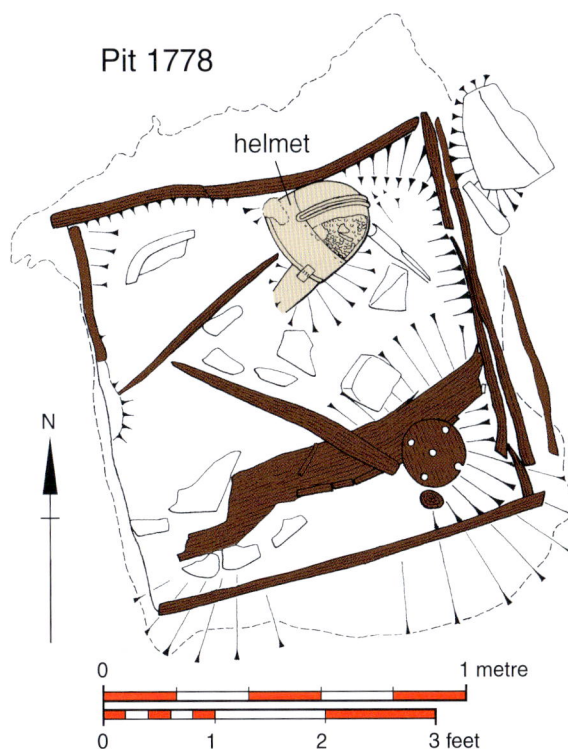

All these features were earlier than a stone spread in the north-west corner of the site incorporating cobbles, limestone rubble and occasional fragments of Roman tile as well as sporadic animal bones (27083; Fig.138), which had been truncated to the south by the construction pit for a later 10th-century building (Structure 5/1, p.614ff). In the base of this cut, however, a small spread of limestone rubble and cobbles 26204 was discov-

Pit 1778

helmet

N

| 0 | | | 1 metre |

| 0 | 1 | 2 | 3 feet |

Fig.148   *Photograph and plan of pit 1778 in which the Anglian helmet was found (for location see Fig.136). Plan scale 1:20*

ered at approximately the same height as 27083, overlying the slumped uppermost fill of pit 27478 (Fig.149). This may indicate that the rubble originally extended north across this area. The rubble 27083 was placed around or was immediately cut by a further series of posts and post-holes (alignment 36660) (Figs 149 and 150) which, like the rubble itself, was concentrated at the west end of the excavated strip.

The post-holes and possible alignments have been extracted from Figure 138 for clarity and are shown separately from the various pits, spreads and intrusions which challenge interpretation; they are shown on Figure 150. This helps to demonstrate that for 7–8m to the east of alignment 36660 there was an area within which there were relatively few contemporary features other than shallow scoops together with a scatter of small, relatively shallow post-holes, all less than 0.2m deep, and a shallow arc of stakes against the northern limit of excavation (30127). A scatter of other stakes, small post-holes and occasional small rubble formed no recognisable features.

Other than an alignment of stakes 30791, discussed with Period 4A, this relatively feature-less area had as its eastern limit another post-hole alignment 33239, made up of two sections, and a cluster of stake-holes (33248, in the northern section) (Figs 150 and 151), which ran back from the modern street line at approximately a right-angle

Fig.149   Limestone spread 27083 and post-hole alignment 36660 over slumped uppermost fill of pit 27478. Scale unit 0.1m

to the street frontage. At one point a noticeable gap approximately 0.75m wide suggested a traverse through the alignment. This was subsequently infilled by some of the stakes in a secondary align-ment (indicated by the white labels on Fig.151) that followed the same course and the more southerly section of alignment 33239. Some of the post-holes in 33239 intercut, and several phases were clearly represented. The post-holes varied in shape and profile, were up to 0.5m or more in width and were mostly 0.2–0.5m deep. Posts, principally of sub-rectangular section, and measuring up to 0.25m x 0.08m, remained in only a few instances, including each of the three northernmost holes in the align-ment where they had been sharpened to points and driven up to 0.23m through the base of the post-hole. Their preservation, along with the absence of any indication of decayed timber in the other post-holes, suggests that the majority of posts had been deliberately removed. The surviving posts, where identifiable, were either of oak (*Quercus*) or alder (*Alnus*), with the occasional hazel (*Corylus*).

Immediately to the east was another series of post-holes 33247, centred up to 1m from 33239 (Fig.150), and with an even wider gap between the northern and southern sections of the alignment. These post-holes, which were also intercut and of at least two phases, were generally rather smaller and shallower than those in 33239; one contained traces of limestone rubble packing. Some were cut into the backfill of a slightly earlier pit, 30630; the entire north-easterly group of pits and scoops, which included 30630 as well as 30675, 30690, 30691 and 33032 (Fig.138), was relatively late in the sequence of features which preceded the post-holes. None of these pits, however, was contemporary with or later than the post-holes, thus emphasising the change of land-use from random pit digging to the establish-ment of early alignments which the stakes and post-holes represent.

To the east of post-hole alignments 33239 and 33247, close to the eastern limit of excavation, other post-holes were discovered, the most northerly being 30743 and the southerly twin posts 30457 and 30458 (Fig.150), and there were also a number of surviving posts and stakes. Some of these are posi-tioned in such a way as to raise the possibility that a rectilinear structure incorporating either 33239 and/or 33247 stood in the north-east corner of the

Period 3

a

alignment
36660

31584

31600   31585

31599

30384   30447   30870   30743

33252   30457/8

30763   30764

30763

31663
31676   30266
31587   31522

0   2   4   6 metres
0   10   20 feet

b

33239
33248

30791

36660   30127

33245
30792   33247

37138

33239

Site
N

N

30791
30792
33239
33245
33247
33248
36660
37138

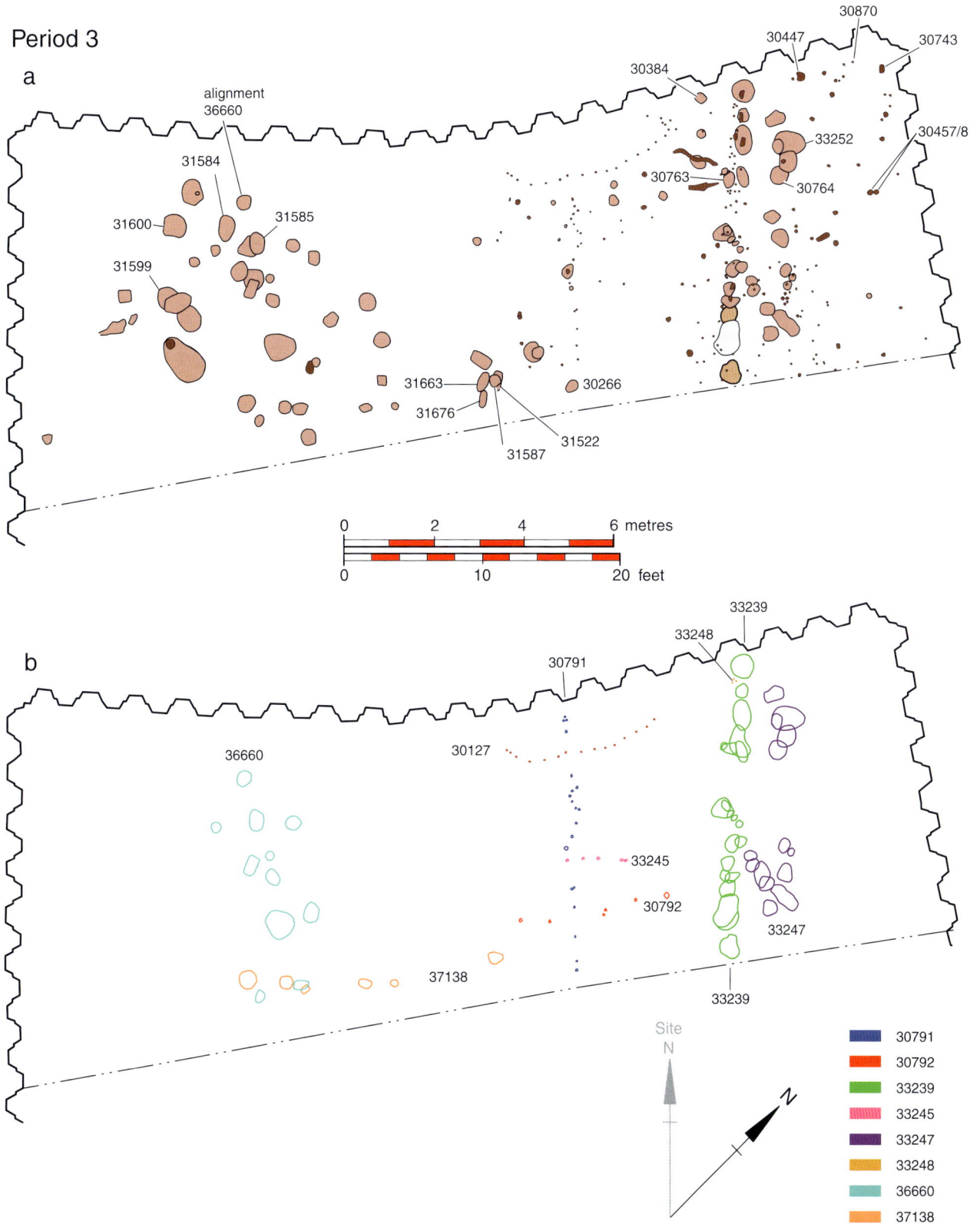

Fig.150   *Plans of (a) Period 3 post-holes; (b) Period 3 alignments. Scale 1:125*

555

excavated area. Perhaps other posts represent an internal division, or just conceivably an eastern wall, although this might more likely lie outside the area of excavation. A row of posts against the north section of shoring, incorporating 30384 and 30447 (Fig.150), might also have conceivably functioned as part of the structure. Many stakes were also planted at this time, although it is impossible to say which were contemporary since they were almost all simply rammed into the ground. They cannot be grouped convincingly into features, although there was a noticeable concentration at the north-east of the excavated area.

The absence of contemporary pits, other than shallow scoops, is particularly noticeable in the 7–8m between alignment 33239 and the alignment/group 36660, and it is possible that either or both of them were part of a structure occupying this area. A probable post-hole alignment (37138) (Fig.150) ran parallel to the Coppergate frontage for a distance

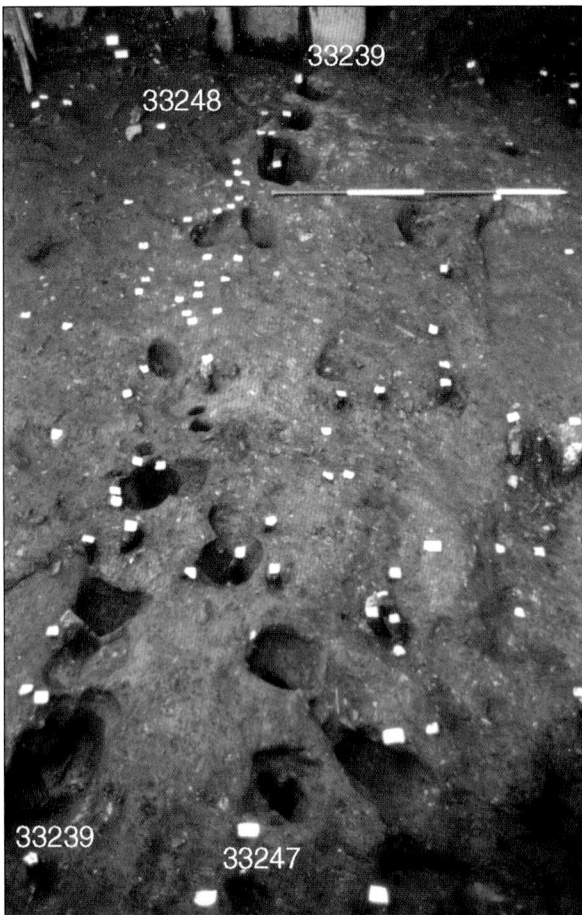

Fig.151   *Post-hole alignments 33239 and 33247 to the east of the street frontage area. Scale unit 0.5m*

of approximately 5.5m, ceasing to be readily identifiable beyond the group of post-holes cut into a shallow scoop 30893 (Fig.138) which includes post-hole 31676 (Fig.150), although there is one post-hole further east, 30266. This could perhaps have formed the southern wall of a structure in this area, although neither floor levels nor any other distinguishing feature was identified 'within' the possible building.

To the south-west was another featureless area, wedge-shaped, curtailed along one long side by the site's perimeter and on the other by a concentration of often intercutting pits. It was, however, considerably disturbed by later intrusions which might, of course, have removed traces of features of Period 3. Once again, there is no supporting evidence to confirm the presence of a building, nor any indication why this area was apparently undisturbed at this time.

Among the features defining the eastern side of this featureless area was 36512 (Fig.138), a short length of a shallow gully, 0.1–0.19m deep, interrupted at both ends by other cuts, and accompanied by stake alignment 36533. Contemporary pits here and to the south were usually sub-circular or sub-rectangular in shape and of varying sizes. Some, e.g. 36081 and 34824 (Fig.138), contained traces of a stake-and-wattle lining, although usually only the stake elements survived. Larger upright posts, sometimes in recognisable pairs or triplets, were also noted in some pits, for example in 36239, 34963 and 36579 (single), while in 32505 there was a cluster of posts (Fig.138). Intercuttings and later intrusions which have removed parts of many of the other pits may have removed similar uprights; this inhibits comparison and hinders interpretation of these post groupings. Furthermore, as the posts appear normally to have been driven rather than placed in post-holes, pits and posts usually cannot be associated firmly through stratification.

Since there are some examples of broadly similar but unexplained post groupings found without any associated pit (for example, that which includes posts 32845–32848; Fig.138), it may sometimes be fortuitous that post groupings are located within earlier pits. Nonetheless, two- or three-post clusters are found within pits with sufficient frequency, both in this period and later, to indicate that they were often deliberately placed there. It is suggested that they may have supported a seat over a cess-pit, and analysis of the pit fills supports this interpretation. Pits 27491 and 31154, both in late Period 4A (see p.561 and Fig.134), are the best examples of pits with post groups.

Another notable feature, found over the top of pit 34824 (Fig.138), consisted of a horizontal setting of timber beams, only part of which was exposed within the area excavated. Two principal elements (34633 and 34636) lay one across the other at right-angles, with a group of other apparently related timbers at their west end. Timber 34636 was 0.12m square in section, with peg-holes of 20mm diameter centrally positioned at intervals varying from 30mm to 350mm, and with a shallow seating 100mm wide cut across its face at one point; a length of 2.19m lay within the excavated area. In contrast, 34633 was circular in section with a diameter of 70mm; only two peg-holes pierced it, one at the point where it oversailed 34636, the other 0.9m further along it. Some 2m to the south were further lengths of timber of similar proportions, again including pieces with peg-holes.

None of the peg-holes in any of the timbers retained pegs in place, and it is not clear whether even the principal members 34633 and 34636 are in their original position, were deliberately re-used here, or simply discarded. Squared timbers with peg-holes like 34636 were noted in later Anglo-Scandinavian contexts, forming either a foundation plate for a wattle wall (see also p.774) or parts of pegged plank pathways found in broadly similar positions relative to the street frontage (see Figs 168 and 176). It is possible that 34633 and 34636 were also the surviving parts of such a pathway, but with so limited and disturbed a fragment visible this must remain speculative. On stratigraphic grounds they seem to represent a late Period 3 or early Period 4 feature.

Towards the back of the site, as described above, lengths of Roman foundations and footings of stone may still have been visible in the south-central area during at least part of Period 3. Just west of the westernmost surviving length of Roman wall were the roots of an elder (18659), a typical urban plant of decayed, derelict, waste or underused land; in spite of this, features believed to be of Period 3 date were recovered in this vicinity. One of these lay within the area of the former Roman building and formed a gently curving cut 26784/28050/28446 (Fig.139), extending for some 14m on a radius of

Fig.152   *Curving ditch 26784/28050 in backyard area. Scale unit 0.5m*

approximately 13.5m (Fig.152). It was 1m across at its widest, and up to 0.8m deep. At its better-preserved western end its upper edge sloped to a point where there was a ledged effect, before the sides were cut near vertically to a flat base, but towards the south-east, where it was shallower, the sides sloped more gently and it had a wider profile. Among the layers it cut was 28558 (not on plan), which contained two sherds of York D ware datable to the 9th/10th century; this was stratigraphically later than the backfill of the trench 28795 dug in the course of robbing the Roman building. The fill of the curving cut, 24939/28020/28197/28477, was a uniform dark grey silty clay loam incorporating some slabby limestone rubble in places. The unweathered angularity of its sides at the western end indicates that either it cannot have remained open for very long, or that it was cut from higher up and therefore did not weather. The backfill was subsequently cut by the large pit 28283 (Fig.139), itself assigned to Period 3, which suggests rapid, if unspecific, development in this area. After the gully had been backfilled, the line of its north-eastern edge was apparently perpetuated by a number of post-holes, including 26014 and 26708–14 (Fig.139), which were irregular in shape, 0.15–0.30m deep, and ranged in size from 0.22m x 0.24m (26709) to 0.3m x 0.5m (26713). Their purpose is uncertain. The course of the cut suggests that it was not a drain, and its plan is more characteristic of a foundation trench for a timber structure. Circular buildings are not, however, characteristic of 9th-century structural traditions, and it is tentatively suggested that this feature defined part of an enclosure of unknown function.

Within the south-central area of the excavation, where the intrusions caused by the foundations for a late medieval building had isolated an area from surrounding stratification, York Excavation Group uncovered patches of cobbles and limestone rubble, such as 3700/3717 and 3731 which should probably be assigned to this period (Fig.139). There were also several pits and other cuts here, including an irregular cut 3706 in which there were remains of a wattlework lining 3786. As it survived, this was sub-rectangular in shape, its greatest 'diameter' being 1.2m. A complex of intercutting pits including 28573, 28585, 32918 and 32973 partially underlie these limestone spreads (Fig.139).

Outside this stratigraphically isolated area and on either side of the gully described above (Fig.139) were two other wattle-lined pits which belong to this period. The first consisted of an oval wattle-lined shaft 36682, 0.9m in maximum width, which could be traced to a depth of 0.7m, and was filled with a very dark grey slightly clayey silty loam 24829. This lay within a considerably bigger construction pit 24950 that averaged 0.95m in width and was 2.05m deep at its greatest depth; at the centre of its base the inward-curving sides dropped abruptly for 0.1m. It contained 26016, a dark-coloured silty sandy peaty clay loam.

The other pit with a possible wattle lining was in the site's south-western corner. Its irregular, sub-circular cut 28794 was some 1.2m in greatest width and was 1.15m deep (Fig.139). Within the backfill were traces of a wattlework lining represented by vertical stakes and interwoven horizontals (28325) which seemed to revet the sides of the cut and had facilitated the insertion of an inner lining, 27231, which in turn rested directly on the bottom of the construction cut. This lining had been hollowed out in one piece from the bole of a tree, and was not a stave-built barrel as might be inferred from *AY* 14/7, 528. The tree was one of the *Populus* family and, given its size, was probably one of the poplars rather than an aspen. It measured 0.8m in height, with a diameter of 0.59m. Above the top lip of the bole, the line of interface between the backfill layer 27194, a black slightly peaty clay loam, and 27418, a dark grey silty clay loam forming the upper layer of backfill in the construction trench, suggests that there was originally an upper part to the lining which had been salvaged in antiquity before the feature was infilled. It is assumed that it originally served as a well; the hollow bole lining is the only one of this construction from the site.

This well lay between two parallel stake alignments (Fig.139), spaced 2m apart, which ran on an approximately south-west/north-east course. That to the north-west, 28199, which included occasional closely set pairs of stakes, was in the same layer, 28195, into which the well was cut. This layer contained Roman pottery and three sherds of undiagnostic hand-made wares, possibly of mid-9th-century date. The other stake alignment, 36683, lay within 28194, a layer identical to 28195, and was close to the edge of 28198, a linear if somewhat irregular layer comprising mostly pebbles with a few tile fragments and larger cobbles all in a dark grey loam matrix. 28198 was set in a steeply/vertically sided cut, 28324, averaging some 0.15m deep, which was traced for some 6.4m beyond a discontinuity of 1.5m to the east. A similar pebble feature, 19831, was recorded on the same axis, running for a further 1.4m.

Period 3 pits

The character and contents of the large, sometimes recut, pits ascribed to Period 3 have been extensively researched by environmental archaeologists (*AY* 14/7), archaeozoologists (*AY* 15/3) and material culture researchers (*AY* 16, 17 and 18) and their findings are published in detail elsewhere (see Table 26).

In summary, however, it is evident that some element of zoning across the site can be identified. In the western part of the Period 3 area of excavation, for example, pits 27288, 27410 and 31636 (Fig.138) indicate a range of human activities close to what was to become the Coppergate street frontage. Pits 27288, 27410 and, to a lesser extent, 31636, were extensively sampled for bioarchaeological data (*AY* 14/7, 514–21) and provided evidence of food plants surviving in the form of seeds and stones and as macro-evidence in human faecal material. They indicate a fibre-rich diet which included apples, sloes, plums and celery. Other pits provide evidence for the stabling of animals, while animal bone assemblages indicate a preference for cattle, along with sheep, goat, pig, a small amount of venison, fish and fowl (*AY* 15/3, table 39).

Small rounded York ware cooking pots which, judging by the heavy sooting on their flat bases and lower body, stood directly on or close to the source of heat, occur as fragments in many of these pits. A few pits also contained sherds of the later, 10th-century, Torksey-type wares, often in upper fills or in pits which are possibly later. Other household utensils included a wooden cup, a lid and a lathe-turned box (*AY* 17/13, *8614, 8638, 8934*), while an example of the lighting for the putative houses in the area was provided by a small stone lamp (*AY* 17/14, *9662*). Iron nails, tacks, staples, plate and strip might have

had more structural purposes, while an iron knife, a bone comb and a bone skate are typical personal possessions.

Not all pits necessarily had the same initial purpose. Pits 27288 and 31636, for example, contained both household rubbish (and a little human waste), while the adjacent 27410 was rich in both human and animal waste, apparently incorporated in hay or livestock litter, but had little else. Although of comparable size and shape to pit 27288, pit 27410 produced only a scrap of glass and a wool fibre in comparison with 50 and 25 individual finds from pits 27288 and 31636 respectively.

Those pits found further along what was to be the Coppergate street frontage, in the north-east corner of the site, which were cut into the glass-melting hearth and which pre-date the various stake and pit alignments, produced faecal material (in pit 30851). This indicated a diet containing wheat/rye bran, sloes, and other fruit, together with field beans (*AY* 14/7, 522–3) deposited in a single fill (30835) which contained three iron nails and tacks, a lead-alloy stud and leather waste. It was cut into by pit 30816 (*ibid*, fig.133) whose insect population suggested that it might have stood open for some time and which contained further ironwork (key, clench bolt, plate, tack, nail) and glass-working waste. Pit 30630 had further glass-working and leather waste and, with the exception of three sherds from the top levels, the contemporary pottery (excluding Roman) from pit 30691 is all York ware.

Further down the site the pattern is much the same (Fig.138). Pit 32706/32505 contained ironwork (needles, strip, clench bolt), glass-working debris and leather waste, together with a rotary quern-stone, but was not sampled for bioarchaeological data. The original purpose of pit 36276 is unclear, but it contained a single sherd of pottery and, from a single sampled fill, what is described as 'backfill material ... rich in durable occupation debris' (*AY* 14/7, 525), while pit 34824 contained significant quantities of leather shoes (e.g. *AY* 17/16, *15379, 15441*), a scabbard (*ibid, 15552*) and working waste. The shoes, which include slip-ons and ankle shoes (Type 4a4), have parallels in southern England and the Continent. Apart from further York ware sherds, pit 34824 produced only two iron strips and what is described as '... rather less substantial evidence ...' for human faeces. Human waste from pit 28542 (Fig.139) provided further evidence for a diet which included field beans, leek, apple, rose-hips, rowan, bilberry and cereals (*AY* 14/7, 525–6); the insect assemblage suggests that the pit was open and exposed over a period of time and contained '... a clear "house" fauna element ...', together with considerable quantities of ironwork (plate, bar and strip fragments, buckles, a barrel padlock, a hammer head, pins, needles and knives, a collar and nails), a lead-alloy ingot, a stone grindstone, a small amount of leather waste but only three sherds of pottery.

Further towards the back of the site the challenge of separating Period 3 deposits from later levels was most acute and some of these pits might belong to, or have continued in use into, Period 4. Pit 32885, for example, was not sampled for bioarchaeological data but produced an antler saw handle, fragments of composite combs, including an early handled type (*AY* 17/12, *7683*, 1934–5), an iron knife, staple, strips, needle, comb tooth and nails, two amber finger rings, a fired clay loom weight and stone weight, while pit 32752 similarly contained ironwork (clench bolt, comb tooth, buckles, arrow and strips) as well as hearth lining and glass-working debris (Fig.138). A leather shoe, a bone composite comb and gaming piece, a fragment of amber waste and a birch wood cup are, perhaps, indicative of a range of Anglo-Scandinavian activities. Pit 28038, at the River Foss end of the site (Fig.139), contained both York ware and Torksey-type wares, together with ironwork (key, strap-guide, plate, knife, clench bolts) and two honestones, a fragment of gold, and a large quantity of leather shoes, strap fragments, and leather waste. The presence of Torksey-type ware and small amounts of leather, an iron awl and a glass bead in pit 24950 might similarly support the idea that some of these pits date from nearer 900 than 850.

Discussion

The interface between Periods 2 and 3, between complete abandonment and renewed activity, cannot be closely dated nor can a precise chronology be ascribed to the different episodes within Period 3. Some hints that activity stretched back into the 8th century is offered by coins, sculpture and pottery (see below), but these are almost invariably found rede-

posited in later levels. This being the case, it is difficult to present a compelling argument that there was occupation, as opposed to activity, on the site before the 9th century.

Anglian evidence, however, has a wider context in this area of the city. It has been suggested, on the basis of possible pagan burials in the Castle Yard/ Clifford Street area (*AY* 7/2, *2*, *11*, *140*, *148–54*) and of two urned cremations recorded as overlying the Roman wall in the Parliament Street/Market Street area (*ibid*, *3*), that Anglian activity in this part of the city might extend back into the 5th or 6th century (*ibid*, 207–8). A thread of continuity from the 6th to the 8th century is hard to find, however, although later Anglian artefacts have been recovered from nearby 6–8 Pavement (*AY* 6/1, 25–8; *AY* 7/2, *73*), from elsewhere along Parliament Street (*AY* 7/2, *82*) and from what is now Clifford Street (*AY* 16/6, fig.238).

Given this body of evidence, and that recovered residually from later levels at 16–22 Coppergate, a strong case can be made for 8th-century activity in the Coppergate/Castlegate area which has left little conclusive mark on the site itself. If there had been 8th-century structures there, then subsequent pit digging, laying out of properties, and the cutting of foundations, followed by demolition and dumping as new buildings were constructed, might well have destroyed the evidence or rendered it unrecognisable. There are, however, pit-free spaces on the site large enough to have accommodated simple halls of the type found at 46–54 Fishergate (*AY* 7/1), whose rectangular pattern of post-holes might have been obscured by the palimpsest of later features. Had they existed, however, perhaps larger assemblages of Fishergate-like material culture might have been expected. Nevertheless, the presence of 8th-/early 9th-century ceramics such as Ipswich ware and foreign imports found residually on the site point to a nearby resident population. This might have been a small community associated with a predecessor of All Saints' church, or with an early burial ground hinted at by the sculptural and burial evidence. The fragments of a late 8th-to early 9th-century cross (Lang 1991, 104) found in the north-east corner of the site in Period 5A levels, close to where two of the early Period 3 burials were recovered (see Fig.146), support this suggestion of a community which might have been focused on the higher ground between what were to become the streets of Ousegate and Coppergate where All Saints' church now stands (Fig.131, **5**).

The early burials might have pre-dated the church foundation as burials were not universally associated with churches at this time (Hadley and Buckberry 2005, 126–7), and these burials are some little distance from the church itself (see Fig.324). The date range given to Skeleton 30944 (AD 690–880) spans almost two centuries, but seen in conjunction with the archaeomagnetic date of 860 (± 20) for the hearth cut by the skeleton's pit, the evidence points to this being a late 9th-century burial as the association between hearth and pit is undisputed. This would allow for the interpretation that this skeleton might have fallen victim to the disruption in the city resulting from the arrival of the Great Army in 866 (Hall 1994, 43–4). It is equally possible, however, that the skeleton represents the summary reburial of a (?recent) corpse encountered during the construction, for whatever purpose, of the early alignments 33247 and 33239 (see Fig.150b). Skeleton 36318 (dated AD 715–885) also has clear signs of disarticulation as if had been disturbed as activity on the site intensified. Perhaps the putative late Anglian community occupying the ridge of higher land had simply used the vacant margins of their settlement for occasional burials, small-scale industrial purposes, and, subsequently through the 9th century, for the digging of refuse pits.

The land downslope towards the River Foss might have been used in a similar manner. Skeleton 30979 is conventionally laid out, but is not in an obvious grave cut or on a conventional alignment. The dates given for this burial and for the skull 32803 found further down the site (both AD 670–780) suggest that this custom of haphazard burial went back into at least the 8th century. This practice has parallels 200m away at Spurriergate where mid-8th-century burials were recovered apparently unassociated with a known church, the nearest being the 'lost' church of St Peter the Little (for which the earliest reference is in the 1120s) which stood some 40m to the north in High Ousegate (Paula Ware, pers. comm.).

If these burials are as early as the earliest C14 determinations allow then it is possible that some of the pits and features downslope in the backyards might also be of 8th-century date. The earliest

features usually contain only Roman pottery and cannot be independently dated, and they are also usually cut about with later features. Early coins recovered from the site include a porcupine sceat (AD 720–40, *AY* 18/1, 3) found in an 11th-century deposit, stycas of Eanred and Aethelred dating to the first half of the 9th century (*ibid, 19, 25, 30*, fig.2) found in Period 3 dumps and backfills, together with a further nine stycas in even later contexts (*ibid*, 17), and their presence supports the case for Anglian activity close by.

A small assemblage of 7th- to 9th-century pottery, usually stratified in later contexts, includes the suite of wares which helped to identify the proposed *wic* site downriver at 46–54 Fishergate (*AY* 16/5). Local coarsely gritted wares, Ipswich-type ware and Maxey-type ware, together with imported Rhenish and northern French ceramic types, were all found at 16–22 Coppergate, albeit on a much more limited scale than at 46–54 Fishergate. The presence in Period 3 at Coppergate of what appears to be a transitional form of hand-made pottery (Type 1) which was not seen at Fishergate might suggest that early occupation on the site of 16–22 Coppergate itself was marginally later than the final phase (Period 3c) on Fishergate (*AY* 7/1, 10). Hand-made Type 1 wares were rapidly superseded by York wares which become the hallmark of the later 9th and early 10th century and were virtually absent on Fishergate (*AY* 16/6, 583).

To summarise, in Period 3 the Coppergate site appears to have been used initially for rubbish disposal, sporadic short-lived industry, as represented by the glass-making hearth, and for haphazard burials, and these activities are followed by an intensification of pit digging especially, but not exclusively, along the street frontage. Cut into the backfills of these pits are the earliest alignments, signalling a change of land use and the initial laying out of properties and structures. Although structures could not be clearly defined, structural elements including alignments of stakes and posts, and laid surfaces of tile and limestone were encountered in these late Period 3 deposits. These, together with the pits containing human cess, food waste and other domestic debris, indicate a nearby population that was expanding through the later 9th century. Evidence for continuing small-scale industrial activity, notably metal working and early leather working, can be convincingly traced back to this same period.

The subsequent watching brief and excavations at 22 Piccadilly discussed on pp.695–700 revealed features such as fences, pits and post-holes which show that the land to either side of the site (see Fig.136) was used in much the same way. Fence lines such as 1960, 2041 and 2165 follow the same axial alignment as the other property boundaries, leading to the conclusion that the pattern of land division is perpetuated in both directions along Coppergate. A pit (1778) located just off the south-western corner of the site contained the Anglian helmet, an item which dates to c.750–75 (*AY* 17/8, 1082), but which was deposited in a pit about a century after its date of production (*ibid*, 1165–7) (Figs 136, 148 and 153). Its concealment there remains a mystery and does little to help understanding of the use and character of the backyards.

On this basis, however, taking into account the new dating evidence and the information from the watching brief, it can be argued that true abandonment of the site relates most convincingly to the 5th to mid-8th century. The findings from the wider Coppergate/Ousegate/Clifford Street area suggest a resident population from the mid/late 8th century onwards although convincing structures were not recovered from Coppergate itself. By the end of Period 3, which equates approximately to the end of the 9th century, the intensification of activity along what was to be the street frontage suggests an expanding population which leads to the developments which characterise Period 4.

Fig.153   *The Anglian helmet: (left) as found, scale unit 10mm; (below) after restoration*

Period 4

Period 4 spans approximately a century from the late 9th century to c.AD 955/56 and represents the first clearly structural phase on the site in the decades following the arrival of the Viking Great Army. Period 4A extends from the late 9th/early 10th century to c.930/35 and Period 4B from c.930/35 to c.955/56), the more precise dates being provided principally by dendrochronological determination from surviving timbers (see Tree Ring Analysis Report, pp.743–4).

Period 4A

The decades either side of AD 900 (Period 4A) mark the transition from the essentially unstructured character of the site in preceding periods to its clear division into properties with buildings and backyards (Period 4B). The earlier (Period 3) post alignments observed in the north-eastern corner of the site (see Fig.150), however they are interpreted, therefore presaged the much more obvious sub-division of the entire surviving street frontage area into plots. By the beginning of Period 4B, the earliest coherent remains of structures occupy these properties, and their positions along the northern edge of the site then remain consistent throughout the Anglo-Scandinavian period and beyond.

The erection of the Period 4A stake and wattle alignments which run at more or less right angles to Coppergate divided the area into plots (Fig.154). The alignments themselves comprised uprights with a maximum cross-sectional dimension not exceeding 50mm and are, in the vast majority of cases, circular in cross-section and with bark in place, and are supplemented with occasional larger posts. The alignments, and the contexts that relate stratigraphically to them, indicate an intensification of activity in the street frontage zone.

Taken overall, the soil layers of Period 4A differed from the cleanish clay loams of Period 3 in containing more patches of ash, charcoal and other inclusions, and in being somewhat siltier. However, it was not possible to follow this distinction with confidence in areas progressively further and further from the street frontage. In this part of the excavated site there were no alignments to help in determining the inception of the Period 4A

horizon, and the frequency of later pits made stratigraphic links rather tenuous. Whatever contemporary deposits may have existed here have therefore been subsumed within the strata assigned to Period 3. Period 4A can, therefore, only truly be distinguished along the street frontage strip.

Pits, together with stake and post alignments, characterise the Period 4A developments at the street frontage, and these begin to form coherent patterns. Figure 154 shows the alignments and other features identified in this area, which constitutes the full extent of Period 4A. For clarity the various alignments (Fig.154b) have been extracted from the cut features (Fig.154a) and it begins to be possible to identify the distinct properties which characterise later periods. The greatest concentration of the recognisable Period 4A deposits was in the eastern part of the street frontage strip, while equivalent levels at the western end had been destroyed by subsequent building operations, notably the construction of Structure 5/1 of Period 5B (see p.614ff).

Some of these alignments appear to represent the ultimate phase of features which had been initiated in Period 3, underlining the seamless progression from this earlier period. Where deposits survive at the western end, alignment 37147 (Fig.154b), set back some 6m from the street frontage, and running approximately parallel to it, for example, includes post-holes 31328, 31332 and 31416 which replace elements in the Period 3 alignment 37138, which had previously occupied the same position (see Fig.150). Post-hole 31328 was cut appreciably later in the period than the other two (although contemporary with a row of stakes which includes 31238) and may indicate the continued existence and piecemeal renovation of an earlier fence or wall.

Another relatively early Period 4A feature in this western part of the frontage strip is the rubble spread 37153 (Fig.154a) which represents a rather more patchy renewal of an earlier spread (27083) (see Fig.138). It comprised a larger percentage of limestone rubble and a smaller percentage of cobbles than did its predecessor, and it also incorporated part of a quernstone (*AY* 17/14, *9733*) which, unusually, was made of oolitic limestone, probably from the Howardian Hills to the north of York. Also contemporary with these features was a scoop

31518, lying at the area's southern edge (Fig.154a), and a few small post-holes, the purpose of which could not be determined.

If these features in the western part of the excavated Period 4A area continue aspects of the site's use from Period 3, other elements represent innovation. Among the earliest of these is an alignment of vertical stakes (sails), 36659, running at 90° to the frontage (Fig.154b) and discernible in the area of the rubble spread (37153). While not so coherent as some other contemporary and later alignments, and without any surviving trace of interwoven horizontal wattle elements (rods) to confirm its course, sufficient of it survived, particularly at its northern end, to lend confidence to its identification as an alignment. A scatter of other stakes spread in an apparently more random fashion to its east defy interpretation.

While these western features remain tantalisingly suggestive of plot layout, features further along the street frontage are easier to interpret. This is certainly true of a large pit 31154, set back some 2m from the street frontage, more or less in the centre of the area excavated (Fig.154a). The pit was approximately 1.6m square and 1m deep, and had been filled with layers of dark grey loam interleaved with layers of 'peaty' material which included human faeces (*AY* 14/7, 535, fig.137). Biological analysis identified substantial numbers of eggs of human intestinal worms in these layers, as well as beetles indicative of foul matter. Substantial posts, one on the north side, two on the south, may have supported a latrine seat, helping to define this as a toilet.

An alignment of stakes, 36594, running at right angles to the street frontage had been inserted into the uppermost layer of this pit, and a further 0.5m to the west a fragment of another alignment (31192) ran on a parallel course (Fig.154b). While alignment 36594 comprised single sails and had no rods surviving, alignment 31192 included some adjoined pairs of sails and did retain vestiges of its rods. They are parallel to and apparently contemporary with a number of horizontal timber beams and vestigial traces of horizontal wattles that could be interpreted as remains of a length of recumbent hurdle, perhaps representing a walkway or collapsed fence.

Also contemporary but at a right angle to these features, and also overlying the backfill of pit 31154, was another alignment of stakes and wattle, 25415 (Fig.154b). There was more variety in the positioning of the sails in this alignment, with a number of pairs juxtaposed either along or across its line, and one instance of a triple group. It ran east–west for a distance of 5.3m before petering out, and neither end is clearly defined, although more substantial vertical posts were located very close to each limit on the alignment's northern side, with another intermediate upright nearer its eastern end. All three of these posts had apparently been driven into position, the intermediate one through the backfill of an irregular scoop 30130 (Fig.154a).

Closer to the street frontage and adjacent to the cess pit 31154 is another, sub-circular, pit 27491 (Fig.154a) which had the same sorts of fill layers and the same axial double-post arrangement, with posts positioned within the pit 0.3–0.6m from the edges. Biological analysis again suggests that this was a cess pit (*AY* 14/7, 535–7). The cutting of pit 27491 truncates the northern course of alignments 36594 and 31192, indicating that it is later than pit 31154. On the other side of pit 31154, a third near-contemporary pit, 31421, lay in part beyond the limit of excavation (Fig.154a). It appears to be of rather smaller proportions than the other two but has a post-hole in a similar position within it.

There are various shallow scoops associated with these pits, of which scoop 30130 was the earliest, but which include 25997 to the north, 26808 and 27473 to the west, and 25984 and 31331 to the south (Fig.154a). The latter were against the southern limit of excavation in these levels, and here a tiny length of another stake and wattle alignment, 25888, was visible, apparently running approximately parallel to 25415, although marginally later in date (Fig.154b). The purpose of the scoops is uncertain but some at least might represent the source of the soil used to cover foul matter in the latrines (*AY* 14/7, 537) while others, such as 25997, might have been caused by the rootling of pigs in the area (*ibid*).

Stake alignment 30791, which has its main axis approximately perpendicular to the frontage, is apparently associated with the shorter alignments 30792 and 33245, which both ran at approximately

Period 4A

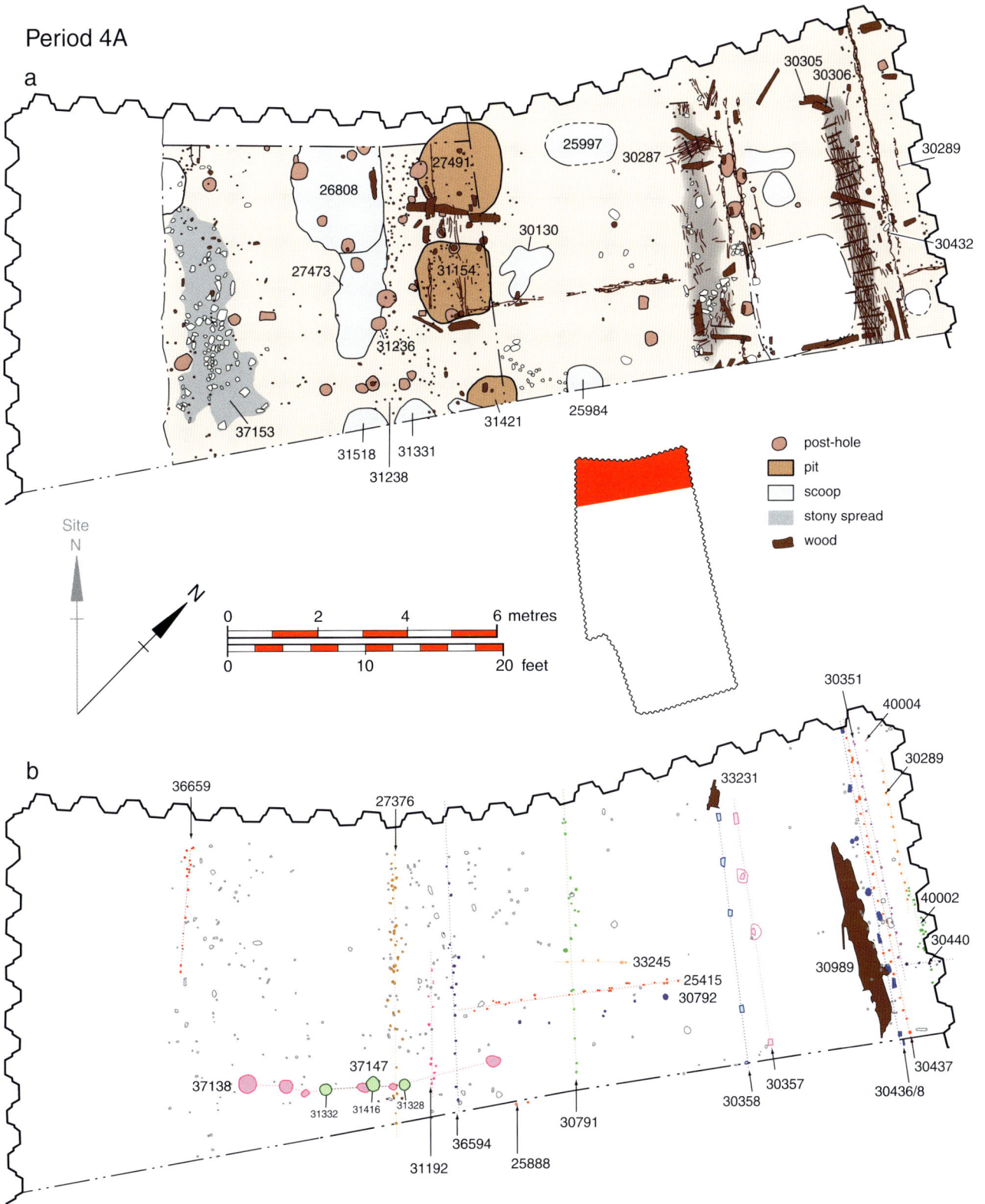

Fig. 154 *Features at the front of the site in Period 4A: (a) all features; (b) alignments. Scale 1:125*

90° to it, about 1m from each other (Fig.154b). Alignment 30792 stretches for 2.7m and 33245 for 1.6m, with a possible gap at the western end of the latter. These two alignments appear to span the distance from, and possibly connect with, the privies and link them to the remnants of what is more convincingly a wattle-covered walkway 30287 (Fig.154a) (see below). As such, the cess pits and the line of 30792/33245 might represent part of a property which extended under the street frontage from the putative community existing along the ridge before the street of Coppergate came into existence.

These early alignments were approximately contemporary with another, 30351, which runs at 90° to them, and to the street frontage at the eastern edge of the area (Fig.154b). This alignment was more instantly intelligible, due to the preservation of some of its rods. It consisted of single-stake uprights (sails), spaced on average approximately 0.3m apart; three driven posts of varying shape and size, to the west and immediately adjacent, appeared to be coeval and to form an integral part of the feature.

Towards the excavated southern limit of 30351 it was adjoined by two virtually contiguous alignments, only 0.1m apart, running east–west. Of these, 30440 (Fig.154b) had no surviving interwoven rods, in contrast with that slightly to the south (not shown on plan). It was not possible to discern any chronological priority between the two, and they may well have been contemporary.

Also associated with alignment 30351 was a length of wattle hurdle 30989 (Fig.154b). This is the lowest of three superimposed such lengths, lying to the west of, and with their main axes parallel to, 30351, separated from it by approximately 0.4m. Hurdle 30989 lay above 30352, a widespread layer which has provided one of the animal bone groups studied in *AY* 15/3 (Group 29, p.143). The wattle hurdle 30989 itself survived in a rather fragmentary form, and subsequently a number of miscellaneous fragments of timber, including 30305 and 30306 (Fig.154a), were placed on top of its remains or along its course, presumably to support and/ or stabilise its replacement 30284 (not on plan). This too had single sails, on average some 0.3m apart, was about 0.5m wide, and was traced for a length of 4.5m. In turn it was superseded by a third

similar hurdle, 30187 (not on plan), which, although substantially intact at its southern excavated limit, became increasingly fragmented as it ran northwards.

The regular superimposition of these wattle features, their coherent, undistorted appearance and the absence of any contemporary, coincident sail bases from which the transverse elements in the hurdles might have snapped, combine to indicate that they were deliberately laid horizontally. They are most readily interpreted as having been laid on the line of a frequently used pathway where it was necessary to provide extra grip and stability on the potentially slippery slope. They are the earliest representatives of a type of feature that was to be seen again in Anglo-Scandinavian deposits on the site. In later contexts at 16–22 Coppergate they were found consistently outside buildings (often immediately outside), and are interpreted as pathways leading to or running immediately adjacent to the buildings. Similar features are known from elsewhere in York, such as Spurriergate (see Fig.322) (Paula Ware, pers. comm.), and have been recognised frequently in the excavations of Viking Age Dublin (Wallace 2001, 40–1).

Probably during the time-span represented by the three superimposed hurdle lengths, alignment 30351 to their east was replaced by alignment 30437 (Fig.154b) which stood some 0.2m to the west of 30351 and was composed of single upright sails usually spaced 0.2–0.3m apart. At approximately the same time a new alignment, 30289, was erected in parallel, some 0.5–0.6m to the east (Fig.154b). Its use was apparently short-lived, and it too survived for the most part as a line of single stakes on the 'standard' 0.2–0.3m spacing, with only the barest vestiges of its original rods.

Recumbent wattlework hurdles were found elsewhere along the frontage strip at this period. Some 3m to the west lay the less well-preserved and smaller example, 30287, referred to above in connection with the possible route down the property to the privies (Fig.154a). Its position was apparently associated with alignment 30358 which ran back at right angles to the street frontage. Alignment 30357 is slightly later and might perpetuate this alignment (it is placed in Period 4B for stratigraphic reasons but is shown on Figure 154b).

The axes of all the alignments referred to above were approximately parallel or perpendicular to the present street line. Furthermore, the majority of the alignments which ran at 90° to the frontage lay either directly or very closely below the course of other later alignments which formed walls or fences in and around the buildings of Period 4B. The only one of the Period 4A alignments at right angles to the frontage which was unique to that period was 30791, suggesting that its purpose proved more transitory. What at later periods could be recognised as the boundaries between Tenements A and B and Tenements B and C were established at this time (see Fig.156), as was a line which was subsequently taken by the eastern wall of the later structure on Tenement D. No demarcation of what was later the division between Tenement C and D was noted in Period 4A levels, although a line just inside what was to become the western wall line of the Period 4B buildings on Tenement D was erected in Period 4A; it was briefly re-used in Period 4B. Thus the evidence indicates that the area was sub-divided at the start of Period 4 very much along the lines which were to crystallise in Period 4B and were then perpetuated for the following millennium. A corollary is that it seems inherently likely that a street or thoroughfare of some sort already existed on the line now taken by Coppergate.

Most of the alignments, whether parallel or perpendicular to the frontage, did not include any more substantial upright elements than stakes. In this characteristic these alignments differ from those that were clearly the wall lines of buildings in subsequent periods, where stake and wattle alignments were very often associated with stouter vertical timbers. Thus, although the alignments of Period 4A which run parallel to the street line indicate further sub-division at the frontage, they should not necessarily be interpreted as the walls of buildings and cannot be taken as proof that the frontages were built up. Indeed, the presence of the large pits 31154 and 27491 underneath some of the alignments indicates that at the start of the period, at least, the entire area was certainly not given over to structures. Their interpretation as cess pits suggests, however, that occupation was taking place not far away, continuing and intensifying the evidence noted in Period 3. Indeed, palaeobiological studies indicate that the proportion of 'house' fauna, indicative of material from within buildings, although

recovered from pit fills and surface deposits, was similar to that recorded for Period 3.

The one exception to this, however, is the presence of posts in alignments 30436/8 and 30358 and in 37138/37147, suggesting that at least some may have served as more than fences. As these alignments were able to bear a greater weight it is conceivable that they represent the walls of otherwise unrecognised buildings. Dendrochronological dates obtained from alignment 30358 demonstrate that the timbers used were felled either late in what is defined as Period 4A or early in Period 4B (AD 921–39), thus possibly representing an early post and wattle building wall line (see Tree-Ring Analysis Report, p.743).

Despite this uncertainty regarding the presence and character of any Period 4A structures, there can be no doubt that the area was being divided into relatively long and narrow properties typical of urban plots. The time when this occurred cannot be ascertained with any precision, but a date centred on c.AD 900, within a range of c.875–920, must be in order. Dating is based on a stratified penny of Cnut dated c.895–903 (*AY* 18/1, 17, *40*) and various dendrochronology dates of isolated timbers and those in the alignments (Table 28).

Table 28 Dendrochronological dating of selected Period 4A timbers.

Timber no.	Alignment no.	Felling date range
8867	isolated	906–41
9026	30358	921–39
9025	30358	921–39
9219	isolated	897–933

In summary, therefore, the intensification of activity along the street frontage would seem to include the erection of the first property divisions in the form of post and wattle fences running at right angles to the street. Whether these fences were substantial enough to be weight-bearing walls seems unlikely except in one or two cases. The laying and successive re-laying of linear wattlework hurdles, reinforced in some cases by larger irregular planks and designed to counteract the natural dampness of the heavy clay soils, suggests regular and frequent footfall along the edges of these fences in at least two cases. In a third case, at the western side of the Period 4A area, the linear spread of lime-stone rubble (37153; Fig.154a) might have had the same purpose alongside the slight traces of another fence line (alignment 36659; Fig.154b).

Some of these alignments of posts perpetuated earlier such sub-divisions, and some are in turn perpetuated into the next period. Those running at right angles to the street frontage might have served as property divisions while those running parallel, effectively sub-dividing the properties, must have served other purposes. The keeping of livestock would require pens, runs and shelter, all of which might have left such traces. Of these parallel align-ments only 37138/37147 and possibly 25415 include substantial posts (Fig.154b).

The clearest evidence of occupation is the exist-ence and use of the two or possibly three privies (27491, 31154, 31421; Fig.154a). The deposits within these cuts included layers of interleaving peaty matter presumably added to cover odours from their foul contents, a suggestion which is consistent with the character of the insect assemblage. While the pit fills contain flies characteristic of cessy matter, the concentration of such evidence was half that of the surrounding levels suggesting that such deposits were covered rapidly. It is tempting to view the irregular scoops which are positioned around the privies (p.564) as the possible source of the covering soils (Fig.154a).

Fig.155   *Early 10th-century dirham with an Arabic inscription, probably a contemporary forgery*

The environmental data gathered from the surrounding Period 4A layers included food remains associated with preparation and storage and there was evidence for '…increases over Period 3 in the amount and diversity of almost all ecological and use groups, notably dyeplants, which became rather more obvious'(*AY* 14/7, 537). There is also a signifi-cant increase in the amount of waste from leather working from the north-eastern part of the site in what was to become Tenement D (*AY* 17/16, tables 360–1), while other crafts broadly reflect the level of activity seen in Period 3. A dirham (Fig.155; *AY* 18/1, 47), recovered from an isolated pit (shown on Fig.133 against the western edge of the shoring behind the street frontage area) and dated to 903–07/08 (*ibid*, 55), attests to wide networks of trade at this time.

When assessing the significance of Period 4A it is essential to remember that the period defines no more than an intensification of activity along the street frontage and that elements of the backyards where thinning deposits were difficult to distin-guish, some ascribed to Period 3 (see Fig.139), are probably contemporary. The continued use of hand-made pottery alongside wheel-thrown York wares is consistent between Period 3 and Period 4A (and even into Period 4B) (*AY* 16/5, fig.152), while techniques of textile production remain unaltered from Period 3, including elements with an Anglian character (*AY* 17/11, 1793–7).

The regularly maintained wattle and rubble walkways which run axially down the site may have linked the well-used privies and putative livestock pens close to the street frontage, with occupation still focused on the slightly higher ground under the present street of Coppergate. Whether these proper-ties were randomly placed, or grouped around an early church on the site of All Saints Pavement, or were longer properties fronting onto High Ousegate, remains uncertain. The closure and abandonment of the privies must be significant, however, as that event is almost certainly associated with the establishment of Coppergate as a street with more clearly defined plot/property boundaries fronting onto it. Putting a precise date on that development is not possible but it is likely to be in the two decades immediately after AD 900, some half a century after the arrival of the Great Army.

Period 4B
Introduction

Period 4B is the most complex in terms of features identified and recorded on site. Fences demarcate properties, dwellings/workshops are aligned gable end to the recently established street of Copper-gate, while pits, gullies, enclosures and laid surfaces occupy the backyard areas. Dating evidence is provided by coins and by dendrological determinations which supply convincing evidence that this intensification of activity belongs to the first half of the 10th century. It was this period that Richard Hall was working on at the time of his death. While no complete text survives for two of the properties, his work was far advanced in terms of the other two, as was the preparation of publication drawings. The description of this period presented below includes fragments of the incomplete text incorporated into a continuous narrative, together with plans, drawings and images, completed by Ailsa Mainman (text identified by grey tone). Richard's most recent broad summary of this period appears in his book *Exploring the World of the Vikings* and provides a useful introductory overview (Hall 2007).

In Period 4B '…houses-cum-workshops … stood at the street frontage of each tenement. Up to the mid-10th century these buildings were single-storey structures, typically at least 7m (23ft) long by about 4.5m (14ft 9in) wide. They are reminiscent of Anglo-Saxon buildings and have nothing particularly Scandinavian about them. Upright posts set into the ground at fairly short intervals along the wall lines supported the thatch roof; the walls themselves were made of wattle withies woven horizontally in and out of stakes set between these posts. Earth benches contained within a revetment of wattlework sometimes ran along the side walls. The only other identifiable fixture in each building was a very large rectangular hearth, its edges defined by re-used Roman tiles or building stones, or by lengths of wood. The floors were simply earth, onto which debris accumulated and into which objects were trampled, thus making them a rich source for the archaeologists. The disposal of rubbish around the houses, and the need to repair and replace the structures every few decades, with consequent dumping of building debris, caused the ground level to rise at the rate of about 10–20mm each year' (Hall 2007, 117).

Artisans and their families worked, and dwelt, in these buildings and the evidence for their activities takes the form of raw materials, unfinished objects and working debris. In some cases the specialist nature of the work implies a non-domestic/commercial scale of production, focused on one or two of the properties; in others the activities are of a more domestic nature and at a scale common to all properties. The scatter of material culture debris implies that some trades or crafts, especially those which required space, were carried out in the backyards while others, which required shelter, were carried out indoors. The evidence for these crafts, and discussion of its significance, is published in detail elsewhere (see Table 26), but is briefly reviewed below, tenement by tenement, together with a summary of the environmental evidence.

Methodology of post-excavation analysis

Interpretation of the numerous posts, stakes and interwoven wattlework that characterise Period 4B has been the single most challenging component of the entire analysis of Anglo-Scandinavian Copper-gate. It has involved the creation of a composite computerised drawing, intended to show all the vertical wooden structural elements (Fig.156) and including all the alignments that were individually identified during the excavation, other alignments (for all Anglo-Scandinavian periods) which were recognised during post-excavation analysis, and other vertical timbers not assigned to any alignment. This has provided an opportunity to re-assess the integrity of the alignments that were defined during excavation, to see if there was good reason to incorporate previously unassigned uprights into any existing alignment, and to define wholly new alignments. The grounds for taking either of these latter steps included issues such as the similarity in shape and dimensions of their potential components, spatial patterning, and relative stratification.

Interpreting the inter-relationship of individual alignments in chronological, spatial and functional terms has involved a number of considerations.

Where alignments or some of their component parts were erected within cut features (post-holes or foundation trenches), their stratigraphic position is reasonably clear. For alignments with upright elements simply rammed into the earth without any preparatory cuts, however, the position is usually much less precise. Such was the complexity and number of the thin, superimposed layers into which many of these alignments were erected that it is usually impossible to link any one of them unambiguously with the inception of a particular alignment, unless there is an especially obvious spatial patterning of adjacent layers. Thus, many of the alignments 'float' in the stratigraphic sequence. If horizontal wattle rods are preserved *in situ*, their lowest strand may provide some indication of the contemporary ground level/floor level, and this assumption has been made here. Where no rods are present, the point at which the excavation of surrounding soil layers made its components become unstable has been taken to indicate the earliest possible time for that alignment's period of use. The alignment's 'life-span' is almost certainly exaggerated in this process; excavating surrounding layers to the point where stakes and posts were liable to collapse suggests what is probably too early a date for that alignment's erection. Conversely, unless there is some very obvious indication otherwise, such as a single clearly recognisable layer occurring on both sides of an alignment at a lower level, the surviving tops of stakes are taken to indicate the approximate level of the ground surface at the time when they went out of use and were broken. If, however, stakes were snapped off above ground level, this too will have led to an exaggeration of the alignment's period of use. Thus even the relatively few quite closely dated artefacts in these layers, notably the coins, may not be associated precisely with particular structural episodes, although they do indicate the period within which the sequence of structures was erected and utilised.

The absence of interwoven wattlework from many of the putative stake/post alignments is itself noteworthy. With the rapid accumulation of deposits against walls and fences, more wattlework might be expected to survive. Perhaps the expectation that wattle would always have been woven from the ground level up is misplaced. An alternative explanation might be that uprights in alignments were pushed further into the ground, and

that what has been excavated represents the subsurface portions of the uprights. The nature of both the stratification and the stratigraphy – i.e. the build up of soil and its recording – generally does not help to resolve this question. The layers themselves were often very similar either side of alignments; if the alignments had not been present, it would often have been difficult to distinguish separate contexts to either side. The very presence of alignments encouraged the giving of different context numbers to material on each side unless there were unusual distinguishing characteristics present to either side which clearly indicated continuity of strata.

Whatever explanation for the absence of wattlework is correct, it does not alter the relative sequences of superimposed alignments but it could affect the interpretation of occupation layers with construction phases.

Dating evidence

There are dendrochronological dates for timber posts in several of these alignments (pp.743–4) and these provide a framework of dates stretching at its widest range between c.925 and c.980 but which are concentrated on the central decades of the 10th century. The coins tell a similar story (p.799), with the last date for a stratified coin in this period being 955 (*AY* 18/1, 57) but again, disregarding obviously residual examples, the coins cluster in the period c.927–950.

Defining major land divisions

Interpreting the overall spatial patterns defined by the alignments has been facilitated by the large size of the excavated area. This has allowed opportunities for a relatively widespread comparison of characteristics in an exercise which is partly one of pattern recognition. Viewed altogether, the twin factors of density of components and periodic replacement appear to identify an ongoing importance for three groups of composite alignments which continue to define the properties emerging in the preceding period. With their northerly portions running back approximately perpendicular from the Coppergate street frontage, each continued down the slope towards the River Foss. They did not all run parallel to each other; the most easterly (dividing Tenements C/D) diverges notably

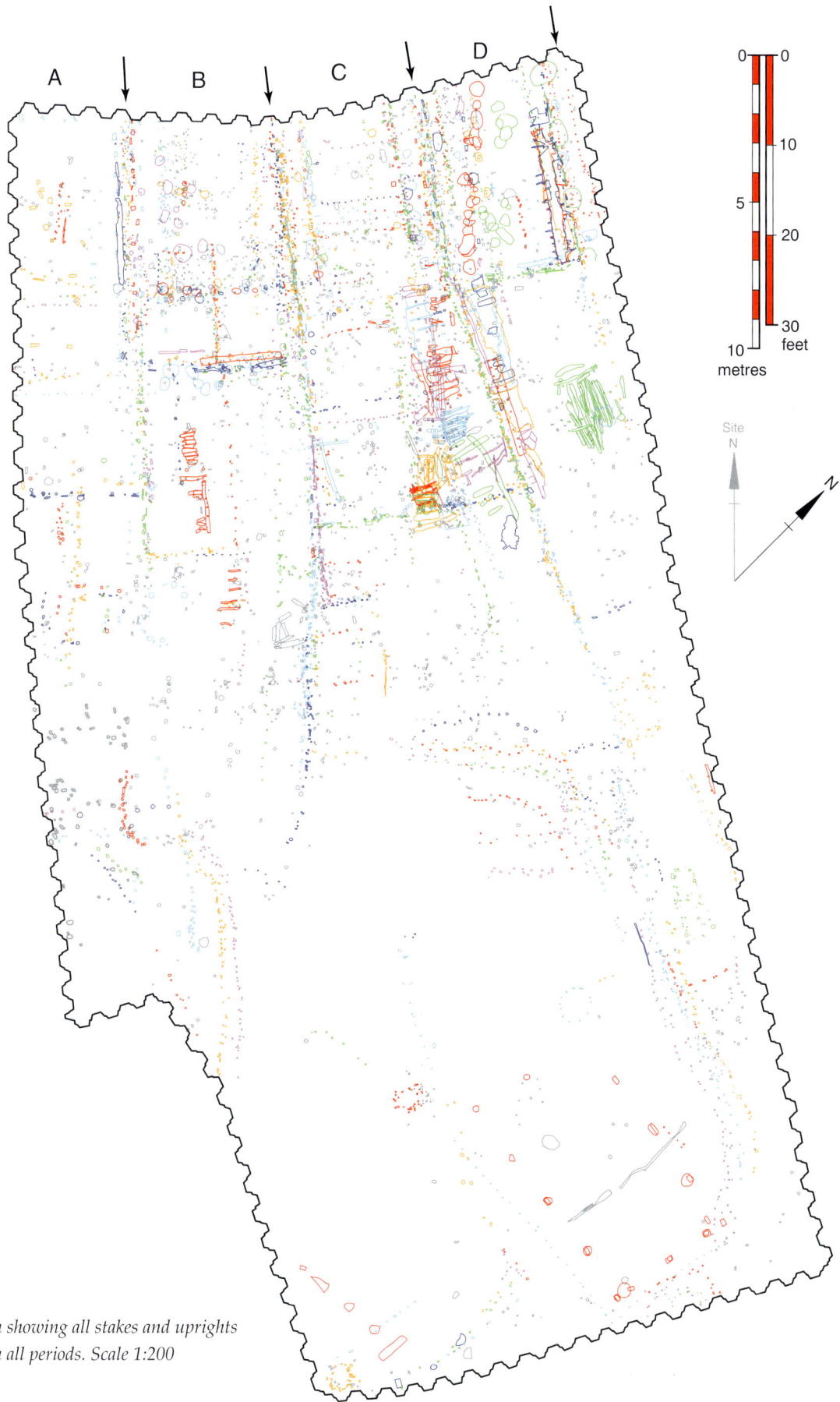

A   B   C   D

0
10
5
20
30
feet
10
metres

Site
N

N

Fig.156   *Plan showing all stakes and uprights from all periods. Scale 1:200*

eastwards from this course, while the central of the three (between Tenements B/C) diverges slightly to the west from approximately 7m south of the excavation's street frontage giving Tenement C a splayed wedge shape, while the most westerly (between Tenements A and B) is the most incomplete, at almost a right angle to the street (Fig.156). These three alignments appear to be property boundaries and represent major sub-division of the site, defining units of landholding which, at the street frontage, each measure approximately 5m (16ft 6in) in width. Each alignment has some characteristics which it does not share with the two others: horizontal boards within the middle one (between Tenements B/C) and a lack of large uprights in the diverging back part of the most easterly (between Tenements C/D). However, each alignment has characteristics in common with other alignments: the most westerly (between Tenements A/B), for example, incorporates many staves, as do various other axial and transverse alignments across the site.

Buildings and structural elements

Buildings are defined as fully enclosed and roofed structures, in permanent use/occupation. Their existence at the street frontage was signalled, among other things, by the presence of regularly spaced hearths, a general absence of pits, and distinctive, more finely laminated stratification indicative of floors. The unusually frequent occurrence within this zone of some artefact and material types is suggestive of both manufacturing premises and domestic premises. Taken together, these indicate the likelihood that buildings stood at the street frontage, although their front part remains under the present street of Coppergate.

Investigating the possibility that fragments of adjacent or contiguous alignments which appear to be stratigraphically concurrent were erected as integral parts of a single structure has taken account of a variety of factors. In a few instances the presence of *in situ* horizontal wattle rods which bind together alignments and which run approximately perpendicular to each other is a firm indicator of their spatial link. These instances apart, however, given the stratigraphical 'flexibility' which can occur when there is no clear evidence to define a construction level, it may theoretically be possible to link many different combinations of alignments

and thereby to hypothesise a variety of different composite structures. In attempting to propose the most likely combinations, there is the risk of a circular argument developing – that because buildings found at the street frontage have a particular set of structural characteristics, these characteristics alone can define buildings elsewhere on the site. This has *not* been assumed here.

Structures are identified through a variety of criteria. These include the presence of structural components believed to be physically capable of supporting such a construction, for example an alignment of large posts in combination with substantial wattlework walls forming a rectangle; however, the presence in an alignment of vertical elements larger than stakes is not in itself a valid criterion for interpreting that alignment as part of a building, for staves occur as components in several alignments which are interpreted as fences. Other characteristics that confirm the possibility that a building existed include the presence of internal deposits compatible with occupation; the general absence of features such as rubbish pits which are unlikely adjuncts to occupation; and the presence of hearths. Interpretation is often supported or refuted by environmental evidence.

The densest overall concentration of timber uprights occurred in a zone up to 10m wide immediately behind and alongside the present Coppergate street frontage (Fig.156). Here there were many distinct alignments consisting of a series of posts/staves, and some of them were in close proximity to stake (and wattle) alignments. There are, however, remarkably few instances of two similarly constructed alignments appearing to form opposing sides of a single building, although occasionally timber from the same tree can be identified as being used in two or more different properties (see pp.743, 744).

Even in the strips where stake and wattle boundaries were replaced on several occasions, and where other, parallel alignments represent structures, the boundaries between layers sometimes lie parallel to but between the various recognised alignments, not contiguous with any of them (see for example Fig.157). The lines of soil changes may coincide with occasional stakes, but these sporadic or isolated timber elements would not themselves qualify as alignments. Such soil boundaries are not represented in the structural plans in this volume, and the question remains as to what determined the line of these soil changes – a physical boundary, in the form, for example, of prefabricated alignments that were removed (almost) *in toto*? If so, the structural sequence is even more complex than that presented here. Or could it be that these soil lines indicate that there was some form of thick cladding to the various alignments that was evident at the time but has now disappeared?

Inter-tenement comparisons

For descriptive purposes, the four axial subdivisions of the site that lay between the three alignments of property boundaries mentioned above are designated, from the west to the east, Tenement A, B, C and D (Fig.158). Tenements Z and E, to the west and east respectively, were identified during

Fig.157 *Alignments 36583, 20671 and 23513 (Period 4B) and 36582 (Period 5A). Scale unit 0.1m*

the watching brief. Backyards behind the structures comprise pits, gullies and various scooped features.

Tenements A and B

The extent of late 10th-century disturbance (Period 5B) at the west of Tenement A hinders interpretation of the earlier 10th-century (Period 4B) features there. To overcome this, and in order to appreciate fully the inter-relationship of various features with Tenement B, it is necessary to review Tenements A and B together, while also taking account of broadly contemporary developments in Tenements C and D.

An undisturbed 'spine' of soil survived between the cuts for the later 10th-century Period 5B Structures 5/2 and 5/3 which subsequently occupied Tenements A and B, and is longitudinally bisected by various alignments; other alignments also run longitudinally on both sides of the medial line (Fig.157). It is noticeable that on either side of the median the innermost alignments comprise staves; each alignment is quite regularly spaced, although that in A (36583) is more closely spaced than that in B (23513) (Fig.159).

The division between these two properties is continued further down the slope by two lines of stakes (27676 and 36649), the one reinforcing or replacing the other (Fig.159); a timber from a small alignment on this same line (27796) had a felling date of AD 937–73 and a small horizontal (timber 9070) on the same alignment was felled during the period 941–59. These dates suggest that division of the land in the middle decades of the 10th century was not restricted to the zones around the buildings but continued downslope.

Some 8m from the northern edge of the excavated area, an alignment of staves (27607) runs transversely across Tenement B (Fig.159), with a setting of four staves in a stone-packed post-hole at approximately its mid-point. Near its eastern end it incorporated a length of plank laid flat, rebated on diagonally opposite sides at either end in order to embrace a stave or staves (Figs 160 and 161). This looks like a door threshold, although if this was originally its function here, the presence of equidistant stakes driven through it suggests that it was later blocked. Nevertheless, it could be suggested that alignments

573

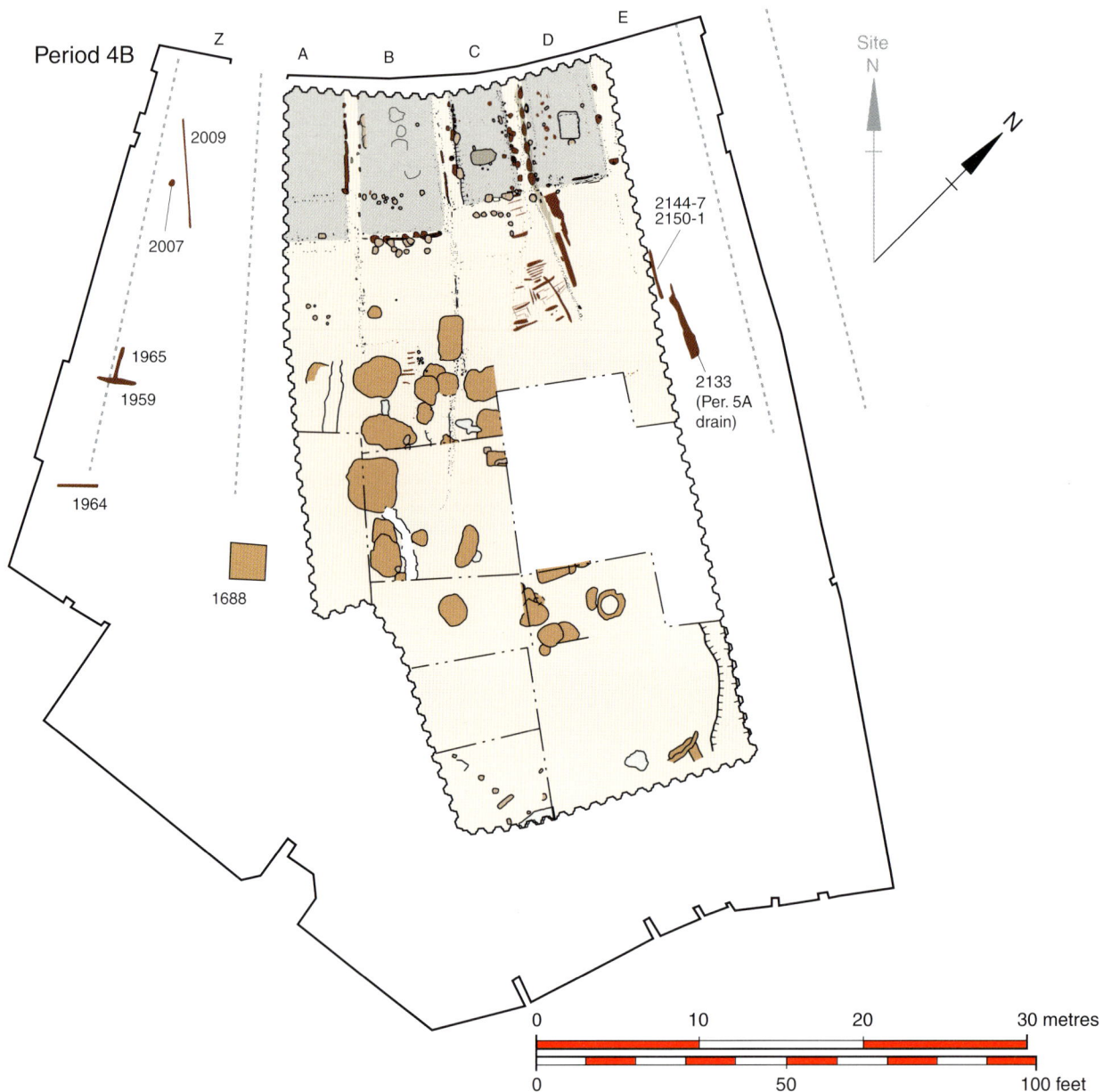

Period 4B

Z

A   B   C   D   E

Site
N

2009

2007

2144-7
2150-1

1965
1959

2133
(Per. 5A
drain)

1964

1688

0   10   20   30 metres

0   50   100 feet

Fig.158   *Plan of Period 4B features across the site, including the watching brief. Scale 1:250*

23513 and 27607 represent the west (side) and south (back) walls of a building, even though an east side wall constructed in the same manner is not recognisable. By extrapolation, the stave line running north–south on Tenement A (36583, Fig.159) could represent the east wall of a Tenement A building otherwise destroyed or unrecognised. A timber in alignment 36583 has a dendrochronological date of after 941 and two in alignment 27607 have dates of 925–47, showing that their construction was broadly contemporary; the fact that another timber in align-

ment 27607 is dated 950–85 emphasises the ongoing repair these buildings required.

Inter-tenement comparisons of the relative positioning of transverse alignments (taking account of the curving line of the street), and analysis of their constituent components, registers several points of similarity. On Tenements B, C and D, for example, there are groups of successive transverse alignments, respectively 8.5m, 6.5m, and 7m back from the street frontage, which seem to represent the

Period 4B

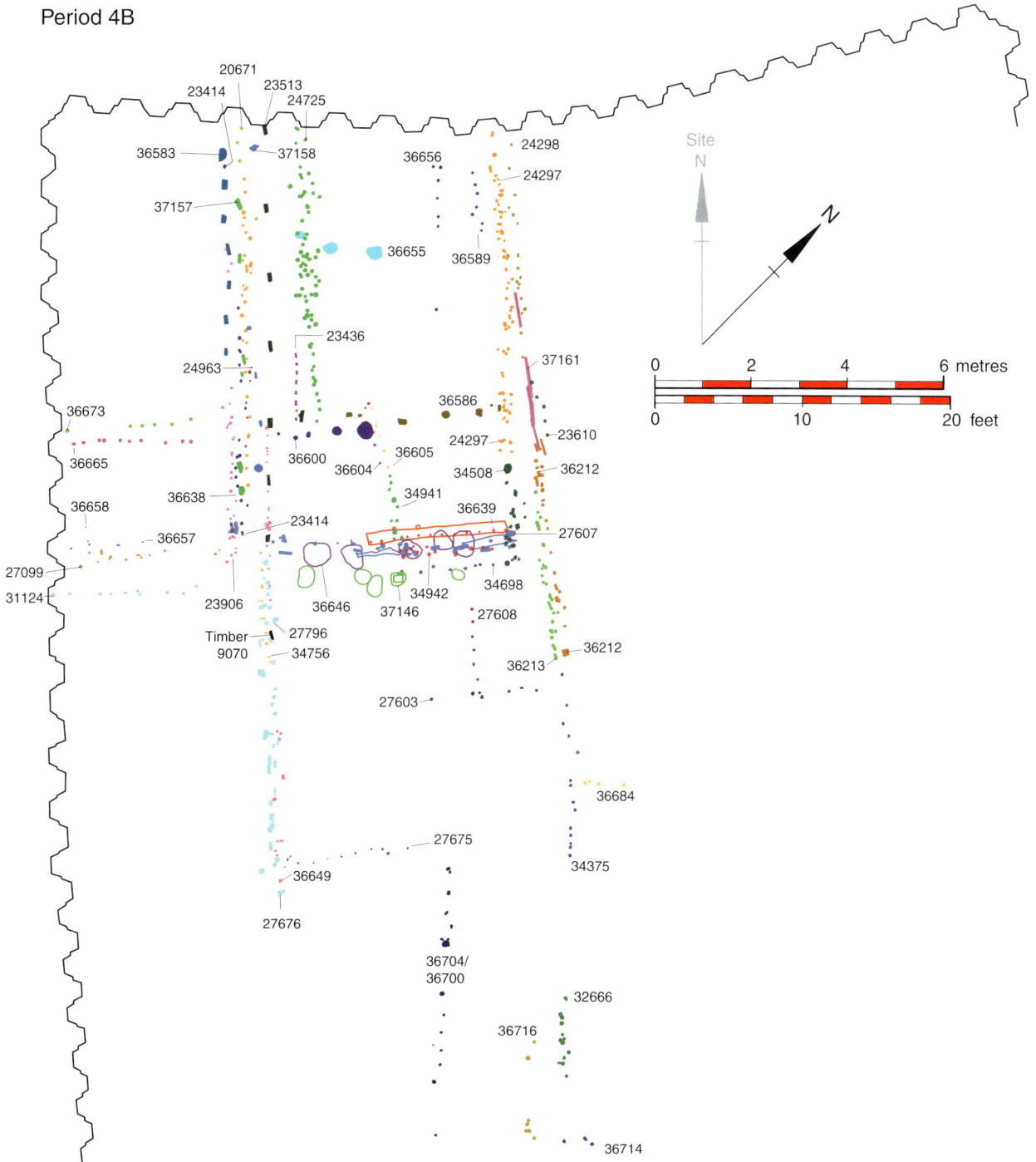

Fig. 159 *Plan of alignments in Tenements A and B. Scale 1:125*

south (back) walls of the buildings. On Tenements B and C they incorporate indicators of doorways, while on Tenements B and D they incorporate horizontal plank elements. The extent of intrusions on Tenement A has removed more evidence than on the other tenements, and there is an absence of the larger upright timbers which are found on B, C and D. There are, however, successive stake alignments some 9.5–10m back from the street frontage in Tenement A (alignments 27099 and 31124, Fig.159), coincident in position with the south wall on Tenement B, and it is conceivable that they represent a south (back) wall on Tenement A.

The northerly zone of Tenement B also shows another trait that may be replicated elsewhere. This

575

Fig. 160 *Threshold of Tenement B, looking south. Scale unit 0.1m*

Fig. 161 *Detail of threshold of Tenement B, looking south. Scale unit 0.1m*

is the existence of another transverse alignment (36586), parallel to and approximately 2.5m to the north of the back wall (Fig.159). There are indications of transverse alignments in a broadly similar position on Tenements A (36673/36665) and C (see Figs 159, 170), but not on D. On Tenement A, in the absence of other surviving features, their purpose is not clear but their position in the other cases suggests possible internal sub-divisions (see p.585).

At the base of the Period 4B deposits, running north–south from the street frontage end, was a discontinuous alignment of small posts without any interwoven wattlework (alignment 37158, Fig.159). Just to its west and apparently accompanying it ran an alignment of stakes and wattlework (24963, Fig.159). There were no obvious reasons why both these should not have extended beyond the relatively limited extent within which they were recorded. A soil change continued the line of 24963 south until it returned to align with the stake and wattlework alignment 27099 (Fig.159); this soil change, however, was slightly later than and 0.4m to the north of the well-preserved stake and wattle-work return, alignment 23906, and its interpretation is uncertain though it might have been a fenced enclosure just outside a putative doorway.

Another, but less favoured, interpretation is that these alignments represent a more substantial, earlier structure. Alignment 23906 and fragments of a similarly aligned 36638 some metres to the north were amongst the stratigraphically earliest Period 4B alignments (Fig.159). The wattlework was rather degraded, perhaps in part a result of somewhat less favourable soil conditions at this time; in its southern 1.2m there was some evidence for later strengthening/patching with a few inserted stakes. Nonetheless, it could clearly be linked with the transverse stake and wattle alignment 27099 which marked its southern extent. No uprights more substantial than stakes were associated with either return of this feature; although in the case of 23906 this might be the result of modern intrusions, there is no such reason for their absence from 27099. Thus, unless it is argued that it was a structure employing different building techniques on different axes, it seems that no larger timbers at all were present.

The transverse alignment 27099 was one of three fragmentary alignments (the others being 31124 and 36657) which ran, virtually parallel, within a strip 1m wide and which appeared to terminate against the main axial alignments which divide Tenement A from Tenement B. Within Tenement B, the course of this strip was continued as the series of alignments which include more substantial uprights and some horizontal timbers which are seen as forming part of the back wall of a building. Although they all appeared within a relatively shallow band of stratification, it was possible to determine the sequence of the three transverse alignments in Tenement A, and to relate them to a short length of axial alignment, 36658 (Fig.159). The earliest was the transverse alignment nearest to street frontage, 36657, a row of stakes without wattle, damaged by the insertion of the later Period 5B building. This was over-ridden by the axial 36658, which had been likewise damaged, and which was either cut by or abutted the transverse alignment 27099. To the south of 27099 was the less

fully preserved parallel alignment 31124, with which it appeared to be approximately contemporary.

The regularly spaced stave alignment 36583, the putative east wall of the Tenement A building, which was positioned towards the west edge of the surviving spine of soil, was erected relatively late in Period 4B, and was cut away towards the south by the insertion of the cellar for Structure 5/1. Beyond the northernmost surviving stave a depression which continued the regular spacing seems to represent the position of another stave. No other alignment was recognised in association with it, and its regularity and off-centre position support the idea of it being part of a building.

Approximately bisecting this spine of surviving deposits was an alignment of stakes and wattle-work, 23414 (Fig.159), which was erected quite early in Period 4B. Alongside it was an alignment of staves (37157), traceable intermittently over virtually the same extent as 20671 (Fig.159). The staves were slightly canted, apparently supporting horizontal edge-set planks (23425, Fig.162) which were themselves canted. All but one of the staves was recorded as having a charred top, but none of the stakes or the horizontal timber showed signs of burning. Nonetheless, all three elements – staves, horizontal timber, and stake and wattle – may have been integral. This group of alignments appeared to have been replaced by an immediately adjacent well-defined stake and wattle alignment 20671, which was easily traced until truncated by a modern wall foundation.

The boundary between Tenements A and B, however, was continued into the backyard by another early alignment, 34819 (not on plan), which was disturbed by a modern well and by a cut (36754); it survived in only a short disconnected length between modern intrusions. It seems to be an earlier version of alignment 27676, for which there is a dendrochronological date of 942–74, and may well be the same as alignment 36649 (Fig.159). Their line was arguably established in Period 4A by alignment 36659 (see Fig.154), but by Period 4B these alignments clearly divide the two properties (Tenements A and B); this division lasts for approximately two generations, disappearing briefly in Period 5A (see pp.605–6) but subsequently re-established and then perpetuated through Period 5B and beyond.

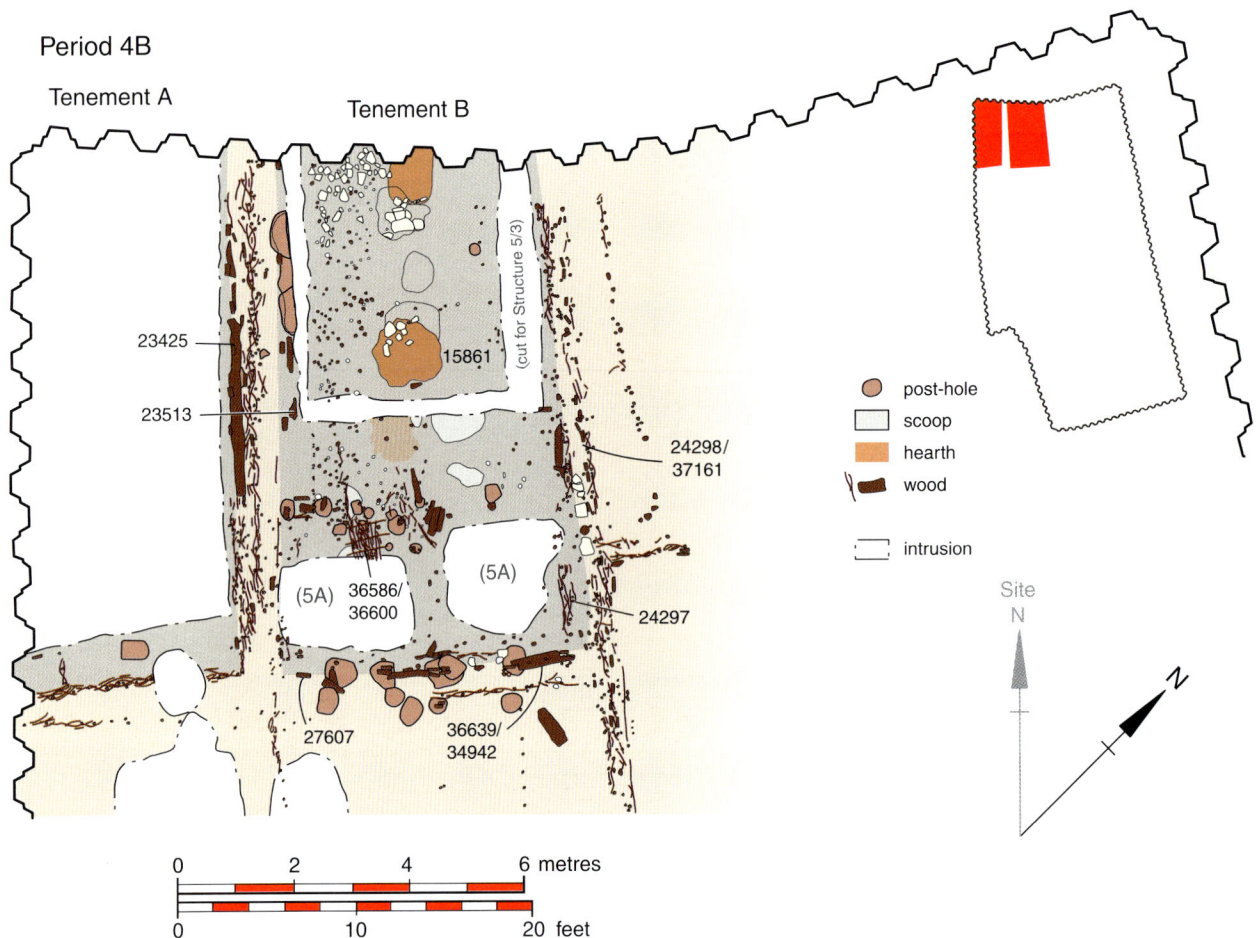

Period 4B

Tenement A

Tenement B

23425

23513

15861

(cut for Structure 5/3)

24298/
37161

(5A)   36586/
36600

(5A)

24297

27607

36639/
34942

post-hole

scoop

hearth

wood

intrusion

Site
N

0   2   4   6 metres

0   10   20 feet

Fig.162   *Plan of Tenements A and B, showing the nature of various features. Scale 1:125*

The backyard features which relate to Period 4B survive best on Tenement B (Fig.166) and show a complex of intercutting pits (e.g. 28334/37084/37027), some of which are wattle-lined (e.g. 28652), together with the remains of plank and wattle walkways. Occasional transverse alignments (e.g. 27675, Fig.159) and axial alignments such as 36704/36700 might have served to demarcate and stabilise the walkways. The remains of timber elements associated with several of the pits in this central area, and the nature of their contents, indicate that many served as cess pits, presumably accessed down the backyards on the observed walkways. Beyond this central zone of pits, the evidence for activity decreases and the occurrence of pits and scoops is less concentrated.

Development of this western side of the site almost certainly goes back to the early years of the 10th century (Period 4A). Before that, in the second half of the 9th century, this same area had been used for refuse pits, limestone spreads and post-holes. By the early decades of the 10th century, however, it seems likely that structures stood aligned to the street of Coppergate in both Tenements A and B. The complex overlaying, replacement and repair of boundary fences, house walls and possibly internal divisions confirm that this was not a single episode of construction but one in which modifications and repairs took place almost continuously. In its latest phase, which tree-ring dates suggest might have been in the 940s, the structure on Tenement B seems to have comprised an eastern wall (24298/37161/23610), a western wall (23513) and a back wall (27607) with threshold (36639/34942) (Figs 159 and 162). The building was damaged by the cut for the later Structure 5/3 (Figs 162 and 163) but despite this there were surviving patches of clay floor (Fig.164) and fragments of hearths, together with further alignments

578

Fig. 163   *Tenement B, showing the Period 4B building damaged by the cut for the later Structure 5/3. Scale unit 0.1m*

and groups of stakes which suggest internal features. Notable amongst these is an alignment of stakes (24725) along the west wall which has been interpreted as a bench or sleeping platform (Figs 159 and 165); a more broken alignment, including a southerly section (24297) might indicate a similar feature on the east wall (Fig.159). Three larger posts (36655, Fig.159) running on a transverse line across the centre on the west are more difficult to interpret, but they pre-date the hearth and possibly the structure. A more

complete transverse line formed by 36586/36600 (Fig.159) might represent some form of internal room division. An internal space whose eastern edge is defined by alignments 36605/36604/34941 (Fig.159) might have been divided off but much of the data was destroyed by a later Period 5A pit (Fig.162). The frequent refurbishment of the lines of posts and stakes which represent the back wall and threshold make this area difficult to disentangle but the position of some of these elements suggests that there might

Fig. 164   *Clay floors in Tenement B. Scale unit 0.1m*

Fig. 165   *Surviving traces of the bench/platform in the Tenement B building. Scale unit 0.1m*

have been an externally supported roof overhang or small porch. Outside the structure, another line of stakes (27608) might, in combination with transverse alignment 27603, suggest some form of fenced enclosure (Fig.159).

The biological remains from the surviving internal deposits on Tenement B (none survived from Tenement A) were sampled and 'suggest fairly tolerable living and working conditions. The floors were probably by no means dry by modern standards, but were generally not so unpleasant that they could not be sat on' (*AY* 14/7, 550). These deposits produced an essentially 'house' fauna in terms of insects, together with sheep parasites which might have arrived with fleece or wool. Evidence of plants of 'outdoor' species suggested that the structure was occasionally open to let in light and air, and a mixture of habitats were identified within the building including those indicative of foul conditions such as deposits of moulding plant debris and, in one case, stable manure (*ibid*, 549).

Surviving external deposits immediately behind the supposed structure on Tenement A (Fig.166) contained cornfield weeds and cereal chaff which might represent the periodic cleaning of floor litter, an interpretation given credence by the presence of human fleas and lice (*AY* 14/7, 545). Little survives of the backyard deposits as these were disturbed by later intrusions, including a long Period 5B gully (2378, Fig.166). Two backyard pits, 27070 (which straddles Tenement A and B) and 18490 (Fig.166), both contained human faeces with large counts of parasite eggs and, in the case of 18490, probable evidence for materials used for sanitary purposes (*ibid*, 545). Both pits contained a wide range of domestic waste including foodstuffs, such as charred bread, fish and various fruits, both wild and cultivated. The small but well-preserved insect assemblage from 27070 suggests that the fills accumulated rapidly. Pit 27070 (Fig.167) was very large, carefully lined with wicker, and as such represents a considerable investment of labour. Its position, just beyond the terminus of the Tenement A/B boundary, begs the question whether it was constructed to serve both households. Pit 18490, by contrast, is smaller and is clearly in the backyard of Tenement A.

Immediately behind the structure on Tenement B further evidence was found for periodic house sweepings, with the area devoid of evidence for human faeces (*ibid*, 551). A red-stained patch resulting from the dumping of dyebath waste (*ibid*, 551) immediately outside the structure is consistent with accounts of dyeplants being recovered from the area. Samples taken from slightly further back, from the area enclosed by the fence (27608 and 27603) described above provided evidence for more general organic food and domestic waste including the fruits from sloe, apple, blackberry and cherry, 'bran' and food flavourings (*ibid*, 551–2). Opposite this area, against the property boundary with Tenement A, pit 36574 (Fig.166) contained further evidence of foodstuffs, together with human and animal faeces, and comparable material was recovered from a pit (37027) further down the backyard (*ibid*, 552–3).

Sherds of pottery from both the small, rounded, flat-bottomed York ware jars and from the wider range of forms produced by potters of Torksey-type ware were recovered from internal floors, external deposits and from pits. External sooting on some suggests they stood in the hearth and internal residues attest to the preparation of food. Domestic activities such weaving, spinning and other stages in the production of textiles and garments appear to have been routine domestic tasks, some of which, including disposal of dyebath waste and laundering, were doubtless conducted out of doors (*AY* 17/11, 1803). The survival of the debris from the lathe-turning of wooden bowls and cups which occurred in all backyards (*AY* 17/13, fig.1045) suggests that this was an outdoor skill common to many of the Coppergate householders. The deposits in and around the houses also produced evidence for small-scale craft production such as the working of imported amber into finger rings and pendants (*AY* 17/14, fig.1224), and turning bone and antler into all manner of items, functional and decorative, the most numerous being antler combs (*AY* 17/12, fig.881). Deposits associated with Tenement B produced considerable quantities of leather-working waste (*AY* 17/16, figs 1582–4). The metal industries, which require a wider range of expertise and some specialist equipment, are most visible in the two other tenements (C and D) but greater amounts of iron smithing slag were recovered from deposits associated with Tenement B (*AY* 17/6); there is also considerable evidence for the working of copper and lead, as opposed to silver (see below), on this tenement (*AY* 17/7, figs 355 and 358).

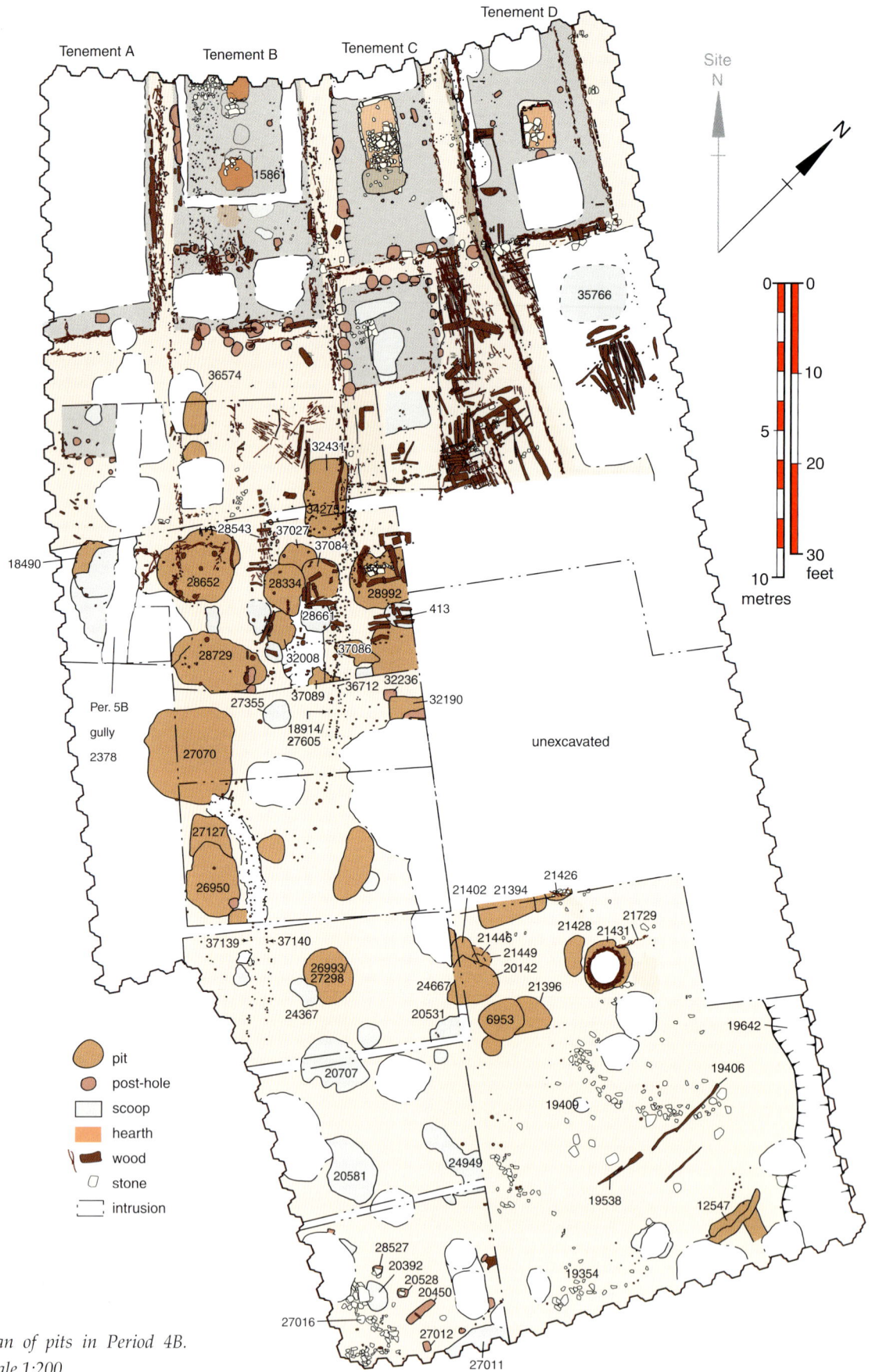

Tenement A   Tenement B   Tenement C   Tenement D

Site
N

15861

36574

35766

32431

34274

18490   28543   37027
37084
28652   28334   28992
28661   413
28729   32008   37086
27355   36712   32236
37089   32190
Per. 5B   18914/
gully   27605
2378   27070   unexcavated

27127

26950

21426
21402 21394
37139   37140   21428   21729
21446   21431
21449
20142
26993/   24667   21396
27298
24367   20531   6953   19642

20707   19406

19400

24949

20581   19538   12547

19354
pit
post-hole
scoop   28527
hearth   20392
wood   20528
stone   20450
intrusion   27016
27012

27011

Fig.166   *Plan of pits in Period 4B.*
Scale 1:200

582

Fig. 167   *Large wicker-lined pit 27070 in the final stages of excavation*

Tenements C and D

The boundary between Tenements B and C (Fig.168) is defined by the much-repaired, reinforced and refurbished series of alignments 23055, 24282, 36645, 27606, 27605 and 36712 (Figs 168 and 169). The boundary curves slightly to the west as it extends into the backyard, where the fence line becomes more patchy before petering out. At various points along their combined course the alignments include stakes, posts, and lengths of timber, but few staves. This boundary was a major one, perpetuating an earlier fence line, and was itself perpetuated for the duration of the Anglo-Scandinavian period.

The walls which define the building at the front of Tenement C (Fig.168) also underwent numerous phases of repair, replacement and strengthening which, over time, has resulted in the east and west walls of the buildings being not obviously matched. The need for repair and extra support for the eastern wall might well have been more acute due to the increasing lateral slope of the land as it falls off to the east (see Fig.134). In several instances it was clear from charring on the top of stakes that here too fire necessitated episodes of full or partial rebuilding of walls, as well as *ad hoc* repairs.

An attempt was made by the excavator to chart the sequence of development of the wattle buildings on Tenement C, the front of which still lies under the present street of Coppergate. The west wall seems, from an early stage, to have comprised a dense line of stakes (25640) and larger posts (33237) (Fig.168). One of the timbers in 25640 produced a felling date of 914–48, and the wall was then successively strengthened and repaired (alignments 33237, 40020, 25320, 22596). The southern (back) wall of the building was defined by a line of stakes (29855) and larger posts (35161), the latter alignment including two timbers with felling dates of after 891. A rear entrance crossed a threshold which led onto an external stabilised ground surface, described below. The east wall of the building is defined by a line of large posts (30770) and

583

Period 4B

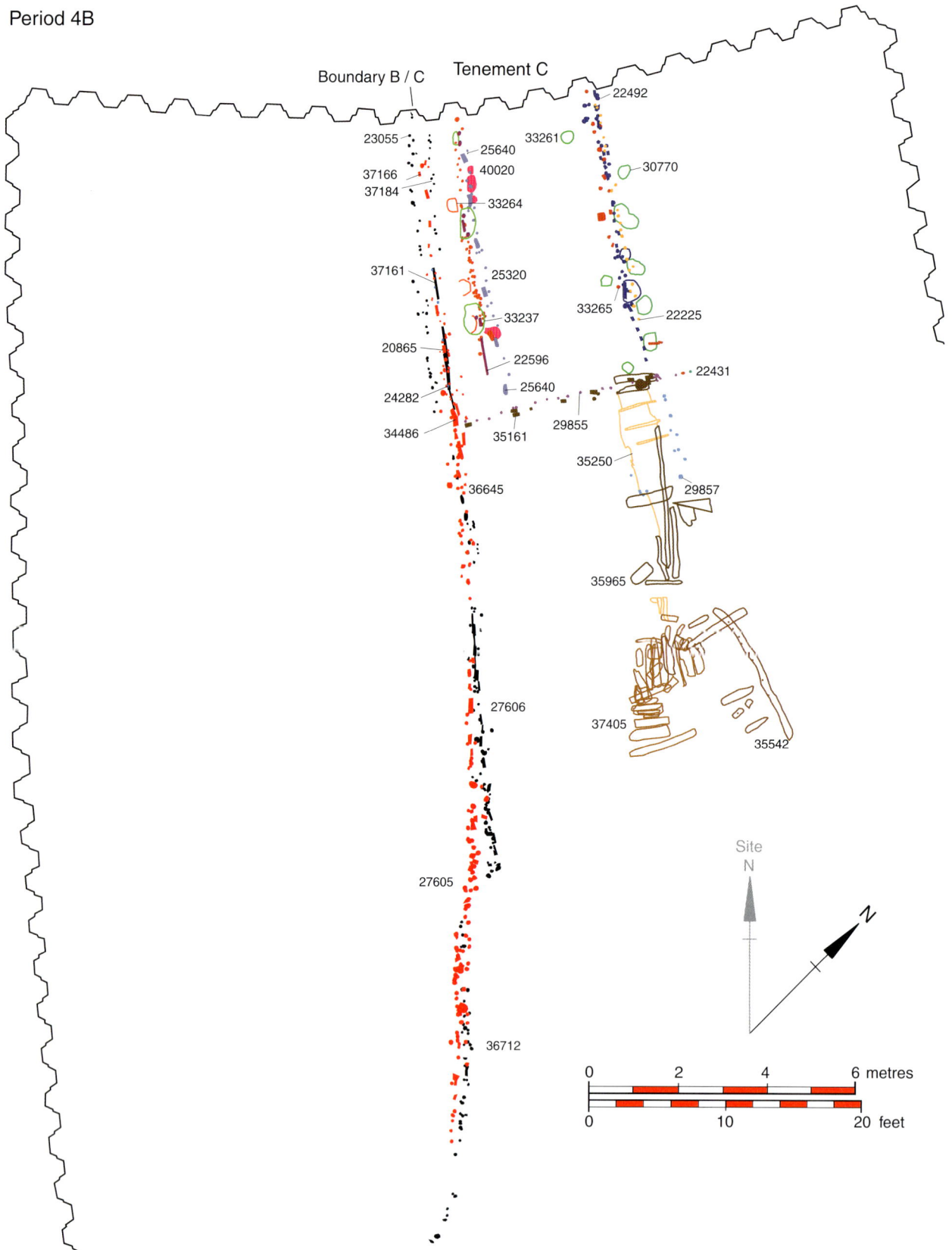

Fig.168   *Plan showing boundary between Tenements B and C, and the major axial alignments on Tenement C. Scale 1:125*

Fig. 169   *The boundary between Tenements B and C from the west. Scale unit 0.1m*

stakes (33265/22492), and they too were periodically augmented by further short alignments (Fig.168).

Early phases of the building included two transverse lines of stakes (25850 and 25775) running parallel to each other and to the back wall. These are shown on Figures 170 and 171i and appear to be contemporary with the earliest phase of the west wall (25640); they pre-date any recognisable hearth. How this line of posts functioned within the building is unclear, other than as a form of room division, although there is no obvious throughway at the level of the surviving stakes. The transverse alignments do not appear in later phases when the layout of the room is established with a central hearth and sleeping platform(s) along the wall(s); they might, therefore, have been associated with its construction.

Another unexplained feature, in the south-west corner of the building against the back wall, is defined by two short parallel lines of stakes (40024/40027, Fig.170); they might have been an early form of bench. The back wall (29855) apparently extends to the west

as far as the boundary wall, beyond its intersection with alignment 25640 (Figs 168 and 170), an extension which is perhaps mirrored by a similar feature to the east. This suggests either that this wall continued as a fence, or more probably that the wall extension supported an overhanging roof. Such support might also have been the purpose of some of the many north–south alignments (for example 37184) running immediately east of the property boundary (Fig.168).

The next phase of development is marked by the disappearance of the transverse alignments and the construction of a succession of large rectangular hearths situated centrally between the east and west walls. Before this there had been no evidence of a hearth, although there were a few scoops and gully-like features within the interior as well as individual stake-holes and small post-holes. In the next phase an area of burned clay 25069/25630, approximately delineated by gullies (22982 and 25068), defines a small hearth (Fig.171ii). This feature was replaced by a large rectangular cut for the subsequent hearth (22720, Fig.171iii). At about the same time the west

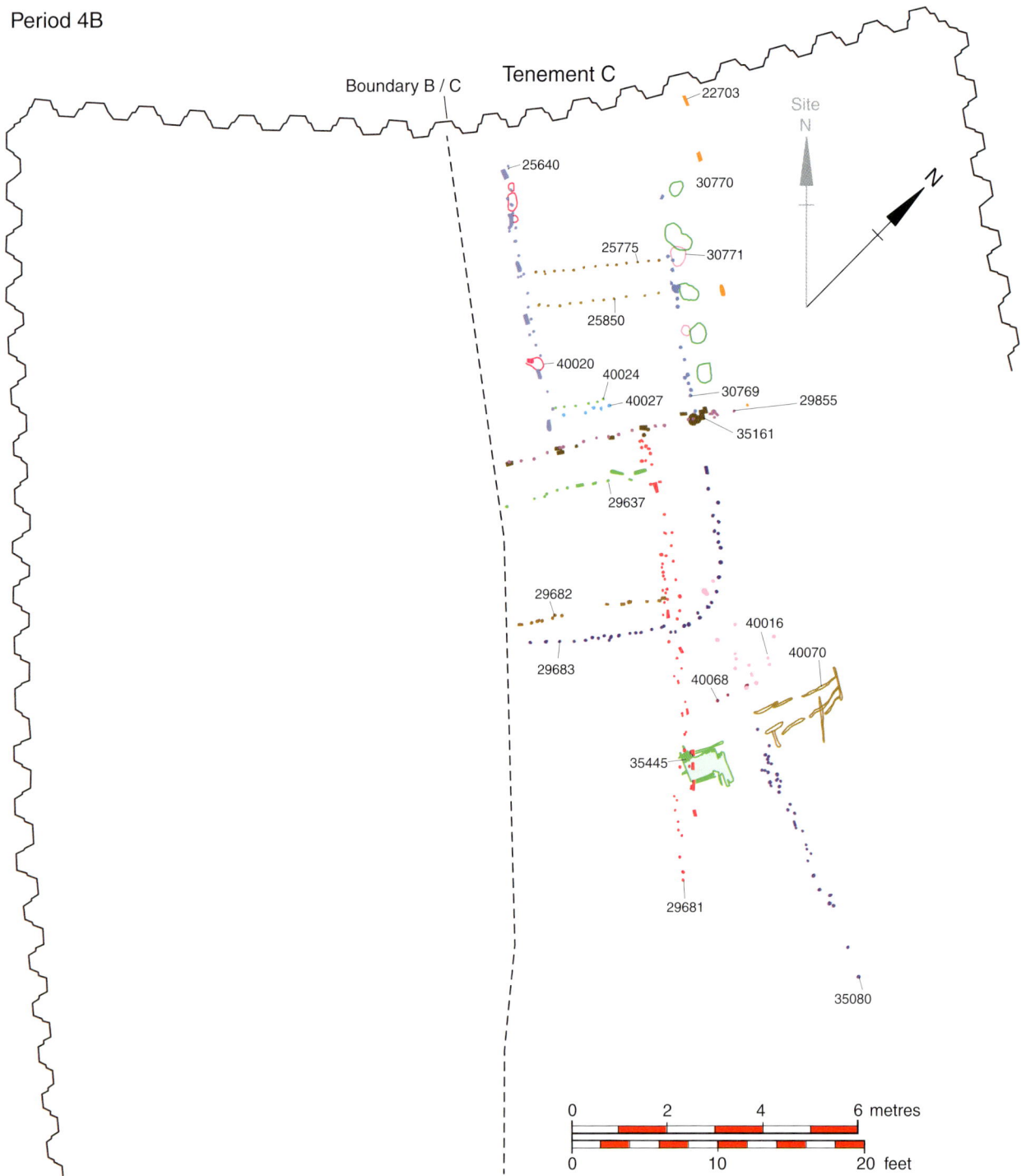

Period 4B

Boundary B / C

Tenement C

22703

Site
N

25640

30770

25775

30771

25850

40020

40024

40027

30769

29855

35161

29637

29682

29683

40016

40070

40068

35445

29681

35080

0   2   4   6 metres

0   10   20 feet

Fig.170   *Plan showing the transverse alignments on Tenement C. Scale 1:125*

wall is strengthened by one or two large posts, while the east wall remains relatively flimsy although reinforced with another alignment of stakes (22492, Fig.171ii). The base of the newly constructed hearth (22720) was lined with irregular pieces of limestone and Roman tile and edged with small limestone blocks (Figs 171iii and 172). At the southern end of the hearth is a scoop (22721) which has limestone pieces in its base, and one or two associated post- or stake-holes. The subsequent hearth (22320) is slightly smaller (Figs 171iv and 173) and is lined with laid timbers (for example 22321, 22322) rather than limestone but retains the scoop (22721), now separated from the clay of the hearth by a row of post-holes (Fig.173). The fills of this feature contained the largest group of beetles and bugs from any of the Anglo-Scandinavian deposits, with one of the highest concentrations of species typical of damp mouldering organic material, and it was suggested that 'the abundant insect and other decomposer organisms, probably living *in situ*, had almost completely broken down what had originally been a large quantity of organic matter' (*AY* 14/7, 558).

The floor of the house was of beaten earth with patches of hardened clay but with one or two depressions or scoops within it, unique to this property, the purpose of which is unclear. One of these (see below) contained what might be the remains of a bee skep (*AY* 14/7, 765–6), while dyeplants remain an important component of the others. Food plants are rare in these scoops and the other species include weeds, mosses, and marshland and woodland plants (*ibid*, 558–9). A pit up against the shoring, but still within the structure, contained either horse or cow dung (*ibid*, 559). The environmental evidence (*ibid*, 554–63) recovered from floors and cut features within the house is, by and large, domestic in character with an insect assemblage representing a typical 'house' fauna, and foodstuffs indicated by nuts, charred grain and edible plants including celery. Human fleas were recovered but only 'hints of a fouler element' (*ibid*, 555) from internal deposits. The exceptions to this generally domestic character include the large number of sheep lice and sheep ked puparia indicative of wool and fleece preparation, and evidence for bee keeping in the form not only of the bee skep but also beeswax and bees themselves which together 'surely represent evidence of apiculture' (*ibid*, 557).

It is likely that there was an entrance to the successive structures on Tenement C on the street frontage, but there was clearly another through the back wall of the building into the backyard. In the earlier phases of the building the area immediately outside the door appears to have been partially enclosed by a curving line of stakes (29683) running east–west, while lines of stakes running north–south (e.g. 29681) suggest subdivisions of this area (Fig.170). The purpose of these various alignments remains obscure, but animal enclosures or defined kitchen gardens are amongst the most likely. Determining which of these lines were contemporary with which phases of the building is hampered by the continuing replacement of different elements of these alignments.

In a later phase of the building the entrance is more clearly defined by the threshold (29855) in the south wall which opens onto a walkway comprising various re-used planks and wattlework (35250, 29857, 35965, 37405, 35542) (Figs 168, 174 and 175), often secured to the ground by stakes in an effort to stabilise the area which took the brunt of footfall. A horizontal plank in group 37405 has a date of after AD 823, suggesting this walkway included recycled timbers that were lying about, which is consistent with the evidence for several stages of patching and refurbishment using planks or pieces of wattlework.

The environmental evidence from the two strips of land either side of the structure, and from the rear of the structure, suggests that it was a trampled and disturbed area on which nettles, brackens, short rushes and mosses thrived. There is no evidence of foul matter behind the structures, the best evidence for cess coming from a pit (37086) (Fig.166) half way down the property on the boundary between Tenements B and C. Foodstuff in the form of nuts, charred peas and grain was found, together with further examples of dyeplants. Pit 32190 (Fig.166), further back down the yard from pit 37086, contained in its various fills flax, oat chaff and dung, together with evidence of what appears to be material cleaned out from a stable or byre.

A large intrusion removed most of what there was in the area beyond the walkway, and it is difficult to tie in the backyard area with the different episodes of occupation in the buildings. Other than the walkways and stake alignments referred to above

Period 4B

(i)

Tenement C

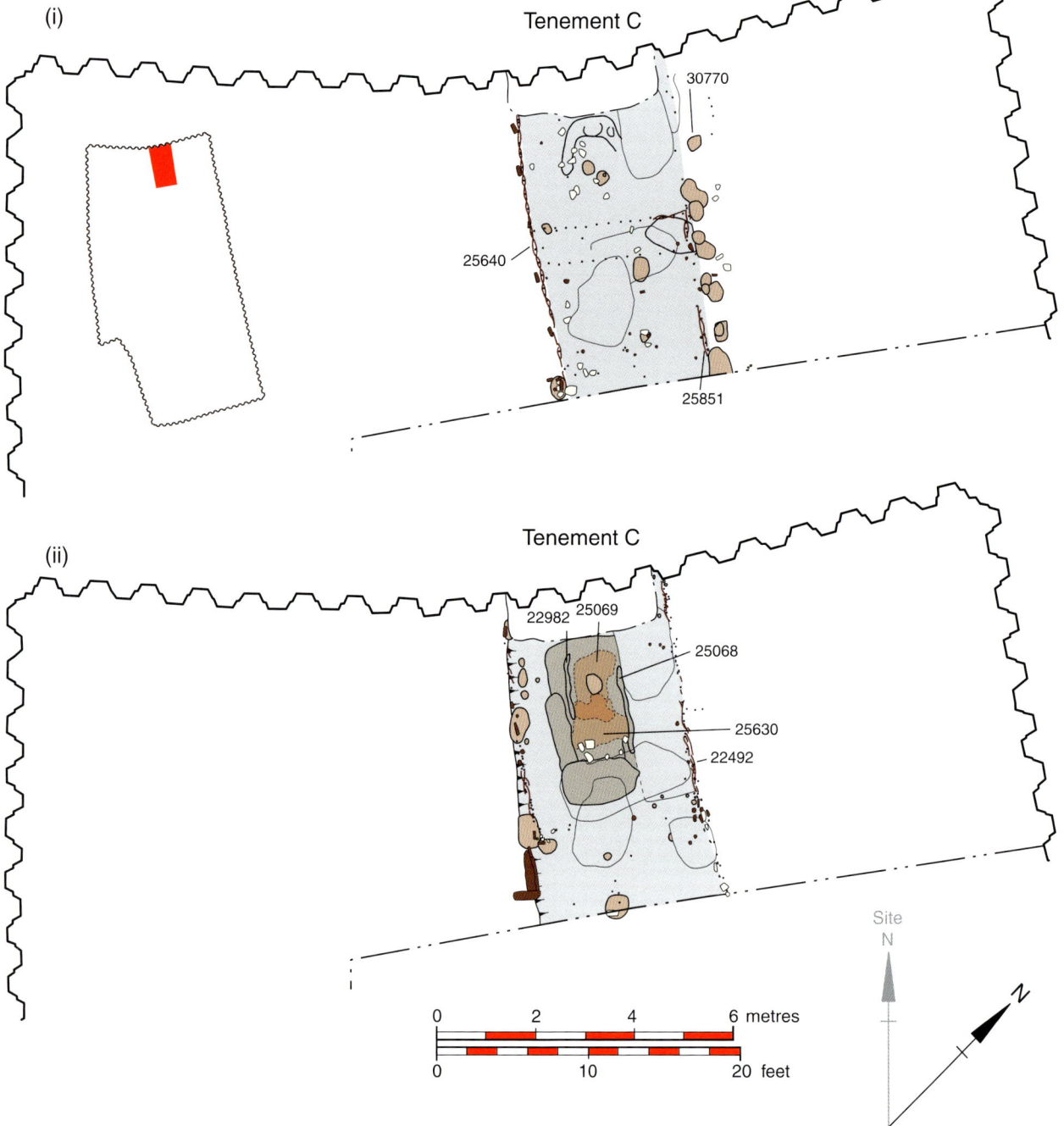

30770

25640

25851

(ii)

Tenement C

22982 25069

25068

25630

22492

0   2   4   6 metres

0   10   20 feet

Site
N

N

Fig. 171   The hearth sequence in Tenement C in Period 4B. Scale 1:125

there are a number of scoops, pits and gullies. Fills in pit 21431, which is neatly wicker-lined and lies to the south of the intrusion (Fig.166), were analysed and found to contain mostly weed plants. That fact, combined with an insect assemblage indicative of wet conditions with little evidence for dumping of plants, led to the conclusion that the pits had contained open

water and stood disused for a considerable time (*AY* 14/7, 567–8), a time during which large numbers of frogs either blundered in, or took up residence there (*ibid*). This would seem to reinforce the suggestion that the River Foss end of the site was not as extensively or intensively used as the central area, and that conditions there were very wet.

Period 4B

(iii)

Tenement C

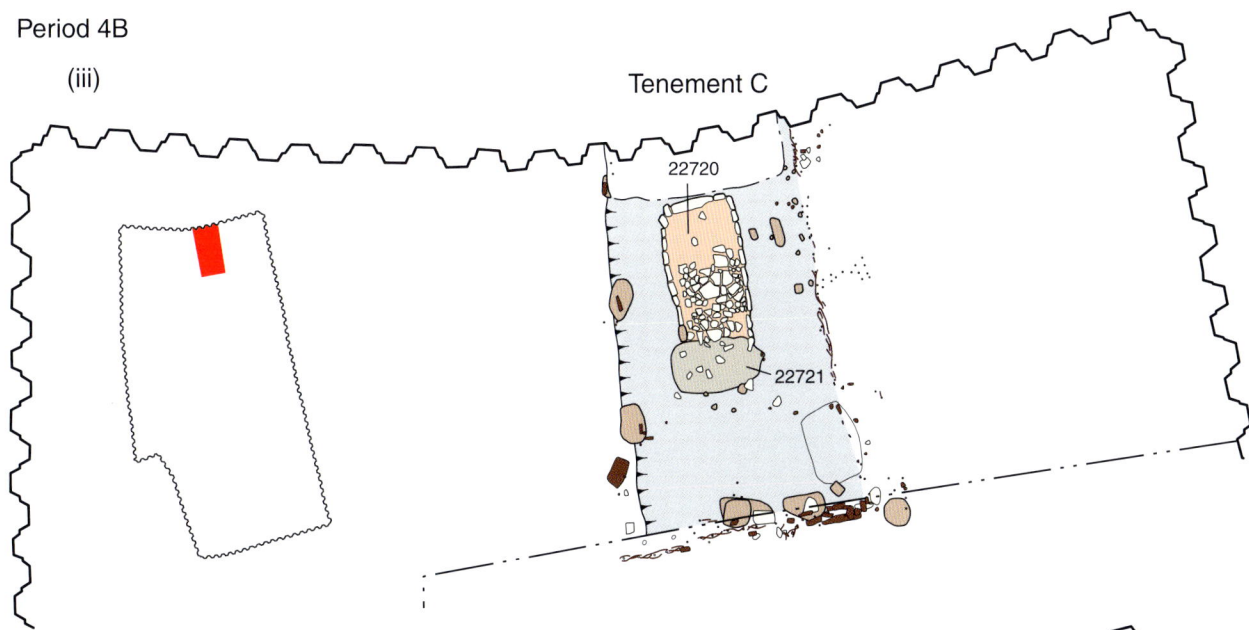

(iv)

Tenement C

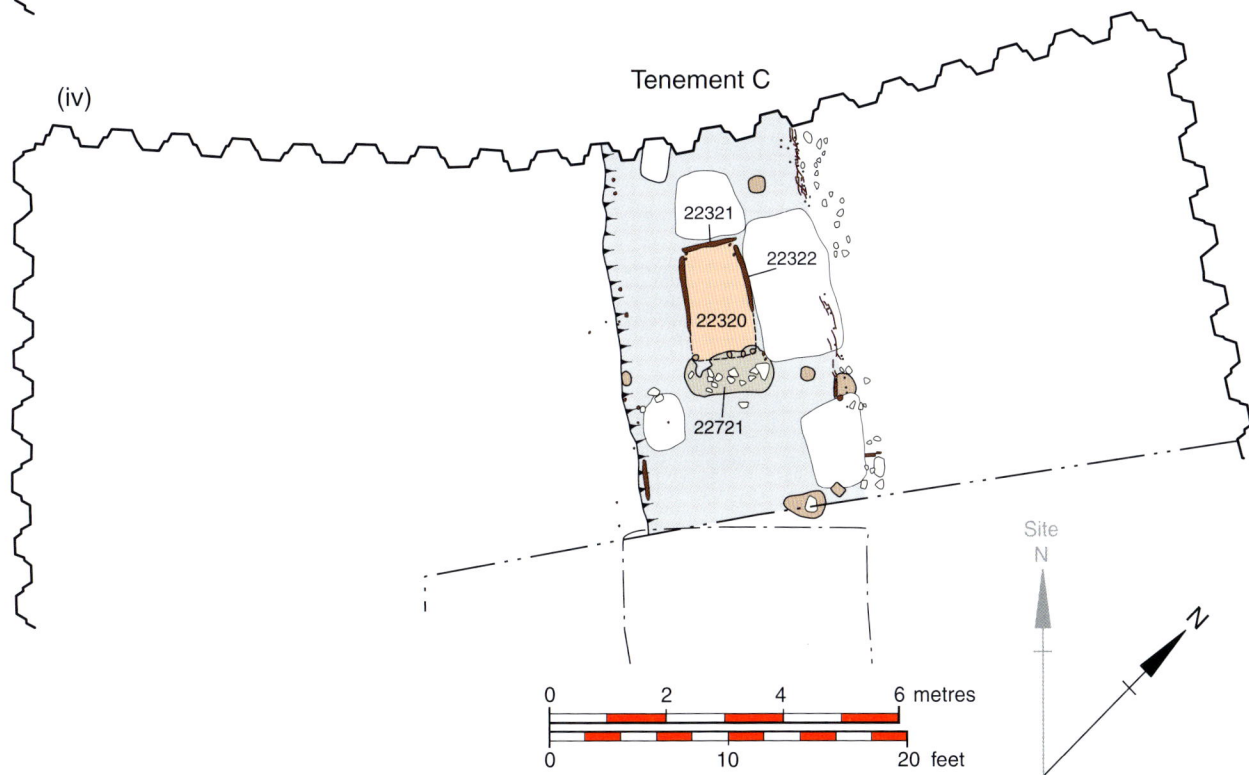

As with Tenement B, the material culture assemblage from both the Tenement C building and from the backyard area indicates a range of domestic and household craft activities. There is copious and diverse evidence for ferrous and non-ferrous metal working, associated no doubt with the frequently refashioned hearth. What part the scooped feature at the hearth's southern edge played is unclear but it might have provided access to the heat source as part of the process. The hazards associated with these high-temperature industries doubtless account for the evidence of charring and the frequent repairs. While the distribution of smithing slag is greatest in Tenement B (*AY* 17/6, fig.177), the distribution

Fig.172 *Hearth 22720 on Tenement C, looking north. Scale unit 0.1m*

Fig.173 *Hearth 22320 on Tenement C, looking west. Scale unit 0.1m*

Fig.174   *Part of the south wall of Tenement C, looking south. Scale unit 0.1m*

of bars, strips and plates (*ibid*, fig.191), objects with plating (*ibid*, fig.179), needles (*ibid*, fig.218), dress fittings and riding equipment (*ibid*, fig.295) is greatest in Tenement C. Other more general-purpose, utilitarian objects, such as knives, are more evenly spread between Tenements C and D. Sharpening stones, both hones and rotary grindstones, occur in some concentration with the greatest number of hones, especially those of schist and phylitte (*AY* 17/14, table 229), coming from this property. Fragments of three rotary grindstones were also recovered from inside the structure.

Just as the concentrations of different biological remains in Tenement B suggested discrete habitats inside the buildings and, by extension, different activities, the distribution of material culture indicates the possible location of different practices. Plated objects, for example, are distributed principally in the south-west corner of the building on Tenement C, raising the possibility that the cluster of stake-holes in that corner (p.585), partly destroyed by a later Period 5A rubbish pit, might represent some sort of work bench situated to take advantage of light from the doorway. The distribution of non-ferrous metal-working evidence in the form of crucibles and other types of debris, while focused on the building on Tenement D in this period (see below), extends also to Tenement C

(*AY* 17/7, fig.329), and the presence of plated objects must be indicative of either co-operative working practices or individuals with multiple skills.

The waste from leather working recovered from the successive phases of this structure and from the area immediately behind is found in almost equal quantities in Tenements B and C (*AY* 17/16, figs 1582–4), although there is more evidence for sheath and scabbard making in Tenement C (*ibid*, fig.1682), suggesting some specialisation. The distribution of antler comb-making waste and amber-working waste is equally spread across all four tenements, but focuses on Tenements B and C (*AY* 17/12, fig.881; *AY* 17/14, fig.1224), while textile and garment production was an activity common to all four tenements.

The structure on Tenement C is narrower than the other Period 4B buildings, but as it is incomplete its length cannot be determined (see Table 29). The large central hearth, together with the scooped feature at the southern end, occupies a great deal of the floor area, and there is no compelling evidence for the benches or sleeping platforms along the walls as seen in Tenement B (and perhaps D, see pp.579 and 595–6). These factors raise the question as to whether, in this later phase, the structure might not have functioned as a dwelling but simply as a workshop, although

Tenement C

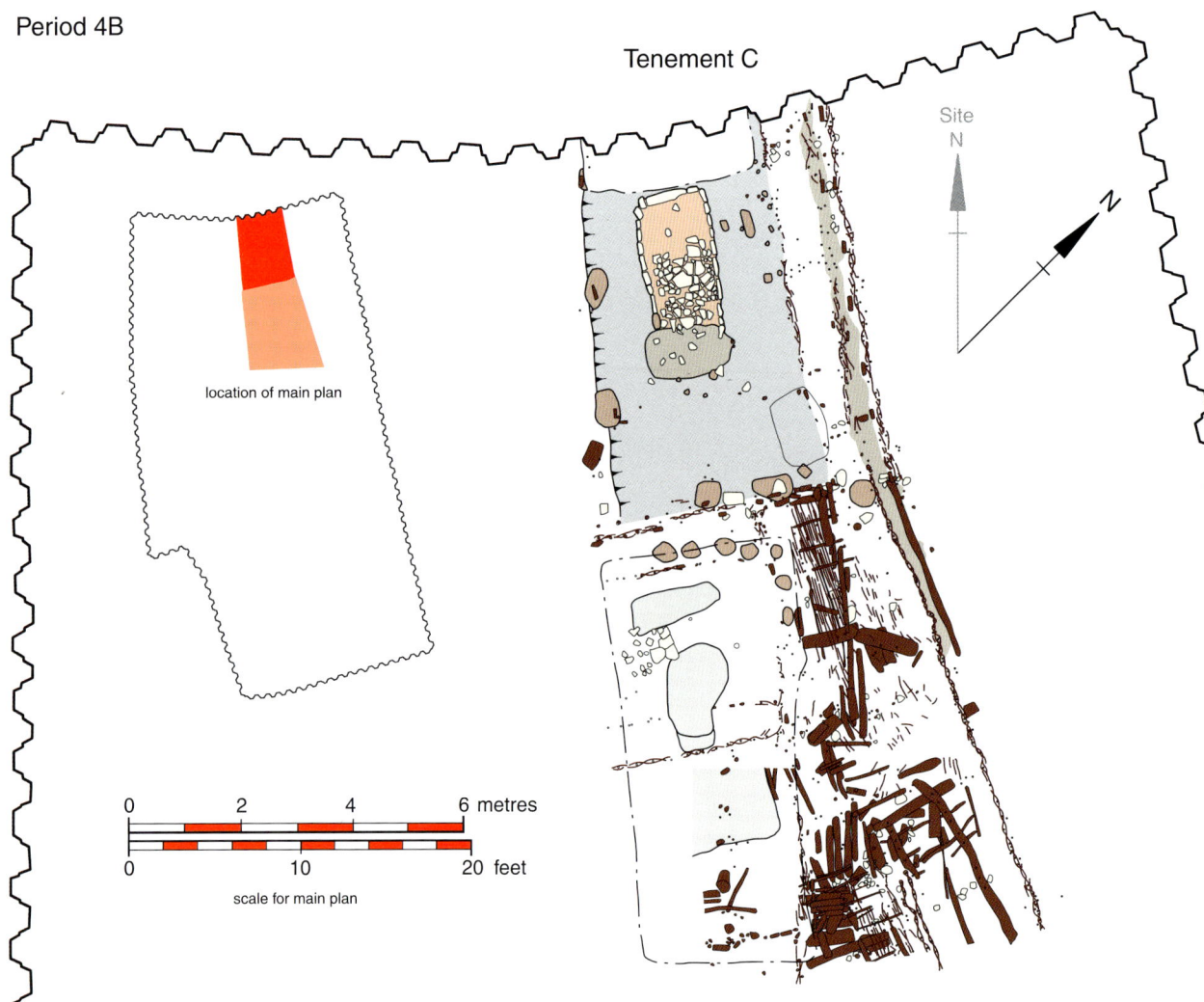

location of main plan

Site
N

0   2   4   6 metres

0   10   20 feet

scale for main plan

Fig.175   *Plan of Period 4B features in Tenement C. Scale 1:125*

the environmental evidence supports continuing domestic activities.

Tenement C perhaps best exemplifies the difficulties in distinguishing domestic activities from commercial pursuits, although the distinction was probably not one that would have been recognised in the 10th century. While the distribution of iron needles (*AY* 17/6, fig.218) reflects the concentration in that building of bars, strips and plates (*ibid*, fig.191), implying they were produced there, this structure also has the greatest concentration of spindle whorls; this raises the question as to whether the needles reflect loss in manufacture or use in textile production. On the face of it, the activities associated with production of iron and copper-alloy artefacts appear incompatible with the preparation of textiles and garments

but the evidence suggests both took place. Textile and garment production are typically domestic activities undertaken by every household (*AY* 17/11, 1821–5), activities comparable to the preparation of food; the latter is also indicated by the persistent presence of York ware cooking pots and, subsequently, Torksey-type and Stamford ware vessels (*AY* 16/5, 494–5 and fig.218), as well as evidence for foodstuffs.

The boundary between Tenements C and D appears to have been as significant and durable as that between Tenements B and C, defining a property on which a similar post and wattlework structure stood gable end to the street frontage (Fig.176). A line of stakes (22431) runs in the narrow space between the buildings, and its continuation (29856) follows through into the backyard. Figure 177 shows how

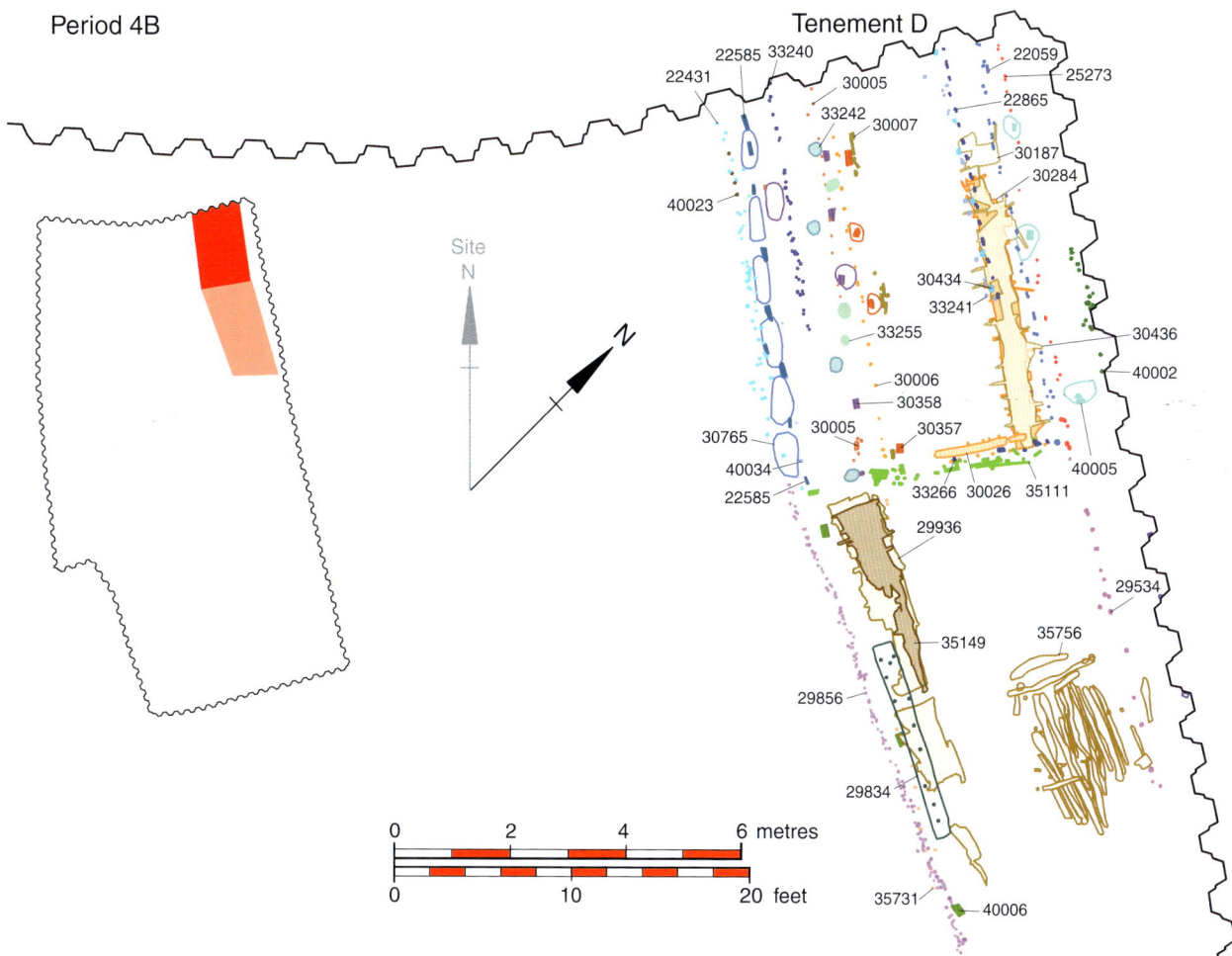

Fig.176   *Plan of alignments on Tenement D. Scale 1:125*

close together these houses were, any overhang of the roofs almost touching, and highlights the difficulty in separating refurbishment of house walls and boundary fences of essentially the same construction.

The building on Tenement D (Fig.176), like the one on Tenement C, was constructed from upright posts, with wattlework woven through to create walls, and once again these were periodically repaired, refurbished and replaced, often falling victim to fire (Fig.178).

The east wall of the structure (Figs 176 and 179) comprised a line of well-spaced squared posts (40005) combined with a line of stakes (25273) and reinforced by an inner line of stakes/post and wattlework (22059, Fig.176); a timber in the latter has a felling date of after AD 933. It is not clear whether all

these alignments were contemporary or were added to strengthen the walls on the natural lateral slope of the land (see Fig.134). The west wall has a similar line of squared posts (22585; Fig.180) and larger posts (30765), together with smaller posts and wattlework (Fig.176). A timber in alignment 30765 has a felling date of after AD 899, while five dated timbers from alignment 22585, including two (possibly three) from the same tree, were probably felled in the period AD 935–37. One of these timbers appears to be from the same tree as a timber found in alignment 30436, referred to above in relation to the interface between Periods 4A and 4B (p.567) on the east side of the structure, while another post from the same tree was identified in alignment 37166 (Tenement B); this once again emphasises the contemporaneity of construction activities in the early decades of the 10th century.

Fig.177   *Looking across the tenements towards Tenement D*

Fig.178   *Detail of the east wall of Tenement D in Period 4B, looking east, showing charred wattlework. Scale unit 0.1m*

Fig.179 *The east wall of Tenement D in Period 4B, looking north-east. Scale unit 0.1m*

The back wall of the building on Tenement D is defined by a line of stakes 33266/35111 and access was over a planked threshold 30026 (Figs 176 and 181). A timber from alignment 35111 has a felling date of after AD 903. As ever, the different methods of construction seen in these three surviving walls, combined with the factors described in the introduction, make it very difficult to determine which of the various elements are contemporary and which represent repairs and replacements. Given the closely packed arrangement of the alignments, there is also the possibility of confusion between lines of stakes refurbishing the Tenement C/D boundary, on the one hand, and repairs or strengthening of the west wall of the Tenement D building on the other.

As in Tenement C a series of hearths occupied a central position within the building, and several phases of refurbishment can be identified (Fig.181). The earliest hearth (30435) was the largest and, like

hearth 22720 in Tenement C was framed with regular rectangular limestone blocks (Fig.182) and re-used Roman tile. Similarly, an associated scooped feature (25453) in Tenement D mirrored that recorded in Tenement C (22721), suggesting similar manufacturing processes in the two buildings. Hearth 30435 was replaced by a succession of smaller hearths (30817 and 30800) in the same position; the final hearth (22441) was also edged but mostly with re-used Roman tile (Fig.183). Limestone blocks provided a firm surface at the western side of the hearth itself, and a cut feature 22881 replaces the scooped feature seen in earlier manifestations of the hearth.

Once again, as in the structure on Tenement B, internal features are suggested by clusters or lines of stakes and occasionally larger posts running parallel to the walls (e.g. alignments 33240 and 33242 on the west side and alignments 33241 and 30434 on the east, Figs 176 and 181iii). Some of these can be interpreted

Fig.180   *The west wall of Tenement D in Period 4B, looking north-east. Scale unit 0.1m*

as benches or sleeping platforms while others might have been associated with industrial processes. The cant stave from a barrel (*AY* 17/13, *8776*) and various other planks and timbers lay along the western wall, and may have been incorporated into the possible sleeping platform (Fig.184). A timber in one of the western alignments, 30357, which runs hard up against the earliest hearth, has a felling date of after AD 908.

The rear entrance to the building is indicated by a threshold which comprises re-used timbers and limestone blocks (Fig.181iii). Although most of the area immediately outside the threshold was cut away by the foundations for the later Period 5B building (Structure 5/8), a narrow deposit along the Tenement C/D boundary survives, and is characterised by a horizontal spread of wattle hurdling (29936, 35149, 29834) pegged to the ground to provide a way across the waterlogged soils of the backyard (Figs 176, 185 and 186). If there were further stake and wattle enclosures, as were recorded in Tenement C, these have been destroyed by the construction cut for Structure

5/8. Traces of a large scooped feature (35766; Fig.166) which survive below a large later intrusion had fills rich in wood and twig fragments including heather and dyer's greenweed with only a little foul matter (*AY* 14/7, 565–6), together with bracken, heath grasses and sheep's sorrel. Adjacent to the scoop and possibly related to it were horizontal laid timbers (for example 35756), presumably used to stabilise the soil on this sloping land (Figs 166 and 176.).

Once again artefacts and ecofacts from within the Tenement D structure and from the surviving parts of the associated backyards provide a rich source of interpretative evidence. Ferrous and non-ferrous metal working was carried out on a significant scale and the environmental evidence from the floors and cut features within the building had an even greater charcoal content than that from buildings in Tenements B and C. Nonetheless, a typical house 'fauna' is also represented by the insect assemblage (*AY* 14/7, 564), suggesting that the floors were kept clean; human fleas and lice occurred only in small numbers and there was no evidence of human faeces

Period 4B

Tenement D

Site N

hearth 1
30435

scoop
25453

0   2   4   6 metres
0   10   20 feet

Period 4B

Tenement D

Site N

hearth 3
30800

hearth 2
30817

0   2   4   6 metres
0   10   20 feet

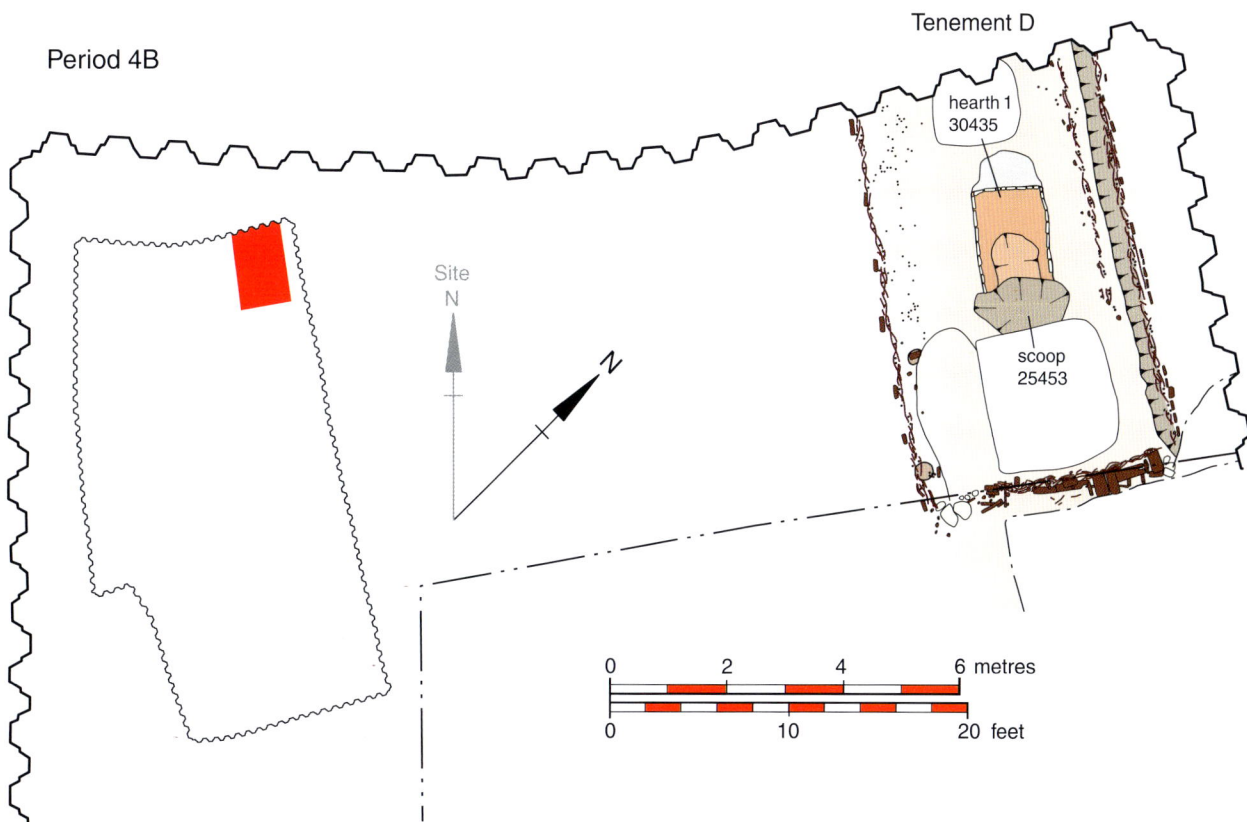

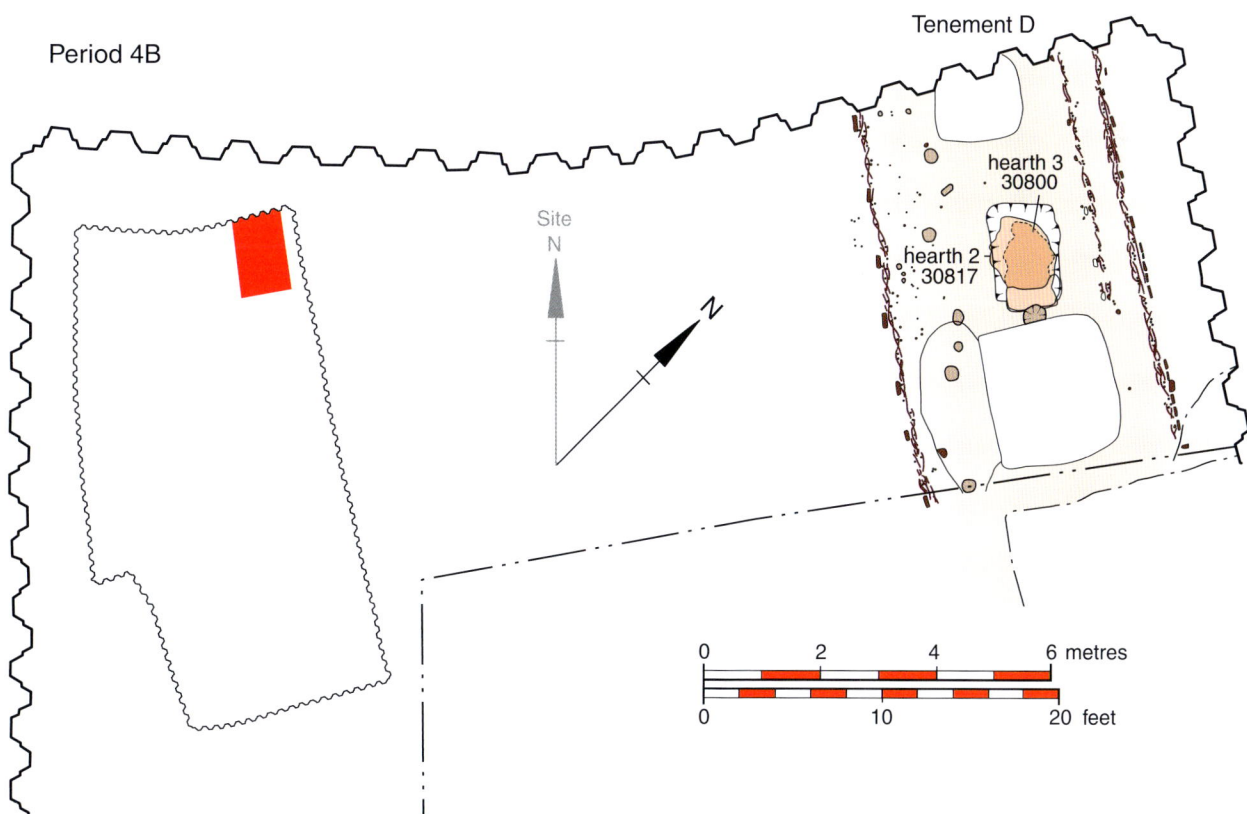

Fig.181   *(above and overleaf) Plans of the Tenement D hearth sequence in Period 4B. Scale 1:125*

Tenement D

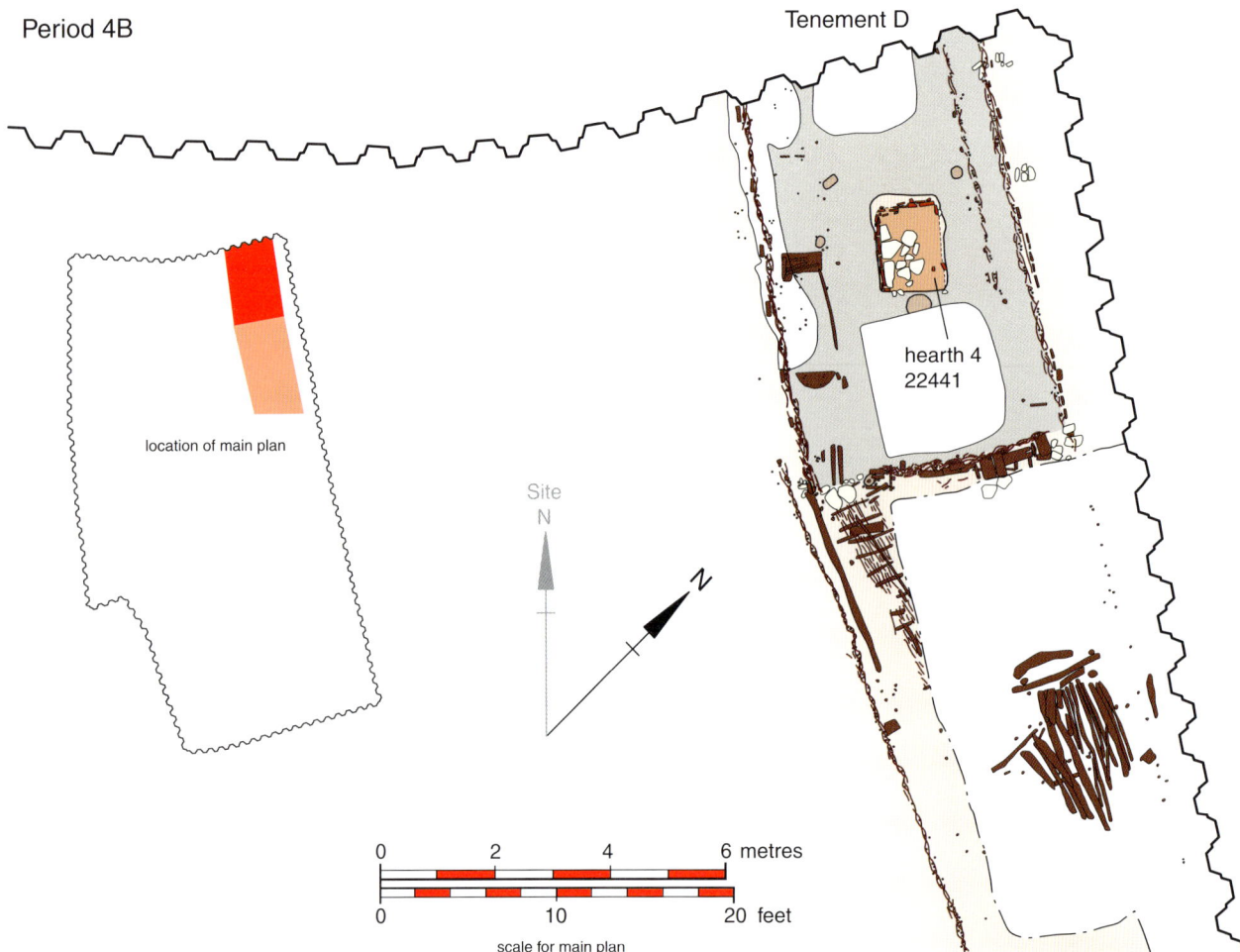

location of main plan

Site
N

hearth 4
22441

```
0          2          4        6 metres
███   ███   ███   ███
0                    10         20 feet
```
scale for main plan

Fig.181 (cont'd)   *Plans of the Tenement D hearth sequence in Period 4B. Scale 1:125*

in the samples. Sheep lice indicative of wool or fleeces, together with evidence for dyeplants, some in local concentrations, once again support other evidence for the manufacturing of textiles (*ibid*, 565) alongside the more noxious metal-working tasks. Four samples produced beeswax and a few bees, but not in the quantities seen in Tenement C (*ibid*, 564). Although some contexts were rich in woodland plants such as mosses, holly and sorrel (*ibid*, 564), others, again localised in particular parts of the building, provide evidence of food plants, as well as food flavouring such as hops, dill, celery, opium poppy, summer savory, cat-mint and carrot. A single grape pip was a rare occurrence (*ibid*, 565). Domestic pottery, including York wares and Torksey-type wares, also indicate food preparation.

The backyard of Tenement D was cut longitudinally by the shoring so its original size and shape cannot be reconstructed. Deposits in this area had also been removed by the cut for Structure 5/8 and by a larger later intrusion further down the backyard. These factors combine to skew the quantitative data for establishing the intensity of activity on this tenement. Although there is numerically less evidence for crafts such as leather working (*AY* 17/16, figs 1582–4), amber working (*AY* 17/14, fig.1224) and antler comb making (*AY* 17/12, 1921, fig.881) than on Tenements B and C, the evidence supports these being carried out and there is, by contrast, more or less the same amount of evidence for the production of face-turned and spindle-turned wooden items in the form of wood-turning cores and other waste (*AY* 17/13, fig.1045).

What is most striking, however, is the evidence for a high level of activity associated with ferrous and, more particularly, non-ferrous metal working.

Fig.182   *Early hearth 30435 on Tenement D. Scale unit 0.1m*

Fig.184   *Period 4B bench/platform on Tenement D. Scale unit 0.1m*

Fig.183   *Later hearth 22441 on Tenement D. Scale unit 0.1m*

Smithing slag was absent from samples in Tenement D (*AY* 17/6, fig.177) and there were fewer examples of bars, strips and plates (*ibid*, fig.191), knives (*ibid*, fig.242) and needles (*ibid*, fig.218) than in Tenement C but all stages of non-ferrous metal working were represented. The greatest concentration of crucibles was focused on Tenement D (*AY* 17/7, fig 329) and the same is true of other forms of silver (*ibid*, fig.354) and copper-alloy working (*ibid*, fig.355), suggesting some form of co-operative working between craftsmen in the two adjacent properties. In this context the almost parallel changes in the sequence and appearance of the hearths in Tenements C and D are noteworthy. The presence of benches/sleeping platforms in Tenement D but not in Tenement C raises the possibility that one building functioned principally as a workshop and that the other doubled as a dwelling, but this suggestion founders on the very clear division perpetuated between the two properties.

Fig.185　　*Wattle walkway on Tenement D, looking south. Scale unit 0.1m*

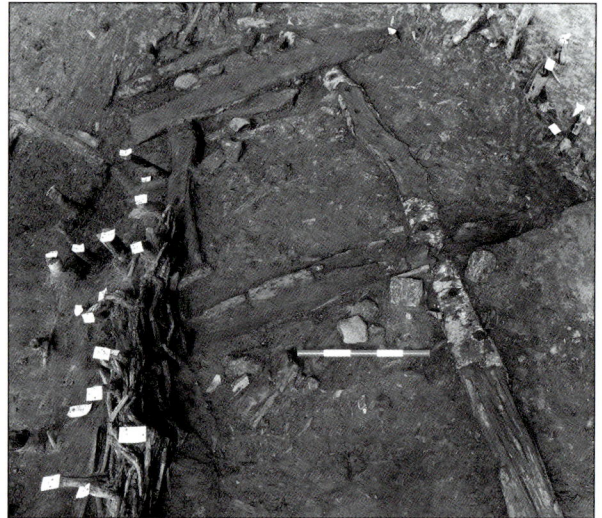

Fig.186　　*Pegged walkway on Tenement D. Scale unit 0.1m*

There is little evidence with which to reconstruct the interior of any of these buildings in terms of fixtures and fittings, other than the position of the hearths and the benches. Structural ironwork recovered from this period includes possible door hinges (*AY* 17/6, *3461–8*) and a wooden bracket for a door fastening mechanism (*AY* 17/13, *9047*, fig.1164). Other structural elements, both of wood and iron, are more generic in nature and could as well relate to boxes and chests as to the structure itself. Parts of such items, and also casks, baskets and other containers, were recovered from inside and outside the structures and form part of the domestic household goods, along with ceramic and metal vessels. Parts of wooden racks or frames (*AY* 17/13, *8945*, *9057*, figs 1128 and 1171) were recovered, together with part of what has been tentatively identified as a dual-purpose stool/workbench (*ibid*, *8946*). The only find which relates directly to a structure is a possible window opening frame (*ibid*, *9058*, fig.1172) found in context 22857.

Discussion

The changes which took place on the site at the beginning of the 10th century were fundamental to how the Coppergate area was to be used for the next millennium. The deliberate laying out of new tenement boundaries and the erection of the post and wattle buildings at the modern Coppergate street frontage provides a rare and important glimpse of early town planning. This, coupled with the opportunity to investigate a large swathe of land behind the buildings, provides a model for how this part of the Anglo-Scandinavian town developed. Despite the challenges in understanding the precise sequence of development on the site during Period 4, the big picture is clear.

For five decades or more, alignments of posts, stakes and staves perpetuated the property divisions which had been laid out soon after c.900. These alignments were irregular in terms of their composition (stakes, staves, posts etc.) and were frequently repaired and replaced, either in isolated patches or along their entire length. The same is true of the structures which occupied more or less the same position along the street frontage throughout this period. The walls were constructed from withies or wattlework interwoven between uprights which included both posts and stakes; there is no evidence for extensive use of daub to cover and insulate them. Walls were periodically strengthened by additional alignments or by the replacement or repair of indi-

600

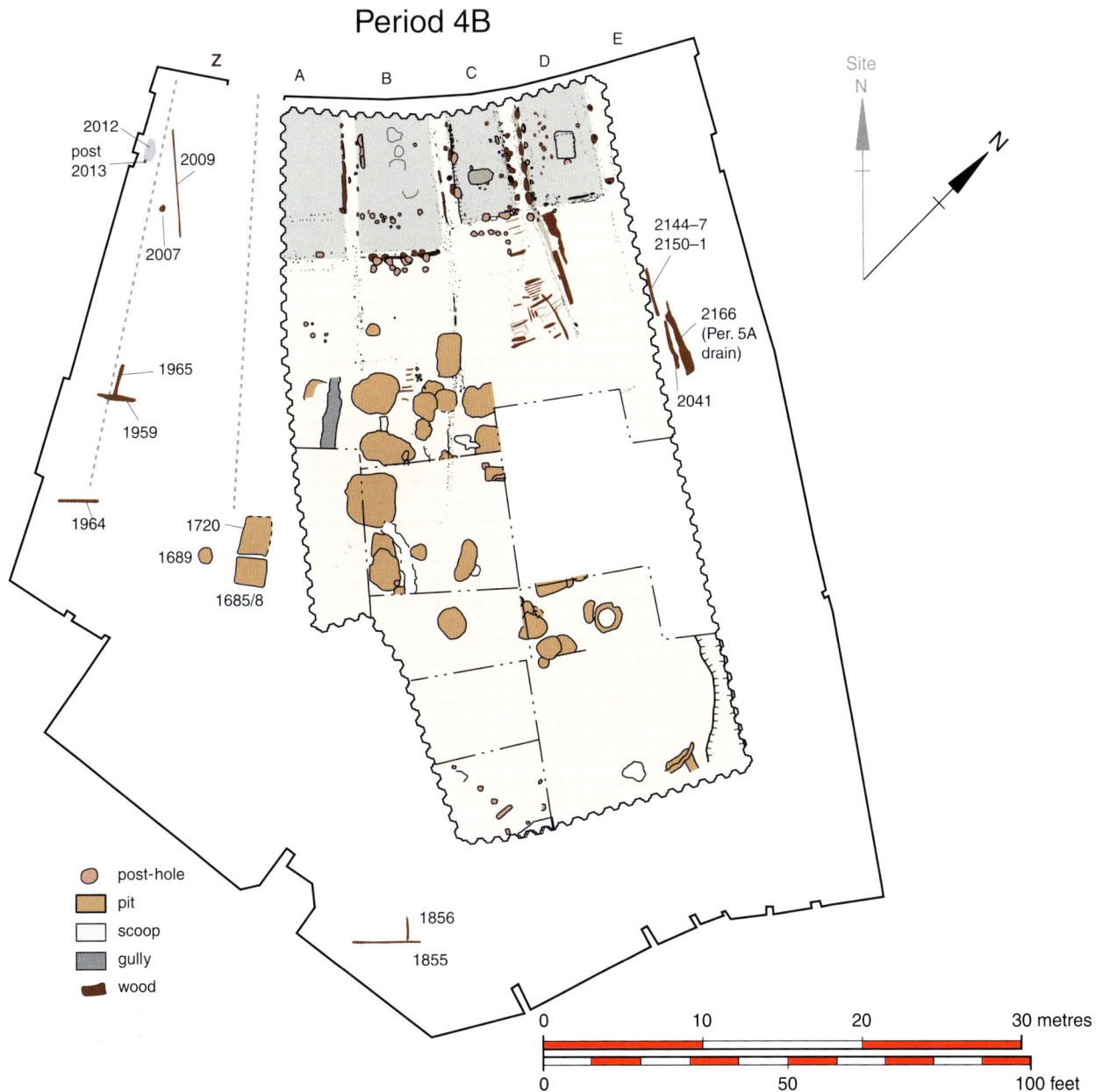

Period 4B

Fig.187   Plan of Period 4B and watching brief features. Scale 1:400

vidual timbers; charred uprights attest to frequent fires. The ordered, regular, layout of the buildings, and their generally consistent construction method, is also indicative of a measure of planning and control, perhaps resulting from common ownership. Behind the buildings, in the backyards, there is more variety in layout although their shape and dimensions remain constant throughout the period. Walkways and paths leading from the back of the houses, renewed and repaired as required, provided access to the backyards and to whatever activities took place there.

The structures on Tenements C and D were better preserved than those on Tenements A and B but the evidence suggests that all four served as both dwellings and workshops, with the possible exception of the Tenement C building. The flimsy character of the walls indicates that these were single-storeyed buildings. Interiors were dominated by central hearths, used for both domestic and industrial purposes, and again these were periodically refurbished and relined to minimise the risk of sparks igniting flammable interiors. Alignments of posts and stakes inside the buildings suggest internal features such as benches or sleeping platforms running along the sides of the walls and, less convincingly, internal subdivisions. Entrances were marked by thresholds in the back walls which might have been matched by entrances on the street frontage, though these could not be excavated, lying beneath the modern street of Coppergate. Nothing was recovered to help elucidate the roof construction and material, though there is evidence for overhangs with some external support.

Deposits on all four properties had, to some extent, been damaged either by the construction of the later (Period 5B) sunken-featured buildings or by more modern intrusions and this was also true of the backyards where later cellars had removed deposits, especially from a large part of Tenement D. Where deposits survived, however, further alignments of stakes and posts defining small pens and enclosures were identified, together with drains and gullies (Fig.166). Pits including cess and rubbish pits, some of which were wicker-lined or with associated postholes, were irregularly positioned behind the buildings further down the site. Although the boundary fences which separated the properties at the street frontage were significant enough to be well maintained, the same is not always true for their continuation into the very rear of the backyards. Intrusions, thinning deposits, and consequently less favourable survival conditions, make definitive statements regarding their extent unreliable, but it would appear that the River Foss end of the site was not as enthusiastically claimed by the owners, or tenants, as was the area closer to the street. This observation raises the question as to whether the River Foss end of the site was in common, or different, ownership. The watching brief and excavations at 22 Piccadilly provided evidence for attempts to stabilise the riverbanks during this time (see pp.697, 700).

The distribution of various forms of debris resulting from craft and industrial practices in and around the structures offers a few, occasionally contradictory, insights into how the backyards were used. Immediately behind the buildings the pattern of debris reflects, more or less, that recovered from

Fig.188   *Evidence for non-ferrous metal working*

Fig.189   *Evidence for iron working*

Fig.190   *Leather shoes and nålebinding sock*

inside the buildings but further back (to the south) this distribution is less clear cut. For example, in the case of the leather waste, there is a focus of activity on Tenement B and, to a lesser extent, on Tenement C (*AY* 17/16, figs 1582–4), and the spread continues half way down the backyard but not beyond. By contrast, the distribution of iron bars, strips and plates, which focuses in the building on Tenement C, continues for the entire length of the backyards, occurring in pits right at the bottom of the site (*AY* 17/6, fig.191) on land not obviously associated with particular properties.

Those pits which lay at the very rear of the site, beyond the obviously divided properties, contained evidence that this area was used for further cess pits, to dump household debris, including dyeplant waste, and to discard animal bone (*AY* 15/3, fig.22). The presence of amphibians, wetland plants, and other taxa typical of ditches and water margins occurred alongside other outdoor species and supports the view that this area was wet and possibly prone to flooding; as such this land was perhaps unclaimed by the occupants along the street frontage who used it for *ad hoc* rubbish disposal and for latrines. There is no evidence that the end of the plots was defined by further transverse alignments, demarcation ditches or gullies.

Once again the watching brief evidence and features observed in the small trenches at 22 Piccadilly indicate that settlement continued on both sides of the main excavation and beyond (p.697 and Fig.187). Post and wattle walls representing further property divisions, and possibly further structures, were observed but only partially recorded due to the circumstances of the their recovery. The backyards too had a similar character, being occupied by rubbish pits and traces of fences which might represent enclosures. Recovery of a fragment of a plough raises the possibility of horticultural practices, while evidence from 22 Piccadilly reveals attempts to stabilise the riverbank.

In summarising the environmental data for this period Kenward and Hall remark that although the range of taxa in Period 4B remains much the same as in Periods 3 and 4A there were 'profound quantitative changes in deposits of Period 4B' (*AY* 14/7, 569) and that serves as a general verdict on the period. The first half of the 10th century was a time of intense activity with evidence for domestic and subsistence activities including animal husbandry, vegetable cultivation, food preparation and textile production taking place alongside the working of bone, antler,

leather, jet and amber on what might have been a semi-commercial scale (Figs 188–90). The quantities of debris relating to wood-turning and all aspects of ferrous and non-ferrous industries suggest a larger scale of production. This was also the period when foreign trade is most evident, suggesting York participated in the great Viking Age trade networks. Continuing contact with Scandinavia is attested by the imported schist and phyllite hones (*AY* 17/14, table 229), steatite bowls (*ibid*, 2541) and Baltic amber (*ibid*, table 233), most of which peak in quantity in this period. Similarly, lava querns from the Eifel region are most common in these early periods, with several fragments also found in Period 3 (*ibid*, table 255). More exotic items such as the silks (*AY* 17/5, 437) belong to this period, and two foreign coins or coin fragments (*AY* 18/1, *45* and *47*) are from Periods 4A and 4B.

Thus the Coppergate/Ousegate area was vibrant and busy in the first half of the 10th century, and this has implications for our understanding of the wider development of the Viking Age city. Although the excavations did not uncover the northern ends of the Period 4B post and wattle buildings, it is presumed that they fronted more or less directly on to a forerunner of Coppergate. The alignments interpreted as walls and fences take account of the curvature of the present street line which, it is assumed, reflects the street's original course. This indicates that when the first post and wattle structures were erected there was already a street in existence on the line of Coppergate. The fact that this alignment, rather than those laid down at the end of the preceding Period 3 (e.g. the earlier post-hole alignment 33239, see Fig.150) or during Period 4A (the superimposed wicker hurdles/pathways 30187, 30284 and 30989, the latter shown on Fig.154), may indicate that the course of Coppergate was already in existence at that time. As the superimposed hurdles/pathways are the only features to respect this alignment at so early a date, however, this can only be speculation.

The carefully controlled reorganisation of this part of York at a high density of occupation in the 920s–930s, half a century or more after the establishment of the Viking kingdom, may indicate a growth in York's population at that time, and an expansion away from a putative nucleus of settlement in the Roman fortress area. To date, however, it has not been possible to chart with accuracy the fluctuations in occupation within and immediately outside the fortress, while the size and location(s) of Anglian York, *Eoforwic*, is still a matter of debate (*AY* 7/1).

The regeneration of the Coppergate area is likely to have been linked to the establishment of a crossing point over the River Ouse on the site of the present Ouse Bridge. A 13th-century source reports the existence of a bridge here in connection with events in 1154 (quoted in *AY* Supplementary Series 1/2, 29); this is generally believed to have been a timber structure, but the date of its erection is unknown. It is also believed that there was a pre-Norman crossing point hereabouts, contrived as a replacement for a Roman bridge that crossed the river some 250m upstream. The date at which the Roman crossing was abandoned is not certain – it has been ascribed to the effects of hypothetical 5th-/6th-century flooding, but more recently the recognition of a group of 8th-/9th-century objects found along the approaches to the south-west bridgehead has been interpreted as suggesting that the Roman crossing point remained in use until late in the Anglian period (*AY* 8/1, 7), while others suggest it might have co-existed with any new crossing into the early Norman period (Rees Jones 2013, 95). With the establishment of a new crossing at the Ouse Bridge site, however, there was the inevitable development of a road system servicing it. To the south of the Ouse, Micklegate's sweeping curve

brings it to the new bridgehead, and to the north of the river the line is continued by Ousegate. Thus Ousegate, with which Coppergate merges beyond the church of All Saints, was a principal thoroughfare (see Fig.322). If a routeway approximating to its line was not already in existence and surrounded by occupation or activity before the creation of the new crossing point, which now seems likely, it would certainly have come into being and have attracted occupation soon after its establishment.

Coppergate appears topographically to be of secondary importance when compared to Ousegate. The properties established on its south-east side may have had an additional value in the Viking Age if they included access to the River Foss, as they did in the later medieval and post-medieval periods; this could not be established in the excavation, however, which did not extend to the river's edge. Alternatively, it is possible that there was common access along the Foss frontage via a road which was submerged or buried in the wake of the creation of *stagnum regis*, the King's Fishpool, by William I, and then re-created in the late 11th–14th centuries (*AY* 10/6, fig.395).

The steady development of the site through the first half of the 10th century which had led to its settled appearance was to come to an end in the middle of that century when the post and wattle buildings were abandoned, backfilled and replaced by a very different form of structure.

Period 5A

The process of repair and refurbishment of the Period 4B wattle buildings continued until the middle of the 10th century when, fairly abruptly, they went out of use. According to a consistent set of dendrochronological dates, this was a single episode affecting all tenements, and took place sometime between 955 and 960. This abandonment episode marks the beginning of Period 5, and has been designated Period 5A. In Period 5B, from c.960, construction began of a very different style of building.

Richard Hall described this early Period 5 episode as a time when '... the remains of the latest phase of post and wattle structures at the street frontage were covered to a depth of up to 1m. This horizon, Period 5A, which was not traced in the yard areas behind the buildings, is interpreted as resulting in part from the upcast in digging out the sunken structures of Period 5B, and partly as a deliberate dump of make-up or levelling material' (Hall 1990, 383).

The timing and likely duration of Period 5A can be established with some accuracy. Dendrochronology shows that initial construction dates for the Period 4B buildings had been focused in the 930s and that alteration of elements of the buildings, and thus their occupation, continued right up until the time when they were abandoned prior to replacement. Abandonment appears to be closely dated to immediately before 955/56 as the felling of timbers used in alignments and features ascribed to Period 5A across several of the properties cluster around that date, indicating that this was a site-wide (street-wide?) reorganisation. The dendrochronological report states 'The archaeological evidence indicates that these timbers are primary material and hence neither re-used nor dumped. There are therefore clear implications for the results from the Period 4B timbers, all of which have felling dates compatible with pre-dating the AD 955/56 felling phase identified in Period 5A. In addition, the evidence from later periods suggests that activity associated with Period 5A is likely to have occurred prior to the early 960s, indicating that this period may well last for only a relatively short time span during the Anglo-Scandinavian phase' (see p.745). Taking everything into account, therefore, Period 5A is likely to occupy a period perhaps as short as a few months, or conceivably as long as five years.

No structures can be ascribed to this period, although there was continuing activity. A barrel-lined pit (31266), and further pits (e.g. 20987 and 20991) clearly cut into Period 4B structures (Fig.191); they contain faecal matter and suggest nearby habitation, perhaps of a less-ordered character. New alignments appear but are short-lived, while other alignments perpetuate old boundaries, arguing for some continuation of the 'old order' in terms of tenancy and ownership.

Tenements A and B

As already stated, much of the relevant evidence in Tenement A had been destroyed by the cut for Structure 5/1. The barrel-lined pit 31266 contained occupation debris which had probably accumulated by dumping (AY 14/7, 573) and clearly cut into the rear wall of the wattle building on Tenement A, signifying that this building had gone out of use. A dated barrel stave from this feature was from a timber felled after AD 906. Two timbers from the backfill of a Period 4B cess pit (28652) on the boundary between Tenements A and B are dated to after 960, perhaps indicating continuity of use of some of these features.

Behind the cut for Structure 5/1, within Tenement A, running transversely across the width of the property some 13m back from the street frontage and interrupted by the later linear ditch 2378/2181, was an alignment (8411) consisting of quite regularly spaced stakes and staves (Fig.192), incorporating vestigial traces of wattlework. Most of the individual uprights were clearly charred; associated layers of ash were attributed to Period 5A and the alignment seems to have burnt down during that period. It may, however, have been erected during the later part of Period 4B.

At its eastern end, alignment 8411 intersected at 90° with uprights which continued the established division between Tenements A and B. The most stoutly constructed of these was alignment 27676

Period 5A

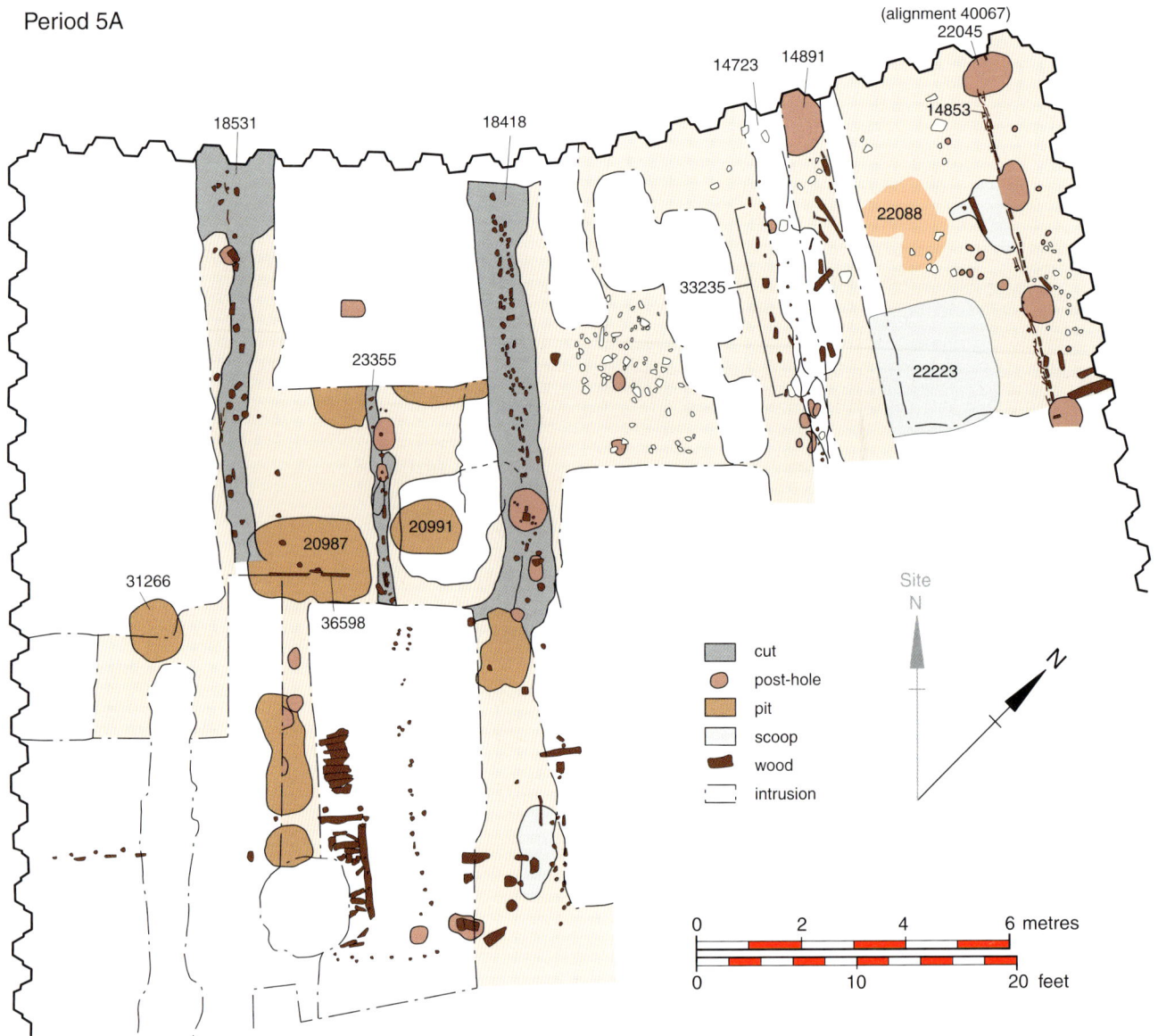

Fig.191   *Plan of Period 5A features. Scale 1:125*

(Fig.192), which had survived from Period 4B and incorporated a variety of staves, posts and stakes. Some of these uprights exhibited clear evidence of charring, like the contiguous alignment 8411. Alignment 27676 finally disappeared, following burning, after some Period 5A deposits had accumulated adjacent to it.

Alignment 27676 was truncated to the south by the insertion of a modern cellar; it is only coincidence that it appears to terminate at the west end of alignment 27675/8152 (Fig.192). The northern limit of 27676 approximates with the corner of Period

4B buildings but practically its northern limit was defined by the northern edge of excavations in 1976.

Some 0.2m to the east of 27676 was an alignment of stakes, 27796, whose original extent is unknown, for it was truncated to both north and south by modern intrusions (Fig.192); it appears to be broadly contemporary with 27676. Approximately 0.2m west of 27676 another alignment of stakes, 27794 (Fig.192), ran parallel with it. 27794 may also have been erected relatively late in Period 4B, but appears to have remained in use into Period 5A, and may have superseded 27796 and 27676.

Period 5A

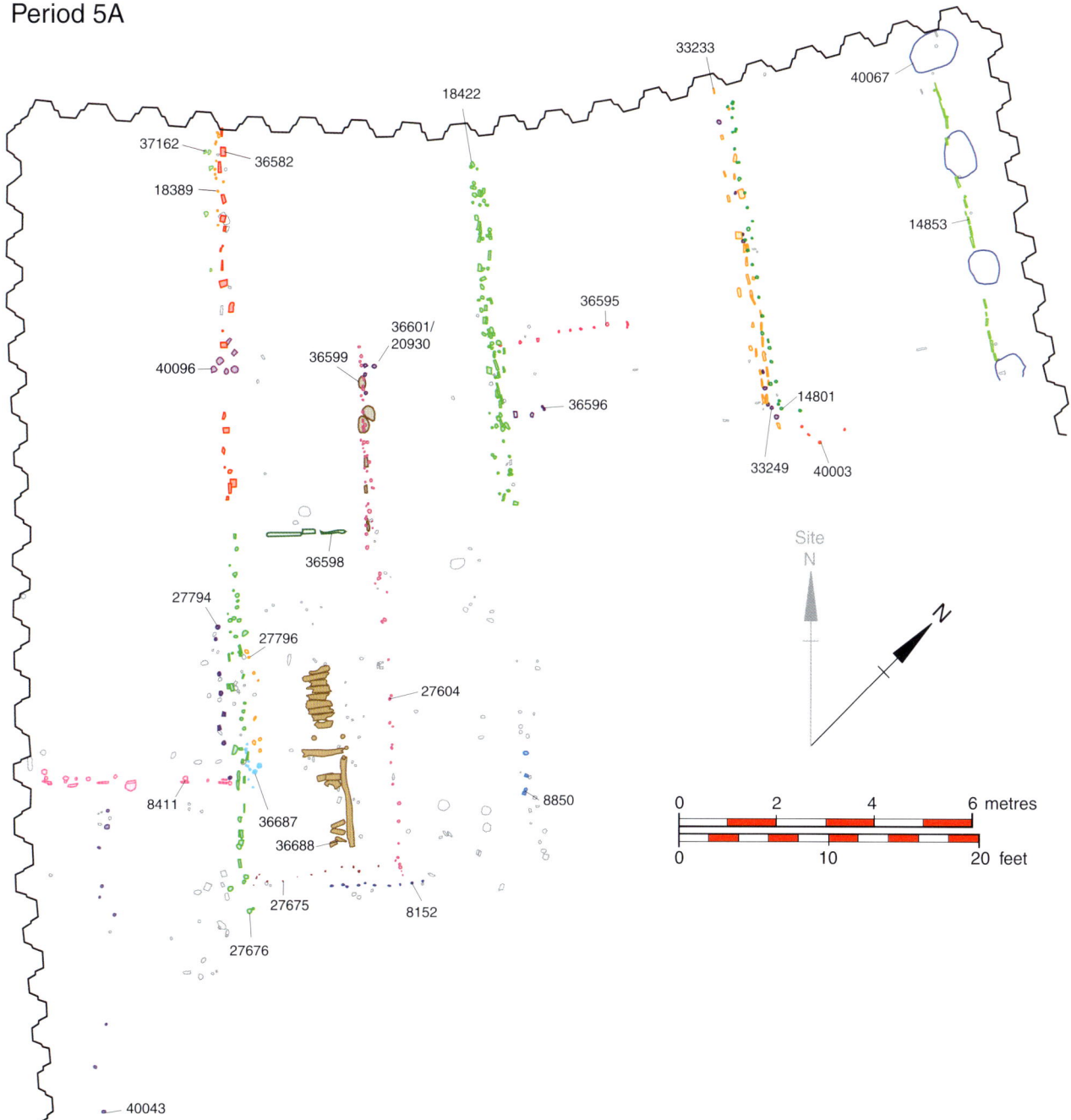

Fig.192   *Plan of Period 5A alignments. Scale 1:125*

The property division between Tenements A and B therefore was perpetuated by alignments which include 36582 (Fig.192) and continues into the backyards along the line of Period 4B alignment 27676 (see Fig.159) which survived the reorganisation along the street frontage. Some 2.8m to its east, however, above the succession of finely laminated Period 4B deposits, was a new alignment of stakes and wattle (20930/27604/36601) (Figs 192 and 193), erected

within a gully (23355) cut into the uppermost Period 4B layers (Fig.191). The cut for Period 5B Structure 5/3 had destroyed the evidence at the very front of the site (Fig.191) but it is possible that the gully continued up to the street frontage. This was a wholly new alignment which ran along the main north–south axis of Tenement B, approximately bisecting its width. Also cut into the top of the Period 4B deposits were two substantial pits, 20987 and 20991 (Fig.191). Both were

Fig.193   Period 5A alignment 20930/27604/36601. Scale unit 0.1m

rather irregular in shape, but each was dug within the area defined between the south (back) and internal walls of the abandoned Period 4B building, one to either side of the axial division represented by the new alignment. These pits were respectively 0.80m and 0.60m deep. Pit 20987 included large amounts of food plant remains, some of them clearly in human faecal material. Palaeoenvironmental evidence from pit 20991 included an extremely rich insect fauna, mostly with a distinct 'house' fauna component, but there was also evidence for some quite foul habitats, and some samples contained noticeable components of aquatic insects and woodland beetles/bugs. Woodland plants from a wide range of soils were also notable in this pit, and it is surmised that all owe their presence to the collection of moss. Heathland taxa were also present, including heather (*Calluna vulgaris*) and other dyeplants, and a clay mineral which may have been used in fulling was also recognised (*AY* 14/7, 576–8).

Both these pits and the intervening new alignment 20930/27604/36601 were covered by a series of strata distinctly different from those of Period 4B. The earliest of these were characterised by a variety of deposits most of which incorporated silty loams.

Individual deposits here were often 100mm or more thick, and some included noticeable amounts of small limestone, tile or cobble rubble and quantities of domestic debris such as animal bone, all indicative of different land use and, perhaps, less ordered practices.

After these deposits had built up to a total average depth of 0.3m, a line of staves (36599; Fig.192) was inserted; three staves survived *in situ*, and the positions of three others were defined by soil disturbance. One of these had a felling date of after AD 940 (see p.744). They are closely adjacent to the parallel alignment of stakes and wattle 20930 which, however, appeared stratigraphically earlier. The alignment was recorded in a limited area; to both north and south Period 5B cellars had destroyed contemporary levels and removed all traces of any continuation. The tops of these staves were charred, and associated with layers which contained notable quantities of ash and charcoal, presumably from the burning down of this feature. Running west from the medial 36599 as far as the line of 36582 (see below) was an alignment (36598) consisting of a stave positioned between two lengths of edge-set horizontal timbers (Figs 191, 192 and 194). Like the intermedial alignment 36599, the timbers in 36598

Fig.194   Alignment 36598. Scale unit 0.1m

were all charred, and these two alignments were contemporary; to the north of 36599 corresponding levels had been destroyed by a modern cellar.

The burnt layers and charred timbers noted above were sealed by a succession of even thicker deposits which are interpreted as deliberately placed dumps of soil. Individually these were up to 0.3m thick, and cumulatively they totalled up to 0.85m thick, comprising predominantly mixed loams with ash, charcoal, clay, and the like.

Within these layers were several other alignments of upright timbers. To the west, running up the undisturbed spine of deposits between the Period 5B cellared buildings in Tenements A and B, was a linear cut (18531; Fig.191). It measured 0.5m on average in width, and its sides sloped to an average depth of 0.20m. Stratigraphically, it appears later than the intermedial alignment 20930. An alignment consisting of posts and staves (36582; Fig.192) ran along its line to the point where modern intrusions had truncated these levels. Some of these posts had been exposed almost immediately after the removal of modern deposits, and a few had even been damaged in that process (see Fig.157). Three dated timbers from the alignments are believed to have been felled in the winter of AD 955/56.

Just to the west of 36582, approximately on the west edge of cut 18531, was an alignment of stakes, 18389 (Fig.192), with decayed fragments of interwoven wattle surviving in places. This appeared to have remained standing into Period 5A, but may have been erected late in Period 4B. It was badly truncated, apparently by the insertion of the 5A gully 18531.

Later within Period 5A another linear cut 15343 (not on plan) was dug approximately along the line of its predecessor 18531, albeit on a more irregular course. Most of the upright timbers in this area clearly lay outside its line, and no alignment can be associated with it. Nonetheless, it does appear to be approximately contemporary with a corresponding but more regular linear cut to the east side of the tenement (18418; Fig.191) where, however, a modern cellar had truncated the southern 4m. Cut 18418 was approximately 1–1.2m wide and 0.25–0.50m deep, with steeply sloping sides. Within this trench was a relatively dense series of varied uprights including stakes, posts and staves, all of which were recorded under the single alignment number 18422 (Fig.192), and one of which was also likely to have been felled in the winter of AD 955/56. Although it is possible that they represent more than one alignment, attempts to distin-

609

guish cohesive sub-sets of uprights, using a variety of criteria, have failed. In the north 4m, where the stratigraphic detail of relationships between timbers has been lost, there was a suggestion that the uprights had been placed in two parallel lines, approximately 0.2m apart, but if this had been the intention it was certainly not rigorously pursued and not clearly recognisable throughout. The trench 18418 returned to the west directly above the line of the south wall of the underlying Period 4B structure, but continued only briefly, to the point where its remains had been obliterated by the Period 5B cellared Structure 5/4. In marked contrast to its northern continuation, there were no upright timbers within this corner forming the return: suspicions that this was a separate but coincident feature are allayed by the distinctive fill layer 8376, a sticky brown clay which ran uninterrupted throughout the trench's entire length.

Behind the line of the transverse return of trench 18418, an alignment of stakes 27604 was exposed in the base of the cellar of 5B Structure 5/4 (Fig.192), continuing the line of 20930 and approximately bisecting the width of the tenement. This alignment continued downslope for about 3m to the point where it intersected with the transverse stake alignment 8152 (Fig.192), which was decayed wattlework *in situ*. It is not clear why 8152 has the limits which it does. No alignments or deposits attributable to Period 5A could be identified with certainty to the south of this point: the insertion of a modern concrete raft as well as various medieval intrusions had removed traces of a 5A continuation. There were, however, remains of a Period 4B stake alignment 36704/36700, only slightly offset from 20930/27604/36599, which continued for a further 5m before petering out. A timber in alignment 36599 was felled after AD 940.These are attributed to Period 4B, as is alignment 27675 which ran transversely, close beside 8152, but they might have continued to exist in Period 5A.

Another stake and wattle alignment continuing the line of the centre of the spine between Tenements A and B was 8491 (not on plan). Only a short length of this was seen, for it had been destroyed to the south by a modern well and a concrete raft foundation, and towards the north by a modern foundation trench; it may be a later version of 27796.

Tenements C and D

The strip of the site along the street frontage in Tenement C shows comparable evidence for an episode of dereliction and abandonment, although the interpretation is limited by the presence of five large Period 5B cuts (14660, 14708/20, 14533, 14652 and 14544 shown as intrusions on Figure 191). The only surviving deposits include a scatter of limestone fragments in burned deposits more or less above where the hearth had stood in the Period 4B building; they presumably derive from it. The biological evidence, taken from surface deposits, provides a similar range of material as that from Period 4B and can be similarly explained (*AY* 14/7, 578), with evidence for deposits which decayed rapidly and involved at least occasionally some standing water (*ibid*). The finds evidence too suggests that much of it is re-deposited Period 4B material.

Two incomplete transverse alignments (36595 and 36596; Fig.192) running parallel to the street frontage 4m and 6m back from it respectively, have no datable elements in them but, on stratigraphic grounds, are believed to belong to Period 5A. Their significance and purpose is unclear.

The various alignments which divided Tenements C and D in Period 4B continued in the same position in Period 5B and it must be the case that whatever fence lines marked this division were visible throughout Period 5A. A linear cut (14723; Fig.191) runs along the eastern side of Tenement C and the scrappy post and wattle alignment 14801 (Fig.192) survives within this cut; both are either late in Period 5A or early in Period 5B. To their west alignment 33233/33235, comprising more substantial posts, equally belong to either Period 5A or to the early phases of Period 5B.

On Tenement D itself a burned spread (22088; Fig.191) above where the hearth had been in the preceding Period 4B building might have functioned as a hearth but there is no evidence that it was within a surviving building. A large rectangular cut (22223; Fig.191), occupying almost half the width of the tenement immediately to the south of the burned area, contained human faecal material, together with 'house' taxa, and abundant evidence for annual

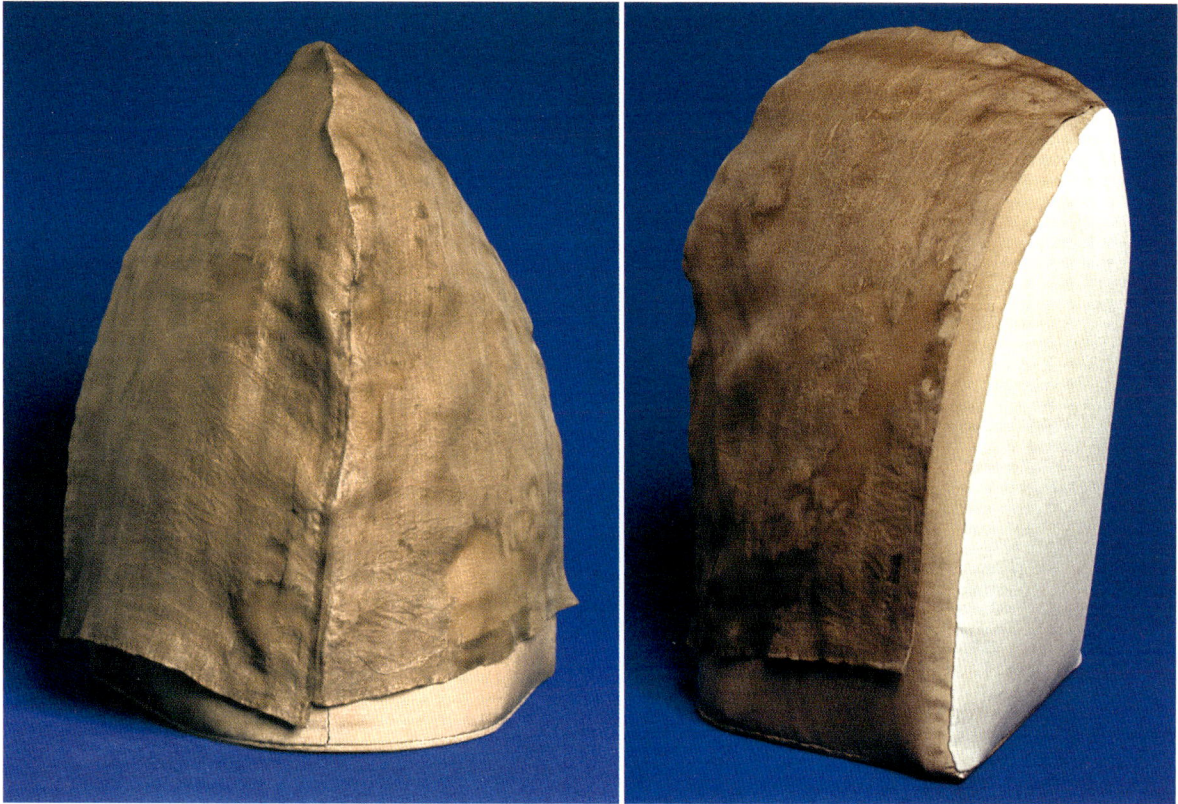

Fig.195   *Silk cap* 1372

weeds (*AY* 14/7, 579). One fill also produced an almost complete silk head-dress (Fig.195) (*AY* 17/5, *1372*) of a type with parallels elsewhere in Scandinavia (*ibid*, 375–7). Lines of posts and staves (14853) and a subsequent line of post pits (40067) (Figs 191 and 192) on the east side of the tenement might either form a boundary division or be the wall of a structure; it cannot be followed far into the backyard. Seven timbers from alignment 14853 are from trees all believed to have been felled in the winter of AD 955/56.

Discussion

After approximately a century of steady development from the mid-9th century onwards, with all the concomitant implications of increasing population and the evidence for intensification of activity, Period 5A marks a break. For whatever reason the post and wattle buildings were abandoned and the old order suspended. From the precision and consistency of dendrochronological data from timbers which chart subsequent post-abandonment development, it appears that this happened across all four tenements

more or less simultaneously, placing this episode in the mid-10th century. The precision is such that it is thought that many of the timbers used in the re-establishment of alignments (or, fleetingly, of new alignments) were felled in the winter of AD 955/56 thus placing the abandonment of the buildings some time, perhaps only a short time, before that winter. This dating, based on revised dendrochronological determinations, places Period 5A some 20 years earlier than the date of c.975 quoted in earlier *AY* publications.

The deposits which have been defined as belonging to Period 5A were only identified along the street frontage, implying that the changes were focused on the buildings themselves. Period 5A deposits appear to have been partly formed by the backfilling of the abandoned Period 4B buildings with domestic refuse and by pit digging, seen most clearly in Tenement B where pits were dug into the southern end of the post and wattle building. These were filled with rubbish, including human cess and sculptural fragments (p.560), and deposits around them contained similar mixed refuse, including a

611

foul element (*AY* 14/7, 573–6). These same deposits were then cut into to create the sunken element of the Period 5B buildings and the upcast material (much of it deriving from Period 4B occupation) was re-deposited in the immediate surroundings and became part of the Period 5A make-up. The sequence of events, therefore, would seem to include abandonment and dumping, followed by the digging out of the sunken element of the next phase of buildings. Features and deposits which relate to this period were not easy to recognise in the watching brief area (p.697) although posts and dump deposits which appear immediately to pre-date the erection of the sunken buildings must be contemporary with this period.

The timescale over which this happened need not have been very long, and a rapid phase of rebuilding would presumably have been desirable. The digging of new Period 5A pits in which human faeces were recovered, and the possibility that some Period 4B cess pits continued in use, indicate that the area was still populated. There is, indeed, no evidence for a corresponding break in the backyard area, suggesting that activities there might have continued throughout the period of disruption at the street frontage. The need to re-house these displaced householders, therefore, or perhaps to house different families, would have been acute, particularly if this reorganisation was on a street-wide or area-wide scale.

This latter point raises the question as to the possible motivation behind the changes. Perhaps practical considerations, a desire to provide better, less-flammable structures, or simply to introduce a new style of building, played a part but as no complete dimensions exist for any of the Period 4B buildings and are known for only one of the Period 5B structures (Structure 5/6) precise comparisons of size are not possible (see Tables 29 and 30). The floor area of Structure 5/6, however, is not substantially bigger than the average floor surface of the earlier wattle buildings so on the face of it a desire to increase size was not a determining factor. The question as to whether the Period 5B buildings supported an upper storey or not is one that is returned to later.

If practical gains provide only part of the motivation for the reorganisation of the street frontage, then other factors must be considered. The simultaneous change across all four Period 4B properties, and supporting evidence from the watching brief, strengthens the case for these plots being in common ownership. Whether the Period 5A changes reflect a decision made by an incumbent landowner or signal a change in ownership, however, cannot be determined. The appearance, and subsequent disappearance, of what has been interpreted as a new property boundary bisecting Tenement B, suggests that the allocation of land was being reviewed, and perhaps disputed. The repeated reference to timbers being felled in the winter of 955/56 focuses attention on that period in York's history. The 940s and 950s saw much political turbulence which culminated in the expulsion of Eric Bloodaxe from York in 954 (see Table 27). How far the subsequent political changes affected the day to day life of Coppergate residents cannot be ascertained, but in the context of the times, changes in land ownership might well be expected.

Period 5B

The episode of upheaval and change which is evidenced in the middle years of the 10th century (Period 5A) was followed by a renewed burst of activity along the street frontage and the re-establishment of a new layout of buildings. Taking into account the watching brief observations, there is now clear evidence for six plots of land. At the far west of the main site there are indications of a property boundary between Tenement A and its neighbour, dubbed Tenement Z, while Tenement E was recognised to the east of Tenement D (Fig.196). The new (Period 5A) property division observed within Tenement B (p.607) was abandoned and the original fence lines reinforced, perpetuating the alignments laid out a century before. A new style of building was introduced, radically different from its predecessors, constructed of posts and planks with lower courses set into cuts dug into the ground and, in

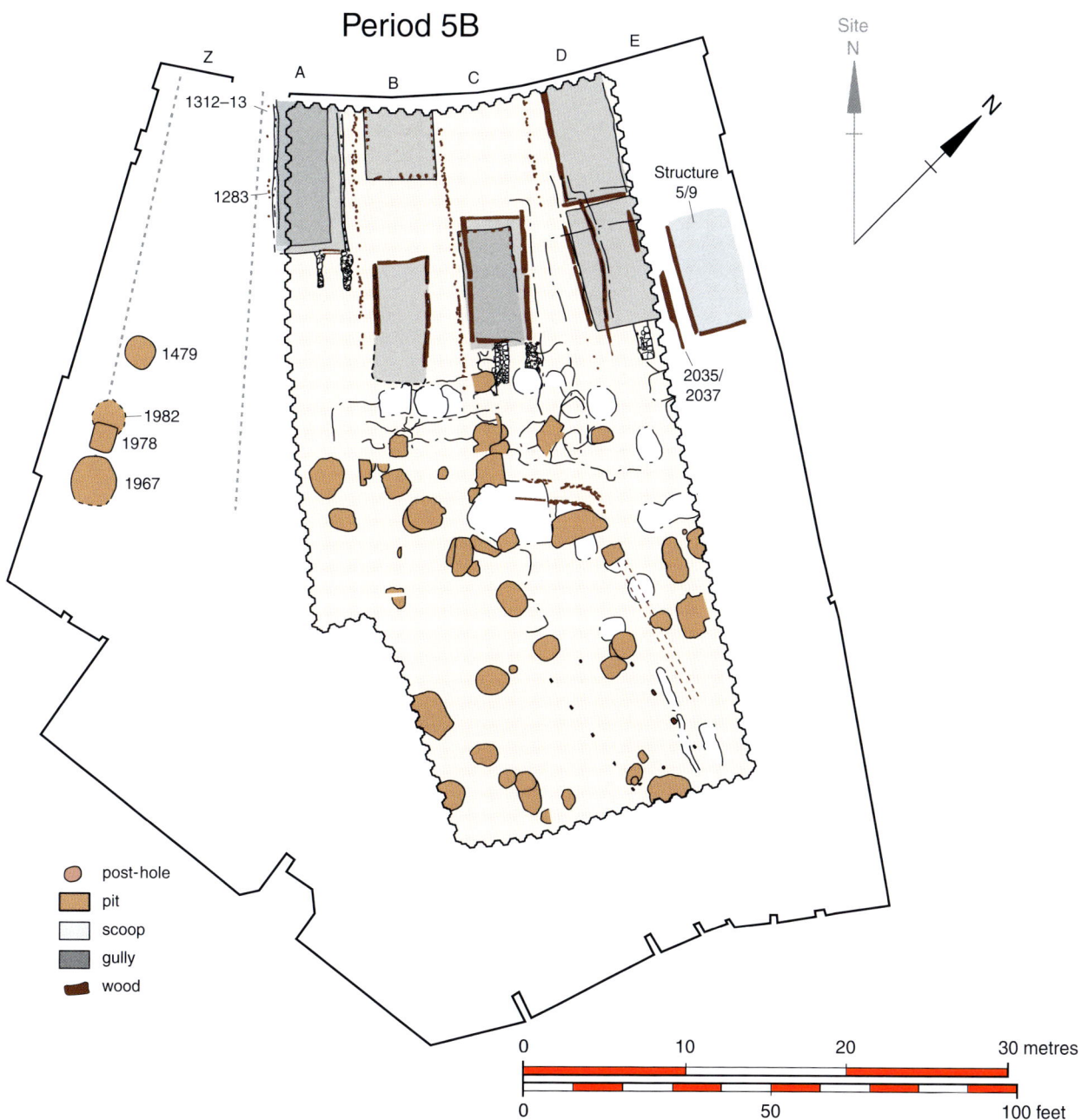

Fig.196   *Period 5B: overall plan, including watching brief features. Scale 1:400*

some cases at least, accessed through a rear stone-revetted entrance. Although several of the buildings burned down or were largely dismantled when they went out of use, survival conditions were such that some walls still stood over 1.5m high, preserving extraordinary details. The backyards continued to be used for rubbish and cess pits, enclosures, gullies and drains (Fig.196).

Fragments of at least thirteen buildings were recovered, nine of which belong to Period 5B, constructed sequentially over the next 50 to 60 years. Once again dendrochronological dates provide a structural sequence which evidently began c.960 and continued into the early 11th century, revealing a dynamic period stretching over little more than two generations. It seems unlikely that more than six structures were in use at any one time as original buildings were replaced, or extended, on the same spot during this period. Unlike the Period 4B post and wattle buildings, their later counterparts do not appear to have been arranged in quite so orderly a manner on the street frontage (see Fig.330). Although later cellars and intrusions have destroyed some of the crucial evidence, there is, for example, no reason to believe that a structure stood on the street frontage in Tenement C during this time, while the building in Tenement B, truncated by the street frontage shoring, appears to have been set considerably further forward than the others. The situation on Tenement D is potentially different again (see pp.663–75). A second rank of buildings behind the street frontage strip is another new development during this period and these too are irregular in their position; the need to take into account the slope of the land and underlying earlier pits no doubt played a part in planning the layout. The terrain has resulted in the various buildings being cut from significantly different heights depending on their position on the site (Fig.197).

Tenement A

This property, and the adjacent Tenement Z in Zone 1 of the watching brief (Fig.196), occupied the highest ground, on the upward slope of the moraine (see Fig.134) as it rose to the south-west before dropping down towards the River Ouse. The advantages of good drainage might have made this a desirable building plot and there is evidence for two successive buildings on the street frontage in

Tenement A. To the west, beyond the site perimeter, the watching brief produced evidence for another property and further features of this date (p.697 and Fig.196). On Tenement A itself the first building, Structure 5/1, was constructed in the early years of the 960s. There is evidence of extensive burning which must have destroyed the building, necessitating its replacement by Structure 5/2, offset slightly to the west, although in the absence of surviving timbers the date of this replacement cannot be established.

Structure 5/1

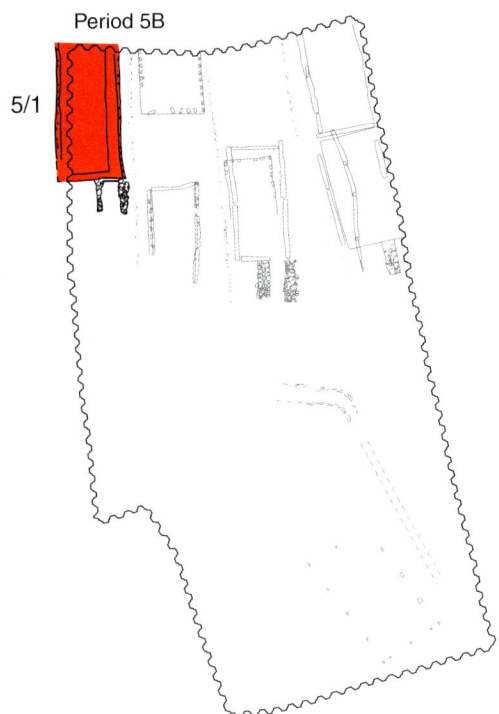

Location of Structure 5/1

Remains of this building, the earlier of the two successive sunken structures on Tenement A, lay in the north-west corner of the excavation. The perimeter piling had cut through the structure at the street frontage and along its western side (Figs 196 and 198). The watching brief recorded much of the line of the west wall (Fig.199 and see p.697) although the south-west corner of the structure was truncated by a modern intrusion. The circumstances of the watching brief allowed only the recording of the positions of timber elements; all the other information about this structure, and its interpretation, is based upon data from the main excavation (Fig.199).

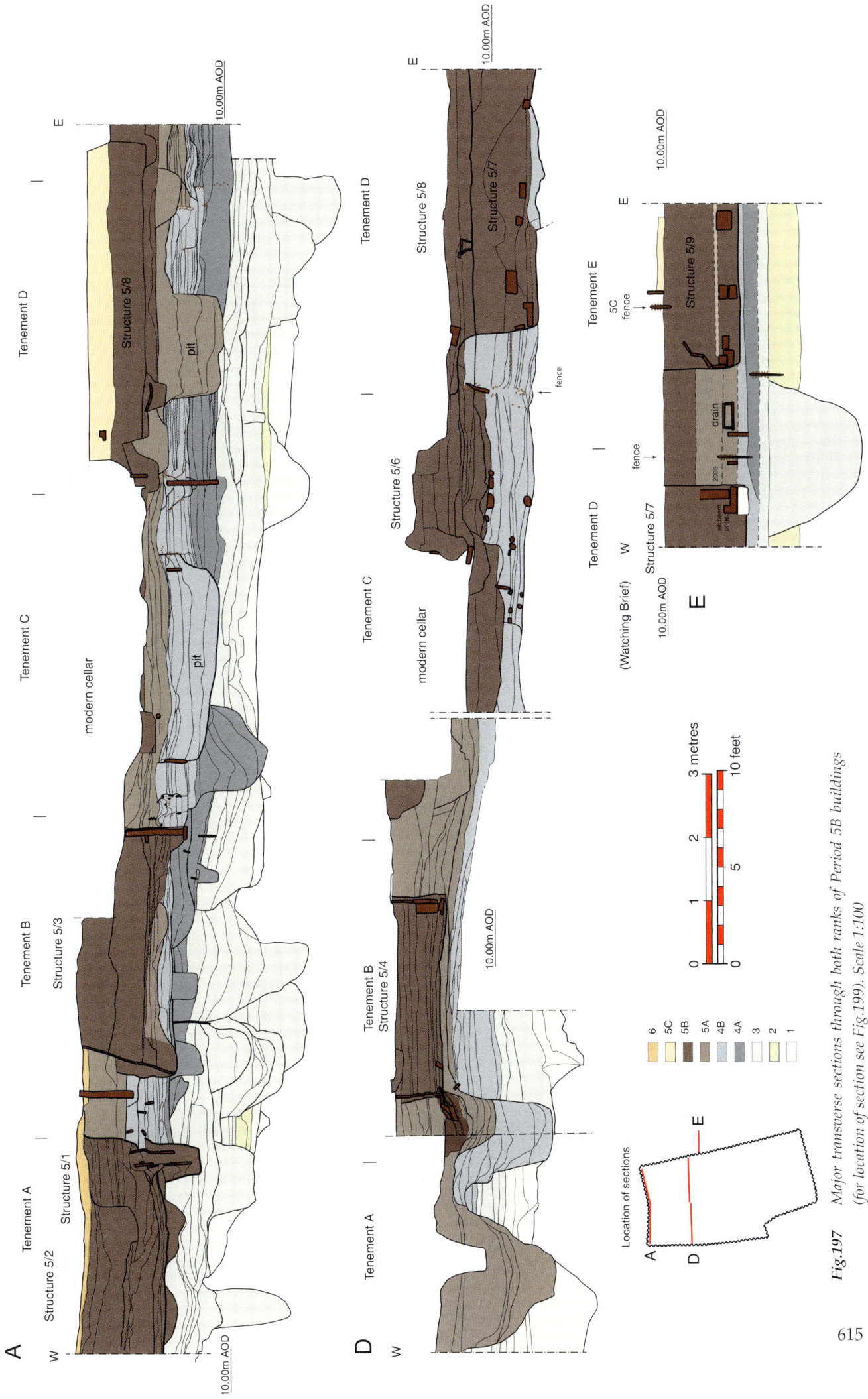

Fig.197 *Major transverse sections through both ranks of Period 5B buildings (for location of section see Fig.199). Scale 1:100*

615

Fig.198   Structure 5/1 fully excavated. Scale unit 0.1m

The structure, which was approximately 4.5m wide and at least 9m long, was erected in a rectangular cutting which dug into earlier levels, cut 15431 (Figs 199 and 200). It survives in places to a height of c.0.8m. Along the east wall line (but not the south) this cut forms a trench (20643, Fig.200) into which the horizontal timbers and uprights were set. The transverse profile of 20643 varied, as did its width (0.65–1.00m) and its depth varied from 0.6m to the north to 0.2m at the south. The timbers occupied the central axis of the trench, i.e. they were not positioned against the outer edge.

Site records show that cut 15431 was dug from approximately 0.90m above the base of the side wall trench 20643 (maximum 1.2m); the profile of its upper lip suggests a slumping of the exposed upper edge. The cut was thus more or less at the contemporary mid-10th-century ground surface. A feature of this structure was the 'cavity wall' construction of both the side walls, which were formed by horizontal planks set either side of upright posts (Figs 199 and 201). The side walls incorporated squared

upright posts of tangentially split oak, with flat bases; several retained tool marks (Fig.202). All rested on the primary silt backfill of the construction trench, with their bases at slightly different levels. The planks averaged 0.25 x 0.08m (virtually all in the range 0.20–0.30m x 0.06–0.10m) with gaps usually of 0.15–0.25m between adjacent uprights. Their positions ensured that at the places where sections of the outer horizontal plank wall cladding abutted, there was an upright directly behind them (Figs 199 and 203). Three of the uprights along the east wall each had a small squarish peg-hole cut into their outer (east) side, near the base, but not necessarily centrally positioned; the remains of pegs survived within them. These uprights (for example, contexts 20738, 20237, 18966; Fig.199) were ones which stood at or adjacent to abutting horizontal wall planks, and it was the function of the peg to support the bottom of the lowest horizontal plank at its correct height (Figs 204 and 205). This technique was not, however, applied to each end of every separate horizontal timber, and the easternmost of the outer timbers was not supported by any pegs.

Period 5B
Structure 5/1

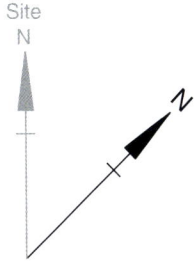

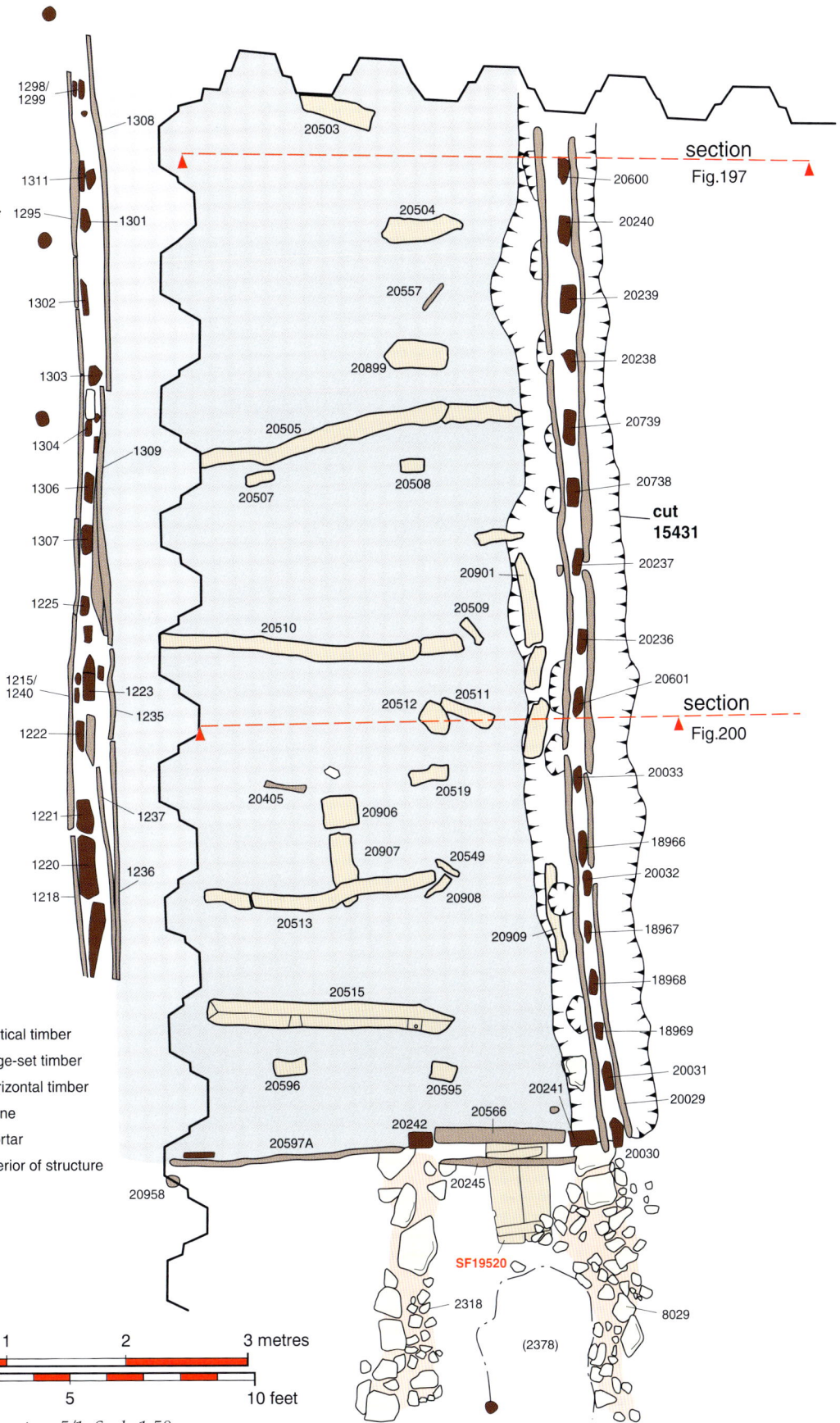

Site N

1298/
1299
1308
1311
1295   1301
1302
1303
1304
1309
1306
1307
1225
1215/
1240   1223
              1235
1222
1221   1237
1220   1236
1218

20958

20503
20504
20557
20899
20505
20507   20508
20901
20509
20510
20512   20511
20405
20906
20519
20907
20549
20908
20513
20515
20596   20595   20241
20597A   20242   20566
            20245
        SF19520
        2318
            (2378)

section
Fig.197
20600
20240
20239
20238
20739
20738
cut
15431
20237
20236
20601
section
Fig.200
20033
18966
20032
18967
18968
18969
20031
20029
20030

8029

vertical timber
edge-set timber
horizontal timber
stone
mortar
interior of structure

0   1   2   3 metres
0   5   10 feet

Fig.199 *Plan of Structure 5/1. Scale 1:50*

617

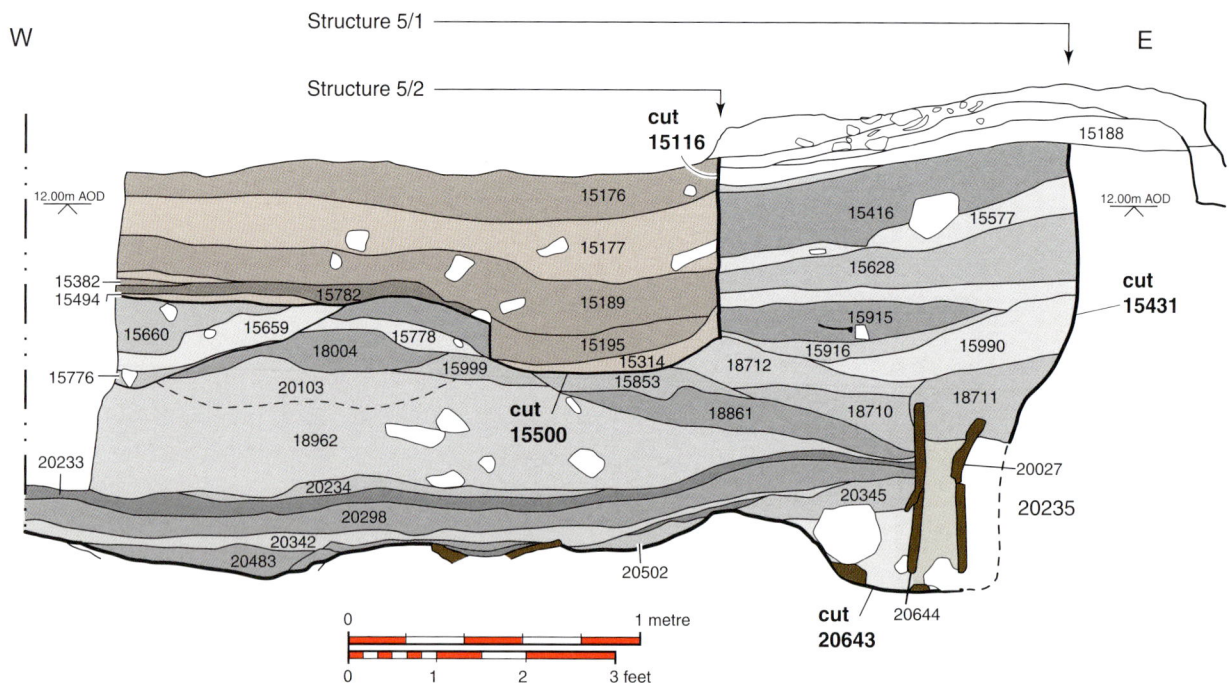

W   E

Structure 5/1

Structure 5/2

cut
15116

cut
15431

cut
15500

cut
20643

12.00m AOD

12.00m AOD

15176

15177

15189

15195

15314
15853

15382
15494

15782

15660   15659

15778

18004

15999

15776

20103

18962

20233

20234

20298

20342

20483

20502

15416   15577

15628

15915

15916   15990

18712

18861   18710

18711

20345

20027

20235

20644

15188

0   1 metre

0   1   2   3 feet

Fig.200   *Section drawing showing Structure 5/1 cut by Structure 5/2 (for location of section see Fig.199). Scale 1:25*

A series of ovoid post-holes, varying from 0.16 to 0.28m in depth and up to 0.4m across, were positioned at irregular intervals along and against the inner face of the inner plank cladding of the east wall (Fig.199). Two of them were so placed that the posts would mask the two abutting joints on the horizontal planks of this face.

The lowest planks of both the inner and outer wall cladding lay slightly above the base of the trench, occasionally resting upon limestone rubble, but normally upon soil. There were a few wooden offcuts in the backfill of the construction trench, and pieces of limestone and gritstone rubble (Fig.206). One of these was part of a small, 10th-century mill-

Fig.201   *Detail of east wall of Structure 5/1 showing charred uprights and outer planking. Scale unit 0.1m*

618

stone grit grave-marker (*AY* 17/14, 2601, *10827*, fig.1298, erroneously published as limestone) (Fig.207).

The outer plank lining is made from tangentially faced oak planks, whist the inner lining, that which formed the inner wall of the structure, was radially faced. The planks measure 0.20–0.30m wide and 0.50–0.80m thick; complete planks varied in length between 0.80m and 3.75m. They appeared to have been chosen and positioned carefully so that, normally, pieces of similar length rested one above the other, their ends forming a vertical edge to each section of walling. Normally, also, the points where adjacent lengths of the inner and of the outer cladding abutted did not coincide. The horizontal planks rested edge upon edge, and were held in place by the upright posts between the two claddings and by the posts that had stood inside the inner cladding (Fig.208). No other securing mechanism (nails, pegs etc.) was employed to give them additional stability. Evidence for up to four courses of horizontal planks survived in some places, to a maximum height of c.1.0m (Fig.209). The inner face of the outer cladding in the east wall was charred

Fig.202   *Detail showing tool marks on east wall of Structure 5/1. Scale unit 0.1m*

for 0.3m below its surviving upper edge (Fig.210); this indicates that the space between the two claddings was not filled with soil or any other material so dense or highly compacted as to inhibit burning. The outer surfaces of both wall claddings were not charred.

The west wall of the building, recovered only during the subsequent watching brief, matched the east wall very closely and the same construction method was applied (Fig.209). The outer planks were supported by uprights at c.0.5m intervals although these, as recovered, were set well back; presumably the uprights retaining the inner planks were removed when the building was demolished. Both sets of planks rested on the ground. Medium-sized limestone blocks were found at various levels between the two sets of planks, presumably part of the infill of the cavity during demolition.

The cut was not observed but its base was at 10.65m OD and the wall survived to 11.70m OD. An irregular layer of moss and brushwood (1244) up to 0.3m thick overlies loam deposits 1253 (up to 0.4m thick) and 1340 which are likely to be backfill deposits or evidence of secondary use of the cut as a rubbish dump. The deposits above c.12.0m OD continue into the area of the sunken building, suggesting the walls were removed down to that point and deposits outside the structure pushed into the cut to level the ground surface. If so, this reduction of the ground surface would have removed all trace of any surface relating to Period 5B.

The south (back) wall of the building appeared to comprise only a single skin of edge-set planking (20597A, Fig.199); its west end had been destroyed by the perimeter shoring. Adjacent to the surviving end was an upright post (20958) which may possibly have been an integral part of the construction (Figs 199 and 211). The east end of the planking abutted the outer face of a squared upright (20242) which was one of a pair, the other (20241) itself abutting the inner end of the east cavity wall (Figs 199, 211 and 212). The gap between them was occupied by a horizontal timber beam (20566) 1.10m long, 0.22m high and 0.12m wide which is interpreted as a sill for a door in this position. Some 0.10m south of this beam was an edge-set plank (20245) of similar length, 0.20m high and 0.11m wide, which lay

Fig.203   *Structure 5/1: detail of east wall showing position of posts and abutting planks. Scale unit 0.1m*

Fig.204   *Structure 5/1: detail of east wall showing position of pegs. Scale unit 0.1m*

Fig.205   *(right) Structure 5/1: detail of peg. Scale unit 10mm*

Fig.206 *Structure 5/1: detail of east wall showing lower planks resting on wood offcut and rubble. Scale unit 0.1m*

Fig.207 *Sculptural fragment 10827 in situ. Scale unit 0.1m*

Fig.208 *Structure 5/1: south end of east wall with inner planks and uprights removed. Scale unit 0.1m*

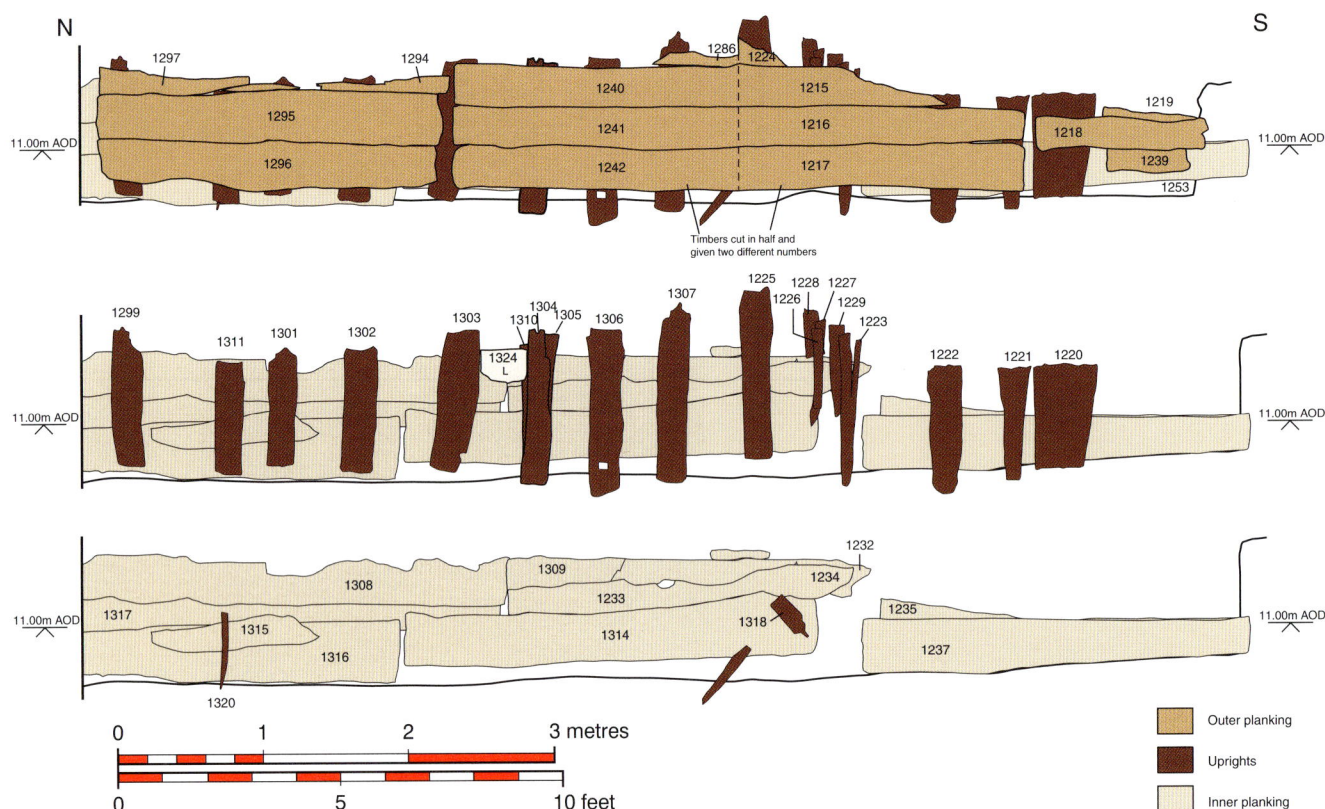

Fig.209 *Structure 5/1: west-facing elevation drawing of west wall. Scale 1:50*

within a linear cut, set at a higher level than the beam, with its base only a few centimetres below the top of the beam and believed to form part of the threshold (Fig.212).

Eleven samples, from both posts and planks, were dated by dendrochronology. They gave consistent results, the most precise of which was a felling date in the winter of 961/62 for the planks and a date range of 961–81 for the posts. A post (8827) from the series of paired posts referred to below (p.626) which are believed to be part of the original construction of Structure 5/1 had a felling date of 946–79 which is consistent with the other dates.

Immediately south of the door was a series of timbers, some of them re-used, which had been used to infill a depression apparently caused by the removal of the earlier (Period 5A) barrel-lined feature (cut 31266) (Fig.213) which was itself repre-sented only by a fragment of a hoop binding made of ash (*AY* 17/13, 2252, *8850*) and several staves.

Above several c.1m lengths of squared timber beam (27214, 27215, 20731, not shown on plan) which lay approximately east–west was a fragmentary barrel lid (20733). On top of this was a composite, rectangular, battened and dowelled wooden item (Figs 199 and 214), identified as a garderobe lid (*AY* 17/13, sf19520, *8951*, fig.1131), which formed part of the construction of the entrance.

To either side of the doorway in the building's southern wall a linear spread of limestone rubble extended down the main axis of the plot. On the site east, and partly overlying the garderobe lid, was 8029 (Fig.199), which was bedded into a layer of mortar; on the western side 2318 was also bedded into a mortar layer which itself covered a further course of limestone rubble (8305, not shown on plan). Both these limestone rubble features were truncated on their outer sides and to the south by modern intrusions; furthermore, a linear ditch (2378, which is ascribed to a later phase in Period 5B, between the demolition of Structure 5/1 and the construction of Structure 5/2) occupied much of

Fig.210 *East wall with inner planks removed (showing charred tops of timbers). Scale unit 0.1m*

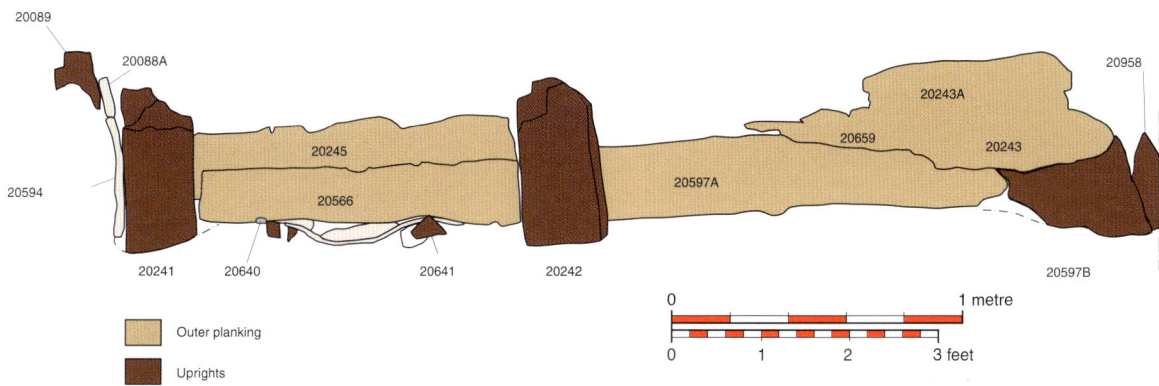

Fig.211 *North-facing elevation of south wall. Scale 1:25*

Fig.212 *Doorway and threshold in south wall. Scale unit 0.1m*

Fig.213 *Period 5A barrel-lined feature 31266 sealed just outside Structure 5/1 threshold. Scale unit 0.1m*

Fig.214 *Wooden garderobe lid. Scale unit 0.1m*

624

Fig.215   *Floor 'joists' in Structure 5/1. Scale unit 0.1m*

the area between them. It is tentatively suggested, on the basis of stratification and position, that these rubble features represent the remains of a revetment for a passageway approaching the putative back door, which had to be cut into the sloping ground surface. Stone rubble revetments were identified in association with other contemporary semi-basement structures on the site (see Structures 5/6 and 5/8).

After the construction pit for this building had been dug out, a cut/hollow within the floor area, up to 0.25m deep, was filled with olive-coloured sand (20502/20589) and immediately over the sand was a widespread thin deposit of dark grey-brown organic silt (20483/4, Fig.200), above which lay a series of four horizontal timbers (20505; 20510; 20513; 20515), truncated to the west by the insertion of perimeter shoring (Figs 199 and 215). They all lay across the main axis of Structure 5/1, spaced at irregular intervals, and all stopped short of the east wall. The northern three were branches, with the bark still adhering in places, and each had a

Fig.216   *Detail of re-used beam with peg in place. Scale unit 10mm*

625

Fig.217   *Floor of Structure 5/1 with paired posts and joists. Scale unit 0.1m*

bevelled or pointed east end; the southernmost was part of a re-used beam, squared and with two joint seatings in its uppermost face, one of them retaining part of a peg in its hole (Fig.216).

A number of vertical post stubs protruded at this level. Six were arranged in fairly regularly disposed pairs (20507 and 20508; 20405 and 20519; 20596 and 20595) up the centre of the building (Fig.199); the southernmost pair (20596 and 20595) was 0.40m inside the south wall, with the other pairs spaced a further 2.20 and 2.40m beyond each other. The gap between the posts in each pair varied from 0.90m to 1.10m (Fig.217). Two other posts (20908 and 20549) formed a V-shaped setting at the east end of one of the transverse beams and another single post was set at an angle to a beam end (20509). The final single post (20557), also set at an angle to the axis of the building, was in an approximately north–south line with the others (Fig.199). These, together with the four horizontal timbers, are likely to have supported some type of flooring which was probably stripped out at the time the structure was abandoned.

Covering the organic silts 2048 (Fig.200), as well as the horizontal beams and vertical post stubs, was a succession of brushwood and related layers which, altogether, were up to 0.2m deep. The earliest component that could be isolated was a scattering of brushwood (20485), overwhelmingly of willow (*Salix*) species, the individual components of which were aligned principally on the north–south axis of the building (Fig.218). Virtually the entire floor area of the building was then covered with a 50–70mm thick layer (20342) consisting largely of mixed imported heathland vegetation (Fig.219). This included appreciable quantities of flowers, capsules, shoot and twig fragments of heather or ling, together with a suite of mosses. It is suggested (*AY* 14/7, 589, 723–4) that imported turf rather than cut vegetation is the most likely source for these remains; the turf could perhaps have been a roofing material. Subsequently, further evidence from sites in York has strengthened the suggestion that turf was used as a roofing material; conceivably, it could have been used as an 'underlay' of some kind for a thatched roof, or as the sole component of the roof (Hall and Kenward in *AY* 8/4, 378–80). Here, this

626

Fig.218   *Earliest layer of twigs and brushwood. Scale unit 0.1m*

Fig.219   *Full extent of brushwood deposit. Scale unit 0.1m*

Fig.220   *Twigs at different alignments. Scale unit 0.1m*

vegetation was sealed by 20–30mm of fine willow brushwood (20298, Fig.200) predominantly aligned approximately with the building's main axis, and then by up to 150mm of coarser brushwood (20233, Fig.200), with components varying from 4mm to 40mm in stem thickness, which lay in more varied alignments (Fig.220). Finally in this succession was a layer (20234, Fig.200) of more limited extent, and only a few millimetres thick; it was described on site as a matted fibrous material, with the appearance of heather, its stems up to 3mm thick, and containing straw-like patches and some ash. Beetle assemblages in this material indicated moist but open-textured decaying matter (*AY* 14/7, 589).

Above this succession of brushwood and related organic deposits, the west/central part of the building was occupied by a layer of very dark grey-coloured sandy silty clay loam (20059/18962/20103), 0.40m thick. A series of small posts, mostly circular, occasionally sub-rectangular,

ran approximately north–south within this deposit (20100, 15506, 15520, 15511 and 20054). This layer (20059) sloped away markedly on the east side of the building, probably resulting from a dumping operation rather than being the edge of a deliberate cut. A succession of subsequent layers (e.g. 15999, 18004, 15778, 15661) may be further dumped constituents of this same operation, with declivities to either side of an axial spine infilled with broadly similar deposits (to the west, 15659/15660; to the east, 18861, 15853, 18710, 18712, 15990, 15916) (Fig.200). The continued build up of relatively thick deposits, also interpreted as part of a succession of dumped deposits above Structure 5/1, was seen in an approximately 1.10m wide strip at the eastern side of the original construction cut dug for Structure 5/1 that was not disturbed by the insertion of Structure 5/2. Here, layers of dark grey clay loam, 0.10–0.20m thick, were most common, interspersed with other deposits of peaty loams, peaty silts, slightly structured peat and a lens of ash.

Structure 5/2

Cut into the deposits that formed the backfill within Structure 5/1 was the hole dug to contain another sunken building, Structure 5/2 (see Figs 197 and 200), although no traces of *in situ* wall timbers were found in this building. Its east wall line was 1.10–1.20m west of the cut for Structure 5/1; its west side and street frontage end were both truncated by the excavation's perimeter shoring, and the east wall by a modern intrusion. The west side of this structure, beyond the perimeter piling, was not detected during the watching brief. Thus only a strip of floor measuring some 2.60m wide by approximately 7m long was available for investigation (Figs 221 and 222). Along the east wall line the base of the construction cut (15116) was deepened to form a trench, 15500, approximately 0.55–0.75m wide and 0.10m–0.20m lower than the internal floor level. At the base of this trench was a pinkish-/reddish-coloured clay which was cut by, and extends beyond, the construction cut 15500, together with pieces of Roman tile and limestone rubble. The inner edge of this trench was revetted at one point by horizontal edge-set timbers (15501/2) which were themselves supported on their east sides by stakes (Fig.222c).

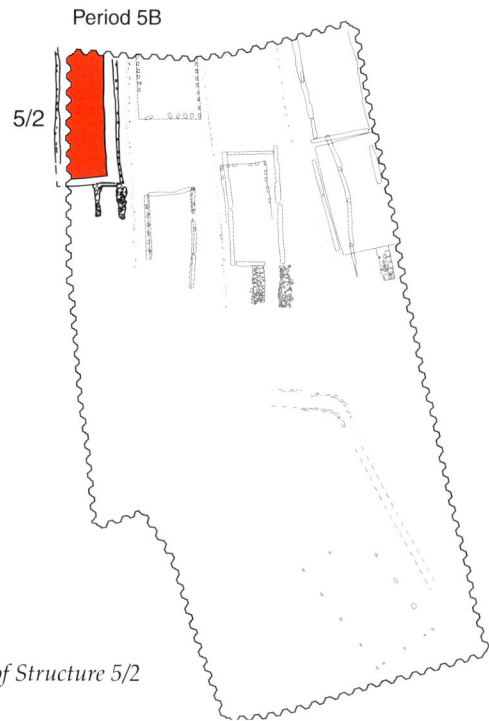

Period 5B

5/2

Location of Structure 5/2

Linear feature 15704 and scooped features (e.g. 37141) appear to belong to the interface between the two buildings (Fig.222a and b) and might relate to construction activities, while inside the building, to the west of the construction trench, was a series

Fig.221   *Structure 5/2: cut for the building. Scale unit 0.1m*

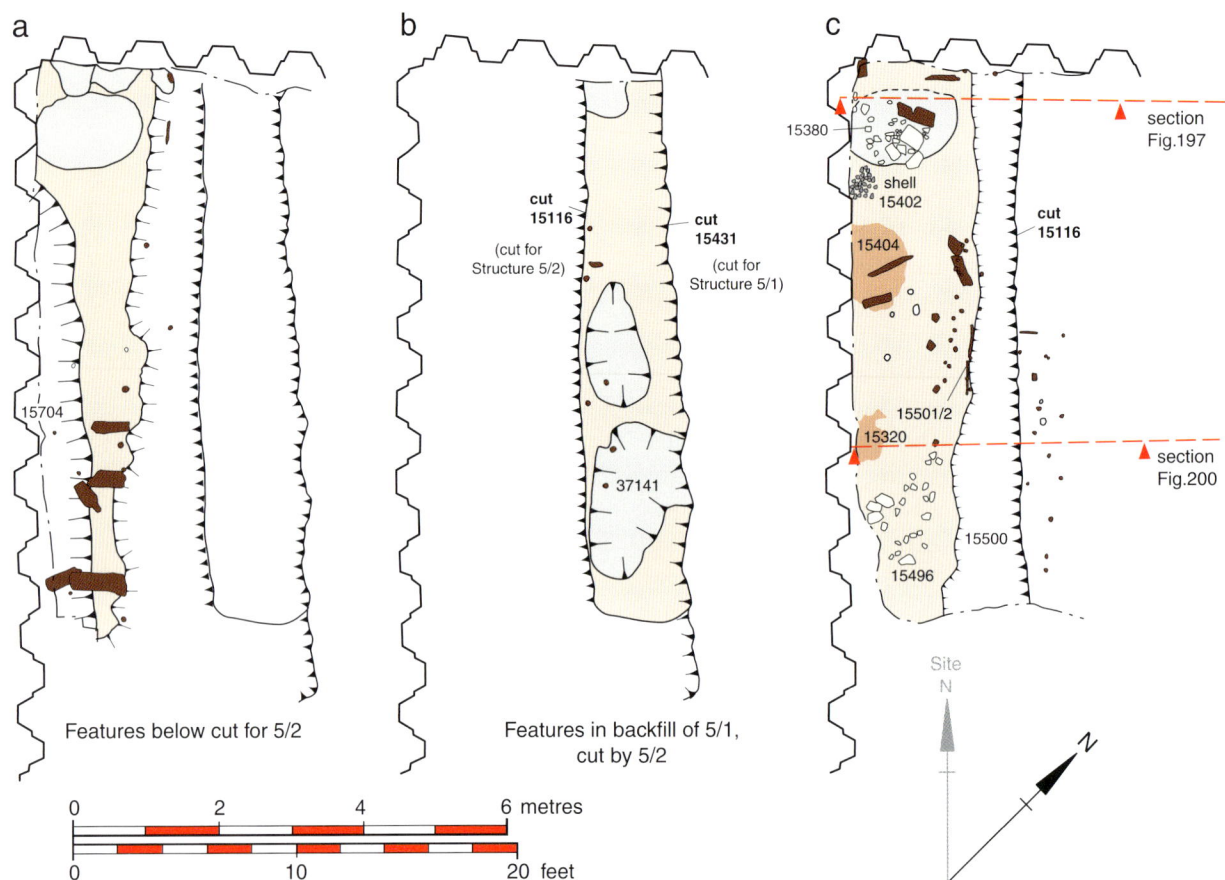

Fig.222 *Plans of Structure 5/2. Scale 1:125*

of relatively thin, horizontal layers and spreads which were stratigraphically later than the deposits infilling the sloping dumped deposits in Structure 5/1. The relationship of these thin layers to the cut for the building is uncertain but, in the absence of other floor deposits, it is suggested that they represent the construction and use of the structure rather than immediately pre-dating it. These layers were essentially dark grey silty clay loams, some with a recognisable organic fraction ('peaty silty clay loams'), and typically incorporating notice-able quantities of burnt clay blobs, oyster shells, small limestone rubble and decayed wood. One of these was sampled (15192) and is described as being consistent with 'a slowly accumulating floor deposit ... (and) ... of a waterproof building probably occupied by humans (*AY* 14/7, 589). This and another layer (15382, Fig.200) contained many fragmentary glass beads.

Within this broadly similar matrix of layers were some smaller spreads that may represent distinct features. These include a small area of dispersed

limestone rubble (15380) and an ashy spread, possibly a hearth (15320), while just to its north there was a 0.5m diameter concentration of oyster shells (15402) which seemed to have been deliberately laid in position (Figs 222c and 223). All of these deposits amounted to no more than 0.1m in depth, but they were sealed by layers of mixed clay loams each

Fig.223 *Deliberately laid deposit of oyster shells. Scale unit 0.1m*

0.10–0.25m thick (15189, 15177, 15176; Fig.200) and totalling 0.40–0.50m in depth. These infilled the cut for the building's construction to its lip, which was in turn sealed by a further broadly similar deposit (13763), and it seems that at least 0.6m–0.7m of wall was below the contemporary ground surface. As no *in situ* timbers survived, but there are layers which are interpreted as floor deposits, it is suggested that the structure was dismantled in antiquity and the timbers re-used.

Tenement B

Two successive buildings stood on Tenement B, one (Structure 5/3) was cut by the site shoring and the other (Structure 5/4) was set back 8m from the street frontage (see Figs 197 and 330).

Structure 5/3

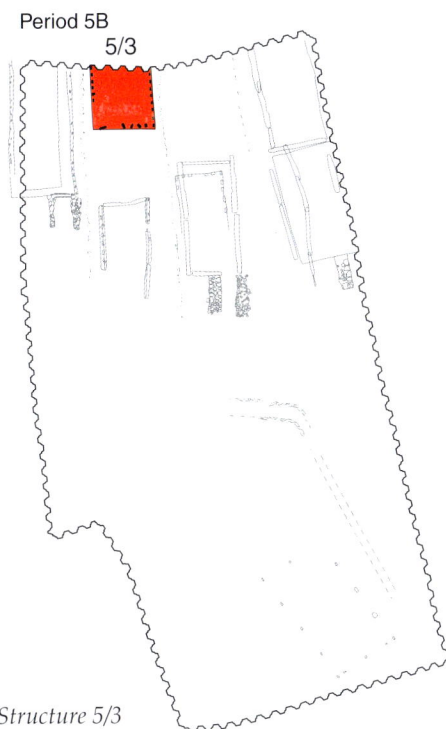

Location of Structure 5/3

Within Tenement B were the remains of Structure 5/3, its street frontage end inaccessible beyond the perimeter shoring (Figs 224 and 225). The sequence of deposits relates to the construction, use and abandonment of this building, and is sealed by layers assigned to the later medieval Period 6.

Approximately one-third of the available internal area of this building had been truncated by a modern cellar (Fig.224) which extended diagonally into the building from near its north-eastern corner and had removed parts of the stratification relating to the abandonment phases of the building.

This building was erected within a rectangular cut approximately 1.2m deep on the east side and about 1m deep on the west side (Fig.226). The structure was 4.25m wide and a surviving length of c.4.5m lay within the excavated area. Along its edges the base of the construction pit had been deepened slightly to form trenches within which the main structural elements were set. The principal wall supports were squared oak box halved or box heart posts, with flat bases, which were found along both the east and west walls. On the eastern side they were regularly spaced with gaps of 0.27–0.30m between them (Fig.224); the base of some rested upon slabs or pads of wood (Figs 227 and 228). The surviving wall top here had been truncated by the modern cellar and survived to 11.65–11.85m AOD, apart from the tallest surviving post (13711), 1.85m long, in the south-east corner of the building (Figs 229 and 230). The western wall posts were more unevenly spaced, the gaps between adjacent uprights varying from 0.19m to 0.28m (Fig.231). None of them rested upon a wooden slab, but some stood in post-holes that were up to 0.20m deep. In addition, one (13706) had a small (0.24 x 0.17 x 0.07m) supporting/bracing post at its base (Figs 231 and 232). The surviving wall top on this side was mostly in the range 12.40–12.50m AOD. No posts that supported the building's south (back) wall remained in position; a number of wooden pads or slabs (eg. 18220–1, 18109 and 18243) found here might have supported posts which were removed when the structure was abandoned. Edge-set plank 18279 survives to mark the position of the wall (Fig.224).

The upright posts in the side walls supported horizontal planks which revetted the sides of the construction cut. As in Structure 5/1, these planks were in quite regular courses abutting each other both vertically and horizontally. There was no evidence for the use of any iron nails, wooden pegs or dowels, or any form of jointing which could have assisted the stability of this construction.

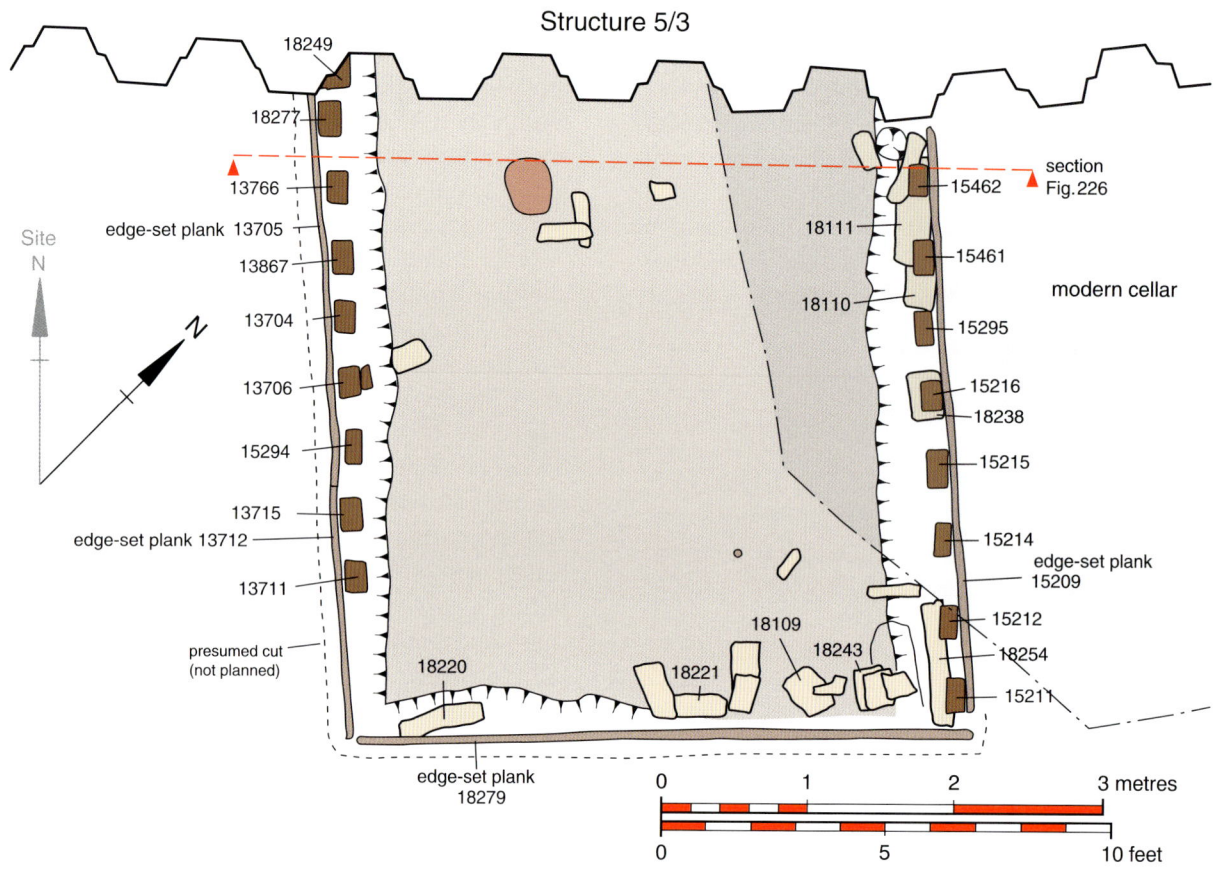

Structure 5/3

18249
18277
13766
edge-set plank 13705
13867
13704
13706
15294
13715
edge-set plank 13712
13711
presumed cut
(not planned)

18220
18279
edge-set plank
18279

18221
18109
18243

15462
section
Fig.226
18111
15461
15295
15216
18238
15215
15214
edge-set plank
15209
15212
18254
15211

modern cellar

Site
N

N

18110

0   1   2   3 metres

0   5   10 feet

Fig.224   *Plan of Structure 5/3. Scale 1:50*

Fig.225   *Structure 5/3 fully excavated. Scale unit 0.1m*

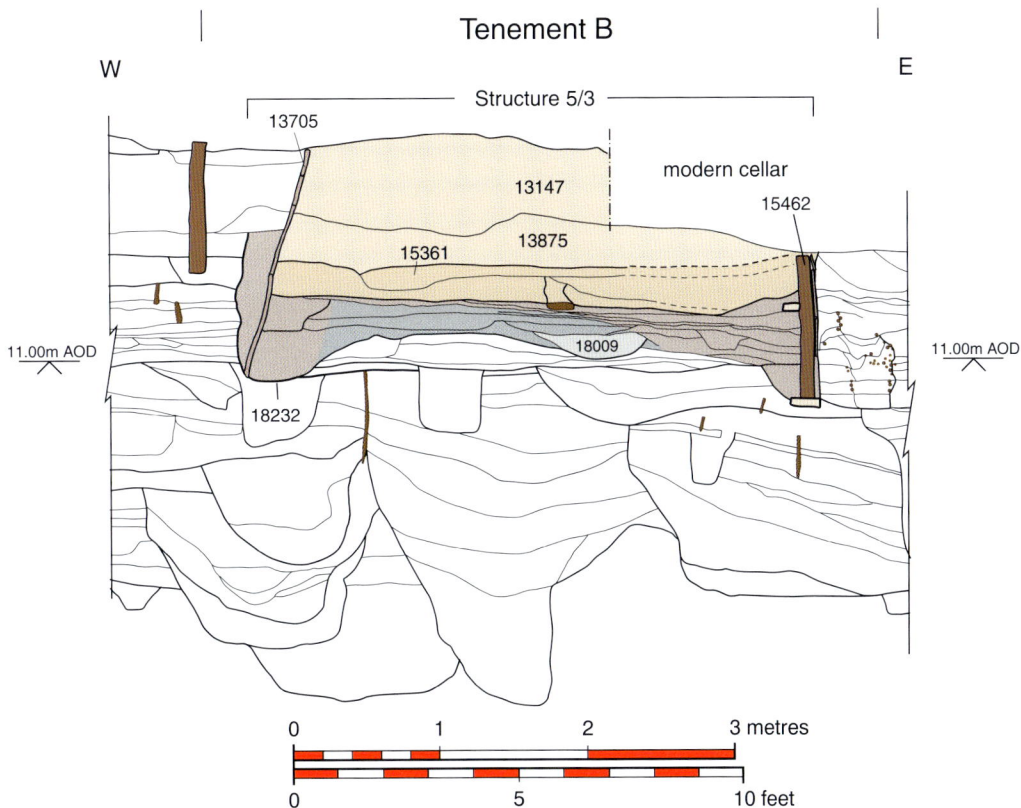

Fig.226 *West–east section through Structure 5/3 (for location of section see Fig.224). Scale 1:50*

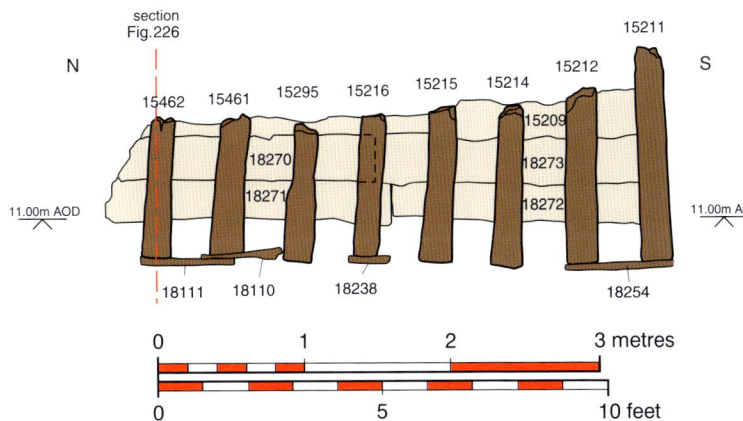

Fig.227 *West-facing elevation, east wall, Structure 5/3. Scale 1:50*

Planks in the west wall varied from 30mm to 70mm in thickness, from 210mm to 480mm in width, and could be up to at least 3.95m in length. Parts of the uppermost three courses of planks were degraded, but the lower three courses were in good condition (Figs 231 and 233). One incomplete and two complete courses of planks (comprising five individual planks) survived in the east wall, generally in good condition (Figs 227 and 234). They were 20mm to 50mm thick, and 280mm to 340mm wide. The two that had not been truncated by the perim-

eter shoring were 1.83m and 1.90m long; the three which had been truncated were 1.76m, 1.97m and 3.02m long.

Relatively few planks from the south wall remained *in situ*. They ranged in thickness from 10mm to 40mm, in width from 200mm to 270mm, and in length from 0.58m to 3.46m. Additionally one plank (15335, not shown on plan), found lying horizontally just below it, is presumed originally to have been part of the wall; it measures

Fig.228   *East wall showing wooden post pads. Scale unit 0.1m*

Fig.229   *South-east corner with corner post in place. Scale unit 0.1m*

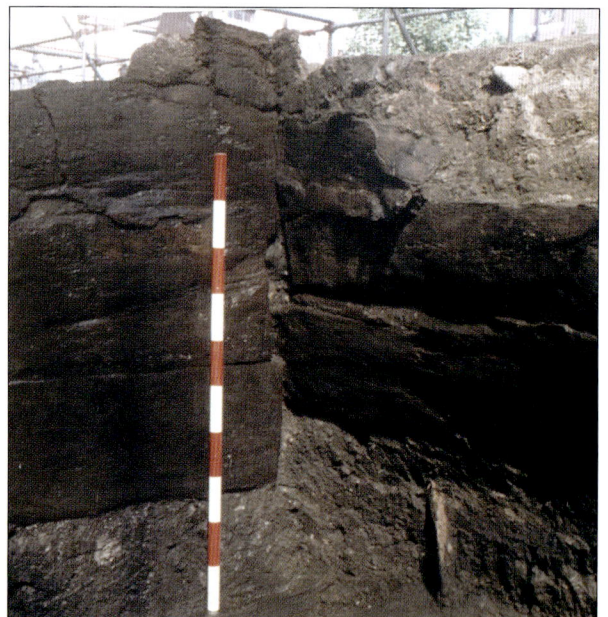

Fig.230   *South-east corner with corner post removed. Scale unit 0.1m*

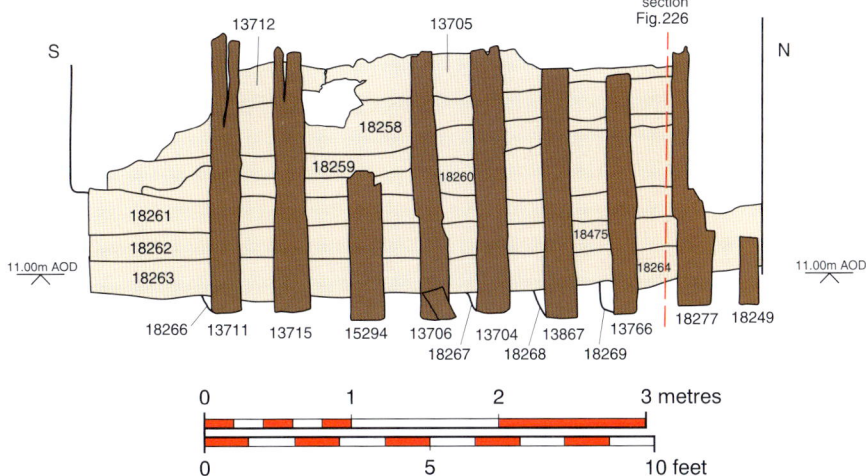

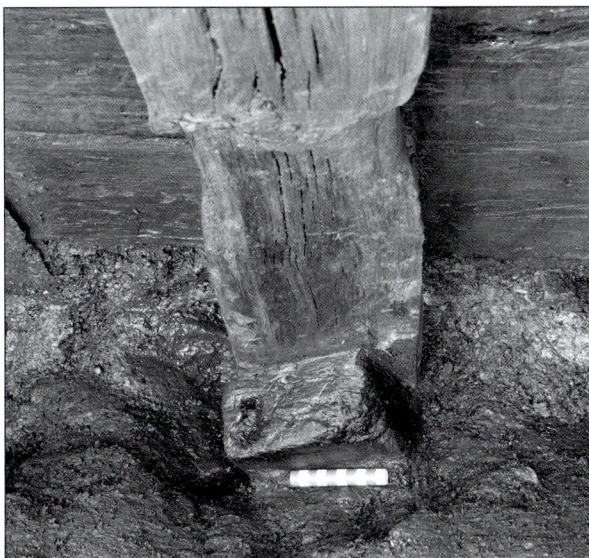

Fig.232   *Upright in western wall held in place by wooden chock. Scale unit 10mm*

0.25 x 0.36 x 3.07m. There is no surviving evidence for an entrance in the back wall of Structure 5/3 as might have been expected on the basis of the other structures; equally there is no surviving evidence for a stone-revetted passageway. This leads to the conclusion that this structure, unlike the others, must have been accessed from the street frontage.

Establishing the stratigraphic points from which and to which the wall trenches were cut was extremely difficult in this structure. Soil changes running parallel to walls, or to parts of walls, which could represent the fills of such cuts, were identified at several different levels within the structure, but were interleaved by other more widespread deposits. The interpretation offered here recognises a succession of thin floor deposits, with a total depth of about 0.1m, consisting predominantly of silty loam. Slightly off the centre of the excavated floor area, the uppermost of these (15561) was cut by a sub-rectangular depression (15578) measuring approximately 1m x 0.80m and 0.20m deep, and with a shallower (0.10–0.15m deep) irregular gully leading into one corner from the side of the building (Fig.235). Both depression and gully were filled with black, slightly peaty silts. These contained an insect assemblage similar to those found on the floors of buildings, a striking and inexplicable variety of lice, and also a component indicating the presence of water, perhaps in the context of use as a soakaway (*AY* 14/7, 595–6).

Sealing these features and the sequence of thin deposits was a succession of distinctly thicker deposits, typically up to 0.10m or more in depth (15530–2). The lower deposits were very dark grey or grey-brown silty loams or peaty (i.e. organic-rich) silts; biological analysis revealed materials that originated both indoors and outdoors, and thereby suggested that these layers may reflect a changing use of the structure, rather than its abandonment (*AY* 14/7, 596–7). Slightly higher up, some broadly similar deposits (15470) contained quantities of wood chips and had a high mineral content; this suggests that slightly foul, 'compost heap'-like organic matter may have been included (*ibid*). This part of the succession was terminated by a 0.30m thick ridge of a similar deposit near the north-western end of the structure (13875, Fig.226), which sloped away quite markedly to both north-west and south-east.

635

Fig.233 *West wall from the east. Scale unit 0.1m*

Fig.234 *East wall from the west. Scale unit 0.1m*

Fig.235 *Sump and gully within Structure 5/3. Scale unit 0.1m*

Upon the essentially concave surface to the south of this ridge lay a deposit of 'brushwood', predominantly willow (*Salix* sp(p).) but incorporating a little alder (*Alnus*). It had been imported with its leaves in place, apparently as whole branches. At its base (15207) was a mixture of fine withies, larger withies and some plank fragments. In the centre of the building the brushwood lay on a variety of alignments, but at its outer edges, where it rose at an angle corresponding to that of the adjacent backfill, it seemed to run in bands parallel to the nearest wall line (Fig.236). Distinguished from it and separately recorded during excavation was an overlying brushwood layer (Fig.237), comprising a higher

Fig.236 Brushwood layer looking north-east. Scale unit 10mm

Fig.237 Brushwood spread in the south-east corner. Scale unit 0.1m

Fig.238 Beam 13876 in Structure 5/3 looking west towards 13879. Scale unit 0.1m

proportion of fine withies. Together, these deposits had a maximum thickness of 0.10–0.15m. As with the similar deposits from Structure 5/1, there is no clear-cut explanation for the presence of this material except that it may form part of a collapsed roof, post-abandonment.

Towards the north of the excavated building, where this brushwood was lying on the upward slope of the underlying deposit, it was partially overlain by a substantial timber beam 13876 (Figs 238 and 239) which ran parallel to the short axis of the building. This beam had a partially charred upper surface, was roughly semi-circular in cross-section and measured 1.77 x 0.19 x 0.11m. Close to the west end of this beam was a shorter (0.57 x 0.2 x 0.11m) length of beam (13879), lying at a steep angle with one end against the remains of the building's west wall; 13879 has a similar cross-section to 13876 and might have been part of it. Near the west end of 13879 was a rectangular perforation, with a smaller, circular hole adjacent which must have played a part in its original function. Given its position it is possible that the timber is a part of the superstructure, perhaps a roof support, which broke as it fell.

Fig.240   Brushwood overlying beam 13876. Scale unit 0.1m

More brushwood (Fig.240) then covered this beam, assuming a convex profile over the underlying 13875.

Above these timber and brushwood layers the building was infilled by very dark grey-coloured silty clay loams (13716, 13367, 13147) containing an admixture of ash, charcoal and clay flecks, and also timber fragments (13712–28). These layers had a combined depth of approximately 1m, and are interpreted as a single operation of deliberate dumping/backfilling.

Dendrochronology results are based on seven surviving planks and four posts from the east wall, all of which have a combined felling date in the range of AD 958–87, and an argument has been presented for construction in AD 966 or shortly after (see p.746).

Fig.239   Beam 13876 in Structure 5/3 looking east with 13879 in the foreground. Scale unit 0.1m

Structure 5/4

Structure 5/4, situated c.4.1m behind the south gable wall of Structure 5/3, was excavated in 1976–77, early on in the excavation campaign (see Fig.197). Its uppermost surviving traces were revealed within days of the excavation commencing, immediately upon archaeological cleaning of the area after the clearance of the 19th-century cellar which had occupied this spot.

It was found that the north (front) end of the building was virtually contiguous with that of modern cellars: a modern wall foundation ran within 0.2m of its west wall; a 19th-century brick-lined well had punctured a c.1.75m diameter hole through its west wall, while a 20th-century cellar had removed evidence for its south gable end (Fig.241). The surviving maximum length of the building, measured from the outer edge of the sill beam, was 8m, and its width was originally 3.7m but following substantial repairs and replacement of walls (see below) became 3.1m. It survived to a maximum height of 0.75m.

Construction had involved digging out the area of the building, with seating trenches around the edges of the cut to contain foundation beams (Fig.241). These trenches were generally c.0.4m to 0.55m wide and c.0.15m to 0.3m deep. The north wall's foundation consisted of a single beam (8743, Fig.242), 2.95m long, 0.25m wide and 0.05m thick, with a simple rectangular cross-section. It was positioned between the ends of the foundation beams for the side walls. The north section of the western surviving beam for the west wall (8614) had been truncated by a modern well; its surviving dimensions were 4.52m x 0.28m x 0.16m. Along its inner edge it had a raised lip (8754), 80mm wide x 30mm high, fashioned from a separate piece of wood and dowelled into place with wooden pegs typically 25mm in diameter and 70mm long. South of the well a number of timber fragments continued the alignment of this wall, one showing the same lipped feature (8969, 8977) and probably part of the same foundation beam (Fig.242). In contrast, the eastern foundation was clearly identifiable for its full surviving length, even where impinged upon by later pits. It comprised an intact northern section (8046/7) (Figs 241, 242 and 243) measuring 6.2m x 0.35m x 0.05m, and an abutting but truncated

Period 5B

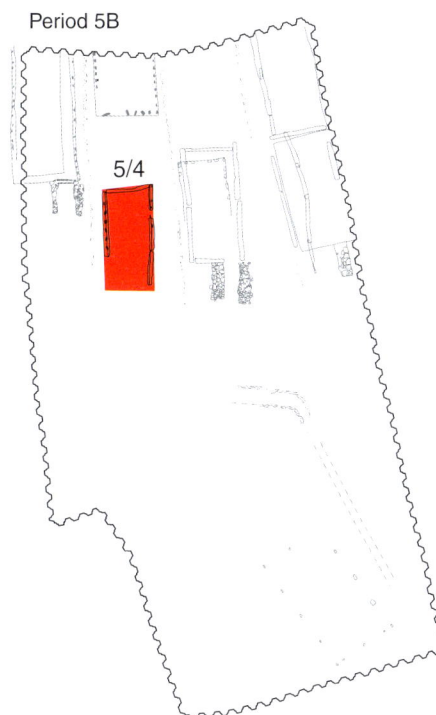

Location of Structure 5/4

Fig.241   *Structure 5/4 in its original layout. Scale unit 0.5m*

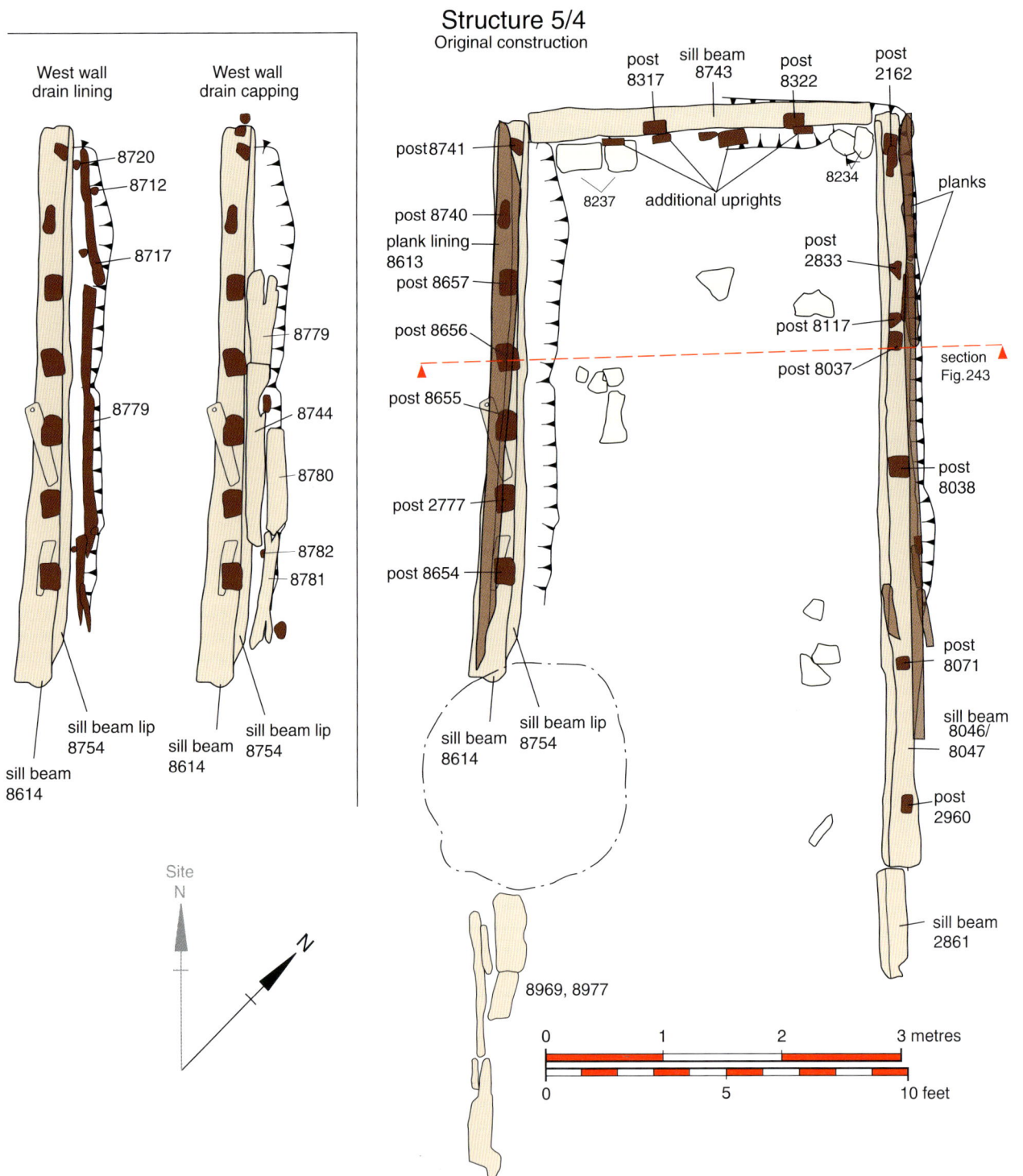

Structure 5/4
Original construction

West wall drain lining

West wall drain capping

8720
8712
8717
8779
8779
8744
8780
8782
8781

sill beam lip 8754
sill beam 8614
sill beam lip 8754
sill beam 8614

post 8741
post 8740
plank lining 8613
post 8657
post 8656
post 8655
post 2777
post 8654

post 8317
sill beam 8743
post 8322
post 2162

additional uprights
8237
8234

planks

post 2833
post 8117
post 8037

section Fig.243

post 8038

post 8071

sill beam 8046/ 8047

post 2960

sill beam 2861

sill beam lip 8754
sill beam 8614

Site N

8969, 8977

0		1		2		3 metres

0		5		10 feet

Fig.242   *Plan of Structure 5/4 showing original and modified south-west wall. Scale 1:50*

southern beam fragment (2861) measuring 0.9m x 0.24m x 0.09m. Both of these beams had been shaped to create a raised lip, standing proud along the inner edge of their upper surface. The lip was typically 60–80mm wide and 20–40mm high.

Dendrochronological evidence indicates that the building was constructed no earlier than 961 (Timber No. 8379, context 8047, sill beam from the eastern wall). A probable original drain capping (Timber No. 8387, context 8744, Fig.242) suggests a more

640

Structure 5/4

E

W

11.00m AOD

2951
2160

post
8037

sill beam
8047

2403

2690
2824

2875
8033
8106

8107

8526

8799

8077

8114

2389

2388

2436
2443

2447

post
8656

plank
8613

8658

sill beam
8614

8572

8666
8730

8730

2445
2451

36676

11.00m AOD

27805

natural

36574

unexcavated

1 metre

0   1   2   3 feet

Fig.243   *Section showing original footing for south-west wall and subsequent modification/replacement. Scale 1:25*

641

precise date, as this timber was felled in the winter or early spring of 972/73; however, this timber may not have related to the original construction of the building. Timber No. 8849 (context 8550), a supplementary drain capping at the south end of the west wall, was felled a little later, 975–1011, and may represent a later repair to the structure (see below).

Several uprights were driven against the internal face of the north sill beam, presumably to prevent it from moving inwards. In the north-west corner of the building were two rubble blocks, one of gritstone and the other of limestone (8237), while in the north-east corner were two limestone rubble blocks, each with a flat upper surface (8234) (Figs 242 and 244). It is suggested that these blocks, unique to this structure, were put in place to support the uprights retaining the north sill beam, and/or possibly to act as stylobates, underpinning additional upright supports which were subsequently removed.

The walls of this structure were formed of horizontally laid oak planks, originally resting edge to edge, and supported by squared oak uprights resting upon the foundation beams (Figs 245 and 246). Along the west beam some of the uprights had thin pieces of wood, such as re-used cask staves wedged between their base and the foundation beam (Fig.247). It is suggested that this was required to ensure an even height at their top ends. It was also recognised that small, relatively thin slabs of limestone rubble, or cobbles, had been used occa-

sionally as filling/packing between the horizontal wall timbers and the side of the cut.

Running parallel to the west wall, inside the building, was what has been interpreted as a drain. This feature was situated approximately 0.10–0.20m east of the west wall's foundation beam and defined by an alignment of short stakes (including 8720, 8712, 8776, 8857–60, 8869, 8870–1, 8782) that supported a series of edge-set, horizontal timbers (8717, 8779/80, 8781) (Figs 242 and 248). These horizontal timbers revetted the eastern edge of a very shallow linear depression, the western side being defined by the foundation beams themselves. Oak plank 8717, measuring 1.07m x 0.14m x 30mm, was distinctive on account of its rebate/s and wooden dowels (Fig.248). One long rebate apparently had a chamfer at one inner corner, corresponding to an instep in the rebate at the other corner and adjacent to one broken end there was a suggestion of another rebate whose purpose is not clear.

A capping to this linear feature was provided by a series of planks (including 8739 and 8744); it is their presence, particularly the lowest ones, and their interpretation as a deliberately placed capping, which promotes the overall interpretation of this entire assemblage of timbers as a drain. For comparable features in other buildings see pp.656, 673. No distinct or characteristic drain fills were recognised, however, and it is possible that the timbers could be considered as revetting for

Fig.244   Rubble blocks in (a) the north-west and (b) north-east corners of Structure 5/4. Scale unit 0.1m

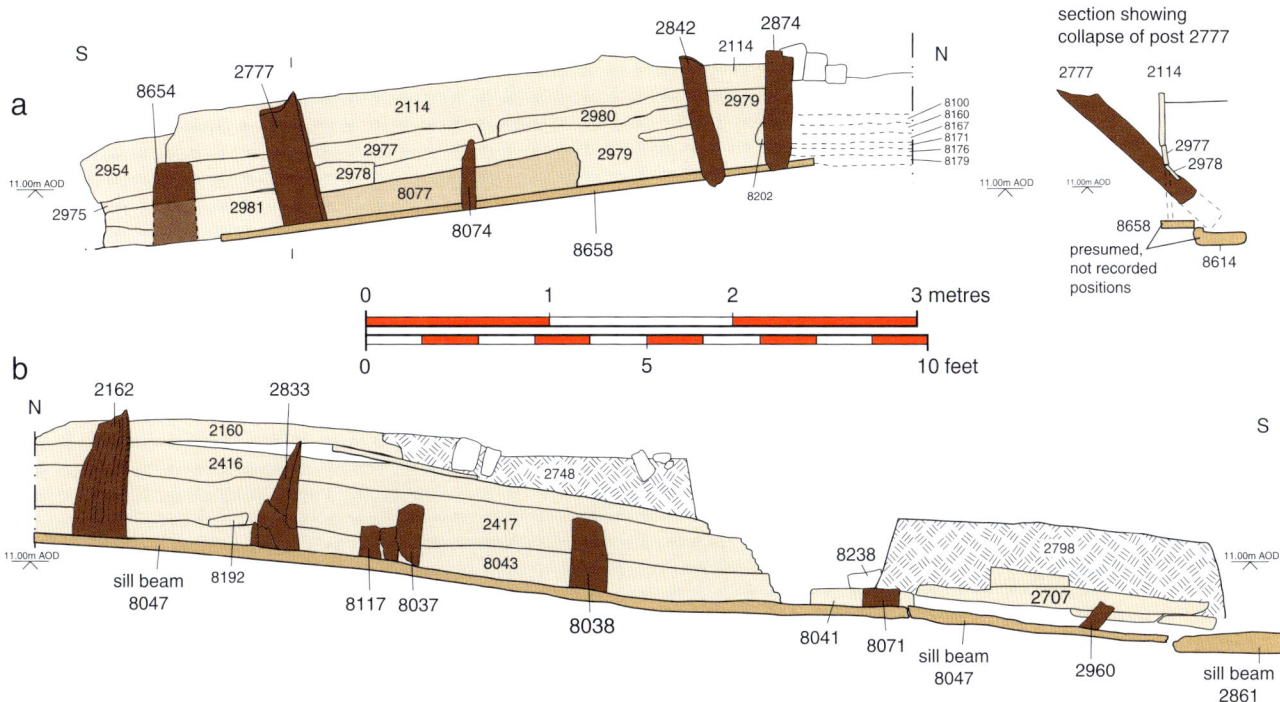

Fig.245 (a) East-facing elevation of west wall of Structure 5/4. (b) West-facing elevation of east wall of Structure 5/4. Scale 1:40

Fig.246 East wall, detail of wall and sill. Scale unit 0.1m

Fig.247 Detail of south-west wall showing use of cask stave and wooden block to level the uprights. Scale unit 10mm

a rather wide slot associated with the insertion of the foundation beam. Another possibility, that the stakes and edge-set timbers represent an earlier 10th-century alignment, pre-dating the phase of semi-basement buildings, is considered less likely, both because the alignment is not in the position of earlier and later fences, and because this is not a structural form associated with the earlier (Period 4B) 10th-century post and wattle buildings. Horizontal timber 8658, measuring 3.26 x 0.2 x 0.05m, overlaid the drain capping timbers and appears to have been a subsequent attempt to reinforce the drain. The line of this timber was continued south of the 19th-century well by timber 8849 (context 8550), which provided the dendrochronological date of 975–1011 referred to above.

643

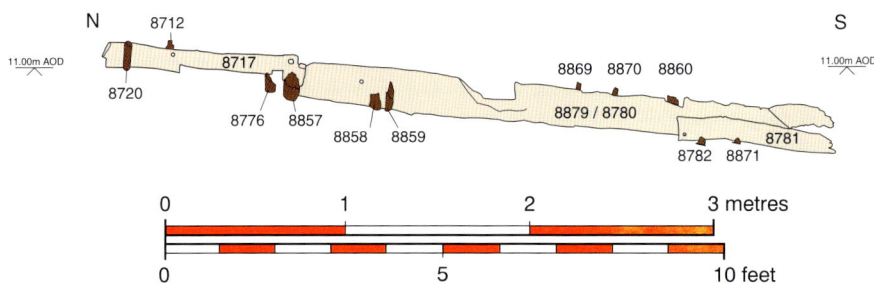

Fig.248 *Elevation of possible drain structure. Scale 1:25*

On the east side of the building, contiguous with or closely adjacent to the inner edge of the foundation beam, decayed traces of what appeared to be a deliberately placed wattle rod were recorded within the deeper cut made to seat the foundation beam (Fig.249). Whatever its purpose – and it seems to have been deliberately laid – there were no stake uprights associated with it, and it cannot have formed either a drain or an effective revetment for the cut.

Remains of the upright timbers, which had originally stood vertically upon the foundation beams, were recorded along all three surviving walls. Often, however, they were in a quite severely degraded and truncated condition; a few were leaning into the building at acute angles (Figs 243, 245, 250 and 251). Along the west wall they had been positioned quite regularly at centre to centre intervals of approximately 0.55m (Fig.242). On the north wall only two uprights were identified (8317 and 8322, Fig.242); their positions were not bilaterally symmetrical, but their spacing with regard to each other and to the ends of the beam was wider than the 0.55m module noted above. The east wall uprights also survived irregularly when compared with those for the west wall; in a couple of instances, however, they could be 'twinned' with ones directly opposite them. The uprights, when not degraded, typically measured c.0.22 x 0.16m and survived to heights of up to 0.7m.

The west wall underwent significant changes during its construction history. The uprights in the west wall had broken c.0.2m above their bases, leaving the wall planks (8077, 2977–81) leaning inwards at up to 45° (Figs 245 and 251). The upper surviving 0.8m of upright 2777 appears to have remained attached to its base and was also left in place (Fig.245). This collapse could well have been provoked by the fact that immediately beneath the

line of the wall are two deep pits (27805 and 36574); the west wall foundations seem to have settled in the pit fills (Fig.243).

Repair of the west wall left a substantial part of the leaning original wall in place, but supported by additional, earth-fast uprights 8073–4, 2842, 2874 north of the well and 2882, 2831 south of the well (Fig.251). New planks, 2114 north of the well and 2883 south of the well, were placed on top of the surviving angled planks and against the new uprights to form a new wall line up to 0.5m east of the original wall line (Figs 251 and 252). The void between the old and the new wall was filled with dumped deposits (2451, 2445, 2447, 2443, 2436; Fig.243).

There were no very obvious floor deposits within Structure 5/4. Layers 8106, 8526 and 8799 (amongst others) are possible floors on the basis of their stratigraphic position, their limited extent and their relative thinness in comparison with the thicker and more widespread deposits above them (Fig.243). None of these yielded particularly informative suites of biological information (*AY* 14/7, 598–601).

The north end of Structure 5/4 had collapsed in antiquity, and a series of plank fragments was found just inside this end, lying across the width of the building (Figs 252 and 253). Notable among these were two (8197, 8201) in which the edge had been rebated for a short length (Fig.254). On both planks the rebates were 180mm long and 40mm deep, but they were not equidistant from the ends of their respective planks. Elsewhere on the site similar but more frequent features were recognised only on floor planks within Structure 5/5; the planks seen here are not interpreted as flooring material, and the function of these rebates remains obscure.

644

Fig.249   *Wattle rod* in situ. *Scale unit 0.1m*

Fig.250   *Acute angle of surviving early phase upright 2777*

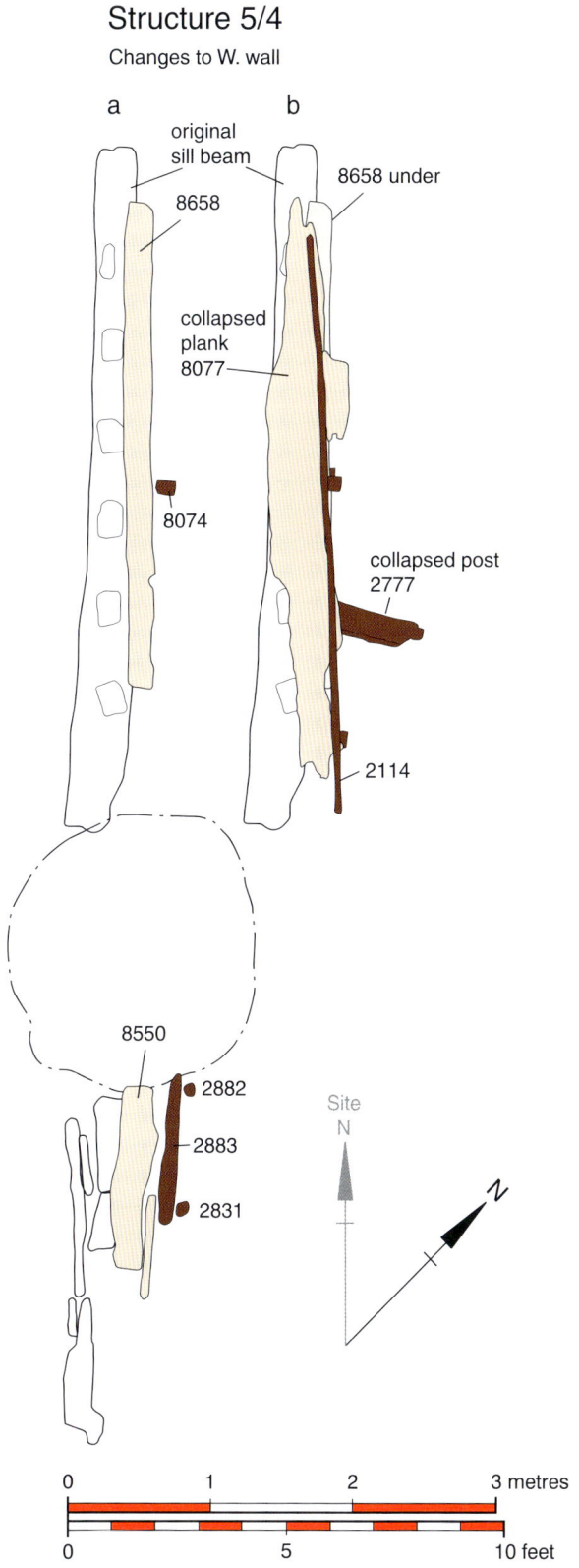

Structure 5/4

Changes to W. wall

a   b

original
sill beam

8658   8658 under

collapsed
plank
8077

8074   collapsed post
2777

2114

8550

2882

2883

2831

Site
N

N

0   1   2   3 metres

0   5   10 feet

Fig.251   *Plan showing collapsed plank 8077 on west wall*
of Structure 5/4. Scale 1:50

Structure 5/4

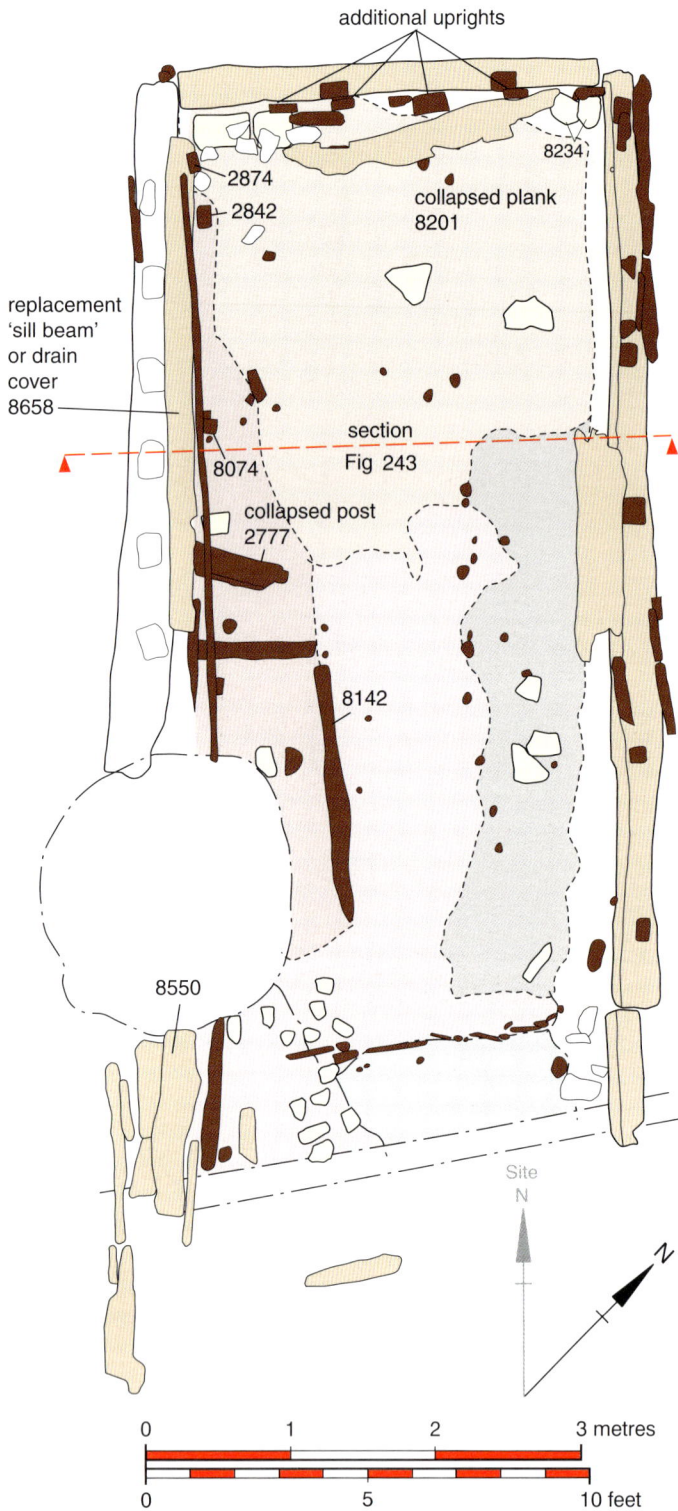

additional uprights

8234

2874

2842

collapsed plank
8201

replacement
'sill beam'
or drain
cover
8658

section
Fig 243

8074

collapsed post
2777

8142

8550

Site
N

N

| 0 | 1 | 2 | 3 metres |

| 0 | 5 | 10 feet |

Fig.252   *Plan of rebuilt Structure 5/4. Scale 1:50*

Above these collapsed timbers were layers of black sandy clay loam 8033; dark brown structured peaty material containing a high degree of wood chips 2875 (Fig.255); very dark grey peaty loam 2824, etc., typically 0.10–0.20m thick, and covering all or most of the building's interior (Fig.243). Occasional lumps of limestone rubble and fragments of wooden plank or beam occurred throughout these layers, which are interpreted as deliberate backfill.

Within this build up of dump deposits was a composite timber object, lying at a pronounced angle of slope (Fig.256). It consisted of two reasonably well-preserved planks (2709, 2710) measuring 1.47 x 0.20 x 0.02m and 1.17 x 0.29 x 0.02m respectively, which abutted along their length. Towards one end were remains of a batten (2711) which lay across their upper surface at right angles, pegged to them with wooden dowels. It measured 0.76 x 0.04 x 0.10m and had three circular dowel holes, c.0.04m in diameter (Fig.257). A fragment of a second dowelled batten (2952), which also contained three dowel holes, lay close by the feature's eastern side; it measured 0.42 x 0.06 x 0.04m. There were adjacent fragments of other planks that might have been part of this feature, but such associations are speculative. Although this object's position respects the building's axes, it is unlikely to be an integral part of its construction – unless the dumped deposits were put into the building quickly while parts of the superstructure still lay around on the surface, awaiting re-use or disposal. Although this is possible, it is equally likely that it originated in some different structure, and its function remains obscure. With no metallic or other fixture – no nails, for example – its totally wooden construction would have decayed to leave perhaps the barest soil-stain in dry soils. It is thus a potent reminder of the degree to which we depend upon anaerobic conditions such as those encountered at Coppergate to allow us a glimpse of contemporary wood-working techniques.

A further build up of deposits, interpreted as dumps within the still visible outline of the building, covered the battened planks before a second series of planks was deposited quite regularly across the building (Fig.258). Severely decayed and friable traces of seven planks were recorded in the northern half of the building on its eastern side; the maximum discernible dimension was c.1.9m x 0.16m. A single more substantial timber beam

Fig.253   Collapsed north wall from the east. Scale unit 0.1m

Fig.254   Collapsed north wall with uppermost timbers removed. Scale unit 0.1m

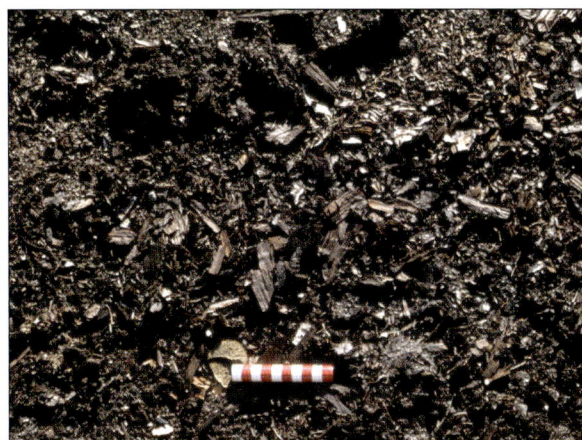

Fig.255   Wood chips. Scale unit 10mm

(2414), lying just within the east wall just south of the planks, appeared to be contemporary with them. It is possible that these timbers are all that remained of a later structure that occupied the area of Structure 5/4 and even made use of the remaining slight depression which signified its former position. This would account for the regularity of these timbers and their respect for the earlier building's axis – they do not have the characteristics of casually discarded debris. These features represent virtually the latest stratification to survive below the 19th-century cellars here.

The destruction of the southern wall of the building means that once again the evidence for an entrance is missing, though in the absence of a break in the extant walls this can only have been at the south end. Conceivably the spread of small limestone fragments which survive some 1.5–2.0m behind the south wall, separated from it by intrusions, might indicate that it too had a stone revetted passageway although this remains unproven.

647

Fig.256 *Battened composite object in dumps. Scale unit 0.1m*

Fig.257 *Detail of composite object. Scale unit 0.1m*

Fig.258 *Planks lying above composite feature. Scale unit 0.1m*

Three late Saxon coins were found in association with Structure 5/4. A fragmentary penny of Eadwig (955–59) (*AY* 18/1, *58*) came from a layer which is the very lowest of the possible floor levels, and could even possibly be the uppermost layer surviving below the construction cut. A *First Small Cross* penny of Aethelred II minted at York in 978–79 (*AY* 18/1, *62*) was found in a layer interpreted as one disturbed during the building's construction; as its date is clearly later than that indicated by dendrochronology for the erection of this structure, it is surmised that the coin was trodden into the exposed underlying layer and thus represents relatively early activity within the structure before deposits accumulated within it. A *First Hand* penny of Aethelred II, struck at York in 979–85 (*AY* 18/1, *64*), was recovered from an unambiguous use deposit.

A plank found in the collapse of Structure 5/4 and possibly part of the structure, together with three timbers in the backfill, have felling dates of AD 993–1029 in the former case and AD 1001 in the latter, raising the possibility that the structure remained in use into the 11th century. This suggests that there may have been modifications to the building in the late 10th or early 11th century, giving a lifespan of some 30 years.

Tenement C

No traces of any sunken structure were recognised at the street frontage on Tenement C. This absence may be accounted for by the intrusion of a modern cellar which impinged upon Structure 5/3 to the west (Tenement B), continued the east wall line of Structure 5/3 with its own east wall, and came within 0.2m of Structure 5/8 on the east (Tenement D). In terms of ground plan, therefore, any structure at the north of Tenement C that had stood directly alongside Structure 5/3 would, depending on the depth to which it was cut, have been obliterated. The modern cellar had removed all deposits down to a depth of approximately 11.5m AOD, whereas the bases of the cuts containing Structures 5/1, 5/2 and 5/3 were at approximately 10.90m, 11.60m and 11.00m respectively, with trenches along the wall lines extending an average of 0.20m deeper. These comparative depths, from two plots slightly higher up the natural ridge occupied by Coppergate, indicate that it is theoretically possible that

the modern cellar cut *could* have removed all traces of comparable building at the north of Tenement C, although the bottom half metre or so of a cut of similar depth might have survived. By the same reasoning, had there been a structure built at ground level in Period 5B, the cellar cut would have removed all traces of it within its limits. Of course, a structure could have been placed further forward on the plot (extending under the present road) but it is possible that this area, for whatever reason, was not occupied by a building.

Structure 5/5

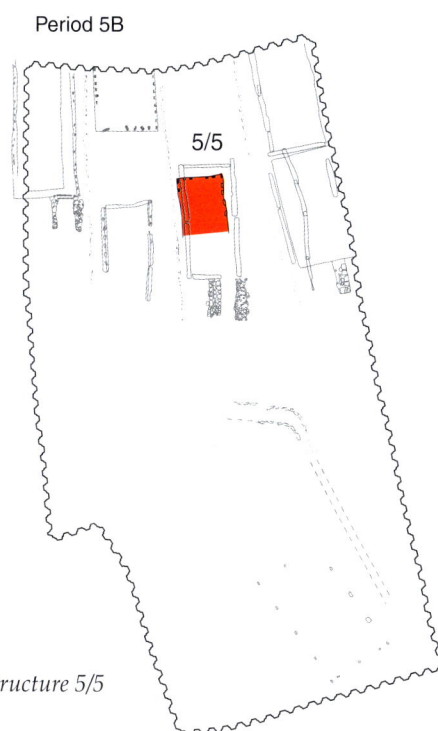

Period 5B

5/5

Location of Structure 5/5

Within Tenement C, but some 7.5m behind the modern street frontage edge of excavation, the fragmentary remains of a plank-built structure (c.3.1m in width; surviving length approximately 3.2m; surviving height 0.5m) were excavated in 1980. This was two years after the excavation and removal of a superimposed plank-built structure (Structure 5/6) and, despite attempts to protect the exposed strata, weathering during this time inevitably resulted in some attrition of the stratification, which complicates interpretation of the detail for the inter-relationship of the two successive structures.

Structure 5/5 appears to have shared several of the characteristics of the broadly contemporary buildings on adjacent plots. Like them, it had been erected within a cut dug into the contemporary ground surface. In this case, however, only a c.0.40m depth of cut was identified, and even this survived only at the building's northern end. A broad sweeping cut had truncated the southerly end of the buildings (see below).

A series of post-holes, spaced at approximately 0.60m centres, was identified along the surviving edges of the construction cut (Figs 259 and 260). Those on the east side were noticeably smaller than those on the north and west sides and rectangular rather than rounded in shape. Some of these post-holes are anomalous with regard to the construction of Structure 5/5 and might relate to an earlier, short-lived or abandoned, building on the same footprint. Within four of the holes along the northern wall and two on the western wall stood the charred bases of squared timber uprights (29562–7). Only one timber (Timber No. 8967; not in timber database: see Table 34) incorporated sapwood, but the available dates from the

surviving timbers give a combined felling date in the range AD 956–79; posts 29562 and 29565 in the north and west walls (Timber Nos 9133 and 9146) probably derive from the same tree.

A single edge-set horizontal plank (29569) (Figs 260 and 261), charred on its inner face, represented the lowest element of the north wall. This plank and its supporting upright posts were canted inwards in places as a result of external pressures, and so too, even more obviously, was the single edge-set plank surviving in part from the lowest course of the west wall (29568, Fig.260). Nothing of the planking in either the east or the south wall survived.

Abutting the base of one of the west wall's upright posts, inside the building, was a horizontal timber (29560) measuring 1.67 x 0.17 x 0.13m, aligned along the structure's long axis. A second similar timber (29561) measuring 1.60 x 0.17 x 0.13m ran parallel, down the centre of the building; it incorporated, on its upper surface, a circular peg-hole, 30mm in diameter x 10mm deep, positioned 1.08m from its north end. The impression or bedding trench for a third timber was equidistant on the other side of the

Fig.259   Structure 5/5 following removal of timbers. Scale unit 0.1m

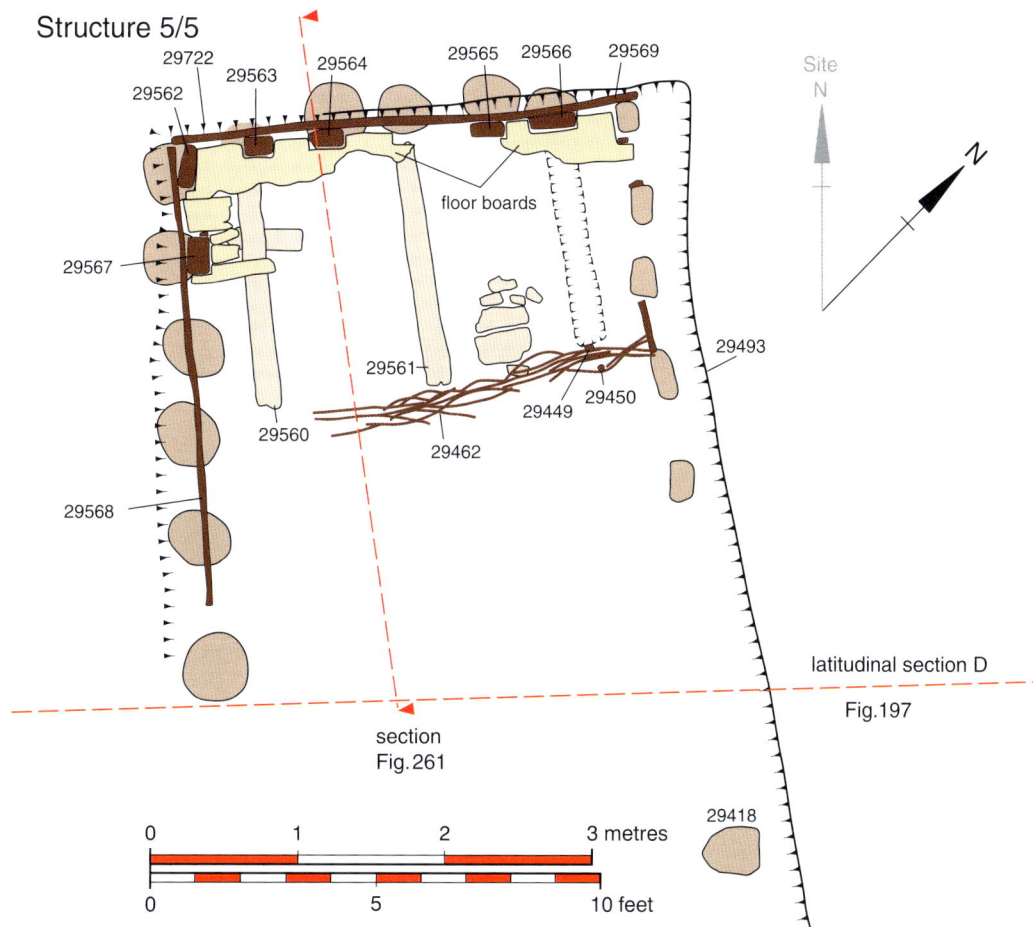

Fig.260 *Plan of Structure 5/5 showing wattlework in burnt material above the structure (Scale 1:50)*

central timber (Figs 260 and 262). All three appeared to have been truncated by subsequent activities that had removed all evidence for the southern part of the structure. These timbers, themselves charred on their upper surfaces, had served as joists, supporting a wooden floor, only charred fragments of which survived at the building's northern end. Floor planks ran west–east across the building from wall to wall; where necessary, their edges had been cut back to accommodate the bases of the upright timbers supporting the horizontal wall planks (Figs 260, 263 and 264).

Covering the remains of the plank floor was a layer of ash and charcoal lumps, some of which were up to 80mm long. Biological investigation revealed that charred plant material, mostly fused masses of bread/club wheat caryopses but also including charred stem fragments of what was probably flax, occurred amongst this (*AY* 14/7, 602). This layer (29465) is interpreted as being part of the debris caused by the building's destruc-

tion by fire, and was up to 0.40m deep against the north wall (Fig.261). It extended back for 2.2m, thinning out in the process, and seemed to have been truncated by a long, raking intrusive cut or cuts (e.g. 29827, 29471, 29493) (Fig.261), in which were further layers distinguished from each other by their varying proportions of charcoal, ash and clay loam. Altogether these conflagration deposits had a maximum total depth of 0.60m. Within them, some 2m behind the north wall line, a 0.20m high length of interwoven wattle comprising up to seven strands (29462) ran across the width of the structure (Figs 260 and 261). Unequivocally sealed within the build up of conflagration deposits, it poses problems of interpretation. Only two stake uprights (29449 and 29450), close together near its eastern end, were recorded in association with it. Even if the wattlework was somehow redeposited here, its presence, unburned, indicates that the fire debris is not a simple *in situ* build up, but has been partly redeposited within the area of the building, as the configuration of cut/tip lines suggests.

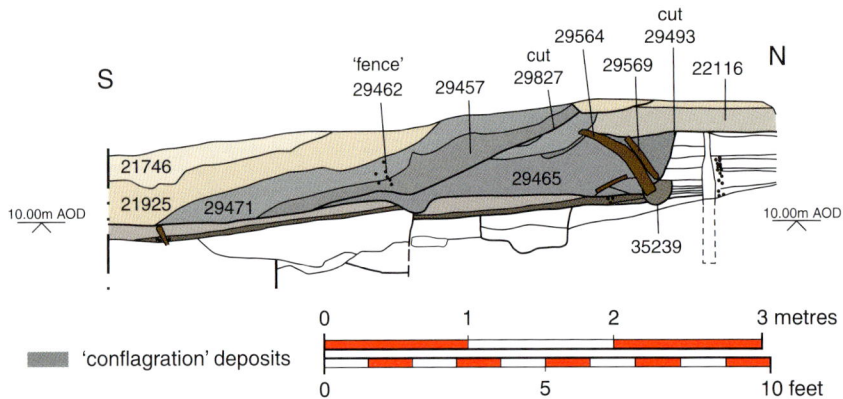

Fig.261   East-facing section through
Structure 5/5. Scale 1:50

Fig.262   Structure 5/5 following removal of overlying Structure 5/6. Scale unit 0.1m

Fig.263   Detail of plank floor in north-west corner of
Structure 5/5. Scale units 0.1m

Fig.264   Detail of plank floor in north-east corner of
Structure 5/5. Scale unit 10mm

Structure 5/6

Period 5B

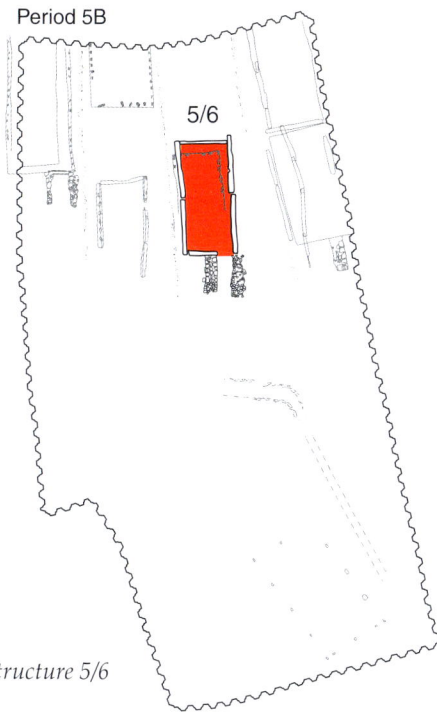

5/6

Location of Structure 5/6

Structure 5/6 was one of the better preserved and most complete of the buildings (7.5m long by 3.7m wide) with walls still standing, if slumped, to a height of almost 1.4m (Figs 265, 266 and 267). The north end of the structure lay c.6.5m behind the north (street) limit of excavation, virtually directly below modern cellar floors, and had been disturbed in places by subsequent intrusions (e.g. at its north-west corner). Its west wall had slumped inwards in antiquity, leaving the previously vertical wall support posts at an angle of 50° (Figs 268 and 269); this created practical difficulties in terms of excavating and recording the stratification oversailed by the leaning wall. However, because these slumped wall timbers had been enveloped by organic-rich deposits dumped within the building, they were preserved to a greater original height than in any other structure. Slumping along part of the lower east wall, towards the building's south-east corner, had formed an obtuse angle between the bottom-most and the penultimate horizontal wall planks (Fig.270). Although much of the surviving timber-work was well preserved, the east wall and an adjacent stretch of the south wall were in a degraded

Fig.265   *Structure 5/6 viewed from the north-west. Scale unit 0.1m*

condition (Fig.271). The north wall, which coincided with the northern limit of the excavation at the time it was investigated, had completely collapsed (Fig.267).

A rectangular cut at least 1.1m deep had been dug to retain the structure; in places along the western side it seemed that this cut had a narrow step part way down it (Fig.267), perhaps to facilitate the construction of the wall. Deeper trenches were dug along each side of the cut's base to contain the foundation beams; the trenches were revetted on their inner sides by pieces of timber, including a re-used cask stave, which were held in position by stakes. In places, for example at the north end of the west beam, limestone rubble slabs were placed in the trenches below the beams, presumably to level them.

The location of a doorway (1.1m wide) was identified at the east end of the south wall line by the absence of a foundation beam, revetting, or any trace of superimposed wall (Fig.267). Its position was also defined by two parallel lengths of limestone rubble walling which demarcated an approach, also 1.1m wide, to the door from the south. In both walls the limestone was bonded with, and lay upon and within, a yellow sandy clay. The western of these two stone walls (5863; Fig.266) was the more obvious, outlined by an edging of larger stones with smaller stones in the middle. It was constructed of two courses, survived to a height of 0.2–0.3m (Fig.272) and ran for approximately 2.20m until interrupted by an intrusion. At this point, however, the feature seemed to indent for 1m across the line of the approach. It then continued on its original axis for a further 2.4m before appearing to terminate in a return (Fig.273). The line of the west side of the narrower approach created by the indent coincided with a series of small posts which may have deliberately continued this alignment downslope for a further 1.6m.

The stonework on the east side of the approach was not so regular, so large, nor so clearly defined. It consisted of small pieces of limestone rubble, without coursing or well-laid edging stones. Nevertheless it formed a distinct feature parallel to 5863 as far as that feature's indentation. Beyond this its line was continued only sporadically by rubble blocks (Fig.266).

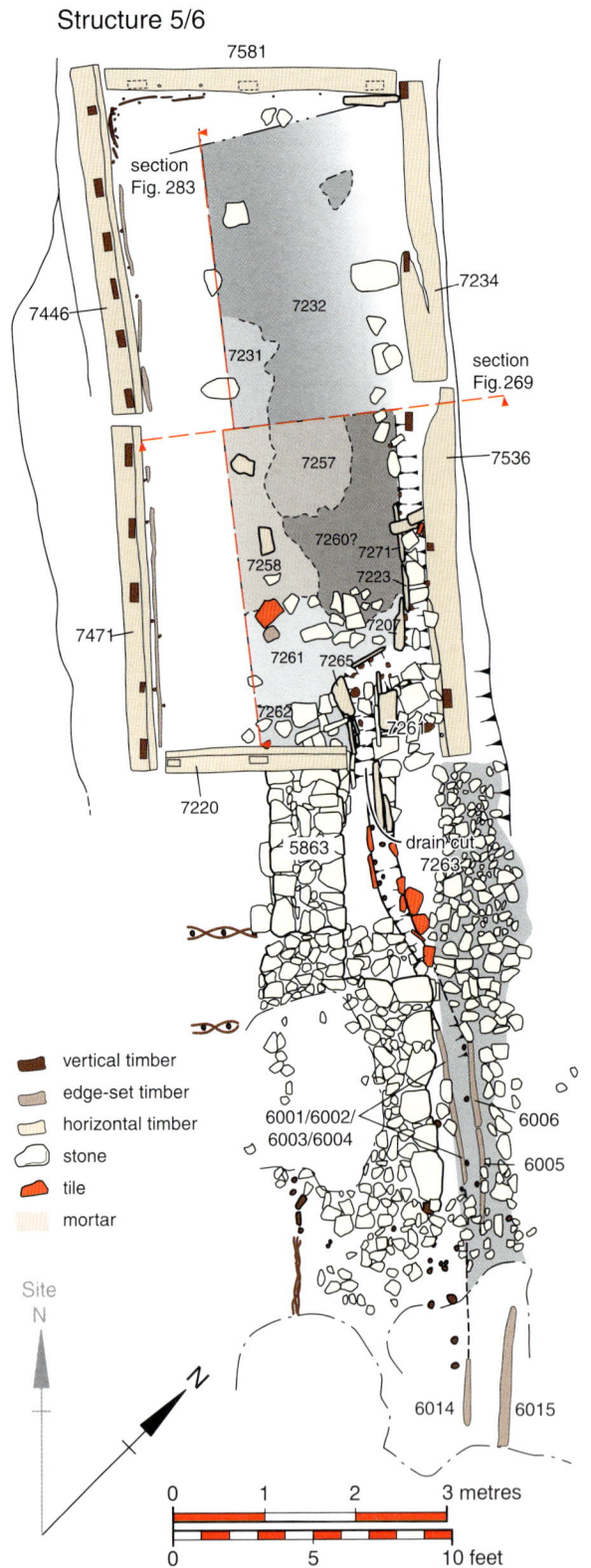

Structure 5/6

Fig.266 *Structure 5/6: sill beams, floor deposits, drain and stone-lined entrance. Scale 1:80*

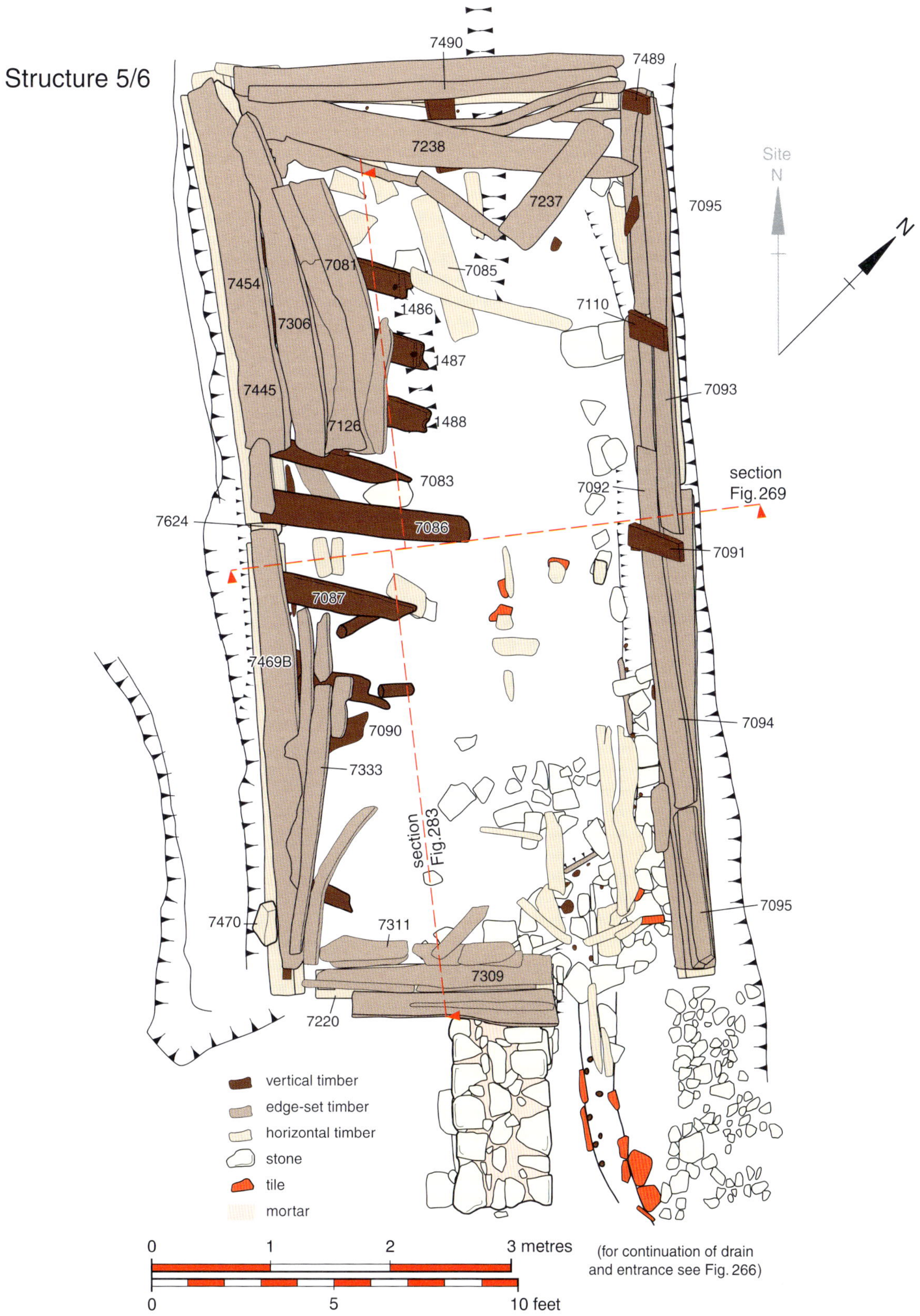

Structure 5/6

7490
7489
7238
7237
7095
7081
7085
7454
1486
7110
7306
1487
7093
7445
1488
7126
7083
section Fig. 269
7624
7086
7092
7091
7087
7469B
7094
7090
7333
7470
7095
7311
section Fig. 283
7309
7220

Site N

N

vertical timber
edge-set timber
horizontal timber
stone
tile
mortar

0	1	2	3 metres

0	5	10 feet

(for continuation of drain and entrance see Fig. 266)

Fig.267 *Structure 5/6 showing collapsed superstructure and stepped cut for west wall. Scale 1:50*

Fig.268   *Slumped west wall of Structure 5/6 showing over-burden of soil. Scale unit 0.1m*

A drainage channel which originated inside the structure (Fig.270) debouched from it down this stone-lined passageway. Within the structure one side of this channel (drain cut 7263; Fig.266) was defined for the most part by the east wall's foundation beam, and on the other side by edge-set planks held in place to either side by rather irregularly positioned stakes and posts. In the northern half of the structure the feature seemed no more than the standard trench revetting associated with the insertion of the foundation beams; it became more recognisable only in the southern half (Fig.274), particularly where it zig-zagged across the south-east corner to flow out of the west side of the doorway and down the west side of the stone-revetted approach (Fig.275).

As the drain ran beyond the structure its edges were defined either by re-used Roman tiles (Fig.276) or by lengths of horizontal edge-set timbers (Fig.277), held in place by stake uprights. Its course curved around the indented west stonework, and it ran beyond the structure's south wall for a total of approximately 7.5m before its line was cut across by a separate, later, wattle-revetted channel. It was covered, presumably deliberately, by an assortment of miscellaneous wood, including barrel fragments (Fig.278). A 'house' fauna insect component was found within the drain fill, but there was little or no primary faecal material (*AY* 14/7, 607).

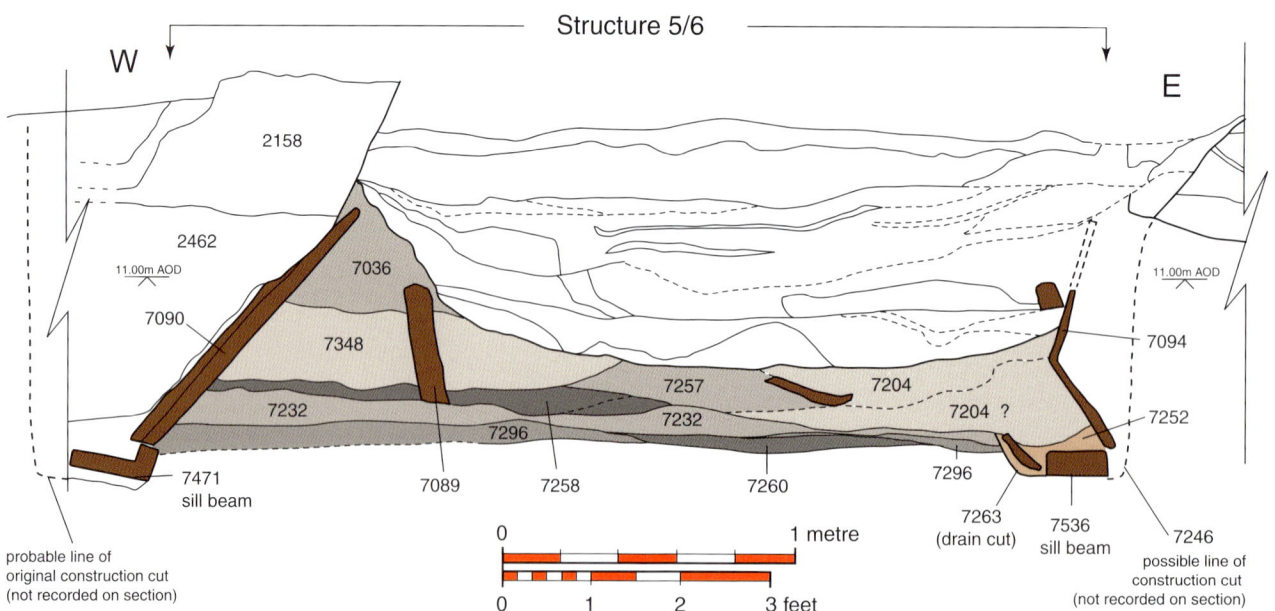

Fig.269   *East–west section through Structure 5/6. Scale 1:25*

Fig.270   *Southern end of east wall showing revetted drain. Scale unit 0.1m*

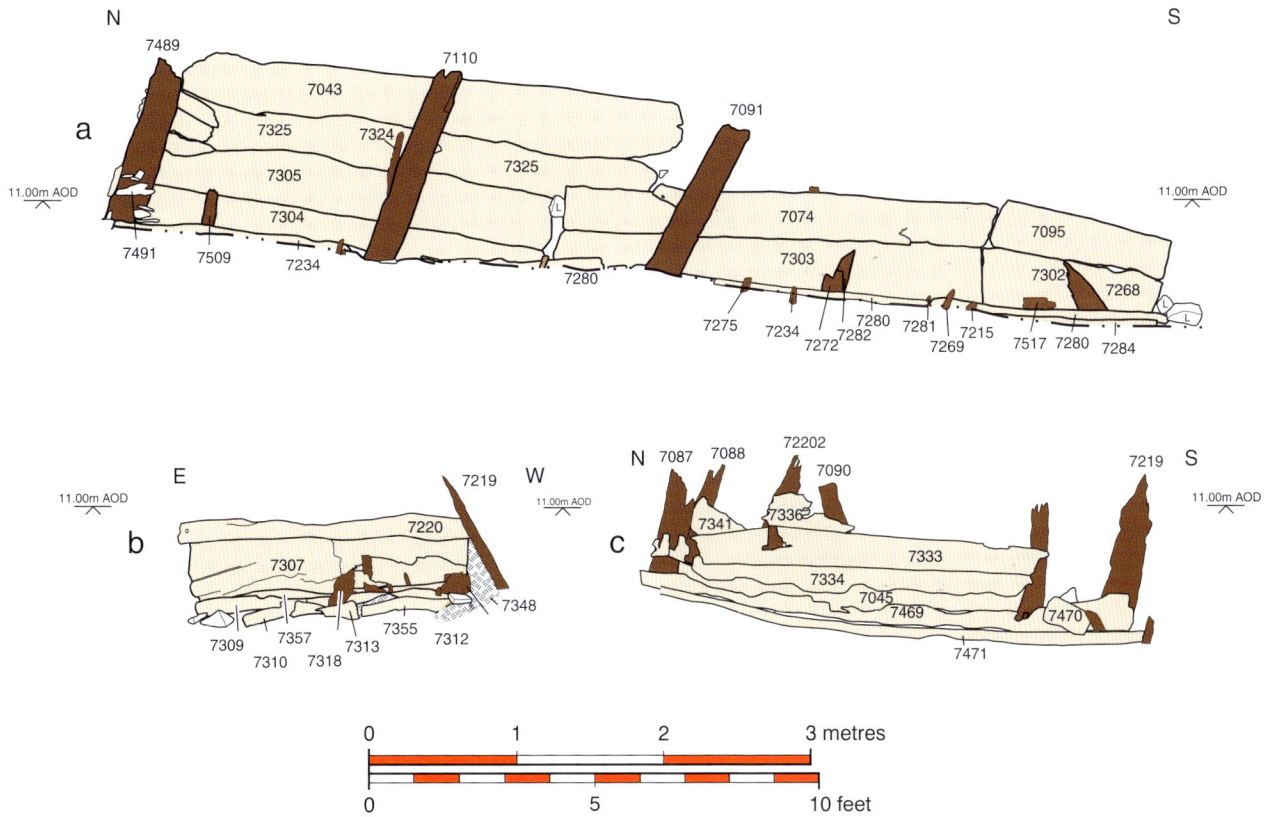

Fig.271   *Elevations of three walls of Structure 5/6: a, west-facing elevation of east wall; b, north-facing section of south wall; c, west-facing elevation of west wall. Scale 1:50*

Fig.272   *Stone entrance to Structure 5/6, looking east. Scale unit 0.1m*

Fig.273   *Stone entrance and spread to the south of Structure 5/6, looking north. Scale unit 0.1m*

The foundation beams of Structure 5/6 broadly corresponded in their positioning to those of Structure 5/5; both the west and east side foundations consisted of two lengths of beam with a narrow (c.0.1m) gap between each pair, and there was a single beam at the north and south ends (Figs 266 and 279).The gap between the two beams in the west wall (7446 and 7471) was underpinned by a length of timber (7624; Figs 266 and 267), 0.88m long and 0.19m wide. The west and east foundation beams were lipped. On the southern of the two east side beams (7536) the lip had been a separate strip of wood, pegged into place; it appeared that the remainder of the lip had sheared off. There was no sign of any lip on the northernmost of the eastern sill beams or on the north wall sill beam. The northern beam in the western wall protruded slightly beyond the northern beam (Figs 266 and 280).

The planks in the west wall (or at least one of them) overlapped the foundation beams for the side walls, as seen in Structure 5/3. The lowest course of the horizontal plank wall cladding rested upon the foundation beams, as in Structure 5/4, and was similar in character to that seen in the other broadly contemporary buildings on the site. Where the supporting uprights had slumped inwards, the

658

Fig.274 *Revetted drain in the south-east corner of Structure 5/6, looking north. Scale unit 0.1m*

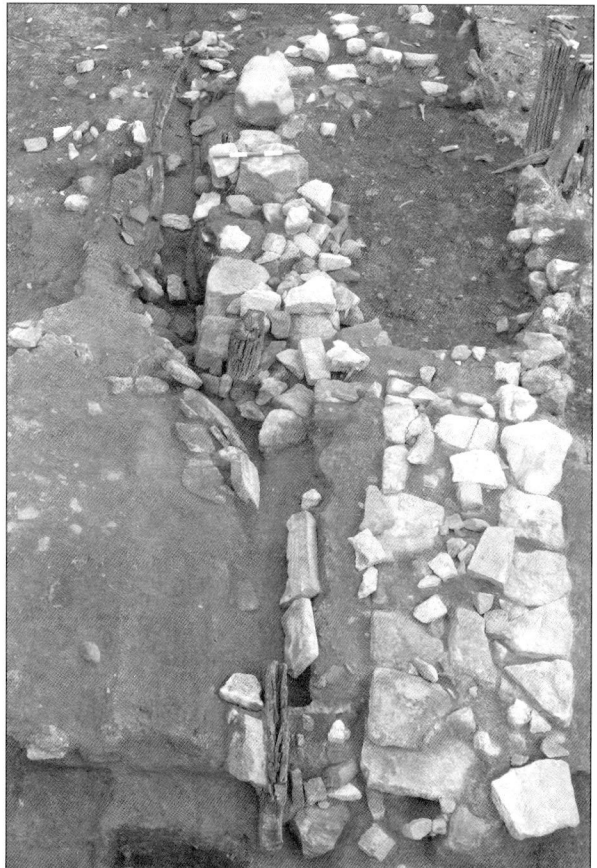

Fig.275 *Continuation of drain downslope south of Structure 5/6, looking south. Scale unit 0.1m*

Fig.276 *Edge-set tiles lining drain running through stone-lined entrance of Structure 5/6, looking north. Scale unit 0.1m*

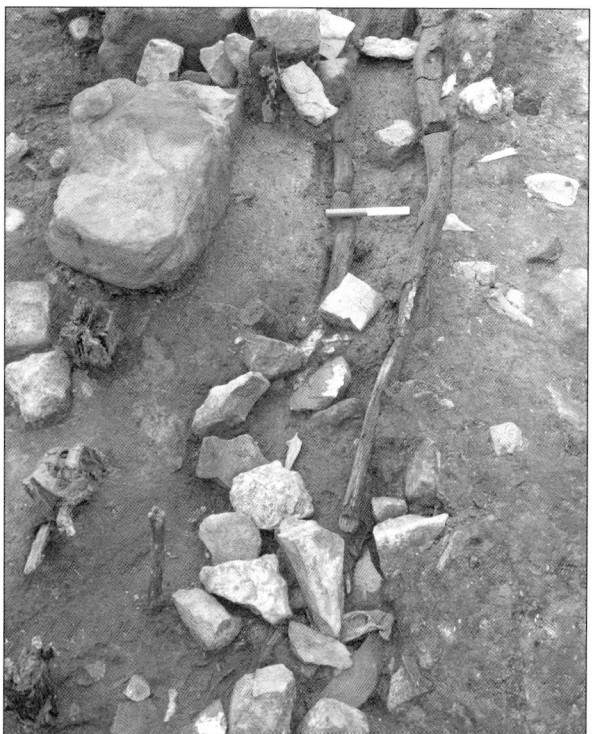

Fig.277 *Wood-lined drain running south of Structure 5/6, looking north. Scale unit 0.1m*

659

Fig.278   *Planks and cask lids covering the drain. Scale unit 0.1m*

horizontal planking appeared in places to overlap the course below, but this is believed to be an accidental product of dilapidation (Fig.281).

Fewer uprights remained in position along the west, east and north sides of this building than in some of the adjacent contemporary structures. Yet slumping had preserved some uprights from the west wall to a greater extent than anywhere else, thereby presenting important evidence for the form of construction and superstructure. On three of the uprights, 1.69m above their bases, and in a central position, a circular hole had been cut through the timber. In two cases where the hole survived intact, it was 40mm in diameter. In these two uprights there were also remains of a joint seating on their outward-facing side, just 30mm above the circular holes (Fig.282). A ledge was formed across the full width of the uprights; the cuts made in creating these ledges were 55mm deep, leaving only a 25mm thickness of wood behind the seatings. Unfortunately, a maximum height of only 45mm of

Fig.279   *Foundation and sill beams in Structure 5/6. Scale unit 0.5m*

Fig.281   *Planks of the west wall viewed from outside Structure 5/6. Scale unit 0.1m*

Fig.280   *Detail of west sill. Scale unit 10mm*

Fig.282   *Details of uprights in west wall. Scale units 10mm*

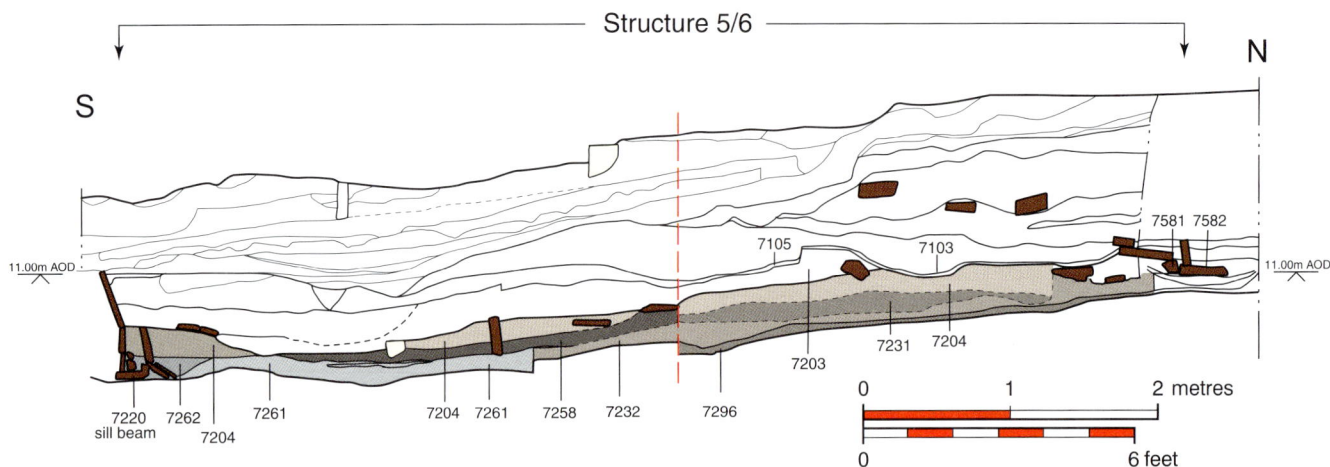

Fig.283   *North–south section through Structure 5/6. Scale 1:50*

this thinner continuation survived, decay having removed an unknown amount of the uprights above this point.

Planks, posts and a sill beam could be dated by dendrochronological analysis, and gave a combined felling date of AD 970–97, suggesting a construction date in the late 10th century (p.747).

A series of layers at the base of the construction cut have been interpreted as floors (e.g. 7260/1) (Fig.283). An important criterion in establishing this interpretation is the stratigraphic position of the drainage channel 7263, for this feature is itself inter-preted as an integral part of the building's use. The drain is recorded as cutting a layer of very mixed dark-coloured sandy loam which had spreads of gravel on its surface, incorporated a range of other material, and included limestone rubble around the door and adjacent portions of the drain (Fig.274). Although the possibility that such a heterogeneous layer may have been an amalgam of many different lenses of deposits was considered, this layer was removed as a single stratigraphic unit, up to 0.15m thick in places. Thus it was not recognised as having the lens-like qualities of some of the more obvious Period 4B floors. Biological analysis identified 'house' fauna and foul matter components within samples from this layer; the processes which led to their incorporation in these deposits are uncertain, however, and they may largely represent imported sediment (*AY* 14/7, 605–6).

Other widespread layers apparently pre-dating the drain and interpreted as successively earlier floor deposits included a very concreted, charcoal-rich layer up to 0.10m thick, described as like a black iron pan (7258, Fig.283), containing human fleas, a 'house' fauna and some charred cereal grain; a clayey surface (7232, Fig.266) that may perhaps represent a deliberately laid floor; and a strongly compacted surface of mortar-like resilience incorporating tile and limestone chips, resembling disaggregated Roman *opus signinum* concrete, and measuring up to 0.10m thick. The only other occur-rence of such a deposit was a patch of flooring in one of the earlier 10th-century (Period 4B) post and wattle structures on Tenement D.

The uppermost identified floor surface (7204, Fig.283) had been disturbed by the bases of two shallow depressions which were recorded as cut into the surface of an overlying layer (7100). At 0.1m or less deep, and without a distinct infill, these may have been surface irregularities or depressions rather than deliberately cut features; they invite notice through their position on the central axis of the structure which might suggest that they are vestiges of inserted central supports for a floor or roof.

Above these floor surfaces was a series of thicker, widespread deposits, typically 0.1–0.3m thick, dark grey-brown in colour and sandy silty clay in texture. Most contained appreciable amounts of charcoal and some were rich in ash; characteristically they had a 'jumbled' lithology and are interpreted as dump deposits infilling the depressions created when the building was dismantled.

Tenement D

Structure 5/7

Set back from the street frontage, and in a position on Tenement D comparable to those of Structures 5/4 on Tenement B and of 5/5 and 5/6 on Tenement C, was a 1.2m deep rectangular cut (29389; see Fig.289) which is the remains of Structure 5/7. On the vacant plot in front of the cut were the remains of a hearth (14348/9, see Figs 292 and 299) whose possible significance is discussed below (p.668). The cut itself was 7.3m long and a maximum width of 5.1m lay within the excavation, though the east wall was beyond the modern shoring; part of it was recovered during the watching brief, however (see Figs 196 and 286).

Two lengths of lipped foundation beam, 2.7 x 0.28 x 0.15m and 4.37 x 0.36 x 0.12m, defined Structure 5/7's west wall line (Figs 284 and 285). The shorter northern stretch of this wall (29518) lay in an almost imperceptible depression, but no such

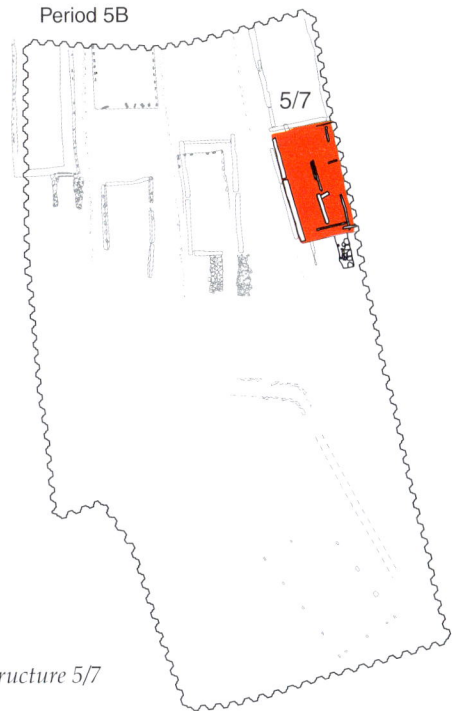

Period 5B

5/7

Location of Structure 5/7

Fig.284 *Structure 5/7 looking north towards the street frontage. Scale unit 0.5m*

Fig.285 *Structure 5/7 looking south towards the river. Scale unit 0.5m*

Structure 5/7

section
Fig.289a

29515   29509
29511
29508
29510
29518
29572
29572
29512
29534
29521
29574
29548
29389
29577
29527
29577
29536
29552
2035
29519
29737
29542
29553
section
Fig.289b
29555
29554
29541
29605
29706
2036
29576
29727
29600
29618
29601
2036

Site
N

N

0   1   2   3 metres

0   5   10 feet

35804

Fig.286   *Plan of Structure 5/7. Scale 1:50*

Fig.287   *Detail of timbers in the south-western corner of the cut. Scale unit 0.1 m*

Fig.288   *Three-sided 'box' arrangement of vertically-set staves. Scale unit 0.1 m*

feature could be discerned containing the southern length of beam (29519) (Fig.286). Transverse timbers underpinned and supported both these beams, regulating a slope from 9.81m AOD at the north to 9.31m AOD at the back – a gradient of approximately 1:16 or 6.25% clearly seen on Figure 134. No trace of corresponding foundation beams was seen on the east side of the structure, and neither were there any at the structure's north or south walls. Lying to the south of the structure, separated by a standing baulk, were the remains of what is believed to be another revetted limestone entrance passage, visible at the lower right on Figures 284 and 286.

Outside the shoring, part of what is believed to be the east wall of the building was recovered during the watching brief. This comprised a short length of sill beam with a raised lip on its west side (2036–8) and an edge-set plank on the east edge (2035) (Fig.286). The planking, but not the sill beam, continued to the south for about 2m beyond the end of the building, perhaps forming a revetment on the east side of the entrance passage which, on the west was revetted by a drystone wall. If correct, this would be a unique arrangement on the site, but details of this eastern side of the building could not be recovered in the context of the watching brief.

Dates for two of the sills and an associated chock in the western wall provide felling dates of after AD 966 and, in the absence of any evidence for re-use, would imply a construction date of shortly after 966, a date that is consistent with the initial building programme on other tenements. That date is repeated by the edge-set timber plank recovered from the putative eastern wall but the lipped eastern sill beam was felled after AD 994 (see p.748). This latter date was initially seen as evidence that this wall must have been part of the back room of the later Structure 5/8 but this cannot be the case as Structure 5/8 is cut from much higher (see Fig.197). That being the case, the length of surviving east wall sill beam must represent a repair, perhaps necessitated by the challenges of building on land sloping in two directions.

Structure 5/7 was exceptional for the number of timbers that lay at its base. Generally they respected the building's main axes, and some had been carefully positioned on top of others (Figs 286 and 287). For example, two edge-set planks were superimposed close to and parallel with the back edge of the cut, the uppermost of which (29600) had a felling date range of AD 957–91. At the north end of the building, at the east side, and truncated by the shoring, there was a single edge-set plank (29509), perhaps in some way an equivalent to that at the south (29618) (Fig.286). Plank 29509 rested upon

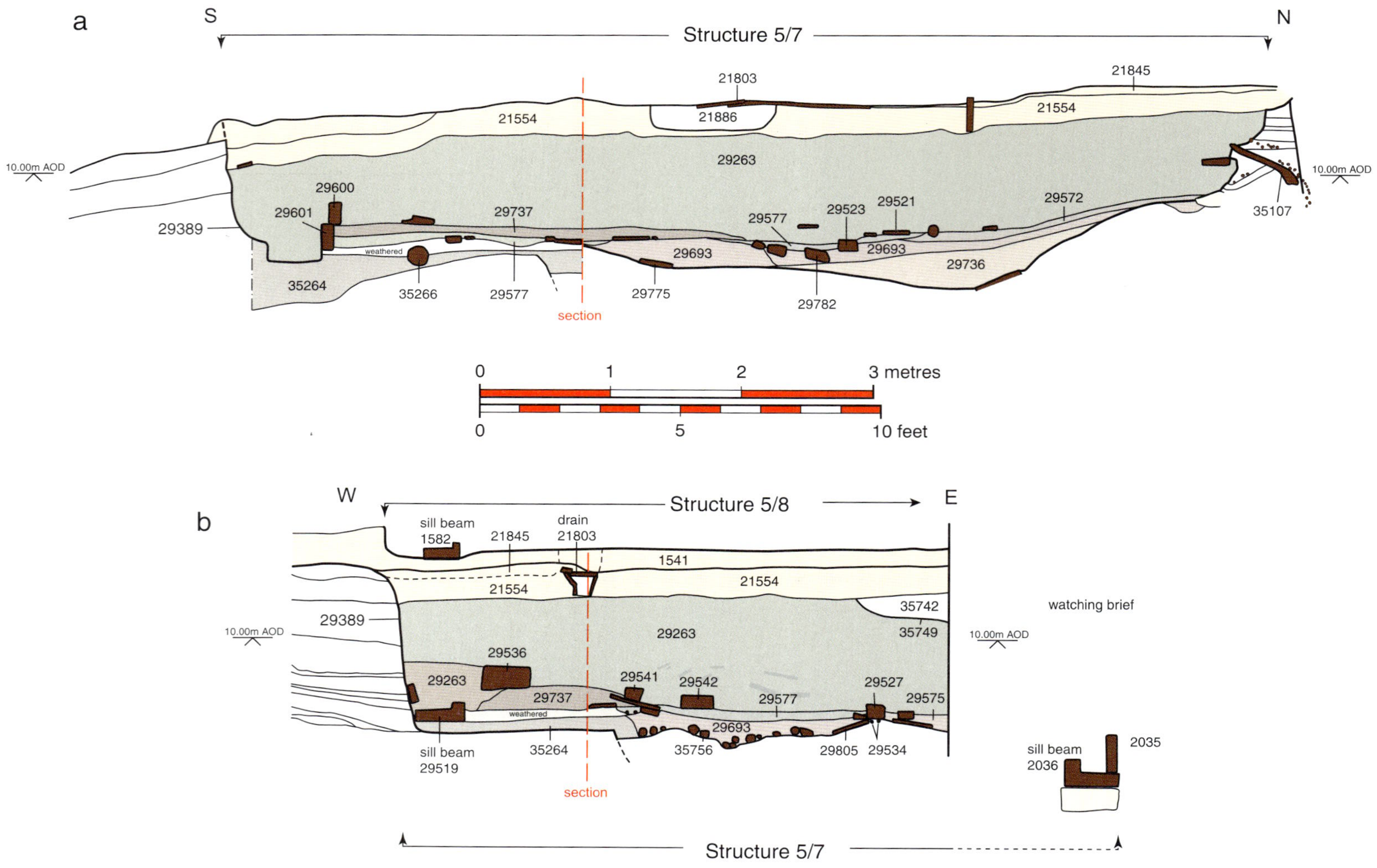

Fig.289   South–north and west–east sections through Structure 5/7. Scale 1:50

a 0.34m long plank fragment (29515, Timber No. 9008) which has a felling date range of AD 954–90 and is from the same tree as a post in Structure 5/3, implying a measure of co-operation in this construction episode, if only in the procurement of resources.

In the south-east corner was a three-sided setting of earth-fast staves (29706) (Figs 286 and 288). The staves were at least 0.70m long, of which the topmost 0.50m protruded above the base of the rectangular cut. Contiguous superimposed edge-set timbers might be interpreted as forming the fourth side of a squarish feature which measured some 0.5 x 0.6m, but as these timbers had a combined depth of only 0.35m, their association with the staves is questionable. Enclosed by these various timbers, but extending down below the lower of the super-imposed edge-set timbers, was a 0.25–0.30m thick deposit of black sandy peaty loam (29576). It lay over a 50mm thick deposit of peaty loam and ash (29724, not on plan), which in turn capped a peaty silt layer (29725, not on plan) incorporating a variety of inclusions and containing a silver penny of King Aethelstan, BMC type v, struck for him at York by the moneyer Regnald, and datable to AD 927–39 (*AY* 18/1, *51*). This layer and its coin pre-date the stave-built feature, and presumably relate to adjacent deposits that were not investigated because of time and resource restraints. Stave 29605 (Timber No. 9020) gave a dendrochronological date of after AD 952, consonant with many of the other timbers lying in this structure. Their date does not, however, rule out the possibility that the stave-built feature was fabricated as part of an earlier building but the fact that it was apparently undamaged by the digging of the rectangular cut mitigates against this interpreta-tion, as does the dendrochronological felling date range of AD 957–91 from the upper of the contig-uous edge-set timbers (29600) apparently forming the south side of the feature.

From approximately 0.3m east of the stave-built feature, a line of four contiguous staves (29727) ran up the building's long axis (Fig.286). They were sandwiched between two horizontal timbers (29553 and 29554; Fig.286), above which they protruded for just a few centimetres. Slightly to their north was another stave. Generically, they may all be grouped with the stave-built feature but, like it, their purpose is unclear.

The only other vertically set timbers were two more substantial posts (29508 and 29511), one at the north-west corner of the rectangular cut and the other close to the shoring (Fig.286). Post 29508 (Timber No. 9003) gave a dendrochronological date of AD 955 which is, once again, consonant with dates from many of the timbers within the building.

Among the timbers lying within the building were some which were very similar in size and shape to identifiable structural members. For example, the large beam 29536 (4.41 x 0.32 x 0.14m) was compa-rable in overall dimensions to the adjacent lipped foundation beam, 29519 (4.37 x 0.36 x 0.12m), and could have served as the basis for making another one (Fig.286). The purpose of a row of three holes in its upper surface is unclear. Nearby, a smaller beam (29541) also had a series of variably spaced holes in its upper surface (p.786), but all the other horizontal timbers were devoid of any supplemen-tary features. None of these horizontal timbers was bedded into the base of the rectangular cut, and there is no indication that they were *in situ* struc-tural remains of the building.

An irregular arrangement of limestone rubble slabs and one fragment of Roman tile which lay above the lips of both foundation beams on the west side of the cut was separated from the beams (and masked on Fig.286) by a thin skim of amorphous peaty loam. Otherwise, the cut had been backfilled with a deposit of dark grey silty clay loam incorpo-rating 15% ash and charcoal (29263), up to 0.8–0.9m thick (Fig.289). A result of its relatively rapid exca-vation was that a series of friable, light-coloured inclusions with a characteristically thin rectan-gular cross-section were seen only in a standing section. Although it has been suggested (*AY* 14/7, 608–9) that these were deposits of ash, their shape may suggest otherwise; it is possible that these are decayed turves (Fig.290). The final dump in the sequence was 21554 (Fig.289) into which a well-constructed drain (21803) associated with the rear room of Structure 5/8 was dug (see Fig.289 and below).

No unequivocal floor deposits were identified within this structure and only one possible floor layer (29577; Fig.289) was sampled for palaeobio-logical analysis (*AY* 14/7, 608). Although it contained elements of what has been suggested to be a 'house

Fig.290   *Possible decayed turves in dumps backfilling Structure 5/7. Scale unit 0.1 m*

fauna', it may represent an early component of the dumps which infilled the building's rectangular cut, and thus may be redeposited.

A stratigraphically equivalent layer (29737; Fig.289) that underlay many of the large timbers contained a very high proportion (<60%) of wood chips. It is possible that the layer accumulated partly as a result of these timbers being worked upon and that they represent abandoned building materials – their suitability for conversion into foundation beams and other structural components, such as rafters, has already been noted. If this was indeed the case, and Structure 5/7 was never completed, there is no obvious explanation for this change of plan. It may reflect directly a change of requirement for the two-room Structure 5/8 (see below), which was in part built above the infilled cut, presumably to make the two rooms structurally compatible.

Whatever the reason for the structure's abandonment, the quantity of worked timbers discarded within it seems remarkable. What appears to represent a profligate waste may be an eloquent testimony to the ready availability of this resource, though this is in contrast to the salvaging of timbers identified in other abandoned buildings (see pp.772–4). It is at least possible, however, that some timbers were salvaged from this structure and re-used in Struc-

ture 5/8. Eight of these timbers in the backfill were dated and have felling dates in the late 10th or early 11th century, with the earliest possible felling date being AD 991, 25 years after the date of the initial sill beams.

Structure 5/7 was replaced by a two-roomed sunken-featured building, Structure 5/8, whose front room occupied the previously vacant street frontage plot. A possible hearth base (14348/9) comprising limestone blocks and a burned area lay approximately 2m back from the front shoring and is stratigraphically immediately below the cut for this Structure 5/8 front room; it is positioned in what would have been more or less a central position (see Fig.299). Initially it was thought that this hearth and two linear cuts 14592 and 14723 belonged to Structure 5/8 but further analysis suggests that they are more likely to be contemporary with Structure 5/7. This raises the intriguing possibility that these features are all that remains of a structure erected on the contemporary ground surface. Whether this putative structure was entirely independent of Structure 5/7, or whether Structure 5/7 provided a cellared element to a two-roomed composite building comprising a surface-built room and rear cellared room can only be the subject of speculation as no other supporting evidence survives. The hearth might equally have been an external feature.

668

Structure 5/8

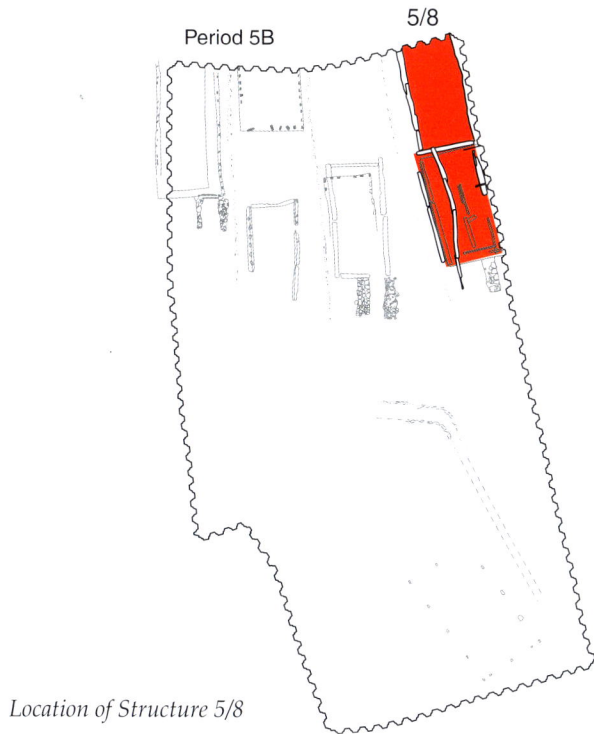

Period 5B

5/8

Location of Structure 5/8

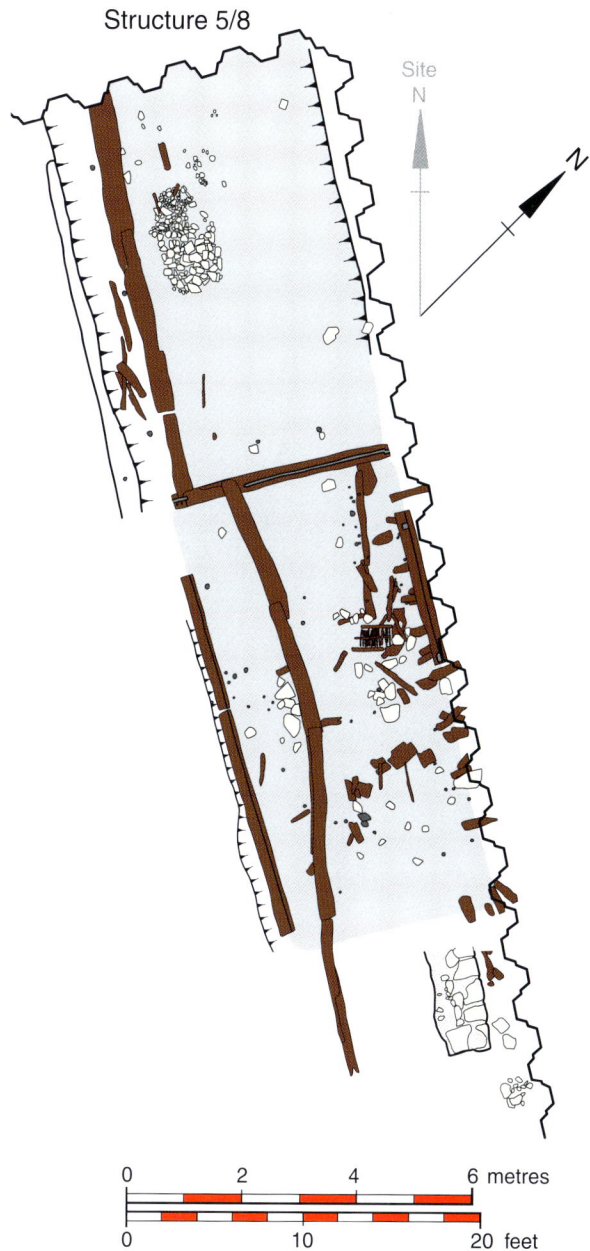

Structure 5/8

Site
N

| 0 | | 2 | | 4 | | 6 metres |
| 0 | | | 10 | | | 20 feet |

Fig.291 *Structure 5/8: overall plan of both rooms. Scale 1:125*

Structure 5/7, in whatever form it took, was subsequently replaced on Tenement D by the two-room Structure 5/8, its more southerly (rear) room overlying the remains of Structure 5/7 (Fig.291). Parts of this room were exposed to view almost immediately after the removal of modern cellar floors in 1976, while the area of the north room was not available for investigation until 1978.

No structural timbers remained in situ in the north (front) room, which was identified by a cut, 14330 (Fig.292), 0.5–0.6m deep, which continued the line of the west wall of the south (back) room as far as the modern street frontage, and also defines the structure's eastern side (Fig.293). In the absence of foundation beams for the side walls, the room's width could not be defined precisely, but at its maximum it was c.4.7m and at its minimum c.4.1m. The beam demarcating its southern end (1600, Fig.292), not excavated until 1978, was 3.92m long and would probably have abutted or rested adjacent to the foundations for the side walls. Just under 7m of this room's length lay within the excavated area.

Several layers identified as possible floor deposits were exposed immediately after the removal of the cut's backfill (14184/14200), including 14293–7, 14299–301, 14574–80 and 14816 (Figs 292 and 294).

One of these (14297) was studied for its biological remains (*AY* 14/7, 609–10) and contained typical house fauna and human fleas. The area had subsequently been infilled with mixed loamy soils (14184/14200; Fig.294), within which were several lengths of squared timbers. These were up to 1.2m

669

Structure 5/8
Front room

section
Fig.294

Site
N

drain
21803

14294
14296
14262

14295

14330

14334

14313

14301

14297

14644

14349

14299

14337

14300

14565

1600

21793

post structure
1620

drain
21804

9587

1599

1587

21801

drain
21805

0   1   2   3 metres

0   5   10 feet

Fig.292   *Plan of the front room of Structure 5/8.*
            Scale 1:50

670

Fig.293   *Cut 14330 for the front room of Structure 5/8, looking north. Scale unit 0.1 m*

long and ranged in cross-section from 80 x 80mm to 90 x 270mm; they may have originated in the demolition of this structure.

The ground level sloped from 11.32m AOD against the modern street frontage to 10.51m at the opposite end of the structure in the back room, a differential of 0.8m over a distance of just over 14m (a gradient of 1 in 17.5; approximately 6%). The structure's south (rear) room lay over Structure 5/7 and had been severely truncated by modern cellars, but was defined by two abutting lengths of lipped foundation beam on the west (1582 and 1587), by a single surviving beam (1599) and other associated timbers to the east, and by a foundation beam (1600) to the north which had separated this room from that at the street frontage (Figs 295 and 296). There was no certain trace of the south wall and there were no layers within this room which could confidently be identified as representing floors. The room measured at least 7.5m x c.4.0m, and the whole structure was thus at least 14m long. Dates provided by the foundation beams suggest that the building was constructed at the very end of the 10th century (i.e. AD 995/96). A chock associated with

the east wall, however, is from a tree felled in the winter of 1008/09 and may represent a modification to the structure some 12–14 years later. All other timber dates were compatible with either of these felling dates.

The north beam in the west wall of the rear room (1587), a boxed oak heart, measured 2.23m x 0.21m x 0.08m, with an inner lip 50mm wide standing 70mm proud of the surface. The corresponding beam surviving on the building's eastern side (1599) lay partly below the edge of excavation (Fig.296). It measured 2.56m in length and did not have an inner lip. It was perforated by a medially positioned 100mm square hole some 0.20m from its northern end, and by a medially positioned, 0.16m long, oval hole at its southern extremity (Fig.297). This beam was supported by a varied series of wooden chocks or wedges that raised its south and north ends to levels respectively 100mm below and 30mm above those of the opposite beam. Although no adjacent beam was found to the south of 1599, the occurrence there of what appear, on the basis of their position, to be more of these wedges, is taken as proof of its former existence and original position.

671

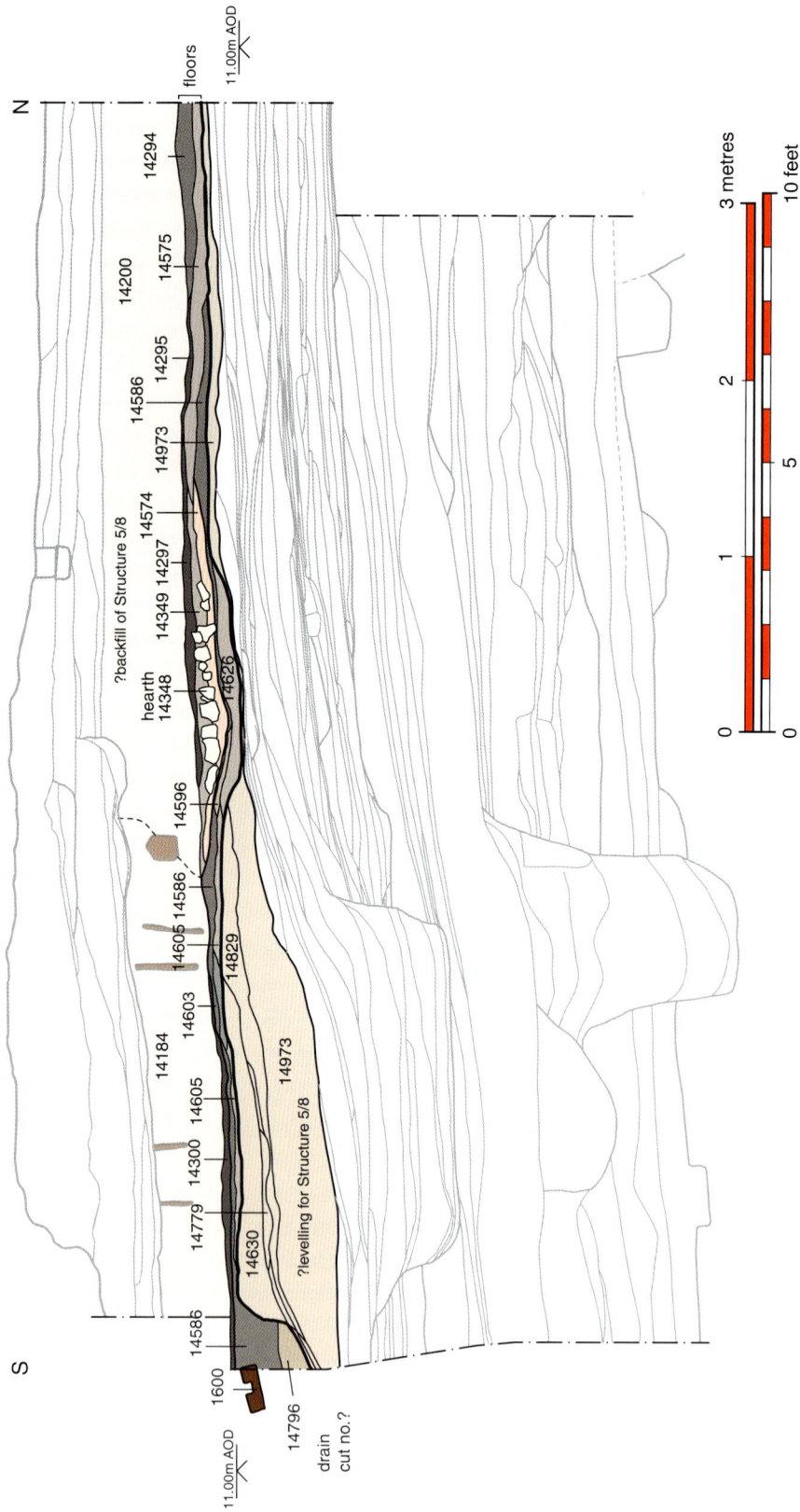

Fig.294   *North–south section through the front room of Structure 5/8. Scale 1:25*

Fig.295 *Foundation beams in the back room of Structure 5/8. Scale unit 0.5m*

This putative beam was matched on the west side of the building by one which measured 4.02m x 0.26m x 0.06m, with a 50mm wide inner lip standing 40mm proud (1582, Fig.296). At a point 0.63m from its southern end the lip was pierced to its base by a cut which widened from 0.12m at the inner side of the lip to 0.15m at its outer side.

A transverse beam (1600) defined the room's northern end. This beam's western end lay on a line continuing the inner edge of the west wall's foundation beam; in contrast, its eastern end lay on a line close to the outer edge of the eastern wall's foundation beam. The foundation beams on both sides of the room did not run right up to the transverse beam but left gaps, the one on the west side of the room being 1.12m, the one on the east being 0.91m wide, and the obvious interpretation of these gaps is that they represent opposed entrances (Figs 296 and 298). These would be the only side entrances noted in any of the Anglo-Scandinavian buildings on the site. Millstone grit blocks (Fig.295) immediately outside the western entrance might have

functioned as a pathway or even been part of steps which mitigated the slope which would have been evident at this point.

Although of similar dimensions to corresponding beams in adjacent buildings the transverse foundation beam 1600 (measuring 3.92m x 0.22m x 0.12m) differed from them in the form of superstructure implied by its upper surface. A squared, central channel, 40mm wide x 40mm deep, extended for 2.62m from its eastern end (Fig.296). There was then a 1.06m wide gap in which the upper surface was unmarked before the channel was continued for the 0.24m to the beam's western end. At that end, on the south side of the medial channel, a rebate 0.21m long had been cut, and this in turn was perforated by two circular holes, each of 20mm diameter. The 40mm wide slots in the transverse beam probably held either planks this thickness or tenons at the base of somewhat wider posts. The slots are not wide enough to hold horizontal baseplates supporting wattlework. The 1.06m wide interruption of this slot presumably denotes the position of a communicating doorway between the two rooms of this structure, and it is possible that the terminal rebate held a door jamb which was pegged into position at its base.

A plank-lined and plank-capped drain (21803, 21804, 21805, 21806) (Figs 292 and 296) was traced for the full length of Structure 5/8, and for a distance beyond it sloping downhill, but was truncated by an intrusion. It ran beneath the floor, and the capping planks were soon covered by soil deposits. Biological analysis suggested that the drain, like that in Structure 5/6, did not receive foul waste (*AY* 14/7, 610). Within the front room its course was virtually straight, but at the point where it ran below the putative doorway in the dividing wall between the two rooms (Figs 292 and 299), (where it was capped by beam 1600 itself), it dog-legged through two right-angled turns and then adopted a gently arcing course for the remainder of its length (Fig.300).

This drain itself was 0.2–0.3m deep and its capping was up to 0.4m wide. As it survived, the drain's cross-section had the shape of either an inverted triangle or a truncated inverted triangle (see Fig.289b); there was no trace of any planked base. The sides were braced apart at irregular intervals, either by circular-sectioned rods that were

Structure 5/8
Rear room

Site
N

14565

1600

21793

drain
21804

9587

post structure
1620

1599

9590

9591

9592
9593

1587

9605

21801

9606
9607

21794

21805

1582

9639

drain
21806

9359

9356

0   1   2   3 metres

0   5   10 feet

Fig.296   *Plan of the rear room of*
Structure 5/8. Scale 1:50

Fig.297   *Sill beam 1599 along the east side of the rear room of Structure 5/8. Scale unit 0.1m*

dowelled into the side planks, or by wedges of truncated triangle shape. The planks lining the sides and forming the capping varied in length from 2.5m to 4.0m (Fig.300).

Dendrochronology indicates that the drain timbers have a combined felling date range of AD 988–1017 (see p.748) and include several parts of the same tree.

Within the rear room there were two fragments of wattle hurdling and various pieces of timber which could be remains of planks and beams following the demolition of the building (Fig.296). The hurdling (21801 and 9639) could have served a variety of functions including internal partitions, flooring or working surfaces. Along the eastern edge of the rear building there was a cluster of posts, some of which

are aligned parallel to the wall, which might have provided a sleeping platform similar to that seen in the earlier Period 4B wattle buildings (see pp.579, 585, 595–6).

The depth to which the building was cut below the surviving ground surface will have influenced the construction methods, and modern truncation has removed the necessary evidence around

Fig.298   *Structure 5/8 showing northerly side entrance, looking east. Scale unit 0.1m*

Fig.299   *The drain and hearth 14349 in front room of Structure 5/8. Scale unit 0.1m*

675

the south room. The north room's base, however, was only some 0.5–0.6m below its surroundings, although it is conceivable that later Period 6 buildings which directly capped that room were themselves both sunk into the ground.

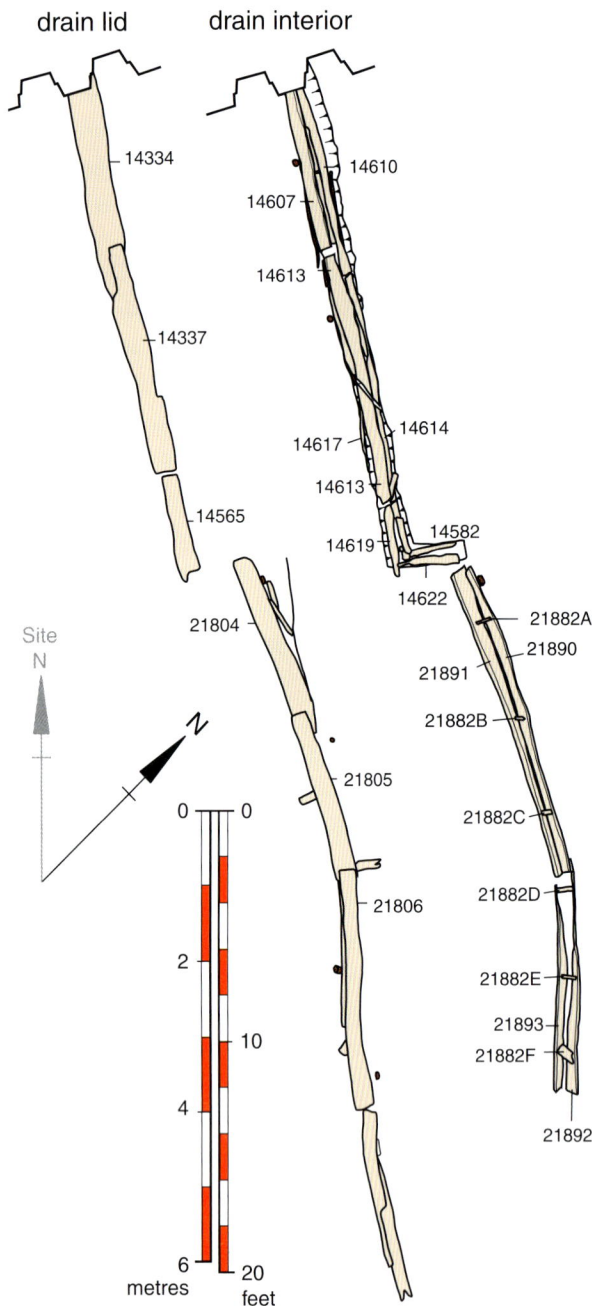

drain lid   drain interior

14334
14610
14607
14613
14337
14614
14617
14613
14565
14582
14619
14622
Site N
21804
21882A
21890
21891
21882B
21805
21882C
0   0
21882D
21806
2
21882E
21893
10
21882F
4
21892
6   20
metres   feet

Fig.300 *Route of drain 21803–6 in Structure 5/8. Scale 1:100*

Structure 5/9

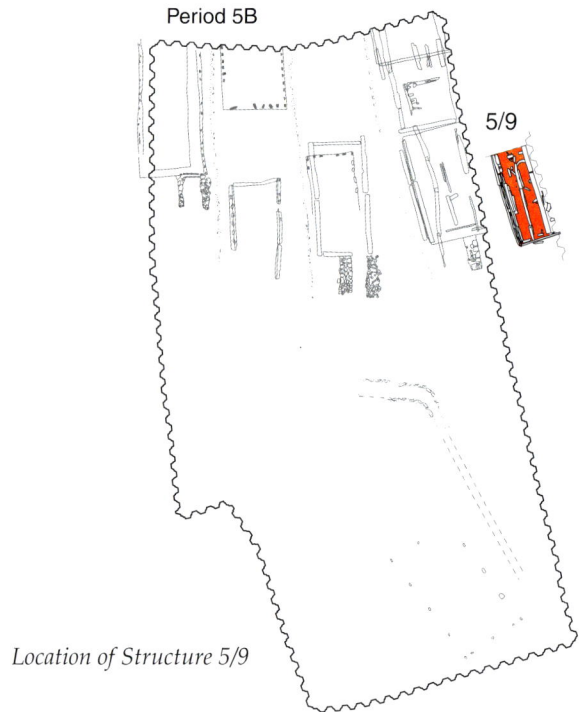

Period 5B

5/9

Location of Structure 5/9

Another sunken structure was found during the watching brief set back from the street in Tenement E. It probably measured 6.2m long and was at least 2.65m wide, and survives to a height of 0.7m. A foundation beam in two sections (2110/2111 and 2109/2152, Fig.301) defined the west side of the structure, and there was a plank wall at the south end (2119, Fig.301). The north end of the structure was not recorded, but the presence of Period 4B–5A features immediately to the north point to its termination some 10m south of the Coppergate frontage. This point was at the boundary of two separate watching brief events, which could mean that the north wall was present but was overlooked. The east side of the structure lay beyond the limit of the watching brief. The rectangular cut dug to accommodate the sunken structure was not identified, but the base was probably at 8.7m AOD at the northern end and sloped down slightly to 8.6m AOD at the southern end. The level of the adjacent Period 5A features indicates that the cut was about 0.8m deep; presumably the upcast from the cut was used to raise the surrounding ground level to at least 10m AOD, the height of the Period 5C ground surface in the vicinity of the building.

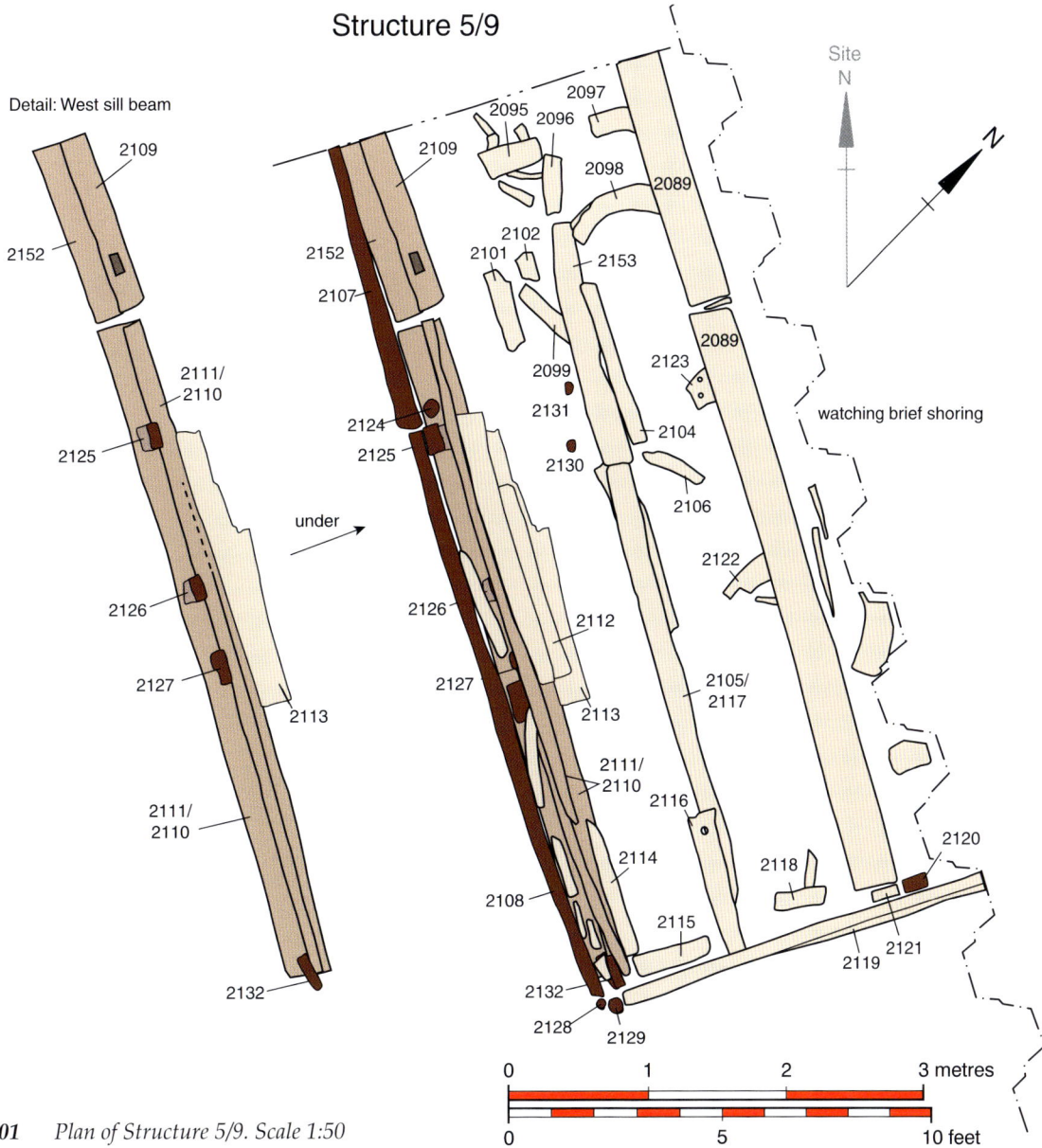

Structure 5/9

Detail: West sill beam

under →

Site N

watching brief shoring

Fig.301 *Plan of Structure 5/9. Scale 1:50*

0 1 2 3 metres

0 5 10 feet

The west foundation beam was formed by two timbers with an overlapped joint, the complete southern element measuring 4.84 x 0.34 x 0.22m; both elements had an attached lip. The two planks forming the lowest course of the wall (2107, 2108) were found *in situ*, apparently resting against the west edge of the cut, although a short length of three superimposed planks is thought to have formed a higher section of wall that had partially collapsed inwards. No retaining posts were seen, although four timber blocks (2125–7 and 2132, Fig.301) found between the bottom plank and the lip and measuring an average of 0.2 x 0.08 x 0.12m indicate that the bottom planks were held in place by chocks as well as posts. Further-

more, at least two small roundwood posts (2128 and 2129, Fig.301) were found associated with the south-west corner and another further north (2124) stood in the west wall sill against the wall planks, indicating that such posts were used to help retain the planks even if they had no load-bearing role.

One plank (2119), measuring 2.72 x 0.27 x 0.09m, is regarded as forming part of the south wall. However, its top edge was 9.37m AOD at the west end but only 9.05m AOD at the east surviving end and so it appears to have been disturbed; one possibility is that it rested on the floor and fell into its current position when the floor was removed. This plank was

677

retained by posts 2120 and 2132, a probable collapsed post (2121), and two horizontal timbers or post-pads (2115 and 2118).

The two internal longitudinal beams (Fig.301) were at spacings of 0.9m, and are interpreted as joists for a plank floor that had subsequently been removed. The uppermost surface of these beams was around 9.04m AOD at the south and north ends but only 8.89m AOD towards their middle, presumably following a slightly concave construction cut base. Consequently, an overlying plank floor would have been around 9.1m AOD at either end but 8.95m AOD in the middle. The eastern of the beams (2089) was the more substantial at 6.45 x 0.2m square and consisted of two elements, whereas the western beam (2116, 2105/2117, 2153, 2096) was at a slight angle to the long axis of the building and was constructed from several superimposed timbers, none more than 0.1m thick; one timber (2116, Fig.301) had a peg-hole, suggesting re-use. Several timber fragments were found partly beneath the east beam and appear to have been used to level it up; one timber (2123) displayed two peg-holes, suggesting re-use. Planks found alongside the west sill (2112–14) could mark the position of another joist.

Numerous smaller pieces of timber found within the structure in the base of the cut, including part of a plank, may well have formed part of the building but their function cannot be determined. They are thought to have been deposited in the structure after the removal of the plank floor.

If the eastern beam was in the middle of the short axis, this structure would have measured 5m wide. Otherwise, it is assumed only a lipped foundation beam lay to the east and the building would have been about 3.9m wide.

Timber 131 (2109) provided a felling date of AD 951–87 (p.748), but bears shallow blind mortices that indicate it had been re-used (p.776). However, as this structure post-dates the Period 5A drain (2133, Timber 172) which is dated to AD 960–94 (p.745), a later construction date is likely anyway.

A sill beam observed to the west of Structure 5/9 (2035/7) is believed to be part of the east wall of Structure 5/7 (see Figs 196 and 286).

Discussion of the buildings and backyards in Period 5B

The nine structures which belong to Period 5B all exhibit some features which help to throw light on their appearance but the dataset is far from complete and reconstruction must remain speculative and open to different interpretations. While some of the buildings met their end in conflagration, others were partially dismantled following abandonment and timbers salvaged for re-use on site and elsewhere. Re-used timbers are identifiable by features such as holes or rebates which have no purpose in their secondary setting (e.g. Fig.216). Differential survival and the evidence for quite substantial repairs has further confused the picture, as has the fact that on three tenements (A, C and D) houses have been replaced on exactly the same spot (Structure 5/2 over 5/1; Structure 5/6 over 5/5, and Structure 5/8 over 5/7) (see Fig.330).

The upright posts set into cuts were supported on post-pads in the cases of Structures 5/1, 5/3 and 5/5, while the other buildings used sill beams; the evidence has not survived for Structure 5/2. Whether this difference is chronological, functional or simply a matter of individual preference is unclear – it might have been found that sill beams gave better stability on the unstable ground. Structures 5/1, 5/6 and 5/7, and possibly 5/4, had rear access through stone revetted passageways, while the incomplete evidence for Structures 5/2 and 5/3 suggests a front entrance. Structure 5/8 might also have had a front entrance but the rear room is unique in having access through the side. The evidence is too incomplete to speculate in the cases of Structures 5/5 and 5/9.

There is evidence that at least some of these structures had plank floors. This is particularly well illustrated by the surviving patch of well-laid flooring neatly cut around uprights in Structure 5/5 (see Figs 260 and 263) but is also indicated by surviving floor joists in Structures 5/1, 5/4, and possibly 5/7 and 5/9. Other stray timbers from this period have been identified as planks but are in pine and silver fir (*AY* 17/13, *9065–6, 2374*) as opposed to the usual oak and, as probably imported material, might have served other purposes. Other *in situ* features within the houses are rare, for the reasons described above, but include timbers demarcating a possible sleeping platform or bench in Structure 5/8 (p.675) similar to those observed in Period 4B (pp.579, 585, 595–6). The recovery of the seat from an oak stool (*AY* 17/13, *8947*, 2303–4) serves as a reminder that there would have been other free-standing furnishings. Similarly, the wooden cist-like structure in the corner of Structure 5/7, whose exact purpose is unclear, must be seen in the context of other boxes, containers and chests which were recovered from the site, some of them (e.g. *AY* 17/13, *8941*, fig.1125) quite substantial. Iron chest fittings, including nails, staples, hinge straps and hasps (*AY* 17/6, 608–46) indicate possible further examples.

No trace of a hearth was found in any of the sunken-featured buildings, and nothing was found amongst the surviving metalwork which might have been part of an above-ground contained hearth or iron brazier. This lack of hearths has always been a matter of some puzzlement: if these structures were dwellings, then a hearth would be fundamental for warmth, for food preparation and for small-scale craft activities. Hearths constructed on top of the wooden planked floors would have been a constant fire risk, and charred *in situ* planks and timbers (notably in Structures 5/1 and 5/5) perhaps attest to catastrophic mishaps. If hearths existed they have left no trace.

The one possible exception to this is on Tenement D where the vestiges of a hearth can be seen below the cut for the front room of Structure 5/8 which, it is speculated on stratigraphic grounds, might be contemporary with sunken-featured Structure 5/7. This raises the possibility that at least some of the sunken elements of these buildings might have served as cellars behind surface-built structures. While this argument might hold for Structure 5/7 it is less compelling for structures which are arranged on the street frontage (Strcutures 5/1–5/3), while no evidence has survived in front of Structure 5/6. In addition to planking, some of the structures were carefully drained (e.g. Structures 5/4, 5/6 and 5/8). This fact does not greatly help in the debate as to whether these sunken elements were cellars or living quarters as both needed to be kept dry.

A discussion of the environmental evidence from the floors (*AY* 14/7, 733–6) indicates that the insect fauna from Period 5B floors is broadly similar to that from Period 4B floors (of what were undisputedly dwellings), although the former does reflect the 'cellar-like' conditions of the Period 5B structures (*ibid*, 734). Human lice which, together with human fleas, are seen as indicative of the building being used as dwellings (*ibid*, 728) were eight times more abundant in the Period 4B floor deposits than in Period 5B deposits, but this might be accounted for by the presence of plank floors which might have been regularly swept. The number of fleas was equally abundant in both periods (*ibid*, 735). There are, in fact, arguments and counter-arguments in every case.

The question as to whether these structures are the sunken components of two-storey buildings or were simply partially sunken single-storey structures also remains open to debate. Allen (see pp.793–8) favours the latter interpretation on the basis of constructional detail and height limitations, and has proposed the composite reconstructions shown on Figures 366 and 367. Richard Hall long wrestled with this issue (Hall 1982, 239; 1984a, 71–7; 1994, 60–4; 2007, 116–17) but latterly favoured the two-storey option with reconstructions perhaps similar to those proposed in London (e.g. Horsman *et al.* 1988, fig.106, d) and Waterford (Hurley *et al.* 1997, fig.6.2), while recognising that the surviving evidence was open to different interpretation. In the absence of his final thoughts on the subject the question remains for future scholars to debate. At present there appear to be three or possibly four options: (1) that these were single-storeyed sunken-featured buildings; (2) that the sunken elements are cellars to two-storey buildings whose superstructure is a matter of conjecture; (3) that in one case (based on the evidence in front of Structure 5/7) the sunken element is the rear cellar to a surface-laid building; (4) that the sunken features were cellars within surface-built structures and were not connected to the superstructure at all. Contemporary ground surfaces, which would have preserved traces of any surface elements, were not identifiable, leaving this possibility unresolved, but it is worth noting that the late 13th-/early 14th-century timber-framed building (Building C6f) on Tenement C had a timber-lined cellar (4.5m x 3.2m in a 1.2m deep cut) accessed through a plank-lined passage (*AY* 10/6, 743–6). Such an model for (some of) the Period 5B buildings might account, for example, for

Period 5B

post-hole
pit
scoop
stony spread
wood

Site N

0   10 metres

0   10   20   30 feet

Fig.302   *Backyards, shown with structures in*
their initial layout. Scale 1:200

14592

14723

fence
7511/29119

drain
7263

fence
5982

fence
1580/5852

6196

5229

29320

6199

15931

21326/
21247

11371

11767

18785

29826

3495

13337

6362

37118

21260

37112

13967

20223

6867

20259

20525

20290

gully
21142

20162

6838/
21190

29809

20050

5760

19306

20161

6953

clay spreads

11534

19638

20371

15058

hearth
15442

19386

15182

19248

15436

19354

20283

skeleton
15548

2181

072/
040

680

the collapse inwards of the west wall in Structure 5/4 and for the subsequent re-use of the rebuilt wall, perhaps indicating that it was not weight-bearing as it did not articulate with the building's superstructure. The debate will no doubt continue, with a recognition that no single explanation need apply to all the Period 5B buildings.

Allen has also raised the intriguing possibility that the buildings might all have originally been double-skinned as was the case for Structure 5/1, the inner layer simply having been salvaged at the point of abandonment in the other buildings. If this was the case, however, then traces of this inner planking might have been expected to survive elsewhere, especially in the slumped wall of Structure 5/6 where salvage might have been a difficult operation. In the case of Structure 5/5, where the burned floor planking is cleanly cut around uprights which support a single skin of planking, no trace of an inner skin survives.

Additional information relating to the appearance of the Period 5B buildings is provided by some surviving elements of material culture. Brackets for door fastening mechanisms were recovered (*AY* 17/13, 2361–4, figs 1164–5, 1167, *9048–9050*) as was an oak fragment of what is considered to be a window opening (*ibid*, 2369, *9059*, fig.1172), similar to that recovered from Period 4B (p.600). The Period 5B example is made from radially split oak board 17mm thick and has the remains of a rectangular or sub-rectangular central opening, two side boards and a wide end. A complete window opening of this kind was found in a 9th- to 11th- century context at Hedeby (*ibid*, 2371). Fragments of three wooden panels (*ibid*, 2371–4, *9062–4*) were found; one of them (*9064*) was decorated with incised lines and is considered to 'have been part of an internal wall panel, a furniture panel such as a chair back or side, or even a chest panel'. These panels serve as a reminder of other internal features which have left no physical trace. Two of the fragments were found together in context 21554, the final dumping levels in Structure 5/7, and might have derived from that structure. Both wooden pegs and trenails (*AY* 17/13, 2375–8) and iron nails (*AY* 17/6, 608–15), some *in situ* in timbers, provide further non-specific structural evidence.

With apparently only small window openings and an open door to admit natural light, the interior of the structures would have been dark although further lighting was provided by small pottery lamps (*AY* 16/5, 440, fig.186) and iron prickets for wax candles (*AY* 17/6, 679, *3678–80*, fig.293). Stone lamps were recovered from contexts that were both earlier and later than Period 5B (*AY* 17/14, 2544–6, *9661–70*), but these were probably used throughout the Anglo-Scandinavian period.

Several suggestions have been put forward as evidence for roofing material. The brushwood layers, comprising mostly willow, which were recovered from abandoned Structures 5/1 and 5/3 (see Figs 219 and 236) are strong candidates for fallen roofing material although other explanations including flooring or animal bedding have been proposed (*AY* 14/7, 723–4). In Structure 5/1 brushwood overlays a deposit rich in remains of heather and other heathland/moorland taxa such as might populate turf, raising the possibility that turf might have served as an alternative roofing material; the fallen beam in Structure 5/3 (see Figs 238 and 239) might have been part of the roof superstructure in that building.

What is clear from examining the individual structures is that within broadly similar constructions there is individual variation both in detail and in their position on the site. The natural slope from the street frontage down to the River Foss and the lateral slope of the land necessitated modifications of some original building plans and ongoing repair throughout the second half of the 10th century. Despite the build up of deposits caused by a century's pit digging and dumping in the backyard area this slope remained a significant feature throughout the Anglo-Scandinavian period and it was not until the deliberate, and massive, dumping and ground-raising operations in the later 11th century (*AY* 10/6, 859) that a serious attempt was made to level this area.

The land clearly required drainage and a number of linear features identified as drains and gullies ran downslope from behind the buildings, draining the land and disposing of liquid craft residues (see below) (Fig.302). In Tenement A, for example, gully 2181, seen only as surviving fragmented sections but stretching at least 10m and with a width of 1m, was extensively sampled and contained richly organic fills, including dyeplant waste. None of the fills produced insect assemblages typical of open water and it has been suggested that the disposal of dyebath liquors was its main function (*AY* 14/7, 591–3). In Tenement C another drain (5229) whose northerly section (7263) originated within Structure 5/6 (see Fig.266) continued downslope some distance beyond the back wall of the structure and might then have taken a dog-leg to link up with a wicker-lined drain (21260) before continuing down slope, its course running parallel with and to the west of gully 21142 (described below; Fig.302). The association between 5229 and 21260 is lost due to later intrusion, but the northerly section (7263) contained abundant 'house' fauna and post-depositional invader insect species (*AY* 14/7, 607). Gully 21260, by contrast, contained an appreciable component of foodstuff but also some faecal matter (*ibid*, 608). Samples taken from deposits elsewhere in the backyard of Tenement C produced evidence of weedy vegetation including *Genista*

Fig.303   *Skeleton 15548. Scale unit 0.1m*

stems (*ibid*), giving some insight into the appearance of the backyards.

The most conspicuous of the drains, 21142 and the adjacent 19638, appear at the division between Tenement C and Tenement D and might, in fact, have served as property boundaries in the lower regions where wattle fences could no longer be traced (Fig.302). There is evidence that both were wicker-lined along at least part of their course. Lining these drains represents a considerable investment of labour and the drains were probably in use over a period of time; environmental evidence, however, indicates that they were periodically colonised by species typical of open, neglected areas and might have dried up during drier seasons.

In addition to the gullies or drains there is evidence for numerous pits in the backyard area, some intercutting to form pit clusters. A number of these, for example pit 29809/29810 at the rear of Tenement D (Fig.302), were clearly latrines and their fills contained a wide variety of evidence for food-plants, many in the abundant faecal concretions, with evidence of moss being used as anal wipes (*AY* 14/7, 613–14). A possible hearth 15442 in the south-west corner of the site (Fig.302) appears to be an external feature unassociated with any structure.

Attempts to stabilise the damp sloping ground, or to produce dry working platforms, are evidenced by patchy spreads of limestone fragments or cobbles. A sizable spread (20259/20162; Fig.302) occupies the central part of Tenement B and might have linked up with the spread to the north (15931) immediately outside Structure 5/4 and served as a pathway down the slope from the back of the structure.

Immediately underneath one such spread (20283) in the south-western corner of the site, and cut by the shoring, the upper part of an undisturbed skeleton (15548; Figs 302 and 303) was unexpectedly discovered. It proved to be that of a mature adult female, just under 1.60m tall and suffering from widespread degenerative joint disease (Table 33) which would have left her possibly on crutches but certainly with a lurching limp. She had been laid on a true east–west orientation with her right arm flexed across her abdomen and her left arm flexed across her lower chest. Radiocarbon dating places her some-

Fig.304   Wooden artefacts

Fig.305   Richard Hall playing the panpipes

Fig.306   Antler-working debris

where between the end of the 9th century and the first decades of the 11th century (c.890–1020), but her stratigraphic position, just below the cobble spread, puts her firmly in Period 5B, above layers which contain 10th-century Torksey-type and Stamford-type wares. Isotope analysis on her teeth showed that the combination of strontium and oxygen isotope ratios would be consistent with her having originated in Scotland, Norway or Sweden (but not Denmark) and that it is highly unlikely that she was born in England (J. Montgomery, pers. comm.).

The circumstances of this isolated burial are unclear; there was no trace of a coffin or even a grave cut and she seemed to have been placed directly on the ground surface. Despite having been carefully laid out, the position of the burial at the bottom of the backyards underneath a spread of limestone cobbles has an almost furtive character. This burial lies almost equidistant between the churches of All Saints Pavement and St Mary Castlegate but is not obviously directly associated with either.

The spread of craft and industrial debris resulting from activities in and around the houses extended from the street frontage over approximately two-thirds of the length of the site, with an emphasis on Tenement C where many of these activities appear to have been associated directly with Structure 5/5 or 5/6. This is certainly the case for both the production of wooden bowls and cups (AY 17/13, fig.1054) (Fig.304) and associated working debris (ibid, fig.1047). A pit behind the structures (6362, Fig.302) also produced a syrinx, a set of boxwood pan pipes (ibid, 9038, fig.1159) (Fig.305) which, upon cleaning,

were still capable of playing a five-note scale (Hall 1984a, 116). Iron-working evidence, which is much more diffuse in Period 5B than in Period 4B, shows a similar focus on this tenement and this more durable evidence is spread the full length of the excavated area although doubtless includes residual material. The distribution of knife blades appears to be focused on Structures 5/6 and 5/7 (or conceivably the rear room of Structure 5/8) on Tenements C and D (*AY* 17/6, fig.242) and the distribution of needles follows the same pattern (*ibid,* fig.218). Amber-working and bone- and antler-working evidence is more widely spread but other forms of debris show this same focus on Tenements C and D (Fig.306). Spinning, weaving and dyeing continued across all properties as before but there is more evidence for fibre processing in this phase, again with the emphasis being on Tenements C and D (*AY* 17/11, fig.845). How much of this can be seen as reflecting real differences in the scale and variety of activities on the different tenements and how much is due to site formation processes and differential survival must, however, remain a matter of conjecture.

Various strands of evidence can be used to give insights into the character and appearance of the backyards. The prevailing wet conditions which are implied by the need for drainage gullies – some drains actually originating within the houses – is supported by the range of insect species described above and is given further credence by the presence of frogs in about one-third of samples taken from Anglo-Scandinavian backyard deposits (*AY* 15/3, 189). Plants typical of disturbed habitats, including mainly weed species such as patches of elder, nettles and dock (*AY* 14/7, 736–9) were common, with few plants gaining permanence on this frequently trampled area. There was no evidence for cultivated garden beds in the backyards but cultivation, or at least exploitation, of certain plants growing as weeds, is likely (*ibid,* 614, 739). Period 5B pit fills include evidence of parsnip and beet, while celery seed is widespread across the site. Perhaps the shovel blades (*AY* 17/13, fig.1135, *8965–6*), spade (*ibid,* fig.1137, *8969*) and various tool handles (*ibid, 8991–3*) recovered from the site should

be seen in the context of small-scale horticulture necessary for maintaining the backyards, while the plough fragment (*ibid,* 2323–4) recovered during the watching brief is suggestive of larger areas of cultivation, not necessarily immediately adjacent.

Alongside the evidence for horticulture, such as it is, it is likely that some livestock was kept in the backyards. Studies have shown that the majority of the animal bones recovered are of cattle (*AY* 15/3, 149–54) but, with the exception of possible milk cows, these would have been brought onto the site for slaughter or as carcasses for butchery. Sheep were the next most frequent species recovered (*ibid,* table 40), valued as much for their wool as for their meat (*ibid,* 171), but they would have been pastured elsewhere. The relative abundance of pig bones rose in Period 5, as the number of cattle fell, suggesting that these animals supplied an increasing amount of the city's meat (*ibid,* 179); samples taken from Structures 5/3 and 5/4 show a high incidence of pig metapodials and other evidence which points to slaughtering and butchering on site. Pigs, however, are one species which might reasonably have been kept in the backyards and there is some evidence for the presence of farrowing sows and their young (*ibid,* 183): surviving post and wattle alignments might have been part of enclosures used to accommodate these animals. The late 10th–early 11th century also saw an increasing diversity of birds brought onto the site but common throughout were domestic fowl, hens and greylag geese (*ibid,* 193, table 55), which could have been kept as a ready supply of both meat and eggs. The relative scarcity of bones of the scavenging black rat in Periods 4B and 5B (*AY* 15/3, 189–91) is perhaps indicative of the intensification of activity in the backyards during the 10th century which would have discouraged their presence.

Period 5C

The end of Period 5 was designated Period 5C and is defined by two buildings at the street frontage in Tenement D (Period 5Cf) and by a post-built structure and a series of dumps at the rear (Period 5Cr). Fragments of an additional contemporary building were recovered during the watching brief on Tenement E.

This period is less well dated by dendrochronology as many timbers used to construct the Period 5Cf buildings are clearly re-used (see below) but dates from underlying structures provide *termini ante quem* for their construction. The end of the period can be identified at the River Foss end of the site (Period 5Cr) by the first in a series of dumps which continue into the 12th century.

Period 5Cf

The remains of two structures (Structures 5/10 and 5/11) were found at the front of Tenement D and a fragment of a further structure (Structure 5/13) was recovered during the watching brief on Tenement E. Evidence for contemporary buildings on the other tenements did not survive due mainly to the truncation of deposits there.

Structure 5/10

Represented only by limited parts of its foundation and a few *in situ* planks, the remains of Structure 5/10 were exposed at the street frontage end of Tenement D, immediately beneath modern debris and overlying the front room of Structure 5/8. The north and east sides of the structure lay beyond the perimeter piling, leaving an internal floor area only 2.7m long (north–south) x 5.0m wide to be examined.

The south foundation comprised a decayed beam (14065; Figs 307 and 308), at least 4.91m long by 0.17m x 0.09m, which was underpinned by at least four transverse timbers c.1.80–2.10m long and a linear spread of limestone rubble incorporating a few pieces of redeposited Roman tile. The transverse timbers included a virtually unworked forked bough (14215), 1.51 x 0.18m diameter; a simple beam (14213), 2.11 x 0.24 x 0.12m; one (14219) 1.84

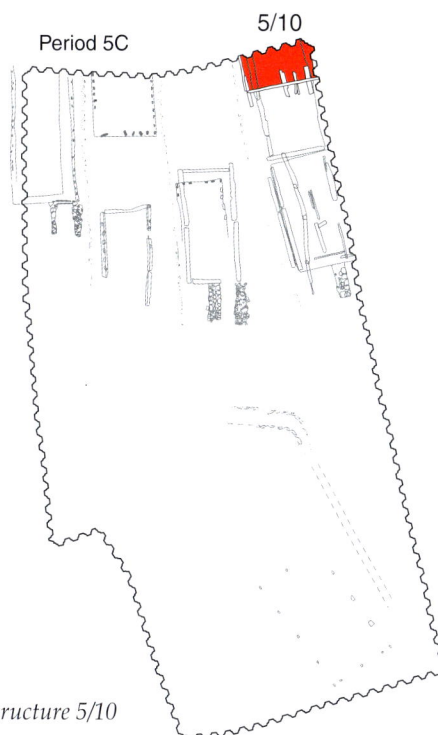

Period 5C   5/10

Location of Structure 5/10

x 0.33 x 0.13m with a rebate-like cut along one long edge (Fig.309); and another (14214) 1.83m x 0.34 x 20mm with a similar rebate but also a series of other rebates and grooves cut into it (Fig.310).

The west side foundations consisted of a decayed beam (14066) measuring 2.20m x 0.14m x 0.10m. A linear soil change, parallel to and just beyond its outer edge, suggested that it had been placed in a cut, but the modern truncation had removed any further evidence for this. The upper surface of this beam was at approximately the same level as that of the southern beam but, unlike the latter, it was not supported by any transverse beams – at least, not within the short excavated length.

Vestigial traces of what appeared to be horizontal edge-set planks were set upon the foundation beams, presumably forming the lowest parts of the two walls.

A series of stake-holes concentrated at the western side of the building are thought to be contemporary with it, although they might be later – their function is not known. No certain floor levels

Structure 5/10

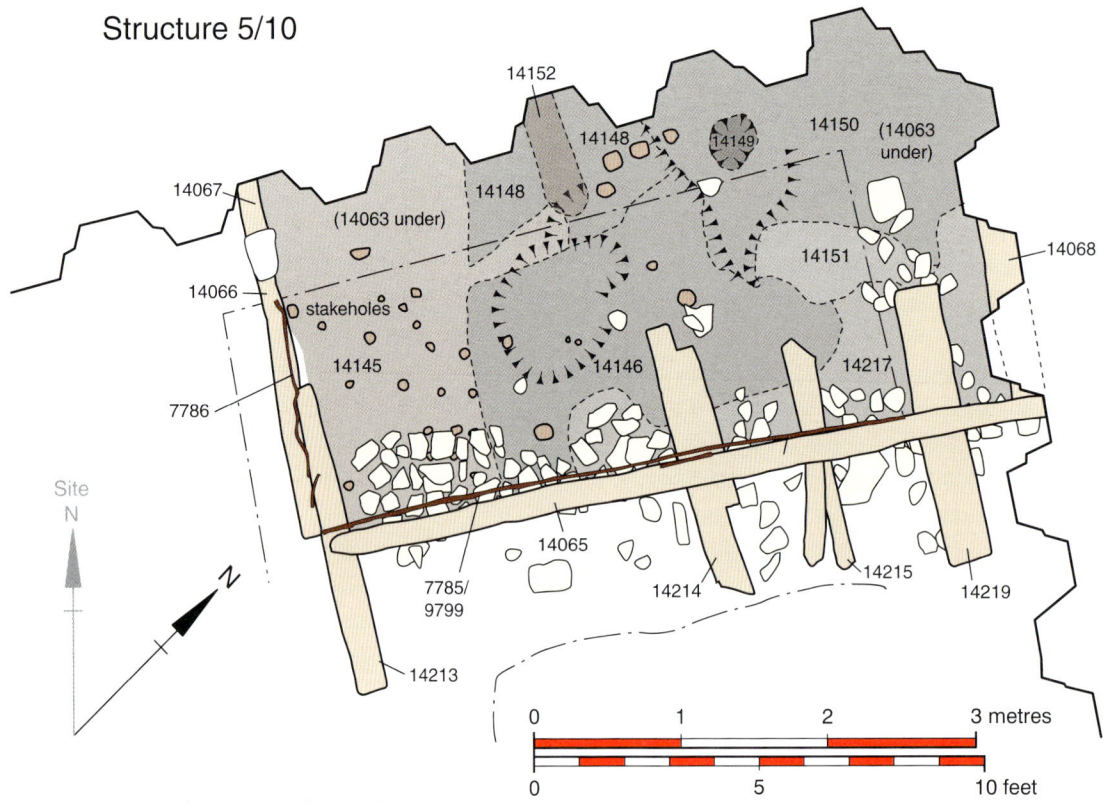

Fig.307   *Plan of Structure 5/10. Scale 1:50*

Fig.308   *Structure 5/10, beam 14065 looking east. Scale unit 0.1 m*

Fig.309   Structure 5/10, beam 14219. Scale unit 0.1 m

were recognised, although possible candidates include 14063, 14145–52, and 14217 (Fig.307). Little useful biological information was gathered that relates to this structure, or to Structure 5/11 (below), but what there was suggested the accumulation of non-specific occupation debris (*AY* 14/7, 619).

Two of the transverse beams provided felling dates of 963–98 and the sill beam 14065 was felled after 944 (p.755); all were evidently re-used. The relationship to the underlying Structure 5/8, however, suggests that the construction of Structure 5/10 must have taken place some time after 1008/09. Only a small amount of pottery was recovered from construction and occupation levels (*AY* 16/5, fig.227) and, although not statistically significant, it shows an increase in Stamford ware which is a regular feature of mid-11th-century assemblages. Pinning the co-called Stamford peak either side of the Conquest, however, has proved difficult (*AY* 16/9, 1176–8).

Structure 5/11

The remains of Structure 5/11 lay immediately south of Structure 5/10, and above the back part of the front room of Structure 5/8. Structure 5/11 was positioned within a 0.15–0.20m deep overall cut

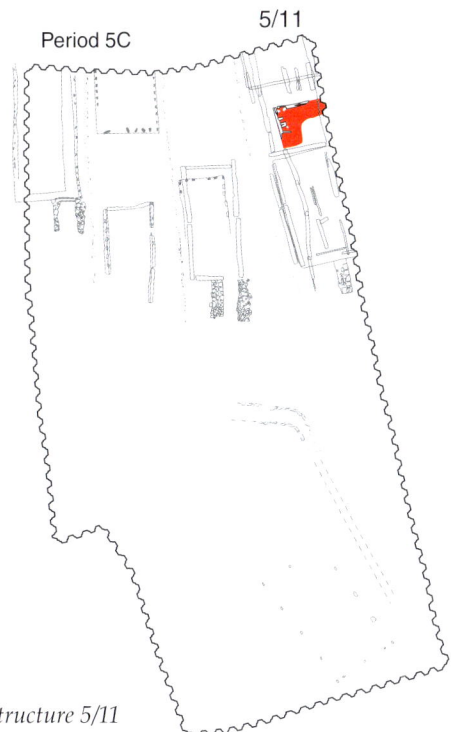

Fig.310   Structure 5/10, beam 14214. Scale unit 0.1 m

Location of Structure 5/11

687

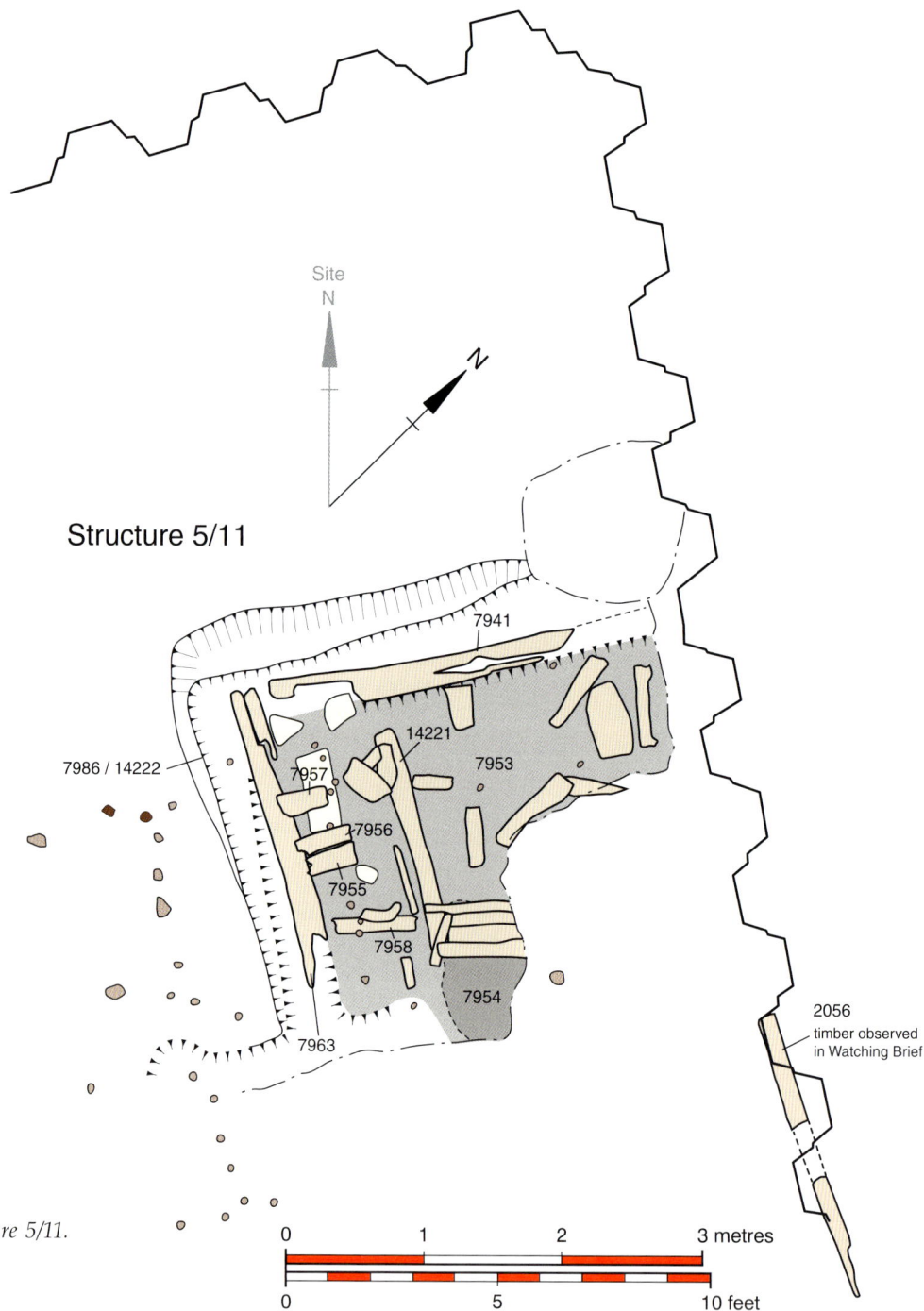

Structure 5/11

Fig.311 *Plan of Structure 5/11.*
Scale 1:50

(7986/14222) so that there was approximately 1.5m between it and the back of Structure 5/10; while the two structures appear broadly contemporary, 5/11 is probably slightly later (*AY* 16/5, 507), and had been severely truncated by a variety of intrusions. Only parts of its north (7941) and west (7963) wall foundation beams survived, defining an area approximately 3.1m x 2.5m (Fig.311). Both timbers 7941 (originally 2.18 x 0.22 x 0.07m) and 7963 (2.08 x 0.18 x 0.1m), which appeared to have been

squared beams abutting one another, were very badly decayed. Within the floor area were several short lengths of wooden board, virtually all of them aligned on one or other of the main axes, and some slightly overlapping the foundation beams (7955–7) (Figs 311, 312 and 313), which are interpreted as the remains of a wooden floor, rather than as collapsed elements of the superstructure. With little of its internal area surviving, only a small number of biological samples were taken in and around the

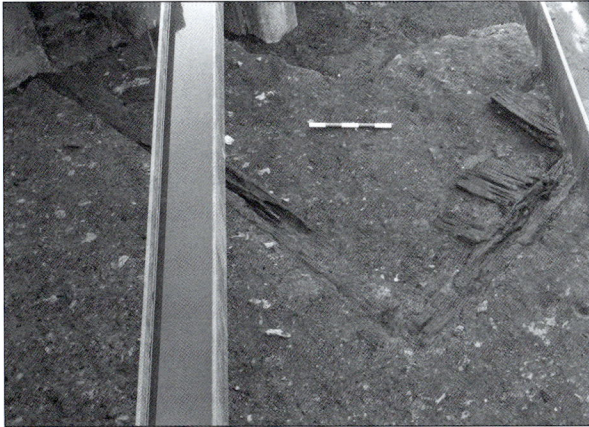

Fig.312   *Surviving elements of Structure 5/11.*
             Scale unit 0.1 m

structure, and they can be interpreted at no more specific level than as occupation debris (*AY 14/7,* 619).

There are no dendrochronological dates for Structure 5/11 but as it is cut into deposits which have built up against Structure 5/10 it must post-date that structure leaving it too with a construction date somewhere in the mid-11th century. Few pottery sherds were recovered from these deposits (*AY 16/5,* 507–8) and other artefacts are similarly uninformative – the most eye-catching, a wooden box lid decorated with bone mounts, is of a type found in both early and late 11th-century contexts (*AY 17/12, 6964*) (Fig.314). This whole phase of occupation can therefore be dated only loosely to the mid-11th century.

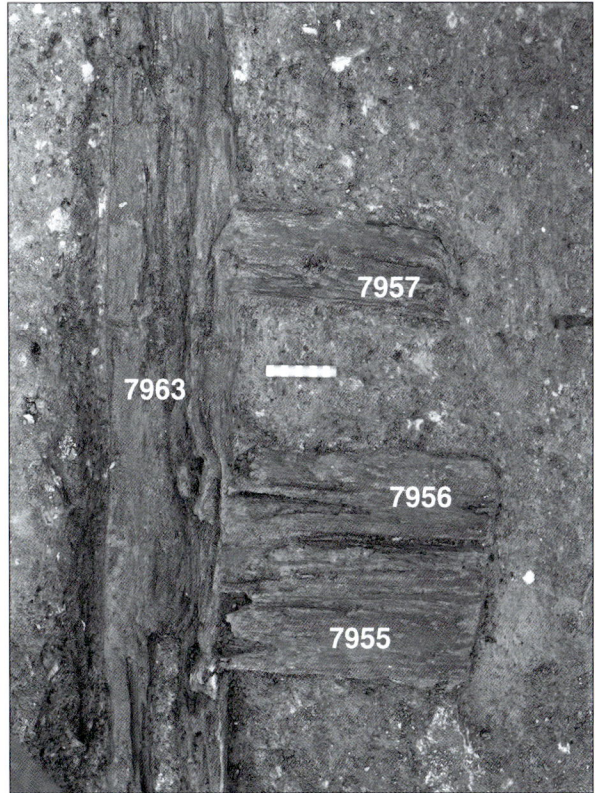

Fig.313   *Detail of timbers of Structure 5/11 (7963, 7957,*
             7956 and 7955). Scale unit 10mm

Please note: Structure 5/12 is considered below (pp.691–2) as it is part of Period 5Cr. It was assigned its number before Structure 5/13 was discovered during the watching brief.

Fig.314   *Wooden box lid decorated with bone mounts* in situ. *Length 336mm*

Tenement E

Structure 5/13

The remains of a timber structure (Structure 5/13) were found during the watching brief in 1982, parts of it overlying Structure 5/9 (Fig.315 and see Fig.319). A c.10m long alignment of posts, edge-set planks and wattle (2055/2088) is thought to have formed the west side of a building with its long axis perpendicular to the street of Coppergate. The planks in the west wall were 1.0–1.5m long and around 50mm thick. This wall terminated to the north with an earth-fast post, apparently in a post-pit packed with stones; an upright immediately to the east suggests a wall return. At the southern end, another return to the east is indicated by a substantial flat-laid plank (2082), with a socket to retain post 2086; these timbers could mark the position of a doorway. The minimum width of this structure was 1.55m. Most of it lay to the east of the limit of excavation and its layout and internal details are unknown.

Brushwood observed on the east side of the main wall could constitute a floor, and organic deposit 2087 to the west may have been a build up deposit. However, the west side of Structure 5/13 was at least 1.4m east of the corresponding wall of Structure 5/9. Furthermore, the limited number of major upright timbers suggests that this was a single-storey structure with an insubstantial roof. It is therefore possible that Structure 5/13 was positioned on the eastern side of Tenement E and was not used for habitation.

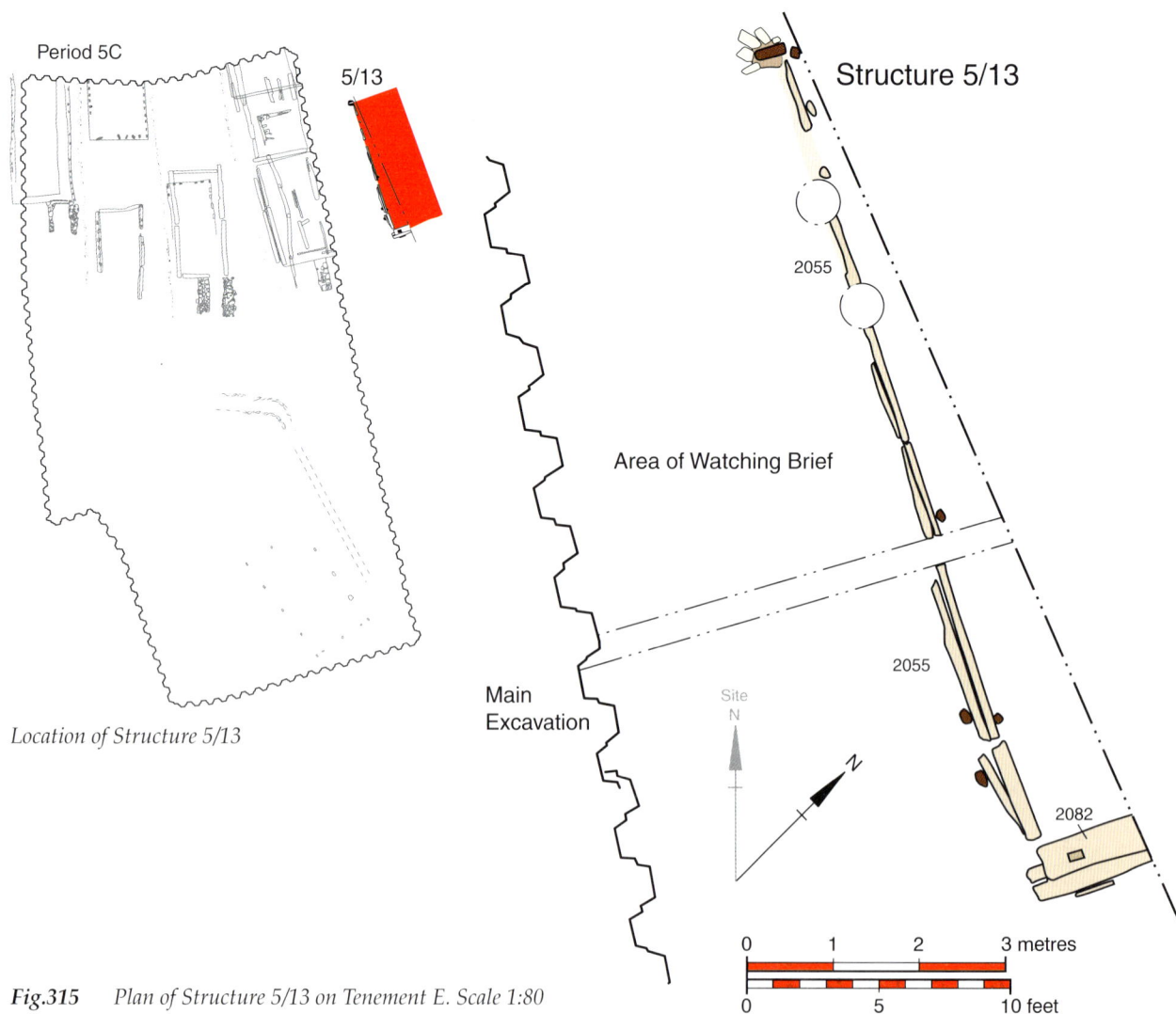

Location of Structure 5/13

Fig.315 *Plan of Structure 5/13 on Tenement E. Scale 1:80*

Period 5Cr

Cut into what was designated a Period 5B backyard deposit (19188) were posts and post-hole alignments which constitute Structure 5/12. The building appears to have been constructed in the early decades of the 11th century and following its abandonment was covered by a series of dumps which continued through the later 11th century.

Structure 5/12

At the extreme south (River Foss) limit of the excavated portion of Tenement C were the remains of the only post-Roman/pre-Norman building recognised at this end of the site (Fig.316). It was set at an angle to the street frontage, with its long axis aligned approximately north-west/south-east. Earth-fast posts or their remains defined an area that measured 8.2m x 4.5m, laid out in four virtually equal bays (Figs 316 and 317). The north corner had been destroyed by a later intrusion, and the three adjacent posts in the north-east wall (19291,

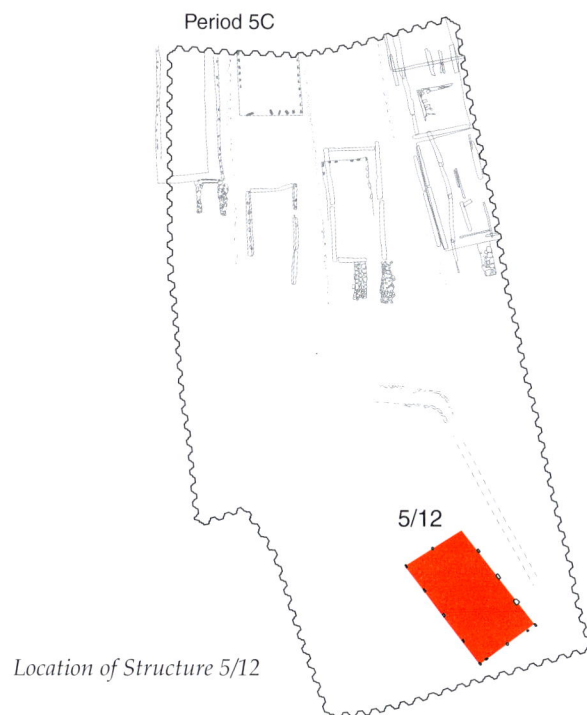

Period 5C

5/12

Location of Structure 5/12

19582 and 19303) had either been removed in antiquity or had rotted away completely to a dark olive-grey-coloured sandy silty clay loam. Other posts

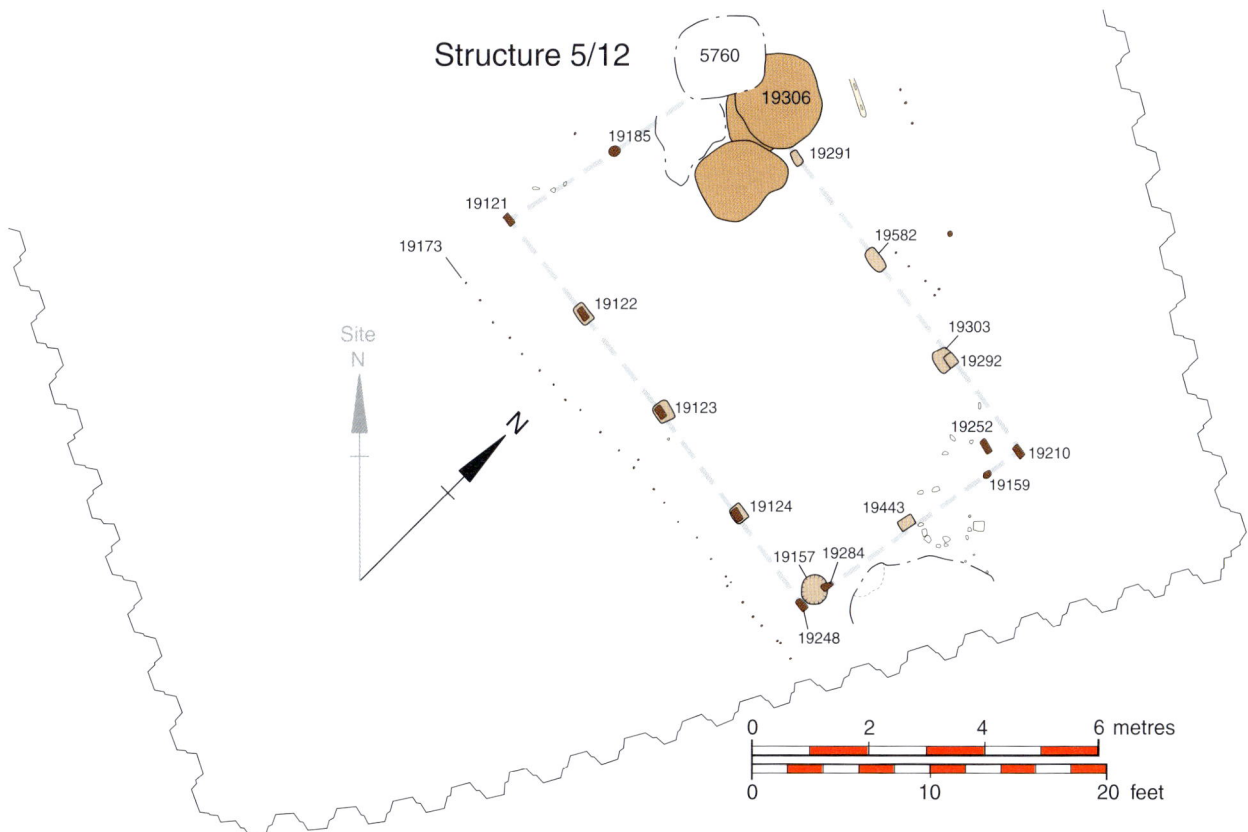

Fig.316   Plan of Structure 5/12. Scale 1:125

691

Fig.317   *Structure 5/12, looking north-west.*
          Scale unit 0.5m

survived, albeit extremely decayed at their upper
limits; their condition sometimes makes certainty
impossible, but nearly all the surviving timbers, all
oak, seem to have been squared off as boxed hearts,
measuring on average 0.21 x 0.13m. Post-holes were
identified for almost all of the uprights; one of those
in the north-east wall (19303/19292) had a clearly
shelving lip (Fig.318). As similar features were not
noted during excavation of the post-holes that still
contained post stubs (19122–4) it is supposed that
this may have been created during the removal of
the post. In the centre of the north-western gable
wall there was an additional post (19185); there was
a similar central post in what is assumed to have
been the south-eastern gable wall (19443), together
with two further uprights, one approximately 0.5m
inside each corner post. There were no recognisable
floor deposits representing occupation or activity
within the building, nor any deposits identifiable as
representing demolition or disuse. The alignment of
the side walls was approximately mirrored by that
of a wattle alignment 19173 which gently converged
with the building as it ran towards the River Foss.

Six of the post stubs were dated by dendrochronology and provide a combined felling date of
AD 1013–49; in the absence of evidence for re-use,
construction must have been shortly after that date
(p.749). A 'porcupine' sceat, c.AD 720–40 (*AY* 18/1,

Fig.318   *Post-hole 19303 in Structure 5/12. Scale unit 0.1 m*

51, *3*), was found in context 19120, a dump deposit
within the area of the building, immediately above
the level at which the post-holes were visible. A coin
of Cnut dated 1029–35 (*AY* 18/1, 58, *65*) was stratified above this structure in what is interpreted as a
residual (post-Norman Conquest) context.

The first phase of dumps over the abandoned
Structure 5/12 contained pottery typical of the late
10th/early 11th century (*AY* 16/5, fig.228), suggesting
that the dumps were largely composed of redeposited
Period 5B material. Features including pits and scoops

692

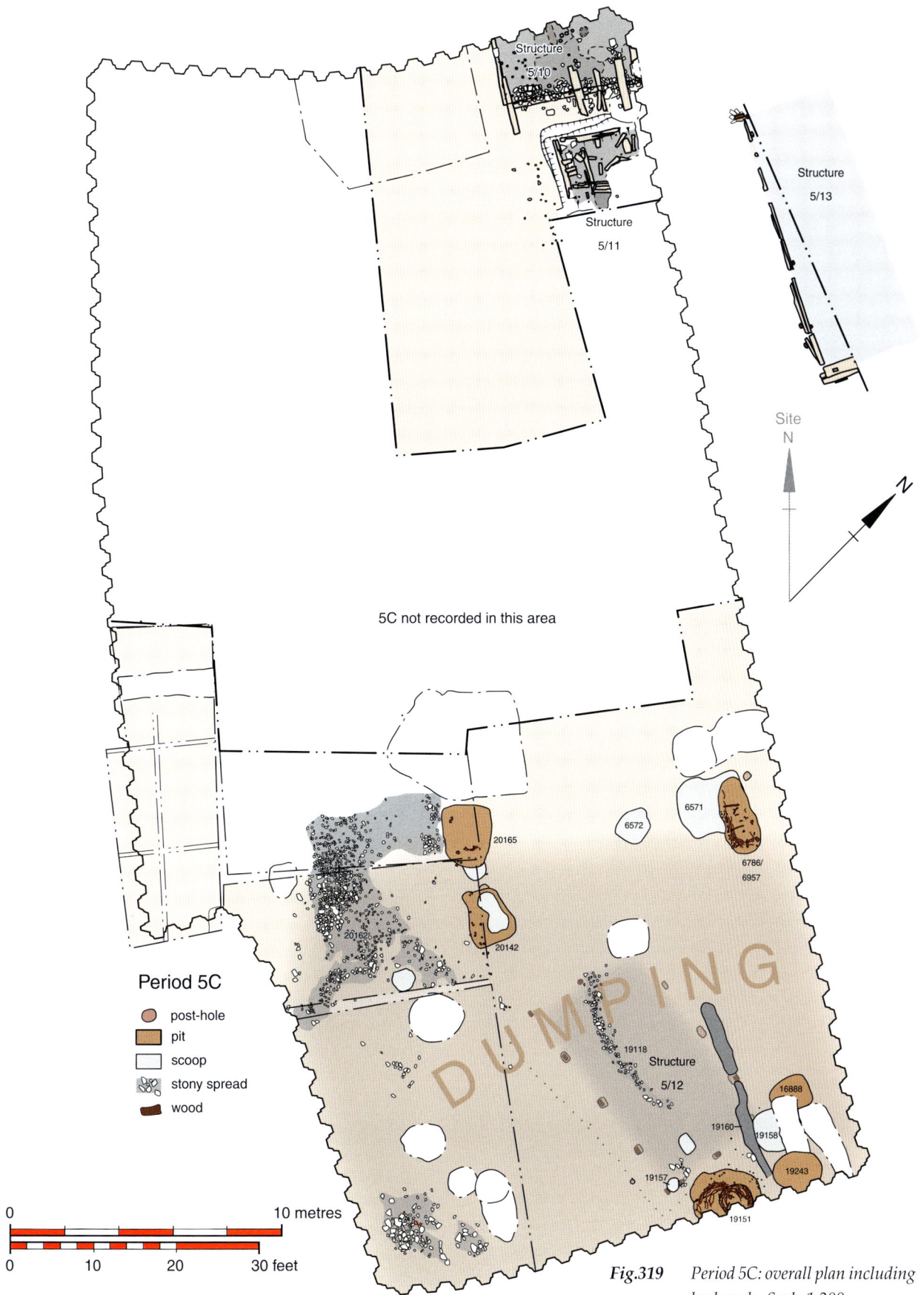

Period 5C

- ● post-hole
- ▬ pit
- ☐ scoop
- ▨ stony spread
- ▬ wood

Structure 5/10

Structure 5/11

Structure 5/13

Site N

5C not recorded in this area

6572

6571

20165

6786/ 6957

20162

20142

DUMPING

19118

Structure 5/12

16888

19160

19158

19157

19243

19151

0   10 metres

0   10   20   30 feet

Fig.319   *Period 5C: overall plan including*
backyards. Scale 1:200

693

which separated initial dumps from the next phase produced a small pottery assemblage which was again marked by the Stamford ware peak indicative of a mid-11th-century date. The second phase of dumps, and features cut into them, showed a more typical late 11th-century assemblage (*ibid*) which belongs to Period 6 (see *AY* 10/6 for further discussion).

The apparently isolated position of Structure 5/12 at the rear of the site represents a significant break with previous practice. Its atypical alignment is perhaps best explained by the builders taking advantage of the topography to place the structure on a relatively flat plateau at the bottom of what had been a challenging slope for their predecessors. The post-holes were cut from 7.15 OD in the north and 7.1 OD in the south suggesting that either deliberate levelling or general build up had resulted in a more or less flat platform on which to build. This meant that it was no longer necessary to cut a flat-based sunken feature prior to erection, although there is evidence from Structure 5/10 that this practice was no longer invariably followed at this period and might have been falling out of fashion. Equally, the simple barn-like appearance of Structure 5/12 might reflect a different function, perhaps as a store or warehouse. There is some evidence that the backyard area was becoming more neglected at this time, especially at the very rear of the site where a more permanent kind of vegetation was now able to become established (*AY* 14/7, 738) (Fig.319). This, coupled with an observed increase in the number of black rat bones (*AY* 15/3, 189–90) in Period 5C might support the idea of less intense occupation at this time. This is borne out by the reduced number of pits and scoops although some, for example 6786/6957 and 19151, are wattle-lined, suggestive of repeated usage. Gully 19160 continued the course of previous Period 5B gullies up until the construction of Structure 5/12.

The position of Structure 5/12, at the bottom of Tenement C, begs the question as to what relationship, if any, it had to the rest of Tenement C. Structure 5/6, higher up that tenement, had been constructed in the late 10th century and might have already been abandoned when Structure 5/12 was built, and no trace was found of a subsequent Period 5C building at the street frontage on Tenement C to match that on Tenement D. Despite modern disturbance truncating deposits along the street frontage, these, where

visible, suggest a slow build up of layers throughout the rest of the 11th century and into the 12th (*AY* 10/6, 716, 727, 756) rather than continuing occupation. The exception was at the front of Tenement D where an insubstantial structure was erected sometime between the later 11th and early 12th century (*AY* 10/6, Building D6x, 771–2).

It is possible, however, that the erection of a building at the lower end of the site is entirely unconnected with anything happening at the street frontage and should not be thought of as belonging to the long-established tenements running back from it at all. The alignments which had sub-divided the site for almost three centuries never reached into the rear third of the site and it has already been suggested that the backyard area might have been in common, or different, ownership. The erection of a new obliquely-angled post and wattle alignment (19173) running parallel with the south-western wall of Structure 5/12 might represent an attempt to define ownership of a property on a completely different alignment to its predecessors (Fig.316). This new position, and its orientation, was subsequently adhered to by a series of buildings and/or building repairs throughout the 12th century (*AY* 10/6, 730–42) until a substantial five-bayed building, Building C6f, dated to the late 13th–early 14th century, was constructed which once again respected the old tenement boundaries through its various subsequent modifications (*ibid*, 743–56). Structure 5/12, therefore, represents an anomalous episode at the very end of the Anglo-Scandinavian period which might be better seen as the beginning of a phase of occupation at the lower end of the site which then continued into the post-Conquest period.

Structure 5/12 might have stood for little more than a decade before it was abandoned and covered by dumped material. Continuous large-scale episodes of dumping characterise the second half of the 11th century, presumably in part connected with the creation of the King's Fishpool in the post-Conquest period. In what was excavated of Tenement A, where the natural slope was most acute, this dumping continued into the 13th century, interleaved by only ephemeral traces of structural activity (*AY* 10/6, 715–16). The first post-Conquest building at the rear of Tenement B (B6b) was erected in the late 12th century (*ibid*, 717–18) and the first at the rear of Tenement D (D6b) in the early to mid-13th century (*ibid*, 762).

The Coppergate Watching Brief and 22 Piccadilly

Please note: True north is used in this section.

The Coppergate watching brief covered the entire 2.02ha area of the Coppergate shopping centre redevelopment and was largely carried out during 1981–82 following the end of the main excavation. Subsequently excavations at 22 Piccadilly in 1987 examined four small trenches (Trenches 1–4) south-east of the main excavation. N.F. Pearson directed both sites and R. Finlayson supervised the latter. Work was funded by Wimpey Construction and Wimpey Property Holdings Ltd.

These observations and excavations established that the highest part of the natural ground surface (at 10.1m OD) was on the ridge occupied by the street of Coppergate. To the north-west, in Zone 7 (see Fig.131, **6**), it fluctuated between 9.1 and 9.4m OD suggesting an undulating surface to the moraine. In Zone 1 (Fig.320), south-west of the main excavation, the natural ground surface was above 9.0m reflecting the ridge of high ground seen on Figure 134. From there the land sloped down steadily eastwards to 6.0m to the east and to c.5m OD in the western part of 22 Piccadilly, representing the floodplain of the River Foss. The deposit at the base of the slope (at about 5.0m OD) was a sandy clay, perhaps alluvial in nature, while the natural clay on the higher ground is glacial till, overlain by post-glacial deposits.

A small valley, possibly the channel for a stream draining the higher ground, was observed immediately south of the main excavation site in Zones 1 and 3 (see Figs 134 and 320), most evident about 30m from Coppergate. At its base it was some 5m wide by up to 1.5m deep and contained alluvial silt and clay. A minor stream further to the west, originating between this valley and St Mary Castlegate, apparently joined the valley, clay laminated with peat forming a stream bed at c.6.0m OD. A slope in the ground surface down to the north-east on the north-east side of 22 Piccadilly (Fig.134) could indicate the position of another stream valley, perpendicular to the River Foss.

Anglian evidence

Across the north-western end of the site, including Zones 1 and 2, as well as the main excavation, was an extensive layer of grey silt loam. It was generally about 0.3m thick but at a point 10m from Coppergate at the base of a small natural terrace it was about 1m thick. A similar deposit 0.6m deep was observed in Zone 1, although not immediately at the street frontage, and appears to be a natural soil which developed prior to the 9th century. Hand-made pottery of Anglian date (8th or 9th century) was recovered at 22 Piccadilly from Trenches 1 and 2 and possibly from Trench 4. The square timber-lined pit (1778) in which the Anglian helmet and other artefacts were recovered (see Figs 136 and 148) was recorded in Zone 1 although the feature is believed to be of later date (*AY* 17/8, 1165–7).

Anglo-Scandinavian evidence

Cobble, stone and crushed stone surfaces encountered in Zone 7 slope in an easterly direction down from 14.4m to 13.9m and might reflect occupation dated no earlier than the 10th century (lower deposits were not excavated). A row of horizontal timbers perhaps mark the position of a fence aligned north-west/south-east. Two rows of inhumations (1931, 1933, 1935 and 1938) proved to be 12th century in date, presumably outliers to All Saints' church burial ground. They seem to have succeeded and preceded occupation, suggesting that the cemetery might have expanded onto an area of settlement but that later the limits of the graveyard were more closely defined.

In Zone 1 clean black silty clay deposits, up to 0.5m closest to the street, perhaps equate to Period 3 on the main site. They were cut by pits (1986 and 2010). Fence 1976 to the south could represent the limit of this activity towards Coppergate. The position of pit 1687 and dump 1857 in the lower-lying area to the north (at c.6.6m OD) suggests that

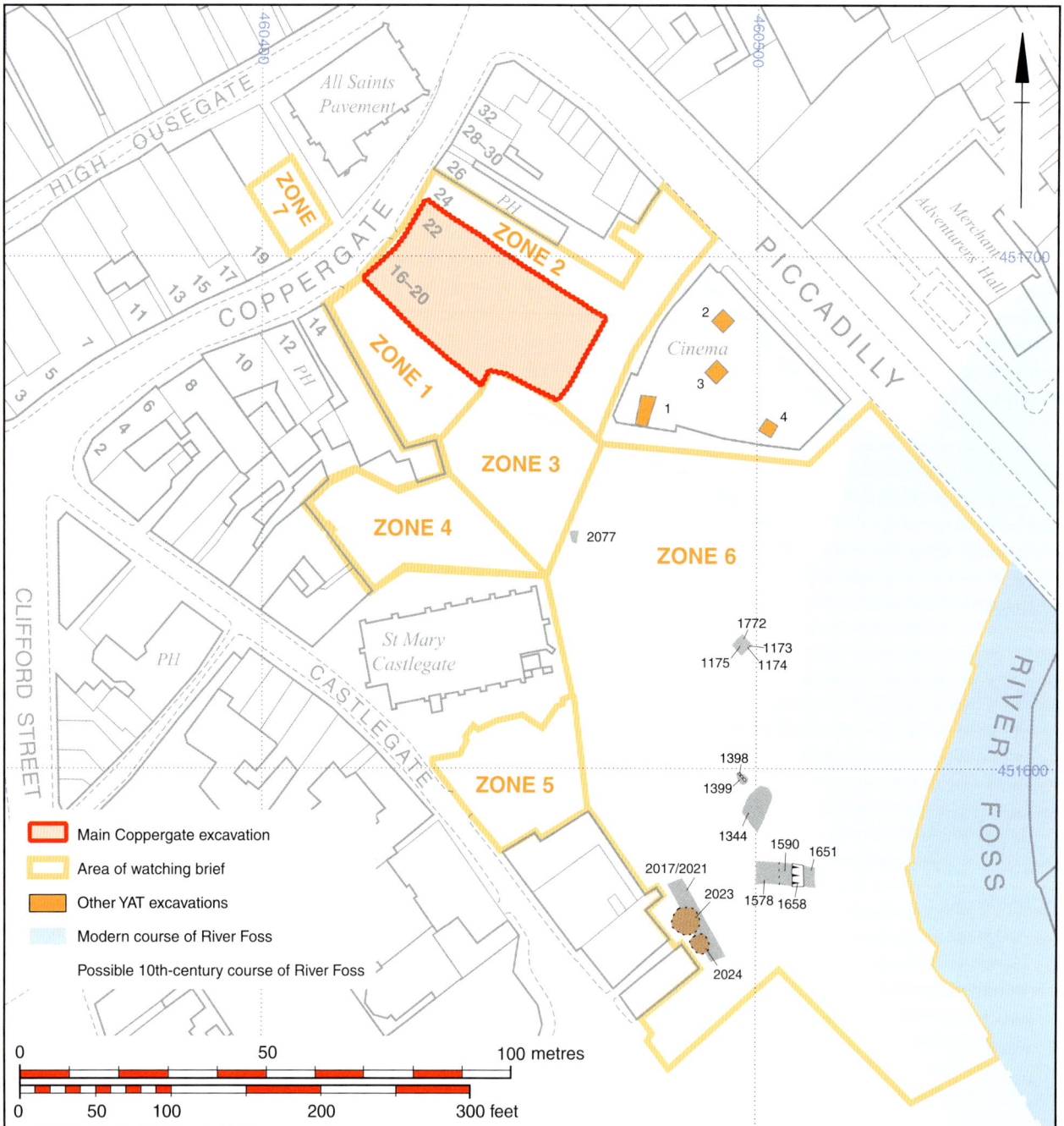

Fig.320   *Features uncovered by the watching brief. Scale 1:1250.* © *Crown copyright 2014 Ordnance Survey Licence No. 100018343*

the stream was no longer active although there is some evidence of further alluviation in the form of a clay deposit some 0.7m thick (1664/7) which is laminated with sandy lenses. These features, limited though they are, appear to be consistent with Period 3 activity seen on the main excavation (see Fig.136).

In Zone 2, to the north of the main excavation, a large circular pit (2061) measuring 2.4m wide by 1.6m deep appears to have had a primary use as a cess pit before being filled with rubbish. Vertical timbers (2062–5) on its south-east side may mark the position of a superstructure and an extensive clay deposit (2066) was perhaps a deliberate capping. Immediately to the north-east of the pit a wicker fence (2165) aligned north-west/south-east survived for a length of 5.2m. A deposit which built up against the fence (2166) contained many leather off-cuts. A second, slightly smaller, cess pit (2002) lay to the north-west and immediately to the north-east of that pit was a short length of wicker fence (2169). These features are believed to equate with 9th-century Period 3 activity on the main excavation (see Fig.136).

Excavations at 22 Piccadilly produced comparable evidence from Trenches 1 and 2 (Fig.321a). In Trench 1 a length of wattle fence (1.5), running parallel to the river, might represent a boundary. An early pit (2.2) observed in Trench 2 contained remains of dyeplants, clubmoss and madder as well as evidence for hemp and apple. In Trench 4 were dumps of domestic waste containing animal bone and oyster shell, 0.4m thick overall (4.3.2).

Features which might equate to Period 4 on the main excavation were observed in Zones 1 and 2 and at 22 Piccadilly although they cannot always be directly related to Periods 4A and 4B. In Zone 1 there is no evidence for structures although early features (possibly belonging to Period 4A) include an alignment of posts (2009) perhaps forming an early property boundary, post (2013), possible collapsed brushwood fence (2012) and post-hole or small pit (2007) towards Coppergate (see Fig.158). Wattle alignments 1965 and 1959 observed about 20m south-east of Coppergate appear to be fences against which rubbish seems to have accumulated, raising the ground level locally to about 10.35m OD (see Fig.158). Some 5.5m further to the south-east of fence 1965 was another wattle alignment (1964), apparently replacing 1976, and between them was an extensive loamy deposit up to 0.55m thick (1977) which contained parts of a wooden plough (2001) (*AY* 17/13, 2323–4, *9178*), raising the possibility of horticultural activity. Much of the area was sealed by an organic dump (2000) which might equate to Period 4B. In the lower lying area of the former valley a little to the north were traces of one, possibly two, timber-lined pits (1685/8 and 1720, see Fig158) with possibly associated posts (1723–9) and a small circular rubbish pit (1689).

Further alignments (e.g. 1855–6), dumps (e.g. 1564) and posts lie to the south of the main excavation in Zone 3 and point to land reclamation in this low-lying area at some time in the 10th century.

In Zone 2 a north-west/south-east post alignment (2144–7, 2150–1) apparently associated with a compacted 'structured peat' deposit (2004, 2094)

could form the south-west side of a building measuring at least 7m long by 3.5m wide (see Fig.158). It was subsequently sealed by mixed clayey dump deposits (2039/2043, 2167). A new alignment (2041), on the same line, might represent a repair, a fence, or the wall of another building. If the latter, it is more likely to be the north-east wall, making the structured peat (2034) observed to the south-west possible occupation evidence; peaty loam (2158) noted to the north-east would then be external build up. By the end of this putative Period 4 activity the ground surface was c.9.0m OD, rising to 9.5m towards Coppergate.

At 22 Piccadilly early 10th-century activity was noted in Trenches 1–3. In Trench 1 dumps containing ash and charcoal (1.6.7) covered the earlier wattle fence which was itself replaced by a more substantial fence and another running at right-angles and to its east (1.8) (Fig.321b). In Trench 2 there is evidence for dumping and flooding (2.4.1), while similar alluvial material in Trench 3 (3.2) was followed by a loose alignment of timbers (3.3), perhaps in an attempt to stabilise the river bank. A dump of clay which reduced the slope to the east might have been similarly employed (3.4).

The mid-10th-century episode of upheaval represented on the main site by Period 5A was difficult to identify during the watching brief. In Zone 1 c.0.2m from the west wall of Structure 5/1 was an alignment of three large driven posts (e.g. 1312–13) which might have formed a Tenement Z/A boundary. Alternatively, an alignment of stakes 0.4m further south-west (1283) might have been the boundary and the larger posts part of a structure not otherwise recognised. Timbers 1251 and 1270 which lie at 11.75m are not believed to be *in situ* structural elements but might relate to activity prior to the construction of the Period 5B buildings. Other deposits to the south-east have been interpreted as dumping of waste and possible horticulture, with further evidence for possible fence lines.

In Zone 2 a short length of wattle work (2168) and a post – possibly part of an alignment – might, on the basis of relative ground levels, represent the top of Period 5A deposits. To their east was a shallow timber-lined and capped drain aligned north-west/south-east (2133, see Fig.158) which survived for a

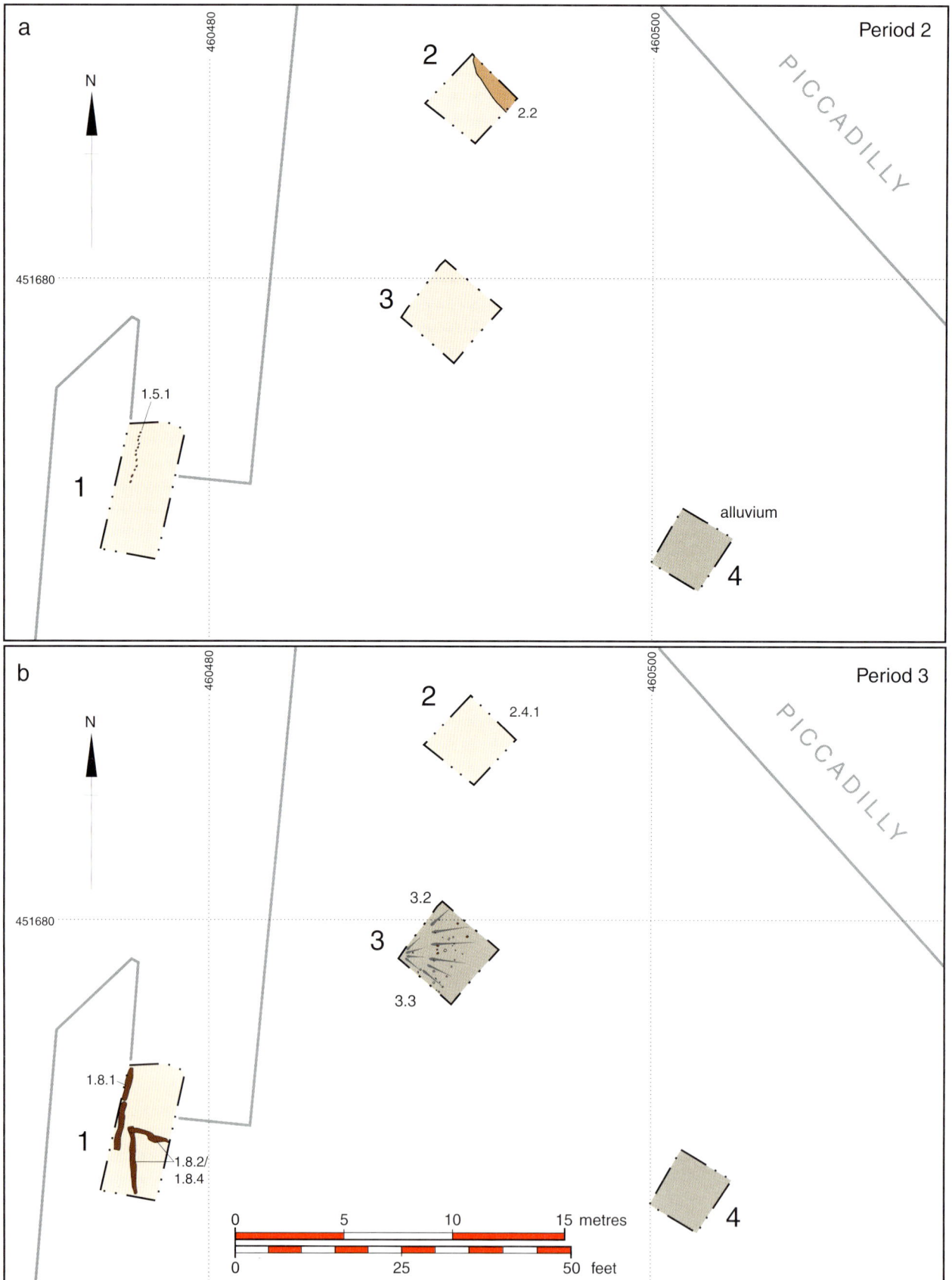

Fig.321 *The four trenches at 22 Piccadilly in Periods 2–4. Scale 1:250*

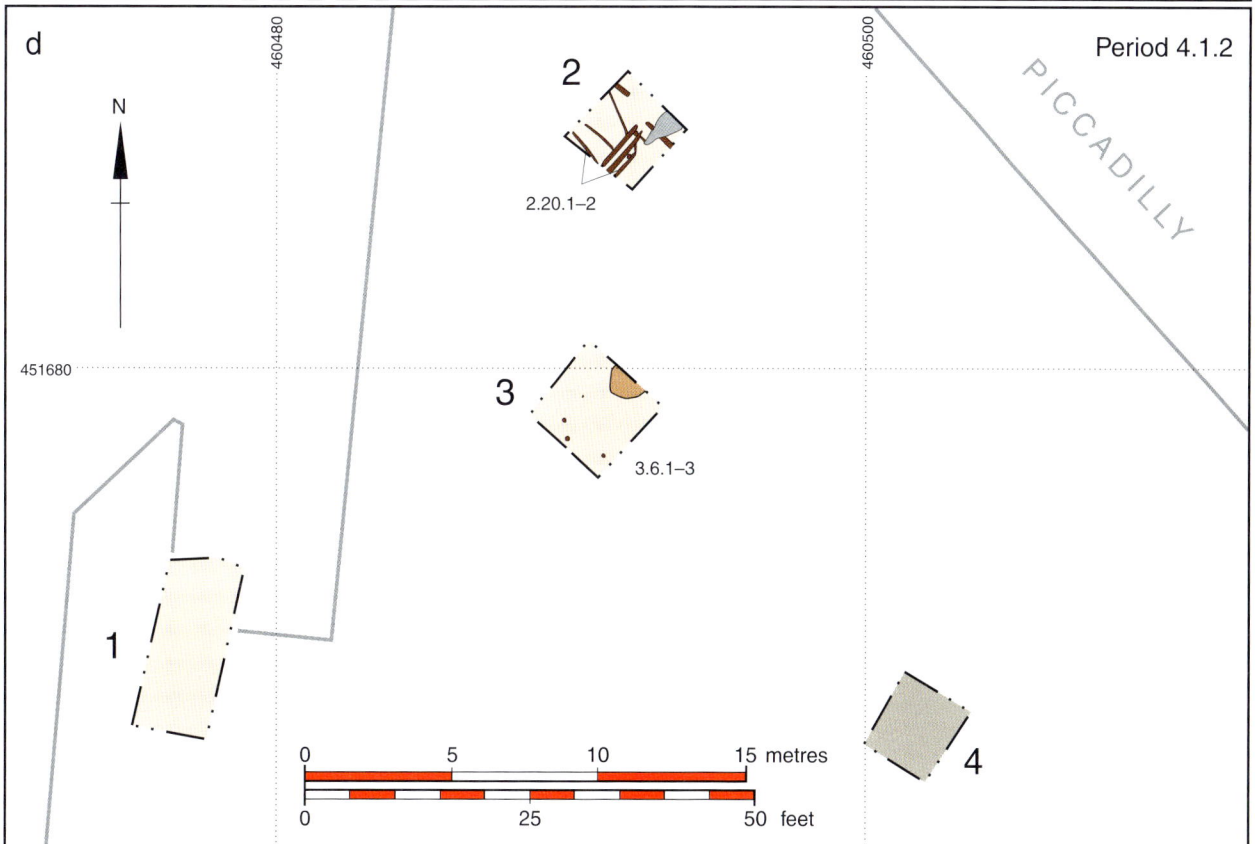

699

length of 4.4m, dated by dendrochronology to AD 960–94 (Timber 172).

Later 10th-century activity, equating to the construction of the Period 5B sunken-featured buildings, was observed in both Zones 1 and 2. In Zone 1 the west wall of Structure 5/1 was recovered and is described with the rest of the building (p.619). In the part of the Tenements A and Z backyards observed in the watching brief there were further intercutting pits (1479, 1982, 1978 and 1967, see Fig.196), some with wattle linings, which might have served as cess or rubbish pits. Lengths of a collapsed wattle fence (1991–2 and 1995), associated with a post (1998) and wattle (1996), might represent a former tenement boundary but appear to have been deliberately laid over pits 1967 and 1978, possibly at a time when the sunken buildings went out of use.

Structure 5/9 was identified in Zone 2 (see Fig.196) and, on the basis of levels and a single dendrochronological date, probably belongs to the initial phase of sunken buildings, and is discussed on pp.676–8. It was associated with a short length of wattlework (2168) and a post which represent either fencing or a possible building between Structure 5/9 and Coppergate.

Activity at the end of the 10th century, designated Period 5C on the main excavation, was only observed as a thin deposit (1259) in Zone 1, while yet another structure (Structure 5/13) was recorded in Zone 2 (see Fig.315). On the basis of levels this building is likely to be contemporary with Structures 5/10 and 5/11 and is discussed with them (p.690). The north-east wall (2056) of Structure 5/11 was also recovered at this time (see Fig.311). Between this wall line and a wattle fence to the north-east (2048) was an extensive organic deposit. That fence (2048) and another length of fence (2047) might have formed the boundary between Tenement D and E.

The River Foss end of the site

The dumping of waste seemed to have continued right down onto the low-lying flood plain east of St Mary Castlegate where an organic deposit (2077, Fig.320) at 6.3m OD more than 65m south-east of the street frontage contained a wide range of finds

and pottery of 9th-/10th-century date. There are also intriguing glimpses of laid surfaces in that area which might represent attempts to stabilise the west bank of the River Foss to facilitate the loading and unloading of ships. A number of limestone and crushed mortar surfaces (1394) at 5.7m OD, an alignment of gritstone/sandstone blocks (1398) associated with another laid surface (1399) and posts (1773–5) at 5.5m OD all point to deliberate manipulation/stabilisation of land adjacent to the river bank (Fig.320). The bank itself was observed as a steady slope down from a flat surface at about 6.35m OD (1590–2, 1658–9) and a spread of cobbles and limestone (1651) might represent an associated quay (Fig.320). This concentration of activity, which includes further cess pits (2023–4) and peaty, possibly occupation deposits, lies only 40m north-east of the street of Castlegate whose line might perpetuate an early thoroughfare which served the waterfront in this area.

The excavations at 22 Piccadilly supplied further evidence for fences perpendicular to the River Foss in Trench 2 (2.4.3 and 2.5.1), perhaps to consolidate the possible south-west bank of the possible stream flowing down to the river; a U-shaped wicker fence in Trench 3 (3.5.9–10) appears to have consolidated the ground towards the River Foss itself (Fig.321c). These fences were sealed by clay deposits and dumps. One of the latter produced substantial evidence for glass bead manufacture, including crucibles and waste. A series of laid wattle hurdles, posts and dumps indicate that attempts to stabilise the ground continued through the 11th century. This activity was concentrated in Trenches 2 and 3, which suggests that it primarily involved the consolidation of the river bank and the possible stream to the north-east, although build up/dumps and a rubbish pit in Trench 3 point to use of the land surface (Fig.321d, 2.20.1–2; 3.6.1). The lack of activity in Trench 4 suggests this area remained marginal land.

The extensive watching brief and the excavations at 22 Piccadilly demonstrated that the broad sequence of development recorded during the excavations at 16–22 Coppergate extended over much of the observed area bordered by the modern streets of Piccadilly, Coppergate and Castlegate. The implications of these findings are discussed further in the general discussion.

General Discussion

The excavations at 16–22 Coppergate were under-taken in a district of York which is a key area for understanding the rebirth of the city following post-Roman decline and abandonment. Past work in the neighbourhood had established the potential richness of the archaeological record there and the opportunity to investigate such a large tract of land, coupled with the extraordinary preservation of the remains, under-pins the enormous value of the project.

The location of the site – on the moraine, on a spur of land defined by the confluence of York's two rivers, some 150m south of the crumbling Roman fortress (Fig.322) – would have made this an obvious place for urban life to redevelop with its easy access to both rivers and to the old Roman centre. The street of Coppergate runs parallel to High Ousegate more or less at right angles to the River Ouse, and crosses the route of Nessgate before dropping down to the river as the modern King Street (Figs 322 and 323). Nessgate itself, which continues nowadays as Castle-gate and runs parallel to the Ouse, is not referred to until the 12th century (*Nessgathe* c.1154 x 1174, *AY* 8/4, 366) but their combined route might perpetuate an earlier thoroughfare which led down towards the confluence of the two rivers where William of Normandy would later build his castle. Modifica-tions to the course of the River Foss in order to create the associated castle moat and the King's Fishpool have masked the original course of the Foss and the natural topography in the area immediately south of the excavations, but given the tidal regime and the low-lying land at the confluence of the rivers the area would have been prone to flooding. A recent sugges-tion that the defensive potential of the spur of higher land now occupied by the Norman castle might have been recognised from an earlier date (Rees Jones 2013, 63–4) emphasises the significance of this area, which was part of what was to become an important market district in the medieval period (*ibid*, 40).

There is no convincing evidence for post-Roman activity in this area during the 5th and 6th centuries with the exception of antiquarian accounts of pagan burials (urned cremations) recovered from the Parlia-ment Street area (*AY* 7/2, 233, *3*) and hints of accom-panied Anglian inhumations from the Castle Yard and Clifford Street area (*ibid*, 232, 236, *2, 11*). There

is similarly little evidence for activity there in the 7th century although by c.627 Edwin, king of North-umbria, had been baptised in a wooden church, presumed to be near the site of York Minster, implying there was some level of activity in the old fortress area. Historic accounts of 7th-century York record the reigns of various kings of Deira and Bernicia, the establishment, loss and then re-establishment of the episcopal see, and the granting of land, probably also in the fortress area, for the foundation of a monas-tery (*AY* 1, *passim*). By the end of the 7th century a community, perhaps including traders, had become established less than a kilometre downriver from Coppergate on the east bank of the River Foss at Fish-ergate (*AY* 7/1) – but these events and circumstances have left no physical traces on the area excavated and observed at Coppergate.

During the 8th century, however, there is some evidence for renewed occupation in the Copper-gate/Ousegate district. Pottery evidence, including Ipswich-type ware, Maxey-type ware and imported Badorf and Tating wares, found in early levels and residually in later deposits suggest that the domestic and commercial activities first recognised at 46–54 Fishergate were, in fact, more widely spread, albeit thinly, in the course of the 8th century (*AY* 16/5, 392–400, 479–83; *AY* 16/6, 557–62, fig.237). The burials from Coppergate, whose earliest possible dates place them in the late 7th or early 8th century, indicate that the site was being used occasionally for the haphazard disposal of the dead, a practice seen from contemporary deposits both nearby at Spur-riergate (Paula Ware, pers. comm.) and across the River Ouse at 1–9 Micklegate (*AY* 7/2, 97, 193, 267). Both the scatter of pottery and the burials provide some evidence for a small resident population in the Coppergate/Ousegate area by the end of the 8th century.

While the difficulties of distinguishing, and independently dating, the homogeneous soils in the initial post-Roman deposits at Coppergate hinder a precise understanding of the physical context of the early burials, the churches of All Saints Pavement and St Mary Castlegate might have provided a spiritual one. Excavation and renovation at St Mary's, which lies 50m to the south of the street of

Minster
St Leonard's Pl.
Aldwark
R. Ouse
Roman river crossing
Market St
Ousegate
Hungate
R. Foss
Micklegate
Ouse Bridge
see inset below
Castle Yard
Castle
Spurriergate
Ousegate
Nessgate
King Street
Clifford St
Castlegate
Coppergate
Pavement
Piccadilly
All Saints
St Mary Castlegate
Micklegate
Ouse Bridge

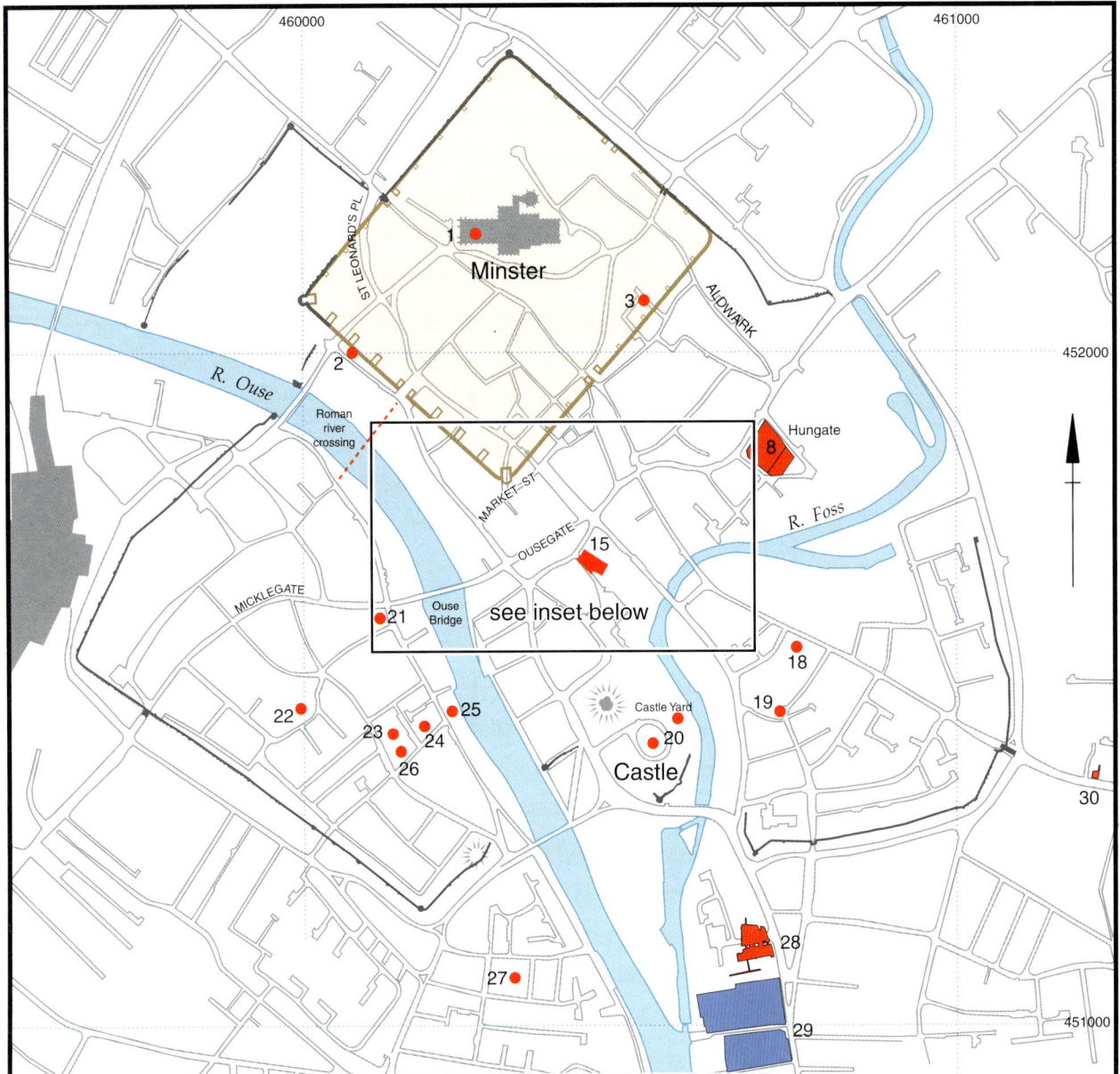

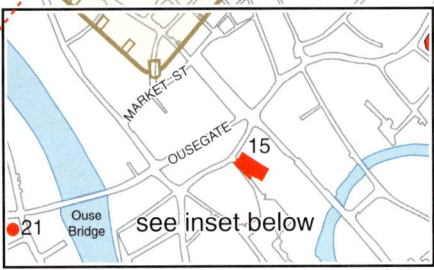

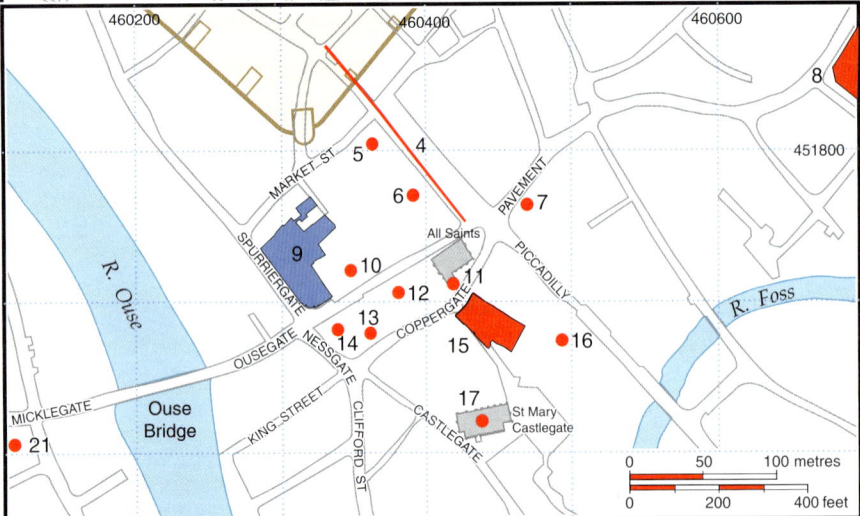

	Roman fortress
	YAT excavations
	Non-YAT excavations
•	Sites mentioned in text

0   100   200 metres
0   300   600 feet

0   50   100 metres
0   200   400 feet

Coppergate, produced architectural fragments paralleled by 7th-century examples at Ripon and Reculver which Richard Hall earlier remarked raises '... the intriguing possibility that there might have been a significant pre-Viking stone church on or near the site of St Mary's ... It is possible, however, that such architectural features remained in fashion until a very much later date, and it would be unwise to date the St Mary Castlegate stones firmly through their similarities with those from Ripon and Reculver' (Hall in *AY* 8/2, 154). Fragmentary crosses and grave slabs of late 9th-/10th-century date (Lang 1991, 96–101) from St Mary's also attest to a long tradition of burial but as the church lies some 50m from the edge of the excavation it is unlikely that the early burials from Coppergate are associated with it.

If the burials *are* associated with a church at all it is more likely to be All Saints Pavement for which there is a growing body of evidence for an early foundation, perhaps as an early Minster church; as such it would have been senior to St Mary Castlegate (Palliser 1996, 207–14; Norton 1998, 27–8). All Saints' church lies at the convergence of the streets of Coppergate and High Ousegate and excavations have demonstrated the presence of a pre-10th-century structure (perhaps a church) on the site (Paula Ware, pers. comm.); again early burials are indicated by the discovery of a late 9th-/mid-10th-century recumbent grave slab built into the church porch (Lang 1991, 80). It is at least possible that the high-quality cross shaft of late 8th- or early 9th-century date (*ibid*, 104–5, illus 337–8, 4), of which fragments were found distributed in Period 5A levels (p.611 and Fig.324) in the north-east corner of the Coppergate excavations, may once have been associated with the church. That institution might also be the source of the three other pieces of sculptural evidence – two 10th-century grave covers (*10827* and *10828*) and an unfinished 10th-century grave marker (*10826*) (*AY* 17/14, 2601–2, figs 1296–8) – recovered from the street end of the site (Fig.324). The two finished examples could be from graves disturbed as the growing settlement encroached on the burial ground or as a result of the later Anglo-Saxon trend for enclosing cemeteries which might have excluded outliers (Hadley and Buckberry 2005, 130). The presence of the unfinished grave marker remains ambiguous.

The early burials from Coppergate need not, however, be associated with either church. As Hadley and Buckberry remark there is '... little to suggest that burial in a cemetery at, or belonging to, a mother church, or indeed any church, was either expected or demanded much before the 10th century' (*ibid*, 126). While skeletons 30944 and 30979 were found in the north-east corner of the site, nearest to All Saints' church, 36318 and 32803 were some distance away, towards the west and centre of the site. The burials are uncoffined, although skeleton 30944 had traces of what might be a shroud, and they appear haphazard insofar as they are incomplete, although in some cases disarticulation has occurred due to subsequent disturbance.

Fig.322 *(facing page) Sites mentioned in the text*

1. *York Minster*
2. *Lendal (1972.5)*
3. *Bedern*
4. *Parliament Street Sewer (1976.11)*
5. *11–13 Parliament Street*
6. *5–7 Parliament Street (1980.1036)*
7. *Lloyds Bank, 6–8 Pavement (1972.21)*
8. *Hungate (2006.5201)*
9. *7–17 Spurriergate (2000.584)*
10. *8 High Ousegate (1977.30)*
11. *All Saints Pavement*
12. *20–21 High Ousegate (1992.172)*
13. *5–7 Coppergate (1974.8)*
14. *28–29 High Ousegate (2002.475)*
15. *16–22 Coppergate (1976–81.7)*
16. *22 Piccadilly (1987.21)*
17. *St Mary Castlegate*
18. *41–49 Walmgate (1999.941)*
19. *St Stephen's Fishergate (2005.3203)*
20. *Castle Yard*
21. *1–9 Micklegate (1988–89.17)*
22. *St Mary Bishophill Junior*
23. *37 Bishophill Senior (1973.15)*
24. *58–9 Skeldergate (1973–75.14)*
25. *Albion Wharf, Skeldergate*
26. *St Mary Bishophill Senior*
27. *Clementhorpe (1976–7.3)*
28. *46–54 Fishergate (St Andrew Fishergate)*
29. *Blue Bridge Lane*
30. *27 Lawrence Street (2006.5202)*

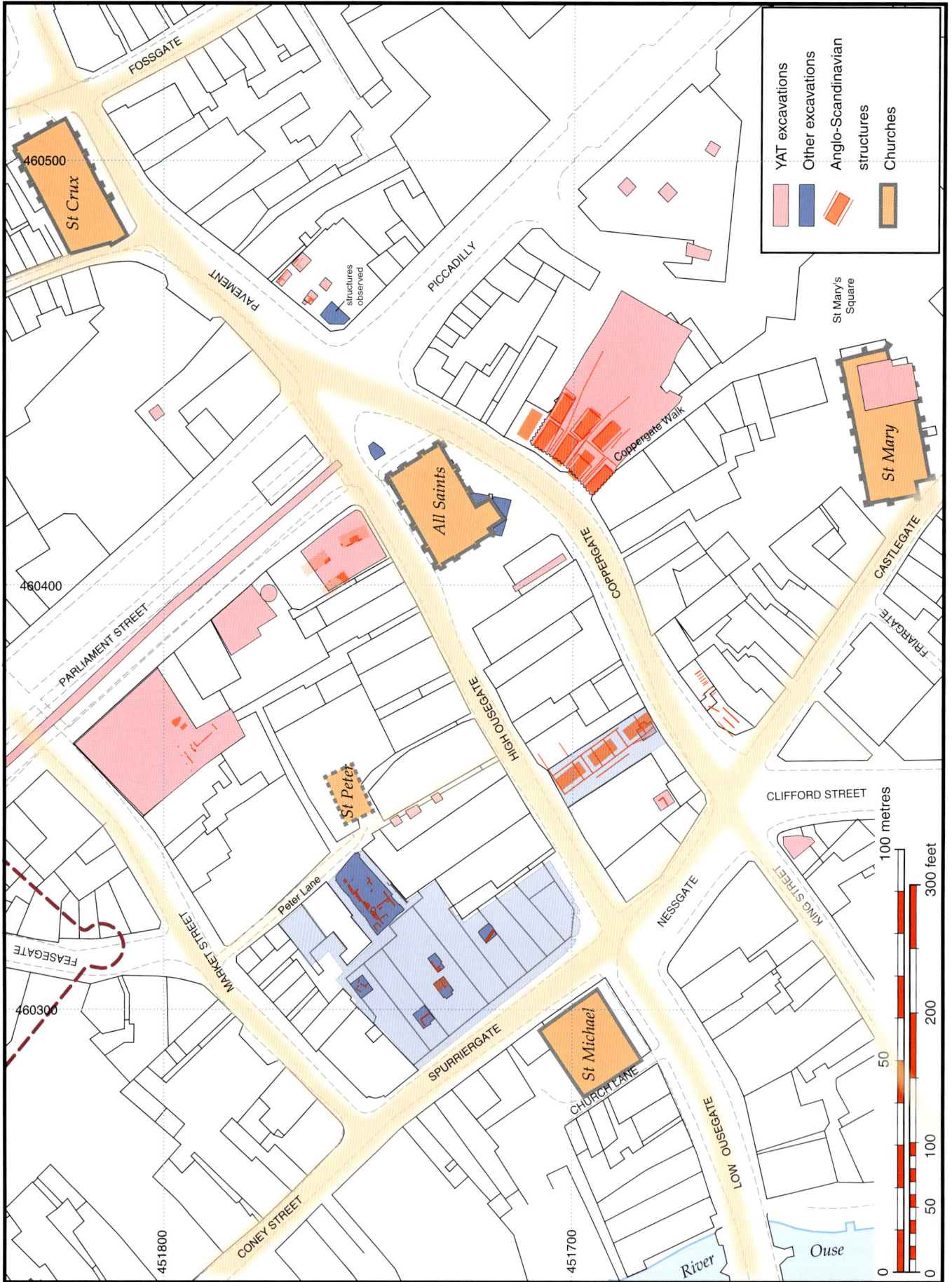

FOSSGATE

460500

St Crux

PAVEMENT

PICCADILLY

structures observed

St Mary's Square

St Mary

Coppergate Walk

COPPERGATE

460400

PARLIAMENT STREET

All Saints

HIGH OUSEGATE

CASTLEGATE

FRIARGATE

CLIFFORD STREET

St Peter

Peter Lane

MARKET STREET

NESSGATE

KING STREET

FEASEGATE

460300

SPURRIERGATE

St Michael

CHURCH LANE

LOW OUSEGATE

451800

CONEY STREET

451700

River Ouse

Legend:
- YAT excavations
- Other excavations
- Anglo-Scandinavian structures
- Churches

Scale: 100 metres / 300 feet

704

Other evidence of 8th- or early 9th-century date includes a Porcupine sceat (c.720–40) (*AY 18/1, 3*) found in an 11th-century context at the rear of the site and four stycas of Eanred (c.810–41) (*ibid, 13, 15, 19, 20*) distributed, in many cases residually, either at the front of the site or in the backyards (Fig.325) (see *AY* 18/1, figs 2–5 for distribution of later coins). A range of other early material culture evidence is summarised here by Nicola Rogers: *The quantity of Anglian artefacts from 16–22 Coppergate is small, and none was recovered from contexts dating from before Period 3. They include 56 finds of glass vessel fragments (AY 17/14, 10006–61) of late 7th- to mid-9th-century date and similarly dated items of non-ferrous metalwork. These comprise a copper-alloy dress pin of 7th- to 8th-century form (ibid, 2578, 10468, fig.1274), a copper-alloy cross brooch of the second half of the 8th to first half of the 9th century (ibid, 2574, 10431, fig.1270), and a silver stud with glass setting, which probably derives from a precious metal bowl, similar to the later 8th-century Ormside bowl (ibid, 2554–5, 10541, fig.1251).*

That there was activity, possibly including occupation, in the Coppergate area from some point in the 8th century is consistent with the, albeit limited, evidence from other sites south of the old Roman fortress. That recovered from downstream at 46–54 Fishergate (*AY 7/1*) and the adjacent site at Blue Bridge Lane (Spall and Toop 2005) has already been mentioned but excavations near the lost church of St Stephen, Fishergate (*AYW 9*), (Fig.322,**19**) also produced features and artefacts which indicate continuity of occupation from the late 7th/early 8th century through into the Anglo-Scandinavian and Anglo-Norman periods, implying that contemporary activity was also spread upstream along the River Foss. The presence of hand-made pottery from 22 Piccadilly (see p.695) on the opposite side of the Foss, on the low-lying land between the Coppergate backyards and the river, suggests that there might have been a strip of riverine Anglian settlement, possibly contemporary with occupation on the higher ground between Coppergate and Ousegate. The same continuity of occupation is suggested at 1–9 Micklegate, on the south side of the River Ouse (Fig.322,**21**), where there are Anglian rubbish pits and evidence of Anglo-Scandinavian structures (*AY 7/2, 267*). Elsewhere there is a thin spread of Anglian ceramics and

artefacts across the city, a distribution which appears to form clusters around, for example, the Aldwark area and St Leonard's Place, and extends along both sides of the rivers (*AY* 16/6, fig.237; *AY* 7/2, fig.116).

This growing body of archaeological evidence is consistent with the picture which emerges from contemporary historical accounts of increasing activity in the city through the 8th century. In 735 York became an archbishopric and in the course of the 8th century documents record the ascension, deposition and deaths of kings and the comings and goings of bishops and archbishops; documents also describe fires which burned the *monasterium* and parts of the city (*AY* 1, *passim*). York's famous 8th-century poet and scholar, Alcuin, refers to the adornment of churches (in the plural) (*AY* 1, 141–4), the founding of a school, a library, and the construction of the architecturally advanced Alma Sophia (in 779/80; *ibid*, 61). Alcuin's 'Poem on the Bishops, Kings and Saints of the Church of York', written around the 780s, describes the city as a place '…destined to attract many settlers by its richness…(where) divers peoples…come in hope of gain, seeking wealth from the rich land, a home, a fortune and a hearth-stone for themselves' (*ibid*, 129–30), while Altfrid's Life of St Liudger (839–49) refers to Frisian merchants expelled from the city and to a population large enough to raise an army (*ibid*, 131).

In this context the possibility of occupation in the Coppergate area reaching back into the 8th century would not be unexpected even though it has been hard to demonstrate conclusively. Some of the postholes, pits and other features which were observed in the Period 3 levels on the site might belong to the late 8th century but in the absence of clear dating evidence they might equally relate to the 9th century. Only three coins, two of Aethelred (c.841–4) (*AY* 18/1 25, 30) and one of Eanred (c.810–41) (*ibid*, 19) were found stratified in Period 3 deposits, all at the street frontage (Fig.325).

There is also an argument that some of the early alignments (e.g. 33239 and 36660) and/or pit-free zones (see Fig.150) attributed to Period 3 might indicate that small timber halls once stood on the high ground at what was to become the street end

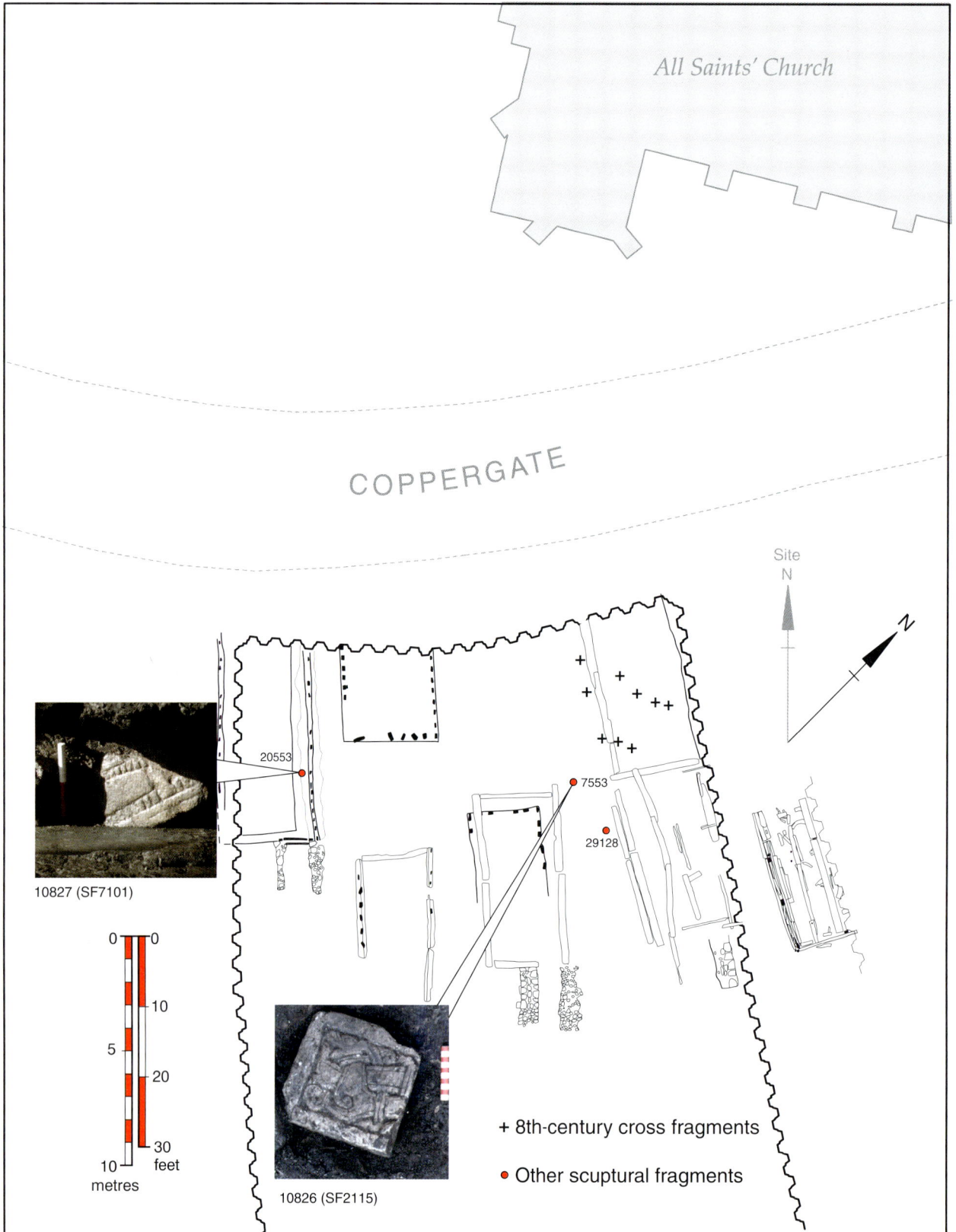

All Saints' Church

COPPERGATE

Site
N

20553

7553

29128

10827 (SF7101)

10826 (SF2115)

0
0

10

5
20

30
feet
10
metres

+ 8th-century cross fragments

● Other scuptural fragments

Fig.324 *The distribution of late 8th-/early 9th-century cross fragments and other sculptural fragments found at Coppergate in relation to All Saints' Church. Scale 1:250*

706

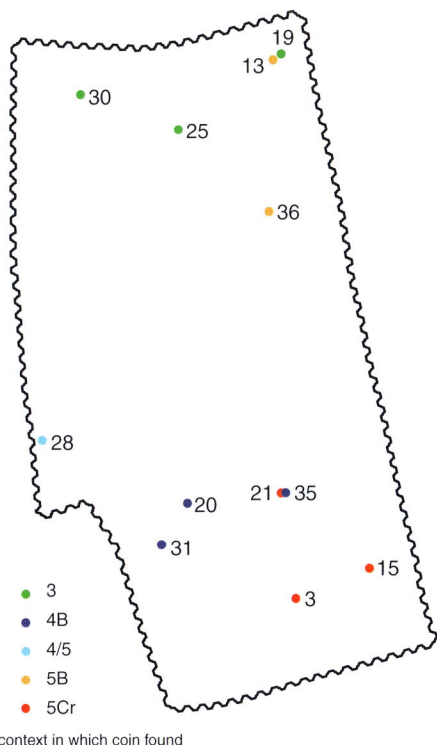

Fig.325 *Distribution of coins dating from before AD 850 found at Coppergate (the numbers are* AY *8/1 catalogue numbers). Scale 1:500*

of the site, but these are more likely to be 9th century in date, and one or two of these alignments presage what was soon to become the established layout of the site.

More precise chronology for the Anglian/Anglo-Scandinavian interface remains difficult; no coins were found on the site between those of Aethelred (c.841–48) (*AY* 18/1, *21, 25, 28, 30, 31*) and that of Cnut (c.895–903) (*ibid, 40*) and there are few other independent dates available. The composition of the ceramic assemblages recovered from Fishergate's Period 3c (early 9th century, *AY* 7/1, 10, table 1) and Coppergate's Period 3 barely overlap, suggesting that there was a real chronological difference between the two sites with a wholly new type of pottery (Handmade Type 1) occurring only at Coppergate – and only briefly there (*AY* 16/5, 396–8). Period 3c at Fishergate is associated with a shrinking settlement which came to an end soon after c.850, and this shrinkage might be linked with a more general re-focusing of settlement around the old Roman centre, perhaps corresponding with an intensifica-

tion of activity in the Coppergate area. Future excavations along the course of York's two rivers might well hold the key to understanding this progressive development.

Without a doubt the single most critical event in late 9th-century York was the arrival of the Viking Great Army and the capture of York in 866/67. 'York's attraction to the Scandinavian invaders was largely its wealth, which was generated by the manufacturing and trading activities of a growing population ... The extensive distribution of successive pottery types and artefacts groups, and the widespread occurrence of settlement, demonstrates how in the two centuries which followed (866–1066) the city grew and expanded into new areas' (Hall forthcoming).

Symeon of Durham records that the invading Vikings '... destroyed monasteries and churches far and wide with sword and fire, and when they departed they left nothing except roofless walls, to such an extent that the present generation can recognise hardly any sign – sometimes none at all – of the ancient nobility of these places' (*AY* 1, 71). Coin hoards deposited c.865 along Coney Street, at St Leonard's Place and Walmgate (*AY* 7/2, 207) all attest to the fear with which this attack was anticipated, and the same explanation might account for the presence of the Anglian helmet which, although made c.750–75, was deposited just to the west of the excavated area c.890 (*AY* 17/8, 1082). It was not until 894, almost 30 years after the arrival of the Great Army, that King Alfred made peace with the invaders (*AY* 1, 72).

Tangible archaeological evidence for these late 9th-century events is hard to recognise although if the latest possible dates for skeletons 36318 and 30944 are accepted (AD 885 and 880 respectively) (p.720) then they might, as Richard Hall first thought, represent 'victims of war or civil disturbance' in the turbulent years of the late 9th century (Hall 1984a, 47).

More settled conditions under the rule of the occupying army might well have been established before the political peace was agreed between Alfred and '...the pagans who inhabit Northumbria...' in 894 (*AY* 1, 72), but approximately 30 more years then elapsed before the property boundaries which characterise the Coppergate site were firmly established.

Fig.326 *a, Reconstruction of a wattle building; b, reconstruction of a post and plank building, Jorvik Viking Centre*

If the date of c.930/35 given for the beginning of Period 4B is correct, then this initial phase of buildings belongs to the period immediately following King Aethelstan of England's recapture of York in 927 (*AY* 1, 165–6). The Period 3 and 4A deposits, therefore, potentially span almost a century, between the early/mid-9th century and c.930/35 when the post and wattle buildings were constructed (Fig.326a). It is entirely possible, of course, that prior to this there was a focus of occupation on the strip of higher land to the north-west of the excavation between what are now the streets of High Ousegate and Coppergate, possibly associated with a precursor of All Saints' church, and that only the latrines and pits containing household debris (Fig.327), together with the enigmatic alignments referred to above, were located in the excavated area.

The establishment and layout of the post and wattle buildings, and their chronology, informs an understanding of the development of the street of Coppergate. The route of the water lane now called King Street (previously Cargate, *Kergathe* 1191 x 1210, *kjarr* meaning 'marsh', *AY* 8/4, 366) continues the line of Coppergate down to the river and runs parallel to Low Ousegate (see Fig.323). The latter linked High Ousegate to a new river crossing, presumably a bridge, which spanned the River Ouse to join with Micklegate on the south bank. The route of Coppergate runs parallel to High Ousegate for about 40m,

before bulging slightly to the south, reflecting the natural contours of the moraine at this point, and then changes course to join High Ousegate just beyond All Saints' church. There must have been a reason why Coppergate did not continue to run parallel to High Ousegate and perhaps the most likely is that such a course would have taken it onto low-lying land, prone to flooding. By joining with High Ousegate the thoroughfare was able to continue along the moraine, following the course taken by Pavement and St Saviourgate.

Modern Coppergate therefore has a curve (see Fig.323) which is mirrored by the arrangement of the Period 4B post and wattle structures along its street frontage, strong evidence that the route of the street was established around the time of their construction in the 930s. Taking the position of the hearths as being in the centre of these early structures, it is likely that they extended several feet beyond the shoring, implying that the Anglo-Scandinavian street was narrower, perhaps little more than a track. The curve might also reflect the position of an early graveyard associated with All Saints' church. Burials encountered in a narrow trench excavated to the south-west of the church have been dated to the 12th century (Zone 7; see Figs 131 and 323) but, as argued above, the area might have been used for burials since the 8th or early 9th century, and conceivably the burial ground might have pre-dated the church itself.

708

Fig.327   York ware cooking pot

Coppergate, therefore, could initially have served as a path around an early burial ground, linking occupation in the area with the river.

The street name Coppergate, formed from the Scandinavian occupational term *koppari* meaning cup maker or turner (*AY* 8/4, 365) combined with *gata*, meaning street, is not recorded until the 12th century, but the activity of wooden cup and bowl making goes back to Period 4B (*AY* 17/13, table 210) and this implies that the street might already have been recognised as a place of specialist production as early as the first half of the 10th century. There is, in fact, no evidence for large-scale wood turning on the site at the time of the first record of the name c.1120 x 1135 (*AY* 8/4, 364), supporting the case for an early coining of the street name.

By the beginning of the 10th century the Coppergate area was about to undergo a period of rapid growth and dynamic change. In little over a century from c.930–c.1030 a sequence of at least eighteen buildings had been erected, abandoned and replaced, their remains recorded during excavation or in the subsequent watching brief. Excavation and observation by archaeologists and antiquaries over the last century glimpsed the same pattern of development elsewhere in the Coppergate/Ousegate area (Fig.323) suggesting that this process of rapid development was replicated throughout the neighbourhood.

Amongst these eighteen buildings, four distinct building styles can be recognised (post and wattle structures; sunken-featured post and plank buildings; surface-laid structures; earth-fast timber buildings). The earliest – the post and wattle structures – were regularly repaired, refurbished and perhaps replaced during their currency (Table 29) and although they have fewer associated dendrochronological dates their construction is likely to be prior to the mid-950s. The identification of timbers derived from the same tree in buildings and fences in both Tenement B and D implies '... contemporaneous construction work in the mid-930s on these two tenements' (p.744), a premise which could reasonably be extended across all four tenements (Fig.328).

The post and wattle buildings are very close to one another, and each building is close to its respective boundary fences (see Fig.330a), a situation which gave rise to the challenges described above in distinguishing between alignments which are house walls from others which are fence lines. The apparently contemporary, even simultaneous, construction of the buildings suggests some measure of organised

Table 29   Dimensions of the Period 4B wattle buildings

	Length	Width	Floor level AOD
Tenement A	*c.*8.9m (incomplete)	*c.*3.8m (incomplete)	11.15–11.40m in north
Tenement B	*c.*8.5m (incomplete)	*c.*4.8m	11.10–11.40m in north; 10.70 and 10.90m in south
Tenement C	*c.*6.8m (incomplete)	*c.*4.2m	10.60–11.25m in north; 10.10–10.70m in south
Tenement D	*c.*7.8m (incomplete)	*c.*4.3m	10.60–11.10m in north; 9.95–10.50m in south

Fig.328   *Aerial view of Coppergate*

planning, perhaps by a single landowner. Whether any putative earlier settlement which might have existed on the higher ground between Ousegate and Coppergate was similarly well ordered, or whether the layout of these new buildings represents an attempt to rationalise an earlier more random arrangement, remains uncertain but such a rationalisation might have included a clearer definition of the street itself.

The occupation, repair and replacement of these post and wattle buildings continued thereafter, apparently uninterrupted by the frequent oscillations between English and Viking political control of the city which characterise the first half of the 10th century. The proliferation of domestic and specialised craft activity based in these dwellings-cum-workshops, with their concomitant need for regular interaction with the hinterland to ensure a supply of raw materials and a market for finished items, suggests the turbulent political events did not significantly damage the operation of commerce. Domestic activities including the maintenance of buildings, preparation of food and clothing, animal husbandry and horticulture in the backyards thrived alongside the more commercial pursuits of metal working (ferrous and non-ferrous), wood turning, amber

and jet working, leather working, bone and antler working, with some raw materials and individual items traded from Scandinavia and other parts of the Viking world (see list of publications on p.540). The continued expansion of the city at this time is charted through the widening distribution of 10th-century ceramic types (*AY* 8/4, fig.119), while the widely dispersed evidence for the operation of other crafts, on a more limited scale than seen at Coppergate (*ibid*, figs.121–8), supports the idea of a prosperous Jorvik citizenry going about its business.

Fig.329   *Coin dies and lead trial pieces*

710

Perhaps most startling of the finds from these early structures is the evidence for coin production (*AY* 18/1, 33–45). A fragmentary trial-piece of Aethelstan (*ibid, 48*), perhaps an episcopal issue of 927–31, was found in a Period 4A deposit in what was to become Tenement D, while one of the earliest Period 4B floor levels of Tenement C produced a die for a Sword St Peter penny (*ibid, 43*), the minting of which is conventionally dated to c.921–27. Further evidence for minting, including the Regnald trial-piece of Aethelstan (*ibid, 50*), current in York c.928–39, came from a later layer in that building together with a range of coins (*ibid, 20*, fig.4). Still more evidence for minting/die-cutting was recovered from the adjacent Tenement D (*ibid*) (Fig.329). These findings are presented and discussed by Pirie and Stewart (*ibid, 33–45*) and the significance of their recovery from apparently flimsy dwellings/workshops is still a matter of debate.

Rees Jones has recently remarked upon the importance of the old Roman *canabae* with its rectilinear pattern of street and burgage plots which largely ignored the earlier Roman pattern and suggests that '... after the late 9th century [the area] was resettled as a planned, market *burh* outside the walls of the former fortress' (Rees Jones 2013, 42), and it is true that the arrangement of the post and wattle buildings has a very regimented appearance perhaps developing from, or imposed upon, earlier occupation in the area. Their occupants – artisans, merchants, traders, perhaps even moneyers – were entrepreneurial and adventurous, bringing silks and other exotic items from the east, raw materials (stone, amber, walrus ivory and, doubtless, furs and skins) from Scandinavia, wine and quern stones from the Rhineland, and participating within the great trading networks of their day.

After approximately 25 years of usage, however, these post and wattle buildings went out of use, perhaps quite abruptly, signalling the end of this vibrant period and heralding the beginnings of Period 5.

What has been ascribed to Period 5A (c.975 in previously published literature) denotes an episode of upheaval before the next major phase of construction. Reconsideration of the dendrochronological dates for timbers recovered from this period allow for

this episode starting perhaps a decade or more earlier than previously thought. The new dates place the abandonment of the wattle buildings immediately before 955/56 which inevitably focuses attention on the politically turbulent 940s and 950s which culminated in the expulsion of Eric Bloodaxe in 954 (*AY* 1, 69). While the precise motivation, or the compulsion, behind the upheavals observed on site remains unclear, the timing might connect this episode with changes in land ownership in the aftermath of political and social turmoil. The fragments of the 8th-/9th-century cross referred to above (*AY* 17/14, *10825*) derive from dumping in the abandoned post and wattle building in Tenement D at this period, while the other sculptural fragments were recovered from deposits which immediately post-date these events (*10827* being in the east wall foundation of Structure 5/1) suggesting that burials, probably associated with All Saints' church, might have been disturbed at this time (see Fig.324).

On site, Period 5A is characterised by an episode of dumping, perhaps backfilling the abandoned structures, and there was a brief and temporary attempt to sub-divide Tenement B. Ephemeral traces of other alignments form no coherent structures although newly-dug cess pits suggest continued human habitation nearby and further rubbish pits were dug into and through the floors of the abandoned wattle buildings. The duration of the period is unclear but dendrochronological dates suggest that it might have been relatively brief (p.745).

These disruptions must inevitably have disturbed the economic activities of Coppergate's inhabitants, not least because for a period they lost their homes and a locus for their indoor activities. Any impact which might have been reflected through material culture, however, has been masked by the reworking of the Period 4B levels both during Period 5A and at the beginning of Period 5B when the sunken elements of the later buildings were dug out and the spoil upcast on the contemporary ground surface. Period 5A deposits cannot be traced into the backyard area where activities continued as in Period 4.

Rees Jones has recently reviewed what can be reconstructed regarding Anglo-Scandinavian land ownership in York in the decades prior to the Norman Conquest, based on urban estates or urban

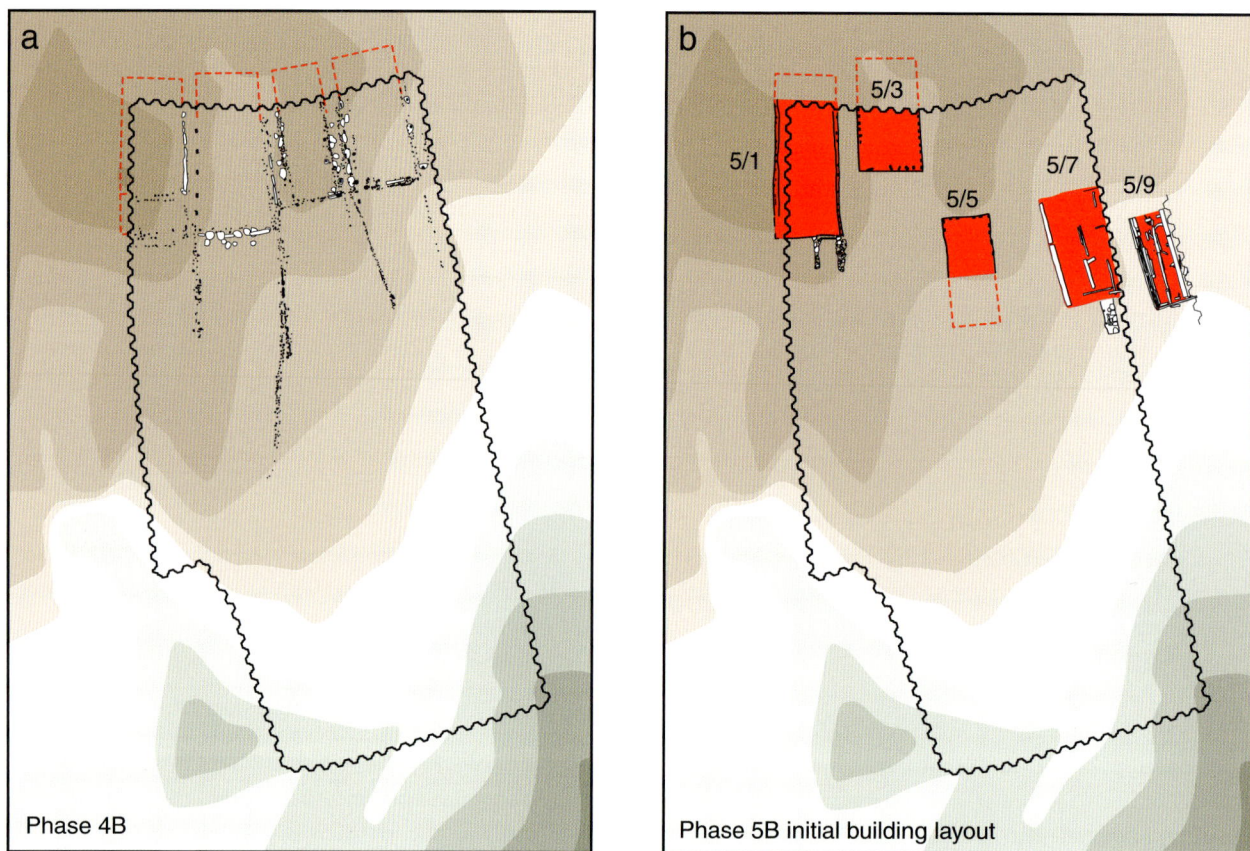

a

Phase 4B

b

5/3

5/1

5/5

5/7

5/9

Phase 5B initial building layout

Fig.330   Four phases of buildings on Coppergate. Scale 1:500

manors comprising landlords with their various sub-tenants and associated privately-endowed churches (Rees Jones 2013, 61–83). The Conquest inevitably brought about changes in ownership, some of which can be surmised from the Domesday records, when William's supporters were given control of tracts of the city as a reward for services and to ensure continuing loyalty. One such example includes the land on which the castle was to be built, and associated properties in the Castlegate area, which was given to the powerful Norman lord William Percy (*ibid*, 62–4). Perhaps the political upheavals of the mid-10th century are similarly reflected in Period 5A. What was observed on site might represent a change or even a temporary loss of control over land ownership during which time there was an attempt to sub-divide at least one of the plots. Following the departure of Eric Bloodaxe York became, in principle at least, part of the kingdom of England, with its rule entrusted to a series of earls sharing power with a succession of archbishops, and changes in land ownership might well be expected.

It is in this context that the next phases of buildings were erected on site. A wholly new type of structure, the sunken-featured post and plank buildings, were constructed from c.960 onwards (Fig.326b). While broadly consistent in style, the nine successive buildings erected on five tenements have some differing features and, on average, seem to have had a life span of 25–30 years although some, due to constructional problems or conflagrations, survived for a shorter period.

The neat arrangement of structures along the street frontage seen in Period 4B was apparently not re-established following Period 5A. The initial layout of Period 5B buildings in the 960s (Fig.330b) shows an uneven spread of construction, with some buildings (i.e. Structure 5/3) extending further into the street while others are set back with possibly vacant zones in front (as on Tenement C). Dendrochronological results allow for the buildings shown on Figure 330b to have been in use at the same time. Timber from the same trees being identified in more than

712

c

5/2

5/8

5/4

5/6

Phase 5B later building layout

d

5/10

5/13

5/11

5/12

Phase 5C building layout

>10.5m
>10m
>9.5m
>8.5m
>8m
>7.5m
>7m
>6.5m
>6m
>5.5m
>5m
>4.5m
>4m
>3.5m

Site
N

N

Building in use

Building possibly in use

0	10	20	30 metres
0	50		100 feet

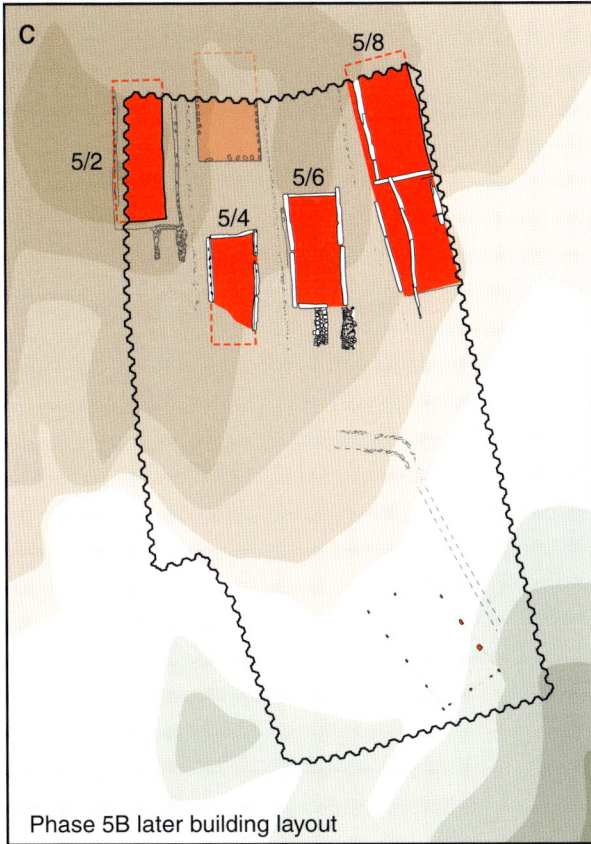

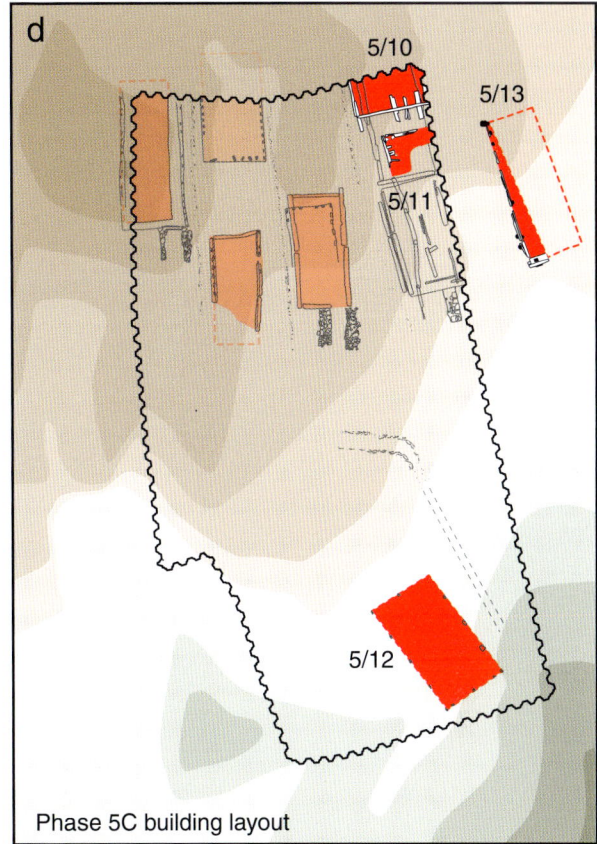

one building emphasises the co-operation involved in what appears to be a contemporaneous initial re-development with little attention paid to what went before, other than perpetuating the property boundaries and erecting structures gable end to the street. Only Structure 5/1 is positioned directly above the preceding post and wattle building while in every other case the initial footprint of the Period 5B buildings is different (Fig.330a and b). For one reason or another the early Period 5B buildings were successively replaced, and by c.980/990 the layout had changed to that shown on Figure 330c. Once again the front of Tenement C is left vacant and, depending on the longevity of Structure 5/3, the same might be true of Tenement B. On Tenement D, by contrast, a two-roomed building replaced the earlier structure with a front room extending into the street (Table 30) and with, for the first time, access through a side entrance into the rear room.

In London it has been suggested that smaller sunken-floored structures served as outhouses set behind principal buildings on the street frontage, and functioned as stores and workshops (Horsman *et al.* 1988). It is worth considering whether the same model might apply here and that this new configuration should be seen as evidence for very long backyards of properties which fronted onto High Ousegate rather than onto Coppergate. If that were the case then Coppergate would have been reduced in status to a thoroughfare cutting across these

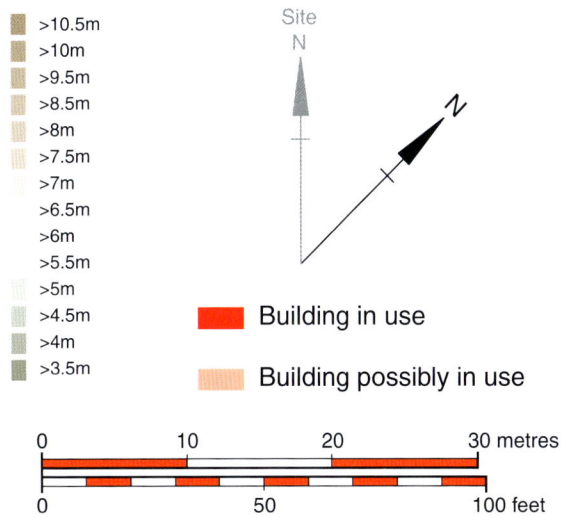

Table 30   Dimensions of the Period 5B and 5C sunken buildings

Structure	Length	Width	Surviving height	Depth of cut	Floor level AOD
Structure 5/1	c.9.0m (incomplete)	c.4.5m (incomplete)	c.0.8m upstanding wall	> 1.2m cut	c.11.05m
Structure 5/2	c.7.7m (incomplete)	c.2.6m (incomplete)	0	c.0.6m	c.11.60–11.70m
Structure 5/3	c.4.5m (incomplete)	c.4.25m	c.1.85m	c.1.2m	c.11.10–11.30m
Structure 5/4	c.8.0m (incomplete)	c.3.1–3.7m *	0.75m	c.1.0m	c.11.10–11.25m at north; c.10.50–10.75m at south
Structure 5/5	c.3.0m (incomplete)	c.3.1m	0.5m	At least 0.3m	c.10.26–10.33m (plank floor at north)
Structure 5/6	c.7.50m	c.3.70m	c.1.7m	> 1m	c.10.26–10.33m at north
Structure 5/7	c.7.3m	c.5.1m (incomplete)	0	c.1.20m	c.9.35m at base of cut
Structure 5/8 (front room)	c.6.6m (incomplete)	> 4.0m	0	0.6m	11.20–11.30m at north; 10.95–11.10m at south
Structure 5/8 (rear room)	c.7.50m (incomplete)	c.4.3m	0	0	Base of cut at c.10.6m
Structure 5/9	6.2m (incomplete)	2.65m (incomplete)	0.7m	0.7m	9.05m (plank floor)
Structure 5/10	c.2.7m (incomplete)	c.5m	0.25m	—	c.11.85–12.10m
Structure 5/11	c.2.5m (incomplete)	c.3.1m	? 0.25m	> 0.3m	? c.12m
Structure 5/12	c.8.2m	c.4.5m (incomplete)	0	0	Posts at c.7.15m (north) and c.7.1m (south)
Structure 5/13	10.05m (? incomplete)	1.55m (incomplete)	0.25m		? c.10.00m

* difference is between base of original and top of repaired wall

properties to link with the water lane (modern King Street) leading down to the River Ouse. While this explanation cannot be ruled out, there are very good arguments against it. Firstly, any burial ground associated with All Saints' church would have occupied at least some of the upper parts of these putative long properties with others abutting very closely to it (Fig.323). Secondly, the buildings encountered by George Benson in 1902–03 which lay between High Ousegate and Coppergate all appear to have been sunken-featured buildings (*AY* 8/4, 294), demonstrating that there at least this style of buildings occupied the street frontages rather than just the backyards. It seems, therefore, that the Coppergate Period 5B structures do indeed represent the principal buildings on properties which continued to be aligned to a Coppergate whose frontage might have been rather more raggedly defined than previously.

The more haphazard appearance of the street continued into the later 10th century. There are no dendrochronological dates to help elucidate the constructional sequence in Tenement A but at some point Structure 5/2 replaced Structure 5/1 which appears to have burned down; Structure 5/2 is sited slightly further to the west but over much of the same footprint (Fig.330c). On Tenement B, after only a few years (c.972/73), Structure 5/4 was erected behind Structure 5/3, and, as there is no reason to suppose that Structure 5/3 was not still standing, it appears that for a period the two buildings occupied different parts of the same plot. The situation on Tenement C is different again: after 10–30 years (somewhere between 970 and 997) Structure 5/5 suffered a fire and was replaced by Structure 5/6, whose footprint entirely covered that of Structure 5/5. The later building has one of the most complete examples of a revetted stone entranceway. The buildings on Tenement D have the most complex constructional history: Structure 5/7, which might have had a surface-built structure positioned in front of the sunken feature, was replaced 'in the very late 10th century' (p.748) by the two-roomed Structure 5/8 which occupied both the street frontage and the original second rank, but which stood for perhaps little more than a decade. Structure 5/9, although perhaps belonging to the initial layout, occupies a second rank position and no evidence survives for a structure in front of it.

Refurbishment, repair and reconstruction of the Period 5B buildings seem to have been almost continuous. Charred posts and planks suggest that fire, whether resulting from domestic or industrial mishap, or from social or political disturbance, played a role in driving these activities, while the difficulties presented by the terrain caused walls to slump, necessitating periodic reinforcement or replacement. Building over early pits and on sloping terrain combined to cause serious constructional problems for some of the builders, notably in the cases of the second rank Structures 5/4 and 5/6 where substantial repairs resulted in a confusing sequence of development.

Only a few years later, in Period 5C, two surface-laid structures (Structures 5/10 and 5/11) were built at the street frontage on Tenement D (Period 5Cf), Structure 5/13 replaced Structure 5/9 on a slightly different footprint, and an earth-fast structure (Structure 5/12) was built at the rear (Period 5Cr) (Fig.330d). Structure 5/10, which might have been arranged with its long axis as opposed to its gable end to the street, survives only as a fragment up against the shoring at the street frontage, replaced the front room of Structure 5/8, and soon afterwards the poorly preserved Structure 5/11 was built immediately behind it. Evidence for the re-use of timbers confuses the dating sequence but it is suggested that the construction of Structure 5/10 dates to after c.1008/09, while no dates are available for Structure 5/11.

The position and alignment of Structure 5/12 marks a completely new departure; it is the first building to be erected at the River Foss end of the site, an event which took place after a felling date of 1013–49 for some of the timbers used in its construction. It is also constructed in a different manner – from earth-fast timbers – perhaps within its own defined area, and begins a sequence of buildings on much the same footprint which continues into the post-Conquest period (*AY* 10/6, 730–42), perhaps

taking advantage of land reclamation noted during excavations at 22 Piccadilly (p.700). Elsewhere on the site, in the later 11th century, the evidence is more patchy but where it survives it suggests that occupation was at a reduced level.

Thus the century from c.930 to c.1030 was a remarkably dynamic period during which there had been only a single interruption (Period 5A) in a rapid sequence of development. Periods 4B to 5C span little more than two generations – a child born in a post and wattle building could conceivably have enjoyed old age in Structure 5/10 – and for much of the period the same activities continued to occupy the 10th- and early 11th-century inhabitants and artisans of 16–22 Coppergate. The distribution patterns left by craft-working debris are less easy to interpret with confidence as time goes by due to decades of deposit disturbance and the consequent problems of identifying and taking account of residuality but it seems that several of the earlier activities continued at a reduced scale. Evidence for precious metal working, for example, is less significant with more of an emphasis on copper-alloy working (*AY* 17/7, fig.327) and debris from other craft activities is generally reduced. Rees Jones remarks that by the medieval period the Coppergate/Ousegate area was '…a place of residence by some of the city's mercantile elite' (*AY* 10/6, 692), a situation that Loveluck sees as extending back into the 10th century, while recognising that the excavated structures are not ostentatious residences (Loveluck 2013, 314). The evidence suggests, however, that this was not a smooth upward progression – the glory days of high levels of production, of gold and silver smithing, moneyers and international trade belong to the second quarter of the 10th century (Period 4) and are diminishing by the third and fourth quarter (Period 5), a decline which might continue into the 11th century when occupation on the site becomes more difficult to follow and interpret.

Production might have been at a lesser scale, and the markets more local or regional, in the later 10th century but household chores and domestic activities including food preparation and textile working all continue. Glass working is one of the few new crafts to be identified in the later 10th century and early 11th century (*AY* 8/4, 474), with substantial evidence coming from 22 Piccadilly (p.700). In the course of the

10th century the ceramic assemblage changes from domination by small gritty York ware cooking pots to embrace the wider repertoire offered by the reduced sandy Torksey-type wares (Fig.331). This change brought the city into a ceramic province which extended from East Anglia up the eastern side of the country (AY 16/5, 442–4; Blinkhorn 2013, fig.10) where similar wares (i.e. Thetford-type wares and other local variants) drew on the same repertoire of forms and decoration, thus illustrating the diffusion of fashion and technology at this period. Experimentation with glazing also emphasises this awareness of technological developments and continued links with Europe (AY 16/5, 444–62).

The increasing density in the distribution of these later wares across the city bears witness to an expanding population (AY 8/4, figs 118–20). There is also now a growing body of Anglo-Scandinavian structural evidence outside the Coppergate/Ousegate area, although nothing comes close to the quality of the evidence and extraordinary preservation seen there. Settlement had spread in the course of the 10th century into what was to become the medieval Walmgate suburb where, for example at 41–49 Walmgate, traces of five timber buildings, dating from the mid-10th to the early 11th century were investigated (AYW 1) and occupation continued

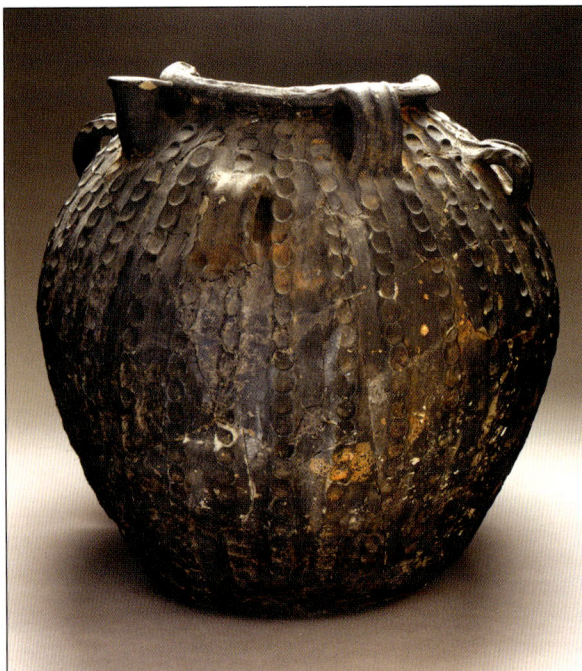

Fig.331   *Torksey ware pot*

along Lawrence Street (see Fig.322 for locations). Traces of structures and occupation have also been recovered on the south side of the River Ouse at Albion Wharf on Skeldergate and at 1–9 Micklegate which complement the burial and sculptural evidence recovered from St Mary Bishophill Junior and Senior (Lang 1991), lending some support to the idea of an early, possibly noble, enclave on the south bank (Palliser 1984, 103; Stocker 2000). The discovery in 2008 of Anglo-Scandinavian buildings of similar construction to those from Coppergate, within defined properties aligned to the street, in the low-lying area of Hungate adjacent to the River Foss (Connelly in prep.) all support an expansion of the city in the later 10th century. These new data add to more fragmentary examples published from both sides of the River Ouse in the 1980s and 1990s (AY 8/1 and 8/3; Hall forthcoming).

The opportunity to excavate, and subsequently observe, a large area in what was an important focus of the re-emergent city has given insights that would not have been achievable in a smaller investigation. Beyond what was recovered from within the main site, the excavations at 22 Piccadilly have located the Anglo-Scandinavian bank of the River Foss where the dumping of waste, numerous fences lines and deposits on and adjacent to the river suggest land stabilisation and/or land reclamation along the west bank of the river. More has also been learned about the lower reaches of the River Foss, close to its confluence with the Ouse, where the watching brief observed laid surfaces adjacent to the modern street of Castlegate – possible hard standing for the loading and unloading of boats; it is all too easy to forget the important role that the River Foss (as opposed to the Ouse) must have played in the lives of the residents of Coppergate. The better understanding of the Anglo-Scandinavian period gained from examining a wide swathe of land, the identification of old stream beds and the charting of the original slope of the land down to the river explains much about the layout of the streets, tenements and structures as well as the drains, gullies and other features preserved in the backyards.

The Coppergate excavations are not unique in terms of providing evidence for Anglo-Scandinavian occupation but they are unique in terms of the scope and quality of that evidence; the extraordinary preservation conditions and deep stratification produced results which continue to set Coppergate apart. Having sufficient time to excavate the site was the consequence of an economic recession, while the subsequent relatively favourable economic conditions allowed post-excavation work to adopt a careful and scholarly approach, supported generously by English Heritage and many other funding bodies. The excavation was hugely successful in engaging public interest on an international scale both during its 5½-year duration and afterwards, and this brought it many supporters, attracting worldwide media attention and leading to the permanent display and interpretation of the discoveries at the Jorvik Viking Centre – which has now welcomed over 17 million visitors.

This report concludes the current research on 16–22 Coppergate although the evidence collected and curated by York Archaeological Trust will provide invaluable research material for generations to come. The last words must be those of Richard Hall, the Director of Archaeology at York Archaeological Trust who oversaw excavation and post-excavation but who was fated not to complete what was the defining work of his career, a life-long commitment and endless fascination (see Hall publications in the Bibliography), to whom this volume is dedicated.

'Of course, there is still much to find out about the Viking Age city; key sites and topics – the Viking Age cathedral, the possible royal and aristocratic residences, the waterfronts, the defences, to name but a few of the most obvious – remain in obscurity. "The Viking Dig" is not an archaeological panacea; but it has been an exciting, ground-breaking, project which has re-written urban history, discovered the lost city of Jorvik and provided a benchmark for future studies of Viking Age towns in Britain ... There was never a dull day at the office on "The Viking Dig"' (Hall 2011, 191–2).

Radiocarbon Dating and Analysis
by Derek Hamilton (SUERC)

A total of 16 radiocarbon measurements are available on six samples of human bone from 16–22 Coppergate. The samples were submitted to the Scottish Universities Environmental Research Centre (SUERC) for radiocarbon dating by Accelerator Mass Spectrometry (AMS).

The samples were pretreated following a modified Longin (1971) method, and combusted as described in Vandeputte *et al.* (1996) with the graphite targets prepared and measured following Naysmith *et al.* (2010). The SUERC laboratory maintains rigorous internal quality assurance procedures, and participation in international inter-comparisons (Scott 2003) indicates no laboratory offsets, thus validating the measurement precision quoted for the radiocarbon ages.

The radiocarbon results are given in Table 31. These are conventional radiocarbon ages (Stuiver and Polach 1977), quoted according to the international standard set at the Trondheim Convention (Stuiver and Kra 1986), and calibrated with the internationally agreed curve of Reimer *et al.* (2009) using OxCal v4.2 (Bronk Ramsey 1995; 1998; 2001; 2009). For each sample, three aliquots were measured and the results were combined using a weighted mean (Ward and Wilson 1978), resulting in high-precision measurements with an error at 1σ of ±19 years. The date ranges in Table 31 have been calculated using the maximum intercept method (Stuiver and Reimer 1986) and are quoted in the form recommended by Mook (1986) with the endpoints rounded outward to 5 years where the errors are less than 25 years, and to 10 years where they are greater than or equal to 25 years. The probability distributions seen in Figures 332 and 334 were obtained by the probability method (Stuiver and Reimer 1993).

Methodological Approach

A Bayesian approach has been adopted for the interpretation of the chronology (Buck *et al.* 1996). Although the simple calibrated dates are accurate estimates of the dates of the samples, this is usually not what archaeologists really wish to know. It is the dates of the archaeological events represented by those samples which are of interest. In the case of the Coppergate burials, it is the overall chronology of the use of the site – when did burial activity begin, when did it end, and for how long did it take place – that is under consideration, not necessarily the dates of individual samples. The dates of this activity can be estimated not only using the scientific dating information from the radiocarbon measurements on the samples, but also by using the stratigraphic relationships between samples.

Fortunately, methodology is now available which allows the combination of these different types of information explicitly, to produce realistic estimates of the dates of archaeological interest. It should be emphasised that the *posterior density estimates* produced by this modelling are not absolute. They are interpretative *estimates*, which can and will change as further data become available and as other researchers choose to model the existing data from different perspectives.

The technique used is a form of Markov Chain Monte Carlo sampling, and has been applied using the program OxCal v4.2. Details of the algorithms employed by this program are available from the on-line manual or in Bronk Ramsey (1995; 1998; 2001; 2009). The algorithm used in the model described below can be derived directly from the model structure shown in Figure 332.

The Samples and the Model

As stated above, three aliquots were measured for each sample submitted. These aliquots were produced from a single homogeneous sample of CO_2 gas derived from combusted freeze-dried collagen.

The radiocarbon measurements from the three aliquots were combined prior to calibration using a weighted mean as described by Ward and Wilson (1978). Only in one instance (SK 36318) did the three measurements not pass the χ^2 test. Given that these measurements do pass at 3σ and are from the same homogeneous sample, they too have been combined to form **mean 1981.7 SK 36318**.

The combined result for SK 15548 (**mean 1981.7 SK 15548**) was thought to be too early given the archaeology. The burial was fully articulated in a context that contained 11th-century pottery, and which overlaid deposits containing 10th-century pottery. Furthermore, it was immediately below what were interpreted as Norman dumps. Given that the material has been around for many years and passed through several hands, there is no way of charting when/if material from these bodies might have been mixed. A fresh sample was submitted and the

Table 31 Radiocarbon dates from 16–22 Coppergate

Lab ID	Sample ID	Material	δ13C (‰)	δ15N (‰)	C:N	Radiocarbon Age (BP)	Calibrated Date (95% confidence)
SUERC-40423	1981.7 SK 36318 (Run 1)	human bone: rib	-21.1	11.6	3.2	1272 ± 32	
SUERC-41066	1981.7 SK 36318 (Run 2)	human bone: rib	-21.1	11.6	3.2	1138 ± 31	
SUERC-41223	1981.7 SK 36318 (Run 3)	human bone: rib	-21.1	11.6	3.2	1243 ± 31	
mean 1981.7 SK 36318		T′=10.1; ν=2; T′(5%)=6.0				1217 ± 19	**cal AD 715–885**
SUERC-40424	1981.7 SK 30944 (Run 1)	human bone: rib	-20.8	10.6	3.2	1251 ± 32	
SUERC-41067	1981.7 SK 30944 (Run 2)	human bone: rib	-20.8	10.6	3.2	1189 ± 31	
SUERC-41224	1981.7 SK 30944 (Run 3)	human bone: rib	-20.8	10.6	3.2	1246 ± 31	
mean 1981.7 SK 30944		T′=2.4; ν=2; T′(5%)=6.0				1228 ± 19	**cal AD 690–880**
SUERC-40428	1981.7 SK 30979 (Run 1)	human bone: scapula	-20.7	12.2	3.2	1305 ± 32	
SUERC-41068	1981.7 SK 30979 (Run 2)	human bone: scapula	-20.7	12.2	3.2	1253 ± 31	
SUERC-41225	1981.7 SK 30979 (Run 3)	human bone: scapula	-20.7	12.2	3.2	1264 ± 31	
mean 1981.7 SK 30979		T′=1.5; ν=2; T′(5%)=6.0				1273 ± 19	cal AD 670–780
SUERC-40429	1981.7 SK 15548 (Run 1)	human bone: rib	-21.0	10.2	3.2	1252 ± 32	
SUERC-41069	1981.7 SK 15548 (Run 2)	human bone: rib	-21.0	10.2	3.2	1159 ± 31	
SUERC-41226	1981.7 SK 15548 (Run 3)	human bone: rib	-21.0	10.2	3.2	1233 ± 31	
SUERC-48324	1981.7 SK 15548 (new sample)	human bone: rib	-20.4	10.5	3.2	1083 ± 38	**cal AD 880–1030***
mean 1981.7 SK 15548		T′=4.9; ν=2; T′(5%)=6.0				1214 ± 19	**cal AD 715–890**
SUERC-40430	1981.7 SK 32803 (Run 1)	human bone: cranium fragment	-21.2	10.8	3.2	1298 ± 32	
SUERC-41070	1981.7 SK 32803 (Run 2)	human bone: cranium fragment	-21.2	10.8	3.2	1239 ± 31	
SUERC-41230	1981.7 SK 32803 (Run 3)	human bone: cranium fragment	-21.2	10.8	3.2	1297 ± 31	
mean 1981.7 SK 32803		T′=2.3; ν=2; T′(5%)=6.0				1278 ± 19	**cal AD 670–780**

* this new, very different, measurement has not been included in the mean for skeleton 15548

result (SUERC-48324) is more consistent with the archaeology. Since both samples likely came from articulate human skeletons, albeit from different graves, both have been retained in the model as they provide important data regarding the overall start, end, and use of the site for burial.

The Bayesian model constructed for this site only assumes that the five burials come from a general period of activity that is relatively continuous. This period of activity, therefore, has both an unknown start and end date, and an unknown duration; these can be estimated using the radiocarbon measurements.

Results

The model has good agreement between the radiocarbon measurements and the model assumptions (A_{model}=96).

The model estimates that burial at 16–22 Coppergate began in *cal AD 5350–775* (*95% probability*; Fig.332; *start: Coppergate*) and probably in *cal AD 655–755* (*68% probability*). The activity persisted for *10–535 years* (*95% probability*; Fig.333; *use: Coppergate*) and probably for *135–375 years* (*68% probability*). Burial activity ended in *cal AD 780–1120* (*95% probability*; Fig.332; *end: Coppergate*) and probably in *cal AD 890–1025* (*59% probability*).

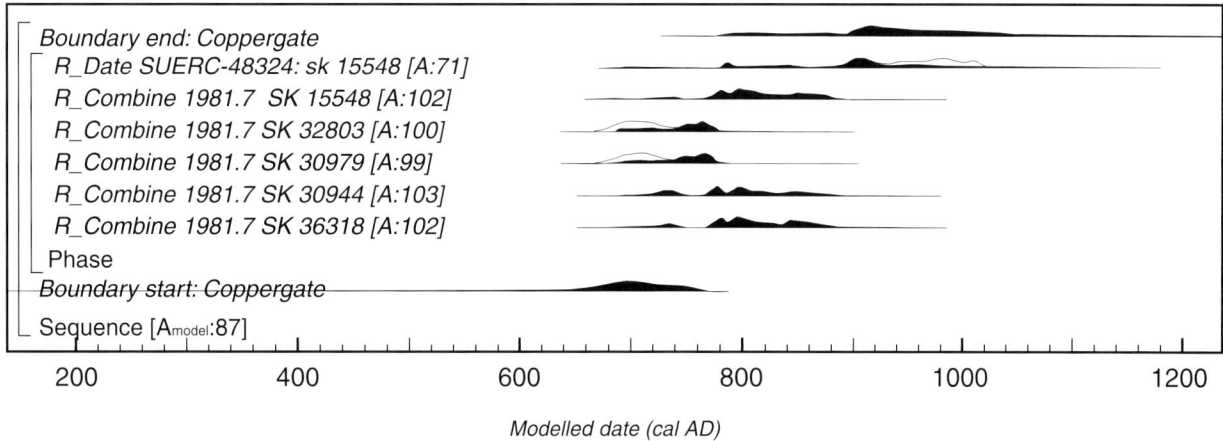

Fig.332 *Chronological model for 16–22 Coppergate. Each distribution represents the relative probability that an event occurred at some particular time. For each of the radiocarbon measurements two distributions have been plotted, one in outline, which is the result of simple radiocarbon calibration, and a solid one, which is based on the chronological model use. The other distributions correspond to aspects of the model. For example, 'start: Coppergate' is the estimated date that burial activity began at the site, based on the radiocarbon dating results. The large square 'brackets' along with the OxCal keywords define the overall model exactly*

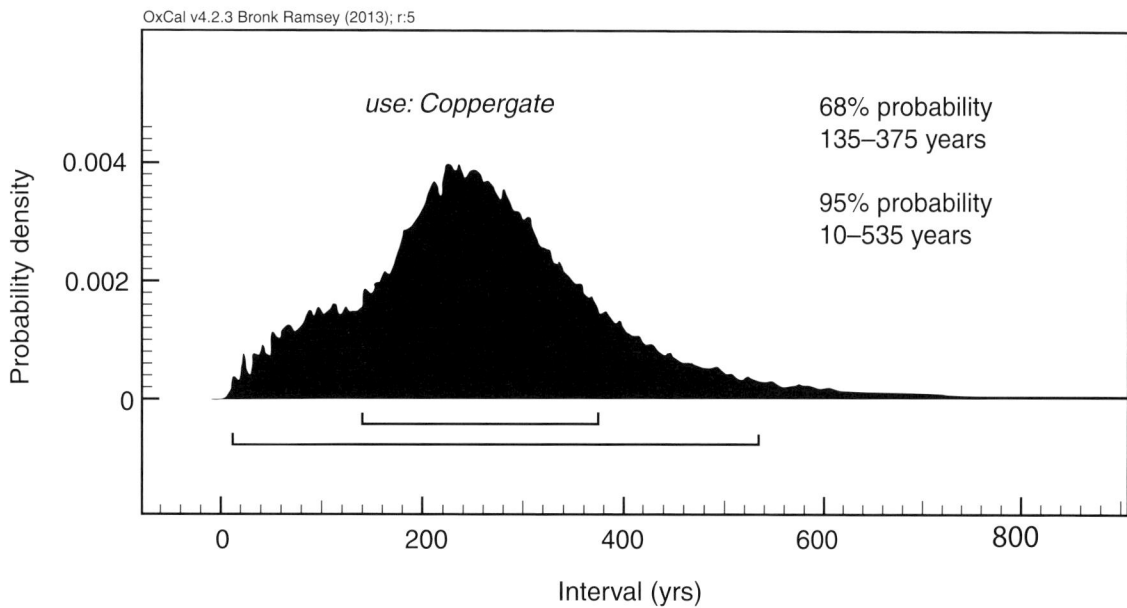

Fig.333 *Span of burial activity at 16–22 Coppergate, as derived from the chronological model in Figure 332*

Discussion

The estimated date probabilities for the start and end of activity at 16–22 Coppergate are likely to be overestimates, especially at 95% probability. The low number of measurements in the model results in lower precision than one might otherwise expect (Steier and Rom 2000). This is further complicated by the fact that the measurements all fall on a portion of the radiocarbon calibration curve that is characterised by a deep wiggle (Fig.334). This can often have the effect of further 'smearing' the results as the radiocarbon age intersects with multiple portions of the calibration curve. The 68% probability ranges are likely more representative of the timing and duration of burial activity.

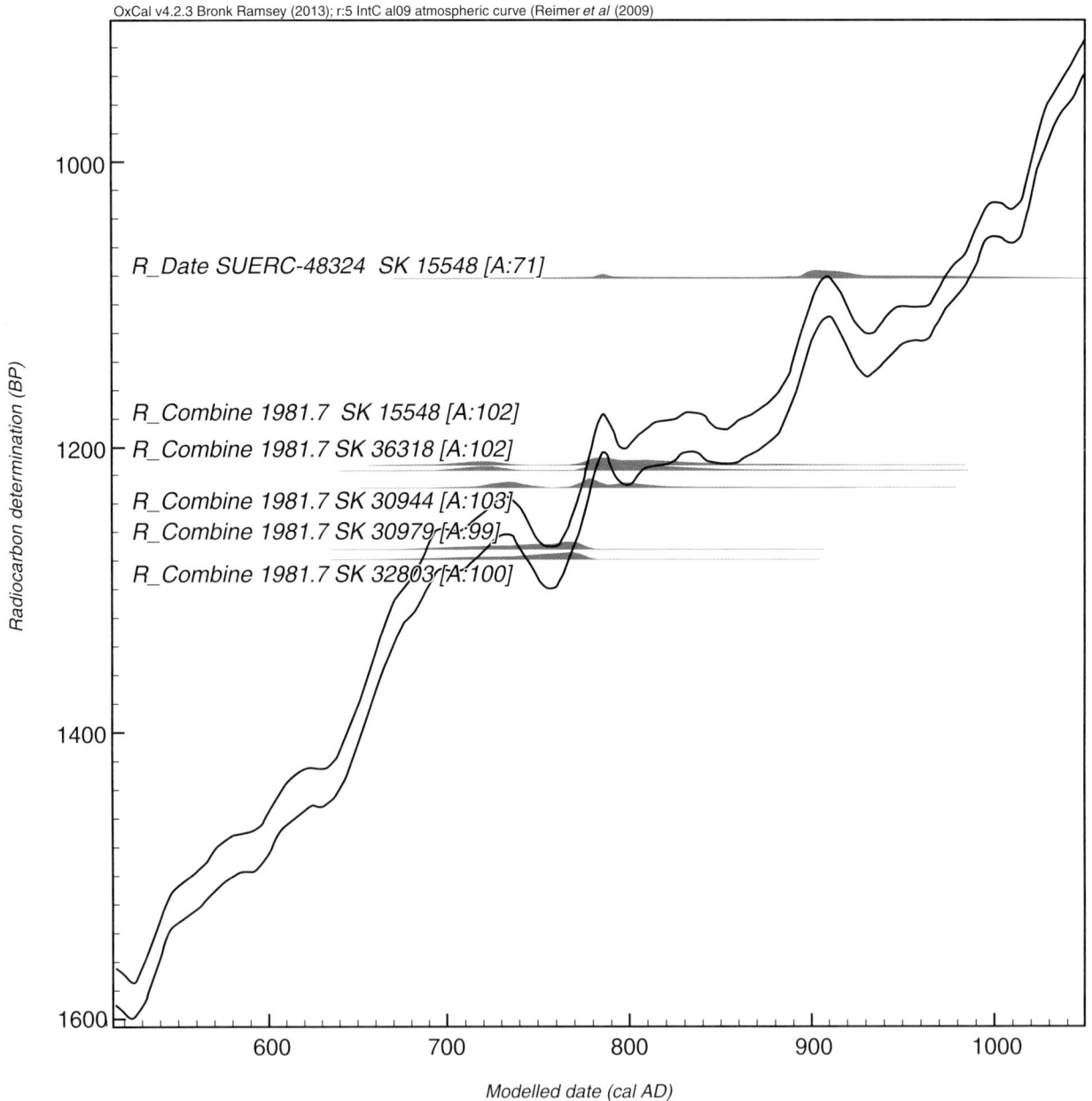

Fig.334   *Plot of the radiocarbon dates against the IntCal09 calibration curve. This plot shows that the dates lie in the area of a wiggle in the curve, which, along with the low number of samples (Steier and Rom 2000), serves to limit the precision of the final results*

722

Osteological Analysis

by Malin Holst, York Osteoarchaeology Ltd

Please note: True North as opposed to Site North is used in this report.

Introduction

The four skeletons which are the subject of this report were recovered during archaeological excavations at 16–22 Coppergate in advance of re-development of the site. At the time this report was initially written, the skeletons were thought to date to the 9th century AD, the Anglo-Scandinavian period, but recent radiocarbon dating has produced dates which allow for the possibility of three of them being earlier (see Fig.146 and Table 31). The aim of the skeletal analysis was to determine the age, sex and stature of the skeletons (Table 33), as well as to record and diagnose any skeletal manifestations of disease and trauma.

It is thought that the population of Anglo-Scandinavian Jorvik was between 9,000 and 18,000 (Hall 1994, 42). Very few remains of the inhabitants of Jorvik have been excavated and, as a result, the skeletons found at Coppergate provide a vital insight into life in the city during this and the preceding period. The few other examples that have been found were at St Mary Bishophill Junior, where two skeletons were interred with grave goods indicative of the late 9th or early 10th century (*AY* 8/2).

Further skeletons at this site and at St Mary Bishophill Senior may also date to the Anglo-Scandinavian period, though their date is less certain (Hall 1994, 45). The 131 early phase skeletons from St Andrew's, Fishergate, date from around the Norman Conquest (*AY* 12/2). Prior to the construction of the Norman Minster in York, a cemetery went out of use beneath it, which contained 155 skeletons dating to the Anglo-Scandinavian period (Hall 1994).

Three of the skeletons from Coppergate were found in close proximity to one another. Skeleton 30944 was complete, though partly disturbed (Table 32) and had been buried in a large pit, either with associated clothing or within a shroud. The skeleton lay with the skull to the north-east in a supine and semi-flexed position, with the left arm bent upwards and the left hand behind the head. Skeleton 30979 lay on a slope or in a large cut only 1.8m from Skeleton 30944; unfortunately the majority of this skeleton was inaccessible. It appears that this individual lay with the head to the south and that the arm was bent in a similar manner to that of Skeleton 30944. The disarticulated remains of Skeleton 36318 were found in a pit 7m to the south of these two burials. Although this pit also dates to the 9th century, as did the features containing the other two skeletons, it is possible that the remains of this individual had been disturbed and removed from an earlier grave.

Table 32 Summary of archaeological information of complete skeletons

Skeleton No	Position	Orientation	Artefacts	Feature Type	Date
15548	Supine, extended. Right arm flexed across abdomen, left arm flexed across lower chest	East–west	None	No cut	cal AD 880–1030
30944	Supine, right leg partly disarticulated; left hand behind skull, right arm flexed beside right side of body, left leg extended, right leg semi-flexed	North-east–south-west	Textile remains adhering to mandible, over chest and below vertebrae and scapulae	Pit	cal AD 690–880
30979	Supine, only parts of left arm, with the upper arm extended beside the head and the forearm bent at an angle to it	South–north	None	Slope or pit	cal AD 670–780
36318	Disarticulated – skull on its side beside the humeri and ribs	—	None	Pit	cal AD 670–780

Finally, Skeleton 15548 was partly truncated by shoring and was located some distance from the others, in close proximity to the River Foss. This individual was buried more formally in a supine and extended position on an east to west orientation, although there was no trace of a grave (see Table 32). It is thought that this burial might be slightly later, dating from the late 9th to early 11th century AD; this has been confirmed by the recent scientific dating.

Notably, five skeletons from nearby Spurriergate were also found in pits. Two of these burials were radiocarbon dated to around AD 760, pre-dating the Viking conquest of York (Holst 2005). The skeletons were buried in south to north or north to south orientations. Three were laid out supine and extended, one was flexed on the right and the fifth burial had been disturbed and was disarticulated, but had probably been prone. It is likely that all of these burials date to the same period.

Osteological analysis

Osteological analysis is concerned with the determination of the demographic profile of the assemblage based on the assessment of sex, age and non-metric traits. This information is essential in order to determine the prevalence of disease types and age-related changes. It is also crucial for identifying sex dimorphism in occupation, lifestyle and diet, as well as the role of different age groups in society.

Preservation

Skeletal preservation depends upon a number of factors, including the age and sex of the individual as well as the size, shape and robusticity of the bone. Burial environment, post-depositional disturbance and treatment following excavation can also have a considerable impact on bone condition. Preservation of human skeletal remains is assessed subjectively, depending upon the severity of bone surface erosion and post-mortem breaks, but disregarding completeness. Preservation is important, as it can have a large impact on the quantity and quality of information that it is possible to obtain from the skeletal remains.

Surface preservation, concerning the condition of the bone cortex, was assessed using the seven-category grading system defined by McKinley (2004), ranging from 0 (excellent) to 5+ (extremely poor). Excellent preservation implies no bone surface erosion and a clear surface morphology, whereas extremely poor preservation indicates heavy and penetrating erosion of the bone surface resulting in complete loss of surface morphology and modification of the bone profile. The degree of fragmentation was recorded, using categories ranging from 'minimal' (little or no fragmentation of bones) to 'extreme' (extensive fragmentation, with bones in multiple small fragments). Finally, the completeness of the skeletons was assessed and expressed as a percentage: the higher the percentage, the more complete the skeleton.

The bone condition in three of the skeletons was excellent (Grade 0), without surface erosion while the fourth skeleton had moderate bone preservation, with some surface erosion (Table 33); a full catalogue of osteological and palaeopathological results can be found online at www.yorkarchaeology.co.uk). Little fragmentation was observed in any of the skeletons. However, they were of varying completeness, between 5% and 95% complete.

Minimum number of individuals

A count of the 'minimum number of individuals' (MNI) recovered from a cemetery is carried out as standard procedure in osteological reports on inhumations in order to establish how many individuals are represented by the articulated and disarticulated human bones (without taking the archaeologically defined graves into account). The MNI is calculated by counting all long bone ends, as well as other larger skeletal elements recovered. The largest number of these is then taken as the MNI. The MNI is likely to be lower than the actual number of skeletons which would have been interred on the site, but represents the minimum number of individuals which can be scientifically proven to be present.

The MNI was four, with four left humeri and scapulae recovered.

Assessment of age

Age was determined using standard ageing techniques, as specified in Scheuer and Black (2000a; 2000b) and Cox (2000). For non-adults, age estimation is based on dental development and eruption, skeletal development (epiphyseal fusion) and long bone lengths (Scheuer and Black 2000b). In adults, age estimation largely relies on the presence of the pelvis and ribs and uses different stages of bone development and degeneration in order to calculate the age of an individual. It can be supplemented though the examination of dental wear (Brothwell 1981).

Table 33 Summary of osteological and palaeopathological results

Skeleton No	Preservation			Age	Sex	Stature (cm)	Dental Pathology	Pathology
	SP	F	C					
15548	0 (Excellent)	Excellent	70%	46+	F	159.32	Calculus, caries, periodontitis, lower left incisor rotated, duplication of upper left second incisor (supernumerary teeth)	Schmorl's nodes, spinal DJD, DJD in clavicles, ribs, scapulae, right first metacarpal, right 5th hand phalanx, right trapezium, hips, right proximal femur, osteoarthritis in right hip, right proximal femur, left distal femur, left proximal tibia, sacrum and L5, congenital hip dysplasia on right side, atrophy of right hip, femur, tibia and fibula, *coxa vara*, spinal congenital anomalies, periosteal reaction at right fibula, bone excavations, enthesopathies
30944	0 (Excellent)	Good	95%	36–45	M	161.5	Calculus, periodontitis, three dental abscesses	Schmorl's nodes, DJD in spine, left scapula, right proximal ulna, hips, ribs, osteoarthritis in T2, T3, L5 and sacrum, bilateral *os acromiale*, congenital anomalies of the spine, manubrium, sacrum, *coxa vara*, periosteal reactions at tibiae and fibulae, *osteochondritis dissecans* at calcanei, bone excavations, enthesopathies
30979	0 (Excellent)	Good	5%	19+	M	173.63	—	Ischemia at ulnar ligament of left humerus, bone excavations
36318	2 (Moderate)	Good	25%	19–25	F	163.47	Calculus	Schmorl's nodes, *cribra orbitalia*, bone excavation

* Preservation: SP = surface preservation, graded according to McKinley (2004); F = fragmentation; C = completeness

Age is split into a number of categories: foetus (up to 40 weeks *in utero*), neonate (around the time of birth), infant (newborn to one year), juvenile (1–12 years), adolescent (13–17 years), young adult (ya; 18–25 years), young middle adult (yma; 26–35 years), old middle adult (oma; 36–45 years), mature adult (ma; 46+), and adult (an individual whose age could not be determined more accurately than that he/she was 18 or over).

Skeleton 15548 was a mature adult (46+ years) who exhibited moderate dental wear, but whose auricular surface and pubic symphysis of the hip suggested a mature age. This was corroborated by widespread degenerative joint disease (DJD).

The age of Skeleton 30944 was more difficult to assess accurately, as the ageing criteria suggested different ages. The dental wear, rib ossification and left auricular surface suggested an age of 36–45 years, whereas the right auricular surface and the pubic symphyses suggested an age of 26–35 years. Considering the widespread degenerative

joint disease in this individual, it was decided that the older age was more plausible, indicating that this was an old middle adult.

It was also difficult to determine the age of Skeleton 30979, as this individual was only represented by one humerus and a scapula. Considering the fact the humerus was fully fused, this individual was aged 19 years old (the earliest age at which a humerus is fully fused; Scheuer and Black 2000b) or older and was therefore an adult.

Skeleton 36318 was a young adult, with a fusing epiphysis of the proximal left humerus, while the right side was still unfused. The humerus fuses between the ages of 16 and 22 years (*ibid*). Parts of the scapula, which fuse between c.18 and 23 years (the acromion processes, borders and angles, *ibid*), had completed development. The fusion suggested that this individual was a young adult, aged between 19 and 25 years. The minimal dental wear observed was also consistent with a young adult age.

Sex determination

Sex determination was carried out using standard osteological techniques, such as those described by Mays and Cox (2000). Assessment of sex relies on the preservation of the skull and the pelvis and can only be carried out once sexual characteristics have developed, during late puberty and early adulthood.

The skull and pelvis suggested that Skeleton 15548 was female. The skeletal measurements implied that she was more robustly built than the average female, but was within the lower range of the undetermined measurements, with the exception of the clavicles, which were as long as those of an average male. The relatively robust nature of her arms may have been related to her pathology, which will be discussed below.

Skeleton 30944 was male, as determined using the skull and pelvis. However, his bone measurements suggested that he was relatively gracile, with very short clavicles for a male.

The sex of Skeleton 30979 could only be estimated based on the size of the humeral head and scapula glenoid. Considering the relatively robust nature of the female and gracile nature of the male, this cannot be considered reliable. However, while the scapula was in the undetermined measurement range, the humeral head suggests a male.

The skull shape and single possible measurement to determine sex of Skeleton 36318 indicated a female, though the young age and the fact that the bones were still fusing would have affected their size and shape.

Metric analysis

Stature depends on two main factors, heredity and environment; it can also fluctuate between chronological periods. Stature can only be established in skeletons if at least one complete and fully fused long bone is present, but preferably using the combined femur and tibia. The bone is measured on an osteometric board, and stature is then calculated using a regression formula developed on individuals of known stature (Trotter 1970).

It was possible to determine the stature of all four skeletons. Skeleton 15548 (mature adult female) was 159.32cm (±3.72cm) tall, based on the length of her left femur. The second female, Skeleton 36318 (young adult female) was 163.47cm (±4.45cm) tall. The female average height was 161cm (5ft 3½in) in the early medieval period, with a range of 152–170cm (Roberts and Cox 2003, 195). Nevertheless, both females were close to the early medieval average in height. The late 8th-century female skeleton from Spurriergate in York was 161.8cm tall (Holst 2005).

The males also differed in height. The more gracile male, Skeleton 30944 (old middle adult) was 161.51cm (±2.99cm) tall, while the incomplete adult male Skeleton 30979 was 173.63cm (±4.05cm) tall. The male mean stature for the early medieval period was 172cm (or 5ft 7¾in), with a range of 170–182cm. While the height of Skeleton 30979 height was close to the early medieval mean, the height of the old middle adult Skeleton 30944 was considerably lower, even than the range of skeletal heights of 996 males from the early medieval period in Roberts and Cox's study (2003, 195).

Measurements of the femora and tibiae are used to calculate the shape of the shafts (Bass 1987). In femora this is termed the meric index, and in tibiae it is the cnemic index. It was only possible to calculate these indices in Skeletons 15548 and 30944. The femora of Skeleton 15548 were different in shape, with the left, healthy bone, being platymeric (broad or flat), while the right femur, which was affected by pathology discussed below, was stenomeric, a shape that is elongated anterior-posteriorly and is usually seen only in pathological cases. The femora of Skeleton 30944 were also different in shape, although neither was affected by pathology. The right femur was platymeric (broad and flat), while the femur leg was eurymeric (more rounded). The right tibia of Skeleton 15548 was mesocnemic (moderately broad), as was the right tibia of Skeleton 30944, while his left tibia was broad (eurycnemic).

The three skeletons whose cranial shape could be measured had very differently shaped skulls. Skeleton 15548 (mature adult female) had a narrow skull (doliocrany), Skeleton 30944 (old middle adult male) had an average shaped head (mesocrany) and Skeleton 36318 (young adult female) had a broad or round head (brachycrany).

Non-metric traits

Non-metric traits are additional sutures, facets, bony processes, canals and foramina, which occur in a minority of skeletons and are believed to suggest hereditary affiliation between skeletons (Saunders 1989). The origins of non-metric traits have been extensively discussed in the osteological literature and it is now thought that while most non-metric traits have genetic origins, some can be produced by factors such as mechanical stress (Kennedy 1989) or environment (Trinkhaus 1978). A total of 30 cranial (skull) and 30 post-cranial (bones of the body and limbs) non-metric traits were selected from the osteological literature (Buikstra and Ubelaker 1994, Finnegan 1978, Berry and Berry 1967) and recorded.

Cranial traits were observed in Skeletons 15548, 30944 and 36318. These included ossicles at pterion (an extra bone on the temple) in Skeletons 15548 and 36318. Skeletons 30944 and 36318 both had incomplete foramen ovale (a small hole at the base of the skull that is split into two). Skeleton 30944 also had ossicle in the lambdoid suture (additional small bone at the back of the head), mastoid foramen extrasutural (a small hole near the ear), a precondylar tubercle (a small protrusion at the base of the skull) and bridging of the supraorbital notch (variation in the shape of the area above the orbit). Skeleton 36318 had parietal foramen (additional small hole towards the back of the head), a double anterior condylar canal (small hole at the base of the skull split into two), accessory lesser palatine foramina (variation in the number of small holes towards the back of the palate) and absent zygomaticofacial foramen (lack of a small hole in the zygomatic bone).

Shared post-cranial traits included bipartite transverse foramina (variation in the shape of holes in the neck vertebrae) in Skeletons 15548 and 30944, and posterior atlas bridging (an extra bony bridge) in Skeletons 30944 and 36318. Skeleton 15548 also had septal aperture (a foramen in the distal humerus), an acetabular crease (a fold in the hip joint), exostosis in trochanteric fossa (a protrusion of bone at a muscle attachment at the proximal femur) and a large third trochanter (a bony lump at the attachment site of the muscle *gluteus maximus* at the femur). Skeleton 30944 had a vastus notch and vastus fossa (notch and depression in the side of the patella), a peroneal tubercle (protruding bone on the medial side of the calcaneus) and absent anterior calcaneal facets (a lack of the anterior facet of the calcaneus).

Conclusion

The osteological analysis of the skeletal remains established that the skeletons excavated from Coppergate comprised a young adult female (Skeleton 36318) and a mature adult female (Skeleton 15548), both of whom were of average height for the early medieval period. Skeleton 15548 was of relatively robust build, though this might have been related to her pathology, discussed below. The pathological conditions also affected the shape of her right thigh bone.

There were also two male adults, one of whom could not be aged beyond stating that this was an adult (Skeleton 30979), while the other male was an old middle adult (Skeleton 30944). While Skeleton 30979 was of average height for the period, Skeleton 30944 was shorter than any of the early medieval skeletons included in Roberts and Cox's (2003) study and was of gracile build. Although the two females and old middle adult male shared some non-metric traits, these were too limited to make suggestions about genetic relationships between the different individuals.

Pathological analysis

Pathological conditions (disease) can manifest themselves on the skeleton, especially when these are chronic conditions or the result of trauma to the bone. The bone elements to which muscles attach can also provide information on muscle trauma and excessive use of muscles. All bones were examined macroscopically for evidence of pathological changes.

Congenital conditions

The embryological development of an individual can be affected by heredity and the environment, leading to the development of a congenital defect or anomaly (Barnes 1994). The most severe defects are not usually seen in archaeological populations as affected babies are usually miscarried or stillborn, or die shortly after birth. However, less severe developmental anomalies are frequently observed in archaeological populations, and in many cases the affected individual will not have been aware of their condition. The frequency with which these minor anomalies occur may provide information on the occurrence of the severe expressions of these defects in the population concerned (*ibid*). The prevalence of minor anomalies may also inform on maternal health, as poor maternal health can lead to increased frequencies of developmental anomalies (Sture 2001).

Congenital hip dysplasia

A severe congenital defect was the congenital dislocation of the hip of the mature adult female Skeleton 15548. Congenital hip dysplasia (CHD) is characterised by the

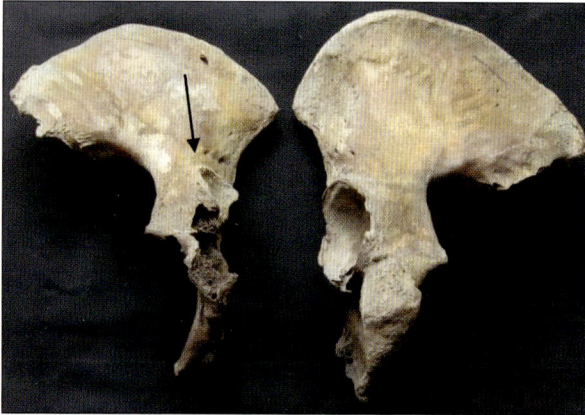

Fig.335   *Skeleton 15548: right hip affected by hip dysplasia, and healthy left hip*

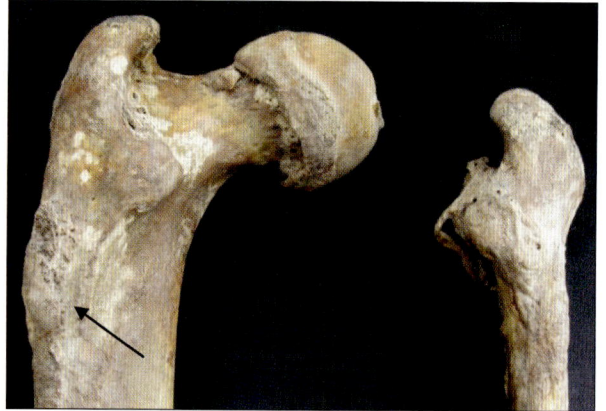

Fig.336   *Skeleton 15548: healthy left femur with muscle trauma and right femur with CHD from the posterior*

loss of the normal relationship between the femur and pelvis at the hip joint. CHD is a genetic disorder, which can be treated today, but in antiquity the condition was often not recognised until the child began to walk, when it was too late for treatment (Roberts and Manchester 1995, 38). As a result, the hip joint becomes displaced, which is subsequently exacerbated by muscle action and can cause an abnormal gait, as well as constant pain (*ibid*). The condition creates false hip joints, flat and oval femoral heads and shortened femoral necks (Aufderheide and Rodríguez-Martín 1998, 69). In Skeleton 15548, the right hip was affected (Fig.335). This had led to the formation of a new hip joint that was half circle shaped and slightly concave and was located supero-laterally to where a normal acetabulum would be. The femoral head and the neck of the femur was not formed (Fig.336) and instead the femur articulated with the hip at the point where normally the intertrochanteric line would be. Although an alternative diagnosis to congenital hip dysplasia must be slipped femoral epiphysis (stress fracture of the femoral neck with downward movement of the femoral head), this is unlikely to have been the case, as no evidence of any original acetabulum could be observed.

The female suffered from considerable secondary complications to the condition. The pseudoarthrosis (newly formed joint) displayed severe eburnation, indicative of osteoarthritis, both at the pelvis (Fig.337) and at the femur. It is clear that the right leg was hardly used, leading to severe atrophy (wasting) of the entire right femur (see Fig.336; including the distal epiphysis), tibia, fibula and also the pelvis. The left leg, on the other hand, seemed much more robust than normal (see Fig.336) and weighed considerably more than the right bone, giving an indication of the much greater bone density in the left

femur. The left femur exhibited muscle trauma in the form of a severe enthesopathy (bony spur at the site of a muscle attachment which can be caused by trauma) for *gluteus maximus*, the main muscle of the bottom that moves the hip (see Fig.336). The proximal femoral shaft was unusually broad medio-laterally. The distal joint with the tibia displayed a tiny area of eburnation, indicative of osteoarthritis, as did the left proximal tibia. The right hip was smaller, lighter and generally diminished compared to the left side (see Fig.335). The evidence suggested that the left leg was used extensively and much strain was put on this limb. The bones of the arms and shoulders were well developed and more robust than those of the average female, suggesting, perhaps, the use of crutches. The spine exhibited unilateral degenerative joint disease on the right side, which was probably associated with the hip dislocation and also the possible use of a crutch or other walking aid.

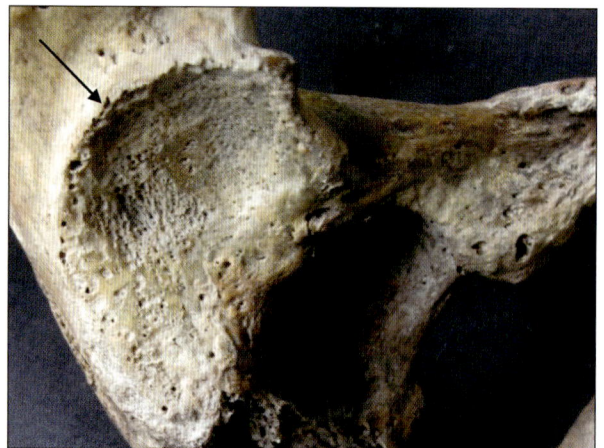

Fig.337   *Skeleton 15548: eburnation and porosity (osteoarthritis) at newly formed hip joint*

CHD tends to be more common in females than males, and occurs most frequently on the left side (Anderson 2000, 213). Early medieval examples of the condition include a male adult from the Golden Minster, St Oswald in Gloucester (Rogers 1999), and another male from Nazeingbury in Essex (Puttnam 1978). Later medieval examples include a middle adult female from Hull Magistrates Court (Holst *et al* 1998) who suffered from bilateral hip dysplasia. An adult female from Jewbury in York had bilateral congenital hip dysplasia, the appearance of which was very similar to the Coppergate case, with atrophy (wasting) of both legs (Brothwell and Browne 1994).

Coxa vara

Coxa vara is a condition where the neck of the femur is short and horizontal and the head of the femur lies below the greater trochanter. It is not present at birth, but develops slowly due to a congenital ossification defect of the femoral neck (Salter 1999). Its cause is still debated, but it may be secondary to rickets, hypothyroidism and osteomalacia (Aufderheide and Rodríguez-Martín 1998, 74). As a result of the defect, the muscles of the hip cannot hold the pelvis level during walking and the individual will have a lurching (although painless) type of limp (Salter 1999). Both Skeletons 15548 (mature adult female) and 30944 (old middle adult male) had *coxa vara*. In Skeleton 15548 only the left side was affected by *coxa vara*, with a horizontal femoral neck. The right side was distorted as a result of the congenital hip dysplasia. Both femoral necks of Skeleton 30944 were affected by *coxa vara*.

Transitional vertebrae

Transitional vertebrae can occur at the borders between different types of vertebra, when a vertebra from one group takes on some or all of the characteristics of an adjacent group (Barnes 1994). The process by which this happens is known as 'border shifting'. Skeleton 15548 (mature adult female) had a first sacral vertebra that had taken on the appearance of a lumbar vertebra at the posterior of the bone. The crude prevalence rate for lumbarisation for the early medieval period was 0.2% (Roberts and Cox 2003, 175).

Cleft neural arches

Cleft neural arches occur when the two halves of the neural arch, which surrounds and protects the spinal cord, fail to unite during development (Barnes 1994). The gap in the bone is filled with a tough fibrous tissue in life, and so the spinal cord remains protected and these defects are asymptomatic. Skeleton 30944 (old middle

Fig.338   Skeleton 30944: cleft neural arch in sacrum and osteoarthritis in articular facets

adult male) had a cleft spinous process of the first sacral vertebra (Fig.338), which is relatively common (*ibid*).

Further vertebral congenital anomalies

Minor congenital anomalies of the spine are very common. Most congenital anomalies, such as the majority of axial anomalies, develop as a result of abnormalities or disruptions during foetal development. Axial defects are commonly observed in archaeological skeletons, and are a result of the impact of developmental disturbances in the first trimester of pregnancy, when the axial skeleton forms.

Both Skeletons 15548 and 30944 had a number of congenital anomalies of the spine. Skeleton 30944 (old middle adult male) had a cleft or bifid first sacral vertebral neural arch, as discussed above. The spinous process of the fifth cervical vertebra was twisted to the left (Fig.339), while the left intertubercular lamella of the transverse process of the seventh cervical vertebra was unusually wide. These were minor congenital anomalies that would not have affected the well-being of this man.

A complete and well-preserved spine is required to determine whether any variation in the expected number of vertebrae in each vertebral group is the result of a genuine extra vertebral segment (i.e. an additional vertebra) or due to a border shift, and if the latter, what kind of shift has taken place. Unfortunately, the spine of Skeleton 15548 was incomplete and as a result it was not possible to identify whether vertebrae were missing post-mortem or were congenitally absent. Skeleton 15548 possibly had only eleven, instead of the usual twelve

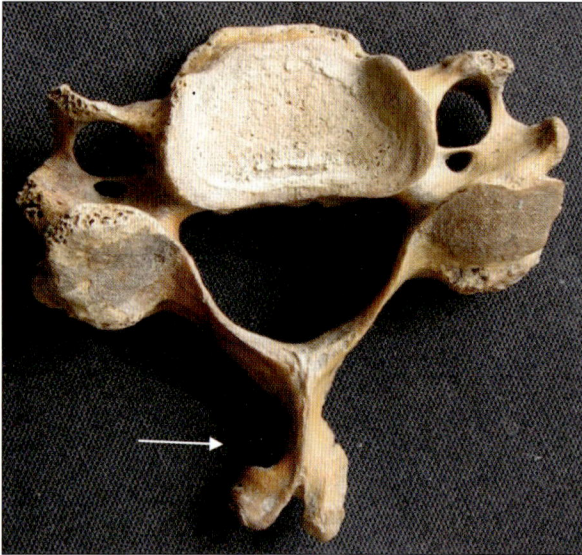

Fig.339   Twisted spinous process in fifth cervical vertebra of Skeleton 30944

Fig.340   Distorted manubrium of Skeleton 30944

thoracic (central) vertebrae. It is, however, possible that one of these vertebrae was lost post-mortem. The superior right articular facets protruded superiorly beyond the left side in the sacrum and the twelfth thoracic vertebra, while the inferior left articular facets protruded inferiorly by 3mm compared with the right side in the third, fourth and fifth lumbar vertebrae. The articular facets on the right side of the ninth, tenth and eleventh thoracic vertebrae were larger than those on the left. The transverse processes of the third, fourth and fifth lumbar vertebrae were twisted and the right sides were smaller than the left. The spinous process of the fourth cervical vertebra was also slightly twisted.

Malformed manubrium

Skeleton 30944 (old middle adult male) also had an unusually shaped manubrium (breast bone), which was 4mm longer at the left half compared with the right half (Fig.340). This would not have had any effect on the individual.

Metabolic disease

Cribra orbitalia

Cribra orbitalia manifests as fine pitting in the orbital roof. It develops during childhood, and often recedes during adolescence and early adulthood. Until recently, it was thought that iron deficiency anaemia was a likely cause of the lesions (Stuart-Macadam 1992), but a recent study by Walker *et al.* (2009) has demonstrated that other types of anaemia, including megaloblastic anaemia and haemolytic anaemia, must be considered instead. Megaloblastic anaemia is a likely cause of the lesions in the New World, and would arise following a diet deficient in Vitamin B_{12} (i.e. plant-based and lacking in animal products) and/or folic acid. Infections and infestations with gut parasites as a result of poor sanitation may have exacerbated such dietary deficiencies (*ibid*). Haemolytic anaemia (e.g. sickle cell anaemia and thalassemia) may have been important in the development of *cribra orbitalia* in areas of the Old World prone to malaria, but in Europe it was suggested that conditions such as scurvy (Vitamin C deficiency) or chronic infections may be more likely causes (*ibid*). *Cribra orbitalia* is often used as an indicator of general stress (Lewis 2000; Roberts and Manchester 2005) and is frequently found associated with agricultural economies (Roberts and Cox 2003).

Cribra orbitalia was present in the right orbit of Skeleton 36318 (young adult female), which indicates this individual had experienced a period of stress during childhood. *Cribra orbitalia* was not observed in the orbits of Skeletons 15548 or 30944. Roberts and Cox (2003, 187) note that 24.6% of orbits (and 7.6% of individuals or 6.1% of sexed adults) were affected by *cribra orbitalia* in early medieval populations. In the early medieval York Minster population, the crude prevalence rate was 10% (*ibid*).

Infectious disease

Bone can respond to infection by depositing new bone at the site of an inflammation. Initially this bone is disorganised and porous, and is termed 'woven bone'; the presence of this type of bone indicates an infection that was active at the time of death. With time, the woven bone deposits are remodelled, becoming smooth and organised 'lamellar bone'. The presence of lamellar bone suggests the infection had healed before death. Bone requires time to respond to infection, so new bone formation only occurs with chronic conditions (i.e. where the person survived for a time before recovery or death). Acute conditions, where the person either died or recovered within a short space of time, will not leave evidence in the skeleton (Roberts and Manchester 2005; Ortner 2003).

Non-specific infection

Identification of a specific infection is difficult in archaeological skeletal remains since the bone changes caused by different infections are usually similar in appearance. The exceptions are tuberculosis, leprosy and treponemal disease (including syphilis), where the changes are distinctive enough to allow these diseases to be recognised (Roberts and Manchester 2005; Ortner 2003). Other infectious diseases are described as 'non-specific' infections, as the bone changes observed are too general to allow diagnosis.

Skeleton 15548 (mature adult female) had distinct striated lamellar bone on the right fibula (Fig.341). She had suffered from a periosteal reaction (inflammatory lesions) of her left lower leg that was healing prior to her death. It is probable that these changes were also secondary to the congenital hip dysplasia and disuse of the right leg.

Both tibiae and fibulae of Skeleton 30944 showed evidence for marked striated lamellar bone at the shafts, suggesting periosteal reactions. The inflammation of the legs was healing at the time of death. Inflammation of the lower legs is a particularly common finding in archaeological populations (Roberts and Manchester 2005), and Roberts and Cox (2003, 235) observed that 14.05% of individuals from the early medieval period were affected.

The same individual also exhibited mild pitting on the outer (ectocranial) surface of the skull, around the sagittal suture at the top of the head. This is probably a periosteal reaction, most likely to be the result of mild scalp inflammation.

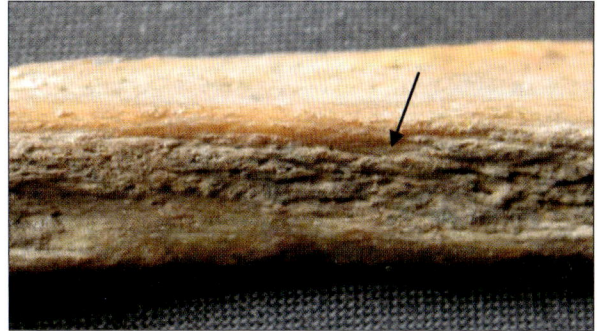

Fig.341   *Periosteal reaction at right fibula of Skeleton 15548*

Joint disease

Schmorl's nodes

Schmorl's nodes are indentations in the upper and lower surfaces of the vertebral bodies caused by the pressure of herniated vertebral discs (Aufderheide and Rodríguez-Martín 1998). Discs may rupture due to trauma, but vertebrae weakened by infection, osteoporosis or neoplastic disease may be more vulnerable (Roberts and Manchester 2005). Schmorl's nodes are often associated with degenerative changes to the vertebral bodies (Aufderheide and Rodríguez-Martín 1998; Hilton *et al.* 1976) and are most commonly seen in the lower thoracic vertebrae (*ibid*).

Schmorl's nodes affected all three individuals with surviving spines. Skeleton 36318 (young adult female) had depressions in the 6th, 9th, 10th, 11th and 12th thoracic vertebrae and the 1st lumbar vertebra. The old middle adult male (Skeleton 30944) had Schmorl's nodes in the 6th, 7th, 9th and 12th thoracic vertebrae and the 2nd, 3rd and 4th lumbar vertebrae. The old middle adult

Fig.342   *Schmorl's node in lumbar vertebra of Skeleton 15548*

male (Skeleton 15548) had Schmorl's nodes in the 8th thoracic vertebra and all lumbar vertebrae (Fig.342). The lesions were mild in the two older adults and mild to moderate in the young adult female. The location of the lesions in the lower part of the thoracic spine and lumbar vertebrae was fairly typical for Schmorl's nodes (Hilton *et al.* 1976). Roberts and Cox (2003, 195) found that 2.9% of individuals and 16.6% of vertebrae were affected by Schmorl's nodes in the early medieval period, which was much less than the prevalence at Coppergate (35.8%).

Degenerative joint disease

The most common type of joint disease observed tends to be degenerative joint disease (DJD). DJD is characterised by both bone formation (osteophytes) and bone resorption (porosity) at and around the articular surfaces of the joints, which can cause great discomfort and disability (Rogers 2000).

The two older adults, Skeletons 15548 and 30944 had DJD in the extraspinal skeleton. Skeleton 15548 (mature adult female) had mild to moderate DJD in the shoulders (scapula right glenoid, both acromiae, both medial and lateral clavicles), ribs, right trapezium (wrist bone), right first metacarpal, right fifth intermediate hand phalanx and left acetabulum. More severe DJD was observed in both auricular surfaces (joints between the hips and the sacrum). Skeleton 30944 (old middle adult male) showed evidence for mild extraspinal DJD in the ribs, right medial clavicle, left scapula glenoid, right proximal ulna, both hip sockets and also the auricular surfaces. Extraspinal DJD was noted in 8.3% of individuals in the early medieval period (Roberts and Cox 2003, 197).

Spinal DJD was not uncommon in the early medieval period, with a crude prevalence rate of 12.1% (*ibid*, 196). Although Skeleton 36318 (young adult female) had a partial spine, no DJD was observed, probably because this individual was so young. Skeletons 15548 (mature adult female) and 30944 (old middle adult male) had DJD of the spine. Skeleton 15548 had mild to moderate osteophytes in the bodies of the 1st, 5th and 6th cervical vertebrae and from the 7th thoracic vertebra to the sacrum (see Fig.342), with osteophytes becoming severe in the upper lumbar vertebrae. Notably, the osteophytes occurred only on the right side of the vertebral bodies. It is likely that the degenerative joint disease of this female was secondary to the disuse of her right leg and the use of a walking aid, such as a crutch, therefore causing unilateral degeneration. Notably, the articular vertebral facets of this individual were not affected by DJD. Skeleton 30944

showed evidence for mild to moderate DJD in the 2nd to 7th cervical vertebral bodies and the bodies from the 4th thoracic vertebra to the sacrum. The articular facets of the 3rd cervical vertebra, 1st, 2nd, 3rd 10th, 11th, 12th thoracic vertebrae and from the 1st lumbar vertebra to the sacrum were affected by DJD.

Osteoarthritis

Osteoarthritis is a degenerative joint disease characterised by the deterioration of the joint cartilage, leading to exposure of the underlying bony joint surface. The resulting bone-to-bone contact can produce polishing of the bone termed 'eburnation', which is the most apparent expression of osteoarthritis. Osteoarthritis can be the result of mechanical stress and other factors, including lifestyle, food acquisition and preparation, social status, sex and general health (Larsen 1997).

Skeleton 30944 (old middle adult male) had mild eburnation on the articular facets of the 2nd and 3rd thoracic vertebrae and severe eburnation in the joints between the 5th lumbar vertebra and the sacrum (see Fig.338), indicative of osteoarthritis. The crude prevalence of spinal osteoarthritis in the early medieval period was 6.1% (Roberts and Cox 2003, 195).

Skeleton 15548 had mild eburnation in the joint between the 5th lumbar vertebra and the sacrum, but similarly to the DJD, only on the right side. Additionally, the left knee (distal left femur, proximal left tibia) was affected by a very small area of eburnation indicative of osteoarthritis and the right hip joint (affecting the pelvis and femur), which was severely malformed as a result of the congenital hip dysplasia forming a new joint (pseudoarthrosis), exhibited severe eburnation. The early medieval prevalence rate of extraspinal osteoarthritis was 4.6% of individuals (*ibid*, 195).

Trauma

Os acromiale

The tip of the acromion process of the scapula, the part of the shoulder blade that projects over the shoulder joint and meets the clavicle, develops as a separate element which fuses to the rest of the scapula as the individual approaches adulthood. In a small percentage of individuals this fusion fails to occur, and the tip of the acromion remains separate, known as *os acromiale*. This developmental anomaly is thought to be caused by severe stress to the rotator cuff muscles during growth, preventing natural fusion of the bones. In modern populations, *os acromiale* was noted in two boxers, where it was attributed to their intensive training during adolescence (Hershkovitz *et al.* 1996, 170). This condition had occurred in both scapulae of Skeleton 30944 (old middle adult male). The frequency of *os acromiale* for the early medieval period was 0.4% of individuals (Roberts and Cox 2003, 203). Failure of this bone to fuse probably results in increased flexibility of the shoulder joint, allowing a greater range of movement without damaging the muscles (Knüsel 2000), and it has been suggested that *os acromiale* is associated with the practice of archery from a young age, or any kind of movement requiring the arm to be rotated over the shoulder (*ibid;* Stirland 2005).

Osteochondritis dissecans

Skeleton 30944 (old middle adult male) had well-defined depressions on the middle articular surfaces of both calcanei (heel bones), measuring 2.7mm in diameter on the right calcaneus and 4.2mm on the left bone (Fig.343). It is likely that a fragment of the joint surface had become detached following death of the bone tissue in that area due to damage to the blood supply, a condition known as *osteochondritis dissecans* (Roberts and Manchester 2005). *Osteochondritis dissecans* usually results in a circular and porous depression in the joint surface. It is a condition that affects young individuals, particularly males (*ibid*, 121). In their survey of health in the early medieval period, Roberts and Cox (2003, 210) observed that 1.5% of individuals had suffered *osteochondritis dissecans*, all in the knee.

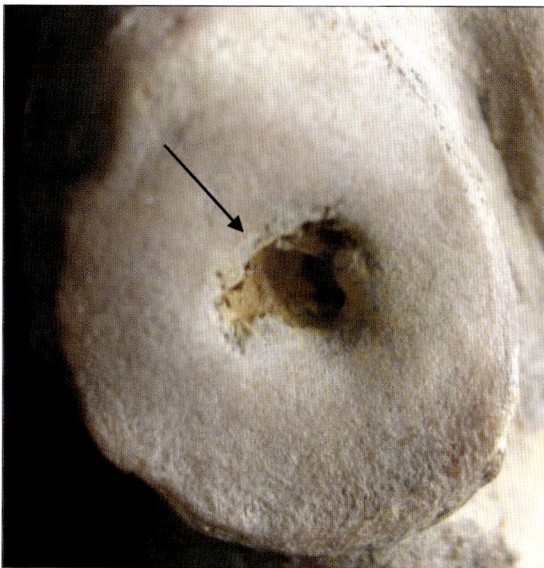

Fig.343   Osteochondritis dissecans *lesion in calcaneus of Skeleton 30944*

Excavated muscle attachment

Skeletons 36318 (young adult female) and 30979 (adult male) had an elongated depression on their left humeri, at the location for the attachment of the pectoralis major muscle. This muscle acts to pull the humerus towards the body (adduction), as well as rotating the humerus inwards (Stone and Stone 1997). Skeletons 15548 and 30944 showed evidence for bone excavations at the right humeri for subscapularis (also on the left humerus of Skeleton 30944) and infraspinatus and Skeleton 15548 also had a bone excavation for supraspinatus. These muscles are part of the rotator cuff and aid in abduction and adduction of the shoulder, lateral and medial rotation of the arm and strengthen the shoulder joint (*ibid*). There was a severe bone excavation for subscapularis on the right humerus of Skeleton 15548, perhaps related to her need for walking aids. The clavicles of Skeleton 30944 had moderate bone excavations for the costoclavicular ligaments. Bone excavations at this site are very common in archaeological populations. There was also an unusual bone excavation at the attachment site for the medial talo-calcaneal ligament at the left talus.

Skeleton 30944 also showed evidence for enthesopathies at the attachments of *rectus femoris* on the left patella; this muscle rotates the hip joint laterally (Stone and Stone 1997, 160). The pelvis exhibited enthesopathies for *semimembranosus,* which extends at the hip and flexes at the knee (*ibid*, 173). A large enthesopathy for *gluteus maximus* was located on the left femur of Skeleton 15548, which was probably related to trauma to that leg.

Circulatory disorders

A smooth depression was located at the left distal humerus of Skeleton 30979 (adult male) between the trochlea and the medial epicondyle. It is likely to be ischemia (restriction of the blood supply) of the anterior part of the ulnar collateral ligament. Knüsel (pers. comm., December 2009) has observed these in the skeletons of the *Mary Rose* as well as skeletons from other periods.

Miscellaneous pathology

Skeleton 30944 (old middle adult male) had a slightly distorted joint of the left fifth metatarsal. The lateral part of the distal joint surface was not smooth, as would be the norm, but undulated and concave. It is not clear what caused this joint change, though this was not related to a degenerative condition and looked more like a crush fracture.

Conclusion

Considering that only four partial skeletons were recovered from the Anglian/Anglo-Scandinavian period at Coppergate, a large number of pathological lesions were observed. Congenital anomalies were recorded in two individuals, with the mature adult female (15548) having congenital hip dysplasia on the right side, which meant that she probably had a severe limp and had to rely on a walking aid, such as crutches. There were numerous secondary complications, including one-sided degenerative joint disease of her spine, osteoarthritis of the lower spine, wasting of the right hip and whole right leg, probably as a result of disuse of the leg, osteoarthritis in the right hip joint, inflammatory lesions in the right fibula, additional strain on the left leg, causing muscular trauma and osteoarthritis in the left knee. Whether the degenerative joint disease in the shoulders, right hand and wrist were complications of her disability was not clear. This female also had numerous minor congenital anomalies of the spine, such as differently sized vertebral joints and possibly also only eleven instead of the usual twelve central vertebrae. In addition, she had a congenital anomaly of the left femur, leading to shortening of the femoral neck, which was also seen in both femora of the old middle adult male (30944). This would have caused a lurching limp.

The old middle adult male also had further developmental defects, such as spinal anomalies and a lopsided breast bone, none of which would have had an effect on his well-being. The male had mild degenerative joint disease of the spine, ribs, shoulders, right elbow and much more severe degenerative joint disease and osteoarthritis in the lower spine. Evidence for trauma was noted in the form of non-fusion of the lateral parts of the scapulae, which has often been associated with requirement for a greater degree of flexibility in the shoulder, as in archery. He also had evidence for muscular trauma. Both of his lower legs exhibited inflammatory lesions which were healing at the time of death.

Both the older male and female and also the young adult female (36318) had depressions in the vertebral bodies termed Schmorl's nodes, which are caused by ruptured discs. Discs can rupture as a result of trauma, axial pressure or through other causes. The young female had lesions in the eye orbits associated with infection or poor nutrition in childhood. Both she and the adult male (30979) also had evidence for muscular trauma. The male had a lesion on the elbow thought to be caused by restriction to the blood supply.

The skeletons from nearby Spurriergate in York were generally incomplete and therefore did not exhibit much evidence for pathology. However, Skeleton 5031, a middle adult female, had degenerative joint disease and osteoarthritis of the spine, a congenital anomaly of the fifth lumbar vertebra and childhood stress lesions in the eye orbits (Holst 2005).

Dental health

Analysis of the teeth from archaeological populations provides vital clues about health, diet and oral hygiene, as well as information about environmental and congenital conditions.

Unusually, Skeleton 15548 (mature adult female) had 33 instead of the usual 32 tooth positions and sixteen of her permanent teeth were present, with the other teeth being lost post-mortem. Skeleton 30944 (old middle adult male) had all his 32 tooth positions but had also lost many teeth post-mortem, leaving twelve teeth to record. A further five teeth were lost ante-mortem. Skeleton 36318 (young adult female) had a full surviving maxilla and all sixteen tooth positions were preserved. However, only three teeth were recovered, the remainder having been lost post-mortem. Skeleton 30979 (adult male) did not have any surviving teeth or jaw bones. In total, 81 tooth positions and 31 teeth were available for study.

Dental wear tends to be more common and severe in archaeological populations than in modern teeth. Severity of the dental wear was assessed using a chart developed by Smith (1984). Each tooth was scored using a grading system ranging from 1 (no wear) to 8 (severe attrition of the whole tooth crown). Dental wear was mild in the young adult female and moderate to severe (3 to 6) in the two older adults.

Dental calculus

Calculus (mineralised dental plaque) is commonly observed in archaeological populations whose dental hygiene was not as rigorous as it is today. If plaque is not removed from the teeth effectively (or on a regular basis) then these plaque deposits mineralise and form concretions of calculus on the tooth crowns or roots, along the line of the gums (Hillson 1996).

Calculus deposits were noted on 29 (93.5%) teeth, suggesting poor oral hygiene. In comparison, 39.2% of teeth were affected by calculus in the early medieval period (Roberts and Cox 2003). As expected, the calculus was worse in the mature adult female (Skeleton 1554) compared with the two younger individuals.

Dental caries

Dental caries (tooth decay) forms when bacteria in the plaque metabolise sugars in the diet and produce acid, which eventually leads to the formation of a cavity in the tooth (Zero 1999). Simple sugars can be found naturally in fruits, vegetables, dried fruits and honey, as well as processed, refined sugar; since the latter three contain the most sucrose they are most cariogenic. Complex sugars are usually less cariogenic and are found in carbohydrates, such as cereals. However, processing carbohydrates, including grinding grains into fine powders or cooking them, will usually increase their cariogenicity (Moynihan 2003).

Dental caries (Fig.344) were only observed in the mature adult female (Skeleton 15548), which was not unexpected since the number of cavities usually increases with age. She had caries in one of her sixteen teeth (6.25%). The prevalence rate of caries at Coppergate was 3.2% and thus lower compared with the frequency of teeth affected by dental caries in the early medieval period, which was 4.2% (Roberts and Cox 2003).

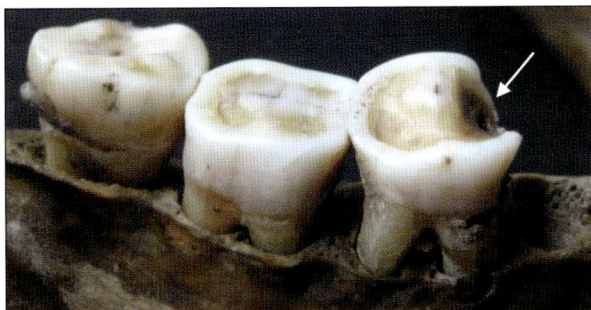

Fig.344   Caries in right mandible of Skeleton 15548

Abscesses

Dental abscesses occur when bacteria enter the pulp cavity of a tooth causing inflammation and a build up of pus at the apex of the root. Eventually, a hole forms in the surrounding bone allowing the pus to drain out and relieve the pressure. They can form as a result of dental caries, heavy wear of the teeth, damage to the teeth, or periodontal disease (Roberts and Manchester 1995).

Skeleton 30944 (old middle adult) was the only individual with dental abscesses. The abscesses concentrated around the upper left first molar and the maxillary right second premolar and first molar. Both abscesses were healed. Notably, both abscesses were associated with ante-mortem tooth loss of the upper first molars. The overall prevalence at Coppergate was 3.7%, which was higher than the early medieval mean of 2.8% (Roberts and Cox 2003, 192).

Ante-mortem tooth loss

Ante-mortem tooth loss (AMTL), or the loss of teeth during life, can occur as a result of a variety of factors, including dental caries, pulp exposure from heavy tooth wear, or periodontal disease (occurring when inflammation of the gums, gingivitis, spreads to the underlying bone). Gingivitis can result when deposits of calculus on the teeth aggravate the gums. Once the tooth has been lost, the empty socket is filled in with bone.

Only the old middle adult (Skeleton 30944) had lost five teeth ante-mortem. The prevalence rate of AMTL at Coppergate was 6.2%, as compared with the early medieval mean, which was 8.0% (Roberts and Cox 2003, 193).

Periodontal disease

Periodontitis (receding gums) was slight to moderate in the maxilla and mandible of the two older adults and may have been caused by the widespread calculus deposits. The young adult female did not have periodontal disease.

Dental anomalies

Remarkably, Skeleton 15548 had 33, instead of the usual 32 tooth positions. Polydontia (or supernumerary teeth) is much less common than congenitally absent teeth. The additional teeth usually take on the shape of the adjacent tooth, and tend to be hidden on the inner side of the mouth (Hillson 1996, 114). However, in this case it appears as if there were two left second incisors beside one another, though unfortunately the teeth were lost post-mortem.

The first left mandibular incisor of Skeleton 15548 (mature adult female) was rotated by approximately 45°, so that the buccal side was located distally and the lingual side medially.

Dental conclusions

Evidence for dental disease was largely restricted to deposits of calcified plaque in all three individuals, which was worse than average for the period and indicative of poor oral hygiene. The mature adult female had a small cavity in a molar. The prevalence of caries was lower than the norm for the period, as was the rate of ante-mortem tooth loss. The prevalence of dental abscesses was, however, slightly higher than the early medieval mean. Dental anomalies included supernumerary teeth in the female with numerous congenital anomalies, as well as a rotated tooth.

Mortuary practice

The presence of these burials in pits or laid on the ground surface in various positions and orientations suggests that these individuals were not interred in a typical Christian manner. Burial of post-Roman skeletons in rubbish pits is relatively rare in the archaeological record. However, examples do exist, such as five skeletons that were found at 7–17 Spurriergate, within 100m of Coppergate. All five skeletons were buried in large pits, though unfortunately truncation by later pits meant that only two of these were almost complete individuals. Two of the skeletons were radiocarbon dated to the late 8th century AD, consistent with the range of some of the Coppergate skeletons.

The position and orientation of these individuals was also varied, with the skeletons in north to south or reversed orientations and supine extended, flexed and prone skeletal positions (Holst 2005).

The majority of burials dating to the 8th and 9th centuries would have been interred in churchyards, such as those at Repton (Derbyshire), Hovingham (North Yorkshire) and Bakewell (Derbyshire) (Hadley 2000, 201). However, according to Hadley, there was much variety in terms of funerary ritual between the 7th and 11th centuries (*ibid*, 202) and it appears that this diversity was widely accepted before the 10th century (*ibid*, 214). Non-churchyard burials from the 7th to 10th century are largely found in barrows. Such burials from the Anglo-Scandinavian period are known from York's surrounding area, at Siward's Howe (Hall 1994, 44) or the Viking barrow cemetery at Ingleby in Derbyshire, which contained cremated remains and is thought to date to the 9th and 10th century (Richards *et al.* 1995).

Alternatively, burials have been found in locations which were later marked by the construction of a church in the 10th or 11th century (Hadley 2000, 211). Examples include Barton-on-Humber, Kellington and Holton-le-Clay (*ibid*). Interments from the period excavated in York

itself tend to be associated with churches, such as the burials excavated at St Mary Bishophill Junior, St Mary Bishophill Senior, York Minster and St Andrew Fishergate (Hall 1994). Notably, there was still much variation, even in church cemeteries, such as the early burials at the Norman Minster, which included charcoal burials, coffins, and even parts of a boat (Hadley 2000, 208).

It is possible that some burials from this period are simply not recognised because of a lack of radiocarbon dating. A mature adult female skeleton interred in a west–east orientation in a supine extended position in an enclosure ditch at Brake's Farm, Sedgefield, County Durham, was thought to date to the Iron Age until radiocarbon dating proved that the individual dated to the late 10th or early 11th century AD (Holst 2009).

Discussion and summary

The osteological analysis of the Anglian/Anglo-Scandinavian period skeletal assemblage from Coppergate has provided an important insight into the lives of these individuals. Two of the skeletons were almost complete, while less than 25% of the other two skeletons survived. (A single skull, 32803, also radiocarbon-dated to the Anglian period was not considered in this study.)Their preservation, however, was excellent, which meant that it was possible to identify much pathology.

The skeletons buried at Coppergate comprised the remains of a young adult female, a mature adult female, an old middle adult male and a possible male adult. All except 15548 were interred in pits, and three of the individuals were buried in close proximity of one another. The mature adult female (15548) was buried some distance away (at a later date), in a formal supine extended position in an east to west orientation (see Table 32). The younger female had been disturbed by a later feature and was therefore disarticulated, while only the left arm of the adult male was recovered, although it is assumed that he had been interred in a south to north orientation and a supine position. The old middle adult male lay with the skull to the north-east and the feet to the south-west in a supine semi-flexed position. His left arm was bent upwards, with the left hand behind his head. Parallels for these pit burials were found in York itself at Spurriergate, only 100m from Coppergate. Here five individuals were interred in large pits in a variety of positions and orientations (Holst 2005). Two of these burials were radiocarbon dated to the late 8th century AD. Although other burials from this period tend to be more formal and are often found in churchyards or under barrows, a similar interment was found near Sedgefield in County Durham, where a mature adult female lay in a west to east orientation in a supine extended position within a large enclosure ditch (Holst 2009).

Two of the individuals showed evidence for a number of congenital anomalies, of varying degrees of severity. The mature adult female, who was of average height for the period, possibly only had eleven thoracic vertebrae (rather than the usual twelve). She also had a number of minor spinal anomalies, such as twisted spinous and transverse processes, lopsided or differently sized articular facets in some vertebrae and lumbarisation of the first sacral vertebra. Her left femoral neck was abnormal, being shortened and horizontal. She also had 33 tooth positions instead of the normal 32. The presence of supernumerary teeth is relatively uncommon. However, the most severe congenital anomaly was the congenital hip dysplasia on the right side, which meant that she would have walked with a severe limp and probably needed a walking aid. The fact that the right hip, femur, tibia and fibula had a severely diminished appearance compared with the left side suggests that the right leg was rarely used for walking. Instead, the left leg was unusually well developed and broad, as were her shoulders and arms, perhaps due to the use of a crutch. Her left leg and arms also displayed evidence for muscular trauma, which was probably related. The left knee showed evidence for this unusual strain in the form of osteoarthritis at the knee and the spine displayed degenerative joint disease and osteoarthritis, which only affected the right side and was also likely to be a secondary complication to her congenital hip dislocation. A new hip joint had formed in the right pelvis and also on the femoral shaft (as the femoral head was not formed). The new hip socket was small and almost flat and severely affected by osteoarthritis. Whether the degenerative joint disease in her ribs, shoulders and right hand were a result of her condition could not be established. However, it is likely that the receding inflammation of her right lower leg was also related to the disuse of that leg. Her dental health was relatively good for her age, with one cavity, mild to moderate plaque concretions and slight to moderate periodontal disease.

The old middle adult male also had congenital anomalies, including the shortened and horizontal femoral necks, as in the female mature adult, which would have caused him to walk with a limp. He also had a twisted spinous process in one vertebra, a cleft spinous process in the first sacral vertebra and an unusually large transverse process in a third vertebra. His breastbone was slightly distorted in shape, which is also a minor congenital defect. He was unusually short for the period and his skeleton was relatively gracile. Evidence for trauma was noted in both scapulae, which had unfused acromiae, a condition that is often seen in those who require increased flexibility of shoulder movement, such as archers. In both heel bones were lesions indicative of problems with his blood supply, causing a small part of the joint surfaces to detach from the joint. He also had lesions indicative of disc herniation in his lower spine and some muscular trauma. Mild degenerative joint disease affected his spine, ribs, shoulders and hips and he had osteoarthritis in the central and lower spine. His lower legs were affected by receding inflammatory lesions. His dental health was moderate, with some ante-mortem tooth loss, widespread dental plaque, moderate periodontal disease and two healed dental abscesses.

The partial skeleton of a young adult female suggested that she was slightly taller than the average for the period. During childhood, she had suffered from stress, perhaps in the form of infection. She suffered from herniation of some of the vertebral discs and showed evidence for muscular trauma. Her dental health was good.

The adult male was slightly taller than the early medieval mean. He had also incurred muscular trauma, as well as circulatory problems in his left arm.

The dental health of the population was moderate, with widespread calculus, indicative of poor oral hygiene. However, while abscesses were more prevalent than the early medieval average, the rate of cavities and ante-mortem tooth loss was lower.

The wider significance of these unorthodox burials remains unresolved but they need to be considered within the context of a growing number of haphazard burials recovered from post-Roman pre-Conquest contexts in the city.

Tree-Ring Analysis of the Anglo-Scandinavian Oak Timbers
by Cathy Tyers and Jennifer Hillam

Please note: The full report referred to below, including all figures, is available at www.yorkarchaeology.co.uk

Introduction

Excavations at 16–22 Coppergate revealed large quantities of waterlogged wood and timber. The dendrochronological investigation was initiated in 1977, since when over 400 timber samples have been submitted for analysis. As the analysis proceeded a series of archive reports were produced for the Anglo-Scandinavian and medieval phases of the main excavation (Hillam 1985; 1987; 1989) and of the watching brief (Groves and Hillam 1986; Hillam 1992a). This report draws together all the results from the timbers associated with the Anglian (Period 2) and Anglo-Scandinavian (Periods 3–5) deposits. The results from the medieval and post-medieval timbers (Period 6) are similarly synthesised in Hillam (2002) and Groves (2002).

Nearly a third (32%) of the samples were rejected as unsuitable for dendrochronological analysis but 200 samples were analysed from Periods 2–5 and 78 from Period 6. Dating proved very difficult initially because of the lack of suitable reference chronologies available in the late 1970s and early 1980s. Consequently the tree-ring dates have been produced over a period of 20 or so years as the network of reference chronologies available has been extended both temporally and geographically. Prior to the production of this report all the Coppergate data were re-analysed, primarily in order to confirm the results previously obtained but also to ascertain whether any additional dating evidence could now be produced. The data have also provided a valuable resource for the investigation of other aspects of dendrochronology, such as the development of cross-matching techniques (Okasha 1987) or the extraction of non-chronological information (Holman nd).

The earliest timbers analysed, assigned to Period 2, were associated with the pit in which the Coppergate Anglian helmet was found (Hillam 1992a). Relatively few timbers were obtained from either this period or Period 3, the earliest of the Anglo-Scandinavian levels. The tenement boundaries were laid down in Period 4, which also saw the erection of post and post-and-wattle structures. The wattle material was clearly unsuitable

for dendrochronology but samples were obtained from some of the posts. Period 5A was a relatively short-lived episode of soil build up resulting from the accumulation of occupation debris, general dumping and the digging out of the foundations of the sunken buildings. Period 5B saw the construction of the sunken buildings and it is from this phase that the bulk of the tree-ring samples come.

When the Coppergate dendrochronological investigation was initiated the primary objective was to provide a precise dating framework. The application of dendrochronology to site-specific archaeological issues was in its pioneer phase and the development of a network of chronologies still very much in its infancy. During the subsequent 20 years the technique has been steadily developed and refined, its potential more widely recognised and its limitations more clearly understood. Current understanding would certainly have affected the way in which the Coppergate dendrochronological investigation was approached and the ability of the assemblage to achieve the primary objective more clearly understood but this can only now been said with the benefit of subsequent decades of experience and hindsight. The ability to provide precise dating evidence is the underlying strength of dendrochronology but the wider potential of the method to provide environmental and socio-economic information is now being increasingly exploited. Consequently the aims of the Coppergate dendrochronological analysis were gradually widened in an attempt to use the basic tree-ring data to provide information concerning the trees from which the timbers were derived, their environment and hence the historic landscape. Such information aids the understanding of past woodland economies, demonstrates the changes in tree utilisation patterns through time, and also indicates the origin of the timbers.

Methods

Professional practice at the Sheffield Dendrochronology Laboratory is described in English Heritage (1998). The following summarises relevant methodological details used for the analysis of the Coppergate samples. Any variations due to the analysis having occurred over an extended period, during which the discipline has made a series of technical advancements, are noted as necessary.

Oak (*Quercus* spp.) is currently the only species used for routine dating purposes in the British Isles, although research on other species is being undertaken (e.g. Tyers 1997a; Groves 1997). Timbers with fewer than 50 annual growth rings are now generally considered unsuitable for analysis as their ring patterns may not be unique (Hillam *et al.* 1987). Thus oak timbers are generally sought which have at least 50 rings and if possible either bark or bark-edge of some sapwood surviving (see below). However, during the course of the study of the Coppergate material some samples with fewer than 50 rings were included for full analysis as part of a collaborative project with the Department of Probability and Statistics at Sheffield University.

The samples were prepared by being frozen for a minimum of 48 hours before their cross-sectional surface was cleaned with a surform plane and scalpels until the annual growth rings were clearly defined. Any samples which failed to contain the minimum number of rings or had unclear ring sequences were rejected. The equipment used to measure the ring widths varied as the analysis progressed (Hillam 1985, 1987, 1989, and 1992a; Groves and Hillam 1986). All the measuring machines were based on travelling stages which allow the sample to be moved from one ring to the next whilst being viewed under a binocular microscope. Ring widths were originally recorded by hand and later typed into the mainframe or microcomputer whereas they are now input directly into the computer using a PC Windows-based measuring system (Tyers 1997b). The sequence of growth rings in the samples selected for dating purposes were measured to an accuracy of 0.1mm, 0.02mm, or 0.01mm depending on when and how the measurement took place. All old system measurements were multiplied by the relevant factor in order to make them compatible with the current system measuring to an accuracy of 0.01mm. On oak, it is usual to measure a single radius as this is considered a reliable representation of the growth pattern of the tree. However, during the initial analysis at Coppergate two radii per sample were frequently measured and averaged to produce a single timber sequence in an attempt to increase the dating potential.

The ring sequences were plotted onto semi-logarithmic graph paper to enable visual comparisons to be made between them. In addition, cross-correlation algorithms (Baillie and Pilcher 1973; Munro 1984) were employed to search for positions where the ring sequences were highly correlated. The Student's *t* test was then used as a significance test on the correlation coefficient and those quoted below are derived from the original CROS algorithm (Baillie and Pilcher 1973). A *t* value of 3.5 or over is usually indicative of a good match (Baillie 1982, 82–5), provided that high *t* values are obtained at the same relative or absolute position with a series of independent sequences and that the visual match is satisfactory.

Dating is usually achieved by cross-correlating, or cross-matching, ring sequences within a phase or structure and combining the matching patterns to form a phase or site master curve. This master curve and any remaining unmatched ring sequences are then tested against a range of reference chronologies, using the same matching criteria as above. The position at which all the criteria are met provides the calendar dates for the ring sequences. A master curve is used for scientific dating purposes whenever possible as it enhances the common climatic signal and reduces the background 'noise' resulting from the local growth conditions of individual trees. Although this method was used for the re-analysis immediately prior to the production of this report it was usually not possible during the initial study to undertake such a structured approach to the analysis because of the complex nature of the site and sample availability. In addition, due to problems encountered during the initial analysis of the Coppergate samples, a collaborative project was initiated with the Department of Probability and Statistics at Sheffield. New analytical programs were developed which, whilst generally based on the CROS program, incorporated other statistical methods (Okasha 1987). The results from these proved to be basically identical to those obtained through the 'traditional' methods, thus providing additional confirmation of the validity of the tree-ring dates.

During the cross-matching stage an additional important element of tree-ring analysis is the identification of 'same-tree' timber groups. The identification of 'same-tree' groups is based on very high levels of similarity in year to year variation, longer-term growth trends, and anatomical anomalies. Such information should ideally be used to support possible 'same-tree' groups identified from similarities in the patterns of knots/branches during detailed recording of timbers for technological and woodland characterisation studies. Timbers originally derived from the same parent log generally have *t* values of greater than 10.0, though lower *t* values do not necessarily exclude the possibility. It is a balance of the range of information available that provides the 'same-tree' link.

The cross-dating process provides precise calendar dates only for the rings present in the timber. The nature of the final ring in the sequence determines whether the date of this ring also represents the year the timber was felled. Oak consists of inner inert heartwood and an outer band of active sapwood. If the sample ends in the heartwood of the original tree, a *terminus post quem* for the felling of the tree is indicated by the date of the last ring plus the addition of the minimum expected number of sapwood rings which are missing. This is the date after which the timber was felled but the actual felling date may be many decades later depending on the number of outer rings removed during timber conversion. Where some of the outer sapwood or the heartwood/sapwood boundary survives on the sample, a felling date range can be calculated using the maximum and minimum number of sapwood rings likely to have been present. The sapwood estimate applied throughout this report is a minimum of 10 and a maximum of 46 rings, where these figures indicate the 95% confidence limits of the range and are applicable to oak trees from England and Wales (Tyers 2000a). Alternatively, if bark-edge survives, then a felling date can be obtained directly from the date of the last surviving ring. In some instances it may be possible to determine the season of felling according to whether the ring immediately below the bark is complete or incomplete. However, the onset of growth can vary within and between trees and this, combined with the natural variation in actual ring width, means that the determination of felling season must be treated cautiously. The delicate nature of sapwood, particularly on waterlogged timbers, increases the likelihood of damage/degradation to the outermost surface of the sample and hence increases the difficulties of positive identification of bark-edge.

The felling dates produced by the technique do not by themselves necessarily indicate the date of the structure from which they are derived. Evidence indicates that seasoning of timber for structural purposes was a fairly rare occurrence until relatively recent times and medieval timber was generally felled as required and used whilst green (e.g. Rackham 1990; Charles and Charles 1995). Physical evidence for the rapid use of trees is widespread in buildings as many show clear evidence of warping or splitting after having undergone conversion. Hollstein (1980) gives examples of use of green timber from earlier periods. However, it is necessary to incorporate other specialist evidence concerning the re-use of timbers and the repair or modification of structures, as well as factors such as stockpiling, seasoning, and transport, before dendrochronological dates can be reliably interpreted as

reflecting the construction date of a structure or phases within it.

The tree-ring dating evidence

Details of the timbers submitted for dendrochronological analysis are given in Tables 34 and 35. Information regarding the dating of most of the individual timbers are given in the archive reports, although some additional timbers have been dated during re-analysis. The dating evidence derived from the dendrochronological analysis is summarised below in terms of the main period subdivisions into which the site's development has been split during archaeological interpretation and also by the four tenement plots recognised within the excavated area. The precise felling dates obtained from timbers with bark-edge clearly show that the development sequence of the site, as represented by preserved timber remains, is intense and extremely compressed, with the bulk of the constructional activity occurring in the latter half of the 10th century. This is, however, based solely on the dendrochronological evidence and consequently excludes other archaeological evidence for activity. Dates of ring sequences for each timber, along with its individual felling date, are set out in Table 34 and are illustrated in the full report. A new Coppergate Anglo-Scandinavian chronology, YORKCPG3, was constructed in 2000 from the dated timbers. It spans the period 460–1011 and includes data from 168 ring sequences. This chronology and its individual components show particularly strong similarities with chronologies from surrounding areas but also, since it is so well-replicated (i.e. data included from many individual samples), it matches well with chronologies over much longer distances (Table 36). A summary of the dating evidence obtained is given in Figure 345 and Table 37. Please note that all dates cited below are AD.

Period 2

The only 'helmet pit' timber that was dated (97) was felled after 586. If this timber is taken to be representative of the date of construction of the pit then the strict dendrochronological interpretation is that the pit was dug and lined after 586. Although the backfill deposits have biological characteristics more similar to those of the Anglo-Scandinavian period, it is relatively unlikely that the timber represents the inner portion of a tree over 400 years old (ie from the 10th century), so this timber appears to date the construction of the pit to the Anglian period. The helmet itself was made c.750–75, and was not new at the time it was put into the pit (*AY* 17/8).

Group

Calendar years

Group			Date range
3	D	isolated	AD904/5
4A	B	isolated	AD906-41
4A	D	alignment 30358	AD921-39
4A	D	isolated	AD897-933
4B	B	alignment 27607	AD925-47
			AD950-85
4B	B	alignment 27676	AD942-74
4B	B	alignment 27796	AD937-73
4B	B	alignment 37166	AD935-7?
4B	B	horizontal	AD941-59
4B	B	discarded	AD930-48
4B	C	alignment 36591/25640	AD914-48
4B	D	alignment 22585	AD935-7
4B	D	alignment 30436	AD935-7?
5A	B	alignment 18422	AD955/6
5A	B	alignment 36582	AD955/6
5A	D	alignment 14853	AD955/6
5A	D	isolated post	AD946-78
5B	A	Structure 5/1	AD961/2
5B	B	pit/cut 27298/26993	AD998-1034
5B	B	Structure 5/3	AD958-87 (966?)
5B	B	Structure 5/4	AD972/3
5B	B	Structure 5/4 supplementary	AD975-1011
5B	C	alignment 33233	AD956/7
			AD964-84
5B	C	alignment 33235	AD955/6
5B	C	isolated	AD940/1
			AD966
5B	C	Structure 5/5	AD956-79
5B	C	Structure 5/6	AD970-97
5B	D	Structure 5/7	AD966
5B	D	Structure 5/7 abandoned	AD957-85
5B	D	Structure 5/8 braces	AD1008/9
5B	D	Structure 5/8 sills	AD995/6
5B	D	Structure 5/8 drain	AD988-1017
5B	D	wb Structure 5/7 or 5/8	AD994-1002
5B	E	Structure 5/9	AD951-87
5Cf	D	Structure 5/10	AD963-98
5Cr	C	Structure 5/12	AD1013-49
wb		drain	AD960-94

AD900   AD950   AD1000   AD1050   AD1100

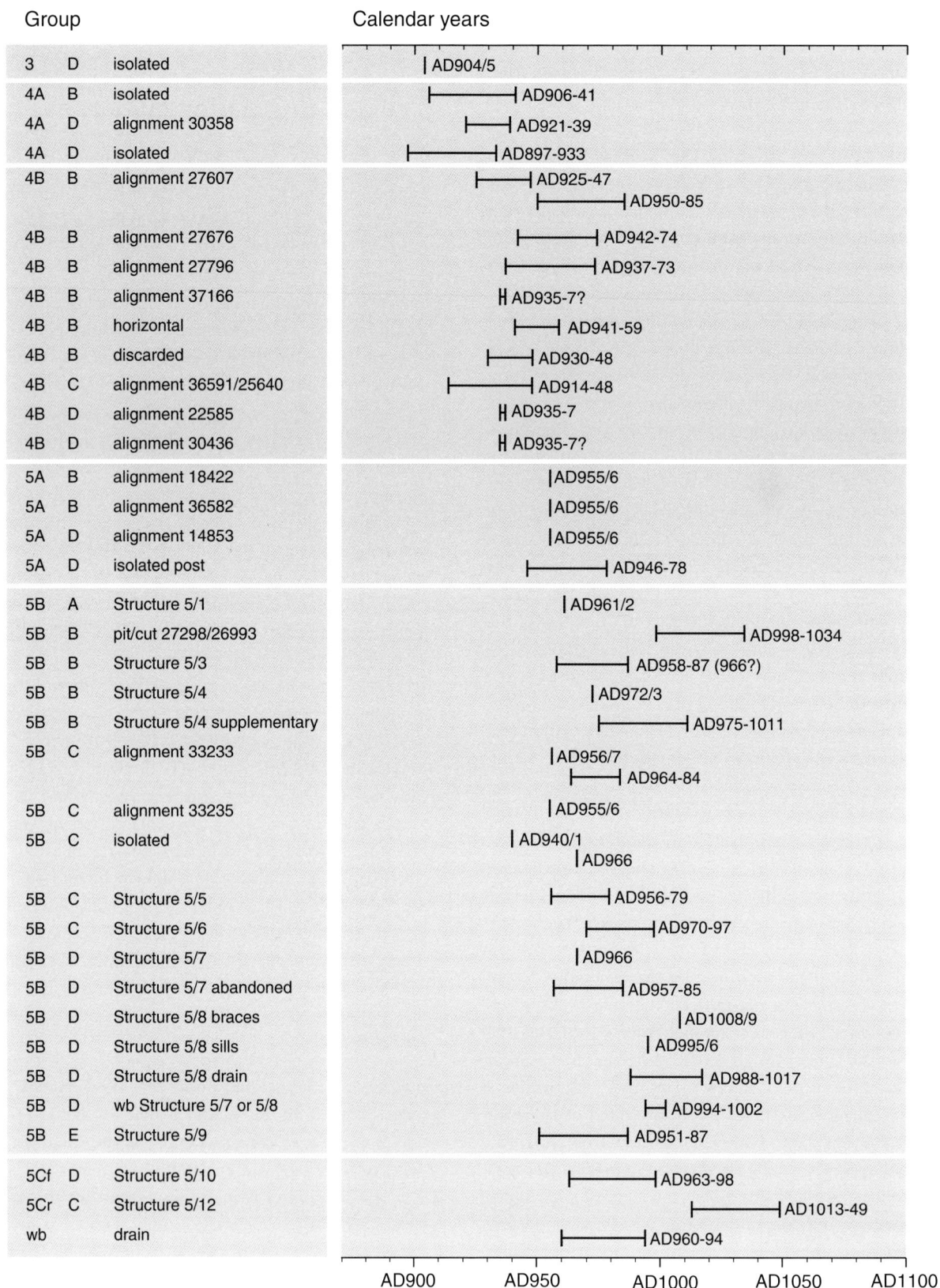

Fig.345   *Summary of the interpreted felling dates or date ranges. Period 2 is excluded, as are all structures for which the results only produced a* terminus post quem *for felling.*

The only other dated timber from Period 2 is 91, an isolated timber found during the watching brief. This was felled some time after 685, and again probably indicates activity in the Anglian period.

The dendrochronological results for Period 2 suggest that there was activity in the vicinity during the Anglian period, though, in the absence of sapwood, precise dating evidence cannot be provided. This evidence is, however, based on only two dated samples.

Period 3

A single isolated timber, 9044, was dated. The outermost measured ring was identified as likely to be that immediately under the bark. This indicates that the timber was probably felled in the winter of 904/05.

The dendrochronological results support other archaeological indications of activity on the site in the very early 10th century, though the evidence for this is provided by only a single timber.

Period 4A
Tenement B

An isolated timber, 8867, was felled during the period 906–41.

Tenement D

Two posts (9025 and 9026) from alignment 30358 were dated. These timbers are components in a clearly defined single alignment and consequently a combined felling date range of 921–39, and a possible construction date, is indicated. An isolated timber, 9219, was felled during the period 897–933.

The dendrochronological results suggest that this period dates to the early/mid-10th century which supports other archaeological evidence. The activity is thought to be continuous and the few dated timbers imply that on Tenements B and D construction work is broadly contemporaneous, though in the absence of bark-edge it is not possible to determine whether these are precisely contemporary or whether the periods of felling are in fact several years apart.

Period 4B
Tenement B

Three timbers from alignment 27607 were dated. The similarities between **9087** and 9088 suggest they are likely to be contemporaneous, indicating a felling date range of 925–47. Timber 9089, however, was felled later during the period 950–85. These results may indicate the date of construction and a subsequent repair or alternatively could indicate the presence of re-used timber within the alignment. There is no other evidence to indicate re-use, however.

Timber 9092 from alignment 27676 was felled between 942 and 974. A single timber from alignment 27796 was dated; this had a felling date range of 937–73, suggesting a construction date in the mid-10th century. The only dated timber from alignment 34486 was felled after 891. The single dated timber, **8978**, from alignment 37166 was felled after 904. However, this timber appears to have been derived from the same tree as timber **8887** from Period 4B, Tenement D, alignment 22585, so it was probably actually felled during the period 935–37. Timber **9070**, a horizontal, was felled between 941 and 959. An isolated timber, **8856**, was felled after 903 and a discarded timber fragment, **9067**, was felled during 930–48.

Ten timbers were dated from Tenement B, the majority of which tend to indicate activity around the mid-10th century, with felling dates potentially as early as the 930s but as late as the 980s.

Tenement C

The only dated timber from alignment 30765 was felled after 899. Two timbers from alignment 35161 were dated; if these are contemporaneous then both were felled after 891. The single dated timber from alignment 36591/25640 was felled during 914–48. An isolated timber, **9215**, was felled after 905. A horizontal in layer 35293 was felled after 923 and another horizontal in path 37405 was felled after 823.

Only one of the seven dated timbers from Tenement C produced a felling date range. This implied activity during the first half of the 10th century. The remaining timbers produced *termini post quem* for felling which range from as early as 823 to as late as 923.

Tenement D

The only dated timber from alignment 22059 was felled after 933. Two timbers (8884, 8885) from alignment 22585 are probably derived from the same tree, with the possibility that a third timber (8886) is also derived from that tree. All five dated timbers from this alignment at the west side of the tenement appear likely to be contemporaneous and were therefore probably felled in the period 935–37 and used shortly afterwards in the construction of the alignment. In addition, 8887 appears to have been derived from the same tree as 8978 (Period 4B, Tenement B, alignment 37166), whereas 8884 and 8885 were probably derived from the same tree as 9041 (Period 4B, Tenement D, alignment 30436).

The only dated timber from alignment 30436, located at the east side of the tenement, has no sapwood and hence has a *terminus post quem* for felling of 900. However, timber 9041 appears to have been derived from the same tree as timbers 8884 and 8885 from alignment 22585 and was thus also probably felled and initially used in the period 935–37. The single dated post from alignment 30357 was felled after 908 and timber 9159, which was embedded in alignment 35111, was felled after 903.

Nine timbers were dated from Tenement D of which the six from alignments 22585 and 30436, lying at the west and east side of the tenement respectively, appear to have been felled in the mid-930s. The remaining timbers produced *termini post quem* for felling in the first third of the 10th century.

Period 4B summary

The dendrochronological results indicate building activity during the mid-10th century on Tenements B, C and D. However, the evidence derived from later periods suggests that the constructional activity in Period 4B occurred prior to the mid-950s (see below). The identification of two timbers derived from the same tree but found on Tenements B and D provides a direct link, implying contemporaneous construction work in the mid-930s on these two tenements.

Period 5A

Tenement A

There were two dated timbers from Tenement A. One from alignment 37253, 8720, was felled after AD 941. The other, a barrel stave from cut 31266, was felled after 906. The cut is for a barrel-lined well/pit which has a well-defined stratigraphical relationship. It clearly pre-dates Structure 5/1 (Period 5B, Tenement A) which cuts into 31266, whereas 31266 itself cuts through Period 4B levels. Consequently it must have been felled before the 961/62 construction date indicated for Structure 5/1 (see below).

Tenement B

The outermost ring on the only dated timber from alignment 18422 dates to 955 and has been identified as likely to be that immediately under the bark. This indicates that the timber was probably felled in the winter of 955/56 and hence may imply construction of this alignment shortly afterwards. The three dated timbers from alignment 36582 (8753, 8759, 8786) appear likely to be contemporaneous. The outermost measured ring of timber 8753 was identified as likely to be that immediately under the bark. This indicates that these timbers were also all probably felled in the winter of 955/56, again implying a possible construction date shortly after felling for this alignment.

The single dated timber from alignment 36599 was felled after 940. Two timbers from the backfill of pit 28652 were dated. The timbers have very different visual characteristics and their ring patterns show no similarity, although the overlap is only 33 years. In the absence of bark-edge and hence the provision of precise felling dates, it is possible that these timbers represent two felling phases both of which probably occur in the second half of the 10th century. The implication is that the pit was probably backfilled some years after these two timbers were originally used. The earliest possible primary use of timber 9056 is 960 which clearly post-dates the 955/56 felling phase obtained for other timbers from Period 5A.

The seven dated Tenement B timbers indicate felling activity in the mid–late 10th century, with two alignments containing timbers felled in 955/56 but with the backfill of a pit containing timber felled after this in the later 10th century.

Tenement D

The seven dated timbers from alignment 14853, two of which are probably derived from the same tree (8807, 8809), appear likely to be contemporaneous. The heartwood-sapwood boundaries date to within a few years of each other with the possible exception of 8951. The outermost measured ring was identified as likely to be that immediately under the bark on timbers 8807 and 8812.

This implies that all seven timbers were likely to have been felled in the winter of 955/56 and hence probably used shortly afterwards in the construction of the alignment. An isolated post, timber 8795, was felled during the period 946–78.

The eight dated timbers from Tenement D again indicate felling activity in the mid–late 10th century, with two timbers from the dated alignment being felled in 955/56.

Period 5A summary

Building activity appears to have occurred on Tenements A, B and D in the mid-10th century, and more specifically Tenements B and D appear to be linked by the presence of timbers felled in 955/56. The archaeological evidence indicates that these timbers are primary material and hence neither re-used nor dumped. There are therefore clear implications for the results from the Period 4B timbers, all of which have felling date ranges compatible with pre-dating the 955/56 felling phase identified in Period 5A. In addition, the evidence from later periods suggests that activity associated with Period 5A is likely to have occurred prior to the early 960s, indicating that this period may well have lasted for only a relatively short time span during the Anglo-Scandinavian phase.

Timber 172 from a covered drain found during the watching brief has a felling date range of 960–94. This felling date range suggests that this timber is most likely to be associated with Period 5A.

Period 5B

The vast majority of the dated timbers (64% or 108/168) are associated with this period.

Tenement A
Structure 5/1

Eight planks were dated, of which six (8675, 8676, 8679, 8702, 8708, 8680) are known to be from the east wall of Structure 5/1 and one from the west wall (0051). Planks 0051, 8675, 8676 and 8680 are probably derived from the same tree. It appears likely that all the planks are contemporary. The outermost measured ring of 8680 was identified as that immediately under the bark, implying that all eight planks were probably felled in the winter of 961/62.

Five posts from the east wall of Structure 5/1 were dated, including two derived from the same tree (8695, 8696). These all appear to be contemporaneous and have

a combined felling date range of 961–81 which is clearly compatible with the 961/62 felling date obtained from the planks.

The results indicate that both the planks and posts from Structure 5/1 are likely to be contemporary so, in the absence of any evidence of re-use, a construction date shortly after felling in 961/62 is indicated for this double-skinned basemented structure fronting Tenement A. This also provides a date before which cut 31266 (Period 5A, Tenement A) must have been made due to their stratigraphical relationship.

Post 8827 is from a series of paired posts within Structure 5/1. This has a felling date range of 946–79 and was therefore potentially felled at the same time as the timbers used in the construction of Structure 5/1. The similarities between this timber and the posts from the east wall of the structure imply that this post was potentially also felled in 961/62 and that the alignment is likely to be contemporary with the erection of Structure 5/1.

The fourteen dated timbers from Tenement A, all associated with Structure 5/1, indicate building work in the latter half of the 10th century, with the construction of 5/1 probably occurring in the early 960s.

Tenement B

A horizontal in pit/cut 27298/26993 was felled between 998 and 1034.

Structure 5/3

Seven planks were dated from the south, east and west walls of this building. 9192 and 9198 are both tangentially converted base planks. These appear contemporary and produce a combined felling date range of 958–91. The remaining five are all radial planks which are thinner than the tangential planks. These have no trace of sapwood and so have *termini post quem* for felling ranging from 883 to 917. The latest rings of the radial planks only overlap those of the tangential planks by nine years. The lack of evidence for re-use suggests that these may well be the inner sections of larger trees. Consequently the five radial planks may be contemporary with planks 9192 and 9198 and hence potentially also felled and used in 958–91.

Four posts from the east wall of the structure were dated. They all appear to be contemporaneous and have a combined felling date range of 952–87 which is clearly compatible with the felling date range obtained from the planks. Post 8556 appears to have been derived from the same tree as timber 9008 which is associated with the Period 5B Structure 5/7 in Tenement D.

If it is assumed that the planks and posts from Structure 5/3 are contemporary they were all probably felled during the period 958–87. In the absence of any evidence of re-use this felling date range reflects the probable construction date of Structure 5/3. However, the same-tree link to a timber in the construction levels of Structure 5/7, possibly a chock, leads to the tenuous suggestion of a construction date of 966 or shortly after for Structure 5/3. Additional weight is given to this suggestion by examination of the quality of the cross-matching between the ring sequences of the Structure 5/3 posts and the Structure 5/7 timbers (see Table 11 in the full report).

Structure 5/4

A post from the west wall (8354) and what is believed to be a drain capping (8387), together with another post from the east wall (8234), were dated. The outermost measured ring of 8387 was identified as likely to be that immediately under the bark. If all three are contemporary, they were probably felled in the winter of 972/73, but it may be that the drain was not part of the original construction. Timber 8379, a sill from the east wall, was felled between 961 and 989, which is clearly potentially contemporaneous with the 972/73 felling date indicated by the posts and drain capping. Timber 8849 appears to be a supplementary sill beam at the south end of the west wall though as a result of modern intrusions this archaeological interpretation must be considered tentative. It was felled during 975–1011. The results suggest that Structure 5/4 was constructed shortly after felling in 972/73, with sill 8849 as a later modification.

One plank found in the collapse of 5/4, and possibly part of the structure, was felled between 993 and 1029. This may indicate late 10th- or early 11th-century repairs or modifications being undertaken on Structure 5/4. Three timbers of uncertain origin found in the backfill associated with Structure 5/4 were dated. These give a combined *terminus post quem* for felling of 1001, thereby indicating that Structure 5/4 remained in use for the rest of the 10th century and was not abandoned until the beginning of the 11th century at the very earliest.

The results from 21 dated timbers from Tenement B indicate constructional work in the later 10th century, with some felling activity as late as the early 11th century associated with Structure 5/4 and pit/cut 27298/26993.

Structure 5/3, which fronts the tenement, appears to have been constructed during the period 958–87, possibly in 966. Structure 5/4, further back on the tenement, appears likely to have been erected in the early 970s and subsequently modified towards the end of the 10th century or possibly the very early 11th century, indicating that it was in use for a minimum of two decades.

Tenement C

Three timbers from alignment 33233 were dated. Two of these (8527, 8599) appear likely to be contemporary and have a combined felling date of 964–84. However, the outermost ring of 8623 was thought to be that immediately under the bark, indicating that it was felled in 956/57. This suggests that the alignment was either constructed in the mid-950s and repaired over a decade later or alternatively that it was constructed shortly after felling in 964–84 using both primary and secondary timber, potentially re-using some material from the short-duration Period 5A.

Two timbers from alignment 33235 were dated. The outermost measured ring of both timbers was identified as likely to be that immediately under the bark. This indicates that they were felled in the winter of 955/56. As this alignment is associated with Period 5B it is suggested that these timbers may have been re-used from Period 5A, though it does raise a stratigraphical issue concerning the transition between the two periods.

The only dated timber from alignment 5852 was felled after 979. Timber 8620 is tentatively associated with fence line 6661 which is located to the rear of Structure 5/6. It was felled after 1017 and hence supports other evidence that this fence line is later than Structure 5/6 (see below). Timber 8832, a horizontal, was felled after 956.

Four isolated timbers associated with this tenement have been successfully dated. Two of these have a *terminus post quem* for felling in the mid–late 10th century. However, timber 8873 was probably felled in the winter of 940/41, whilst timber 8921 has a felling date in the summer of 966. A horizontal, possibly associated with path 37403, was felled after 946. Two (8897, 8899) of the three dated horizontals from path 37404 are likely to be derived from the same tree and were therefore both felled after 919. The third timber, 8903, was felled after 950.

Structure 5/5

Five posts, one of which is from the north wall of the structure, were dated. Two of the posts (9133, 9146) may have been derived from the same tree. These all appear to be contemporaneous and have a combined felling date range of 956–79. In the absence of any evidence of re-use this felling date range reflects the probable construction date of Structure 5/5.

Structure 5/6

Three planks (8213, 8215, 8293) from the west wall were dated. These appear likely to be contemporaneous and could have derived from the same tree, so were therefore all felled after 951. In addition, one plank from the east wall was dated which has a *terminus post quem* for felling of 895. This may indicate that it has been trimmed heavily, resulting in the loss of a large number of outer rings or alternatively it could be a re-used timber, although no evidence for this was noted. Two posts, also from the west wall, were dated. One has a *terminus post quem* for felling in the late 9th century whilst the other was felled during the period 961–97. The dated sill from the north wall was felled during the period 970–1003. If the planks, posts and sill are contemporaneous a combined felling date of 970–97 is indicated which, in the absence of any evidence for re-use, suggests a construction date for Structure 5/6 in the late 10th century.

Two timbers associated with the collapse of Structure 5/6 both have a *terminus post quem* for felling in the 950s, and could consequently be contemporary with the 970–97 felling date indicated for the timbers from the primary construction of Structure 5/6. Four timbers were dated from the backfill of Structure 5/6. Timber **8156** was felled during the period 901–37, whilst 8067 was probably felled in the period 958–94. Of the remaining two dated timbers, 8071 is probably derived from the same tree as 8067 and was thus also probably felled in 958–94, whilst 8075 was felled after 961. These are broadly contemporaneous with, or even earlier than, the suggested construction date of Structure 5/6 and are consequently unable to assist in determining when the structure was abandoned.

Timber 8240, a horizontal from the drain in Structure 5/6, was felled after 963 which shows that the drain could be broadly contemporary with the initial construction of Structure 5/6.

Thirty-five timbers were dated from Tenement C, the majority of which tend to indicate activity in the later 10th century, though there are a number of outliers. One of the isolated timbers (8873) was felled in 940/41 and is thought likely to be re-used in this context, whilst timber 8156 has a felling date range in the first half of the 10th century

but is from the backfill associated with Structure 5/6. In addition, the felling date of 955/56 obtained for the two timbers from alignment 33235 is precisely that obtained for a number of timbers associated with Period 5A which suggests that these may be re-used in this context. This re-use theory is supported by the identification of two felling phases for the timbers used in alignment 33233, one of which was felled in 956/57. The only other obvious outlier is timber 8620, from fence line 6661, which was likely to have been felled in the 11th century. Structure 5/5, the earliest of two superimposed buildings on Tenement C, was probably constructed between 956 and 979. Structure 5/6 which overlies 5/5 was erected no more than 40 years later, and more likely only around 15–20 years later, during the period 970–97.

Tenement D

Timber 8845, a horizontal, was felled after 958.

Structure 5/7

Two sills (9002, 9027) and an associated chock under a sill (9029) were dated. The outermost measured ring of timber 9002 was identified as likely to be that immediately under the bark, indicating that this sill was probably felled in the summer of 966. The remaining two timbers are clearly contemporaneous and were therefore also likely to have been felled in 966. Post 9003 was felled after 955 which is clearly compatible with the 966 felling date. In the absence of any evidence of re-use, the above results imply a construction date for Structure 5/7 shortly after felling in 966.

Timber 9008, is a scrap of wood, possibly a chock, found in the construction levels, although on archaeological grounds not necessarily part of the construction. It has a felling date range of 954–90. However, it appears to be derived from the same tree as post 8556 from Period 5B Tenement B Structure 5/3, and so was actually probably felled in the period 958–87 (see above). It is clearly broadly contemporary with the erection of Structure 5/7 and consequently may also have been felled in 966.

The seven dated timbers lying apparently abandoned in the base of the construction cut appear to be contemporaneous and have a combined felling date of 957–85. The ring sequences from some of these timbers show good similarity with the timbers associated with the construction of Structure 5/7 and may therefore be contemporary with the 966 felling phase (see Table 12 in the full report). Timber 9020, from the stave-built box, was felled after 952.

Eight timbers from the backfill were dated. Three of these (8892, 8947, 8979) have felling dates in the late 10th or early 11th centuries, whilst the remaining samples have *termini post quem* for felling ranging from the early to the mid-10th century. The earliest possible felling date for timber 8947 is 991 which suggests that the backfill episode occurred sometime after this date. In addition, timber 8947 may have been derived from the same tree as timber 8359 from the construction levels of Structure 5/8 which lies directly above Structure 5/7. This same-tree link implies that the abandonment of Structure 5/7 and subsequent construction of Structure 5/8 directly above it are basically contemporaneous.

Structure 5/8

One (8882) of the two dated braces from the east wall has a *terminus post quem* for felling in the mid-10th century whilst the other, 8888, was felled in the winter of 1008/09. Three sills associated with Structure 5/8 were dated. Two (8392, 8394) have *termini post quem* for felling in the mid–late 10th century, whilst one (8393) was probably felled in the winter of 995/96. These therefore could all be contemporaneous. Sill 8394 is likely to have been derived from the same tree as brace 8882. The 995/96 felling date indicated by sill 8393 is obviously earlier than that of 1008/09 indicated by brace 8888, whilst all other dated structural timbers from 5/8 are compatible with either of these felling dates. This could imply that the construction of 5/8 took place in the very late 10th century, with repair work being undertaken some twelve to fourteen years later, or alternatively that the structure incorporates re-used timbers although there was no evidence of re-use.

The dated timber from the construction levels associated with Structure 5/8 was felled between 988 and 1024 and is clearly broadly contemporary with the either late 10th- or early 11th-century date for the demolition of 5/7. It may have been derived from the same tree as timber 8947 from the backfill of Structure 5/7 in which case it must have been felled after 991 but probably before 1024.

Six planks from the dog-leg drain associated with, and believed to be contemporary with the construction of, Structure 5/8 were dated. Planks 8858 and 8863 are clearly derived from the same tree, as are 8859 and 8860. It appears probable that all the planks are contemporary. They were therefore felled, and probably used in the construction of the drain, during the period 988–1017. This clearly demonstrates that the drain is broadly contemporary with Structure 5/8 but in the absence of

bark-edge cannot assist in determining whether Structure 5/8 was constructed in the very late 990s or towards the end of the first decade of the 11th century.

Two timbers from the watching brief were dated that are clearly from the same structure, but stratigraphically it is not possible to determine whether this was Structure 5/7 or 5/8. Timber 123 is probably an edge-set horizontal plank, part of a classic sunken-structure wall, and was felled between 966 and 1002. Timber 122, interpreted as a lipped sill beam, was felled after 994. The evidence that these two timbers are from the same structure implies that this is more likely to be the later Structure 5/8, though the quality of the cross-matching between 122 and 123 and the timbers from Structures 5/7 and 5/8 is inconclusive (see Table 13 in the full report).

The majority of the 36 timbers dated from Tenement D indicate activity in the second half of the 10th century, though some felling is identified in the early 11th century. A construction date shortly after felling in 966 is suggested for Structure 5/7 which is stratigraphically the earliest structure on Tenement D and is located under the rear room of Structure 5/8. Structure 5/8 contains timbers felled in the late 10th century and the early 11th century. This implies that Structure 5/7 was in existence for a minimum of nearly three decades before being replaced by Structure 5/8.

Tenement E
Structure 5/9

Timber 138, possibly a joist or an abandoned timber related to construction, was felled after 913. Timber 131, interpreted as a sill beam, was felled between 951 and 987. In the absence of any evidence for re-use the results suggest a construction date in the latter half of the 10th century but this is based on the felling date range obtained from only one timber.

Period 5B summary

Building activity seems to have taken place on these Period 5B tenements in the latter half of the 10th century and the early 11th century which supports other archaeological evidence indicating that the occupation associated with these buildings continued into the early 11th century. The early 960s date indicated for Structure 5/1 provides further evidence for the short duration of Period 5A, at least on Tenement A. It appears to be the earliest Period 5B structure, whilst Structure 5/8, built at least 34 years later, is the latest. A probable same-tree link between Tenement B Structure 5/3 and the Tenement D Structure 5/7 construction levels implies a connection between the two tenements and may suggest that Structures 5/3 and 5/7 were constructed at the same time. Re-use of timber from Period 5A is also highlighted as a possibility in some structures.

Period 5Cf

Tenement D
Structure 5/10

The similarities between the two dated bracer beams indicate that they are likely to be contemporary. Both were therefore felled and initially used in 963–98. Sill 8456 was felled after 944 and therefore could be contemporary with the two bracer beams. Both bracer beams show signs that they have been re-used in this context so the felling date obtained indicates the construction of an earlier building and not Structure 5/10. Structure 5/10 clearly post-dates Structure 5/8, which it overlies, indicating that the former is likely to be constructed sometime after 1008/09. This shows that the bracer beams were re-used at least a decade after their initial use and probably significantly longer.

The dendrochronological results show felling activity in the mid–late 10th century. However, Structure 5/10 overlies part of Structure 5/8 from Period 5B for which a construction date in the very late 10th or early 11th century is indicated by the dendrochronological evidence. Evidence for the use of secondary (re-used) timber resolves this apparent incompatibility.

Period 5Cr

Tenement C
Structure 5/12

Six stubs were dated. The dates of the outermost measured heartwood rings are within five years of each other which suggests they are likely to be contemporary and thus have a combined felling date of 1013–49. In the absence of any evidence for re-use a construction date shortly after felling is indicated.

The dendrochronological results indicate constructional activity in the first half of the 11th century at the riverward end of Tenement C.

Discussion

The following discussion attempts to place the Coppergate dendrochronological analysis in its historical perspective and provides a revised overview of the major issues raised in earlier archive reports.

The historical perspective

Coppergate was one of the first complex urban archaeological sites in England to employ dendrochronology in order to attempt to clarify the complex and stratigraphically obscure inter-relationships between dense clusters, or even intermingled alignments, of timbers. It remains one of the largest single-site sources of tree-ring data in this country outside London, along with the Roman site of Annetwell Street in Carlisle (Groves 1990). The analysis of the Coppergate assemblage was valuable in developing appropriate strategies with which to handle large diverse groups of excavated timbers. Such strategies are designed to maximise the archaeological potential of the assemblage, whilst enabling efficient yet comprehensive analysis.

The Coppergate samples arrived at Sheffield in numerous batches stretching over a period of many years. Due to the complexity of the archaeological remains, timbers from different periods were extracted simultaneously and enclosed within these batches. It was therefore not possible to examine the samples in a logical order, structure by structure and period by period. The relationship between the requirement for dendrochronological sampling and issues of conservation and display had only just started to be addressed so initially some timbers were held back in their entirety and only became available for analysis at a later date. With hindsight, and also using accumulated experience subsequently gained from the excavation and analysis of other urban waterlogged timber assemblages, it is clear that a more carefully planned strategic approach may well have led to a more efficient dendrochronological analysis.

The fact that Coppergate was a complex urban site with timber structures spanning a millennium brought its own complications since dating timbers from such a site is very different to dating a group of timbers from, for example, a single-phase standing building. In the latter case the process is relatively easy because not only are all the samples from a phase available at once, but also more often than not the timbers appear to have originated in a single woodland stand. When the Coppergate analysis began, it very soon became apparent that the timbers came from a diverse woodland source since there was often relatively poor cross-matching between timbers from the same structure. As a consequence it initially proved difficult to construct site master curves. This made dating more difficult, as did the fact that there were very few reference chronologies in the late 1970s against which to test the Coppergate ring sequences. During the subsequent decades many of these problems were overcome as the technique was developed and refined, the network of reference chronologies hugely extended, and advances in computer technology allowed large amounts of tree-ring data to be analysed far more rapidly than in the late 1970s.

Dating precision

The dendrochronological analysis reported here has successfully provided a basic framework for the development of the Coppergate tenements over a period of about a century. A number of structures have been precisely dated, thus providing a series of fixed points within the complex stratigraphical sequence (Figure 345). This has assisted in the estimation of the duration of each period and has also provided an indication of how long some structures were in use within a period. However, the relative scarcity of timbers that were recognised as having retained bark-edge and the sheer complexity of the timber remains combine to prevent the analysis providing the detailed chronological framework that had perhaps been originally envisaged or hoped for. In some instances the dendrochronology has also raised questions concerning possible re-use of timber and the transition phases between periods.

The analysis has proved remarkable in that the success rate, as indicated by the number of dated samples as a percentage of processed samples, is 84%. This compares favourably with medieval Coppergate at 53% (Hillam 2002) and the usual 50–60% success rate on complex urban archaeological excavation assemblages (e.g. Groves 1990; 1996a). It also exceeds the 72% success rate for medieval and post-medieval standing buildings (Groves 2002).

The presence of sapwood and bark-edge on timbers is vital in the production of detailed dating evidence. In order to maximise the potential of any large assemblage careful sampling within a well-defined sampling strategy is essential to the future success of the analysis and should thus be undertaken in close consultation with the dendrochronologist. Sampling of timbers must be focused on the section of a timber likely to provide the greatest number of annual growth rings but must also take into account the presence of bark-edge or any trace of sapwood, which may occasionally result in a timber being sampled twice. It is possible that sites such as Coppergate, excavated in the late 1970s and early 1980s, may not have had their potential fully exploited. Sites excavated from the mid-1980s onwards have seen a noticeable increase in the presence of sapwood on samples: compare Trig Lane, London (1974–78; Tyers 1992), The Lanes, Carlisle (1978–82; Groves 1993a; Groves 1996a; Groves 1996b), and Billingsgate, London (1982; Hillam 1988; Hillam 1992b), to Fennings Wharf, London (1984; Tyers forthcoming), Annetwell Street, Carlisle (1981–84; Groves 1990), and No. 1 Poultry, London (1995–96; Tyers 2000b). However, sapwood is notoriously friable and will degrade rapidly if the waterlogged conditions required for preservation are not maintained. If sapwood is preserved it is usually extremely fragile and it may well have suffered crushing prior to excavation that can make the recognition of bark-edge or heartwood/sapwood boundary very difficult or make the outermost rings unmeasurable. The process of sampling and subsequent cleaning can also inadvertently exacerbate this problem, however carefully the timbers are handled.

Crushing and the resultant distortion of the outermost rings was certainly a recognised problem at Coppergate, particularly with planks on which the area of likely bark-edge is very small (Hillam 1987). Of the processed timbers 92 (46%) have either some sapwood or the heartwood/sapwood boundary; only 15 (7.5%) samples have retained the bark-edge; this is a very low percentage considering the number of structures sampled but it is typical of other excavations of this date. It is possible that with two decades of accumulated experience of the analysis of waterlogged timbers bark-edge or the heartwood/sapwood boundary, even if crushed, would have been more confidently recognised on more of the Coppergate timbers during either sampling or analysis. Timbers 8798, 8810, 8811 from alignment 14853 in Period 5A Tenement D, for instance, all look to have only one or two rings missing to the bark-edge. These are all tangentially converted planks which appear likely to have suffered slight damage to the outermost surface resulting in the crushing/loss of the outer ring(s), preventing the recognition of bark-edge. Timbers 8692 and 8693, posts from Structure 5/1, Tenement A, Period 5B, also appear likely to have suffered slight damage which has prevented recognition of the presence of bark-edge. The dates of the outermost measured heartwood rings on the stubs from Period 5Cr Structure 5/12 in Tenement C range from 997 to 1003, with the heartwood/sapwood boundary on **8649** also dating to 1003. Such a narrow range of end dates implies that the stubs are only missing the sapwood rings and that the outermost measured ring is likely to mark the heartwood/sapwood boundary. If this assumption is correct then it has the effect of slightly narrowing the felling date range to 1013–43. The same is true for the group of abandoned timbers in Period 5B Structure 5/7 in Tenement D whose outermost heartwood rings range from 938 to 945.

In an attempt to refine the felling date ranges given for many of the structures and timbers and hence the overall dating framework a sapwood estimate based on the Coppergate data was produced. The number of measured samples with complete sapwood was only fifteen, too few for a statistically reliable estimate to be created (see Figure 3 in the full report). This number was increased to 37 by assuming that all timbers with some sapwood or the heartwood/sapwood boundary were felled simultaneously in those structures where one or more timbers had bark-edge, thus creating a pseudo-sapwood estimate (see Figure 4 in the full report). The 95% ranges based on skewed distribution are 11–40 and 11–38 which, considering the small sample size, are not felt to be sufficiently different from the 10–46 range standardly employed to warrant any re-interpretation of the Coppergate results.

Timber source and trade

The quality of the intra-site cross-matching obtained is variable, though this is now known to be not uncommon on large urban complexes. The cross-matching between timbers within some structures (e.g. Period 5B, Tenement C, Structure 5/5; see Table 14 in the full report) is uniformly very good, whilst in others it is variable or poor (Period 4B, Tenement D, alignment 22585; Period 5B, Tenement C, Structure 5/6; see Tables 15 and 16 in the full report). This variation could be due to the use of discrete woodland sources and/or extensive re-use of timber resulting in the mixing of timbers from different sources within a structure. Evidence for re-use from the excavation records is scarce, though this does not entirely exclude the possibility. Re-use can be difficult to recognise without direct evidence provided by non-functional carpentry features, such as mortices or peg-holes for instance, which may well be trimmed off during secondary conversion, thus

removing vital evidence of prior use. However, the dendrochronological results also imply that re-use is not widespread. On sites where re-use is extensive, such as The Lanes, Carlisle (Groves 1993a; 1996a; 1996b), there is no distinct progression of the dates of the outermost rings through the various phases. At Coppergate the outermost rings of the assemblage show a clear progression through the periods. In addition, there are recognisable changes between periods in the characteristics of the timbers, relating to age and size of trees (see below), that also suggest that re-use is unlikely to be extensive.

The cross-dating of the site master chronology and its individual components with reference chronologies from throughout the British Isles and elsewhere in Europe (Table 36) shows no evidence of long-distance importation of timber. They match particularly well with other reference chronologies from York and its surrounding region and thus the timbers appear likely to be of local origin. Coppergate and other sites in the York environs have highlighted that this is an area in which trees do show wide variation in their growth patterns over relatively short distances. This, combined with the evidence from other large urban sites of either Roman or medieval date, suggests that the timber was derived from an extensive area of woodland in the surrounding region rather than a series of discrete sources. This implies that the inhabitants of Coppergate and the rest of the rapidly expanding York had relatively open access to the entire surrounding woodlands. Large urban settlements have a considerable requirement for timber and other woodland products and are therefore automatically exploiting extensive areas of woodland.

The identification of a same-tree pair of timbers in Period 4B on Tenements B and D and also in Period 5B on Tenements B and D implies synchronous construction work, as does the common felling date of 955/56 indicated in Period 5A also on Tenements B and D. This suggests co-operation between the occupants at some level but whether the development as a whole was the product of an organised municipal arrangement or on an *ad hoc* basis remains to be seen. If timber was being obtained through a single central supply route it would be reasonable to suggest that there should perhaps be more same-tree pairs and higher overall levels of similarity (*t* values) between tenements. In addition, the construction work might have been expected to be more intense, with a whole series of structures being erected perhaps over a couple of years rather than decades apart. Conversely there does seem to be a potential link between the occupants of Tenements

B and D. In general though, the dendrochronological results can neither confirm nor refute the possibility of a central timber supply. The likelihood or otherwise of this depends on the social organisation in place, whether individuals were entirely self-reliant for construction and repair work or whether there was communal co-operation.

Trees and woodland composition

As indicated above, the results attest to the use of local timber. Consequently the timber assemblage must give some reflection of the woodland available for exploitation. The dendrochronological analyses can clearly not reconstruct a woodland as the analysed assemblage is only a very small percentage of the woodland product. However, it can add valuable information to a multi-disciplinary approach aimed at landscape reconstruction.

The Anglo-Scandinavian timbers indicate that they were derived from trees which had a wide variation in both age and size. This variation is demonstrated in Figures 5a and 6a in the full report, though it must be noted that the ring sequence length is generally an underestimate of tree age due to the lack of both pith and bark-edge on the majority of the assemblage. It has previously been proposed that the timbers used in the Anglo-Scandinavian phases were derived from two main classes of tree:

1. Those producing radially split planks. They have diameters of at least 500mm and sometimes over 1m. The trees were often over 200 years old when felled and occasionally over 300 years. Sapwood was frequently removed and, in some cases, heart-wood rings as well.

2. Those producing the tangential planks or trunks which had been trimmed, halved or quartered. They are usually less than 500mm in diameter, generally under 100 years old and never more than 150 years when felled. This is the type of oak tree which one might get in the classic coppice-with-standards woodland (e.g. Rackham 1980, frontis-piece; Rackham 1990).

However, there is no distinct grouping of the material apparent in Figure 5 in the full report and the overall assemblage probably represents a mature natural or semi-natural multi-aged woodland. This is likely to contain

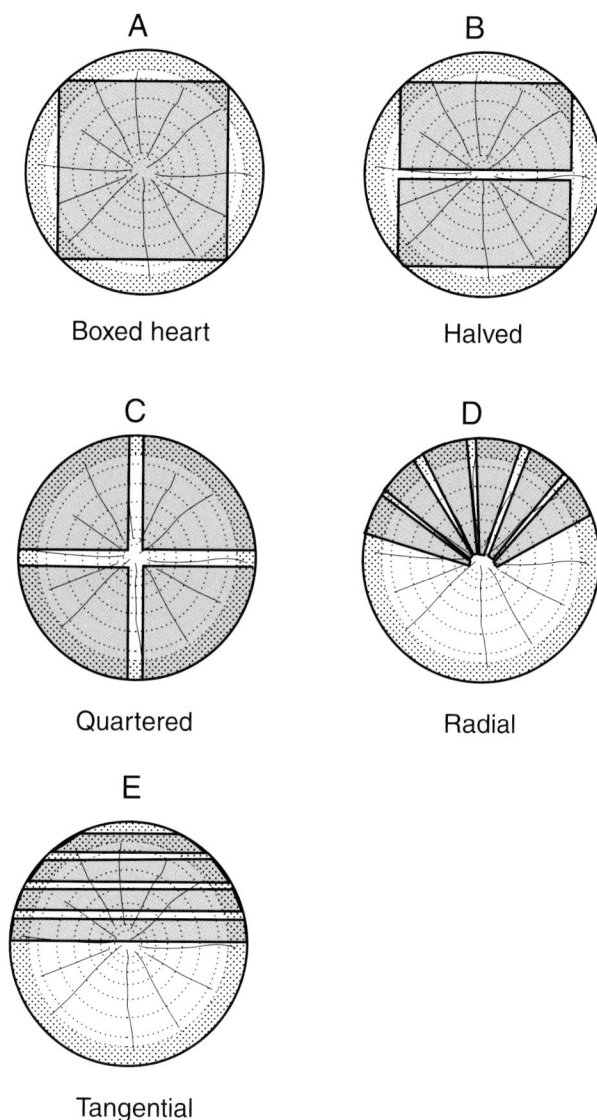

Fig.346   *Typical conversion types found in wooden structures*

trees ranging from fast-grown young trees, perhaps on the peripheral areas where the canopy is more open, to slower-grown long-lived trees in denser areas of the same extensive woodland. Consequently the apparent grouping is more likely to be a result of selection for function prior to conversion into structural elements and then the method by which the conversion was undertaken rather than the use of two discrete sources.

This grouping is perhaps over emphasised in the assemblage as a whole by some structures. Structure 5/1 for instance contains a series of radial planks which are clearly derived from trees in the order of 250–300 years old and in excess of 0.5m diameter when felled, though it should be noted that four of these planks are derived from the same tree. However, the posts, all halved or quartered sections, and the tangentially converted planks tend to be derived from trees that were probably about 100 years old and less than c.0.4m diameter when felled. The selection process has potentially ensured efficient use of the available resource with minimal working and minimal wastage. The ring sequences do show more similarity within the groups but also show some similarity between groups and therefore are all likely to have been derived from the same, though potentially very large, area of woodland (see Table 17 in the full report). Structure 5/3 shows a similar selection process where the trees used as posts are likely to have been selected for their size and subsequently required minimal working, as have the tangentially converted base planks. The radial planks appear to represent the inner sections of longer-lived trees which have been more heavily trimmed, possibly resulting in the production of small but structurally useful outer sections. In general, however, it appears that when planks are required they are usually derived from a small number of large trees, perhaps suggesting that the long-lived large trees may have been perceived as a valuable resource. The possible exception to this are the posts from Structure 5/5 which are derived from relatively long-lived slow-grown trees that have been heavily trimmed during conversion.

The age range distribution does appear to be more uniform in the earlier periods than in Period 5B which has a higher proportion of short-lived material (Figures 5b and 6b in the full report), though direct comparisons are difficult due to the small number of dated timbers from the earlier periods. This increase in the use of young trees could be due to exploitation of woodland that has regenerated (i.e. secondary woodland) on areas previously cleared or heavily exploited during the early Anglo-Scandinavian periods. Intense exploitation has the effect of opening up woodland, decreasing the competition for the remaining trees, and allowing a flush of regeneration which would potentially result in the availability of young relatively fast-grown material in the later 10th century. There is no clear evidence from the dendrochronological analysis to indicate deliberate management of the woodland resource but other archaeological sources may provide further information. Within Period 5B it is also noticeable that Tenement D has proportionally fewer longer-lived timbers than Tenements A, B and C (Figures 6c and 7 in the full report). This presumably may reflect the lack of survival of planks associated with the walls of structures rather than indicating increased exploitation of secondary woodland.

Conclusion

The dendrochronological analysis of the Coppergate timbers played an important role in the development of the dendrochronological approaches currently employed on complex archaeological assemblages. This analysis proved successful in that 84% of the timbers were dated, providing independent dating evidence for structures associated with the intense activity on the tenements during the 10th and early 11th centuries. The resultant site chronology spans the period 460–1011 and is particularly well replicated during the mid-8th to mid-10th centuries. The timber appears to be derived from multi-aged natural or semi-natural woodland some of which, by the latter part of the Anglo-Scandinavian phase, may be young secondary woodland. The apparent diversity of the timber indicates that the area of exploitation was likely to encompass an extensive area of the surrounding region as would now be expected for any large urban development. Links have been identified between some tenements but on current evidence from this site and other large urban excavations there is little to indicate whether the supply of timber is already becoming a specialised occupation within the social organisation of an increasingly urbanised settlement.

Table 34 Details of tree-ring samples. wb – watching brief; +mn – unmeasured outer rings (unmeasured inner rings are not recorded); ARW – average ring width; HS – heartwood-sapwood transition; B – bark edge; fs – outer ring incomplete and not measured, indicates summer felling. Timber conversion types – see Fig.346

Timber no	Context no	Period & Tenement	Function	Total no of rings	Sapwood rings	ARW (mm)	Timber conversion	Dimensions (mm)	Date span (AD)	Felled (AD)
0004	1218	5B A	5/1 plank	120	–	1.73	D	235x40	788–907	after 917
0032	1306	5B A	5/1 post	48 +10	–	1.99	CX	135x120	–	–
0051	1308	5B A	5/1 west wall plank	208	–	1.16	D	275x35	730–937	after 947
0055	1313	5B A	5/1 post	86	–	1.78	CX	150x125	–	–
0090	1715	2 (wb)	isolated timber	77	–	2.15	D	180x70	–	–
0091	1716	2 (wb)	isolated timber	141 +11	–	1.23	DE	225x30	524–664	after 685
0095	?	2	helmet pit	72	–	1.74	D	?x?	–	–
0096	?	2	helmet pit	53	–	1.49	DE	85x20	–	–
0097	?	2	helmet pit	117	–	1.26	D	150x20	460–576	after 586
0098	?	2	helmet pit	69	–	1.99	DE	145x30	–	–
0099	?	2	helmet pit	63	–	1.99	DE	135x25	–	–
0100	?	2	helmet pit	106	–	1.27	DE	135x20	–	–
0101	?	2	helmet pit	114	–	1.27	CX	150x40	–	–
0103	?	2	helmet pit	73	–	1.57	DE	120x30	–	–
0104	1956	wb	post & wattle alignment	48	5	1.36	E	155x50	–	–
0121	2036	wb	covered drain 2133	82	–	1.87	CX	195x110	–	–
0122	2037	5B D (wb)	5/7	80	–	1.97	CX	165x155	905–984	after 994
0123	2035	5B D (wb)	5/7 or 5/8	72	9	2.37	E	295x65	894–965	966–1002
0131	2109	5B E (wb)	5/9 sill	68	6	1.21	CX	115x85	880–947	951–87
0135	2110	5B E (wb)	5/9 sill	91 +27	–	2.75	CX	280x180	–	–
0138	2089	5B E (wb)	5/9 joist/construction	157	–	1.53	CX	300x230	747–903	after 913
0172	2137	5A (wb)	covered drain 2133	61	12	2.20	E	260x65	900–960	960–94
0187	2153	5B E	5/9 sill beam	50	7	2.22	CX	170x105	–	–
8065	2970	5B B	5/4 backfill – plank	82	–	2.52	D	210x30	910–991	after 1001
8066	2955	5B B	5/4 backfill – plank	121	–	1.07	D	135x30	867–987	after 997
8067	7025	5B C	5/6 backfill	97	HS?	1.43	D	?x?	852–948	958–94?
8071	7047	5B C	5/6 backfill	78	–	1.07	CX	140x100	848–925	after 935
8075	7096	5B C	5/6 backfill	58	–	1.32	CX	80x60	894–951	after 961
8105	2876	5B B	5/4 backfill	54	–	1.61	D	90x20	827–880	after 890

Table 34 *(cont'd)*

Timber no	Context no	Period & Tenement	Function	Total no of rings	Sapwood rings	ARW (mm)	Timber conversion	Dimensions (mm)	Date span (AD)	Felled (AD)
8156	7085	5B C	5/6 backfill	84	10	1.39	BX	210x100	818–901	901–37
8157	7240	5B C	5/6 collapse	72	–	1.43	CX	120x80	871–942	after 952
8213	7081	5B C	5/6 west wall plank	143	–	1.18	DE	180x35	799–941	after 951
8215	7319	5B C	5/6 west wall plank	171	–	1.52	D	250x40	771–941	after 951
8221	8201	5B B	5/4 collapse	64	10	2.04	BX	280x65	930–993	993–1029
8234	8038	5B B	5/4 east wall post	102	–	1.11	B1	200x105	835–936	after 946
8240	5228	5B C	5/6 drain	81	–	2.08	DE	190x50	873–953	after 963
8275	7091	5B C	5/6 east wall post	50	??	2.37	BX	240x120	–	–
8293	7306	5B C	5/6 west wall plank	228	–	0.90	D	210x40	709–936	after 946
8316	7448	5B C	5/6 collapse	109	–	1.15	CX	140x110	840–948	after 958
8319	1488	5B C	5/6 west wall post	84	4	1.79	E	260x100	872–955	961–97
8320	1487	5B C	5/6 west wall post	74	–	2.56	CX	190x100	812–885	after 895
8330	7088	5B C	5/6	68	–	1.38	AX	170x170	–	–
8340	7095	5B C	5/6 east wall plank	46	–	2.54	DC	285x110	840–885	after 895
8354	2777	5B B	5/4 west wall post	144	–	0.79	AX	220x130	775–918	after 928
8359	9403	5B D	5/8 construction	55	3	2.08	AX	210x140	927–981	988–1024
8360	7547	5B C	5/6 west wall post	78	–	0.91	CX	210x90	–	–
8362	8658	5B B	5/4 west wall	98	?5	1.74	DC	180x70	–	–
8376	7581	5B C	5/6 north wall sill	56	13	1.87	E	205x55	915–970	970–1003
8379	8047	5B B	5/4 east wall sill	73	18	1.69	BX	280x70	889–961	961–89
8387	8744	5B B	5/4 drain capping	76	30 ?B	1.64	E	250x65	897–972	972/3?
8392	1582	5B D	5/8 west wall sill	57	–	2.22	BX	275x140	892–948	after 958
8393	1600	5B D	5/8 partition sill	58	28 ?B	1.99	A1	210x120	938–995	995/6?
8394	1587	5B D	5/8 west wall sill	61	–	1.98	AX	240x160	901–961	after 971
8456	14065	5Cf D	5/10 sill beam	60	–	1.47	AX	190x80	875–934	after 944
8464	14214	5Cf D	5/10 bracer beam	76	?3	2.37	BX	330x120	880–955	962–98
8465	14219	5Cf D	5/10 bracer beam	71	–	2.23	BX	320x140	883–953	after 963
8470	14257	5B D	backfill of 5/8	73	–	1.12	BX	200x90	–	–
8527	14391	5B C	alignment 33233	65	21	1.19	AX	150x110	895–959	959–84
8539	14607	5B D	5/8 drain	70	–	2.65	D	195x20	–	–
8543	14614	5B D	5/8 drain	148	HS	1.33	D	200x30	830–977	987–1023

Table 34 (cont'd)

Timber no	Context no	Period & Tenement	Function	Total no of rings	Sapwood rings	ARW (mm)	Timber conversion	Dimensions (mm)	Date span (AD)	Felled (AD)
8551	14582	5B D	5/8 drain	165	2	1.01	D	185x30	809–973	981–1017
8556	15211	5B B	5/3 east wall post	45	–	2.18	A1	200x125	895–939	after 949
8559	15215	5B B	5/3 east wall post	41	–	2.99	AX	200x115	884–924	after 934
8562	15461	5B B	5/3 east wall post	56	?3	2.98	BX	190x110	889–944	951–77?
8563	15462	5B B	5/3 east wall post	62	–	1.61	A1	190x110	881–942	after 952
8599	14089	5B C	alignment 33233	66	18	1.76	BX	210x70	899–964	964–92
8620	6631	5B C	fence line 6661	90	–	1.59	EX	250x100	918–1007	after 1017
8623	14724	5B C	alignment 33233	47	22 ?B	1.63	BX	165x70	910–956	956/7?
8647	19122	5Cr C	5/12 west wall stub	71	–	1.62	A1	210x140	927–997	after 1007
8648	19123	5Cr C	5/12 west wall stub	83	–	1.65	A1	210x130	919–1001	after 1011
8649	19124	5Cr C	5/12 west wall stub	98	8	1.48	AX	250x150	914–1011	1013–49
8653	19210	5Cr C	5/12 south-east corner stub	73	–	1.63	CX	140x130	931–1003	after 1013
8654	19121	5Cr C	5/12 west wall stub	82	–	1.55	A1	220x140	921–1002	after 1012
8655	19248	5Cr C	5/12 west wall stub	69	–	1.58	AX	240x140	932–1000	after 1010
8675	20025	5B A	5/1 east wall plank	230	HS	1.34	D	370x30	713–942	952–88
8676	20644	5B A	5/1 east wall plank	123	HS	3.38	D	400x30	826–948	958–94
8680	20646	5B A	5/1 east wall plank	239	21 Bw	1.19	DE	285x40	723–961	961/2
8679	20645	5B A	5/1 east wall plank	80	5	2.67	D	210x35	875–954	959–95
8690	18466	5A B	alignment 36598	279	HS?	0.96	D	300x120	–	–
8692	20033	5B A	5/1 east wall post	82	26	2.01	B1	300x100	880–961	961–81
8693	20601	5B A	5/1 east wall post	66	13	2.06	CX	150x100	895–960	960–93
8695	20237	5B A	5/1 east wall post	57	HS	2.10	BX	210x120	885–941	951–87
8696	20738	5B A	5/1 east wall post	65	11	2.19	BX	235x100	887–951	951–86
8701	20600	5B A	5/1 east wall post	53	4	2.13	CX	120x110	894–946	952–88
8702	20029	5B A	5/1 east wall plank	142	–	2.54	D	360x45	777–918	after 928
8708	20735	5B A	5/1 east wall plank	57	12	2.61	B1	330x80	895–951	951–85
8720	20705	5A A	alignment 37253	139	–	1.54	DX	200x90	793–931	after 941
8741	18404	5A B	alignment 18422	46	16 ?B	2.40	E	210x80	910–955	955/6?
8745	14478	5B C	alignment 33235	63	13 ?B	1.70	E	210x70	893–955	955/6?
8746	14688	5B C	alignment 33235	73	32 ?B	1.15	E	190x70	883–955	955/6?
8753	20691	5A B	alignment 36582	52	15 ?B	2.72	CX	150x100	904–955	955/6?

Table 34 *(cont'd)*

Timber no	Context no	Period & Tenement	Function	Total no of rings	Sapwood rings	ARW (mm)	Timber conversion	Dimensions (mm)	Date span (AD)	Felled (AD)
8759	18558	5A B	alignment 36582	59	18	1.77	E	210x90	896–954	954–82
8786	18464	5A B	alignment 36582	54	15	1.44	E	230x60	901–954	954–85
8795	14638	5A D	isolated post	64	14	1.74	AX	220x160	883–946	946–78
8798	14640	5A D	alignment 14853	39	18	1.78	EX	210x60	915–953	953–81
8807	14639	5A D	alignment 14853	47	23 ?B	2.04	E	220x60	909–955	955/6?
8809	14636	5A D	alignment 14853	53	15	1.90	E	260x60	897–949	949–80
8810	14641	5A D	alignment 14853	35	14	3.15	E	260x80	919–953	953–85
8811	14637	5A D	alignment 14853	56	17	1.59	E	200x80	899–954	954–83
8812	14774	5A D	alignment 14853	54	19 ?B	2.22	E	220x60	902–955	955/6?
8827	20519	5B A	5/1 internal paired post	68	13	1.70	CX	130x120	879–946	946–79
8832	21459	5B C	horizontal	58	–	1.29	AX	170x120	889–946	after 956
8833	20405	5B B	post associated with 5/1	85	–	1.51	D	140x50	–	–
8845	21522	5B D	horizontal	53	–	3.10	DE	180x70	896–948	after 958
8847	25676	4B C	alignment 30765	109	–	1.48	CX	180x140	781–889	after 899
8849	8550	5B B	5/4 west wall supplementary sill	183	1	1.28	DX	250x100	784–966	975–1011
8851	27300	5B B	horizontal in pit/cut 27298/26993	145	4	1.61	D	250x80	848–992	998–1034
8856	28509	4B B	isolated	88	–	1.40	CX	170x130	806–893	after 903
8858	21806	5B D	5/8 drain	186	–	1.26	DE	250x25	785–970	after 980
8859	21890	5B D	5/8 drain	61	1	4.11	D	270x40	918–978	987–1023
8860	21891	5B D	5/8 drain	66	HS	3.46	D	230x30	913–978	988–1024
8863	21892	5B D	5/8 drain	143	–	1.61	DE	245x20	812–954	after 964
8865	21797	5B D	5/8	60	1	0.80	AX	170x110	–	–
8867	27553	4A B	isolated	129	11	1.52	DE	220x70	778–906	906–41
8873	21959	5B C	isolated	50	18 ?Bw	1.62	A1	160x140	891–940	940/1?
8877	21867	5B C	horizontal in ?path 37403	39	–	2.55	E	250x40	898–936	after 946
8882	21794	5B D	5/8 east wall brace	59	–	2.20	BX	220x110	899–957	after 967
8884	22293	4B D	alignment 22585, west side of D	252	–	0.98	D	270x90	637–888	after 898
8885	22291	4B D	alignment 22585, west side of D	194	22	1.32	D	270x100	742–935	935–59
8886	22514	4B D	alignment 22585, west side of D	115	–	1.33	D	210x70	767–881	after 891
8887	22294	4B D	alignment 22585, west side of D	140	37	1.50	D	240x70	789–928	928–37
8888	21796	5B D	5/8 east wall brace	67	30 Bw	1.05	A1	140x90	942–1008	1008/9

Table 34 *(cont'd)*

Timber no	Context no	Period & Tenement	Function	Total no of rings	Sapwood rings	ARW (mm)	Timber conversion	Dimensions (mm)	Date span (AD)	Felled (AD)
8892	29097	5B D	5/7 backfill	64	HS?	2.32	D	150x30	908–971	981–1017?
8897	29106	5B C	horizontal in path 37404	215	–	1.14	D	270x35	695–909	after 919
8899	29107	5B C	horizontal in path 37404	152	–	1.30	DE	340x40	757–908	after 918
8903	29120	5B C	horizontal in path 37404	141	–	1.01	E	260x50	800–940	after 950
8905	29127	5B D	horizontal sealing 5/7	76	25	1.26	AX	200x130	–	–
8917	22424	4B D	alignment 22585, west side of D	220	31	0.65	EX	210x70	715–934	934–49
8921	21958	5B C	isolated	59	14 ?Bs	1.49	A1	150x150	908–966	966?
8922	21976	5B D	5/7 backfill	187	–	1.18	DX	230x110	734–920	after 930
8945	8163	5A B	alignment 36599	85	–	2.69	D	280x30	846–930	after 940
8947	29460	5B D	5/7 backfill	54	5	1.62	E	220x60	933–986	991–1027
8948	29263	5B D	5/7 backfill	101	–	1.48	D	170x130	805–905	after 915
8949	29464	5B D	5/7 backfill	76	–	1.46	BX	230x100	889–964	after 974
8951	22117	5A D	alignment 14853	67	1	1.71	AX	190x120	856–922	931–67
8952	25960	4A D	isolated	158	28	1.38	D	230x50	–	–
8953	29469	5B D	5/7 backfill	41	–	3.78	DE	210x70	900–940	after 950
8958	29056	5B C	alignment 5852	56	–	2.04	DE	130x60	914–969	after 979
8967	29567	5B C	5/5 post	216	4	0.72	BX	240x120	722–937	943–79
8971	29546	5B D	5/7 abandoned	54	–	1.92	BX	230x70	885–938	after 948
8974	29542	5B D	5/7 abandoned	51	–	2.17	BX	260x120	889–939	after 949
8978	20845	4B B	alignment 37166	92	–	2.01	D	185x70	803–894	after 904
8979	29626	5B D	horizontal associated with 5/7	66	8	2.11	EX	200x80	903–968	970–1006
8980	29600	5B D	5/7 abandoned	77	12	2.47	CX	190x100	881–957	957–91
8984	25422	4B C	alignment 36591/25640	53	12	1.90	BX	180x90	862–914	914–48
8987	31268	5A A	cut 31266	133	–	1.12	D	145x20	764–896	after 906
8988	31270	5A A	cut 31266	88	–	1.56	D	135x20	–	–
8992	29555	5B D	backfill of 5/7	103	–	1.72	CX	170x100	844–946	after 956
8995	29537	5B D	5/7 horizontal	100	–	1.18	D	230x25	–	–
8997	29539	5B D	5/7 abandoned	87	2	1.19	B1	135x110	855–941	949–85
9000	29564	5B C	5/5 post	184	–	1.16	D	220x70	751–934	after 944
9002	29518	5B D	5/7 sill	106	35 ?Bs	1.05	AX	220x160	861–966	966?
9003	29508	5B D	5/7 post	51	–	3.38	BX	290x130	895–945	after 955

Table 34 (cont'd)

Timber no	Context no	Period & Tenement	Function	Total no of rings	Sapwood rings	ARW (mm)	Timber conversion	Dimensions (mm)	Date span (AD)	Felled (AD)
9007	29512	5B D	5/7 abandoned	65	–	2.56	B1	260x100	874–938	after 948
9008	29515	5B D	5/7 construction – ?chock	53	2	2.47	DX	130x45	894–946	954–90
9010	25576	4B D	alignment 30357 post	69	–	1.79	CX	150x130	830–898	after 908
9011	29543	5B D	5/7 abandoned	63	–	2.31	B1	230x110	879–941	after 951
9020	29605	5B D	5/7 stave built box	99	–	1.99	D	210x40	844–942	after 952
9025	25485	4A D	alignment 30358 post	119	HS?	1.01	CX	220x100	775–893	903–39?
9026	25478	4A D	alignment 30358 post	105	14	1.80	CX	180x120	817–921	921–53
9027	29519	5B D	5/7 sill	82	8	2.20	E	330x100	878–959	961–97
9029	29773	5B D	5/7 associated chock under sill	70	17	3.18	D	210x70	891–960	960–89
9036	30008	4A D	isolated	69	–	2.67	D	190x80	–	–
9040	25820A	4B D	alignment 22059	118	–	1.55	D	190x60	806–923	after 933
9041	25824	4B D	alignment 30436, east side of D	277	–	0.91	DX	250x80	614–890	after 900
9044	30461	3 D	isolated	50	21 ?Bw	1.89	A1	150x105	855–904	904/5?
9055	32165	5A B	pit 28652 backfill	52	–	1.93	E	210x70	886–937	after 947
9056	32166	5A B	pit 28652 backfill	54	8	3.66	D	210x90	905–958	960–96
9067	31478	4B B	discarded timber fragment	224	28	0.95	D	210x60	707–930	930–48
9069	8612	4B B	alignment 27796	170	3	1.47	D	240x110	761–930	937–73
9070	34378	4B B	horizontal	220	28	1.14	D	250x50	722–941	941–59
9073	19750	3 C	isolated	92	1	1.39	BX	240x110	–	–
9087	8315	4B B	alignment 27607	143	4	1.85	D	290x80	763–905	911–47
9088	8919	4B B	alignment 27607	155	–	1.75	D	270x60	761–915	after 925
9089	8920	4B B	alignment 27607	57	11	2.04	E	250x60	894–950	950–85
9092	2992	4B B	alignment 27676	89	14	1.37	CX	130x80	854–942	942–74
9102	29418	5B C	isolated	144	–	1.77	DX	260x130	794–937	after 947
9106	35009	5B C	isolated	63	–	1.64	D	170x25	907–969	after 979
9117	34538	4B B	alignment 27607	161	–	1.41	D	230x50	–	–
9119	21929	5B C	isolated	72	8	2.49	CX	190x110	–	–
9133	29562	5B C	5/5 post	210	–	1.37	D	280x110	728–937	after 947
9134	29563	5B C	5/5 post	189	–	1.19	D	210x100	715–903	after 913
9139	35209	4B C	horizontal in path 37405	103 +40	(+25)	1.59	D	210x80	–	–
9146	29565	5B C	5/5 north wall post	196	–	1.29	D	240x100	751–946	after 956

Table 34 *(cont'd)*

Timber no	Context no	Period & Tenement	Function	Total no of rings	Sapwood rings	ARW (mm)	Timber conversion	Dimensions (mm)	Date span (AD)	Felled (AD)
9159	35104	4B D	embedded in alignment 35111	87	–	1.22	D	250x20	807–893	after 903
9162	35264	5B D	5/7 abandoned	64	3	2.91	CX	190x120	882–945	952–88
9164	35300	4B C	horizontal in path 37405	63	–	3.37	D	210x30	751–813	after 823
9170	34471	4B B	alignment 34486	99	–	2.58	D	250x80	783–881	after 891
9179	35320	4B C	horizontal in layer 35293	85	–	2.44	D	190x20	829–913	after 923
9189	15210	5B B	5/3 south wall plank above 9190	45	–	1.26	D	165x30	829–873	after 883
9190	18278	5B B	5/3 south wall plank above 9192	110	–	1.54	DX	230x40	798–907	after 917
9192	18279	5B B	5/3 south wall plank	60	11	2.13	E	270x60	899–958	958–93
9194	15209	5B B	5/3 east wall plank above 9195	126	–	1.92	D	320x30	757–882	after 892
9195	18270	5B B	5/3 east wall plank above 9198	137	–	2.33	DE	335x25	740–876	after 886
9198	18272	5B B	5/3 east wall plank	54	9	2.32	E	295x55	901–954	955–91
9203	18260	5B B	5/3 west wall plank	66+10	–	1.11	D	95x25	812–877	after 897
9212	35507	4B C	post in alignment 35161	56	–	2.16	CX	130x120	826–881	after 891
9215	35517	4B C	isolated	105	–	1.74	DX	190x90	791–895	after 905
9216	35725	4B C	post in alignment 35161	74	–	2.22	DX	170x80	804–877	after 887
9219	30011	4A D	isolated	191	9	1.40	D	260x40	706–896	897–933

Table 35 Details of the tree-ring samples which were unsuitable for dating purposes.
Timber conversion types – see Fig.346

Timber no	Context no	Total no of rings	Timber conversion	Dimensions (mm)
8214	7089	30	A	90x90
8314	–	–	BX	220x80
8430	8841	44	B1	210x110
8453	13863	37	CX	140x100
8460	14213	45	AX	250x130
8471	14184	37	AX	140x100
8475	7557	37	BX	230x100
8509	14048	43	AX	180x140
8528	14422	26	A1	190x120
8601	14721	33	D	210x40
8605	14728	35	D	200x40
8650	6956	33	D	240x50
8656	19230	30	A	90x80
8668	6863	20	A	140x100
8669	6861	26	A	140x120
8671	6883	30	B	190x100
8678	–	–	–	310x60
8737	20881	35	BD	170x60
8754	18533	41	AX	140x130
8775	23489	40	CX	160x140
8799	23682	27	CX	160x70
8814	20820	41	C1	170x70
8828	20295	34	C1	140x120
8846	26871	26	CX	130x80
8850	27009	28	BX	200x100
8857	25022	28	D	210x60
8864	28168	45	BD	140x60
8876	27612	38	A1	150x120
8879	25423	22	CX	230x80
8930	18777	39	B1	180x120
8931	27361	21	A1	240x240
8946	25642	37	C1	170x110
8975	29536	49	AX	310x165
8977	25286	44	B	170x70
8985	31167	24	CX	160x130
8990	28547	38	CX	125x85
9006	27908	39	CX	120x70
9016	29781	36	BD	190x50
9017	29782	26	B1	200x80
9023	25575	43	AX	180x120
9024	25477	47	C1	150x150
9028	29601	42	CX	140x100
9030	29813	37	DE	205x50
9032	30306	19	A	150x120

Table 35   *(cont'd)*

Timber no	Context no	Total no of rings	Timber conversion	Dimensions (mm)
9035	–	knotty	CX	240x150
9042	22264	35	AX	160x120
9048	31446	24	B1	170x80
9051	27314	knotty	A	240x200
9053	27302	38	A1	200x150
9054	27303	36	A1	200x150
9057	27306	32	A	260x200
9058	6637	47	AX	190x150
9064	8353	31	B1	220x80
9065	18767	15	A	140x120
9090	32465	28	D	200x40
9107	34197	30	C1	170x75
9110	35011	knotty	CX	210x180
9122	35133	36	AX	260x110
9124	29890	knotty	X	200x100
9125	34591	17	A	140x120
9128	35124	25	AX	210x190
9140	35071	42	C1	170x80
9144	29882	knotty	BX	160x100
9148	35269	41	B1	180x90
9154	35267	39	C1	200x90
9163	35200	knotty	BX	210x150
9178	35276	20	A1	140x70
9188	35720	knotty	CX	140x120
9193	12259	knotty	CX	160x140

Table 36 Results of comparisons between some relevant reference chronologies and the 168-sample Coppergate site master chronology, YORKCPG3, at 460–1011 inclusive (all dates AD unless specified)

Region	Reference chronology	Date span	*t* value
Cambridgeshire	Peterborough Cathedral nave roof (Tyers 1999)	887–1225	8.12
Cumbria	Carlisle The Lanes southern (Groves 1993a)	917–1193	5.14
	Carlisle The Lanes northern (Groves 1996c)	892–1275	5.45
Hampshire	The Brooks, Winchester (Hillam 1992c)	443–1128	6.27
London	Barking Abbey (Tyers 1988)	413–793	5.44
	Fennings Wharf (Tyers forthcoming)	802–1435	4.69
N Lincolnshire	Barton on Humber Coffins – interim (Tyers 2000c)	811–1130	9.27
Staffordshire	St Mary's and Eastgate (Groves 1987a; 1987b)	884–1189	6.71
West Midlands	Tamworth (Baillie, pers. comm.)	404–825	5.46
Yorkshire	Dyer Lane, Beverley (Groves and Hillam 1985)	903–1183	5.76
	Eastgate, Beverely (Groves 1992)	858–1310	7.23
	Lurk Lane, Beverley (Groves and Hillam 1991)	885–1124	5.80
	Skerne (Hillam unpubl)	440–647	9.09
	Queens Hotel, York (Groves 1993b)	769–1036	12.95
	Swinegate, York (Tyers and Bagwell unpubl)	749–986	12.11
Ireland	Dublin (Baillie 1977)	855–1306	5.26
Ireland	North horizontal mills (Baillie, pers. comm.)	358–894	4.19
Ireland	South horizontal mills (Baillie, pers. comm.)	261–881	4.98
Denmark	West Denmark (Bonde, pers. comm.)	109 BC–AD 1986	5.48
Germany	Trier region (Hollstein 1980)	546 BC–AD 1975	5.58

Table 37 Summary of the tree-ring dates. wb – watching brief; only the latest felling date(s) indicated for backfills are given

Period	Tenement	Structure or Timber	Felled (AD)
2	–	helmet pit timber **97**	after 586
		isolated timber **91**	after 685
3	D	isolated timber **9044**	904/05?
4A	B	isolated timber **8867**	906–41
	D	alignment 30358, timbers **9025–6**	921–39
		isolated timber **9219**	897–933
4B	B	alignment 27607, timbers **9087–9**	925–47 and 950–85
		alignment 27676, timber **9092**	942–74
		alignment 27796, timber **9069**	937–73
		alignment 34486, timber **9170**	after 891
		alignment 37166, timber **8978**	after 904 (probably 935–37)
		horizontal timber **9070**	941–59
		isolated timber **8856**	after 903
		discarded timber fragment **9067**	930–48
	C	alignment 30765, timber **8847**	after 899
		alignment 35161, timber **9212**	after 891
		alignment 36591/25640, timber **8984**	914–48
		isolated timber **9215**	after 905
		horizontal in layer 35293, timber **9179**	after 923
		horizontal in path 37405, timber **9164**	after 823
	D	alignment 22059, timber **9040**	after 933
		alignment 22585, timber **8885/8887**	935–37
		alignment 30357, timber **9010**	after 908
		alignment 30436, timber **9041**	after 900 (probably 935–37)
		embedded in alignment 35111, timber **9159**	after 903
5A	A	alignment 36583, timber **8720**	after 941
		cut 31266, timber **8987**	after 906 (probably before 961/62)
	B	alignment 18422, timber **8741**	955/56?
		alignment 36582, timber **8753**	955/56?
		alignment 36599, timber **8945**	after 940
		pit 28652 backfill, timber **9056**	960–96
	D	alignment 14853, timbers **8807/8812**	955/56
		isolated post **8795**	946–78
	D/E wb	covered drain, timber **0172**	960–94
5B	A	Structure 5/1 plank, timber **8680**	961/62
		Structure 5/1 post, timber **8692**	961–81 (probably 961/62)
		Structure 5/1 internal post, timber **8827**	946–79 (possibly 961/62)
	B	horizontal in pit/cut 27298/26993, timber **8851**	998–1034
		Structure 5/3 planks, timbers **9192/9198**	958–91 (probably 958–87, possibly 966)
		Structure 5/3 posts, timbers **8562/8563**	952–87 (probably 958–87, possibly 966)
		Structure 5/4 post, timber **8234**	after 946
		Structure 5/4 drain cap, timber **8387**	972/73?
		Structure 5/4 sill, timber **8379**	961–89 (probably 972/73)
		Structure 5/4 sill replacement, timber **8849**	975–1011
		Structure 5/4 collapse, timber **8221**	993–1029
		Structure 5/4 backfill, timber **8065**	after 1001

Table 37 *(cont'd)*

Period	Tenement	Structure or Timber	Felled (AD)
5B	C	alignment 33233, timbers **8527/8599**	956/57? and 964–84
		alignment 33235, timbers **8745–6**	955/56
		alignment 5852, timber **8958**	after 979
		horizontal timber **8832**	after 956
		isolated timbers **8873, 9102, 8921, 9106**	940/41?, after 947, 966?, after 979
		horizontal in path 37403, timber **8877**	after 946
		horizontals in path 37404, timber **8903**	after 950
		fence line 6661, timber **8620**	after 1017
		Structure 5/5 posts, timbers **8967/9146**	956–79
		Structure 5/6 planks, timbers **8213/8215**	after 951 (probably 970–97)
		Structure 5/6 post, timber **8319**	961–97 (probably 970–97)
		Structure 5/6 sill, timber **8376**	970–1003 (probably 970–97)
		Structure 5/6 collapse, timber **8316**	after 958 (possibly 970–97)
		Structure 5/6 backfill, timber **8067/8075**	after 961, 958–94
		Structure 5/6 drain, timber **8240**	after 963
	D	horizontal timber **8845**	after 958
		Structure 5/7 sill/sill chock, timber **9002**	966?
		Structure 5/7 post, timber **9003**	after 955 (probably 966)
		Structure 5/7 construction (chock?), timber **9008**	954–90 (probably 966)
		Structure 5/7 abandoned, timber **8980/8997**	957–85 (possibly 966)
		Structure 5/7 stave-built box, timber **9020**	after 952
		Structure 5/7 backfill, timber **8947**	991–1027
		Structure 5/8 brace, timber **8888**	1008/09
		Structure 5/8 sill, timber **8393**	995/96?
		Structure 5/8 construction, timber **8359**	988–1024 (possibly 995/96 or 1008/09)
		Structure 5/8 drain, timber **8551**	988–1017 (possibly 995/96 or 1008/09)
	D wb	Structure 5/7, timber **0122**	after 994, 966–1002
	E wb	Structure 5/9 construction (joist?), timber **0138**	after 913
		Structure 5/9 sill, timber **0131**	951–87
5Cf	D	Structure 5/10 bracer beams, timbers **8464–5**	963–98
		Structure 5/10 sill, timber **8456**	after 944 (possibly 963–98)
5Cr	C	Structure 5/12 stubs, timber **8649**	1013–49

The Woodworking Technology of the Anglo-Scandinavian Timbers from 16–22 Coppergate

by S.J. Allen, with a note on the retrieval and conservation by J.A. Spriggs

Introduction

The structural timbers from the Anglo Scandinavian levels at 16–22 Coppergate are derived from a number of structures of different phases identified and recorded during the excavation. Principally these consist of structures on five parallel tenements (A–E). During the first half of the 10th century buildings and fences were constructed on the contemporary ground surface with vertical rods and horizontal sails forming wattle curtain walls (Period 4B), with some posts set alongside the curtain walls to support the roof. From the 960s onwards, these were replaced by structures cut into the ground, constructed using vertical posts and horizontal planks (Period 5B). The remains of the post and plank and related structures are considered here; records of wattle structures and surface-laid buildings do not permit analysis of species, sources or woodworking evidence; the associated wooden structural fittings and woodworking tools were published in 2000 (*AY* 17/13).

The study of the timbers has been possible through examination of the site and conservation records, in written, graphic and photographic form. Much of the work became possible in the winter of 2000–01 when, during the refurbishment of the Jorvik Viking Centre, it was necessary to remove timbers from public display to assess their condition and clean them for reinstatement in JORVIK (Allen and Spriggs 2002). During this time the opportunity was taken to record timbers from various structures through record sheets and annotated scale drawings, the latter following existing guidelines (Allen 1994; Brunning and Watson 2010). The work was extended to those timbers previously conserved and held in store by York Archaeological Trust and then to those that survived only as paper records, leading to the compilation of a database detailing all the information that could be gathered about each timber.

So far as is possible, the timber numbers cited refer to individual original timbers. It was obviously difficult, given the damage suffered by the timbers prior to and during burial, to identify during the excavation which parts originally fitted together to make one timber. This was a particular problem with boards that had buckled and broken during burial. Thus in some cases, one shattered plank might have been assigned up to three or four different context/timber numbers.

All the parts which originally made up an individual timber are counted in this report as one timber; thus although, for example, planks from the watching brief excavation of Structure 5/1 were cut up for lifting, and assigned different context and timber numbers for tracking during subsequent treatment, they are reported here as the single plank they originally formed.

Retrieval and Conservation
by J.A. Spriggs

The Coppergate excavations produced one of the largest assemblages of structural wood material ever excavated in Britain. The potential of this material for study and display was quickly appreciated, and great efforts were made to retrieve and save as much as possible during the course of the excavations. The process of lifting, making preliminary records and storing this large volume of wood underwater required much planning and resourcing (Spriggs 1980); and the urgent need for a replica of one of the structures (Structure 5/3) for the 1981 'Vikings in England' exhibition necessitated a special *in situ* moulding process to be devised and implemented (Spriggs 1992). The provision of laboratory and workshop facilities for the conservation treatment of the timbers also quickly became a priority and, by the end of the excavations in 1981, the new laboratories in Galmanhoe Lane were being fitted out (Spriggs 1982). Experimental work leading to a choice of treatment for the timbers was instigated (Spriggs 1984) so that timbers were ready to mount for display in the new Jorvik Viking Centre which opened in 1984 (Spriggs 1991).

This early experience in the stabilisation of large timbers at YAT led to the formation of the York Archaeological Wood Centre which, in collaboration with English Heritage, formally opened as a national facility in 1993 for the conservation of waterlogged wood from all sources. A range of innovations in connection with the recording and treatment of archaeological wood were introduced, such as assessment methodologies prior to large-scale freeze-drying (Panter and Spriggs 1997) and the novel adaptation of swimming pool technology for maintaining sterility in the polymer treatment tanks (Spriggs 1994; Vere-Stevens *et al.* 1999).

Only those timbers that were required for display in the Jorvik Viking Centre were conserved initially, the remaining 60 or so structural timbers still being in store underwater. The decision was taken in 2000 to conserve all the remaining Copper-gate wood material, which provided a good opportunity to re-observe and record a large body of Anglo-Scandinavian wood still in the wet state, and to make moulds, photographs and drawings of tool marks and other fine detail, which was found still to be in pristine condition. The decision to close the Jorvik Viking Centre in 2000 for a major refit also provided an opportunity to re-observe all the timbers previously on display. Remedial conservation was required on those timbers which were to be incorporated in the new JORVIK displays, offering a chance to study the effects of the display environment on wood over a 15-year period (Allen and Spriggs 2002).

Function of timbers as found

None of the superstructures of the Coppergate buildings survived. They had either been destroyed, or more probably robbed and recycled when disused. The evidence is restricted to those parts of certain structures which were at or below the contemporary ground surface and which have remained in waterlogged anaerobic conditions since burial.

These timbers may be classified by function into posts, planks/boards, plates and stakes.

Posts are timbers, normally of rectangular cross-section with flat bases, set vertically on end, with roughly squared, not pointed, lower ends. The upper ends of the posts do not generally survive, only three posts having enough evidence to suggest the form of their original upper end. These upper ends are defined by deliberately cut joints, damaged but still visible on the photographs taken whilst the timbers were still *in situ* (Fig.347). These

Fig.347   *Partly collapsed wall of Structure 5/6 showing near-complete post tops. Scale unit 0.1m*

posts retain tiers of planks and boards, laid horizontally on edge, which provide the lining for the below-ground space within the building. Many of the posts themselves sat on other pieces of wood, either for levelling or stabilisation purposes. In some cases, these consisted of no more than offcuts of boards or planks under individual posts. In other cases, the posts sat on continuous plates with a raised flange or lip carved from the solid along the inside edge. This lip seems to have acted to prevent the feet of the posts slipping forward into the structure.

Planks and boards were extensively used. Medieval documents define planks as being more than 1½in (38mm) thick and boards as being less than 1½in thick (Rackham 1982, 215). The dimensions of the Coppergate examples suggest that the term 'board' should be used for most of the material present. In addition to lining the walls and floors of the buildings, boards were also used to line and cover surface drains on the site. Some short battens were utilised to support the wooden lids of these drains. Boarded pathways were also noted, such as 37404, made of offcuts, some of which (8896, 8897 and 8899) have small redundant pegs or peg-holes that might indicate a former use.

768

There are indications that several of the Coppergate buildings had wooden floors, resting on horizontal *plates or joists*, 'floor timbers'. These are lengths of timber laid generally at right angles to the axis of the structure, on the earth floor, to support a boarded floor. Some of these floors survived *in situ*.

Finally there are *piles or stakes*, with cut, pointed lower ends intended to be driven into the ground, usually to help pin other timbers such as plates or joists in position and also to provide supporting uprights for fence lines. Few of these were adequately recorded or retained for conservation and in consequence they are not included in the discussion below.

Wood species and conversion

The surviving structural timbers are from a single species (*AY* 14/7, 722,), Oak (*Quercus* spp.), with one exception of an Alder (*Alnus* spp.) plank (8546) in the lining of the Structure 5/8 drain. Oak is the primary tree exploited for structural timber in most of Great Britain and its extensive use here is not a surprise. Oak was also used for those pegs that survived *in situ*.

Most of the planks and boards appear to have been created by splitting the parent log tangentially, i.e. into parallel slices, or radially, into segments. There are indications that tangential and radially faced planks may have been selected for different purposes (see p.792).

The posts are generally boxed conversions, cut to give sub-rectangular cross-sections, as are the plate and floor timbers. Some relatively thin posts, such as some of those from Structure 5/6, are tangentially faced and suggest that more than one post was cut from the same halved timber.

Very few of the boxed heart timbers have pith which is absolutely in the centre of the timber after conversion. Some of the boxed heart posts have hearts which are significantly offset towards one face of the timber. Other timbers have a particularly irregular or 'wandering' heart. One such is the sampled section of a plate 135 (Fig.348), which at its thickest end (truncated by dendrochronological sampling) is box halved. Some 2.5m away, at the surviving original end, the conversion is boxed heart. In this timber the latter end is the top of the parent log relative to the original tree. The trunk has been begun as a box halved conversion but towards the top of the tree the log narrows and there is less usable timber. The cutting

Context 2110
Timber no 135

Sill beam, Structure 5/9

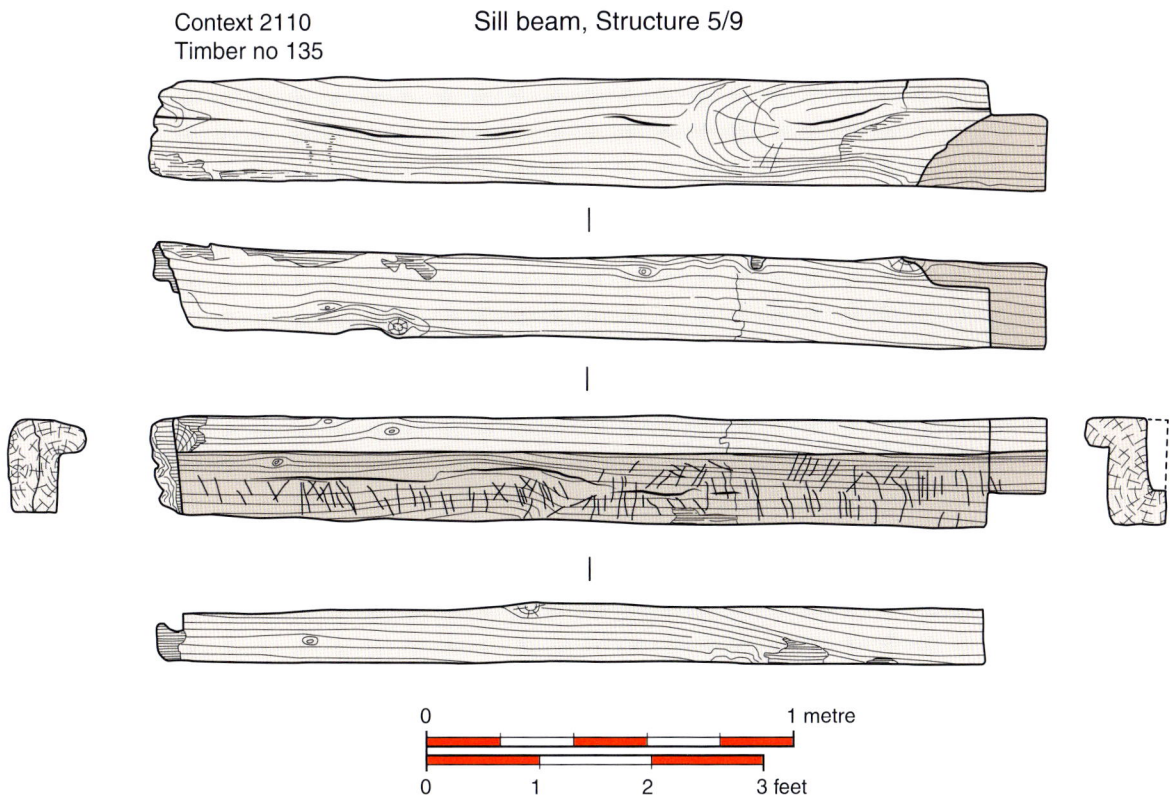

Fig.348   *Drawing of plate **135**. Scale 1:20*

Structure 5/1

20027

22.02
plank

20737

22.30
post

modern
saw cut

22.21
plank

8705
plank

22.27
plank

8709
plank

20739

8697
post

20513

8662
floor timber

8696
8695

8700
8699

Structure 5/3

18262

18270

18261

0   1   2   3 metres

0   5   10 feet

13711

15215

13704

8564
post

8559
post

8568
post

8665
post

8556

9205/
9206
plank

9195
plank

9204
plank

15211

9196
9195
9190

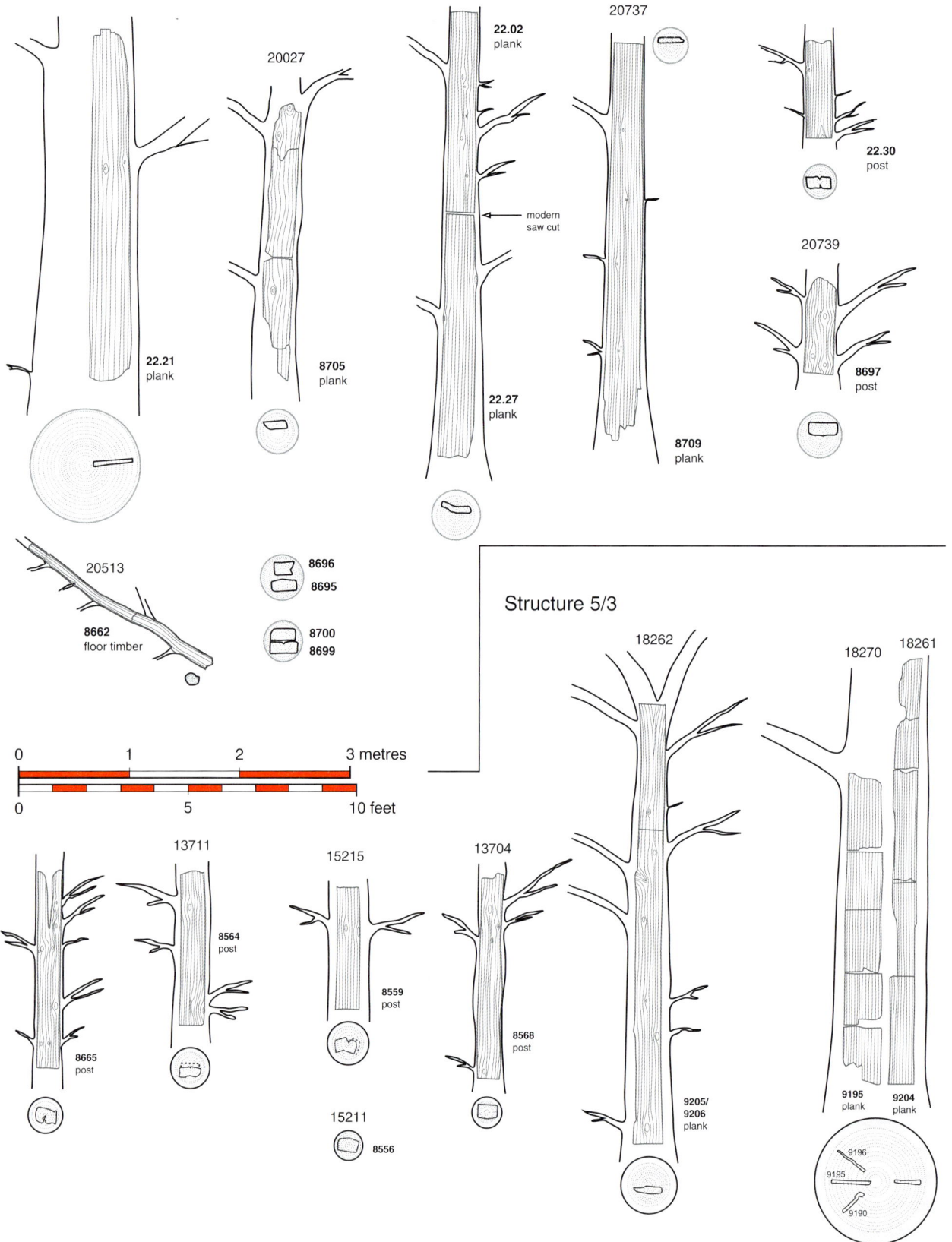

Fig.349   *(above and facing) Parent logs of timbers from Coppergate: Structures 5/1, 5/3 and 5/6. Scale 1:50*

770

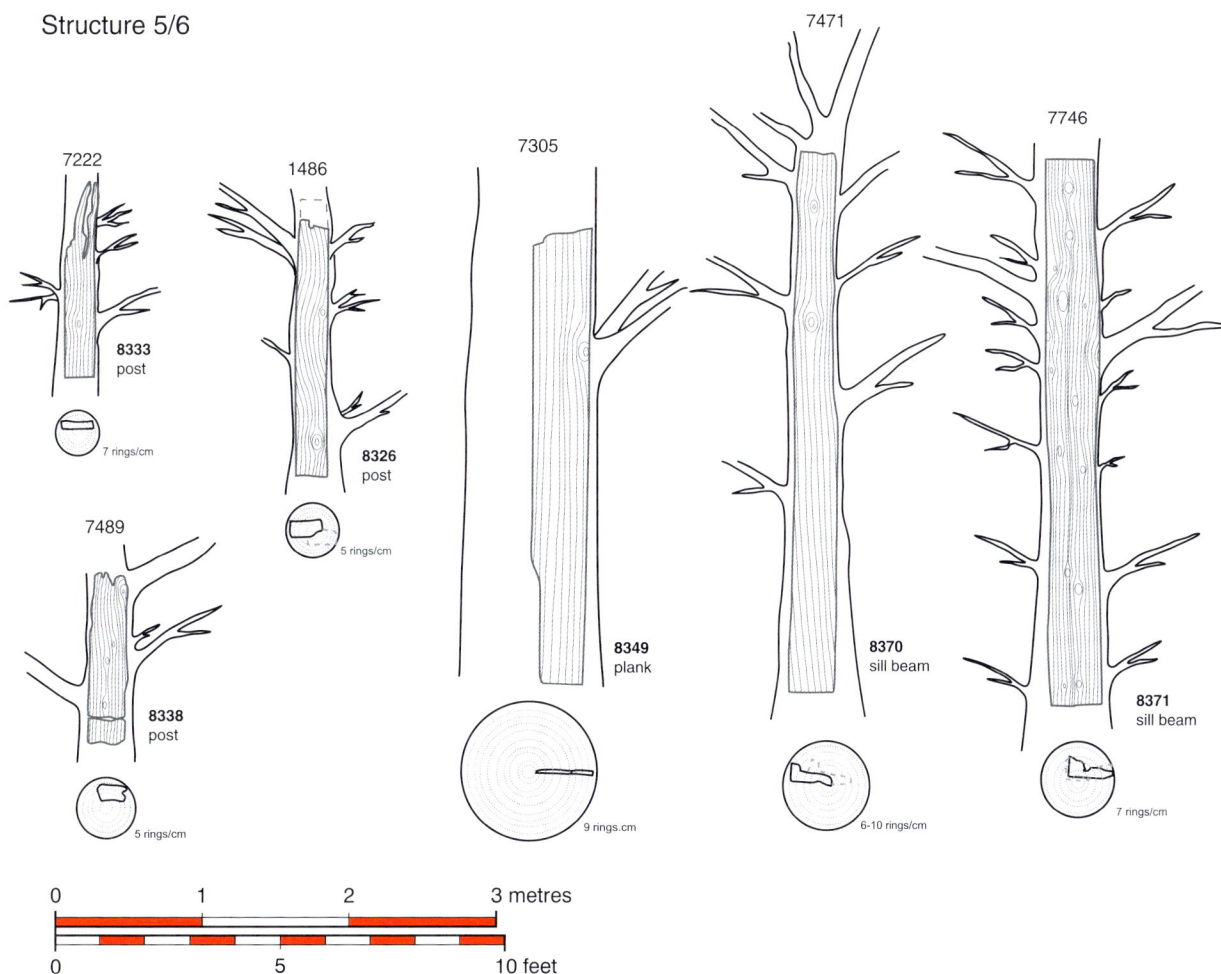

7222

8333
post

7 rings/cm

7489

8338
post

5 rings/cm

1486

8326
post

5 rings/cm

7305

8349
plank

9 rings.cm

7471

8370
sill beam

6-10 rings/cm

7746

8371
sill beam

7 rings/cm

| 0 | 1 | 2 | 3 metres |
| 0 | | 5 | 10 feet |

of this piece therefore took in wood from the 'other' half of the log to maintain a usable thickness of timber. This emphasises the point that the carpenters made the best use of what timber was available.

Sources of timber and wood

Wood is known to have been imported into York in the Roman and medieval periods. Though not themselves necessarily imported, boat planks identified as possibly Baltic in origin, derived from large slow-grown trees with exceptionally straight grain, were re-used in a revetment from medieval Coppergate itself (Goodburn 2000, 238; *AY* 10/6). At Hungate, recent work has identified boat planking originating in south-east England (Tyers 2009). Given the extensive trading contacts of York with north-west Europe and Scandinavia, it would be difficult to believe that no timber was imported to York in the Anglo-Scandinavian period. However, there is no evidence from this period at Coppergate for the structural timber being anything other than grown and obtained locally.

By recording the structure of the individual pieces of timber, an attempt may be made to reconstruct the parent log and tree from which the timber was obtained. This approach is not new, having been used by Rackham in his study of the timbers of 'The Grundle', a 15th-century house in Suffolk (Rackham 1972), of the roof timbers of the Gloucester Blackfriars (Rackham *et al.* 1978) and by Goodburn in his study of the timbers of London's medieval waterfront (Goodburn 1992). Although the range of structures and types of timbers are much more limited on the Coppergate excavation than on other sites, some suggestions as to the forms of the parent trees represented in the Coppergate cellars are presented here (Fig.349).

The plates were cut from mature, slow-grown oaks, around 200 years old, with moderate-sized branches along much of their length. They would seem to comprise much if not most of the trunk of the tree, starting from the butt end and cut off at or just below the main limb junctions. None the less, these plates are quite knotty and the parent trees would seem to have been growing in fairly open woodland, where low-springing branches were able to develop.

The planks and boards also appear to have been obtained from mature oaks. Again, these were taken from the lower part of the trunk, at or just below the springing of the larger branches. The tangentially converted planks would seem to indicate again that the trees were generally medium to slow growing, c.0.25–0.35m diameter and c.80–100 years old, from an open woodland. The radially faced planks are more difficult to source; however, these trees were clearly of much greater girth than those from which tangentially faced boards were obtained, being slow grown, 0.8–1.0m diameter, perhaps up to 200–300 years old.

In so far as it is possible to determine, the posts in all of the structures were cut from top logs, i.e. that part of the trunk which is highest in the living tree. Though it is possible that some were cut from the thickest branches of very large mature trees, those which have been examined do not have pith which is markedly off centre, or any other signs of stress wood usually observed in branch wood, while retaining a fairly straight grain. Most of the posts are cut from logs c.200–300mm diameter (excluding bark) and 50–100 years old.

The trees which were used were selected so as to be just large enough for their intended purpose, whether as planks, posts or plates. This minimised the amount of subsequent working needed to finish them to the form required. Many have sapwood on the corners and/or edges. Some knotty wood was tolerated, though it cannot

be determined whether the degree of this affected the conversion methods practised.

It appears that a range of tree sizes was exploited, from small, moderately fast-grown trees up to large slow-grown trees as they were required. Size and shape, rather than age or growth rate, were the primary criteria for selection. This in turn influenced the quality of the material produced. Though these types of trees might be found in the same woodland, the younger trees around the edges and on the fringes of clearings and the older in the middle of the wood with less light and more competition, it is possible that more than one woodscape was being exploited. One of these would be a fairly open, intensively managed wood with trees felled on a regular basis; the other appears to be denser, developed woodland, not perhaps a remnant of the ancient wildwood, but abandoned woodland not intensively exploited since the late Roman period. Such woods are believed to have been exploited in south-east England at around this time (Goodburn 1992, 118) and the evidence from Coppergate suggests the existence of similar woodland in the hinterland of York.

Re-use of timbers

Several of the buildings incorporate timbers which have evidence of a former use, as indicated by the presence of redundant features. It must be emphasised that due to subsequent robbing and the accidents of preservation in the ground, there were probably more re-used timbers in the structures than can now be identified. Certainly the spread of timbers datable by dendrochronology suggests a probable re-use of some timbers in each building though

Context 20515
Timber no 8661

Re-used floor timber, Structure 5/1

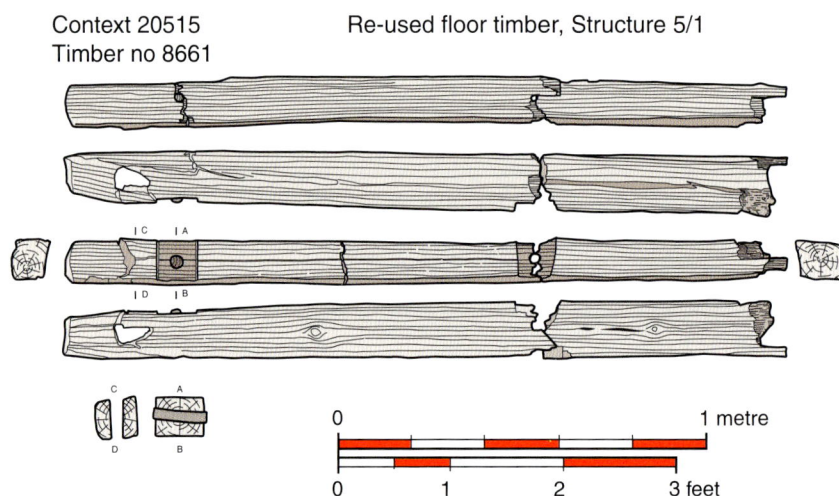

Fig.350   *Re-used floor timber 8661, Structure 5/1. Scale 1:20*

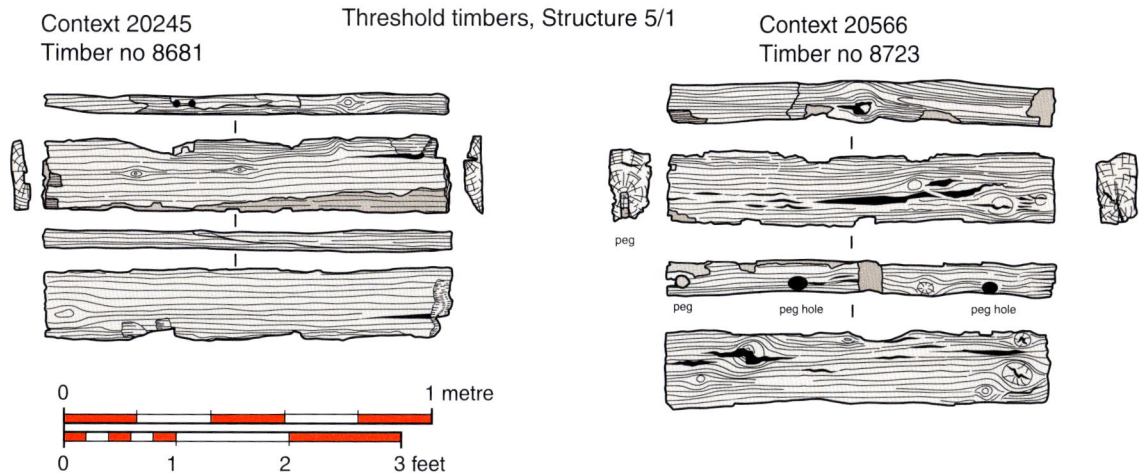

Fig.351   *Re-used threshold timbers 8681 and 8723, Structure 5/1. Scale 1:20*

very few now have redundant features that would allow them to be identified positively as such.

One of the floor timbers of Structure 5/1 (8661, Fig.350) is unusual in being the only such with a pair of pegged lap housings in the upper face as found. These are unlikely to relate to the planked floor of the structure. The same timber has a pair of through mortices cut through the edges. These mortices were buried in the ground when the floor was in use. This timber would seem to be derived from a dismantled frame. Each of the remaining floor timbers (8662–4) was a roughly trimmed length of roundwood with no indication of joints or fixings. The timbers used to revet steps down into this structure were also re-used: 8681 and 8723 each have a pair of redundant peg-holes in one edge and 8723 has a third peg-hole across the end with a truncated peg present (Fig.351).

One of the post-pads of Structure 5/3 (8577) may have had the remains of a joint at one end but it is not now possible to be sure of this. The offcuts used to level the floor timbers in Structure 5/7 include a number of re-used timbers such as 8972 which, although having peg-holes in its upper face as found, also had two other timbers overlying it, and cannot have been pegged to any floor planks. The inverted dovetail lap housing in plate 8392 and the pegged lap housing in the partition plate 8393 may be related to actual use, rather than re-use.

A plate from Structure 5/9 is certainly re-used. This (timber 131, Fig.352) has the remains of three blind mortices cut into one face and two more cut into the adjacent edge, all redundant. As well as being a rare example of morticing in an Anglo-Scandinavian context at Coppergate, the spacing of these mortices is of the

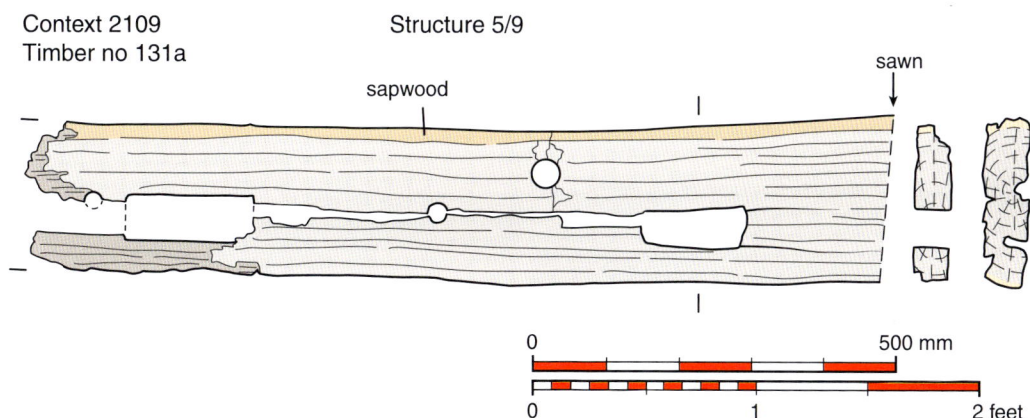

Fig.352   *Re-used morticed plate 131, Structure 5/9. Scale 1:10*

same order as the spacing of the wall posts. Plates do not have mortices at Coppergate and it is therefore possible that this timber once formed part of a ground-level plate, tying the tops of the wall posts and supporting the roof timbers.

Pegged features

Most of the redundant features evident on the posts of these structures are pegs and the holes cut to house them (Fig.353). These pegs and holes do not relate to the structures as found and do not consistently face into or out from the boards of the wall. There are no pegs which pass through a plank into a post nor are there any peg-holes in posts which correspond to peg-holes in boards. Those pegs which do survive are all cut off flush with the surface of the timber into which they have been driven. Thus no pegs fasten timbers together. As found, the planks are retained by gravity or by the pressure of soil backfilled behind them. If small nails were employed none can now be identified.

It was initially thought that these features indicated re-use of the timbers concerned and by the usual criteria this would be the case. However, a number of factors suggest that this may not be so. Firstly there is the consist-

Fig.353   *Peg hole in post 1982.22.34*
           Scale length 100mm

ency of the features concerned. Across the site, in different walls in different structures single peg-holes have been cut into a single face of a post, 150–250mm above its butt end. Had these timbers been re-used, more variety in the number and distribution of the peg-holes would be expected.

Secondly, each of the holes has been cut into what would have been the outermost face of the parent log. Dendrochronological analysis suggested that two of the posts concerned (8695 and 8696) were cut from the same tree (see p.745). When these two posts were physically checked subsequently, it was found that they are indeed two halves of the same parent log, split in two and each half then cut to a rectangular cross-section. When refitted into their original orientation within the tree it was also noticed that the two peg-holes were almost exactly opposite each other. It would appear that the peg-holes were cut and the pegs inserted before the timber was halved.

It therefore appears that these pegs relate to the handling of the timbers before they were installed in the structure. They act either as lifting handles or, more probably, attachment points for cordage or rope used around the end of a timber when it was being moved. They were not necessary in the structure and would have hindered the placement of the posts and boards, so were either extracted or cut off flush with the surface into which they had been driven. A possible parallel for this practice was recorded in the late 12th-century millpond drain at Bordesley Abbey, Worcestershire (Allen 1993, 96), where the hollowed out log forming the base of this feature had a pair of such pegs left *in situ* at one end, and redundant peg-holes elsewhere. Until quite recent times in Norway such methods were still used for hauling felled and trimmed logs out of woodland (pers. comm., Tom Gangstøe, Stiftelsen, Bryggen).

Woodworking and tool evidence

The few woodworking tools recovered during the excavations at Coppergate cannot be related directly to the timbers found there, being stratigraphically later than the structures in which they were discovered. Nor can the corroded cutting edges be accurately matched against surviving toolmarks. Although the timbers have all suffered some degree of deterioration before and during burial, evidence for the toolkit employed can be seen and/ or extrapolated.

Most of the evidence associated with the initial stages of woodworking, i.e. felling, stripping of bark or rough shaping, has been removed by subsequent working. Hewn kerfs on the bases of occasional posts (8700) are all that survive from felling of the tree but do show that this was carried out with axes. Significant branches may have been lopped at the felling site but the stumps of surviving side branches have been subject to subsequent trimming. No marks survive from debarking, nor are there marks from any wedges that could have been used to split the parent logs during conversion.

There is extensive evidence for the trimming and dressing of timbers to the required shape and length. The pattern of hewing and angle of the signature marks to the stop mark indicates that most of this was done with axes of varying sizes and forms. Axes were used for cross-cutting timbers to the required length, as shown by two abandoned cross-cuttings on posts 8320 and 8326, and a completed cross-cutting with surviving wide kerf on the base of post 8694 (Fig.354). Axes were used to prepare the faces of the posts, to cut joints, to truncate pegs, to trim the faces of planks and boards after conversion and in the shaping of plates. None of the toolmarks indicates the use of adzes or saws, all of which are known to be much later developments in structural carpentry (Goodburn 1992, 113).

Fig.354   Completed cross-cut with wide kerf on post 8694
Scale length 100mm

Some evidence survives to indicate the sizes of the tools concerned. No individual timber had evidence for more than one tool being used for a particular purpose. Unfortunately, the tool signature marks are too limited for conclusive matches to be made between timbers of the same or of different structures.

Of those buildings with extensive surviving remains, Structure 5/1 had complete blade widths of 94mm, 66mm and 60mm present on the bases of posts, suggesting at least three axes of the same type were being used to square off their ends. One complete axe mark of 100mm width and a partial axe mark more than 110mm wide show that at least two trimming axes were in use at the same time. Structure 5/3 had no complete axe marks, but blades more than 60mm wide were used to dress ends, while axe blades more than 140mm wide were used to dress the faces. Structure 5/6 again had no complete blade widths present, and the bases of the posts were in poor condition, but axes of more than 160mm width are represented on the trimmed areas of planks.

The evidence shows that smaller axes producing deep cuts were used for cross-cutting and shaping the end grain of timbers, while larger axes making wide shallow cuts were employed to finish the surfaces of planks and posts. This reflects the two principal types of axe used in this period for finishing structural timbers (Goodburn 1992, 112): a felling axe with a compact blade and short width normally used for cross-cutting and a 'T'-axe with a long light blade used to remove finer shavings along the grain to produce flat faces and edges. The only two axes contemporary with these structures from Coppergate (*AY* 17/13, 2105, *2255* and *2256*, Periods 5A and 5B respectively) cannot be related to the toolmarks. Although *2255*, a felling axe, might produce a facet around 70mm wide comparable to some of the felling axe marks, the trimming (or 'shaping') axe *2256* is represented only by a fragment of the socket.

The hewing patterns on the faces of the planks and boards show that they were not made by splitting a log in two and then hewing the two halves down to the required thickness. Examination of the end grain of the wood indicates that the parent logs were split either into radial sections (radially faced) or into parallel slices (tangentially faced). The hewing marks on their faces are very localised (Fig.355). This is consistent with the removal of raised areas of wood resulting from uneven splitting during conversion, especially around knots, or to reduce raised areas of wood resulting from irregular splitting to a more even surface.

The step cut into the upper face of the plates was also hewn out. The plates have been finished off with a trimming axe worked along the face, but these surfaces were very abraded and the marks were indistinct. In contrast, the step in plate 135 (Fig.348) had been roughly

Timber no 22.3   Structure 5/1

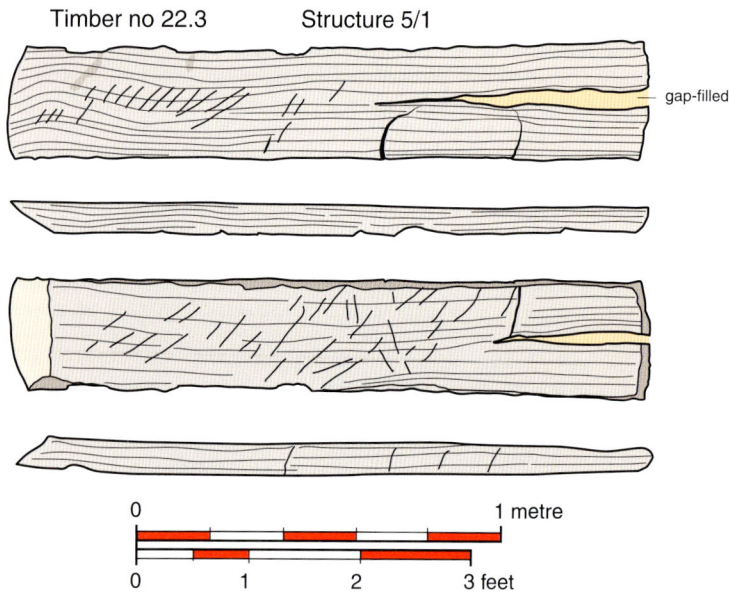

Fig.355 *Localised hewing on tangentially faced*
plank 1982.22.3. Scale 1:20

gap-filled

0   1 metre

0   1   2   3 feet

hewn out but not completely finished. A series of steep, almost vertical cuts, by a blade up to 110mm wide, had been delivered into the upper face of the timber, splitting off wood as further cuts were made. From the angle of the cuts it appears that a felling axe swung into the timber whist it lay on what is now its inner edge was employed. Had the timber been finished, a dressing axe would have been used along the length of the surface to tidy up the rough-hewn surface.

Peg-holes were cut with augers. Wherever a blind peg-hole had been cut, the surviving profile indicates that the tool used was of spoon bit form. The blade widths of those used at Coppergate vary from 13 to 37mm in diameter, though most are around 30mm or slightly less. The auger used to cut below the joints on posts 8319, 8320 and 8326 produced holes of 30mm diameter. Those spoon-bit augers found at Coppergate (*AY* 17/13, 2113) would cut holes from 9mm to 35mm diameter, but not all of these, especially the smaller sizes, would necessarily have been employed in structural carpentry.

Few joints were observed. The three posts (8319, 8320 and 8326, Fig.356) that survived to full height in Structure 5/6 terminated in unpegged bare faced tenons, hewn out with an axe. In the absence of the timber(s) with which these tenons articulated, little can be said with certainty about the joint. The form is very unlikely to be a scarf to continue the post up above ground level, as there are no fastenings through the tenon to secure it. The joint should therefore have articulated with a horizontal tie or

plate linking the tops of the posts in the same wall either through very close fitting lap housing or more securely into a mortice. The peg-hole below the joint might have taken cordage to tie the joint but there are no wear marks to support this suggestion. It is equally possible that the peg-hole is one of those redundant pegged features discussed earlier.

The through mortices in a re-used floor timber 8661 had been cut by having their corners drilled out by spoon bit augers before the waste was removed. The plates were cut leaving a raised flange or lip on their inner edge, retaining the feet of the posts forming the wall. No fixings were used to fasten the posts to the plate and no sockets or mortices were employed to anchor them. The blind mortices present on 131 (Fig.352) are of some interest. They are short and narrow, with sloping ends, having been hewn out with a chisel-like tool. There is some indication that the mortices were started by drilling holes with a spoon-bit auger at each end before removal of the waste. The few lap housings seen (8661 and 8393, both with pegs, also 8392; Fig.350) had been hewn out with axes which must have been done before any pegs were inserted.

The lower edge of the lowest tier of boards rested either on the ground surface, on the upper face of any plates present or on the floorboards. These boards were not fastened to each other and nor were the posts physically fastened to the planks of the wall by any method that can now be observed. Pressure of backfilled soil

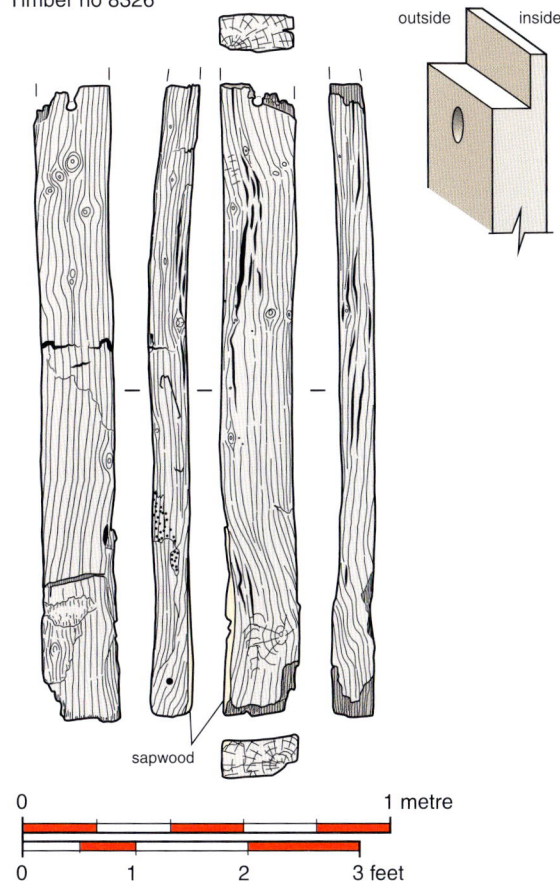

Context 1486
Timber no 8326

Structure 5/6

outside   inside

sapwood

Fig.356   *Surviving post top 8326 from Structure 5/6. Scale 1:20*

would have held the outer lining boards in place. The lower tier of the inner linings evidently relied on gravity; whether any higher tiers were nailed in place or relied on some other form of fastening or fixing that we cannot now identify must be a matter of speculation.

The only surviving floorboards (8962, 8963, 8965, Structure 5/5) were carefully cut to fit around the feet of the wall posts (see Figs 263 and 264). While the pegs or peg-holes in some floor timbers hint that some floorboards were been pegged in place, rather than just resting on them, no floorboard has actually been found with a peg-hole nor were any floorboards found in articulation with pegs or peg-holes in the underlying timber.

Utilisation of timber and provisional construction dates

The following tables and figures summarise the surviving evidence and how different types of timber were utilised in the Period 5 buildings. Plotting the extensive dendrochronological results for this phase, study of the timbers and a critical review of the location and stratigraphic sequences allows the probable construction dates of many of the buildings to be defined within certain parameters (Fig.357).

Tenement A, Structure 5/1 *(Fig.358)*

Table 38   Summary of surviving evidence for use of timber in Structure 5/1

Timber	Roundwood	Boxed heart	Box halved	Boxed radial	Box quartered	Tangentially faced	Radially faced	Unknown
East wall outer lining						6	2	
East wall posts		2	14		1	1		
East wall inner lining							7	1
South wall posts					2			
South wall lining		2				1	1	
West wall outer lining						10		
West wall posts		7	7					
West wall inner lining						1	11	
Floor timbers	3	1						

80 timbers

Most of the east and south walls were recovered and recorded in 1979, while the rest of the south wall and most of the west wall were excavated in 1982. The north wall lies beyond the limit of the excavations. The building was at least partially destroyed by fire. Box converted timber is used for all of the posts. It is noteworthy that the inner linings are almost exclusively high-quality radially faced timber, the outer linings poorer-quality tangentially faced boards. One of the floor timbers is re-used, as are the two thick planks revetting the steps into the south wall. Three posts in each of the west and east walls have single blind auger holes in a face, some with truncated pegs. Two of

777

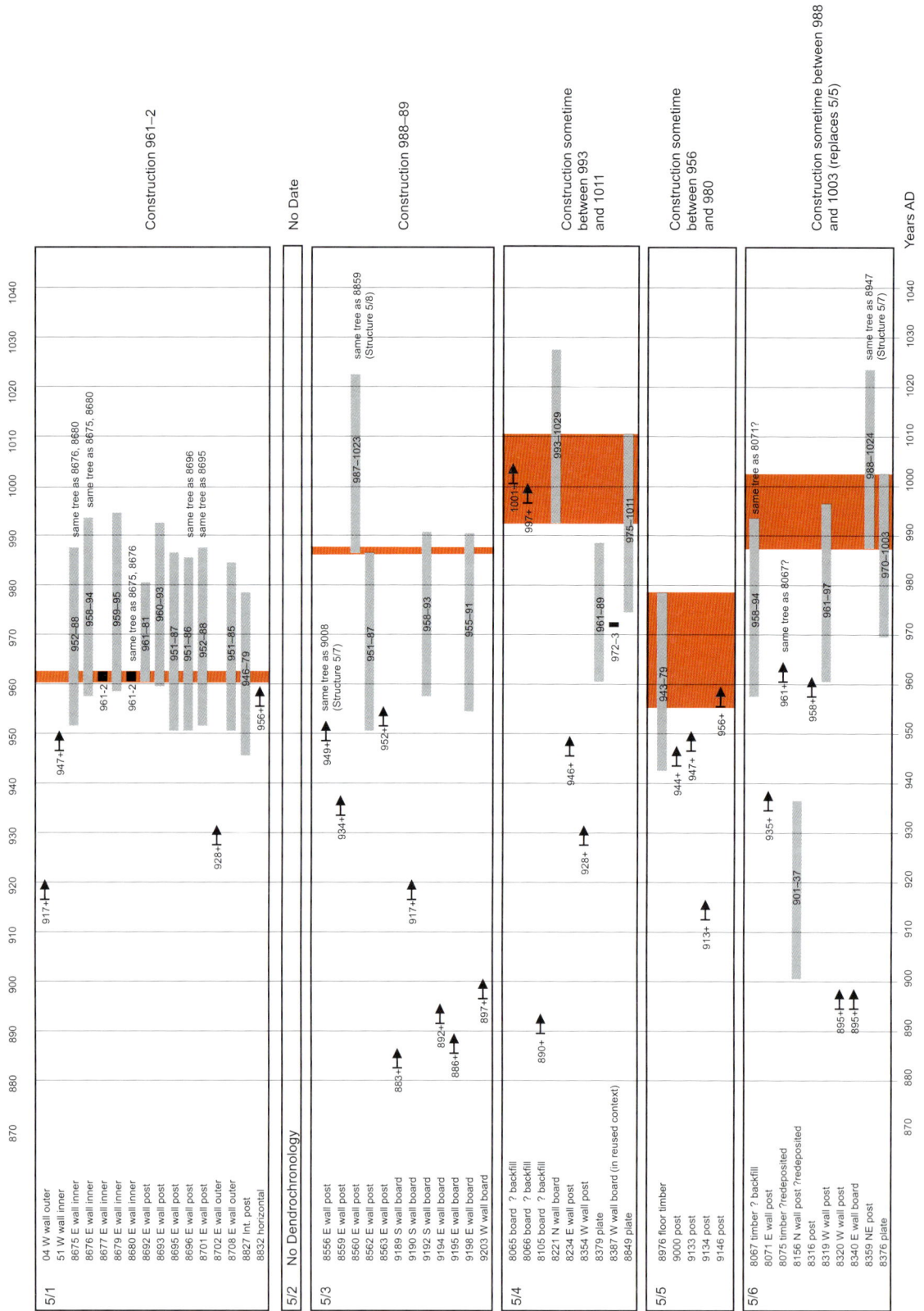

Years AD

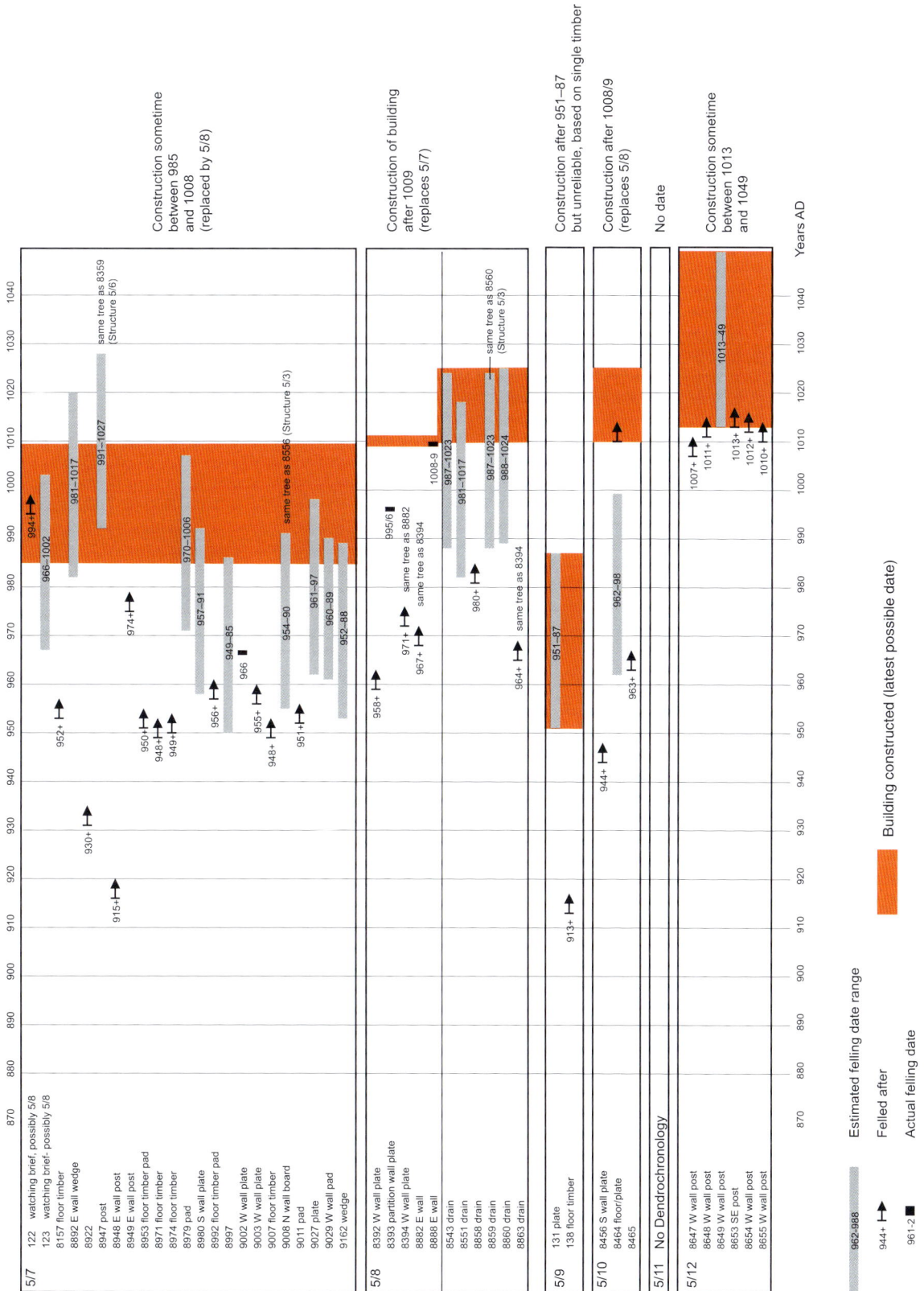

Fig.357   Chart showing dendrochronological information for Period 5 Structures 5/1–5/12

779

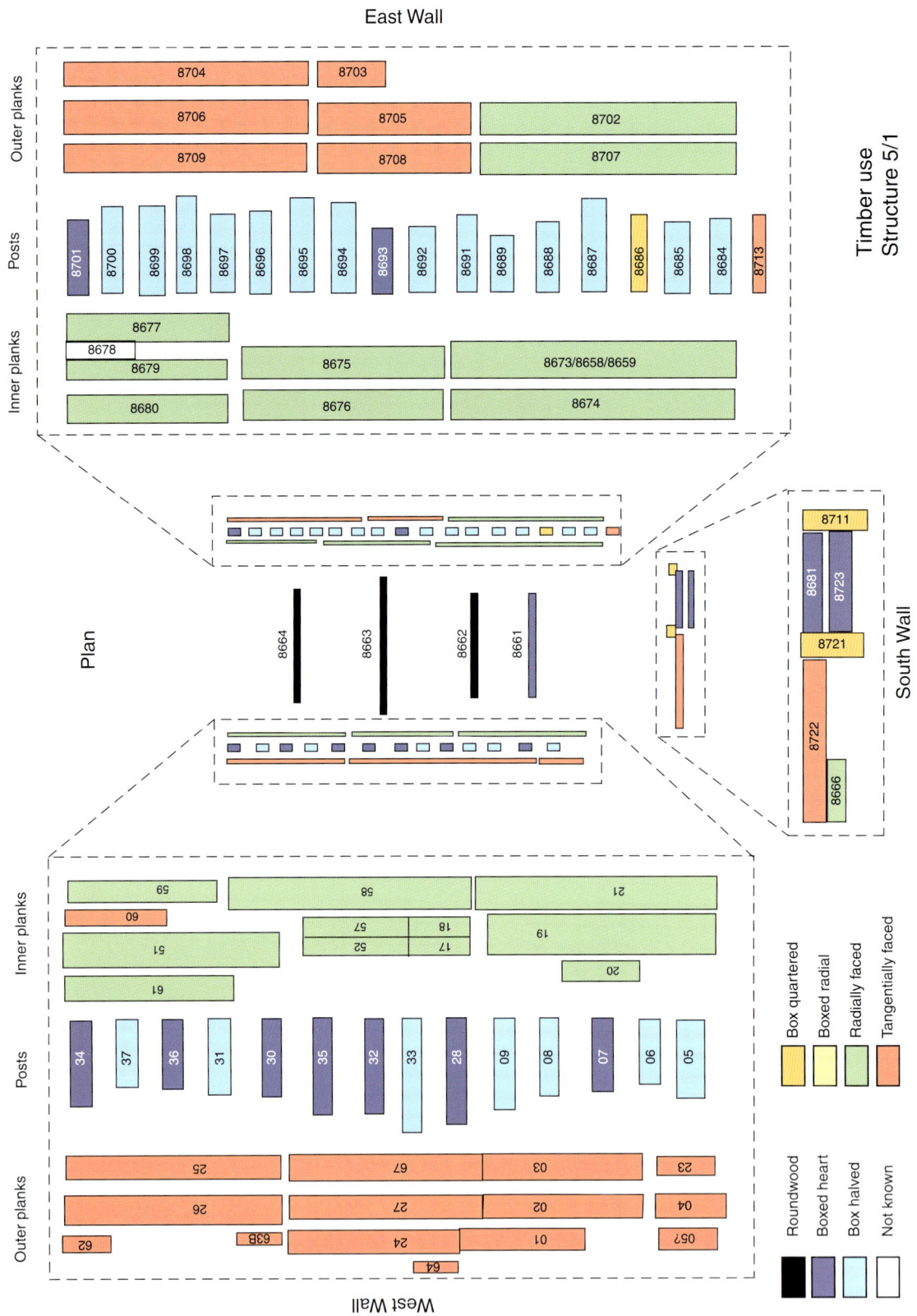

East Wall

Outer planks: 8704, 8703, 8706, 8705, 8702, 8709, 8708, 8707

Posts: 8701, 8700, 8699, 8698, 8697, 8696, 8695, 8694, 8693, 8692, 8691, 8689, 8688, 8687, 8686, 8685, 8684, 8713

Inner planks: 8677, 8678, 8679, 8675, 8673/8658/8659, 8680, 8676, 8674

Timber use Structure 5/1

Plan

8664, 8663, 8662, 8661

South Wall

8711, 8681, 8723, 8721, 8722, 8666

West Wall

Inner planks: 59, 58, 21, 60, 57, 18, 19, 52, 17, 51, 20, 61

Posts: 34, 37, 36, 31, 30, 35, 32, 33, 28, 09, 08, 07, 06, 05

Outer planks: 25, 67, 03, 23, 26, 27, 02, 04, 62, 63B, 24, 01, 05?, 64

Box quartered Roundwood
Boxed radial Boxed heart
Radially faced Box halved
Tangentially faced Not known

Fig.358 *Timber use diagram Structure 5/1. Timber numbers are used in this and following illustrations. See Table 34 on p.754–60 for a concordance of timber numbers and context numbers*

the east wall posts (8695, 8696) are from one tree, and three of the east wall boards (8675, 8676, 8680) are also same-tree matches (see p.745). Examination of the whole timbers concerned has confirmed this.

Dating: Constructed AD 961–62 or immediately thereafter.

Tenement A, Structure 5/2

Table 39 Summary of surviving evidence for use of timber in Structure 5/2

Timber	Roundwood	Boxed heart	Box halved	Boxed radial	Box quartered	Tangentially faced	Radially faced	Unknown
Stakes								18
Horizontals								3

21 timbers

Known only from a site plan, uncompleted context sheets and context lists. No timbers received timber numbers or were retained for recording.

Dating: No dendrochronology available.

Tenement B, Structure 5/3 (Fig.359)

Table 40 Summary of surviving evidence for use of timber in Structure 5/3

Timber	Roundwood	Boxed heart	Box halved	Boxed radial	Box quartered	Tangentially faced	Radially faced	Unknown
East wall lining						2	3	
East wall posts			6	2				
South wall lining						1	3	
West wall lining						2	6	2
West wall posts			7	2				
Post pads				1			10	3

50 timbers

The south wall and southern ends of both the east and west walls were recorded, recovered and excavated; the north end of the building lies beyond the limit of excavation. Although pads for the five or more posts of the south wall were identified, the posts themselves had been robbed. All of the pads were in the form of offcuts from planks or boards. The planks have been arranged with the lowest planks of each wall being tangentially faced and the upper planks being radially faced. Several of the planks are believed to be contemporary (9194, 9195, 9196, 9190, 9191 and 9192) (see p.745). Five of these are radially faced and might be cut from the same parent log, but one is tangentially faced and must be from a different tree. Dendrochronology also suggests that one of the boxed heart east wall posts (8556) may be from the same tree as a tangentially faced plank (9008) in a wall of Structure 5/7 (see p.747) and a second such post may be from the same tree as a tangentially faced board (8859) from the drain in Structure 5/8.

Dating: Construction date proposed in the dendrochronological report is 958–87, possibly after 966, but the latest possible date is c.AD 988/89 or immediately thereafter

Tenement B, Structure 5/4 (Fig.360)

Table 41 Summary of surviving evidence for use of timber in Structure 5/4

Timber	Roundwood	Boxed heart	Box halved	Boxed radial	Box quartered	Tangentially faced	Radially faced	Unknown
East wall lining						6		1
East wall posts		1	3	2		1		3
East wall plate			1					1
North wall lining						?14	2	
North wall posts	1		1		1	2		
North wall plate				1				
West wall lining						4	3	
West wall posts		3	1	2				
West wall plates				1				
West wall 'revetment'							3	
Unknown location						1	4	3

66 timbers

This was a badly disturbed building entirely within the area of excavation, incorporating an internal drain. A number of stakes were used to support the planks of the drain but none was assigned a timber number

781

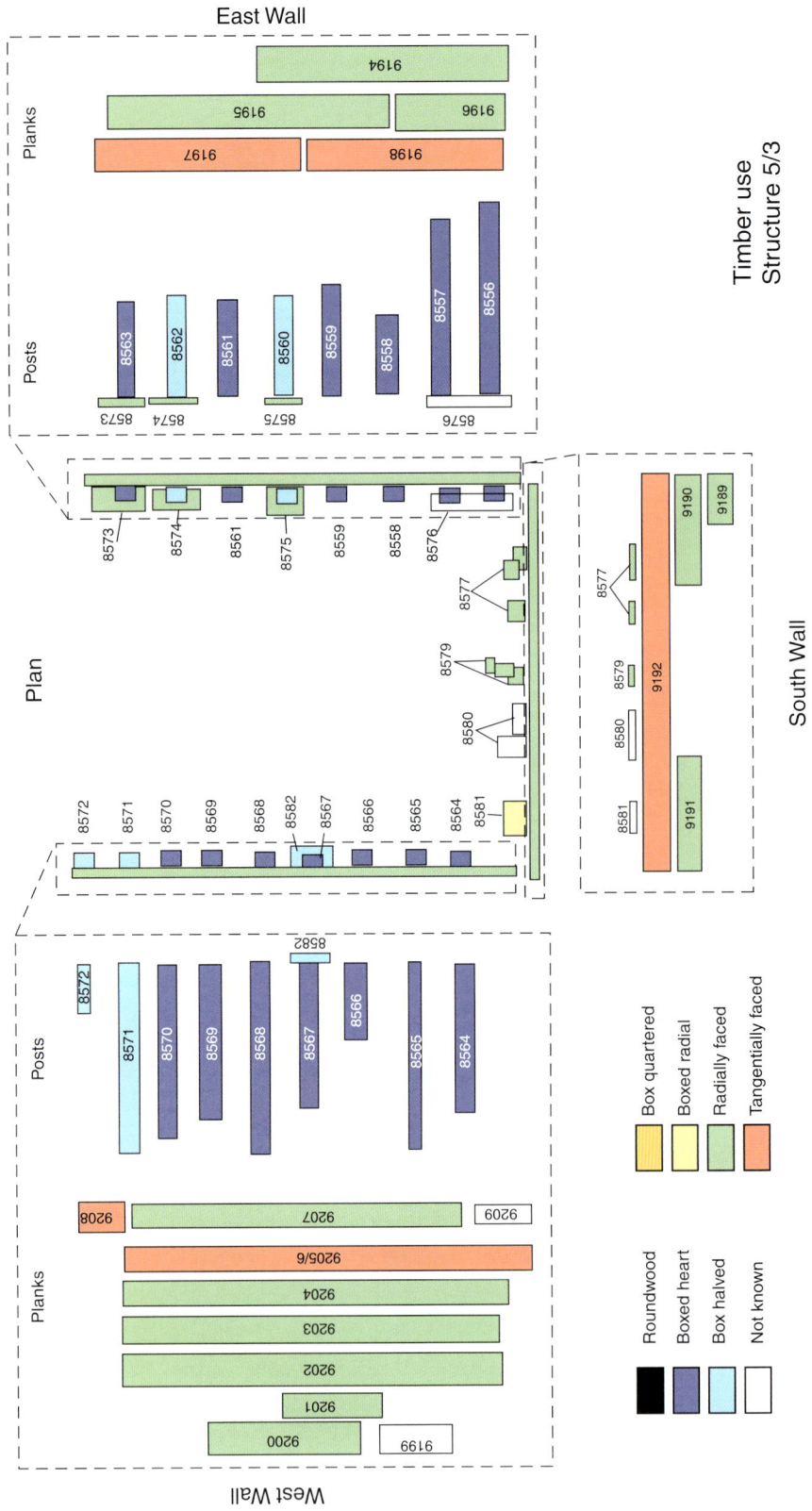

East Wall

Planks

9194
9195
9196
9197
9198

Posts

8563 8562 8561 8560 8559 8558 8557 8556
8573 8574 8575 8576

Timber use
Structure 5/3

Plan

8573 8574 8561 8575 8559 8558 8576

8577

8579

8580

8572 8571 8570 8569 8568 8582 8567 8566 8565 8564 8581

South Wall

9190 9189
8577
8579 9192
8580
8581 9191

West Wall

Posts

8572
8571
8570
8569
8568
8567
8566
8582
8565
8564

Planks

9208 9207 9209
9205/6
9204
9203
9202
9201
9200 9199

Box quartered
Boxed radial
Radially faced
Tangentially faced

Roundwood
Boxed heart
Box halved
Not known

Fig.359   Timber use diagram Structure 5/3

782

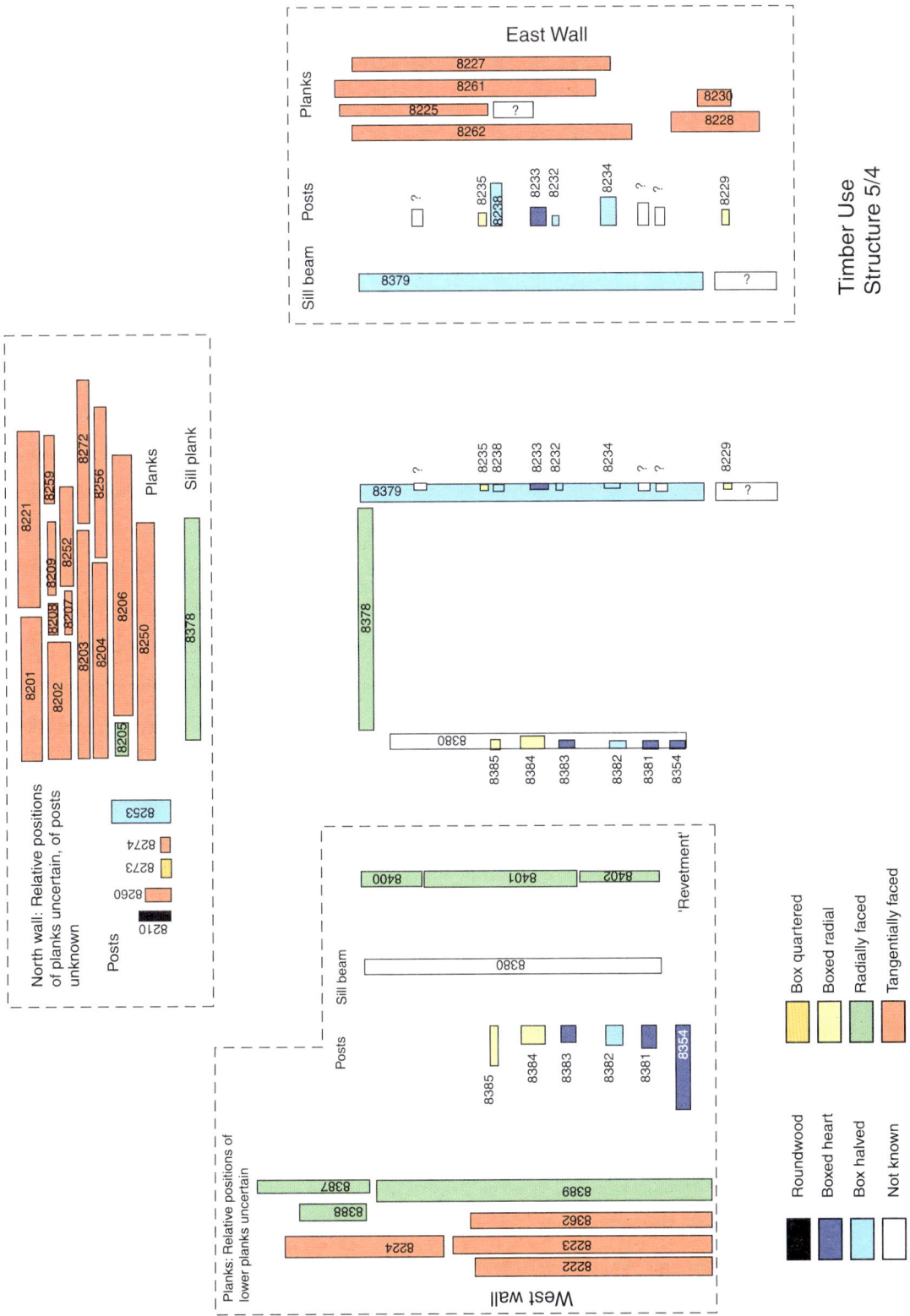

East Wall

Planks
8227
8261
8225   ?
8230
8228
8262

Posts
?   8235 8233 8232   8234 ? ?   8229
8238

Sill beam
8379   ?

Timber Use Structure 5/4

North wall: Relative positions of planks uncertain, of posts unknown

Planks
8221 8259 8272 8256
8209 8252
8203 8205 8207 8206 8250
8201 8202 8204

Sill plank
8378

Posts
8253
8274
8273
8260
8210

8379
?   8235 8233 8232   8234 ? ?   8229
8238

8378

8380
8385 8384 8383 8382 8381 8354

'Revetment'

8400 8401 8402

Sill beam
8380

Posts
8385 8384 8383 8382 8381 8354

Planks: Relative positions of lower planks uncertain

8387
8388   8389
8362
8224   8223
8222

West wall

Box quartered
Boxed radial
Radially faced
Tangentially faced

Roundwood
Boxed heart
Box halved
Not known

Fig.360   *Timber use diagram Structure 5/4*

783

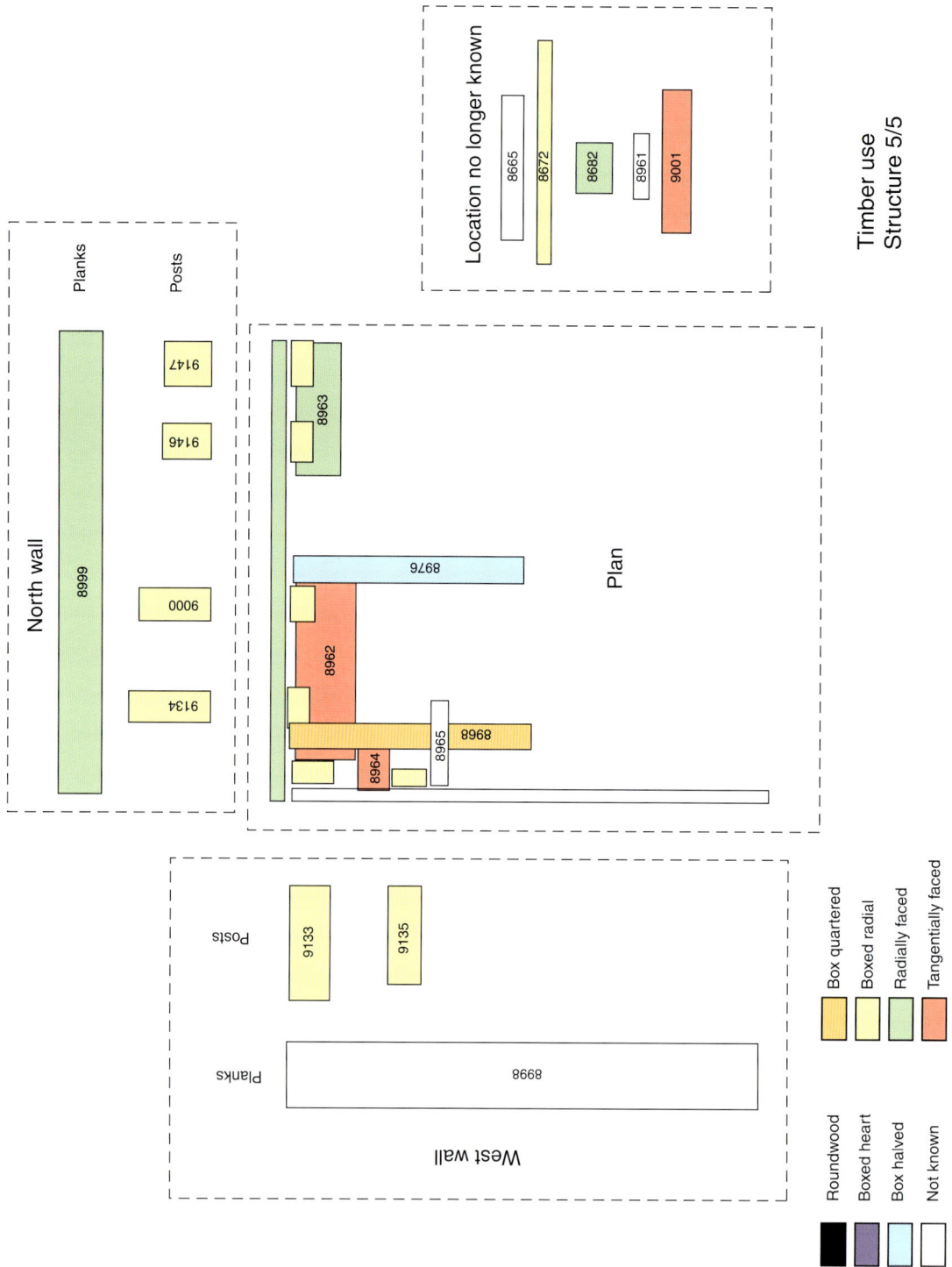

Timber use Structure 5/5

Location no longer known: 8665, 8672, 8682, 8961, 9001

North wall: Planks — 8999; Posts — 9147, 9146, 9000, 9134

Plan: 8963, 8976, 8962, 8968, 8965, 8964

West wall: Posts — 9133, 9135; Planks — 8998

Conversion (key): Box quartered, Boxed radial, Radially faced, Tangentially faced, Roundwood, Boxed heart, Box halved, Not known

Fig.361   *Timber use diagram Structure 5/5*

784

or recorded. Most of the boards are tangentially faced with radially faced examples. Those on the east wall are exclusively tangential facings but it is impossible to tell how the relative conversions relate to each other in the other walls. The plates are relatively thin and might be better classed as planks rather than plates. The posts are little more than stumps: only one is taller than 1m and most are less than half this height.

Dating: Construction date proposed by dendrochronological report is soon after 972/73 but the latest date could arguably be sometime between AD 993 and 1011.

Tenement C, Structure 5/5 *(Fig.361)*

Table 42 Summary of surviving evidence for use of timber in Structure 5/5

Timber	Roundwood	Boxed heart	Box halved	Boxed radial	Box quartered	Tangentially faced	Radially faced	Unknown
North wall posts				4				
North wall planks						2	1	
West wall planks						1		1
West wall posts				2				1
Floor planks						3	1	1
Floor joists			1		1			
Location unknown				1		2	1	4

27 timbers

This building had been almost entirely removed by the subsequent insertion of Structure 5/6. Prior to this the structure had been largely destroyed by fire. The floorboards run across the long axis of the building while the 'joists' run along the short axis. Floorboards were cut to fit around the feet of the wall posts and thus were fitted after the insertion of the outer lining and posts. All the posts here are boxed radial conversions and dendrochronology indicates that two of these (9133, 9146) may be from the same tree (see p.746–7). One of the joists (8976) has a single peg-hole in its upper face which might relate to the fastening of an overlying floorboard. A door jamb (8625/7) with nails is noted from this building.

Dating: Construction sometime between AD 956 and 979.

Tenement C, Structure 5/6 *(Fig.362)*

Structure 5/6 lay entirely within the area of excavation. The three northernmost posts of the west wall (8319, 8320, 8326) survive almost to their full height, owing to the collapse of the west wall, with upper ends terminating in bare faced tenons. The east and west walls sit on two plates each side, with one further plate for the north wall and one for the south. The posts are relatively slender and of varying conversions. In the north, west and south walls tangentially faced boards are used in the lower tiers with radially faced board appearing higher up the wall, a situation reversed for the east wall. Dendrochronology suggests that three of the radially faced planks (8213, 8215, 8293) from the west wall may be from the same tree (see p.747). Though they cannot be physically refitted, their conversions confirm that each could be a radial split from the same parent log.

Dating: Construction in the late 10th century, probably between 988 and 1003.

Table 43 Summary of surviving evidence for use of timber in Structure 5/6

Timber	Roundwood	Boxed heart	Box halved	Boxed radial	Box quartered	Tangentially faced	Radially faced	Unknown
East wall planks						5	5	3
East wall posts		2			1	2		2
East wall plates								2
North wall posts		2	2					1
North wall planks						1		2
North wall plate						1		
West wall planks						9	3	6
West wall posts		2	3	3		4		
West wall plates			2					
South wall posts	1	1						3
South wall planks						3	1	3
South wall plates			2					1
'Drain' timbers						2	2	3
Unknown	1	1	2	2	1		1	2

95 timbers

Records indicate a board-lined or lidded drain associated with this building but only one possibly re-used component was retained for recording and conservation and the exact relationship with the building is uncertain.

Tenement D, Structure 5/7 *(Fig.363)*

Table 44 Summary of surviving evidence for use of timber in Structure 5/7

Timber	Roundwood	Boxed heart	Box halved	Boxed radial	Box quartered	Tangentially faced	Radially faced	Unknown
North wall lining						1		
North wall post			1					
South wall plates and 'step'			2		1			
West wall plates	1	1						
'Joists'	1	3	2					4
East wall ?posts								4
East wall plates								2
Pads and wedges for plates/'joists'	1	3	1	1		2	3	9
?pit lining						1	1	4
Location/function unknown	1	1			2	1	2	
Drain							1	

56 timbers from building, 1 from drain

This was a badly damaged building. Parts of the west and south walls, along with some fragments of the east wall, were recovered and recorded, albeit robbed to plate level. Most of the east wall appears to have lain beyond the limit of the excavation while the north wall and northern ends of the east and west walls seem to have been destroyed by the later construction of Structure 5/8. A drain (discussed under Structure 5/8) bisects the building along its axis, adding to the damage suffered. The west wall stood on two plates. The south wall stood on what may have been a very narrow plate or a very long post-pad (8980). What appears to be the east wall seems to have consisted of a set of uprights with their bases secured between two parallel timbers running along the wall line. Several timbers in the interior of the structure suggest a planked floor, with longitudinal plates (8983, 8975) having peg-holes cut into their upper face as found. Both appear to have been wedged or levelled, with stray pads, offcuts and other pieces of wood placed beneath their ends and are thus in their intended position, rather than having collapsed from a higher part of the structure.

Dendrochronology suggests that a tangentially faced plank (9008) may be from the same tree as one of the boxed heart east wall posts (8556) of Structure 5/3 (see p.747).

Dating: Construction date proposed in the dendrochronology report is soon after 966 but arguably this could be as late as between AD 985 and 1008; directly replaced by Structure 5/8.

Tenement D, Structure 5/8 *(Fig.364)*

Table 45 Summary of surviving evidence for use of timber in Structure 5/8

Timber	Roundwood	Boxed heart	Box halved	Boxed radial	Box quartered	Tangentially faced	Radially faced	Unknown
East wall pads	1	1					2	3
East wall plates	1							
East wall retaining stakes?								8
Partition wall plate	1							
West wall plates	2							
West wall lining								2
Unknown building	2							1
Drain boards/lids						3	12	5
Drain braces/wedges	4						3	3
Unknown								5

24 timbers from building, 30 from drain, plus 5 unattributed

This was a poorly preserved structure robbed down to its plates and associated with a contemporary board-lined drain. The north end of the building is entirely lost owing to the insertion of Structure 5/9 while the south wall has been completely robbed out. A plate (8393), used to support a transverse partition wall between the north and south ends of the building, is unusual in having a shallow groove cut into its upper face along its length, with one interruption (see Fig.292). A plate (8392) from the west wall has a shallow inverted lap dovetail housing cut into the lip/flange, which may indicate transverse floor timbers for a planked floor.

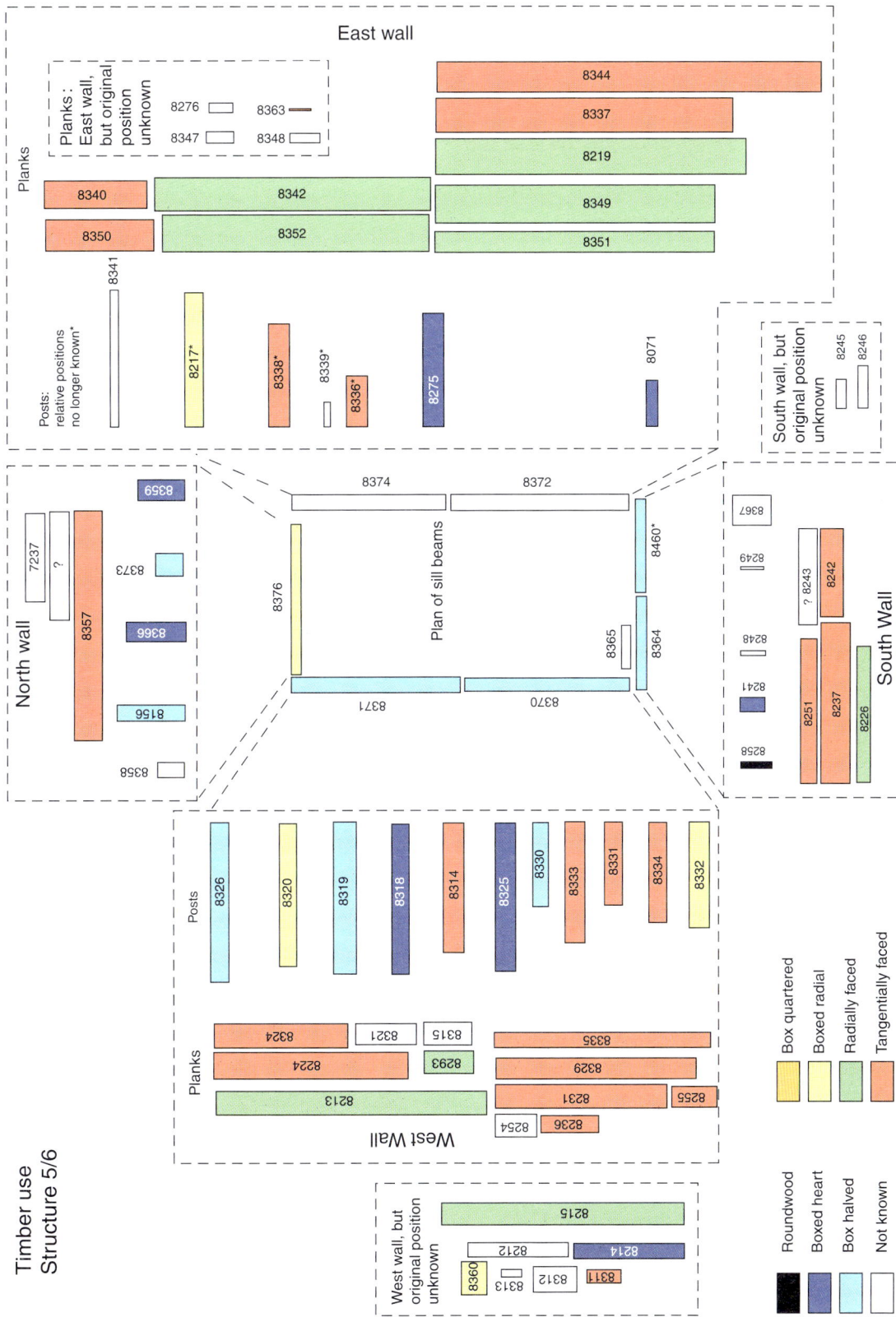

Fig.362   Timber use diagram Structure 5/6

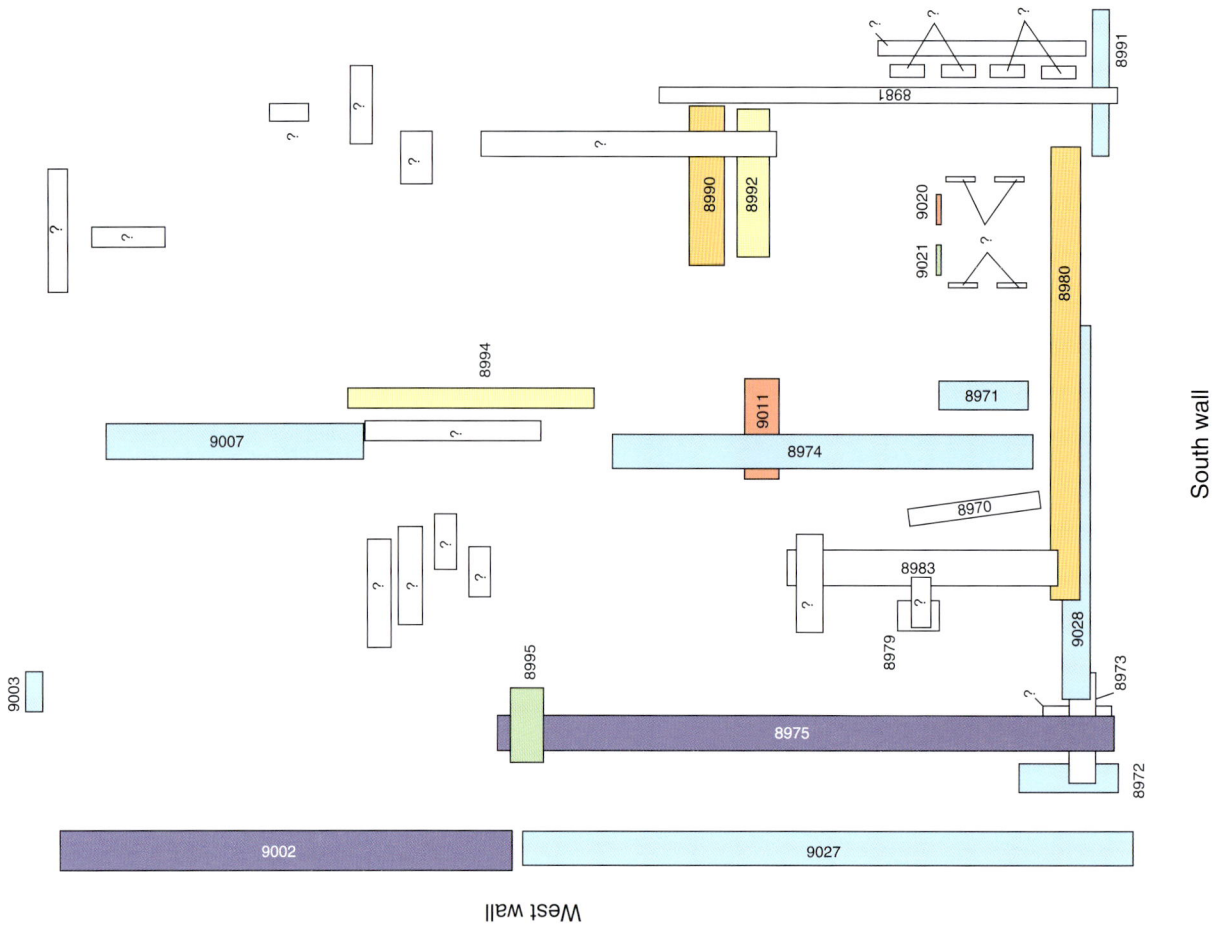

Timber use
Structure 5/7

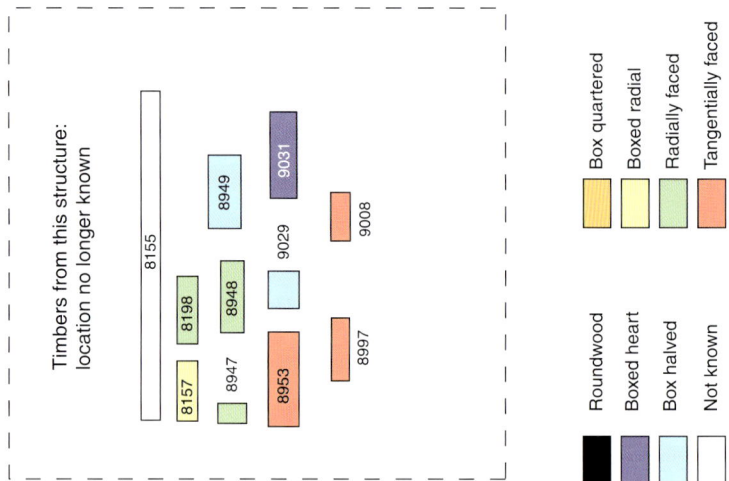

South wall

West wall

Timbers from this structure:
location no longer known

Box quartered
Boxed radial
Radially faced
Tangentially faced

Roundwood
Boxed heart
Box halved
Not known

Fig.363   *Timber use diagram Structure 5/7*

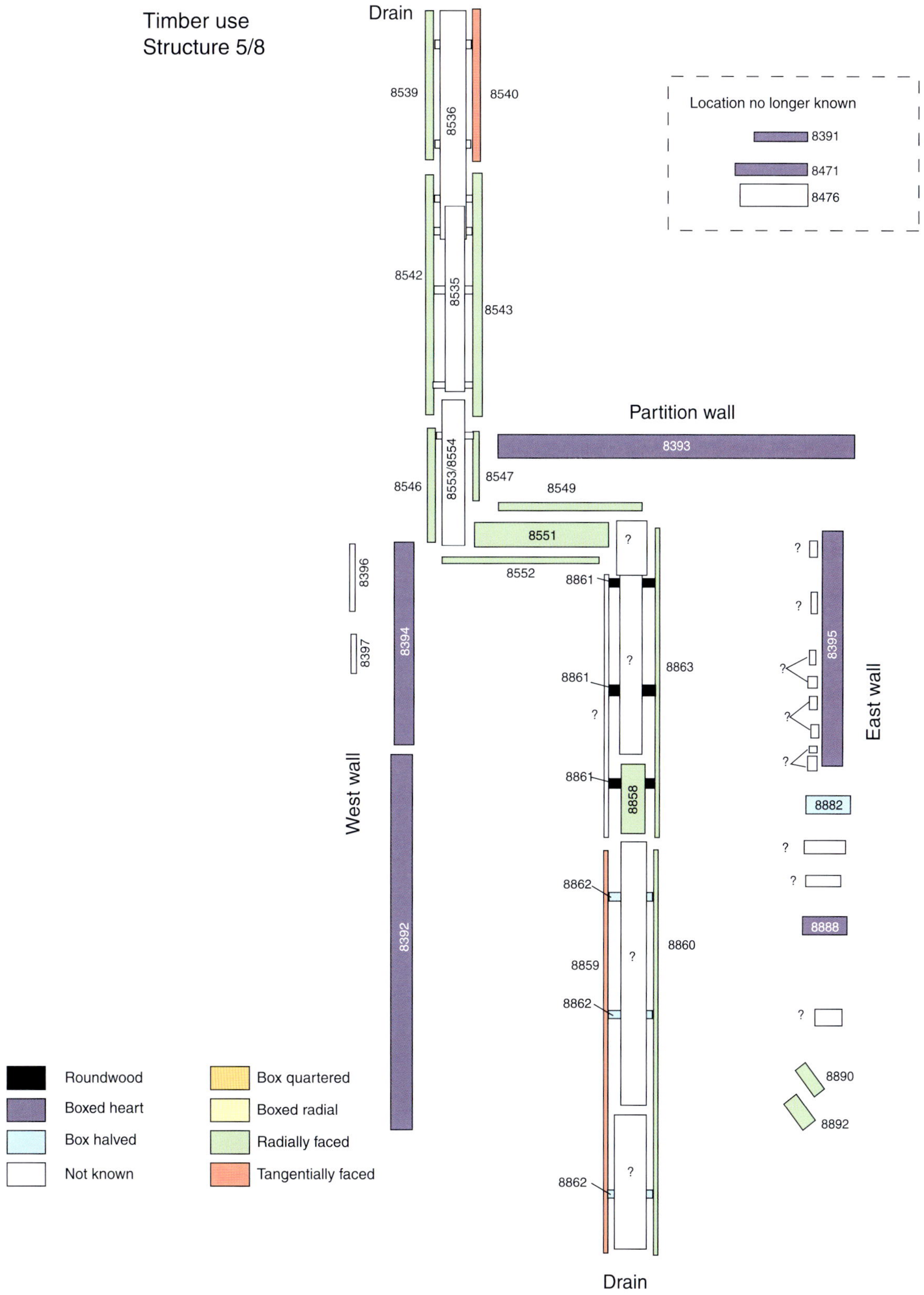

Timber use
Structure 5/8

Drain

8539   8540

Location no longer known

8391
8471
8476

8536

8542   8543

8535

Partition wall

8393

8553/8554   8547

8546   8549

8551

8396   8552

8861

8397   8394   ?   8863

8861

?

8861

8858

West wall   8882

?

8862   ?

8888

8859   8860

8392   ?

8862

?

8890

8892

East wall   8395

8862   ?

Drain

Roundwood   Box quartered

Boxed heart   Boxed radial

Box halved   Radially faced

Not known   Tangentially faced

Fig.364   *Timber use diagram Structure 5/8*

789

Dating: Construction date proposed in dendrochronology report is late 990s but arguably this could be as late as 1008/09 or immediately thereafter. Replaces Structure 5/7.

The board-lined and lidded drain provides two same-tree matches (8858+8863, 8859+8860; see p.748). One further board from this drain may be a same tree match to an east wall post (8560) of Structure 5/3 suggesting re-use. Drain dates to the construction of the building or soon thereafter.

Tenement E, Structure 5/9

Table 46 Summary of surviving evidence for use of timber in Structure 5/9

Timber	Roundwood	Boxed heart	Box halved	Boxed radial	Box quartered	Tangentially faced	Radially faced	Unknown
South wall posts								2
South wall planks								1
South wall pads								2
West wall posts		1						10
West wall planks								5
West wall stakes	3?							1
West wall 'debris'	2							5
West wall plates		1				1?	1	2
Floor timbers						1		1
Unknown			1?					2

42 timbers

Structure 5/9 was partially exposed in the watching brief stage of the excavation and evidently only parts of the south and west walls were identified. It was very fragmentary, only one post and one partial plate being retained. 'Floor' timbers may be from the floor or collapsed planking from the walls, but in the absence of most of the timbers little can be said about this structure. One of the west wall plates (131) may have been a re-used timber, with a number of shallow blind mortices, redundant as found.

Dating: Constructed after AD 951–87 but dates based on a single timber so potentially much later.

Tenement D, Structure 5/10

Only the south end of this structure was identified. It is unclear whether the 'horizontal' timbers are plates, floors or planking from the sides or indeed whether some of the plates are floor timbers and *vice versa.*

Dating: Constructed after 1008/09.

Table 47 Summary of surviving evidence for use of timber in Structure 5/10

Timber	Roundwood	Boxed heart	Box halved	Boxed radial	Box quartered	Tangentially faced	Radially faced	Unknown
South wall plates		1?						
South wall plates or floor timbers	1		2					
Unknown 'horizontal timbers'								2

6 timbers

Tenement D, Structure 5/11

Table 48 Summary of surviving evidence for use of timber in Structure 5/11

Timber	Roundwood	Boxed heart	Box halved	Boxed radial	Box quartered	Tangentially faced	Radially faced	Unknown
West wall plate								1
West wall plank or plate								1

2 timbers

Only a fragment of the west wall appears to have been identified. Neither timber was longer than 0.4m. [Other timbers, from the fragmentary north and east walls, were subsequently recovered.]

Dating: No dendrochronology available.

Tenement C, Structure 5/12

Structure 5/12 was set at an angle to the axis of the tenement at the very south end of the excavated area and was apparently mostly of earthfast post construction. Dendrochronology suggests this is one of the latest buildings in this phase, its timbers being felled sometime after the second decade of the 11th century. Most of the building except for the north-east corner was excavated, but it appears to have been extensively robbed, very few timbers being identified on plan or from the records.

Dating: Constructed 1013–1049 or soon after.

Table 49 Summary of surviving evidence for use of timber in Structure 5/12

Timber	Roundwood	Boxed heart	Box halved	Boxed radial	Box quartered	Tangentially faced	Radially faced	Unknown
West wall Posts		5						
South wall posts		1?		1?				
Unknown plank						1?		

8 timbers

Discussion

The timbers of the Coppergate structures provide first-hand evidence for the supply of timber to Viking Age York. The presence of same-tree matches between different timbers within the same building, sometimes (8695+8696, 8699+8700, 8213+8215+8293) in the same wall, is not a coincidence. It argues that timber for a building was selected and brought to the site for a specific building project as and when it was needed. Those timbers with seasoning shakes (splits) have them running from the centre of the tree to the nearest surface, whether a face or edge. Sapwood has not been preferentially attacked by woodworm before conversion. This must therefore have happened after the timber had been shaped; the timbers have been worked when freshly felled. There is no evidence that timber was felled and stockpiled on a speculative basis before being sold on to the carpenters who required it.

Some same-tree matches were obtained between timbers from different buildings: a boxed heart post (8556) in Structure 5/3 and a tangentially faced board (9008) in 5/8, and a boxed halved post (8860) in Structure 5/3 with a tangentially faced drain plank from Structure 5/8. The overall earlier dendro dates for Structure 5/3 imply that Structures 5/7 and 5/8 may have been partially built from re-used salvaged timbers from the former building. Re-used timbers are normally identified from the presence of redundant features but their immediate origin is not apparent. This attests to the salvaging and re-use of timbers which might not be recognised as such as they lack obvious redundant features.

Little in the way of woodworking debris was recovered or recorded from the site, with the exception of the wood chips observed in Structure 5/4 (see Fig.255). Primary working (the branches lopped, bark removed, and conversion into roughly boxed logs of approximately the required length) must therefore have been conducted off site. Final conversion would be carried out on site according to the needs of the carpenters and the nature and quality of the timbers concerned, and any necessary joints cut on site as and when they were required. Thirteen wooden wedges of a type suitable for cleaving/splitting timbers during conversion were recovered as part of the small finds assemblage from the site (*AY* 17/13, 2106) though their significance in an urban context has not been recognised. Had timbers been fully converted at the felling site, these wedges would not have been present at Coppergate. They were either brought in for the final conversion of timbers just before installation or they were used to break up larger pieces of wood for use in the small-scale woodworking trades practised on the site within and around the buildings.

The nature of the wood which survives shows that the carpenters had selected pieces which were just large enough for the intended purpose, minimising the amount of additional work needed to prepare them. Furthermore, there is good evidence for the selection and use of particular qualities in timber for specific purposes. The knottier tops of the logs were detached and earmarked for making posts. The lower parts of the trunk, at or just below the springing of the principal limbs, were set aside for planks and boards. Although the carpenters were quite capable of splitting through knots to make planks, it appears that a combination of economy of effort and economy in the use of resources (any boards obtained would be thinner and narrower from this smaller diameter part of the trunk) determined what function a piece of raw timber would play in the structure.

A further inference from this particular choice has implications for the construction of the buildings. Wherever it was possible to identify the orientation of a post relative to its position in the tree, it was observed that these posts had been placed butt end down. The end of the timber which was closest to the ground when the tree was growing was the end which was placed lowest in the structure. The logs used were just large enough for their intended task, and often incorporate sapwood into the cross-section of the finished timber. The proportion of sapwood in a timber increases towards the top of a tree and this is directly reflected in the increasing proportion of sapwood present towards the top of the posts. For the Coppergate structures this means that these posts would have to terminate at or around the contemporary ground surface.

Had the posts continued any higher then in most, if not all, cases, sapwood would have made up more than one-third of the cross-section of the wood. Sapwood is more prone to insect and fungal attack than heartwood and is structurally weaker. Whilst one or two weak posts might be tolerable, having a structure composed predominantly of weak posts would compromise the integrity of the building and endanger any inhabitants. It also implies that the posts used to support the walls did not continue up to support the roof as well. At the level of the contemporary external ground surface, the carpenters would have been running out of usable, viable timber height. For this reason it is suggested that the superstructure of the buildings would have to be set either on a ground-level plate which also served to stabilise the wall posts, or perhaps on a separate foundation across or outside the footprint of the cellar. It should be noted that the narrowness of the tenement plots and the width of the surviving buildings argues against this latter suggestion.

Two main styles of construction are used for the building walls, defined by the method used to keep the posts in position. The first is the simplest: pads of timber, usually offcuts from trimming larger timber or boards, are placed below the butt end of individual posts. This allows any variation in the height of the posts to be adjusted, by using thinner or thicker pads as necessary to create posts of equal height. The second uses long plates or plates set along the axis of the wall upon which the butt ends of the posts rest. The posts that articulate with these plates always have butt ends hewn to a flat surface – slightly

more irregularity was tolerated in the pad-supported posts. The change in construction appears to be chronological: it can be shown that those buildings constructed using post pads (Structures 5/1, 5/3 and 5/5) pre-date AD 989, while those built using baseplates (Structures 5/4, 5/6, 5/7 and 5/8) all post-date AD 988 (if the latest construction dates are accepted). Construction dates from dendrochronology for plate buildings 5/9, 5/10 and 5/11 are uncertain or unknown but Structures 5/10 and 5/11 are stratigraphically later than Structure 5/8. Structure 5/12 is not only later but of earthfast post construction and surface laid. The Coppergate evidence suggests that in the years either side of AD 990 there was a change in construction styles between walls with posts set individually in pits (with or without post-pads) and walls with posts set on horizontal plates.

Some sophistication is evident in the use of radially and tangentially faced planks in the wall cladding. This is most evident in the remains of Structure 5/1 where both outer and inner linings survived. Here, the outer plank lining, against the earth side of the construction pit, is made from tangentially faced planks, whist the inner lining, that which formed the inner wall of the structure, was radially faced (Fig. 358). In dating terms, the two claddings are contemporary, within the date range offered by the dendrochronology. In functional terms there is no clear reason for this choice. Radially faced oak allows less moisture transmission than tangentially faced oak; it is for that reason that staves intended for coopered vessels are generally radially faced. Radially faced planks are less prone to cupping, the cross-sectional curved distortion produced as a plank or board shrinks as it seasons.

In the case of Structure 5/1 the use of different qualities of planking is probably connected with the visual appearance of the finished structure. Across the site, the tangentially faced boards are more irregular than the radially faced ones and are not especially easy to fit together edge to edge. They would warp slightly across the grain as they dried out and seasoned *in situ*. The poorer-quality planks are employed for the cladding which would be hidden from view. The radially faced boards are more regular, have a smoother, more even appearance and would be less prone to distortion. These higher-quality boards are employed as a cladding which would be seen inside the structure.

Where the original location and position of particular boards can be identified, there is a similar distinction in the use of radially and tangentially faced boards in the surviving portions of other buildings. In Structure 5/3 the outer lining included boards with both conversions, but the tangentially faced ones are used at the base of the walls, the radially faced ones higher up (Fig.359). In Structure 5/6 the arrangement is the same, but the proportions (and locations) of the two types are reversed in the east and west walls (Fig.362).

The carpentry and the use of timber evident in the buildings under discussion demonstrate that they were not casually put together but carefully assembled. There is no evidence of prefabrication although the structures which survive would hardly have required it. The nature of the structures, their timbers and working methods all suggest that the components were fashioned and assembled in the place where they were erected as the building was being constructed. This is most obviously demonstrated by the floor planking of Structure 5/5 as the boards are cut to fit closely around the feet of posts which must therefore already have been set in place, giving an implied order of assembly.

Published comparative evidence from elsewhere informs aspects of construction details but not as yet of close dating. Sunken-floored buildings in contemporary London (Horsman *et al.* 1988) are broadly dated by ceramic assemblages to the late 9th to late 11th centuries but not closely within that frame by dendrochronology. Those examples from Billingsgate and Cheapside seem to have been less deeply set into the ground than those in York. A wider variety of wall types was identified including posts set on pads (stone and wood) and plates. Preservation was variable, some pieces surviving as timber, others as soil stains or decayed fragments which preclude close comparison with the York Period 5B structures but finds such as this and a similar baseplate from Billingsgate Lorry Park (Brigham 1992, 92, *6516*) confirm that very similar structures were being built in London at around this time. Sunken-floored buildings have been identified at Lower Bridge Street, Chester (posts without baseplates: Mason 1985, 8–10), and Westgate Street, Gloucester (posts set on plates: Heighway *et al.* 1979, 169). An example from Christchurch Place, Dublin (CP356/1, Murray 1983, 67), is broadly 10th-century in date but shallower and more crudely constructed; two more from Dublin are wattle- rather than plank-lined or have a board lining set vertically on end (*ibid*, 76, 84, 169–75). The evidence confirms the widespread use of similar technology and practice across much of the country, perhaps reflecting a common woodworking heritage and not one confined to those areas with strong Scandinavian influence.

The study of the woodworking technology of these structures has informed ideas about the way timber was supplied to Coppergate, how the timbers were worked, how the structures were put together and how they may have related to the missing part(s) of the structures. The importance of scale drawing and recording of timbers for archive purposes, extensive sampling for tree-ring as well as dating evidence has been made repeatedly elsewhere (Goodburn 1992, 115; Brunning 1995). The Coppergate structures were excavated at a time when the study of wood from archaeological sites was in its very early stages; although the project may indeed have used one of the earliest systems for recording wood features in the United Kingdom, much still remained to be learned about studying timbers in the late 1970s. That the current study has been possible at Coppergate is due to the far-sighted decision made to retain and conserve many of the timbers from the site for archive and public display.

Implications for the reconstruction and appearance of the Coppergate buildings

The only evidence for the form of the buildings at Coppergate comes from their excavated remains. The extensive survival of the buildings at Coppergate – and indeed elsewhere in York – has perhaps overshadowed an aspect of the preservation that has hitherto not received much attention. The one aspect of these buildings which has not been emphasised is that they are not complete. This is not an accident of the burial conditions or a result of the method of excavation. The extensive waterlogging of the Coppergate site which has resulted in the preservation of organic materials is partly the product of the extensive flooding following the creation of the moat around York Castle in the later 11th century and a consequent rise in the local water table, and partly the build up of later deposits sealing earlier ones. This was less than a century after the first of the Period 5 buildings was erected. None the less, the burial environment at Coppergate is such that, had the buildings simply been left to decay and collapse, the excavation team would in some cases have been up to their waists in fragments of collapsed timber buildings.

That this was not the case is because the buildings were extensively robbed and salvaged as soon as they were disused. Timber was the predominant building material in York until the later medieval period and the extent to which parts of buildings were robbed and

Earlier (pre-AD 990) wall

Rafter resting on wall plate

Lap joint with wall plate

Peg-hole

Inner face

Tangentially faced boards

Radially faced boards

Post

1.8m

Tangentially faced floorboard

Truncated peg in blind hole

Joists

Individual post-hole with timber post-pad

Later (post-AD 990) wall

Rafter resting on wall plate

Lap joint with wall plate

Peg-hole

Inner face

Mixed radial and tangentially faced boards

Radially faced boards

Post

1.8m

Truncated peg in blind hole

Tangentially faced floorboards

Joist

Sill beam in continuous cut

0 — 0
1
2
1 — 3 feet
metre

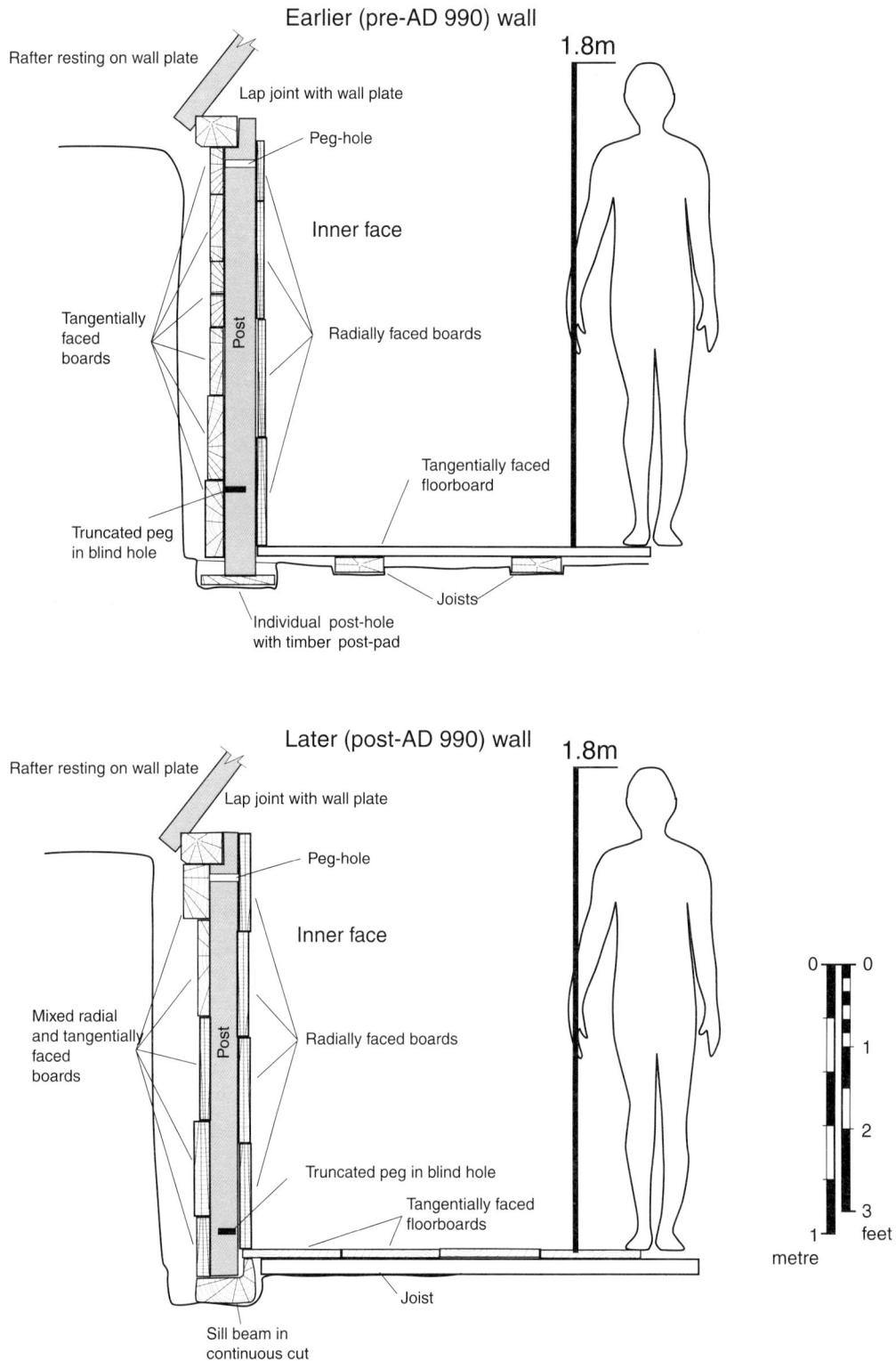

Fig.365   *Provisional reconstructed cross-sections based on Structures 5/1 and 5/6. Scale 1:25*

recycled is not reflected in the surviving, relatively high-status, standing structures. Whilst wattle structures could be replaced every time the coppice cycle came round, timber was a resource that would take much longer to regenerate. Recycling and re-use of as much material as

it was practical to extract would have been preferable to abandoning everything that was there and starting again with fresh timber. This need not mean that building timbers were re-used in other buildings. Evidence from waterfront excavations shows that building timbers could be reshaped and used to make structures such as quaysides, wharves and revetments of varying sizes and forms. The key point is that timber could be and was recycled whenever practical.

This explains why there is not one single timber from Coppergate that can be ascribed to a roof or superstructure (with the possible exception of beam 13876 in Structure 5/3; see Figs 238 and 239). All of these pieces – potentially of good quality and certainly with worked joints – were removed for re-use when the building was abandoned. This robbing extended to as much of the below-ground structure as could be conveniently reached, whether posts or boards.

Of the nine buildings of Period 5B, two stand out in particular as having elements not present in the others. Structure 5/1 has an inner cladding of high-quality boards and Structure 5/5 has surviving floorboards. Though tangentially faced, these latter are also of very high quality, having regular cross-sections and very consistent thickness. It might be thought that this means that these two buildings were constructed in a different form to the others on the site but this is almost certainly not the case. These two buildings have one further common feature, having been destroyed by fire. In Structure 5/1 the tops of the posts and the inner boards are heavily charred to within 0.25m of the base of the posts (see Fig. 201); all of the inner boarding is to a greater or lesser extent burnt. In Structure 5/5 the burning extends down to the floor-boards themselves, whose upper faces are very heavily charred (see Fig.263). The inner boarding of Structure 5/1 and the floorboards of Structure 5/5 survive *in situ* only because they have been burnt beyond use.

'Joists' or horizontal timbers positioned to support floorboards are present in Structures 5/1, 5/2, 5/5, 5/7 and 5/10, with Structure 5/4 badly disturbed, and drains cut through the floors of Structures 5/6 and 5/8. Structure 5/9 may have had floor timbers but this is uncertain. It can be argued that all of these buildings originally had floorboards that were recovered and removed for recycling when the buildings were dismantled. If correct, this would also account for the apparent lack of occupation deposits within the buildings, boarded floors being easier to keep clean than earth floors and less prone to the build up of trampled deposits (see p.679 and *AY* 14/7, 733–6 for discussion of possible floors).

If the inner cladding were removed from Structure 5/1 the outer cladding and posts would be no different in appearance to the other buildings from Coppergate. The inner cladding is the only feature that marks out this building as being different from Structure 5/3 or 5/5, and had plates been used as foundations for the posts, it would have looked just the same. It is therefore reasonable to suppose that most, if not all, of these buildings had boarded floors and inner linings of good-quality timber; this would affect our notions of the use and environment within them.

As discussed above, there are compelling reasons to believe that wall posts terminated at or just above the contemporary ground surface. This in turn affects the reconstruction of the building superstructure. The initial interpretation of the buildings (Hall 1984a, 71) was as sunken-floored structures. A revised interpretation would have the buildings possessing internal 'upper' floors at the contemporary ground level as a working/living space, with the sunken areas forming a basement for storage purposes. It is argued here that the initial interpretation was correct. There are two lines of reasoning which lead to this conclusion.

Firstly there is the problem of headroom. The highest surviving complete posts in Coppergate are those from Structure 5/6 (8319, 8320, 8326) which have survived due to the partial collapse and toppling inwards of the wall and which consequently survived to their full height, terminating in unpegged lap housings which would have to engage with a horizontal plate at ground level. Their butt ends rest on plates set into shallow construction trenches and so are at or below the contemporary floor level. From butt end to top, the posts are no more than 1.688m high (post 8326). Even if no allowance is made for the thickness of a boarded floor and even if it is assumed that an inserted floor were set above the tops of the posts a figure of 1.7m is very low for storage or working space. Anyone moving or working in such a space would have to do so whilst bent almost double. A space with such low headroom is too large for insulation and too impractical for use, quite apart from the problems of lighting such an environment.

Secondly there is the problem of access. Where reasonably intact end walls have survived, the entrance to these spaces was through a revetted passage attached to the shorter, gable walls, either ramped or at least partially stepped down to the internal floor level. The door space required uses at least a quarter of the length of the gable wall which is a significant opening. Access to an 'upper' floor would need a similar opening cut though the wall,

Fig.366 *Cut-away view showing a possible interpretation of the earlier (pre-AD 990) buildings of Period 5. Not to scale, though the posts are shown approximately 1.7m tall and the doorway is a nominal 2.0m high. Main feature is the setting of post bases in shallow individual post-holes, resting on offcuts from planks or boards. Floorboards are cut to fit around the post bases; orientation of floorboards based on Structure 5/5. Small internal posts supporting a 'collar' in the roof structure are based on surviving stumps. The tops of the wall posts engage with lap housings cut into the edge of the ground-level plates to which the rafters are fastened*

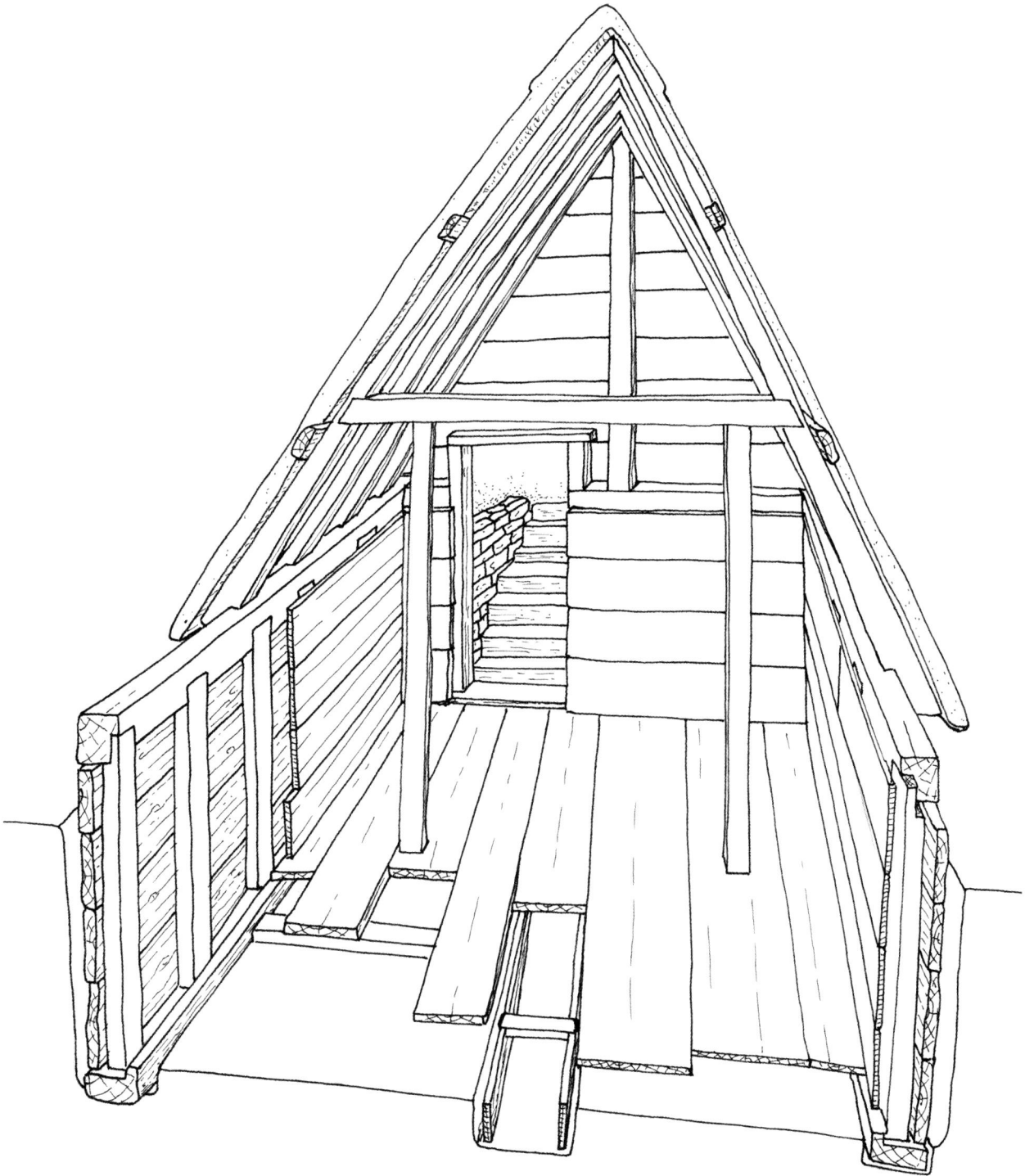

Fig.367 *Cut-away view showing a possible interpretation of the later (post-AD 990) buildings of Period 5. Not to scale, though the posts are again approximately 1.7m tall and the doorway is a nominal 2.0m high. Main feature is the setting of post bases resting on sill beams in a shallow cut around the edge of the construction pit. Floorboards are cut to fit around the post bases; orientation of floorboards based on orientation of joists in Structure 5/6. Small internal posts supporting a 'collar' in the roof structure are based on surviving stumps, repeating the arrangement in the earlier buildings. The tops of the wall posts engage with lap housings cut into the edge of a smaller wall plate above the level of the contemporary ground surface, to which the rafters are fastened. A board-lined and lidded drain is shown running the length of the building. Drains vary in position, sometimes axial, sometimes set against the foot of the wall, often changing direction and usually exiting the building via the revetted entrance passage through the gable end to the lower ground nearer the river*

resulting in perhaps half of the gable wall being made up of doorways rather than walling. This would require additional framing for a second doorway and take up more space for a door in an already small building. There is no indication that a second threshold was present on any of these buildings, nor is there any trace of steps leading up from the outside in order to access a floor higher than the ground surface. Ladder or step access inside the building from the 'upper' floor to the basement might have been possible, with the evidence removed when the buildings were robbed out, but such access would have taken up a significant amount of the floor area, creating dead space on two floors which could not have been used for any other purpose. It must be concluded that there was only ever the one doorway in the gable end and this led through to the only floor in the building.

Tie beams spanning the building at wall top height would also restrict headroom and though there are possible pairs of posts in opposing walls, none is sufficiently distinct to suggest that they rather than any other posts supported such a timber. A tie or collar set between the principal rafters of the building would, however, allow reasonable headroom inside and provide additional lateral stability to the structure. Provisional reconstruction drawings of the cross-sections of Structures 5/1 and 5/6 (Fig.365) show the minimum internal structural timbers required for this interpretation of these buildings.

Such a sunken-floored building need not have been of low status, nor necessarily squalid and uncomfortable and suggested reconstructions are shown here (Figs 366 and 367). Even if the eaves came down almost to ground level, a pitched roof of around 60° needed to throw rain off the thatch would have made the structures appear quite imposing as well as creating accessible space in the rafters for storage. A boarded, rather than an earth floor with internal cladding to the walls might not have been the height of luxury but it would have been a practical solution to the need for shelter in a dense urban environment.

Appendix: Provisional construction dates for the Period 5B buildings

The following dates are derived from the dendrochronological work undertaken by Tyers and Hillam, from examination of the timbers themselves, their stratigraphic location and from those site records relating to them. This list summarises the tabulated data in Fig.357.

961–62:	Tenement A, Structure 5/1
988–89:	Tenement B, Structure 5/3
993–1011:	Tenement B, Structure 5/4
956–80:	Tenement C, Structure 5/5
988–1003:	Tenement C, Structure 5/6 (replaces Structure 5/5)
1013–49:	Tenement C, Structure 5/12 (no stratigraphic link between this and Structure 5/6)
985–1008:	Tenement D, Structure 5/7
1008–09:	Tenement D, Structure 5/8 (replaces Structure 5/7)
1008/09–24	Tenement D, Structure 5/8 drain
Constructed after 1008–09:	Tenement D, Structure 5/10 (replaces Structure 5/8)
Constructed after 951–87 (single dated timber):	Tenement E, Structure 5/9

List of coins from 16–22 Coppergate

Catalogue number	SF number	Coin	Context	Period
19	12042	Eanred c.810–41. Styca, Irregular, temp.	30693	3
25	14287	Aethelred, c.841–48. Styca. Moneyer: Monne	30882	3
30	10866	Aethelred, c.841–48. Irregular, temp. Moneyer: Eardvvlf	27819	3
40	9862	Cnut, c.895–c.903. Penny	27440	4A
47	10582	Sihtric I (Sihtric Caoch), 921–27. Copper dirham, comtemporary forgery, A.H.290–95, AD 903–7/8, Mint: Samarkand	27915	4A
48	11133	Aethelstan, King of all England, 924–39. Lead trial piece, BMC type iv, of the York mint, Moneyer: Adelbert	30274	4A
20	8289	Eanred c.810–41. Styca, Irregular, temp.	24520	4B
31	8266	Aethelred, c.841–48. Styca, Irregular, temp. Moneyer: Eardvvlf	20470	4B
42	7600	St Peter coinage of York. Penny, first issue, without sword: second (light-weight) phase	22416	4B
43	9351	St Peter coinage of York. Iron die for obverse of St Peter Penny; second issue, with sword	25630	4B
44	9539	Sihtric I (Sihtric Caoch), 921–27. Penny, contemporary imitation of the Sword/Hammer issue	26247	4B
45	10614	Sihtric I (Sihtric Caoch), 921–27. Silver penning (fragment), Danish proto-penny, c.850. Mint: attributed to Hedeby, Jutland	22714	4B
49	13993	Aethelstan, King of all England, 924–39. Iron die, cylindrical 'cap' of hardened metal, c.928–39, from the obverse of a penny	35524	4B
50	8563	Aethelstan, King of all England, 924–39. Lead trial-piece. Moneyer: Regnald of York, c.928–39	25350	4B
51	14105	Aethelstan, King of all England, 924–39. Penny, BMC type v. Moneyer: Regnald of York	29725	4B
52	7997	Aethelstan, King of all England, 924–39. Penny, BMC type via, c.?939. Mint: Chester. Moneyer: Wulfstan	22803	4B
53	7996	Aethelstan, King of all England, 924–39. penny, BMC type i, c.?939. Moneyer: Willuf	22803	4B
54	7999	Anlaf II Guthfrithsson, 939–41. Penny, Raven, c.939–40. Mint: York. Moneyer: Aethelferd	22803	4B
55	7995	Anlaf II Guthfrithsson, 939–41. Penny, Raven, c.939–40. Mint: Lincoln? Moneyer: Odeler	22803	4B
56	12817	Sihtric II (?Sihtricsson), 941–42. Penny, Triquetre/Standard. Mint: York? Moneyer: Farman	19719	4B
57	7755	Eadred, 946–55. Penny, fragment, BMC type i. Moneyer: Werstan?	22523	4B
28	5400	Aethelred, c.841–48. Styca. Moneyer: uncertain (Fordred?)	3608	4 / 5
35	8644	Uncertain attribution. Styca. Fictitious moneyer	21143	5A
46	13574	Sihtric I (Sihtric Caoch), 921–27. Charles the Bald, King of the West Franks, 843–77. Obolus (half denier); Palace mint, 864–77	22127	5A
62	2372	Aethelraed II, 978–1016. Penny, First Small Cross, 978–79. Moneyer: Styr of York	8801	5A
13	3849	Eanred c.810–41. Styca. Moneyer: Cudhard. Base silver	14297	5B
15	9542	Eanred c.810–41. Styca. Moneyer: Eadvini. Base silver	16881	5B
36	10191	Uncertain attribution. Five fragments of styca-sized coins. Unidentifiable	29125	5B
58	1927	Eadwig, 955–59. Penny, 9 fragments, BMC type i. Most likely moneyer: Heriger	8526	5B
59	4622	Eadwig, 955–59. Lead, trial-piece for penny, BMC type id, obverse and reverse dies for moneyer Frothric	7743	5B
60	4349	Eadgar, 959–75. Penny, Circumscription Small Cross, BMC type iii. Moneyer: Fastolf	15472	5B
61	4439	Eadgar, 959–75. Penny, Circumscription Small Cross, BMC type iii. Moneyer: Fastolf	15550	5B
63	8715	Aethelraed II, 978–1016. Penny, First Hand, 979–85. Moneyer: Fastolf of York	26240	5B
64	1078	Aethelraed II, 978–1016. Penny, First Hand, 979–85. Moneyer: Outhgrim of York	8225	5B
3	6081	'Porcupine' sceat. c.720–40	19120	5Cr
21	6232	Aethelred, c.841–48. Styca. Moneyer: Alghere	6789	5Cr
65	4838	Cnut, 1016–35. Penny, Short Cross, 1029–35. Moneyer: Thurgrim of York	17103	6

Acknowledgements

York Archaeological Trust and the authors are grateful for the assistance of a wide range of institutions and individuals who have supported this project over a long period. York City Council's decision to facilitate archaeological excavation on the site led to one of the nation's most important discoveries which, in turn, has done much to raise interest in the city and its past. In the final stages of the excavation the site's development contractors Wimpey Property Holdings Ltd. and their constructional firm Wimpey Construction Ltd. were also extremely sympathetic to archaeological requirements. They continued this policy throughout the archaeological watching brief which accompanied construction work and during the excavations at 22 Piccadilly.

The excavation was funded in part from the rescue archaeology budget of the Inspectorate of Ancient Monuments at the Department of the Environment (now English Heritage) whose successive Inspectors and their superiors responded sympathetically to the project's requirements. In parallel the Trust carried out a major fundraising campaign under the patronage of the Prince of Wales, Queen Margrethe II of Denmark, King Carl XVI Gustaf of Sweden, Crown Prince Harald of Norway and Kristjan Eldjarn, President of Iceland. Chaired by Magnus Magnusson and enthusiastically supported by the relevant British ambassadors, this enlisted support from a wide range of donors in Britain, the Nordic countries and the United States (see list below).

Within York Archaeological Trust Richard expressed his thanks to the permanent excavation team who worked continuously beside him for the five year duration of the excavation and in particular to the Area Supervisors including Dave Evans (1976–81) who helped see this project through to completion, Shahed Power (1976–79), Mick Humphreys (1976–78) and Ian Lawton (1978–81) who also assisted in the early years of the post-excavation work. The watching brief was staffed by Peter Bolton, Chris Gallagher, Lawrence Manley and Russell Marwood. It was overseen by Nicholas Pearson who did the initial post-excavation work on this aspect, which was completed by Kurt Hunter-Mann who also brought together the results of the excavations at 22 Piccadilly conducted and reported on by Rhona Finlayson.

A great many specialists have contributed to understanding this complex site and the full list of their reports is on p.540. The ground-breaking work undertaken by the Environmental Archaeology Unit and the YAT Conservation Laboratory was particularly notable and helped to push their respective disciplines forward, while facilitating the work of other specialists and a legion of subsequent scholars. The authors are grateful to those specialists whose work is included here and on-line.

The radiocarbon dates were funded from the Richard Hall Memorial Fund through the Friends of York Archaeological Trust.

York Osteoarchaeology Ltd would like to thank Christine McDonnell, Richard Hall and Dave Evans of York Archaeological Trust for their help and support.

The dendrochronology was funded by English Heritage and before that the Department of Environment. Cathy Tyers and Jennifer Hillam are also grateful to Richard Hall, Dave Evans and Kurt Hunter-Mann for information and lengthy discussion about the site and its timbers and all those dendrochronologists, too numerous to mention by name, who allowed them access to unpublished data during the course of the Coppergate project.

Steve Allen is grateful to the members of staff and many students and volunteers working in the Conservation Department who all did their bit over the years to help to preserve the assemblage of Coppergate timbers for the appreciation of future scholars and enthusiasts. He also wishes to thank the many firms who have from time to time contributed equipment, materials and services to the laboratories and is grateful to the many colleagues within the profession, both at home and abroad, who have shared their knowledge and experience to develop waterlogged wood treatment approaches and methods.

A great many individuals have contributed to the post-excavation process including Dave Evans, Kurt Hunter-Mann, Jane McComish and Neil Oakey, with assistance from Kaye Howarth, Jenny Kestle and Katie Jones. The photographs reproduced here are the work of M.S. Duffy with others by S.I. Hill and M. Andrews, the latter being invaluable in helping with the production of this volume. The illustrations are all by Lesley Collett with the exception of those in the specialist reports which are by the respective authors. YAT's curatorial team, led successively by Arthur MacGregor, Dominic Tweddle and Christine McDonnell, have helped to secure the material culture of the site for the future, while Christine Kyriacou has done the same for the documentary archive. The summary was translated into French by Tony Mathews, into German by Hannah Linington and into Norwegian by Unn Pedersen.

The authors would like to thank the Trust's former director Dr Peter Addyman for his support throughout the entire duration of the project, and his more recent encouragement in seeing it through to completion. Pulling together the incomplete report left mid-progress due to Richard Hall's ill-health was achieved with the support of YAT's Board of Trustees and with the continuous sympathetic support of Dr Peter Wilson of English Heritage. The publication could not have been achieved without the professionalism of the editor, Frances Mee, and the book design and production skills of Lesley Collett. Project management was by Ailsa Mainman.

List of Donors
Financial contributions to York Archaeological Trust 1976–82

Aksjebelskapet Freia
Arrid Nordquist
Association of Norwegian
    Students Abroad
Association of Voluntary Guides
    of York
Aurelius Charitable Trust
Bergen Bank
Bikuben Forvalten A.F.D.
A.S. Boyle
B.P. Olie-Kampaginet
The British Academy
British Railways Board
C. Carlson
Central Bank of Iceland
Chloride Group Ltd
Claxton & Garland Ltd
Courage Charitable Trust
Den Dansk Bank
Drapers Charitable Trust
East Asiatic Company
Fairways Charitable Trust
Finansbanken
Forenede Chocolade Grossist
The Foundation for the Preservation of
    the Archaeological Heritage Inc.

General Accident Fire and Life
    Assurance
Handelsbank
HRH Prince Peter
Hustru Emma Jorck's Fund
ICI Charity Trust
ICL Discretionary Trust
Illustrated Newspapers
Isaac Jackson Charity
Yvette and Hermione Jacobson Trust
Jan Lanrasbraten
Lloyds Charities Trust
Low & Bonar Charitable Fund
Lutheran Brotherhood
Magnus Magnusson
Mercers Charitable Fund
A. Moe
Samuel Montague & Co.
Mulberry Hall
Nidor A/S
North Yorkshire County Council
Norwegian Coppergate Appeal
Egmont H. Petersen's Fund
Dame B. Philpotts Memorial Fund
Portakabin Ltd
Privatbanken

Provinsbanken
Queen Margrethe and
    Prince Henrick's Fund
Josef Rank Charity
Sir James Reckitt Charity
Rowntree Macintosh Ltd
Scandinavian Bank
Scandinavian Studies Grant
S.F. Air Treatment Ltd
Shepherd Building Group
C. Ian Skipper
B.R. Snell
John & E. Sturge Ltd
Tay Charitable Trust
Joseph Terry & Sons Ltd
Tetra Pak
Tjæreborg Group
Tuborg Foundation
Twenty-Seven Foundation
Union Bank of Finland
Wallenberg Foundation
Westminster Press Ltd
F.H.Woodward Discretionary Settlement
York City Council
Yorkshire and Humberside Tourist Board

Summary

Excavations at 16–22 Coppergate uncovered a large swathe of York's late Anglian and Anglo-Scandinavian townscape on a spur of land between the Rivers Ouse and Foss. The report charts the establishment and subsequent development of four urban properties, demarcated by fence lines, which were still recognisable into modern times. A total of seventeen structures, some of them still standing almost 2m high, were excavated on these properties, arranged gable-end to the newly established street of Coppergate or on land immediately behind. Excavation of the backyards of the plots, which extended behind the buildings down towards the River Foss, revealed them to have been used for cess-pits, rubbish pits, and small-scale animal husbandry and horticulture, accessed from the structures along wattle or plank pathways.

The site was abandoned in the immediate post-Roman period and was then used for small-scale industrial activities, rubbish disposal and for casual burial in the Anglian period, before there was clear evidence for occupation there. Property boundaries were established c. AD 900 and post and wattle structures were erected on each building plot in the following decades. A period of upheaval in the mid-10th century was characterised by the abandonment of these buildings, a brief hiatus in occupation, followed immediately by the erection of semi-sunken plank-built structures arranged in single or double ranks at the street end of the site. These underwent episodes of repair and replacement over the next 50 years until they too were abandoned and replaced by surface-built structures for which only ephemeral traces survive on a single property.

Anaerobic conditions on the site resulted in extraordinary preservation not only of the various structures but also of evidence for domestic and industrial activities and for living conditions; these have been fully reported in other fascicules of *The Archaeology of York* series (p.540). The survival of wood allowed for a very large number of dendrochronological dates to be established and these, augmented by other scientific dates and a sequence of coin dates, provide a detailed chronological framework for the site.

A subsequent watching brief and small-scale excavation on an adjacent site revealed evidence for further properties and structures of the same character. These findings, combined with the detailed evidence from the main excavation, facilitated an unparalleled examination of a large tract of York's townscape which includes early churches and the west bank of the River Foss, and charts the rebirth of urban life in York in the pre-Conquest period.

Résumé

Des fouilles à 16-22 Coppergate ont découvert une grande étendue de la topographie citadine de York datant de la fin de l'époque anglo-saxonne et anglo-scandinave et située sur une crête entre les rivières Ouse et Foss. Cette communication décrit la formation et la suite du développement de quatre propriétés urbaines, délimitées par des lignes de clôture, qui pouvaient être encore visées jusqu'à l'époque moderne. En toutes, dix-sept structures, dont quelques-unes avaient encore presque 2m de hauteur, ont été fouillées sur ces propriétés dont le côté du pignon donnait sur la rue Coppergate qui avait été récemment établie ou sur du terrain qui se trouvait juste derrière. La fouille des arrière-cours des parcelles, qui s'étendaient derrière les bâtiments en descendant vers la rivière Foss, a démontré qu'elles servaient en fosses à purin, fosses à ordures et pour l'élevage des animaux à petite échelle et pour l'horticulture, dont l'accès à partir des structures était fourni par moyen des passages construits de clayonnage ou de lattes.

Le site a été abandonné juste au début de la période post-romaine et était utilisé pour des activités industrielles modestes, pour déposer les ordures et éventuellement pour l'enterrement pendant la période anglo-saxonne, avant l'existence indiscutable de signes d'habitation. Des limites de propriétés ont été établi vers 900 apr. J.-C. et des structures de poteaux et de clayonnage ont été érigées sur chaque parcelle de construction pendant les décennies suivantes. Une période troublée au milieu du 10ème siècle se distinguait par l'abandon de ces bâtiments, une courte interruption dans l'habitation, suivie immédiatement par la construction de structures à demi enfoncées et fabriquées de lattes qui étaient placées à unique ou à double rang au bout du site donnant sur la rue. Ces structures ont été éventuellement réparées et remplacées au cours des 50 ans qui suivaient jusqu'au moment où elles aussi ont été abandonnées et remplacées par des structures construites à surface dont il ne reste que des vestiges éphémères sur une seule propriété.

Des conditions anaérobiques sur le site ont conduit à une conservation extraordinaire, non seulement des structures différentes mais aussi des indications d'activités domestiques et industrielles et des conditions d'habitation; le tout a fait sujet de rapport dans les autres fascicules de la série *The Archaeology of York* (p.540). Du bois existant encore à récupérer, on a pu établir un nombre important de dates dendrochronologiques et celles-ci, en ajoutant les autres dates scientifiques et une séquence de dates de pièces de monnaie, ont produit une gamme chronologique précise pour le site.

Un programme suivant de surveillance et de fouille à l'échelle modérée sur un site attenant ont découvert des indications d'autres propriétés et de structures du même type. Ces résultats, ajoutés aux indications détaillées de la principale fouille, ont permis l'étude sans pareille d'une grande partie de la topographie citadine de York qui comprend plusieurs des premières églises et la rive occidentale de la rivière Foss, et décrit la renaissance de la vie urbaine à York pendant la période avant la Conquête.

Zusammenfassung

Die Ausgrabungen in 16 – 22 Coppergate, York haben auf einer Landzunge zwischen den Flüssen Ouse und Foss einen Großteil des späten anglischen und anglo-skandinavischen Stadtbildes freigelegt. Der Bericht befasst sich mit der Gründung und der folgenden Entwicklung von vier städtischen Grundstücken, deren Grundstücksgrenzen auch jetzt noch nachvollziehbar sind. Insgesamt wurden siebzehn Gebäude, einige davon nochimmer fast zwei Meter hoch, ausgegraben. Die Gebäude sind mit der Giebelseite zur neu gebauten Straße, Coppergate, ausgerichtet oder befinden sich auf Grund, der direkt dahinter liegt. Die Ausgrabungen der Hinterhöfe, welche hinter den Gebäuden bis zu dem Fluss Floss hinunter reichten, ergaben, dass diese als Sickergruben und Abfallgruben Verwendung fanden, sowie auch der Haltung von landwirtschaftlichen Nutztieren oder dem Gartenbau dienten. Zugang von den Gebäuden zu diesen Hinterhöfen wurde über Flechtwerkbrücken oder Holzplanken ermöglicht.

Der Standort wurde während des poströmischen Zeitalters verlassen um dann in der anglischen Ära für Kleinindustrie, als Abfalldeponie oder für informelle Beerdingungen genutzt zu werden. Erst später gibt es eindeutige Beweise für eine Besiedelung dieses Ortes. Grundstücksgrenzen wurden ungefähr 900 n. Chr. gezogen und während der folgenden Jahrzehnte wurden auf jedem Grundstück Gebäude aus Flechtwerk und Lehm errichtet. Als Folge eines Umbruches in der Mitte des 10. Jahrhunderts, wurden diese Gebäude verlassen und es gab einen kurzen Zeitraum, in dem der Ort unbewohnt blieb. Kurz darauf wurden Gebäude auf halb-versunkenen Holzbalken gebaut, die ein- oder auch zweireihig an dem, der Straße angrenzendem Ende der Ausgrabungsstätte, angeordnet waren. Diese wurden über die nächsten 50 Jahre immer wieder Reperaturen unterzogen oder wurden neuerbaut. Danach wurden diese Bauwerke durch Gebäude ersetzt, die nur auf der Oberfläche gebaut wurden. Von dieser neuen Art Gebäude sind jedoch nur auf einem einzigen Grundstück vereinzelte Spuren zu finden.

Die anaeroben Bedingungen, die auf der Ausgrabungsstätte herrschen, haben zu einer außergewöhnlich guten Erhaltung nicht nur der veschiedenen Gebäude geführt, sonder auch zu der Erhaltung von Hinweisen auf handwerkliche Tätigkeiten und den damaligen Lebensumständen. Diese sind ausführlich in anderen Faszikeln der *"The Archaeology of York* series" (p.540) aufgeführt. Die gute Erhaltung des Holzes hat es uns ermöglicht, eine große Anzahl dendrochronologischer Daten zu ermitteln. Diese und weitere wissenschaftliche Daten, sowie eine Reihe datierter Münzen, liefern einen detaillierten chronologischen Rahmen für die Ausgrabungsstätte.

Eine anschliessende Kontrolle und eine kleine Ausgrabung auf einer angrenzenden Ausgrabungsstätte legte weitere Grundstücke und Gebäude des gleichen Typs offen. Diese Funde, zusammen mit den detaillierten Hinweisen von der Haupt-Ausgrabungsstätte, ermöglichte eine unvergleichbare Untersuchung eines riesigen Teils von Yorks damaligen Stadtbild, das frühe Kirchen und das westliche Ufer des Flusses Foss sowie Urkunden über das Wiederaufkommen städtischen Lebens in York im Zeitalter vor der Eroberung mit beinhaltet.

Sammendrag

Utgravninger i 16–22 Coppergate avdekket en bred stripe av Yorks sent angliske og anglo-skandinaviske bylandskap på en landtunge mellom elvene Ouse og Foss. Denne rapporten beskriver etableringen og utviklingen av fire urbane eiendommer, avgrenset av gjerder som fremdeles kunne gjenkjennes i moderne tid. Totalt sytten strukturer ble utgravd på eiendommene, noen av dem bevart i nesten to meters høyde. De var plassert med gavlen mot den nyetablerte gaten Coppergate, eller på områder umiddelbart bak. Utgravninger av bakgårdene på parsellene avslørte at de var brukt til latrinegroper, avfallsgroper, småskala dyrehold og hagebruk. Bakgårdene, som strakte seg bak bygningene og ned mot Foss, var tilgjengelig fra bygningene via gangveier av flettverk eller plank.

Lokaliteten ble forlatt like etter Romerrikets fall, og ble deretter brukt til småskala håndverksaktivitet, avfallshåndtering og enkelte begravelser i den angliske perioden, før det igjen er tydelige spor etter bosetning. Eiendomsgrenser ble etablert ca. 900 e.Kr. og det ble reist stolpe- og flettverksstrukturer på hver enkelt tomt i de følgende tiårene. En periode med omveltninger på midten av 900-tallet kjennetegnes av forlatte bygninger og et kort avbrudd i bosetningen, umiddelbart etterfulgt av oppføringen av delvis nedgravde plankebygde strukturer, som sto i enkle eller doble rekker mot gate-enden av lokaliteten. Bygningene ble reparert og utskiftet i løpet av de neste 50 årene, inntil de også ble forlatt og erstattet av overflatebygde strukturer, som det kun finnes spredte spor av på én enkelt eiendom.

Anaerobe forhold har ført til ekstraordinær god bevaring, ikke bare av de ulike strukturene på lokaliteten, men også av rester etter husholdningsaktivitet, håndverk og levevilkår. Funnene er fullt ut beskrevet i de øvrige bind i serien *The Archaeology of York* (s.540). Bevart treverk ga mulighet for et stort antall dendrokronologiske dateringer, og sammen med andre naturvitenskapelige dateringer og myntdateringer, gir de et detaljert kronologisk rammeverk for lokaliteten.

Etterfølgende overvåkning og småskala utgravning på tilgrensende lokaliteter avslørte spor etter flere eiendommer og strukturer av samme karakter. Disse funnene, kombinert med de detaljerte resultatene fra hovedutgravningen la til rette for en undersøkelse uten sidestykke av en stor del av Yorks bybilde. Undersøkelsen inkluderer tidlige kirker og vestbredden av Foss, og kartlegger gjenfødelsen av urbant liv i York forut for den normanniske perioden.

Bibliography

Addyman, P.V., 1975. 'Excavations in York, 1972–73, First Interim Report', *Antiq. J.* **LIV Part II**, 200–31

Allen, S.J., 1993. 'The Mill Pond Drain' in Astill 1993, 95–8

Allen, S.J., 1994. *The Illustration of Wooden Artefacts: An introduction and guide to the depiction of wooden artefacts*, Association of Archaeological Illustrators and Surveyors Technical Paper **11** (Oxford)

Allen, S.J. and Spriggs, J.A., 2002. 'The Redisplay of Viking House Timbers in JORVIK, York' in P. Hoffman *et al., Proceedings of the 8th ICOM Group on Wet Organic Archaeological Materials Conference* (Stockholm)

Anderson, T., 2000. 'Congenital conditions and neoplastic disease in palaeopathology' in Cox and Mays (eds) 2000, 199–225

Astill, G.G., 1993. *A Medieval Industrial Complex and its Landscape: The Metalworking Watermills and Workshops of Bordesley Abbey,* Council for British Archaeology Research Report **92**

Aufderheide, A.C. and Rodríguez-Martín, C., 1998. *The Cambridge Encyclopedia of Human Paleopathology* (Cambridge)

AY. Addyman, P.V. (ed.). *The Archaeology of York* (London and York)

1 D.W. Rollason, with D. Gore and G Fellows-Jenson, 1998. *Sources for York History to AD 100*

3 *The Legionary Fortress:*

  3 P. Ottaway, 1996. *Excavations and Observations on the Defences and Adjacent Sites, 1971–90*

6 *Roman Extra-Mural Settlement and Roads*:

  1 D. Brinklow, R.A. Hall, J.R. Magilton and S. Donaghey, 1986. *Coney Street, Aldwark and Clementhorpe, Minor Sites and Roman Roads*

  2 P. Ottaway, 2011. *Archaeology in the Environs of Roman York: Excavations 1976–2005*

7 *Anglian York (AD 410–876):*

  1 R.L. Kemp, 1996. *Anglian Settlement at 46–54 Fishergate, York*

  2 D. Tweddle, J. Moulden and E. Logan, 1999. *Anglian York: A Survey of the Evidence*

8 *Anglo-Scandinavian York (AD 876–1066):*

  1 D. Tweddle and J. Moulden, 1986. *Anglo-Scandinavian Settlement South-West of the Ouse*

  2 Wenham, L.P., Hall, R.A., Briden, C.M. and Stocker, D.A., 1987. *St Mary Bishophill Junior and St Mary Castlegate*

  3 P.V. Addyman and R.A. Hall, 1991. *Urban Structures and Defences. Excavations from Lloyds Bank, Pavement, and Other Sites*

  4 R.A. Hall, D.W. Rollason, M. Blackburn, D.N. Parsons, G. Fellows-Jensen, A.R. Hall, H.K. Kenward, T.P O'Connor, D. Tweddle, A.J. Mainman and N.S. H Rogers, 2004. *Aspects of Anglo-Scandinavian York*

10 *The Medieval Walled City North-East of the Ouse:*

  6 R.A. Hall and K. Hunter-Mann, 2002. *Medieval Urbanism in Coppergate: Refining a Townscape*

12 *The Medieval Cemeteries:*

  2 G. Stroud and R.L. Kemp, 1993. *Cemeteries of the Church and Priory of St Andrew, Fishergate, York*

  3 J.M. Lilley, G. Stroud, D.R. Brothwell and M.H. Williamson (eds), 1994. *The Jewish Burial Ground at Jewbury*

14 *The Past Environment of York:*

  4 A.R. Hall, H.K. Kenward, D. Williams and J.R.A. Greig, 1983. *Environment and Living Conditions at Two Anglo-Scandinavian Sites*

  7 H.K. Kenward and A.R. Hall, 1995. *Biological Evidence from 16–22 Coppergate*

15 *The Animal Bones:*

  3 T.P. O'Connor, 1989. *Bones from Anglo-Scandinavian Levels at 16–22 Coppergate*

  5 J.M. Bond and T.P. O'Connor, 1999. *Bones from Medieval Deposits in York*

16 *The Pottery:*

  4 J.R. Perrin, 1990. *Roman Pottery from the Colonia: Tanner Row and Rougier Street*

  5 A.J. Mainman, 1990. *Anglo-Scandinavian Pottery from Coppergate*

  6 A.J. Mainman, 1993. *Pottery from 46–54 Fishergate*

  8 J. Monaghan, 1997. *Roman Pottery from York*

  9 A.J. Mainman and A. Jenner, 2013. *Medieval Pottery from York*

17 *The Small Finds:*

  3 A. MacGregor, 1978. *Anglo-Scandinavian Finds from Lloyds Bank, Pavement, and Other Sites*

  5 P. Walton, 1989. *Textiles, Cordage and Raw Fibre from 16–22 Coppergate*

  6 P.J. Ottaway, 1992. *Anglo-Scandinavian Ironwork from Coppergate*

7 J. Bayley, 1992. *Non-Ferrous Metalworking from Coppergate*

8 D. Tweddle, 1992. *The Anglian Helmet from Coppergate*

11 P Walton Rogers, 1997. *Textile Production at 16–22 Coppergate*

12 A. MacGregor, A.J. Mainman and N.S.H. Rogers, 1999. *Bone and Antler from Anglo-Scandinavian and Medieval York*

13 C.A. Morris, 2000. *Wood and Woodworking from Anglo-Scandinavian and Medieval York*

14 A.J. Mainman and N.S.H. Rogers, 2000. *Finds from Anglo-Scandinavian York*

15 P.J. Ottaway and N.S.H. Rogers, 2002. *Medieval Finds from York*

16 Q. Mould, I. Carlisle and E. Cameron, 2003. *Leather and Leatherworking from Anglo-Scandinavian and Medieval York*

18 *The Coins:*

1 E.J.E. Pirie, M.M. Archibald and R.A. Hall, 1986. *Post-Roman Coins from York Excavations 1971–1981*

The *Archaeology of York* Supplementary Series

1 *The Medieval Buildings of York: The Pictorial Evidence*

2 B. Wilson and F. Mee, 2002. *'The Fairest Arch in England'. Old Ouse Bridge, York, and its Buildings*

The *Archaeology of York* on the web:

AYW **1** N. Macnab, *Anglo-Scandinavian, Medieval and Post-Medieval Urban Occupation at 41–49 Walmgate, York*

AYW **9** J. McComish, *Roman, Anglian and Anglo-Scandinavian activity and a medieval cemetery on land at the junction of Dixon Lane and George Street, York*

Baillie, M.G.L., 1977. 'Dublin Medieval Dendrochronology', *Tree Ring Bulletin*, **37**, 13–20

Baillie, M.G.L., 1982. *Tree-Ring Dating and Archaeology* (London)

Baillie, M.G.L. and Pilcher, J.R., 1973. A simple cross-dating program for tree-ring research, *Tree Ring Bulletin*, **33**, 7–14

Barnes, E., 1994. *Developmental Defects of the Axial Skeleton in Palaeopathology* (Niwot, Colorado)

Bass, W.M., 1987. *Human Osteology: A Laboratory and Field Manual* (Columbia)

Bayley, J., 1987. 'Viking glassworking: The evidence from York', *Annales 10e Congrès de l'Association Internationale de l'Histoire du verre*, 245–54

Berry, A.C. and Berry, R.J., 1967. 'Epigenetic variation in the human cranium', *Journal of Anatomy* **101** (2), 361–79

Binns, J.W., Norton, E.C. and Palliser, D.M., 1990. 'The Latin inscription on the Coppergate Helmet', *Antiquity* **64**, 134–9

Blinkhorn, P., 2013. 'No pots please, we're Vikings: pottery in the southern Danelaw, 850–1000' in D.M. Hadley and Letty Ten Harkel (eds), *Everyday Life in Viking-Age Towns: Social Approaches to Towns in England and Ireland, c.800–1100* (Oxford), 157–71

Brigham, T., 1992. 'Reused House Timbers from the Billingsgate Site, 1982–83' in Milne 1992, 86–105

Bronk Ramsey, C., 1995. 'Radiocarbon calibration and analysis of stratigraphy: the OxCal program', *Radiocarbon*, **37**, 425–30

Bronk Ramsey, C., 1998. 'Probability and dating', *Radiocarbon*, **40**(1), 461–74

Bronk Ramsey, C., 2001. 'Development of the radiocarbon calibration program', *Radiocarbon*, **43**, 355–63

Bronk Ramsey, C., 2009. 'Bayesian analysis of radiocarbon dates', *Radiocarbon*, **51**(1), 337–60

Brothwell, D.R., 1981. *Digging Up Bones* (New York)

Brothwell, D.R. and Browne, S., 1994. 'Pathology', in *AY* 12/3, 457–94

Brunning, R. and Watson, J., 2010. *Waterlogged Wood. Guidelines on the recording, sampling, conservation and curation of waterlogged wood* (English Heritage)

Buck, C.E., Cavanagh, W.G. and Litton, C.D., 1996. *Bayesian approach to interpreting archaeological data* (Chichester)

Buikstra, J.E. and Ubelaker, D.H. (eds), 1994. *Standards for Data Collection from Human Skeletal Remains* (Fayetteville)

Charles, F.W.B., and Charles, M., 1995. *Conservation of timber buildings* (London)

Connelly, P., in prep. Early Medieval Hungate, York

Cox, M., 2000. 'Ageing adults from the skeleton', in Cox and Mays (eds) 2000, 61–82

Cox, M. and Mays, S. (eds), 2000. *Human Osteology in Archaeology and Forensic Science* (London)

English Heritage, 1998. *Dendrochronology – guidelines on producing and interpreting dendrochronological dates* (London)

Finnegan, M., 1978. 'Non-metric variation of the infra-cranial skeleton', *Journal of Anatomy* **125**, 23–37

Goodburn, D.M., 1992. 'Woods and Woodland: carpenters and carpentry' in Milne 1992, 106–130

Goodburn, D.M., 2000. 'Re-used medieval boat timbers found at Coppergate' in *AY* 17/13, 2379–82

Groves, C., 1987a. *Tree-ring analysis of timbers from St Mary's Grove, Stafford, 1980–84*, Ancient Mon Lab Rep, **132/87**

Groves, C., 1987b. *Tree-ring analysis of timbers from Eastgate Street, Stafford, 1982–84*, Ancient Mon Lab Rep, **135/87**

Groves, C., 1990. *Tree-ring analysis and dating of timbers from Annetwell Street, Carlisle, Cumbria, 1981–84*, Ancient Mon Lab Rep, **49/90**

Groves, C., 1992. Tree-ring analysis of timbers in D.H. Evans and D.G. Tomlinson, *Excavations at 33–35 Eastgate, Beverley, 1983–86*, Sheffield Excavation Report, **3**, 256–65

Groves, C., 1993a. *Dendrochronological analysis of timbers from The Lanes, Carlisle, Cumbria, 1978–82: Volume 1*, Ancient Mon Lab Rep, **21/93**

Groves, C., 1993b. *Tree-ring analysis of oak timbers from Queen's Hotel, York, Yorkshire, 1988–89, part 2*, Ancient Mon Lab Rep, **38/93**

Groves, C., 1996a. Dendrochronological analysis of timbers from the northern area of 'The Lanes', Carlisle, Cumbria, 1978–82: Volume 2, unpublished report

Groves, C., 1996b. Dendrochronological analysis of medieval oak timbers from the northern area of 'The Lanes', Carlisle, Cumbria, 1978-82: Volume 3, unpublished report

Groves, C., 1997. 'The dating and provenancing of imported conifer timbers in England: the initiation of a research project', in A. Sinclair, E. Slater and J. Gowlett (eds), *Archaeological Sciences 1995: proceedings of a conference on the application of scientific methods to archaeology*, Oxbow Books Monogr Ser, **64**, 205–11

Groves, C., 2002. Tree-ring analysis of imported medieval timbers from 16–22 Coppergate, York, North Yorkshire – section 2 in *AY* 10/6, 835–8

Groves, C. and Hillam, J., 1985. *Beverley: Dyer Lane 1982, Dendrochronology*, Ancient Mon Lab Rep, **4691**

Groves, C., and Hillam, J., 1986. *Coppergate Dendrochronology. III Analysis of the timbers from Coppergate Development*, Ancient Mon Lab Rep, **4846**

Groves, C. and Hillam, J., 1991. Dendrochronological analysis of oak timbers in P. Armstrong, D. Tomlinson and D.H. Evans, *Excavations at Lurk Lane Beverley 1979–82*, Sheffield Excavation Reports, **1**, 237–8

Hadley, D., 2000. 'Burial practice in the Northern Danelaw, c. 650–1100', *Northern* History **36**, 199–216

Hadley, D.M. and Buckberry, J.L., 2005. 'Caring for the dead in later Anglo-Saxon England' in F. Tinto (ed), *Pastoral Care in Late Anglo-Saxon England*, Anglo-Saxon Studies **6** (Woodbridge), 121–47

Hall, R.A., 1976. *The Viking Kingdom of York*

Hall, R.A. (ed.), 1978a. *Viking Age York and the North*, Council for British Archaeology Research Report **27** (London)

Hall, R.A., 1978b. 'The topography of Viking York' in Hall 1978a, 31–6

Hall, R.A., 1981. 'Markets of the Danelaw', in E. Roesdahl, J. Graham-Campbell, P. Connor and K. Pearson (eds), *The Vikings in England and their Danish Homelands*, Anglo-Danish Viking Project (London), 95–9

Hall, R.A, 1982. '10th century woodworking in Coppergate, York, in S. McGrail (ed.), *Woodworking Techniques before A.D. 1500*, BAR Internat. Ser. **129**, 231–44

Hall, R.A., 1984a. *The Viking Dig* (London)

Hall, R.A., 1984b. 'A Late Pre-Conquest Urban Building Tradition, in P.V. Addyman and V.E. Black (eds), *Archaeological Papers from York presented to M.W. Barley* (York), 71–7

Hall, R.A., 1988. 'The Making of Domesday York' in D. Hooke (ed.), *Anglo-Saxon Settlements* (Oxford), 233–47

Hall, R.A., 1989. 'The Five Boroughs and the Danelaw: a review of present knowledge', *Anglo-Saxon England* **18,** 149–206

Hall, R.A., 1990. *Viking Age archaeology in Britain and Ireland* (Princes Risborough)

Hall, R.A., 1991. 'Sources for Pre-Conquest York' in I. Wood and N. Lund (eds), *People and Places in Northern Europe 500–1600* (Woodbridge), 83–94

Hall, R.A., 1994. *Viking Age York* (London)

Hall, R.A., 1996. *English Heritage Book of York* (London)

Hall, R.A., 1999. 'York' in M. Lapidge, J. Blair, S. Keynes and D. Scragg (eds), *The Blackwell Encyclopaedia of Anglo-Saxon England* (Oxford), 497–9

Hall, R.A., 2000. 'Anglo-Scandinavian Attitudes: archaeological ambiguities in late ninth- to mid-eleventh-century York' in D.M. Hadley and J.D. Richards (eds), *Cultures in Contact: Scandinavian Settlement in England in the Ninth and Tenth Centuries*

Hall, R.A., 2001a. 'A Kingdom Too Far –York in the early 10th century' in N.J. Higham and D.H. Hill (eds), *Edward the Elder 899–924* (London), 188–99

Hall, R.A., 2001b. 'Anglo-Saxon and Viking-Age York' in P. Nuttgens (ed) *History of York* (Pickering), 39–67

Hall, R.A, 2002. 'Blood of the Vikings – The Riddle at Riccall', *Yorkshire Archaeology Today*, **2**, 5

Hall, R.A., 2004a. 'Jorvik – A Viking-Age City' in J. Hines, A. Lane and M. Rednap (eds), *Land, Sea and Home*, Society for Medieval Archaeology Monograph Series **20**, 283–96

Hall, R.A., 2004b. 'Drengs, Vikings, Countrymen: raiding, conquering and settling in ninth- and tenth-century England' in S. Lewis-Simpson (ed.), *Vinland Revisited. The Norse World at the Turn of the First Millennium. Selected Papers from the Viking Millennium International Symposium*, 37–44

Hall, R.A, 2005. 'The Case of the Missing Viking', *Yorkshire Archaeology Today*, **9**, 1–4

Hall, R.A., 2007. *Exploring the World of the Vikings* (New York)

Hall, R.A., 2008a. 'York' in S. Brink (ed.), *The Viking World* (London), 379–84

Hall, R.A., 2008b. 'York im Zeitalter der Wikinger' in *Die Wikinger* (Historisches Museum der Pfalz Speyer/Munich), 224–5

Hall, R.A., 2011. 'Erik Bloodaxe Rules OK': "The Viking Dig" at Coppergate, York' in J. Schofield (ed.), *Great Excavations: Shaping the Archaeological Profession* (Oxford), 181–93

Hall, R.A., forthcoming. 'Anglo-Scandinavian York', Historic Town Atlas: York (Oxford: Oxbow)

Heighway, C.M., Garrod, A.P. and Vince A.G., 1979. 'Excavations at 1 Westgate Street, Gloucester, 1975', *Medieval Archaeology* **23**, 159–213

Hershkovitz, I., Bedford, L., Jellema, L.M. and Latimer, B., 1996. 'Injuries to the skeleton due to prolonged activity in hand-to-hand combat', *International Journal of Osteoarchaeology* **6**, 167–78

Hillam, J., 1985. *Coppergate Dendrochronology. I: Tree-ring analysis of timbers from the sunken buildings*, Ancient Mon Lab Rep, **4556**

Hillam, J., 1987. *Dendrochronology of the wattle phase timbers from 16–22 Coppergate, York*, Ancient Mon Lab Rep, **236/87**

Hillam, J., 1988. *Billingsgate Lorry Park, City of London, 1982. Tree ring analysis of the Period V timbers*, Ancient Mon Lab Rep, **94/88**

Hillam, J., 1989. *Tree-ring analysis of medieval and post-medieval timbers from 16–22 Coppergate, York, North Yorkshire*, Ancient Mon Lab Rep, **136/89**

Hillam, J., 1992a. Tree-ring analysis, in *AY* 17/8, 870–5

Hillam, J., 1992b. Tree-ring analysis of oak timbers, in K Steedman, T. Dyson and J. Schofield (eds), *Aspects of Saxo-Norman London: III. The Bridgehead and Billingsgate to 1200,* LAMAS special paper **14**, 143–73

Hillam, J., 1992c. *Tree-ring analysis of timbers from The Brooks, Winchester, Hampshire*, Ancient Mon Lab Rep, **69/92**

Hillam, J., 2002. Tree-ring analysis of medieval and post-medieval timbers from 16–22 Coppergate, York, North Yorkshire – section 1, in *AY* 10/6, 826–34

Hillam, J., Morgan, R.A., and Tyers, I., 1987. Sapwood estimates and the dating of short ring sequences, in R.G.W. Ward (ed), *Applications of tree-ring studies: current research in dendrochronology and related areas*, BAR Internat Ser, **333**, 165-85, Oxford

Hillson, S., 1996. *Dental Anthropology* (Cambridge)

Hilton, R.C., Ball, J. and Benn, R.T., 1976. 'Vertebral end-plate lesions (Schmorl's nodes) in the dorsolumbar spine', *Annals of the Rheumatic Diseases* **35**, 127–32

Hollstein, E., 1980. *Mitteleuropäische Eichenchronologie* (Mainz)

Holman, N., nd. Coppergate tree-rings revisited: a fresh look at the 10th century sunken buildings and a discussion of the 'non-chronological' potential of tree-ring studies at this and similar sites, unpublished manuscript

Holst, M., 2005. 'Osteological Analysis, Spurriergate, York', York Osteoarchaeology, No. **1405**, Unpublished Osteological Report

Holst, M., 2009. 'Osteological Analysis, Brakes Farm, Sedgefield, Country Durham', York Osteoarchaeology, No **0909**, Unpublished Osteological Report

Holst, M., Isaac, L. and Boylston, A., 1998. 'Hull Magistrates' Court', Unpublished Osteological Report, Calvin Wells Laboratory, University of Bradford

Horsman, V., Milne, C. and Milne, G., 1988. 'Aspects of Saxo-Norman London: 1 Building and Street Development near Billingsgate and Cheapside', *London and Middlesex Archaeological Society Special Paper* **11**

Hurley, M., Scully, O. and McCutcheon, S. (eds), 1997. *Late Viking Age and Medieval Waterford, Excavations 1986–1992* (Waterford)

Kennedy, K.A.R., 1989. 'Skeletal markers of occupational stress', in M.Y. Işcan and K.A.R. Kennedy (eds), *Reconstruction of Life from the Skeleton* (New York), 129–60

Knüsel, C., 2000. 'Activity-related change', in V. Fiorato, A. Boylston and C. Knüsel, *Blood Red Roses: The Archaeology of a Mass Grave from the Battle of Towton AD 1461* (Oxford), 103–18

Lang, J.T., 1991. *Corpus of Anglo-Saxon Stone Sculpture* **3**: *York and Eastern Yorkshire* (Oxford)

Larsen, C.S., 1997. *Bioarchaeology: Interpreting Behavior from the Human Skeleton* (Cambridge)

Lewis, M., 2000. 'Non-Adult palaeopathology: Current Status and Future Potential', in Cox and Mays (eds) 2000, 39–57

Longin, R., 1971. 'New method of collagen extraction for radiocarbon dating', *Nature*, **230**, 241–2

Loveluck, C., 2013. *Northwest Europe in the Early Middle Ages, c.AD 600–1150: A Comparative Archaeology* (Cambridge)

Mason, D.J.P., 1985. 'Excavations at Chester, 26–42 Lower Bridge Street 1974–76. The Dark Age and Saxon periods', *Grosvenor Museum Archaeological Excavation and Survey Reports* **3** (Chester)

Mays, S. and Cox, M., 2000. 'Sex determination in skeletal remains', in Cox and Mays (eds) 2000, 117–30

McKinley, J.I., 2004. 'Compiling a skeletal inventory: disarticulated and co-mingled remains', in M. Brickley and J.I. McKinley (eds), *Guidelines to the Standards for Recording Human Remains. IFA Paper No. 7* (Southampton and Reading), 14–17

McMahon, M., 2002. 'Early medieval settlement and burial outside the enclosed town: evidence from archaeological excavations at Bride Street, Dublin', *Proc. Royal Irish Academy* **102c**, 67–135

Milne, G., 1992. 'Timber Building Techniques in London c.900–1400', *London and Middlesex Archaeological Society Special Paper* **15**

Mook, W.G., 1986. 'Business meeting: Recommendations/Resolutions adopted by the Twelfth International Radiocarbon Conference', *Radiocarbon*, **28**, 799

Moynihan, P., 2003. 'Diet and dental caries', in J.J. Murray, J.H. Nunn and J.G. Steele (eds), *The Prevention of Oral Disease* (Oxford), 9–34

Munro, M.A.R., 1984. An improved algorithm for cross-dating tree-ring series, *Tree Ring Bulletin*, **44**, 17–27

Murray, H., 1983. *Viking and Early Medieval Buildings in Dublin*, BAR Brit Series **119** (Oxford)

Naysmith, P., Cook, G.T., Freeman, S.P.H.T., Scott, E.M., Anderson, R., Xu, S., Dunbar, E., Muir, G.K.P., Dougans, A., Wilcken, K., Schnabel, C., Russell, N., Ascough, P.L., Maden, C., 2010. '14C AMS at SUERC: Improving QA Data with the 5MV Tandem and 250kV SSAMS', *Radiocarbon*, **52**(2), 263–71

Norton, C., 1998. 'The Anglo-Saxon Cathedral at York and the Topography of the Anglian City', *J. Brit. Archaeol. Assoc.*, **151**, 1–42

Okasha, M.K.M., 1987. Statistical methods in dendrochronology, unpublished PhD thesis, Sheffield University

Ortner, D.J., 2003. *Identification of Palaeopathological Disorders in Human Skeletal Remains* (Amsterdam and San Diego)

Palliser, D.M., 1984. 'York's West Bank: Medieval Suburb or Urban Nucleus?' in P.V. Addyman and V.E. Black, *Archaeological Papers from York Presented to M.W. Barley* (York), 101–8

Palliser, D.M., 1996. 'Review Article: The "Minster Hypothesis": A Case Study', *Early Medieval Europe*, **5**(2), 207–14

Panter, I. and Spriggs, J.A., 1997. 'Condition Assessments and Conservation Strategies for Waterlogged Wood Assemblages', *Proceedings of the 6th ICOM Group on Wet Organic Archaeological Materials Conference* (York), 185–202

Puttnam, G.G., 1978. 'Analysis of the skeletal material', in P.G. Huggins, 'Excavation of a Belgic and Romano-British Farm with Middle Saxon Cemetery and Churches at Nazeingbury, Essex, 1975–76', *Essex Archaeology* **10**, 29–117

Rackham, O., 1972. 'Grundle House: the question of timber in certain East Anglian buildings in relation to local supplies', *Vernacular Architecture* **3**, 3–8

Rackham, O., 1980. *Ancient Woodland* (London)

Rackham, O., 1982. 'The Growing and Transport of Timber and Underwood' in S. McGrail, *Woodworking Techniques before AD 1500*, BAR Internat Series **S129**, 199–218

Rackham, O., 1990. *Trees and woodland in the British Landscape*, 2nd edn (London)

Rackham, O., Blair, W.J. and Munby, J.T., 1978. 'The thirteenth-century Roofs and Floor of the Blackfriars Priory at Gloucester', *Medieval Archaeology* **22**, 105–22

Radley, J.D., 1971. 'Economic aspects of Anglo-Danish York', *Medieval Archaeol.* **15**, 37–57

Rees Jones, S., 2013. *York: The Making of a City 1068–1350* (Oxford)

Reimer, P.J., Baillie, M.G.L., Bard, E., Bayliss, A., Beck, J.W., Blackwell, P.G., Bronk Ramsey, C., Buck, C.E., Burr, G.S., Edwards, R.L., Friedrich, M., Grootes, P.M., Guilderson, T.P., Hajdas, I., Heaton, T.J., Hogg, A.G., Hughen, K.A., Kaiser, K.F., Kromer, B., McCormac, F.G., Manning, S.W., Reimer, R.W., Richards, D.A., Southon, J.R., Talamo, S., Turney, C.S.M., van der Plicht, J. and Weyhenmeyer, C.E., 2009. 'INTCAL09 and MARINE09 radiocarbon age calibration curves, 0–50,000 years cal BP', *Radiocarbon*, **51**(4), 1111–50

Richards, J.D., Jecock, M., Richmond, L. and Tuck, C., 1995. 'The Anglo-Scandinavian barrow cemetery at Heath Wood, Ingleby, Derbyshire', *Medieval Archaeology* **39**, 51–70

Roberts, C.A. and Cox, M., 2003. *Health and Disease in Britain from Prehistory to the Present Day* (Stroud)

Roberts, C.A. and Manchester, K., 2005. *The Archaeology of Disease* (3rd edition) (Stroud)

Rogers, J., 1999. 'Burials: the human skeletons', in C. Heighway and R. Bryant, *The Golden Minster. The Anglo-Saxon Minster and Later Medieval Priory of St Oswald, Gloucester* (York), 163–82

Rogers, J., 2000. 'The palaeopathology of joint disease', in Cox and Mays (eds) 2000, 163–82

Salter, R.B., 1999. *Textbook of Disorders and Injuries of the Musculoskeletal System*

Saunders, S.R., 1989. 'Non-metric variation', in M.Y. Işcan and K.A.R. Kennedy (eds), *Reconstruction of Life from the Skeleton* (New York), 95–108

Scheuer, L. and Black, S., 2000a. 'Development and ageing of the juvenile skeleton', in Cox and Mays (eds) 2000, 9–22

Scheuer, L. and Black, S., 2000b. *Developmental Juvenile Osteology* (San Diego)

811

Scott, E.M., 2003. 'The Third International Radiocarbon Intercomparison (TIRI) and the Fourth International Radiocarbon Intercomparison (FIRI) 1990–2002: results, analysis, and conclusions', *Radiocarbon*, **45**(2), 135–408

Smith, B.H., 1984. 'Patterns of molar wear in hunter-gatherers and agriculturalists', *American Journal of Physical Anthropology* **63**, 39–56

Spall, C.A. and Toop, N.J. (eds), 2005. Blue Bridge Lane and Fishergate House, York. Report on Excavations: July 2000 to July 2002, (http://www.archaeological-planningconsultancy.co.uk/mono/001/index.html)

Spriggs, J.A., 1980. 'The Recovery and Storage of Materials from Waterlogged Sites in York', *The Conservator* **4**

Spriggs, J.A., 1982. 'The Conservation of Timber Structures in York – A Progress Report' in D.W. Grattan (ed), *Proceedings of the ICOM Waterlogged Wood Working Group Conference* (Ottawa)

Spriggs, J.A., 1984. 'Treating the Coppergate Structures – A Quest for Anti-shrink Efficiency' in P.V. Addyman and V.E. Black V.E. (eds), *Archaeological Papers from York Presented to M. W. Barley* (York)

Spriggs, J.A., 1991. 'The Treatment, Monitoring and Display of Viking Structures at York' in P. Hoffmann (ed), *Proceedings of the ICOM Waterlogged Wood Working Group Conference* (Bremerhaven)

Spriggs, J.A., 1992. 'Lifting a Viking Structure at Coppergate, York' in R. Payton (ed.), *Retrieval of Objects from Archaeological Sites* (Archetype Publications), 77–84

Spriggs, J.A., 1994. 'Field Trials with copper: silver ionisation disinfection of PEG wax solutions' in P. Hoffmann (ed), *Proceedings of the 5th ICOM Group on Wet Organic Archaeological Materials Conference* (Bremerhaven)

Steier, P. and Rom, W., 2000. 'The use of Bayesian statistics for 14C dates of chronologically ordered samples: a critical analysis', *Radiocarbon*, **42**, 183–98

Stirland, A., 2005. 'Human remains', in J. Gardiner and M.J. Allen (eds), *Before the Mast: Life and Death Aboard the Mary Rose. The Archaeology of the Mary Rose* **4** (Portsmouth), 516–44

Stocker, D.A., 2000. 'Monuments and Merchants: Irregularities in the distribution of stone sculpture in Lincolnshire and Yorkshire in the 10th century' in D.M. Hadley and J.D. Richards (eds), *Cultures in Contact: Scandinavian Settlement in England in the 9th and 10th centuries*, 179–212

Stone, R.J. and Stone, J.A., 1997. *Atlas of Skeletal Muscles* (London)

Stuart-Macadam, P., 1992. 'Anemia in past populations', in P. Stuart-Macadam and S. Kent (eds) *Diet, Demography and Disease: Changing Perspectives of Anemia* (New York), 151–70

Stuiver, M. and Kra, R.S., 1986. 'Editorial comment', *Radiocarbon*, **28**(2B), ii

Stuiver, M. and Polach, H.A., 1977. 'Reporting of 14C data', *Radiocarbon*, **19**(3), 355–63

Stuiver, M. and Reimer, P.J., 1986. 'A computer program for radiocarbon age calibration', *Radiocarbon*, **28**(2B), 1022–30

Stuiver, M. and Reimer, P.J., 1993. 'Extended 14C data base and revised CALIB 3.0 14C calibration program', *Radiocarbon*, **35**(1), 215–30

Sture, J.F., 2001. Biocultural Perspectives on Birth Defects in Medieval Urban and Rural English Populations, Durham University, Unpublished PhD thesis

Swanton, M. (ed. and trans.), 1996. *The Anglo-Saxon Chronicle* (London)

Trinkhaus, E., 1978. 'Bilateral asymmetry of human skeletal non-metric traits', *American Journal of Physical Anthropology* **49**, 315–18

Trotter, M., 1970. 'Estimation of stature from intact limb bones', in T.D. Stewart (ed), *Personal Identification in Mass Disasters* (Washington D.C.), 71–83

Tyers, I., 1988. *Dendrochronology report: Barking Abbey 1985/86 Saxon timbers*, MoL EAS Dendro Rep, **01/88**

Tyers, I., 1992. 'Trig Lane: New Dendrochronological Work' in G. Milne, *Timber building Techniques in London c.900–1400: An archaeological study of water-front installations and related material*, LAMAS Special Paper, **15**, 64–5

Tyers, I., 1997a. *Dendrochronological analysis of beech timbers from the Magor Pill I wreck, Gwent*, ARCUS Rep, **261**

Tyers, I., 1997b. *Dendro for Windows program guide*, ARCUS Rep, **340**

Tyers, I., 1999. *Tree-ring analysis of oak timbers from Peterborough Cathedral, Peterborough, Cambridgeshire: Structural timbers from the Nave Roof and North-West Portico*, Ancient Mon Lab Rep, **9/99**

Tyers, I., 2000a. *Tree-ring analysis and wood identification on timbers excavated on the Magistrates Court Site, Kingston upon Hull, East Yorkshire*, ARCUS Rep, **410** (revised edition)

Tyers, I., 2000b. *Archive report on the tree-ring analysis of Roman timbers from Number 1 Poultry, City of London*, ARCUS Rep, **517**

Tyers, I., 2009. 'Tree-ring spot-dates of archaeological samples: Hungate, York (site code YORYM 2006.5201), *Dendrochronological Consultancy Ltd Report* **227**

Tyers, I., forthcoming. Appendix 2 Tree-ring analysis of the Roman and medieval timbers from medieval London Bridge and its environs in B. Watson, *Excavations at medieval London Bridge 1984*, MoLAS Archaeology Series

Vandeputte, K., Moens, L. and Dams, R., 1996. 'Improved sealed-tube combustion of organic samples to CO_2 for stable isotope analysis, radiocarbon dating and percent carbon determinations', *Analytical Letters*, **29**(15), 2761–73

Vere-Stevens, L., Crawshaw, A., Panter, I. and Spriggs, J.A., 1999. 'Further Research into the Copper/Silver Ion Sterilization System as applied to the treatment of Archaeological Oak Wood in PEG Solutions' in C. Bonnot-Diconne, X. Hiron, Q.K. Tran and P. Hoffman (eds), *Proceedings of the 7th ICOM Group on Wet Organic Archaeological Materials Conference* (Grenoble), 95–104

Walker, P.L., Bathurst, R.R., Richman, R., Gjerdrum, T. and Andrushko, V.A., 2009. 'The causes of porotic hyperostosis and cribra orbitalia: a reappraisal of the iron-deficiency-anemia hypothesis', *American Journal of Physical Anthropology* **139**, 109–25

Wallace, P. F., 2001. 'Ireland's Viking Towns', in A-C. Larsen (ed.) *The Vikings in Ireland* (Roskilde)

Ward, G.K. and Wilson, S.R., 1978. 'Procedures for comparing and combining radiocarbon age determinations: a critique', *Archaeometry*, **20**, 19–32

Waterman, D.M, 1959. 'Late Saxon, Viking and Early Medieval Finds from York', *Archaeologia* **97**, 59–105

Zero, D. T., 1999. 'Dental caries process', *Dental Clinics of North America* **43**, 635–64

Index
by Pam Scholefield

Note: Page numbers with 't' are tables; figures are in italics

The Archaeology of York

Reports on the work of the York Archaeological Trust for Excavation and Research are published as separate parts or fascicules making up a series of twenty volumes entitled **The Archaeology of York**:

1   Sources for York History to AD 1100 (*AY* 1)

2   Historical Sources for York Archaeology after AD 1100 (*AY* 2)

3   The Legionary Fortress (*AY* 3)

4   The Colonia(*AY*4)

5   The Roman Cemeteries (*AY* 5)

6   Roman Extra-mural Settlement and Road (*AY* 6)

7   Anglian York (AD 410-876) (*AY* 7)

8   Anglo-Scandinavian York (AD 876-1066) (*AY* 8)

9   The Medieval Walled City south-west of the Ouse (*AY* 9)

10   The Medieval Walled City north-east of the Ouse (*AY* 10)

11   The Medieval Defences and Suburbs (*AY* 11)

12   The Medieval Cemeteries (*AY* 12)

13   Post-medieval York (*AY* 13)

14   The Past Environment of York (*AY* 14)

15   The Animal Bones (*AY* 15)

16   The Pottery (*AY* 16)

17   The Small Finds (*AY* 17)

18   The Coins (*AY* 18)

19   Principles and Methods (*AY* 19)

20   History of Properties in York (*AY* 20)

Supplementary Series
1   The Medieval Buildings of York: The Pictorial Evidence

For further information on all York Archaeological Trust publications please see
http://www.yorkarchaeology.co.uk/pubs.htm